P9-DVA-976

Left and below: Even today
firepower is often used as a
substitute for accuracy, as in
the case of the Marine F4U
rocketing Okinawa in June
1945. The converse is shown by
the single AIM-7M Sparrow
fired from a two-seat F-15 of the
USAF and heading with unerr-
ing precision against a clearly
visible target at higher level.

AMERICAN WARPLANES

Above: In 1928 the USS Saratoga, *the Martin T4M-1 and the P&W Hornet engine were all new. Navy squadron VT-2B was one of the world's first air units equipped to sink the largest ships.*

PUBLISHED BY

SALAMANDER BOOKS LIMITED

LONDON

Right and below: The US Navy has never forgotten the vital importance of organic seagoing airpower. The SBDs and F4Fs on a CVE (escort carrier) were off North Africa in 1942. The F-14s and A-7s were aboard the mighty Sara off Libya in 1986.

AMERICAN WARPLANES

A full-color technical directory of 200 of the most important combat aircraft to serve the United States

BILL GUNSTON

A Salamander Book

Published by Salamander Books Ltd,
129-137 York Way, London N7 9LG,
United Kingdom.

© Salamander Books Ltd 1986, 1997

All rights reserved. No part of this book may
be reproduced, stored in a retrieval system
or transmitted in any form or by any means,
electronic, mechanical, photocopying,
recording or otherwise, without the prior
permission of the copyright owner.

All correspondence concerning the content
of this volume should be addressed to
Salamander Books Ltd.

ISBN 0-7651-9211-X

This edition distributed by
SMITHMARK Publishers,
a division of U.S. Media Holdings, Inc.,
115 West 18th Street, New York, NY 10011

9 8 7 6 5 4 3 2 1

SMITHMARK Books are available for bulk
purchase for sales promotion and premium
use. For details write or call the manager
of special sales, SMITHMARK Publishers,
a division of U.S. Media Holdings, Inc.,
115 West 18th Street, New York, NY 10011
(212) 532-6600

Credits

Editor: Ray Bonds
Designer: Philip Gorton

Color profiles: © Pilot Press Ltd., and
Ray Hutchins © Salamander Books Ltd.
Line drawings: © Pilot Press Ltd., and
Ray Hutchins © Salamander Books Ltd.
Picture research: Jonathan Scott Arms

Filmset by the Old Mill, England.
Color reproduction: Trend Add Ltd., and
Melbourne Graphics Ltd., England
Printed in Spain

The Author

Bill Gunston, OBE, FRAeS, is a former RAF
pilot and flying instructor, and he has spent
most of his working life accumulating a
wealth of information on aerospace technology and history. Since leaving the
Service, he has acted as an advisor to sev-
eral aviationcompanies and become one of
the most internationally respected authors
and broadcasters on aviation and scientific
subjects. His numerous books include the
Salamander titles *Warplanes of the Future*,
*The Illustrated Encyclopedia of Combat
Aircraft of World War II*, *The Illustrated
Encyclopedia of the World's Modern Military
Aircraft*, *The Encyclopedia of the World's
Combat Aircraft*, *The Illustrated
Encyclopedia of the World's Rockets and
Missiles*, *Soviet Air Power* (with Bill
Sweetman), and many of Salamander's suc-
cessful illustrated guides to aviation sub-
jects. He has also contributed to the author-
itative *Advanced Technology Warfare*, *The
Soviet War Machine* and *The US War
Machine*, by the same company, and carries
out regular assignments for technical aviation periodicals. Mr. Gunston is also an
assistant compiler of *Jane's Aero-Engines*
and was formerly technical editor of *Flight
International* magazine and technology editor of *Science Journal*.

Acknowledgements

The publishers wish to thank
wholeheartedly the many organizations in
the aerospace industry, various historical
archives and the audio-visual
departments of the United States
Department of Defense, as well as many
individuals, who have all been of
considerable help in the preparation of
this book. A list of photograph credits
appears on page 216.

Contents

Left and below: A single F100 engine from an F-15 (inset, 49th TFW on Exercise Reforger) costs several times as much as the entire US Army Air Corps 27th Pursuit Squadron's Boeing P-12Es cost in 1932. Statistics of this type are perhaps startling, but have little meaning.

Introduction

THE UNITED STATES was just eight years old when man first ventured into the air, in a hot-air balloon. Three-quarters of a century later balloons played a significant role in several battles in the Civil War, but thereafter public attention was increasingly focussed on the possibility of heavier-than-air airplane flight. Success in this challenging field continually proved elusive, so that by the 1890s it was almost universally accepted that any constructor of a flying machine was at best a crank, and at worst a plain fraud.

Then along came a man of substance with a solid reputation: Dr Samuel Pierpont Langley, Secretary (head) of Washington's august Smithsonian Institution, besides being a famed astronomer. In 1891 he began building exquisite model airplanes, and by 1896 had achieved sustained flights with models up to 13ft (4m) span. The Army and Navy naturally showed interest. Suddenly airplane flight looked not only respectable, but just around the corner.

In 1898 outbreak of war with Spain triggered off more positive interest. Airplanes might be useful in war, certainly for scouting and possibly even as carriers of weapons. The US Government agreed to vote the money if Dr Langley would build a full-scale airplane. Langley agreed, and $50,000, then a tremendous sum, was made available. On 7 October 1903 Langley's airplane was all ready on its launch mechanism erected atop a houseboat on the Potomac. It cleared the rail and then simply dived into the water.

Rebuilt, it took off again on 8 December; this time there was immediate structural failure, and Langley's gifted engine designer and test pilot, Charles Manley, was almost drowned in the icy water.

How this repeated fiasco was received by the public and Congress was predictable. The *New York Times* summed it up: "The flying machine which will really fly might be evolved by the combined and continuous efforts of mathematicians and mechanicians in from one to ten million

years . . .". Just over a week later there came a garbled message from the wind-swept dunes at Kitty Hawk, claiming that two bicycle makers from Ohio, Wilbur and Orville Wright, had flown in some kind of machine. Most newspapers ignored the story. A few carried it in a vague way, and it was universally a subject for laughter.

By late 1904 the brothers had made many flights back in Ohio, mastering the art of piloting and reaching the stage

Above: The world's first military airplane, resting behind its technological predecessor. Before it was accepted, on 2 August 1909, it had to demonstrate "demountability; that is . . . to fit into an Army wagon". This was accomplished by folding the front and rear sections against the wing.

Below: Hair-raising experiments with a proposed shipboard launching cable for the first airplane in the Navy, the Curtiss A-1. Ordered on 11 May 1911, this was a seaplane version of the established Curtiss pusher, with a 75hp V-8 engine. With wheels added it became the Triad.

where they had a practical and useful airplane. In January 1905 they wrote their Congressman to enquire whether the US Government might be interested. They made no request for money, but merely wished to know whether the Government would be interested in buying a Flyer, or of building some for itself. For the next ten months they failed to penetrate the closed minds in Washington who, ignoring what the brothers had actually written, said they did not wish to provide funds for would-be designers of flying machines. It is easy to dismiss Washington as "a bunch of asses' (as a great glider pioneer, Octave Chanute, called them). The world *knew* that man could not fly. Despite this, there inevitably grew the belief that those Wright boys from Dayton must have accomplished something. Hundreds of people claimed to have witnessed their

flying. On 1 August 1907 the Army established within the Signal Corps an Aeronautical Division. A little later Wilbur Wright called and found a perceptible change in the atmosphere. He was invited to bid on a contract to supply an airplane. Tenders were invited from other inventors, and there were 41 offers! Predictably, 40 dropped out and, after prolonged negotiations, the Army signed the world's first contract for a military airplane on 10 February 1908.

THE FIRST MILITARY AIRPLANE

The Wrights, who had not yet formed a company, undertook to deliver an airplane that would carry a pilot and passenger for ten miles at 40mph (64km/h). They knew they had a practical airplane but had not flown for two years,

so in spring 1908 they returned to Kitty Hawk to brush up their flying. Then, while Wilbur went to France, Orville took the second Model A to Fort Myer, where he flew the acceptance tests under Signal Corps supervision in September 1908. This airplane was finally accepted in August 1909, and the Wrights began training Army officers, first at Dayton and from 1911 at the Army's own school at College Park, Maryland.

Meanwhile, Glenn Curtiss, a famed racing motorcyclist and builder of powerful engines, had become a successful member of the 1908 Aerial Experiment Association at Hammondsport, NY. He quickly outstripped the Wrights in the performance and diversity of his airplanes, and in winter 1910-11 he set up a school on North Island, San Diego, and offered to teach Army and Navy officers for free! In January 1911 the Navy's first aviator, Lt "Spud" Ellyson, qualified on a Curtiss having started flying at Hammondsport. And by this time the handful of officer pilots were experimenting with implements of war. At an air meet at Sheepshead Bay, NY, in 1910, Lt Fickel had gone up with Curtiss and, merely sitting on the lower leading edge (with no strap or hand-hold) proceeded to fire a rifle at a ground target, which he repeatedly hit. A few weeks later Lts Beck and Crissy had gone to an air meet at the Tanforan racecourse, San Francisco, and caused consternation by tossing out extremely successful home-made bombs!

On 14 November 1910 Eugene Ely, Curtiss' demo pilot, took off from a quarterdeck platform aboard the cruiser USS *Birmingham.* On 18 January 1911 he landed on a similar platform on the battleship *Pennsylvania,* and then took off again. Just a month later Curtiss himself flew an A-1 seaplane to the same battleship, taxied alongside, was entertained in the wardroom and took off again. On 1 July 1911 Curtiss flew the first Navy airplane, another A-1. Subsequently there was intensive effort to perfect methods of taking off from ships and landing back on board, including tests by Ellyson with a catapult derived from the standard pneumatic torpedo launcher.

Above: The world's first landing on a ship was made by Eugene Ely with this Curtiss pusher aboard the armored cruiser **Pennsylvania** *(the official caption supplied with this photo calls it "the USS Peuva"!) Here we see the subsequent takeoff, the second from a ship.*

Below: The first shipboard operations were made by Eugene Ely, a Curtiss pilot using a company demonstrator earlier than the first A-1 bought by the Navy. Here Ely poses before taking off from the **Pennsylvania** *on 18 January 1911. He is wearing a lifejacket.*

THE FIRST AIR WEAPONS

In early 1912 a former Army officer, Riley E. Scott, visited College Park with his own invention of a bombsight. Consisting of a pivoted telescope and various graduated scales, it proved far more accurate than merely dropping bombs by hand, but there was no official interest. Later his invention won the Michelin Prize of $5,000 in France, and was the basis for World War I bombsights. In the same way, Col Isaac N. Lewis, who brought his new machine gun to College Park in June 1912, faced a stone wall of disinterest. It was decreed that, if by any unlikely chance a machine gun should be needed on Army airplanes, that gun must be the Benet-Mercier, the standard issue. The fact that this gun had rigid projections on both sides for ammunition feed and case ejection, so that one side or the other got in the way of the pilot's control column, was ignored. Lewis found a better reception in Belgium, and when World War I began his new plant at Liège was ready to supply all the Allied air forces. His gun, originally American, became virtually the standard weapon for all pivoted mountings.

Despite a 1914-17 campaign against Mexico, the growth of Army and Navy aviation was modest indeed. There was virtually no pressure to create an airplane industry, apart from the natural business interest of Curtiss who swiftly became leading constructor. Neither the Army nor Navy had ever had any kind of program for the future of aviation, and when the United States entered World War I on 6 April 1917 not only did strong armed forces have to be created almost from scratch but so did an industry to build the hardware. On 24 May 1917 French Prime Minister Ribot sent a cable to President Wilson recommending that, by spring 1918, the US send to the Western Front 4,500 airplanes; Ribot calculated that, excluding training types, US industry should deliver 16,500 airplanes in the first six months of 1918. When this message was received, the US Army actually possessed just 55 airplanes, classed as 51 obsolete, four obsolescent and one modern trainer. The Navy had 54 obsolescent trainers, one free balloon, one kite (tethered) balloon and one highly unsatisfactory dirigible (airship).

START OF AN INDUSTRY

Something had to happen, and fast. The Curtiss JN "Jenny" was recognized as a satisfactory primary trainer, and the same company was also building good patrol seaplanes. There had never been an American airplane designed for fighting or bombing, and to save time it was decided that foreign designs should be adopted. In June 1917 11 experts headed by Col R. C. Bolling sailed for Europe to visit England, France and Italy and see how the US effort should be organized. Back in Washington they left noisy Allied Air Commissions each eager to point out that its own country's airplanes were the only ones worth having.

Earlier in the year Col Edward A. Deeds had taken a decision whose long-term importance was enormous. He recognised that engines take even longer to develop than airplanes, and decided that the US should produce a single standard type of engine for use in all kinds of combat airplanes. It took time for this to be approved. At last, on 29 May 1917, Deeds practically imprisoned Jesse Vincent of Packard and E. J. Hall of Hall-Scott in his room in the Willard Hotel in Washington. Two days later Vincent and Hall came downstairs carrying the plans for the Liberty engine. The planned 225hp eight-cylinder version was overtaken by events, but the 12-cylinder was soon to be made in colossal numbers and to be by far the most important engine in US military airplanes until the mid-1920s, a few remaining in service well into the 1930s.

The Bolling Commission recommended licence manufacture in the US of the British Airco D.H.4 designed by Capt de Havilland (who later formed his own company), and the French Spad XIII. The latter

was a single-seat scout, and Gen Pershing, US Commander in France, ordered that this class could be left to the French, so the US Spads were canceled. The DH-4 (American designation) was made in large numbers, and though it was commonly criticized because of the fuel tank separating the pilot and observer, being dubbed "The Flying Coffin", it had a most successful career with many other countries. The only valid reason for exchanging the positions of the fuel tank and the observer, as was done in the DH-4B, was to improve communication between the two men. Many other European types were made prior to the Armistice, including Handley Page O/400 heavy bombers sent for final assembly in England.

Long before 1917 Elmer Sperry had been considering aeronautical uses for the gyroscope, and hit on the idea of a pilotless flying bomb (today called a cruise missile). A similar concept was worked out by Charles Kettering of the Delco firm. Sperry's own programs, one for pilotless Curtiss N-9 airplanes and the other for small biplane missiles, failed to achieve success. The Army-sponsored Kettering "Bug", however, was another matter. Made mainly of wood-reinforced papier-maché, and powered by a 30hp engine mass-produced by Ford, it weighed 310lb (136kg) empty and carried the same weight of HE. Many hundreds were built, and they only just missed being deployed by the Army in France in 1918.

There were large numbers of American pilots who both trained and flew with other Allied air forces, but the AEF (American Expeditionary Force) Air Service itself grew swiftly. The 94th (hat in ring) Pursuit Squadron swept into action on Sunday 14 April 1918, to be followed by dozens of other units by the Armistice. On 29 May 1918 the Air Service was set up as the aviation arm of the Army itself, no longer a mere sub-section of the Signal Corps. It was divided into two branches, the Division of Military Aeronautics for operations and the Bureau of Aircraft Production for all procurement and training. By November 1918 Air Service strength had topped 200,000, with 45 squadrons on the Western Front — almost all flying European-built airplanes — and 55 more in training.

THE NAVY'S PART

For various reasons the Navy got operational in Europe long before the Army. At the very start in spring 1917 it sent large numbers of pupils to Canada, England and France, where they not only learned to fly but also learned about bad weather, how to stay alive in operational duties, and how to speak French — of a sort. These early months were enormously aided by such famed educational centers as Yale and MIT, which raised massive training units. Balloon and airship training was set up with Goodyear's help at Akron, Ohio.

The Navy's main role was coastal patrol and anti-submarine operations. NASs (Naval Air Stations) were built all round the North Atlantic, some on the US seaboard and others in France and England.

The first to become operational was NAS Le Croisic, near St Nazaire, France. Using French Tellier flying boats, flying began on 13 November 1917, and armed patrols five days later. As early as 22 November a machine was lost at sea, the crew being rescued after three days clinging to their damaged Tellier which sank minutes after they were picked up. Messages were sent by pigeons in such circumstances, but navigation was vague, to put it mildly, and, especially in winter, a rescue might well come too late.

At the Armistice the Navy had 18,000 personnel and 517 US-built airplanes on active duty in Europe. Navy and Marine units equipped with DH-4s and big Capronis formed the Northern Bombing Group on the Western Front, and many other Navy fliers had served with Allied units, notably Lt David S. Ingalls who in just over a month with RAF No 213 Sqn gained four victories, shared in others and also downed a balloon (later he was Assistant Secretary of the Navy).

While the spirit and accomplishments of the United States in the hectic 19 months of participation in World War I were outstanding, it was generally felt that the aircraft industry had inevitably suffered. From almost nothing it had been

catapulted in a matter of weeks into becoming one of the largest in the world, but making the airplanes of others. There was still very little experience or strength in design, and the close bureaucratic control from Washington did little to help. Indeed, the Navy had set up its own Naval Aircraft Factory at the Philadelphia Navy Yard. In summer 1917, when NAF was feverishly being built, it seemed a natural thing to do. After the Armistice the NAF remained as a major design and production center which, to a considerable degree, competed with the struggling industry.

From the days of the Wright brothers and Curtiss, who respectively had worked with the Army and Navy, the US aircraft manufacturers had become allied with one or other of the US armed services. Rivalry between them was not confined to

Below: The most important US airplane in World War I, the Airco D.H.4 was known in the Army as the de Havilland 4 or Liberty Plane. Of 4,846 delivered, 1,213 reached France, along with hundreds of trained aviators. Here the AEF (American Expeditionary Force) 11th Bombardment Squadron are seen at their operational base at Maulan shortly before the Armistice. Color was khaki-brown.

the football field. It was to endure through the years of peace, continue at a heightened level through World War II, and remain at an intense level in the days of the Cold War. In industrial contracting, in financial appropriations, and above all in missions, the Army/Navy, and later Air Force/Navy, rivalry was to divert attention from the need to compete with the nation's real enemies, and often to cause damage to the nation's military posture.

MITCHELL'S CRUSADE

Such rivalry was a major national topic in the early 1920s. Gen "Billy" Mitchell, the Air Service commander in France during the war and one of the greatest popular heroes, was an uncompromising advocate of Air Power, with capital letters. Unfortunately, he was led to adopt unconstitutional methods. Increasingly he felt that to tread softly, or to recognize that budgets had to be trimmed, or that airplanes were as yet still puny and unreliable, or that the procurement officials were not to the last man guilty of treasonable negligence and criminal incompetence, was merely to betray the cause of air power and become one of his enemies. In June and July 1921 Mitchell's

big MB-2s dropped bombs on captured German warships. Former Navy Secretary Daniels proclaimed he would "stand bareheaded" on any battleship's bridge attacked by airplanes. He emphasized how quickly bombers would be shot down in any real war, whereupon the MB-2 crews clamored for the Navy to shoot back whilst they made their runs.

The tests resulted in the sinking of a U-boat, a destroyer and a cruiser. But the attention of the world was focussed on the mighty *Ostfriesland*, allegedly the most "unsinkable" battleship ever. Ignoring a "rule" limiting him to 600lb bombs Mitchell put 2,000 pounders aboard his Martins, and on 21 July 1921 they sent the great ship to the bottom. Four simmering years followed, punctuated by massive public attacks by Mitchell on all those who refused to understand Air Power. Inevitably, Mitchell's campaign culminated in his court martial. It is doubtful that any real good came of the bitter conflict.

Indeed the 1920s and 1930s were marked by slow and halting progress in US military aviation, despite a succession of investigations, boards, hearings and committees. One of the most important supposed architects of future air power, the Morrow Board of 1924-25, advocated con-

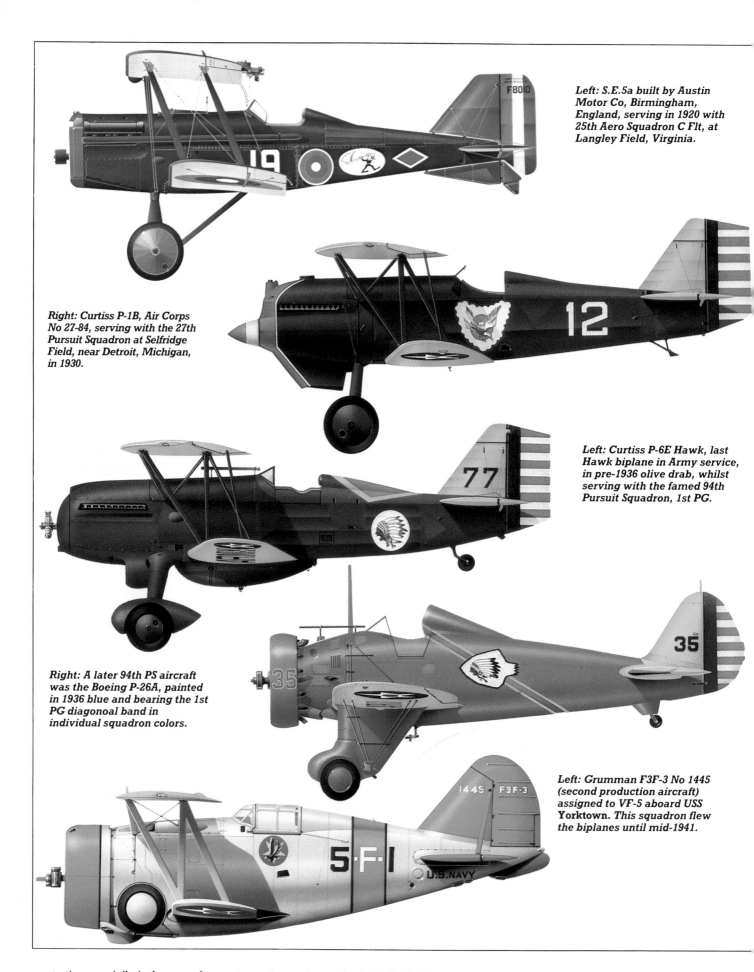

Left: S.E.5a built by Austin Motor Co, Birmingham, England, serving in 1920 with 25th Aero Squadron C Flt, at Langley Field, Virginia.

Right: Curtiss P-1B, Air Corps No 27-84, serving with the 27th Pursuit Squadron at Selfridge Field, near Detroit, Michigan, in 1930.

Left: Curtiss P-6E Hawk, last Hawk biplane in Army service, in pre-1936 olive drab, whilst serving with the famed 94th Pursuit Squadron, 1st PG.

Right: A later 94th PS aircraft was the Boeing P-26A, painted in 1936 blue and bearing the 1st PG diagonoal band in individual squadron colors.

Left: Grumman F3F-3 No 1445 (second production aircraft) assigned to VF-5 aboard USS Yorktown. This squadron flew the biplanes until mid-1941.

centration on civil airplanes and exports "so as to lessen the number of planes which the Government must order to keep the industry in a strong position".

A particular bone of contention of the struggling planemakers was that both the Army and Navy bought rights to each new design that the contracting firms produced. If prototype testing proved the type to

be a winner, the job of building the production run(s) was put out to general tender. Invariably the contract went to the low bidder, and very often this was not the original company which designed and built the prototype. Sometimes the low bidder was able to undercut his rivals by having a bigger and better-equipped plant, while on other occasions it was the

need to recover the high cost of the design and prototype construction that knocked out the original firm. When the Army at last decided it had to start ordering new post-war pursuits after 1918 it picked the Thomas-Morse, but the low bid on the 200 production airplanes came from a rank outsider in the Pacific northwest called Boeing. Likewise, in 1929

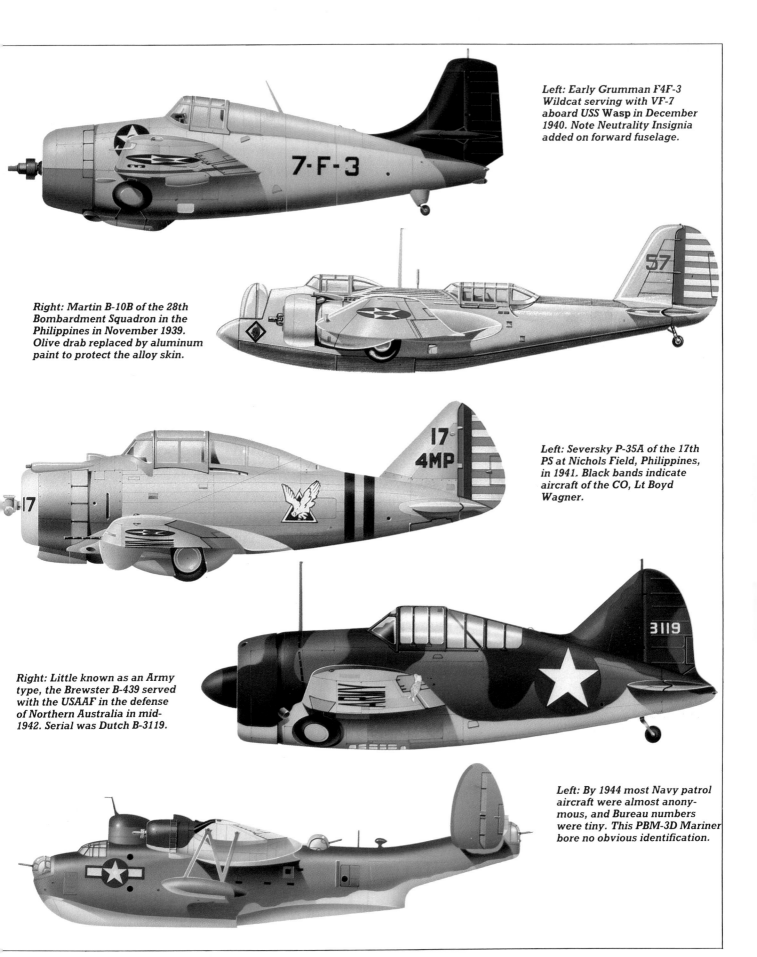

Left: Early Grumman F4F-3 Wildcat serving with VF-7 aboard USS Wasp in December 1940. Note Neutrality Insignia added on forward fuselage.

Right: Martin B-10B of the 28th Bombardment Squadron in the Philippines in November 1939. Olive drab replaced by aluminum paint to protect the alloy skin.

Left: Seversky P-35A of the 17th PS at Nichols Field, Philippines, in 1941. Black bands indicate aircraft of the CO, Lt Boyd Wagner.

Right: Little known as an Army type, the Brewster B-439 served with the USAAF in the defense of Northern Australia in mid-1942. Serial was Dutch B-3119.

Left: By 1944 most Navy patrol aircraft were almost anonymous, and Bureau numbers were tiny. This PBM-3D Mariner bore no obvious identification.

the Navy put out the job of building the great Consolidated XPY-1 monoplane flying boat and the low bidder was Martin, so the production machines were P2Ms and P3Ms.

This policy had a serious adverse effect on stability and security within the Army and Navy airplane manufacturers, which was accentuated by the virtual non-exis-

tence of a market for new civil airplanes. Until the late 1920s airlines hardly existed, and the ex-military pilots who tried to eke out a living by barnstorming — putting on a one-man show in any field near a town, and then offering joyrides for a few dollars — would never dream of buying a new ship when wartime Jennies could be had for $50. In 1920, for example, the

Loughead (Lockheed) brothers failed to attract a single customer for their new light airplane, and temporarily had to suspend operations. Yet in the same year a certain Donald W. Douglas set up a drawing office in the back of an LA barber shop, rented a loft as the assembly hall, and built his first airplane. Soon he was in the almost unique position of selling to

both the Navy and Army, his first airplanes for the latter being specially designed to fly round the world in 1924. Four set out, and two made it the whole way.

This world trip gave the Army brief headlines. Others came from a grueling 27-hour non-stop flight across the US in 1923 by an Army Fokker T-2 transport, and a year later an equally tough crossing of the continent between dawn and dusk in just under 22 hours, with many refueling stops, by a Curtiss pursuit. Lt Russell Maughan, the Curtiss' pilot, gained time by traveling West with the Sun. One factor that made the Curtiss faster than the old Liberty-engined machines was its powerful and streamlined Curtiss D-12 engine, and this was the key to the successful participation of both the Army and Navy in major races — for example, for the Pulitzer and Schneider trophies — in the first half of the 1920s. The Navy won the 1923 Schneider event and the Army the 1925 race. No European competitors appeared in 1924, yet — in contrast to what Britain did in 1931 — the US sportingly canceled that year's race, even though three consecutive wins meant keeping the famed trophy in perpetuity.

Schneider experience suggested that streamlined water-cooled engines made airplanes go faster. This belief was founded on what seemed obvious experience, but in fact it was misleading. Contemporary air-cooled radial engines were crudely instaled, being merely fastened to the front of the fuselage or nacelle. Moreover a practical military airplane could not use streamlined surface radiators to cool the water, and the projecting radiator matrix and massive plumbing added greatly to instaled weight and drag. By the early 1920s engineers were fast learning how to design good air-

cooled cylinders, and the President of Wright, Frederick B. Rentschler (previously a wartime officer in charge of Army engine production), took over the little Lawrence company and developed its J-series engines into the Wright Whirlwind. This enabled Wright to move on from its massive water-cooled engines, and apart from gaining fame as the engine that took Lindbergh to Paris in May 1927 it led to the bigger Cyclone family which powered tens of thousands of airplanes from 1928 to 1958.

Even more important, Rentschler left Wright and in 1925 formed Pratt & Whitney Aircraft. He did this in order to design a new engine, the Wasp. It was planned to be the best engine in the world in the 400hp class, and before starting the company Rentschler assured himself that at last the market was growing. The Army was building up squadrons of new airplanes, and phasing out the old "de Havillands" and other wartime models. The Navy was building two giant flat-tops, USS *Lexington* and *Saratoga,* the first in the world completed as uncompromised carriers from the keel up. Once the Wasp was in the sky, in such new 1926 types as the Curtiss Hawk, Boeing F2B and Vought Corsair, a new era had dawned. The Liberty was out, water-cooled engines were out, and US airpower surged ahead with engines that were more compact, lighter and far more reliable.

AN ARMY AIR CORPS

The Air Corps Act of 2 July 1926 created the Army Air Corps, which had been a pre-requisite to the big re-equipment program. Budgets increasingly permitted research into new technologies, mainly at McCook Field. Subjects includ-

Above: The first air refueling hook-up, on 27 June 1923, between a special DH-4B-1 tanker and a DH-4 receiver with an extra tank with a giant filling funnel. Soon a duration record was set at 37.25h.

ed variable-pitch propellers (marketed by Hamilton from 1931), crude forms of inflight refueling, turbosuperchargers (pioneered by General Electric), high-output engine cylinders and improved fuels, wheel brakes, auxiliary power systems (electric, hydraulic and compressed air), and better cockpit instruments. Under the last heading came blind-flying instrumentation, sponsored by the Guggenheim Foundation, which made such progress that in 1929 Jimmy Doolittle — already by far the best-known Army aviator — was able to make a complete 15 min flight "under the hood" from before takeoff until after the landing.

Other fundamental changes were revolutionizing the entire design of airplanes. Such companies as Northrop, Boeing and Martin were more farsighted than those in Britain and accepted the costs of changing over to all-metal stressed-skin construction. This opened the way to cantilever monoplanes with wings much thinner than the old Fokkers, at last sounding the death-knell of the biplane. Harlan D. Fowler and others patented high-lift flaps that enabled wing loading to be doubled and then doubled again, while the US also led the world in the introduction of all-weather paved runways that were essential for the new generation of heavily-loaded fast-landing monoplanes. The NACA (National Advisory Committee for Aeronautics) played a major role in assisting such advances, together with the development of long-chord cowlings that transformed the aerodynamics of radial engines.

In parallel the rapid growth of airlines resulted in the establishment of recognized air routes between all major US cities. These routes were bid for by the airlines who were franchised to carry the US Mail. At first the routes were marked at night by flashing lights or even bonfires at intervals of some 25 miles (40km), but by 1930 the Radio Range was being rapidly introduced. This provided an aural indication in the pilot's headset, letter A in Morse on one side of the airway, N on the other, and a continuous tone down the center. The airlines entered the 1930s reasonably well equipped to fly across the US or even tackle the formidable 2,400 miles (3,860km) of ocean between Oakland and Hawaii. No Army bomber could think of such flights, and great efforts were made to increase their range, and add the new radio navigational aids.

The problem was all too obvious when in February 1934 Postmaster James Farley canceled existing Mail contracts with what he considered high-priced airlines. General Foulois, Commander of the Air Corps, was asked whether his squadrons could carry the mail. He could hardly announce that they could not, so from 19 February 1934 the Army was carrying the US Mail. On paper it sounds easy, but in practice it meant flying to a timetable over some of the toughest terrain in the world, in some of the worst weather in the world. The airplanes were not modern — the first Martin Bomber was four months in the future — but mostly open-cockpit biplanes. They had none of the new electronic aids, and most carried mail instead of even a radio. A high proportion of the pilots were inexperienced Reserve officers, and none had ever flown the routes before. By the time the airlines worked out a new agreement, on 16 May, there had been dozens of crashes, and numerous deaths or serious injuries. The weather had been some of the worst in living memory, and the only positive result was that the Air Corps gained enormously in experience and set about becoming a night and all-weather force.

INTER-SERVICE CONFLICT

The simmering debate over Army/Navy missions was largely resolved by an agreement of January 1931 between Gen Douglas MacArthur and Admiral William V. Pratt, which looked like a win for the Army. The Air Corps was given sole responsibility for land-based air defense of the US coastlines and US possessions. The Navy's air power was to be part of the Fleet and fly from carriers at sea. Indeed there was still widespread belief that airplanes did not amount to much. Many admirals still felt like Admiral Benson, Chief of Naval Operations in the early 1920s, who proclaimed "I cannot conceive of any use the Fleet will ever have for aircraft". Even in 1934 the Baker Board, convened to plan the future of the Air Corps, concluded that "independent air missions have little effect upon the issue of battle, and none upon the outcome of war".

This was directly contrary to the basic idea of Air Power as championed by Billy Mitchell, by Britain's Lord Trenchard, and

Above: Seen over the Caribbean on 21 October 1937, this B-10B bears an uncanny resemblence to the Maryland and Baltimore of World War II. These later Martin bombers were used only by America's Allies.

by the enormously influential Italian General Douhet. From time to time the Army had managed to scrape together enough money to build a gigantic heavy bomber to put its ideas of Air Power into practice. Not long after World War I the Army Engineering Division had designed the "Barling Bomber" (named for the head designer), which was actually completed in August 1923 as the Wittman-Lewis NBL-1. It proved unable to climb over the Appalachians to reach Washington, so hardly ever flew. In 1933 the Materiel Division at Wright Field conceived Project A for a bomber to carry a ton of bombs 5,000 miles (8,000km); the result was the Boeing XBLR-1, later redesignated XB-15, flown in October 1937. In 1935 plans were drawn up for a far bigger bomber still, the XBLR-2, and this flew in June 1941 as the Douglas XB-19. The magnitude of the expenditure on these monsters testifies to the deep underlying wish of the Air Corps to deploy real Air Power, to the extent prophesied by Douhet which "would render traditional land and sea forces unnecessary".

One recommendation of the Baker Board was that a General Headquarters, Air Force, should be set up. GHQ/AF was to deploy long-range striking power. It was to be relieved of any responsibility for supporting the Army ground forces, a task which was to be handled by tactical squadrons. GHQ/AF also deployed its own reconnaissance and pursuit squadrons, but in a time known as the Depression many Congressmen fought every

cent devoted to defense, and asked "Who are you going to fight?" There was no obvious enemy, so the objective of the bombers was defense against a hypothetical invasion fleet somewhere far out at sea. The first modern instrument of war allocated to GHQ/AF was the Martin Bomber, whose retractable landing gear could be replaced by seaplane floats to give added flexibility in the coast-defense role. The first assignment of GHQ/AF to hit the headlines was a mission by the brand-new Martins, under Lt-Col "Hap" Arnold, future Chief of Staff, from Wright Field, via Washington, to Alaska, and back via Washington to their base at March Field, California. This mission, in July/August 1934, was the first time US warplanes had attempted any kind of demonstration of strategic power.

Lt Col Arnold had previously driven up to the seemingly limitless Mojave Desert, where after prolonged effort he secured a large parcel of real estate for the Government. He desperately wanted a bombing range — even the Pacific ocean was off-limits, thanks to the Navy — and here at last a range could be set up. There was nothing there but a small settlement whose name was that of a leading inhabitant, Corum, spelt backwards. Here was gradually constructed the greatest bombing range in the world, from which tens of thousands of bombardiers went to demonstrate their skill in all corners of the Earth in 1942-45. There also grew up a fantastic complex of airfields, which in the early post-1945 era proved of incalculable value in thrusting the US ahead into a new supersonic era.

As soon as they got their new Martins, at first B-10s and later B-12s, the 1st Wing in California roared into exercises against new P-26 pursuits. There was not much difference in speeds, and the Martin had no significant blind spot in defense, though the firepower against an attacking fighter was hardly ever more than one of the three 0.30in guns. A tight formation, however, could offer mutual firepower protection, and in conjunction with the Tactical School at Maxwell Field, Alabama, these exercises began to confirm the possibility of making massed strategic bombing missions in daylight. It was clear, however, that greater speed and greater defensive firepower would be needed.

In May 1934 the Air Corps issued a requirement for a new multi-engine bomber. "Multi-engine" was one way of

saying "twin-engined", but the design team out in Boeing's plant at Seattle took a broader view. Wright and P&W had engines in the 1,500hp class coming along, but these were not yet ready. With available 750hp Cyclones or Hornets the Army requirements could only just be met; but what a difference resulted from using four engines! The extra power was needed purely to give more speed and altitude. The result was the prototype Boeing 299, precursor of the B-17. This was the first of many Boeing prototypes to represent a financial risk much greater than the net worth of the company, and also the first of many to provide a colossal increase in US strategic striking power.

Between 1935 and 1942 the B-17 gradually grew in combat capability, and especially in defensive firepower, until large formations really did confront hostile fighters with hundreds of large-caliber rounds per second. Self-sealing tanks and armor, and flak jackets for the crew, all helped these great bombers to survive. At the same time, while the introduction of turbocharged 1,200hp Cyclone engines had upped cruising speed to near 250mph (400km/h) in 1939, the sheer weight of the mass-produced wartime B-17s reduced this to about 170mph (275km/h), and pulled down the altitude. All this was far in the future as, in 1937, the Air Corps played with its shiny

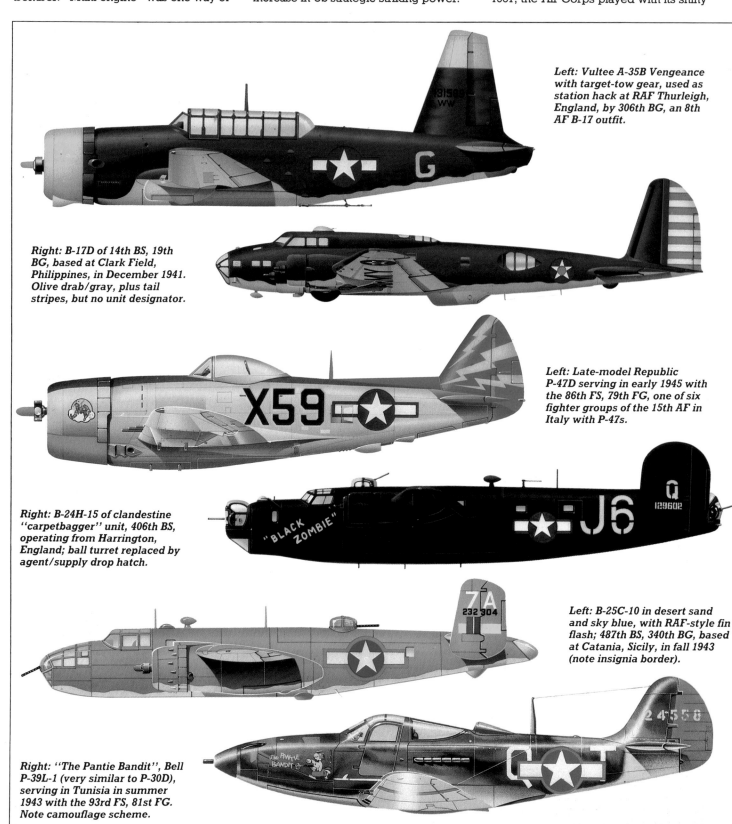

Left: Vultee A-35B Vengeance with target-tow gear, used as station hack at RAF Thurleigh, England, by 306th BG, an 8th AF B-17 outfit.

Right: B-17D of 14th BS, 19th BG, based at Clark Field, Philippines, in December 1941. Olive drab/gray, plus tail stripes, but no unit designator.

Left: Late-model Republic P-47D serving in early 1945 with the 86th FS, 79th FG, one of six fighter groups of the 15th AF in Italy with P-47s.

Right: B-24H-15 of clandestine "carpetbagger" unit, 406th BS, operating from Harrington, England; ball turret replaced by agent/supply drop hatch.

Left: B-25C-10 in desert sand and sky blue, with RAF-style fin flash; 487th BS, 340th BG, based at Catania, Sicily, in fall 1943 (note insignia border).

Right: "The Pantie Bandit", Bell P-39L-1 (very similar to P-30D), serving in Tunisia in summer 1943 with the 93rd FS, 81st FG. Note camouflage scheme.

new Y1B-17s and learned how to navigate over long distances, setting records on every trip. It also learned night flying, and accurate high-altitude bombing.

THE SEARCH FOR ALTITUDE

A major tool in high-level bombing was the Norden bombsight, highly classified from 1936 until near the end of World War II and popularly said to be able to "put a bomb in a pickle barrel". But accurate bombing was just one of many problems encountered as the Army, rather more than the Navy, sought to operate at ever greater altitudes. One officer, Capt O. A. Stevens, had pioneered high-altitude

photography using special developments of the old DH-4M, and in 1935 had gone aloft with Capt Orvil Anderson in a mighty balloon-lifted pressurized sphere and reached 72,395ft (22,066m). A year later the Air Corps bought the Lockheed XC-35 with turbocharged Wasp engines and a pressurized fuselage. On 13 February 1938 the chief Air Corps test pilot, Maj Stanley M. Umstead — later one of the few men to fly the B-19 — was engaged in instrument tests at Chicago, in weather that grounded other airplanes. Louis A. Johnson, at that time Assistant Secretary of War, was stuck in Chicago but urgently needed in Washington. Umstead invited him aboard the XC-35

and took him at 32,000ft (9650m) at a ground speed of over 300mph (483km/h). This showed what the man in the street might enjoy ten years later in the same maker's Constellation.

It also helped Boeing plan its pressurized Model 345 heavy bomber, which was the next generation after the unsuccessful XB-15, carrying the same bombload the same distance but at twice the height and twice the speed, and with dramatically better defensive armament. Turning the Model 345 into the B-29, at a time when the official US Government view was that the B-17 represented the ultimate limit in what was needed in bomber design, was the second time Boeing risked more than its

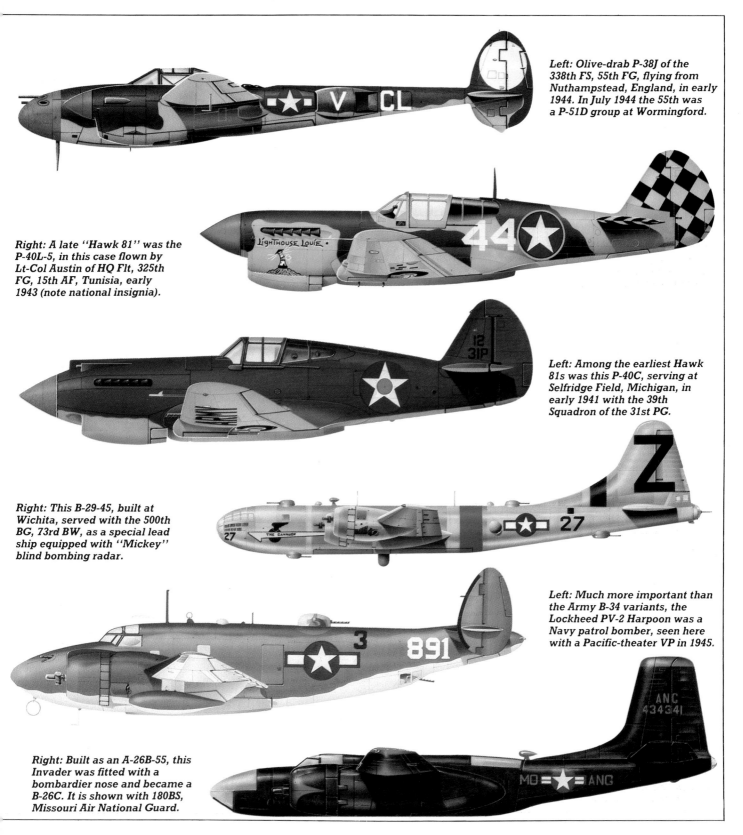

Left: Olive-drab P-38J of the 338th FS, 55th FG, flying from Nuthampstead, England, in early 1944. In July 1944 the 55th was a P-51D group at Wormingford.

Right: A late "Hawk 81" was the P-40L-5, in this case flown by Lt-Col Austin of HQ Flt, 325th FG, 15th AF, Tunisia, early 1943 (note national insignia).

Left: Among the earliest Hawk 81s was this P-40C, serving at Selfridge Field, Michigan, in early 1941 with the 39th Squadron of the 31st PG.

Right: This B-29-45, built at Wichita, served with the 500th BG, 73rd BW, as a special lead ship equipped with "Mickey" blind bombing radar.

Left: Much more important than the Army B-34 variants, the Lockheed PV-2 Harpoon was a Navy patrol bomber, seen here with a Pacific-theater VP in 1945.

Right: Built as an A-26B-55, this Invader was fitted with a bombardier nose and became a B-26C. It is shown with 180BS, Missouri Air National Guard.

net worth. It was becoming evident by the late 1930s that the increasing complexity of combat aircraft was inevitably stretching out the development timescale. Whereas in 1918 a new airplane, or even a new engine, might be with the front-line troops six months after starting the drawings, 20 years later six years was not unusual. This fact was often unknown to politicians, who fondly imagined that in any time of sudden crisis all the nation need do was build a lot more airplanes. Had the Air Corps not boldly planned back in 1940-41 for mass-production of the B-29, not only by Boeing but also by Bell, Martin, Fisher Body and others, the huge armadas of these incredibly advanced bombers would never have happened in time.

Just as Hitler's Luftwaffe was to concentrate on twin-engine tactical bombers, because these could be produced in more impressive numbers than large strategic bombers, so did the Air Corps have to fight endless battles to get its B-17s. The general body of opinion in the War Department was that, as two Martins cost less than a B-17, it was ridiculous to buy the B-17. As for the wish to plan for the next-generation B-29, this was refused point-blank, the US Adjutant-General sending a minute on 13 May 1938 decreeing that "No military requirement exists for the procurement of experimental pressure-cabin bombers in Fiscal Years 1939 or 1940, of the size and type described. The Chief of the Air Corps has been informed that the experimentation and development for the Fiscal Years 1939-40 will be restricted to that class of aviation designed for the close-in support of ground troops, and for the production of that type of airplanes such as medium and light attack, pursuit and other light aircraft."

THE RESTRICTED NAVY

Nor did the Navy have it all its own way, and indeed at that time it never even considered trying to deploy Air Power in the Mitchell sense. It did buy one or two big transport airplanes, some of them being needed by the Marine Corps (which until very recent times always felt it was fobbed off with hand-me-downs cast off by the Navy, which did Marine air procurement). Apart from this the only large Navy airplanes were flying boats, which developed methodically between the wars and in 1935 threw up an exceptionally good design in the Consolidated Model 28 (PBY) which by 1945 far outnumbered all other patrol seaplanes in the world combined. All other Navy airplanes were small, and in accord with the MacArthur/Pratt agreement they went to sea with the Fleet. Some were seaplanes, catapulted from battleships and cruisers for scouting purposes. The rest were landplanes based aboard carriers.

Apart from the old *Langley*, which had been converted from a collier and received its first airplane in October 1922, the Navy's first carriers were the mighty CV-2 *Lexington* and CV-3 *Saratoga*. Both had been started as battle-cruisers, and unlike *Langley* they were among the fastest vessels in the Navy. Both were commis-

sioned in 1927, and with 90 aircraft each they set the Navy off on the long road that was to lead to not only global ship power but also global air power. In 1922 the Washington Naval Treaty had stipulated a limit on displacement of 22,000 long tons (24,640 US tons) for any new carrier. Many in the Navy considered CV-2 and -3 much too big (later these ships were to prove invaluable), and the first purpose-designed carrier was an unimpressive vessel of only 14,500 tons. CV-4 *Ranger* nevertheless carried 75 aircraft, but only at the expense of protection, speed, seaworthiness and armament. She commissioned in 1934.

On 16 June 1933 two new carriers were authorized, and these at last got the balance right. CV-5 *Yorktown* and CV-6 *Enterprise* each had a displacement of 25,500 tons at full load and carried 85 aircraft at high speed. They were followed by CV-7 *Wasp,* which was smaller to comply with treaty limits, and then in 1938 work began on CV-8 *Hornet,* of 29,100 tons. All these fine ships were in service when the Japanese struck at Pearl Harbor on Sunday morning, 7 December 1941. By sheer chance no carriers were in the harbor on that fateful day.

Thanks also to the rise of Germany as a formidable power, and especially as an air power, the US had begun to build up its air strength long before December 1941. It had been assisted in an oblique way by the US airplane industry's increasing success as an exporter. Such customers as Brazil, China and even Republican Spain had kept up employment during the lean 1930s, and from 1938 they were joined by Britain and France. Recognizing that their efforts to avoid war were going to fail, these European nations placed frantic orders on a scale the US had not seen since 1918. Such companies as Lockheed, North American, Douglas, Boeing, Martin, Consolidated, Curtiss,

Below: By 1935 the Navy had seagoing airpower exceeding that of any other nation. Here the carriers Lexington *and* Ranger *are seen, looking aft across the Boeing F4B-4 fighters of VF-6B ranged aboard USS* Saratoga.

Wright and Pratt & Whitney stopped laying off workers and instead began building vast extensions. By 1940 the orders were coming in floods, and on 16 May of that fateful year President Roosevelt, just starting his unprecedented third term, called for US industry to produce 50,000 warplanes a year.

It is difficult from 45 years later to recall how astronomically impossible such a figure seemed. Admittedly Henry Ford replied that his industrial empire could build 1,000 airplanes *a day,* but bearing in mind that the total national output in 1939 had been 921 military aircraft, including trainers, 50,000 caused some debate. World War II was so gigantic in all its dimensions that it cannot possibly be covered here comprehensively, but the fact remains that in the calendar year 1944 the Department of Defense, in its vast new Pentagon building, formally accepted 95,272 airplanes. Again, while in 1940 the Air Corps was staggered to be able to plan to graduate pilots at the rate of 7,000 per year (compared with 120 a few years earlier), in the last year of the war the actual output of very highly trained pilots (Army alone, not Navy) was 105,000.

ARSENAL OF DEMOCRACY

A few further statistics will give a small flavor of the Herculean round-the-clock effort that won World War II. Whereas in the 1930s a galaxy of very advanced liquid-cooled engines were being planned by Continental, Wright, Pratt & Whitney and Lycoming, all were eventually canceled and the war was fought and won with traditional radial engines — but developed to give 2,000, 2,500 and finally 3,000hp. Pratt & Whitney provided half the horsepower for all the American Army and Navy, and 35 per cent of the power for the British Commonwealth forces. With its licencees it delivered during the war itself a total of 363,619 engines, putting out 603,814,723hp!

Meanwhile the Navy coolly planned a force of 32 giant new carriers all of one class. The lead-ship of the class, CV-9 *Essex*, was laid down in 1941 and in the

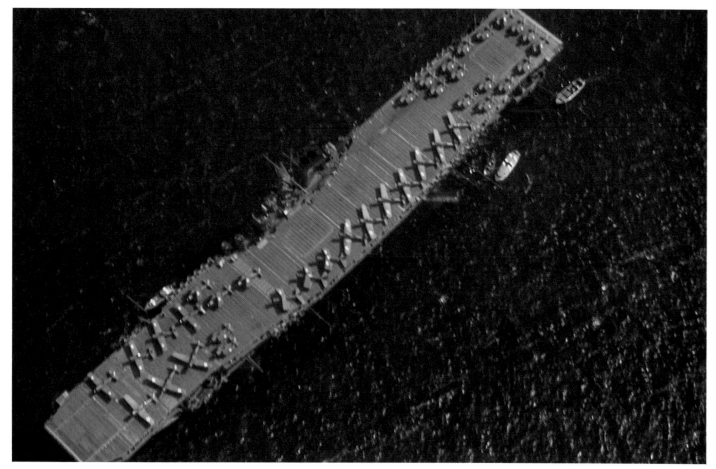

Pacific by May 1943. A ship of 39,800 tons full-load, she benefited from earlier war experience in having not only 12 radar-controlled 5in (127mm) dual-purpose guns but also 68 AA guns of 40mm calibre and 52 (later 70) of 20mm. Aircraft complement was 80, of types far more formidable than before: F6F, TBF, SBD. Behind her came 23 more at frequent intervals, the last eight being canceled. Not for nothing was the US called "the arsenal of democracy".

In general the war was fought and won with the airplanes that existed at the time of Pearl Harbor, the only significant exceptions being the B-29 (which first flew in September 1942, though planned years earlier) and Waco CG-4 assault glider. In the field of pursuits, which increasingly became "fighters" and were redesignated as such from 1948, the dominant type at the start was the Curtiss P-40 for the Army and Grumman F4F for the Navy/Marines. Whereas the F4F held the line aboard Navy carriers totally un-aided throughout the Pacific war until 31 August 1943, the P-40 was swiftly over-taken by better fighters, though large numbers served on all fronts in the tactical attack role. Indeed, Curtiss produced a series of indifferent aircraft — some, such as the SB2C Helldiver, being made in large numbers — and from 1940 went rapidly downhill from its position as No 1 US military and naval planemaker and built its last airplane in 1948. Equally surprising was the fact that not one of the prolific crop of new fighter prototypes flown during the war — most of them highly advanced and unconventional, and powered by all the varied new high-power engines — could equal the existing conventional fighters, the Republic P-47 and North American P-51, the latter

having been designed in 1940 for the British.

In early 1941 the AAF and NACA began studying jet propulsion, and organized the Durand Committee to make recommendations. The result was that Allis-Chalmers received a contract for a tur-bofan engine, General Electric for a tur-boprop, and Westinghouse for a turbojet, all using axial compressors. Within days of the committee being convened AAF Gen "Hap" Arnold was in Britain. To his amazement he was told confidentially of the turbojet developed by an RAF officer, Frank Whittle, which within days was to fly in a new research airplane. Arnold had a Whittle engine (one of two which existed) and drawings sent to Washington, and the very next Allied jet to fly was the Bell XP-59A on 1 October 1942, five months before its British counterpart the Meteor.

ON THE OFFENSIVE

During the war many types of guided bomb and stand-off weapon were developed, and several were used in combat. Remembering the pioneer "cruise missiles" of 1917-18, there was prolonged study of the economics of pro-ducing thousands of modernized missiles for use by both the AAF and Navy, but in the end the idea was rejected. Possibly the gross inaccuracy of the German "V.1" flying bomb of 1944 could be argued to justify that decision.

Be that as it may, the biggest single part of the US air war effort was devoted to the AAF's deployment of Air Power in the form so long believed in. Based in England, the 8th Air Force was establish-ed only a month after Pearl Harbor as the AAF's strategic arm in the European

Above: Taken in 1940, this near-vertical view shows CV-7 USS Wasp with her entire embarked air wing on deck. Most of the aircraft are the F4Fs of VF-7 and the SB2Us of VS-71 and -72. The carrier was to have a distinguished career before being sunk in November 1942.

theater. It was to become the largest single element in an autonomous, though not independent, US Army Air Force created a few months earlier on 20 June 1941. The AAF had the same people in the same uniforms but was organizationally able to continue its amazing expansion until in 1944-45 it exceeded 2,200,000 peo-ple, deployed all over the globe along with over 64,000 front-line airplanes.

Not one reader of this book can be unaware of the titanic campaign fought by the 8th AF in daylight over Hitler's Europe. Day after day B-17s and B-24s by the hundred thundered in formations big-ger than the world had ever seen on long missions to targets as far distant as Czechoslovakia and Berlin, proclaiming their progress by broad white contrails and running the gauntlet of hundreds of deadly interceptors and massive concen-trations of flak. At the start the British said it could not be done, and on occasion losses were grievous; but the sheer might of the 8th, and especially its ability from December 1943 to guard the bombers with long-range P-51 fighters which had the range to go all the way to the target and back, gradually all wore down the Luft-waffe's defences.

A similar outfit was set up in the 15th AF in the Mediterranean, and the 10th AF handled the "forgotten" CBI (China/Bur-ma/India) theater, while the 5th AF operated in the SWPA (southwest Pacific area). Whereas the 8th used mainly the B-17, the strategic units in other theaters

were equipped with the B-24 almost exclusively. Alongside them grew gigantic tactical air forces, which received not only large numbers of P-38s, P-39s, P-47s and P-51s but also thousands of the AF's outstanding twin-engine bombers: A-20s, B-25s, B-26s and, from 1944, A-26s. In the development of night fighters much help was received from the British, notably including the vital new invention of the magnetron which made possible radar operating at centimetric wavelengths. The British also handed over Beaufighters for use until the all-new P-61 became operational in England and the Pacific in July 1944.

Centimetric radar in the most compact form was developed by the Navy to fit into two of the greatest of the wartime single-seat fighters, the F6F and F4U. Many consider the latter the greatest of all piston-engined fighters, but most unfortunately it was thought to have unacceptable deck-landing qualities, and from February 1943 it went into action only with the island-based Marines. The Navy appeared not to notice that its British counterpart, the Fleet Air Arm, was not only using the F4U with great delight but operated a *clipped-wing* version from *small escort carriers*. In April 1944 the Navy ran a further series of trials and decided at last there was no reason why this outstanding warplane should not go to sea, but by that time the F4F and F6F had done most of the hardest work. There just remained the rather unexpected assault by *Kamikaze* suicide aircraft, which among other things rammed home the need for armored carrier flight decks and spurred the urgent development of America's first SAMs (surface-to-air missiles).

EAGLES AND AVGs

Long before Pearl Harbor, American flyers had fought on the side of the Allies. Many had joined Britain's RAF and formed "Eagle squadrons"; after Pearl Harbor these were incorporated into the AAF, and in September 1942 the three Eagle Squadrons became the 8th AF's 4th Fighter Group, soon to be the most famed of all P-45 outfits and, after the pioneer 56th, the top-scoring FG with 583.5 air victories (its combined air and ground-strafing score of 1,052.5 was the highest

Above: Greatest of all winners of the Pacific air war were the Grumman F6F-3 and Douglas SBD, which combined to destroy Japanese power in the air and on the sea. These great airplanes are seen aboard USS Essex in 1943.

of any US unit in history). On the other side of the world from the red noses of the 4th FG were the shark-nosed P-40s of the 23rd FG. This unit had started nearly a year before Pearl Harbor as the AVG (American Volunteer Group) in China, led by the legendary Claire L. Chennault. To give these irregular mercenary pilots something to fly, in their mission to help China put up at least some resistance to the Japanese invader, the US diverted 100 P-40Bs originally earmarked for the RAF. From then until the AVG was absorbed into the AAF as the 23rd Group on 4 July 1942 its score amounted to 286 Japanese aircraft for the loss of 23 pilots. The 23rd became the nucleus of the CATF (China Air Task Force), which in turn became the nucleus of the 10th AF previously mentioned. Finally the CATF again became the nucleus of yet another new AF, the 14th. Until final victory this fought doggedly over China's vast landscape, scoring on average 8:1 against the increasingly desperate Japanese.

There were other Air Forces, too: the mighty 9th was the tactical AF in north-

west Europe, the 7th which moved from Hawaii through dozens of Pacific islands, the 11th in the blizzards of Alaska and the Aleutians, and the 13th which began in the bitter fighting of New Guinea and New Caledonia, and then moved north to Japan. But the last AF to form was the one that abruptly ended the war.

From before Pearl Harbor a growing team of Allied physicists had been working on the possibility of an atomic bomb, based on the predicted chain reaction through a sufficiently large mass of fissile Uranium-235. The first atomic pile (reactor) was constructed under the seating at a stadium at the University of Chicago, and next came stupendous uranium isotope separation plants at Hanford, Washington, and Oak Ridge, Tennessee. This was something not foreseen when the B-29 was created, and this mighty warplane went to war dropping conventional bombs but over wholly unprecedented distances. At first there were severe problems with engine fires, runaway propellers, and many other items, and the distances flown by the inexperienced crews were roughly half what Boeing predicted. Gradually the hardware and the crews got better, and on 4 April 1944 the 20th Air Force was formed purely to deploy this mighty weapon against Japan. At first the new B-29 squadrons had to use airfields in India and China in order to reach targets in Japan, and they flexed their muscles against Bangkok.

MAKING A RISING SUN SET

Setting up major B-29 bases in China was a Herculean task. Hundreds of transports — C-47s, C-46s and various transport and tanker versions of the B-24 — shuttled around the clock flying "over the Hump" of the Himalayas under unbelievably arduous conditions. They brought in men and tools, bulldozers and runway materials, food and fuel. Gradually the bases were brought to the high stan-

Below: SBD-3s, each with a single bomb, positioning for free takeoff from USS Ranger in October 1942. The tail at lower right belongs to an F4F-4. Gray rectangles just beyond the flight deck are armor plates on a row of 20mm anti-aircraft cannon. They had plenty to do that year.

dard needed by a bomber more advanced than any other airplane in the sky. On 15 June 1944 Japan was hit, and by this time the Mariana Islands, newly captured, were converted into five gigantic airbases each able to house a wing of 180 B-29s. From then on Japan's cities and industries were doomed.

On 20 January 1945 the 20th Bomber Command was taken over by a dynamic new Commander, Gen Curtis LeMay. He revitalized the whole command, and among other things changed the mission entirely. Instead of bombing with HE from a formation at 30,000ft (9150m) by day, he ordered a gentle stream of bombers to cross the target at night at only 5,000 to 8,000ft (1,500-2,450m) using incendiaries. This saved fuel and defensive ammunition, roughly doubled the bombloads, and resulted in absolute devastation. The first such mission, on 9 March 1945, left one-quarter of Tokyo gutted, 84,000 Japanese dead and a million homeless, and caused more damage than any other air raid before or since. LeMay's bombers incinerated every major city in Japan, and 57 minor ones. But the fanatical Japanese were fighting savagely and desperately, and something special was needed to bring peace.

The A-bomb provided it. On 6 August 1945 a single B-29 named *Enola Gay* dropped a U-235 type bomb dubbed "Little Boy" on the city of Hiroshima. In a light like a thousand Suns the centre of that city was seared and blasted, and the world entered a new age of awesome power. Three days later another B-29, *Bock's Car*, dropped a Pu-239 type bomb dubbed "Fat Man" on Nagasaki. Just five days later B-29 crews returning from a 3,650-mile (5,875km) round-trip mission to the Nippon Oil Co heard that Japan had surrendered.

The war was won by all the armed forces of all the Allies, but never again would any sane observer underplay the central role of air power in human conflict. And never again would the US let its air power decline relative to other nations as it had between the two World Wars.

TECHNOLOGICAL RACE

After 1945 Britain's new Labour government adopted a different stance. It rated defense almost nowhere on its scale of priorities, exported its most powerful (and world-beating) Nene jet engine to the Russians but made no effort to put it into production for the RAF. In contrast Washington recognized that the nation was engaged in a technological race every bit as serious as war itself. The technical staffs in the Pentagon, at Wright Field, at the Navy Bureau of Aeronautics, in the US industry and at many research centers were not run down but expanded. Captured German aerodynamic data on swept wings were eagerly combed, sifted and put to use in such vital new projects as the XP-86 Sabre and XB-47 Stratojet. Jet engines were developed under the highest priority, and so was the even newer technology of guided missiles.

Though the armed forces were run down in a planned manner to approximately one-tenth of the wartime peaks,

this still left air units many times stronger than in 1940, and the single factor of nuclear weapons — at that time possessed by the United States alone — multiplied roughly a thousandfold the striking power of strategic bombers. This could have been used as an excuse for cutting back such airplanes to a mere handful, but instead the wise decision was taken to create a force with global capabilities called Strategic Air Command (SAC). This came into being on 21 March 1946 as part of a master plan by Arnold's successor as Chief of Staff, Gen Carl "Tooey" Spaatz, which combined AAF combat power into three great commands resembling those of the wartime RAF: Strategic, Tactical and Air Defense.

Even deeper changes were afoot. Back in the war yet another committee had studied the US command structure and in 1945 recommended that a US Air Force be established, coequal with the Army and Navy under a single Department of Defense. This did not bother "Ike" Eisenhower, victor in Europe and from November 1945 Army Chief of Staff, but it was bitterly fought by the Navy. President Truman, however, told the old Navy and War Department that change was inevitable, and the AAF planned in great detail for the Air Force yet to come. On 26 July 1947 President Truman was handed the documents of the 80th Congress' unification bill as he climbed aboard his VC-54C *Sacred Cow* to fly to his dying mother in Missouri. At 15,000ft (4,570m) he signed the National Security Act, as well as Executive Order 9877 defining the roles of the three services, and appointing the disgruntled Navy Secretary James Forrestal as the first Secretary of Defense.

Above: After 6 August 1945 the world was never to be the same again. While the blasted city of Hiroshima was to become a shrine visited by seekers for peace, the nuclear deterrent was to play the central role in preventing major war — at least it has to date.

Below: This B-29-24-BW nose — of interest in view of the combat history there recorded — is representative of the most advanced and complex airplane of World War II, jets notwithstanding. In terms of development and production effort the B-29 story has few parallels.

The United States Air Force came into existence on 18 September 1947, and eight days later Spaatz was sworn in as Commander in Chief wearing the new blue uniform. The Air Force started small, but almost from the first day it was destined to grow. This was not through any imperialist aspirations but because of the increasing might and belligerence of a former ally, the Soviet Union, which through espionage soon came to possess not only the U-235 and Pu-239 fission bombs but also the vastly more powerful fusion, or hydrogen, bomb. Thanks to its "capture" of three B-29s belonging to its supposed wartime ally it also had the means of delivery.

THE COLD WAR

The first of many indications of Soviet policy in what was to become "the Cold War" was started gradually in occupied Berlin in early 1948. Berlin was an island of democracy set in a Communist sea. As such it was regarded by the Russians as an affront, a dangerous center of Western ideas that could infiltrate and pollute its own people. Stalin decided to get the Allies out, but perhaps the Kremlin failed to think the thing through, or it reached a faulty conclusion regarding the will of the Western allies. Following a long period of harassment, all road, rail and canal links to Berlin were shut by the Russians on 24 June 1948. They explained that the railroads needed "repairs", and tore up the tracks to prove it! What followed was the Berlin Airlift, an effort without parallel in history. Nobody knew whether it would be possible to sustain the 2,500,000 Berliners solely by air, though Gen LeMay sounded confident when asked.

It was calculated that 4,500 tons of provisions had to be brought in each day. Gradually the USAF, RAF and civil air carriers gathered aircraft and crews, got the handful of available airfields ready for the traffic, set up rules for the traffic in three crowded air corridors, and started hauling food, military supplies, engineer equipment, cement, coal, sheep and cattle on the hoof, and much more besides. Despite occasional dangerous harassment by red-starred fighters the transports got through, and the tonnage climbed until by May 1949 the daily total was not 4,500 tons but twice this amount. The one thing Russians respect is demonstrable strength, and at midnight on 12 May 1949, the blockade was lifted.

This had a significant effect in showing that the Cold War was no figment of the imagination. It also focussed attention on the long-appreciated fact that small airplanes with a sloping (taildragger) floor and side door were hardly ideal for trucking purposes. The biggest airplane on the airlift had been the C-74, but this was very difficult to load. What was obviously wanted was a high wing joined to an unobstructed cargo hold with a level floor at convenient truck-bed height. Fairchild had provided this with the wartime C-82, but this was slow, unpressurized and had a rear door fairing that could not be opened in flight (though it could be removed and left on the ground). In 1952 Tactical Air Command issued a requirement for a

new transport, and the result was the C-130. To describe this as the DC-3 of the modern era puts this classic design in perspective. Lockheed's advertising claims that this very old airplane "keeps acting newer and newer", and it has outlasted a succession of planned replacements and has a long way to go yet.

SWEPT WINGS

While the USAF had produced a crop of excellent pioneer jet bombers, these were essentially tactical rather than strategic in nature, though a little later the Boeing B-47 really knocked the world for six. Deliberately delayed in order to incorporate wings and tail swept back at 35°, this amazingly bold design also introduced engines mounted in single and twin pods outside the airframe. With drag far below estimate, it could fly missions useful to SAC, especially after Boeing had developed its method of inflight refueling using a rigid boom "flown" into a receiver socket by an operator in the tanker. It so happened that the first production B-47 for SAC flew on the same day that the army of North Korea invaded their neighbors to the south. The resulting war had a profound effect on US military procurement; indeed, never again was it to fall to the low levels of 1946-50.

Korea caught the US off-balance, at the

Above: Seen here taking off from the test center at Moses Lake with the aid of inbuilt rockets, the XB-47 was a glimpse of the future. Its emergence in a piston-engined era can be imagined.

lowest ebb in its military strength since before Pearl Harbor. Worse, the bulk of the air strength was still made up of piston airplanes. A further factor was that, while the few new jets were very fast, they did not take kindly to the short bumpy airstrips, the heat of the Korean summer, and the insistent demands for more bombs and rockets and greater range and endurance. Moreover, because of completely misguided appreciations of Soviet design capability, it was a terrible shock when an unknown swept-wing adversary was encountered on 1 November 1950. This was the MiG-15, made possible by Britain's haste to send Nene engines to Moscow. No Allied fighter could tangle with it, with one exception: the North American F-86 Sabre, the production version of the XP-86 mentioned earlier. This superb fighter was to develop in many forms, the most numerous being the world's first automatic radar-directed all-weather interceptor (which also replaced guns by rockets, salvoed under computer control towards the box of sky where the enemy would be when the rockets reached it). Evenly mat-

Above: Perhaps even more startling, the mighty Northrop XB-35 was developed into a later bomber with eight jets, but (as related overleaf) failed to join the USAF. It was an ancestor of the future ATB.

ched against the MiG, the F-86 dominated its opponent because of great disparity in pilot quality. It thus played a central role in bringing North Korea to the conference table in 1953, and bringing North American Aviation to the top of the league of US defense contractors in 1956.

By this time NAA was also in production with the F-100, the first supersonic fighter in service apart from the MiG-19. Korean experience had resulted in much lobbying by a few senior USAF pilots who were frustrated at being beaten in angle and rate of climb, and high-altitude maneuverability, by the lightweight MiG-15. They said they would trade anything — even the ejection seat, gunsight or fuel — to get on top. One result was the first Mach 2 fighter, the F-104, but in other respects this small-wing airplane showed that the "performance at any price" philosophy was mistaken. A member of the supersonic "Century series" of USAF fighters, which included the F-100, the big twin-engined F-101, all-weather F-102 armed with guided missiles, and the tremendous F-105 "Thud" fighter/bomber, the F-104 kept the Air Force in the limelight,

boosted recruiting and helped to stay on top of the Navy, which had had the effrontery to take the World Speed Record in 1953 with a carrier-based airplane.

In fact the Navy had long been looking at airplanes much bigger than the XF4D that took the record. The biggest ships laid down in World War II had been three carriers of the Midway class, named for the great Pacific battle of July 1942 which, with Stalingrad, marked the turning point of the entire war. With full-load displacement of 62,200 tons, they were almost 1,000ft (300m) long, and could handle aircraft bigger than anything attempted hitherto (the 1942 Doolittle raid on Tokyo using B-25s making free takeoffs from *Hornet* was very far from being normal or even safe practice). Having tasted the fruit of devastating airpower, which far more than anything else crippled the power of Japan, the Navy suddenly saw that it alone had the capability to deploy Air Power in the Mitchell sense against any point on Earth. Jet engines and nuclear weapons served to multiply the possibilities.

Even single-engine airplanes had been transformed by the ability of Pratt & Whitney and Wright to produce more powerful engines. At the Battle of Midway the standard torpedo airplane had been the TBD, with much less than 1,000hp. At the same battle the first six TBFs had gone into action, with 1,600hp, an internally

stowed torpedo and a defensive turret. By the end of the war the 3,000hp Wasp Major engine had made possible the XF8B, AM and TB2D. The TB2D, for example, named Skypirate, is today almost forgotten but it showed what had become possible. Its 70ft (21.3m) wing and massive contra-rotating propellers sufficed to lift *four* 2,000lb (907kg) torpedoes in an internal weapon bay, besides giving it a speed of 350mph (563km/h). Despite this, the mighty Skypirate, along with the smaller BTD Destroyer, remained prototypes while Ed Heinemann went back to his prolific drawing board and created the immortal Skyraider.

Compared with its predecessors the Skyraider was a one-man air force, but the Navy was thinking far ahead. With the Midway carriers it could deploy bigger attack aircraft, and the first generation of these materialized as the AJ Savage, with two powerful piston engines and a jet. For the longer term the Navy wanted a bigger carrier still, and big jet bombers. In 1948 the Navy obtained funds for CV-58 *United States,* bigger than even the Midway class at 65,000 tons and with flush funnels and a retractable bridge to give an absolutely clear deck for the new airplanes. The latter were already being designed by Heinemann's team at Douglas and would emerge in 1952 as the A3D Skywarrior. Predictably such moves generated a powerful reaction by the USAF, and by SAC in particular. Furious battles developed, centered on Capitol Hill, and the outcome was that the new carrier was canceled. In turn, this provoked furious reaction in what was called "the Admirals' Revolt".

SAC was strongly on the upgrade. Back in early 1941 the Air Corps had studied the prospects for the situation following a British defeat. Isolationist or not, there did not seem to be room for the Nazis and the US on the same planet, and the inevitable conclusion was that a way had to be found to bomb Germany from the USA. Airplane technology was just reaching the point at which such a mission was possible, but when the specification was found to require a bombload of 10,000lb (4,536kg) for a radius of 5,000 miles (8,000km) and subsequent return without refueling, the designers whistled. It meant the world's biggest airplane, and the required maximum bombload of 72,000lb (32,659kg) could easily be accommodated. Convair got the job, but wartime pressures delayed the first XB-36 until after the war.

CHOOSING A "BIG STICK"

By this time the B-36 had a rival, and it was one of the most remarkable airplanes ever built. Jack Northrop had always championed the cause of the so-called "flying wing", making the seemingly obvious point that eliminating the fuselage and tail saved weight and drag. After testing various small flying wings Northrop received 1942 contracts for two XB-35s and 13 YBs, the first XB flying on 25 June 1946, six weeks ahead of the XB-36. Whereas the conventional Convair needed six pusher R-4360 engines , the all-wing Northrop needed only four, and on almost every count it appeared to be

Left: Lockheed F-94B-5 Starfire, armed only with four 0.5-in guns, serving with Air Defense Command, USAF, in 1953. Anti-dazzle black ahead of cockpit.

Right: J65-engined Fury, built as an FJ-3M (Sidewinder-equipped) and redesignated MF-1C in 1962. In 1957 this Fury was serving ashore with squadron VF-142.

Left: 25-year-old Martin EB-57B Canberra ECM jammer with the Vermont ANG's 134th Defense Systems Evaluation Sqn. Red is deliberately conspicuous.

Right: This USAF Skyraider was built as Navy AD-5N No 134989 for night attack, and is seen as A-1G No "34989" serving with 1st Special Ops Wing in 1964.

Left: A Grumman F9F-2 Panther, No 123616, rebuilt in 1953 as one of the first missile target drones, designated F9F-2KD. GMGRU-1 was a research unit.

Right: The TF-102 Delta Dagger was subsonic, but served as a combat-proficiency trainer with the "Deuce" squadrons, without unit insignia.

more efficient. It promised almost equal bombload and range, and seen through modern eyes it had a much greater advantage in being a remarkable example of "stealth" design, with absolutely nothing to break the smooth profile of the wing except thin slit cooling inlets in the leading edge and four contra-rotation (later, single-rotation) propellers at the trailing edge.

At the end of the day the B-36 won because it vaguely was thought to present less technical risk, to have more development potential and to offer the opportunity of carrying its own fighter defense in

the form of a tiny McDonnell XF-85 Goblin folded up inside one of its weapon bays. Northrop's brilliant bomber was so good that an initial 200 were ordered from Martin's Omaha plant, which had been building B-29s, but these were canceled. One YB-35 was converted into a YB-49 with eight jets, arranged in two rows of four between two pairs of small fins added to give yaw stability previously provided by the propellers. This flew on 21 October 1947, and was soon joined by a second. An order was then placed for 30 reconnaissance RB-49s, but these were also canceled, as was the EB-35B with four

10,400hp Northrop-Hendy T37 turbo-props. Only one more variant was flown, the YRB-49A of May 1950 with two pairs of J35s of a more powerful type in the wing and two more in single external pods beneath.

Though the B-36 beat the B-35, it had only a fairly brief career as the "big stick" of SAC, despite being updated with four turbojets in outer-wing pods. The airplane that beat the B-49 was not the monster from Fort Worth but a completely new monster from Seattle, the B-52. This had started life in the immediate post-war years, and by January 1948 was under

Left: Air Force 56-032 was built as an F-101C and rebuilt as an RF-101H, seen in the latter form with the 192 TRS from Richards-Gebaur AFB, Missouri.

Right: Identified by its dorsal spine as a Thunderstick II conversion, F-105D 61-0047 served the 563 TFS, 23 TFW at McConnell before joining the ANG's 457 TFS.

Left: F-4B No 152234 served aboard Independence *in the early 1960s with VF-84 Jolly Roger squadron. Tail code AG denoted CVW-7 carrier air wing.*

Right: Now being replaced by the AV-8B Harrier II, this A-4M Skyhawk II serves with VMA-324 from MCAS Beaufort, Maryland. Later painted for low visibility.

Left: An A-7E Corsair II in one of the Navy's experimental low-vis camouflage schemes. This A-7E served aboard Enterprise *with VA-27 Royal Maces Sqn.*

Right: First Pacific AF F-16 outfit was the famed "Wolf Pack" 8th TFW, based at Kunsan AB, South Korea. The stencils have since been toned down.

contract; but at this time it was a turbo-prop rather like the Soviet "Bear". It was Pratt & Whitney's promise of reduced specific fuel consumption from the high-compression J57 engine (an engine of overwhelming importance for fighters and transports as well) that made it possible for the first time to meet SAC's range requirements with a jet — admittedly, a very big jet, with eight of the powerful new engines. The first Stratofortress to fly was in fact the No 2 airplane, the YB-52, on 15 April 1952. At the time this seemed important enough, but nobody then had the slightest idea that the B-52 would not only

be delivered to SAC in eight major versions, but would late in life be required to fly entirely at the lowest safe level, to carry colossal loads of conventional bombs, and finally have various kinds of missiles hung inside and outside whilst being repeatedly gutted and fitted out with totally new avionic systems. When the first B-52 production order was placed in 1951 it was planned that this great airplane would be replaced, possibly by a supersonic bomber, in ten years or less. Today, 35 years later, the B-52 is slated to remain in front-line SAC squadrons well into the 1990s!

During the late 1950s there was much research and study into a CPB (chemical-powered bomber) and an NPB (nuclear-powered bomber). The latter would have had a flight endurance measured in weeks or months, but though Pratt & Whitney and General Electric tested fantastic nuclear turbojet engines, and an operating reactor flew in an NB-36 test-bed, the NPB itself was never built. The CPB, however, became firmer as Weapon System 110A. The problem was the old one of how to get enough range. During the first half of the 1950s Convair had broken a vast amount of new ground in creating the B-58, a SAC bomber with an unrefueled range exceeding 5,000 miles (8,000km) and able to reach Mach 2. This was developed at great cost and equipped two SAC wings, but had a brief active career. In contrast WS-110A finally led to an airplane longer, more powerful, noisier and more costly than anything the world had seen; and it only just missed having the highest speed, longest range and greatest sustained ceiling. The XB-70 Valkyrie was rolled out from the North American (Rockwell) plant at Palmdale in May 1964. This was much later than had been planned, and an unsympathetic Secretary of Defense had already decided against procurement of such a very costly vehicle. A production model would have been designated RS-70, for reconnaissance/strike. The former role could be handled by the even faster "Blackbird" created by Kelly Johnson and Ben Rich at Lockheed's "Skunk Works", while for most of the strike missions SAC could use ICBMs.

The possibility of developing an ICBM (intercontinental ballistic missile) had rather suddenly become apparent as the result of the Teapot Committee under Dr John von Neumann in 1954. The USAF swiftly created a Western Development Division (because most of the contractors, including the specially formed Ramo-Wooldridge company, were in California) headed by a brilliant officer, Brig-Gen Bernard A. Schriever, to manage its biggest project yet. In remarkably short order SAC deployed squadrons and wings of Atlas, Titan I and II, and Minuteman I, II and III. These had a major influence on procurement, not least being that their astronomic cost came out of appropriations that might otherwise have bought airplanes.

SUPERCARRIERS BUILT

Such developments were not unnoticed by the Navy. The Admirals' Revolt alone might have had little effect on Congress, but it so happened that only a few months later, in 1950, the United States found itself involved in a war in remote Korea. Airplanes could get there fairly quickly, but the rapid advance of the North Korean army made it impossible to set up permanent defending airbases. There was only one way to deploy airpower: from the carriers out at sea. Suddenly, carriers were seen as absolutely crucial in getting airpower to the scene of any aggression, even if there were no airfields. An urgent reassessment of the situation resulted in the Navy being authorized to build a fleet of even bigger carriers, and the first batch were CV-59 to -62, commissioned as *Forrestal* in 1955, *Saratoga* in 1956, *Ranger* in 1958 and *Independence* in 1959. Subsequent construction has given the Navy CV-63 *Kitty Hawk* in 1961, CV-64 *Constellation* in 1961, the mighty nuclear powered CVN-65 *Enterprise* in 1961, CV-66 *America* in 1965, CV-67 *John F. Kennedy* in 1968, and the biggest warships ever seen, the nuclear-powered CVN-68 *Nimitz* in 1972, CVN-69 *Dwight D. Eisenhower* in 1977 and CVN-70 *Carl Vinson* in 1982.

Above: North American's F-107 was called "the best plane we ever canceled" by the USAF. The Navy said the same thing, at the same time (1957), about the XF8U-3, which had a similar J75 engine.

Below: As described at left, the XB-70 was in every way a mind-boggling aircraft. This photo was taken minutes before the No. 2 airplane was destroyed in a mid-air collision with the red-tail F-104.

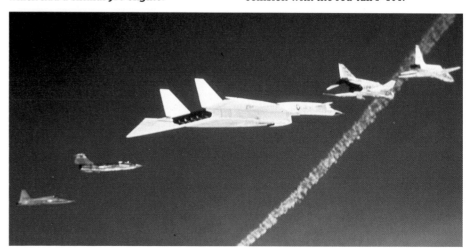

Each of these stupendous vessels is a highly integrated and computerized floating city, with a population of some 6,300 and a cost in current dollars of some $2 billion. They are the supreme example of the deployment of fixed-wing airpower over the world's oceans. Of course they are not indestructible, and the Soviet Union has taken great care to arm its naval attack airplanes with nuclear missiles tailored to precisely that task. Moreover, the point has been made that in the weather encountered by the British task force in the South Atlantic in May 1982 this kind of conventional airpower would have been unable to operate, because there have to be safe weather minima, whereas the British Harrier V/STOLs could recover back to their small unequipped decks in blind conditions.

In due course, in 1961, the original instrument of Navy striking power, the Skywarrior, was succeeded by a supersonic attack airplane, the A-5 Vigilante. This broke almost as much new technological ground as the Air Force's B-58, but it saw only brief service as a bomber because the Navy was spending most of its "strategic" money on a totally new invention, the SLBM (submarine-launched ballistic missile). This has been developed from the Polaris of 1960 through Poseidon to two generations of Trident, and the SLBM is still widely regarded as the only survivable form of deterrence.

This is not to suggest that the Navy has the slightest doubt of the ongoing need for powerful attack airplanes. After all, missiles with self-contained guidance are useless except against fixed targets whose geographic position is precisely known, such as airfields. No sane person would attack a well-defended airfield with a vulnerable manned airplane, because the airplanes are needed instead to hit transient or mobile targets such as armies and navies. In the same way, the development in the 1950s of many families of SAMs in no way lessened the need for the continuing development of fighters, which must intercept intruders and report their identity, destroy hostile airplanes where there are no SAMs (for example, deep in hostile airspace) and collaborate with airborne surveillance and control airplanes and EW (electronic-warfare) jammers in achieving overall control of contested airspace.

Almost unbelievably, the British were so misled by the development of missiles that in April 1957 they announced that manned military airplanes were obsolete. The only British supersonic airplane, the Lightning interceptor, was described as having "unfortunately been developed too far to cancel". It took the best part of ten years for the British to dare to speak of new fighters and bombers, and in fact when the Harrier was invented it had to be built at first as a pure research airplane because warplanes were supposed to have been replaced by missiles. Fortunately none of the US forces came anywhere near following suit, though at just this time one very large and costly fighter, the North American F-108 Rapier, did get axed, partly because of profound difficulty with its proposed ethyl borane "zip fuel" which had also been planned, in a version of the same J93 engine, in the much bigger XB-70.

In the early 1950s the new ability to fly faster than sound seemed to lead naturally to hypersonic warplanes, able to reach Mach 3 to 5. Republic spent much of the 1950s working on the stainless-steel XF-103 interceptor, planned to reach Mach 3.7 (2,446mph, 3,936km/h), but this would probably have ground to a halt even if Wright had not failed to develop the massive tandem turbojet/turboramjet engine. It is a fundamental law of mechanics that an airplane can travel very fast or maneuver, but that it cannot do both at the same time. This is not to suggest that high speed may not occasionally be of great advantage in air warfare, but in any kind of air combat the speed seldom exceeds 450mph (724km/h), and the large excess engine thrust is needed for superior maneuverability in both horizontal and vertical planes.

F-4 YES; TFX MAYBE

It so happened that, as a result of dogged persistence by McDonnell Aircraft, the Navy was persuaded to buy two prototypes of the Phantom II, at the time of first flight in 1958 called XF4H-1s. As the cliché has it, "the rest is history". This large twin-engined, two-seat airplane proved to be so greatly superior to anything in the Air Force that it was bought in enormous numbers for the Navy, Marines and Air Force simultaneously, and became virtually the standard fighter, attack and reconnaissance airplane of 1960-75, a period which encompasses the Vietnam war. This is despite the fact that in the late 1950s the Air Force (TAC) drew up plans for a totally different airplane which was planned to be a "do everything" replacement for the F-100, F-101, F-102, F-104, and F-105, and was confidently expected to be adopted by almost every Allied air force. When the Kennedy administration took office in 1960 the SecDef, Robert S. McNamara, decided that this TFX requirement had much in common with the Navy requirement for a new fighter, and, against the wishes of the customers, he forced through the concept of a common program. The result was the F-111, and this emerged as the world's best all-weather long-range interdiction and attack airplane. It never became a fighter at all, the Navy version being canceled, and this potentially great aircraft, which pioneered today's method of blind first-pass attack on surface targets, had to weather criticism in a hostile press and an unprecedented succession of aerodynamic, propulsion, structural and systems problems before settling down in service not only with TAC/USAFE but also with SAC, as a replacement for the B-58 and early B-52s on limited-radius missions.

A key feature of the F-111 was its variable-sweep "swing wing", which is obviously desirable for any multirole fighter/attack/reconnaissance airplane. Surprisingly, the ebb and flow of fashion began to flow against the VG wing almost as soon as the F-111 reached the Air Force, so that whereas in the early 1960s it

was fashionable to proclaim its advantages, by 1970 this stance had been replaced by concentration on the supposed penalties. It has for 15 years been taken for granted, at least by anyone ignorant of the facts, that a swing-wing airplane must in some way be unacceptably heavy, costly, and operationally inferior. The last VG fighter/attack airplane bought by the US was the Navy's F-14 Tomcat, first flown in 1970 and even today having capabilities far exceeding those of any other interceptor. The F-14 also has considerable attack capability which is not used, whereas the airplane actually used for fighter and attack missions by the Navy and Marines, the F/A-18 Hornet, has fixed-geometry straight wings.

This is not the place for a technical dissertation on aerodynamics and other engineering aspects of airplane design, for the most up-to-date treatment of which readers are refered to a companion volume, *Warplanes of the Future*. But even the most general overview of US military procurement could not fail to comment on the strange results of fashion, which may be harmless when practised by a small country, but which strongly influence the rest of the world when practised by the United States.

Certainly the greatest area for urgent discussion concerns the vulnerability of airfields. In 1953 NATO planning staffs first drew attention to this, and within months a specification was drawn up — a Basic Military Requirement — for a light attack fighter which could operate from any reasonably level area of firm soil, so that in the event of war it could be dispersed away from known airfields. The competition was won by the Fiat G91, which was promptly refused by most NATO air forces and in any case spent its combat career on paved airfields. While the G91 was in service the number of such airfields housing NATO European combat units fell by more than half, to a total of 72, compared with over 4,700 in the same geographical areas in 1945. When this number is compared with the number of warheads on Soviet missiles targeted on those airfields — and airfields are the most obvious and ideal targets for missiles — the answer probably lies in the region of 50 warheads per airfield.

This is surely cause for not mere concern but panic? In the early 1960s the NATO nations addressed themselves a second time to the problem, this time with

requirements for a jet-lift V/STOL tactical airplane and a V/STOL transport to support it. Dozens of proposals were received, and for a while it looked as if NATO nations really were going to deploy air-power that might survive at least for a few days in any future war. For reasons that have never been explained the US posture was to regard the Europeans' concern as misguided, and to ignore the vulnerability of airfields, except for the ridiculous idea that all an enemy might do would be to make a few craters in runways. The whole idea of air-power that can disperse away from airfields has been officially scorned by the US for 20 years and, because the US dominates NATO, this is also the official view of the European NATO nations whose airfields would be the ones that would instantly disappear.

BELIEF IN AIRFIELDS

Instead of recognizing the true situation, the Air Force has instead gradually begun to study ways of "taking off between the craters" – whilst saying rather less about the more difficult problems of landing between the craters. As this is written, in 1996, the Air Force has staked everything on the Lockheed Martin F-22A as its next-generation multirole fighter. There is no question that the F-22 will be an outstanding combat aircraft, providing that it always enjoys runways and taxiways built to a high standard. Apart from the vague claim that its thrust/weight ratio of about 1.2 confers "short takeoff", nothing has been said about how this aircraft, central to the fighting capability of the Air Force in the next century, is going to cope when no suitable runways are available. If in the year 2020 the United States were to be faced with a remote conflict (such as was Britain in retaking the Falklands) the F-22 could not play any part.

The actual required field length of the F-22 is classified, but the figure accepted in the US technical press is 1,500ft (457m). This figure is often accompanied by press releases with artwork showing craters nicely arranged to give a clear

Below: 1984 artwork from McDonnell Aircraft supporting the belief that, with foreplanes and 2-D nozzles, a STOL F-15 could operate from blasted airfields. The author prays for commonsense to emerge.

run of the required length between them, and the use of special electronic landing aids and steep approaches are hoped to enable fighters to land with extreme accuracy, touching down just beyond the first crater and pulling up before meeting the next. Much effort has been expended on rapid runway repair, using precast concrete beams and aluminum matting. Should the craters be too close or too numerous the proposal has been entertained of procuring large numbers of large air-cushion vehicle transporters, on to which airplanes could be loaded and secured. The ACV transporter could then slide over the craters on take-off, the airplane being released just before rotation. So far, landing back on the same transporter has not been suggested. The entire question of base vulnerability seems to the author to betray a staggering lack of imagination of what would actually happen in a real war.

Provided one can shut off one's mind to this, the future of Western airpower looks bright indeed. In the F-15 and F-16 the Air Force still has two of the best tactical aircraft in the world, both with superb air-combat and attack capability and being progressively updated with better avionics and engines. The Navy is sticking with Grumman's excellent F-14 and A-6, but again in improved forms with new avionics and engines, and together with the Marine Corps has built up formidable strength with the F/A-18 Hornet, the first aircraft in history designed to be equally good at both fighter and attack missions. Almost everywhere US airpower goes it is protected, guided and supported by E-2, E-3, E-4, E-6 and E-8 electronic platforms, which as a class are possessed by no other country.

NEW-TECHNOLOGY AIRCRAFT

After the entry to service of the B-52 in 1955-56 the Air Force spent enormous sums wondering where to go next. It spent years evaluating the notion of a Nuclear-Powered Bomber, but never flew a prototype. It looked even harder at the Chemically Powered Bomber, built costly XB-70 prototypes which cruised at Mach 3 burning ordinary fuel, and eventually consigned the survivor to the Air Force Museum, where it is the biggest exhibit. The B-58, which reached Mach 2, did equip two Bomb Wings, but was costly to operate and deficient in radius of action and so had a very short life.

For 20 years various kinds of strategic bomber were studied until the B-1 went ahead in 1970. Seven years later this was cancelled, and only four prototypes were flown. This was immediately after the US had left Vietnam, when weapons were unpopular. President Carter was easily able to claim that a hideously expensive new bomber could be replaced by cruise missiles carried by the B-52. By 1982 the mood had changed, and President Reagan was able to announce that the B-1B – outwardly almost identical but inwardly very different from the original B-1 – would go into production.

What the President did not then announce was that back in 1978 work had begun on a truly fantastic Advanced-

Above: Is this X-29 the future? If so, several current "future fighter" designs are going to be also-rans. In any case, all future warplanes are going to be 100 per cent stealth designs needing no fixed-base airfield.

Technology Bomber, which became the B-2. Since then the nuclear stand-off of the Cold War has been ended by Strategic Arms Limitation Treaties and the dissolution of the Soviet Union in 1991. Today USAF Strategic Air Command has been reorganized as part of Combat Command, and the venerable B-52H is likely to soldier on in that command alongside its new-technology successors far into the Millenium. Equipped with new defensive and offensive avionics and new weapons the B-52 may well serve the USAF for an incredible 80 years, during which time they could (in theory) be flown by four generations of the same family!

The B-2, by far the most expensive aircraft ever put into production, is the ultimate expression of LO (low observables), better known as "stealth" technology. The fact that aircraft could be specially designed to be less visible on enemy radars was known to Sir Robert Watson Watt in 1936. Amazingly, almost nothing was done to make aircraft more stealthy until the 1960s, and then all the running was made in "black" (highly secret) programmes in the United States. The first aircraft to enter service with deliberate stealth features to reduce radar signature was the SR-71, though this also used speed and altitude to accomplish its mission. A totally different form of LO technology was seen in the YO-3A Q-Star, in which aural signature (its noise) was reduced to the level of "rustling leaves".

In the UK there has been plenty of laboratory effort on LO technology but very little money. However, the British-led technology of vectoring the thrust of jet engines has demonstrated that warplanes can go to war even where there is no airfield. As explained earlier, this can also be the key to their survival, because even a sophisticated enemy may not know where jet-lift STOVL (Short Take-Off, Vertical Landing) aircraft are based and so cannot destroy them on the ground.

Today the two technologies of stealth and thrust vectoring have been blended in what must surely be the most important single warplane project in the Western world, the Joint Strike Fighter. This was launched in 1991 as the Navy SSF (STOVL Supersonic Fighter) to replace the AV-8B and F/A-18. Via USAF programmes JAST and CALF it was merged into the JSF in 1995. By early 1997 the announced requirements were: USAF, 2,036 to replace the F-16; USN, 642 to replace the F-14 and A-6; US Marine Corps, 300 to replace the AV-8B; British Royal Navy, 60 to replace the Sea Harrier; total 3,038.

This total easily exceeds that of any other military aircraft for the next century, and is almost certain to be increased to over 5,000 by export sales. The participation for the airframe was narrowed to Boeing (with some Dassault input), Lockheed Martin (with some Yakovlev input) and a team led by McDonnell Douglas and including Northrop Grumman and British Aerospace. All three contenders selected the Pratt & Whitney F119 (engine of the F-22) as first choice, but later contracts were awarded to General Electric to provide an alternative, the YF120-F. Rolls-Royce/Allison also share in the propulsion and lift systems.

As planned, one airframe team was eliminated in November 1996. What was unexpected was that the losing team was that led by McDonnell Douglas, the only team with experience of jet-lift STOVL aircraft in worldwide service. Boeing and Lockheed Martin are now each building two full-scale prototypes of the X-32 and jet-lift X-35. Boeing's STOVL version has a delta wing and a huge chin inlet to a main engine of "three-poster" type with three swivelling nozzles, while Lockheed's design has a trapezoidal wing and sloping lateral inlets to a main engine with a single Rolls-Royce vectoring nozzle and a shaft drive to an Allison lift fan behind the cockpit. These prototypes will be used for testing from airfields, followed by carrier testing and demonstrations of STOVL and hovering. British Aerospace expects to participate, and McDonnell Douglas has said it will take part if requested.

The Directory

There have been many hundreds of types of American warplane. During World War II, for example, US forces pressed into service thousands of former civil airplanes, nearly all of which were assigned official military designations. Quite often the same designation applied to groups of inter-related aircraft of which no two were completely alike. Foreign airplanes were often bought individually for use by Air Attachés at foreign embassies, and during the war front-line units overhauled and put into use captured enemy airplanes of dozens of types, ranging from the lightweight STOL Fieseler Storch to the massive Italian S.M.82 Canguru transport.

To have included every aircraft ever used by US forces would have been counter-productive. We had to set some limits on what was in any case a considerable task, and the responsibility for the final choice is accepted by the author, who apologizes for perhaps omitting any reader's favorites. In general, if the aircraft got into any kind of US military service and shot bullets or dropped bombs, then it is in these pages.

In addition most of the important patrol and transport airplanes are here, and certainly all the recent ones. So too are virtually all the significant reconnaissance airplanes, which used to be known as Observation airplanes. Even some of the most important trainers are here, especially if they served in a FAC or Co-In role, as well as the original Wright biplanes which it was felt merited inclusion on historical grounds. Lighter-than-air aviation is covered by two entries, one non-rigid on "blimps" and the other on rigid airships, both inserted in the year 1931.

This leads to the question of the basic arrangement of the book. There were several obvious choices. We could have attempted subdivision into "Fighters", "Bombers" and so forth, but not only have the names of the missions changed but many of the most important airplanes simply do not fit such rigid compartmentation. Where do we put the few dozen variations of the C/KC-135? Is the F-111 a fighter or a bomber? Or, we could have chosen a straightforward alphabetical listing by maker: but then one company alone (Chance Vought, Vought, Vought-Sikorsky and LTV) is enough to highlight the difficulties. We could have brutally split the book into "Army", "Navy", "Air Force", Marine Corps" and "Coast Guard" (yes, we did not ignore the USCG, who have to be ready for various kinds of war and once bombed and sank a U-boat). This obviously leads to' duplication.

We chose instead a straightforward chronological sequence, based on date of first flight. One problem here is that some important types flew a long time before they became US warplanes. No airplane has done more for the US armed forces than the DC-3 in its many forms, but when if flew on 17 December 1935 it was not even the DC-3 but the DST, the Douglas Sleeper Transport. Yet this was clearly the "right" date to choose, because one of our objectives was to slot each type into a reasonable timeframe, putting it in the context of the technology of the times and facilitating comparison with its contemporaries. Thus, the B-17 is seen as four years earlier in design than the B-24, at a time of rapid technical development. Yet, while sticking with the 1,200hp Cyclone engine, Boeing succeeded in developing the older bomber so that in World War II there was not much difference between them in mission effectiveness.

The last major point to be mentioned is that we have not included foreign imports, or foreign airplanes used by US units in the two World Wars. This is a book about *American* warplanes, and under such a heading we found we could not exclude the DH-4 variations and the B-57.

Above: Over 40 years ago the skies reverberated to the sound of giant colorful armadas, such as the USAAF 447th BG's B-17Gs forming up for another mission.

Above: Today attacks are often delivered by single items of ordnance, which hit the target. An example is this GBU-15 glide bomb from a PACAF 3 TFW F-4E.

Wright Flyers

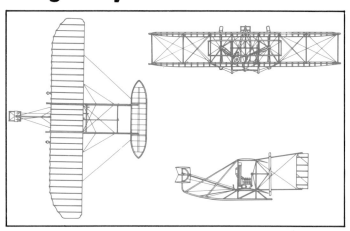

Curtiss R series

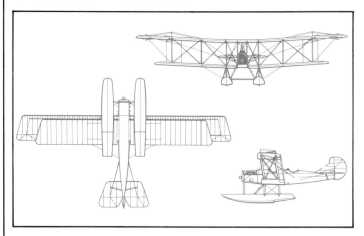

Origin: Wilbur and Orville Wright (from December 1909, Wright & Co.), Dayton, Ohio.
Type: Trainer/observation; data for Model A.
Engine: One 21hp (approx) Wright 4-cylinder water-cooled inline.
Dimensions: Span 41ft (12·5m); length 29ft (8.84m); height (excluding launch rail) 9ft 7in (2.9m); wing area 510sq ft (47.4m²).
Weights: Empty 710lb (322kg); maximum about 1,050lb (476kg), depending on occupants.
Performance: Maximum speed 39-44mph (63-71km/h); range c80 miles (129km) in 2h 25 min.
Armament: See book Introduction.
History: See below.
Users: Army, Navy.

In early 1905 the Wright brothers wrote to the US War Department offering to supply airplanes for scouting purposes. What happened is described in the Introduction to this book. Not until 1908 did the Army show interest, and at last a Model A was brought to the Army at Fort Myer, near Washington, in

Above: The Wright Model A, the world's first military airplane, has been restored and hangs in Washington's National Air and Space Museum.

August. On 3 September Orville made the first public flight in the United States. Over the next two weeks Orville flew intensively, often with a passenger and sometimes airborne for over an hour. On 17 September bigger propellers had been fitted, and these caught a vibrating wire. In the ensuing crash Lt Thomas B. Selfridge was killed.

The Model A was rebuilt and later accepted by the Army, which went on to buy two Model Bs (with elevator moved to the rear), seven dual Model Cs and an F. The Navy bought seaplanes, just able to rise from smooth water: three C-H (similar to Model B), a G Aeroboat and a K (which, like the Army F, had a proper fuselage). All retained warping wings and twin chain-driven propellers, and the basic technology of these famous biplanes was soon overhauled by others.

Origin: Curtiss Aeroplane and Motor Co, Buffalo, NY.
Type: Observation.
Engine: One V-type water-cooled, see below
Dimensions: Span 57ft 1¼in (17.4m); length (R-6L) 33ft 5in (10.19m); height (L) 14ft 2in (4.32m); wing area 613sq ft (56.95m²).
Weights: (6L) empty 3,325lb (1,508kg); maximum 4,500lb (2,041kg).
Performance: Maximum speed (6) 88mph (142km/h); (6L) 100mph (161km/h); service ceiling (typical) 11,000ft (3,350m); range (6L) 565 miles (910km).
Armament: Some fitted with pivoted Lewis (or other) machine gun; many fitted to carry light bombs, and (1919) one torpedo.
History: First flight (R-2) 1915, (R-6) 1917.
Users: Army, Navy (and British RNAS).

The Curtiss R-2 appeared in 1915 as a conventional two-bay biplane with a 150hp Curtiss V-X and the observer seated ahead of the pilot. The Army took 12 and 100 went to

Above: Best-known of the family was the R-6, seen here as a float seaplane. The engine was the 200hp Curtiss V-X-X, a water-cooled V-8 (R-6L, Liberty engine).

the RNAS. The Navy R-3 had span increased from 48ft 4in to the figure given above to support extra weight, mainly because of the twin floats. The Army received 55 improved R-4s with the short wings and 200hp Curtiss V-X-X or V-2-3, a water-cooled V-8 like the V-X. These saw action on the Mexican border against Pancho Villa.

In 1918 the Army received 12 Liberty-engined R-4L, followed by 18 R-6 with the 200hp engine but long-span wings. The Navy received 158 R-6, which were in combat duty at Ponta Delgada, Azores, from January 1918. Almost all Navy machines were seaplanes, and over 130 were re-engined as R-6Ls with the powerful 400hp Liberty. The Navy received 40 R-9 bombers, ten being passed to the Army as landplanes.

The Naval Aircraft Factory PT (patrol torpedo) series mated R-6L fuselages and tails with the long-span wings of the Curtiss HS-1L (PT-1, 15 built) or HS-2L (PT-2, 18 built).

Below: The Army bought at least this example of the R (Roadster) of 1910, without a front elevator.

Bottom: Lt Lahm with Orville Wright and the rebuilt Model A on 27 July 1909.

Below: Pouring gas from an open bucket through a giant funnel into a 200hp R-6 in 1918.

Curtiss H series ("Large America")

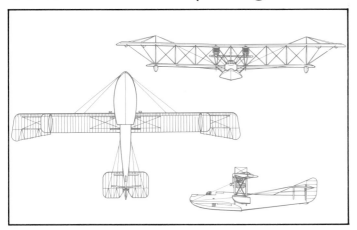

Origin: Curtiss Aeroplane and Motor Co, Garden City, NY; also made by Naval Aircraft Factory, Philadelphia, Pennsylvania.

Type: Maritime patrol flying boat with crew of four; data for H-12L.

Engines: Two 330hp Liberty 12 12-cylinder vee water-cooled.

Dimensions: Span 92ft 8in (28.25m); length 46ft (14m); height 16ft 9in (5.1m); wing area 999sq ft (92.81m²).

Weights: Empty 5,800lb (2,631kg); loaded 7,989lb (3,624kg).

Performance: Maximum speed 85mph (137km/h); climb to 5,000ft (1,524m) in 15 minutes; service ceiling 10,800ft (3,292m); range at 75mph (121km/h) 450 miles (724km).

Armament: Two 0.30in or 0.303in Lewis machine guns in bow cockpit, single Lewis in rear gunner's cockpit between wing spars; racks under lower wing for four 100lb (45kg) or two 236lb (107kg) bombs.

History: First flight (H-8) probably July 1916; (H-12) probably late 1916; first delivery (H-12) February 1917; final delivery (H-16) October 1918.

User: Navy.

Cdr John C. Porte, one of the pioneer pilots of the British Royal Naval Air Service, resigned his commission in 1913 and joined the American Curtiss company, a pioneer of flying boats. His immediate objective was to fly Rodman Wanamaker's special flying boat, "America", being built to try to win the £10,000 prize offered by the *Daily Mail* newspaper for a flight across the Atlantic. War prevented the flight and Porte rejoined the RNAS. He soon persuaded the Admiralty to order two Curtiss boats similar to "America".

Eventually 64 were bought, 58 made in Britain; all eventually had the 100hp Anzani engines instead of the original Curtiss OX-5. Even so, they were nothing like powerful enough and so Curtiss was asked to build what became the "Large

Right: A-774 was one of the 19 production examples of the H-12 built for the US Navy. This model had a very broad planing bottom which terminated under the wings. All later models had it continued right aft.

Above: The first production model was the H-12, with a wooden hull with a short planing bottom and two 200hp Curtiss engines. Some had an open cockpit.

America" boats. The first was the H-8, with 160hp engines delivered in July 1916. In Britain 275hp Rolls-Royce Eagles were substituted and a batch of 50 was ordered. Though still bad sea boats, the H-12s were excellent in the air and soon established a great reputation.

On 14 May 1917 one shot down a

Above: Seen on takeoff, No 767 was the fourth H-12 built for the US Navy in 1916-17. Standard engine of the USN H-12 was the 200hp Curtiss V-X-X.

Zeppelin over the North Sea, the first aircraft ever to fall to an attack by a US-built machine. It was only six days later than another H-12 scored the first aerial victory against a submarine.

In January 1918 the RNAS began to receive improved H-12Bs and 20 were supplied to the US Navy, the

final engine being the Liberty, which changed the designation to H-12L.

Best Curtiss of all was the H-16, with an efficient two-step hull designed by Porte, and more guns and bombs. The RNAS had 75 with 345hp Eagle engines and the US Navy chose the 400hp Liberty.

Curtiss' plant could not meet the demand for these excellent boat seaplanes, and eventually the Naval Aircraft Factory built 150 and Curtiss 124. A few remained in service until 1928.

Above: An H-16 of the US Navy photographed (at NAS Rockaway, NJ?) in late 1919.

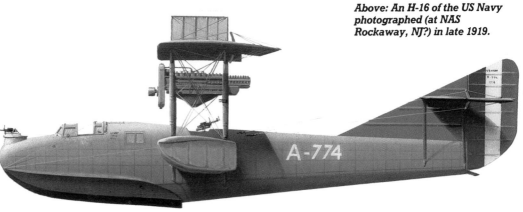

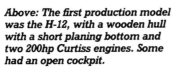

A-774

Curtiss HS series

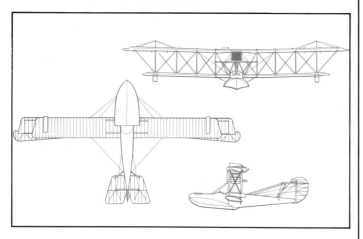

Naval Aircraft Factory F-5L

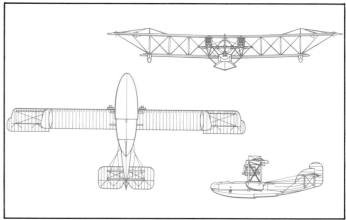

Origin: Curtiss Aeroplane and Motor Co, Garden City and Buffalo, NY; other builders see below.
Type: Patrol flying boat.
Engine: (except HS-1) one 350/375hp Liberty V-12 water-cooled.
Dimensions: Span (1) 62ft 1in (18.92m), (2) 74ft (22.57m); length 38ft 6in (11.73m); height 14ft 7in (4.27m); wing area (1) 653sq ft (60.66m²), (2) 803sq ft (74.6m²).
Weights: (2L) empty 4,300lb (1,950kg); maximum 6,432lb (2,918kg).
Performance: Maximum speed (1L) 88mph (142km/h), (2L) 82.5mph (133km/h); service ceiling (all) about 5,200ft (1,585m); range (2L) 517 miles (832km).
Armament: One or two 0.30in Lewis machine guns aimed from bow cockpit, two depth bombs of (1L) 180lb (81.6kg), (2L) 230lb (104kg).
History: First flight (H-14) late 1916, (1L) 21 October 1917.
User: Navy.

Among the great diversity of Curtiss wartime products the HS series stand out as actually seeing combat duty in the greatest numbers, operating from ten stations on the French coast. The H-14 boat seaplane (flying boat) was powered by

Below: The HS series were the most numerous Navy patrol aircraft of World War I, and they also pioneered the operational use of the Liberty engine. This is an HS-2L (unit unknown).

Above: The Curtiss HS-2L (along with the -1L) was by far the most important Navy patrol airplane in the European theater. It helped start Boeing and Lockheed.

two pusher 100hp Curtiss OXX-2 V-8s, but its poor performance was improved after its conversion as the HS-1 (H Single-engine) with a 200hp Curtiss VX-3.

In summer 1917 the Navy received 16 HS-1s, but on 21 October one was used as testbed to fly the new Liberty 12. Performance was so improved that this became standard, designation becoming HS-1L. A colossal manufacturing plan was quickly devised, and by the Armistice on 11 November 1918 Curtiss had delivered 675 HS boats, while a further 475 had been supplied by Standard, Willard and Fowler, Gallaudet, Boeing and Loughead (Lockheed).

HS boats were tough and serviceable. Different builders introduced small variations, notably in control surface balance (Boeing omitted lower-wing ailerons). HS-1Ls had a cylindrical fuel tank above the upper wing, and the crew comprised the bow gunner/observer and side-by-side pilots further aft. Early in production an extra 6ft (1.83m) panel was added on each side of the centre section to enable the anti-submarine bombload to be increased (the smaller bombs having proved ineffectual against submerged U-boats). The resulting -2L became the standard type, serving until 1926.

Origin: Naval Aircraft Factory, Philadelphia, Pennsylvania; other builders see text.
Type: Patrol flying boat.
Engines: Two 400hp Liberty 12A V-12 water-cooled.
Dimensions: Span 103ft 9¼in (31.63m); length 49ft 3¾in (15.03m); height 18ft 9¼in (5.72m); wing area 1,397sq ft (129.8m²).
Weights: Empty 8,720lb (3,955kg); maximum 13,600lb (6,169kg).
Performance: Maximum speed 90mph (145km/h); service ceiling 5,750ft (1,750m): range 830 miles (1,335km).
Armament: Six/eight 0.30in Lewis guns and four 230lb (104kg) bombs.

Above: Even a keen spotter would have to look carefully to tell an F-5L from an earlier H-16. Differences included hull form, ailerons and vertical tail.

History: First flight 15 July 1918.
User: Navy.

The Curtiss H-12 and -16 were developed at Felixstowe, England, into the F series under the direction of Sqn Cdr John C. Porte, RNAS. A major improvement was a new hull with wide sponsons on each side giving better seaworthiness and faster takeoff. The Navy decided to take the story full circle and adopt

DH-4 Liberty Plane and O2B

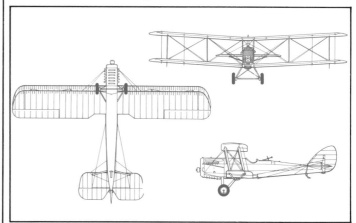

Origin: Based on Airco D.H.4; main production by Dayton-Wright, Fisher and Standard, followed post-war by many companies and Army depots, including Boeing, Fisher Body, Atlantic (Fokker) and Naval Aircraft Factory.
Type: Observation, bomber and many other duties.
Engine: Almost always 400/420hp Liberty V-12 water-cooled.
Dimensions: Span 42ft 5in (12.94m); length (typical) 29ft 11in (9.12m); height (typical) 9ft 8in (2.95m); wing area 440sq ft (40.88m²).
Weights: (Typical 4B) empty 2,939lb (1,333kg); maximum 4,595lb (2,084kg).
Performance: (Typical 4B) maximum speed at sea level 123mph (198km/h); service ceiling

Above: DH-4 versions formed by far the most numerous type of American military airplane until well into the 1930s.

14,000ft (4,270m); range 550 miles (885km).
Armament: As originally built, usually two 0.30in Marlin guns fixed above forward fuselage, two similar guns on Scarff ring in rear cockpit, and underwing bombload of 322lb (146kg).
History: First British airframe imported 15 August 1917 and flown with Liberty engine 29 October 1917; retirement of last DH-4M-2P 1932.
Users: AEF, AS, AAC, Navy, Marine Corps.

No US military type was subjected to more modifications and conver-

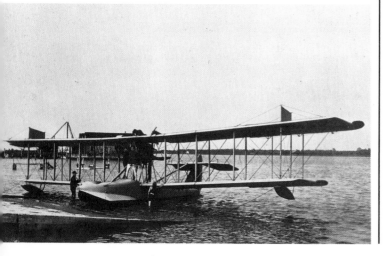

Above: The F-5L was a British design adapted to mass-production in the USA. This one is seen post-war (national insignia dated from August 1919).

Right: This F-5L was one of a batch of 60 built by Curtiss. It is seen after the Armistice, possibly in the post-1922 period when it had become a PN-5.

the British F-5 as successor to the H-16. On 15 March 1918 an RNAS officer arrived at the NAF with F-5 plans, and these formed the basis for the Navy F-5L with Liberty engines. Compared with the H-16 the new boat had greater span, parallel-chord ailerons with large tip horn balances, and extra rudder balance area under the horizontal tail. Orders were placed in hundreds, and though most were

canceled at the Armistice the NAF still delivered 134, Curtiss 60 and Canadian Aeroplanes 30. Four more were assembled from spares at NAS Hampton Roads and San Diego. Two F-6Ls had redesigned vertical tails with curved fin and top rudder balance, and most post-war F-5Ls were rebuilt thus, being redesignated as PN-5s. They were standard throughout the 1920s and led to the later PN series.

---

sions than the famous "de Havilland 4", which was picked in April 1917 as a major warplane for US construction. In fact there was then no de Havilland company, the D.H.4 being a high-speed two-seat bomber by the Airco firm. Made of wood, it had an excellent performance but suffered from shortcomings, notably the long distance separating pilot and observer. In the US the heavy fuel tank between the cockpits was also criticized on grounds of safety.

Despite this the basic airplane was superb, and its tremendous success in British hands was linked with its obvious suitability for the Liberty engine. On 25 May 1917 the first war procurement program included 1,700 "Liberty Planes", a number soon raised to 9,500. No fewer than 3,227 were delivered by 11 November 1918, at which date 628 were with AEF squadrons at the Western Front, the first mission being flown on 2 August 1918. Another 15 were with the 9th and 10th Marine Squadrons at Dunkirk.

Altogether the three original makers delivered 4,846 DH-4s. From July 1918 the DH-4A introduced an improved fuel system, and in October 1918 production switched to the DH-4B in which the pilot changed places with the tank, the landing gear was moved forward and the fuselage was fully plywood-skinned. In the fund-starved post-war era the DH-4B remained by far the most important US warplane, and from 1923 the

Army authorized a major rebuild program which mated the wings, tail and other parts with a completely new fuselage of arc-welded steel tube. Boeing developed the fuselage and delivered DH-4M-1s (M for modernized), while Atlantic (Fokker) built DH-4M-2s.

In the 1920s there were well over 100 sub-variants of 4Bs and 4Ms including models for photo-reconnaissance, ambulance (casevac), transportation, dual training, gas/smoke spraying, target towing, inflight refueling and many other tasks. The O2B-1s were Navy/Marines observation airplanes built by Boeing in 1925. Strangest rebuilds were the Twin DH-4s built in 1919 by LWF for the US Post Office. Ten of this model, with two 200hp Hall-Scott engines mounted between the wings and with a triple-fin tail, went to the Army.

Above: Another British wartime design, the DH-4 was made in vast numbers and served into the 1930s. This was one of the DH-4Bs passed to the Navy in 1918.

Below: This Army DH-4 (British rendering was D.H.4) shows how the fuel tank between the cockpits made it difficult for the pilot and observer to communicate.

Martin MB-1/MT

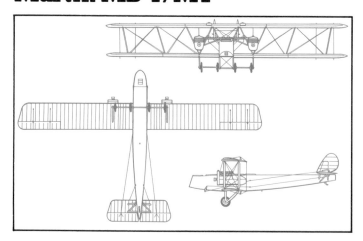

Origin: Glenn L. Martin Co, Cleveland, Ohio.
Type: Bomber, reconnaissance and (MT) torpedo carrier.
Engines: Two 400hp Liberty 12A V-12 water-cooled.
Dimensions: Span 71ft 5in (21.77m), (MT) 74ft 2in (22.6m); length 44ft 10in (13.67m); height 14ft 7in (4.45m); wing area 1,070sq ft (99.4m²).
Weights: Empty (MB) 6,702lb (3,040kg); maximum (MB) 10,225lb (4,638kg), (MT) 12,098lb (5,488kg).
Performance: Maximum speed 105mph (169km/h); service ceiling 10,300ft (3,140m): range (MB) 390 miles (630km).
Armament: Usually twin 0.30in Lewis or Marlin in nose, two in rear dorsal cockpit and one in rear ventral hatch, plus bombload under wings and fuselage of 1,040lb (472kg).
History: First flight 17 August 1918, (MT) 1920.
Users: AS, Navy, Marine Corps.

Glenn Martin, one of America's pioneer aviators, withdrew from the Wright-Martin company in 1917 and set up on his own. He was ask-

Above: Slight anhedral of wings was an optical illusion; they were horizontal. In its day the MB-1 was just called the GMB.

ed to design a bomber better than the British Handley Page O/400, and on 17 January 1918 the Army contracted for ten GMBs (Glenn Martin bombers). Better known by company designation MB-1, these were good and tractable machines, their relatively small size resulting in small bombload but good performance and versatility. Provision was made for a crew of four, or five if an engineer sat beside the pilot.

The Army received 22 GMBs, one being completed as the GMT (transcontinental) with extra fuel, and another as the GMC (cannon) with a 37mm gun in the nose cockpit. The Navy procured two MBTs (bomber torpedo) followed by eight MTs (torpedo), which had the larger wings of the NBS (MB-2). Later designated TM-1, the MTs were used by the Marines, one duty being parachute training from wing platforms. The Martins' most famous exploit was sinking battleships in 1922 (see Introduction).

Above: This contemporary painting shows the wing-tip protection skids, and the unusual pairs of V-struts carrying the engines.

Below: Martin is standing (left) near the nose of the 21st GMB, which is factory fresh. Note the wartime wing insignia.

Navy/Curtiss NC-1 to NC-10

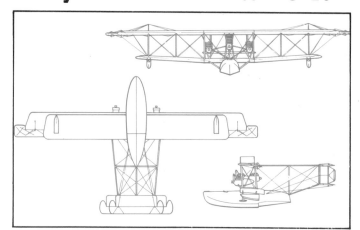

Origin: Joint design by Curtiss at Garden City, NY and NAF at Philadelphia, Pennsylvania.
Type: Patrol and ASW flying boat.
Engines: Three or four 400hp Liberty V-12 (see text).
Dimensions: Span 126ft (38.4m); length 68ft 3in (20.8m); height 24ft 6in (7.47m); wing area 2,380sq ft.

Above: The transatlantic NC-4, which had three tractor engines and one pusher engine.

Weights: (NC-4) empty 15,8740lb (7,200kg); max 27,386lb (12,422kg).
Performance: (NC-4) maximum speed 85mph (137km/h); service ceiling 4,500ft (1,370m): range

Above: NC-4 was by far the most famous, though the less-powerful NC-1 flew with 51 people on board.

about 1,500 miles (2,400km).
Armament: Seldom fitted.
History: First flight (1) 4 October 1918, (others) 1919-20.
User: Navy.

In September 1917 the Navy issued a requirement for a giant flying boat able to fly across the Atlantic, by stages, and go straight into action against U-boats. Curtiss built the first four, with assembly at NAS Rockaway. Ten of the monsters were built, all having a short hull of laminated veneers, with a spruce

Thomas-Morse MB-3

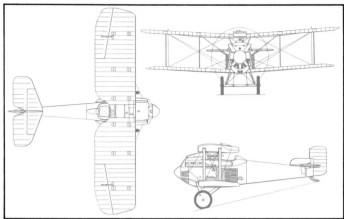

Origin: Thomas-Morse Corporation, Ithaca, NY.
Type: Single-seat scout, data for Boeing MB-3A.
Engine: One 300hp Wright-Hispano H-3 V-8 water-cooled.
Dimensions: Span 26ft (7.92m); length 20ft (6.1m); height 7ft 8in (2.34m); wing area 228.5sq ft (21.2m²).
Weights: Empty 1,716lb (778kg); maximum 2,539lb (1,152kg).
Performance: Maximum speed 141mph (227km/h); service ceiling 19,800ft (6,040m): range 270 miles (435km).
Armament: Two synchronized machine guns, usually one 0.30in and one 0.50in.
History: First flight 21 February 1919, (3A) June 1922.
Users: AS, Marine Corps.

Above: Despite its lumpy appearance the MB-3A was fast and agile, especially with its production type tail (illustrated).

Above: This MB-3M trainer was rebuilt at Fairfield Air Intermediate Depot, hence the "FAID" on the rudder.

Below: Left side of the same MB-3M, showing the insignia of the 43rd School Squadron at Kelly Field, Texas, in 1926.

To meet the urgent demand for fighting scouts the French Mission to the US designed the Packard Le Pere LUSAC-11 but only 25 production models of this speedy machine were built. Orenco produced the Model D, which was even faster, and the Army bought 50 production models from Curtiss.

Loening's high-wing monoplanes led to the PW-2, but only ten were ordered.

In the long term the chief contract winners were Thomas-Morse and a little known firm in the far northwest called Boeing. In spring 1918 T-M was in production with S-4 advanced trainers when it was asked to produce a scout (fighter) better than the Spad XIII. A traditional wood/fabric machine, it used virtually the same engine as the Spad, with the radiator flush inside the upper center section. It proved fast, and four prototypes were followed by 50 MB-3s despite the glut of aircraft in 1919. In 1920 the Army ordered 200 more; putting the job out to tender the low bidder proved to be Boeing. The resulting 200 MB-3As had radiators moved to the fuselage sides, most had Boeing four-blade propellers and the final 50 had much larger fins. All were delivered by December 1922, and a few survived as MB-3M trainers until 1927.

T-M hung on through the 1920s and at last secured major Army orders for the O-19 family of observation biplanes. These began as metal versions of the Douglas O-2.

framework carrying the biplane tail with two or three fins.

All had similar unequal-span wings, but NC-1 had three tractor Liberty engines and the two pilots sitting in the central engine nacelle. NC-2 had two push/pull tandem engine nacelles with the pilots in a third nacelle between them. NC-3 and -4 moved the pilots to the hull and had three tractor engines and one pusher. NC-5 and -6 had two tractors and one pusher, and -7 to -10 were similar to -3. They saw little active duty, but on 16 May 1919 three departed from Trepassy Bay, Newfoundland, to cross the Atlantic. NC-4 made it, via the Azores and Lisbon, to Plymouth. NC-3 reached the Azores, taxiing the last 200 miles (320km) to Horta harbor, where it remained. NC-1 was also forced down but sank, the crew being rescued.

Right: Close-up showing the arrangement of the four Liberty engines in the NC-4.

Martin MB-2/NBS

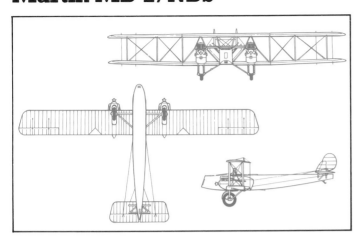

Origin: Glenn L. Martin Co, Cleveland, Ohio; other builders see text.
Type: Night bomber.
Engines: Two 420hp Liberty 12A V-12 water-cooled.
Dimensions: Span 74ft 2in (22.61m); length 42ft 8in (13m); height 14ft 8in (4.47m); wing area 1,121sq ft (104.14m²).
Weights: Empty 7,269lb (3,297kg); maximum 12,064lb (5,472kg).
Performance: Maximum speed at sea level 99mph (159km/h);

Above: Though others built similar bombers, only Martin's were called MB-2s. The triangular sections at the trailing edge folded to allow the complete wings to fold.

service ceiling 8,500ft (2,590m): range 558 miles (900km).
Armament: Usually two pairs of 0.30in Lewis or Marlin in nose and rear cockpits and single gun in rear ventral hatch, plus bombload of up to 3,000lb (1,361kg) with

Above: Army Air Service cadets receiving instruction on the new General Electric turbo-superchargers on one of the Curtiss NBS-1s, with service ceiling close to 20,000ft (6100m).

internal stowage for 1,800lb (816kg) and external racks for single bombs of 1,650lb (748kg) or 2,000lb (970kg).
History: First flight 1920; service career March 1921 to August 1928.
Users: AS, AAC.

Above right: Parachutists are standing behind the interplane struts of this NBS, ready to be pulled off by the slipstream on pulling the rip cord. The bomber would have been olive drab.

Martin improved the MB-1 by slightly increasing span, rearranging the struts, mounting the engines on the lower wing, shortening the fuselage, simplifying the landing gear and providing internal bomb stowage. The wings were arrang-

Douglas DT-2

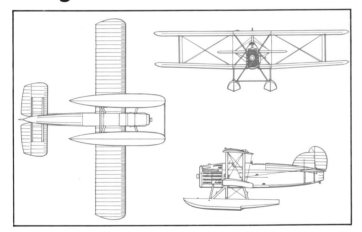

Origin: The Douglas Company (later Douglas Aircraft Co), Santa Monica, California.
Type: Torpedo bomber.
Engine: One 400hp Liberty V-12 water-cooled.
Dimensions: Span 50ft (15.24m); length 34ft 2in (10.42m), (seaplane 37ft 8in, 11.48m); height 13ft 7in (4.14m), (seaplane 15ft 1in,4.6m); wing area 707sq ft (65.68m²).
Weights: (DT-2 land) empty 3,737lb (1,695kg); maximum 6,502lb (2,949kg).
Performance: (DT-2 land) maximum speed 101mph (163km/h); service ceiling 7,800ft (2,378m): range with torpedo 293 miles (472km).
Armament: One 1,835lb (832kg) torpedo.
History: First flight November 1921; service delivery mid-1922.
Users: Navy, Marine Corps.

Donald Douglas left Martin to build the Cloudster biplane for wealthy

Above: The two-seat DT-2 was the first production Douglas. Most spent most of their life as float seaplanes, and there were conversions to other engines, as described below.

David R. Davis. In 1921 Davis withdrew his backing and Douglas struggled to set up on his own. Quickly he modified the Cloudster into a torpedo bomber and persuaded the Navy to order three. The bluff DT-1 had a steel-tube fuselage and folding wooden wings, and attachments were provided for wheels or floats. Only the first was delivered as a DT-1, the Navy asking for a second cockpit for an observer. The Douglas proved an excellent machine and was the foundation of the new company. The 41 built in an old movie studio were augmented by 20 built by LWF and six by the Naval Aircraft Factory. They served in many roles until 1926, some being converted

Above: Letting go a "tin fish" from a DT-1 in February 1923. The sturdy DTs were built in an abandoned movie studio at the corner of Wilshire and 24th Street. Wives sewed the fabric.

as DT-4s or -6s with other engines, while Dayton-Wright converted three as SDW-1 long-range scout seaplanes. These carried extra fuel in an even deeper fuselage keel passing under the wing.

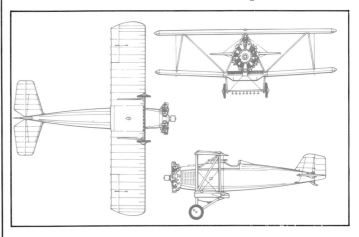

Naval Aircraft Factory TS/F4C

ed to fold backwards, like the Handley Pages. Speed and man-euverability were deliberately sacrificed for a much heavier bombload, the MB-2 being planned for night raids only. The first order was 20 was placed in early 1920, MB-2 being the accepted designation; but from the sixth aircraft the new NBS-1 designation (night bomber, short range) was introduced. Range was actually longer than for any other Army type, no "NBL" ever being delivered. A follow-on

for 100 was canceled, but Aero-marine delivered 25, Curtiss 50 (the final 20 with turbosupercharged engines) and LWF 35 (the final four with dual controls). The NBS-1 had a long and successful career, mainly in the Canal Zone, Hawaii and Philippines, but its high point came on 21 July 1921 during Gen "Billy" Mitchell's controversial bombing of former German capital ships to prove his point against the Navy: the *Ostfriesland* was sunk with 2,000lb (907kg) bombs.

Origin: Naval Aircraft Factory, Philadelphia, Pennsylvania; production by Curtiss.
Type: Carrier-based fighter.
Engine: One 200hp Wright (Lawrance) J-4 nine-cylinder radial.
Dimensions: Span 25ft (7.62m); length 22ft 1in (6.73m); height (land) 9ft 7in (2.9m); wing area 228sq ft (21.2m²).
Weights: Empty 1,240lb (562kg); maximum 2,133lb (967.5kg).
Performance: Maximum speed 123mph (198km/h); service ceiling 16,250ft (4,950m): range 482 miles (775km).
Armament: One (provision for two) forward-firing 0.30in Browning gun.
History: First flight May 1922; carrier service December 1922.
User: Navy.

Above: Shown here as a landplane, the TS-1 was the first US airplane designed for operation from a carrier.

The little TS-1 was the first post-war Navy fighter and the first designed in the US for carrier operation. All-wood, with fabric covering, it had the fuselage placed midway between the wings, and floats could replace wheels. The NAF built five, followed by 34 from Curtiss. They served aboard *Langley* and, on floats, from warship catapults. The NAF built two TS-2s with 210hp Aeromarine U-8D V-8 engines, and two TS-3s with the 180hp Wright-Hispano which became TR thin-wing racers used as trainers by the Navy 1923 Schneider team. Curtiss built two metal TS-1s, which in the new designation system emerged as F4C-1s.

Above: Another practice torpedo drop, each torpedo weighing 1,835lb (832kg). Only the first aircraft (no 6031) was a DT-1, and it was converted into the first two-seat DT-2.

Below: Five DT-2s ready for a formation takeoff, without torpedoes. This aircraft led to the DWC (Douglas World Cruiser) used by the Army to girdle the globe in April-September 1924.

Above: BuAer No A-6689 was the first of two Curtiss-built F4Cs, which were metal framed derived aircraft with the same J-4 radial engine. Note the wing struts.

Below: One of the 34 Curtiss-built TS-1s, seen here on a land airfield. It was finally concluded that fighters needed engines giving over 200hp.

Curtiss PW-8

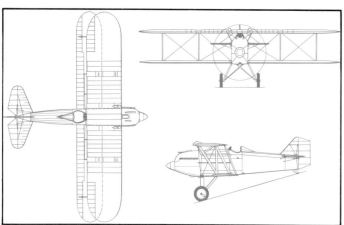

Origin: Curtiss Aeroplane and Motor Co, Garden City, NY.
Type: Single-seat pursuit.
Engine: One 435hp Curtiss D-12 V-12 water-cooled.
Dimensions: Span 32ft (9.75m); length 23ft 1in (7.04m); height 8ft 10in (2.7m); wing area 279.3sq ft (25.95m²).
Weights: Empty 2,191lb (994kg); maximum 3,155lb (1,431kg).
Performance: Maximum speed at sea level 171mph (275km/h); service ceiling 20,350ft (6,200m); range 440 miles (710km).
Armament: Two 0.30in Marlin mounted above cowling.
History: First flight late 1922; service delivery June 1924.
Users: AS, AAC.

The prototype L-18-1 (much later given Type Number 33) was a private venture pursuit based on the R-6 and other Curtiss racers. It had similar thin untapered wood/fabric wings and welded steel tube fuselage, finely cowled D-12 engine and flush surface radiators in the upper wing. In April 1923 the Army ordered three of what promised to be a very fast airplane, and the first (23-1201), later designated XPW-8, was delivered on 14 May 1923. Following various changes to landing gear and cowl, removal of elevator balance and addition of struts joining the ailerons, the PW-8 entered production, 25 being turned out. The No 2 (24-202) had a turbosupercharger, while No 4 was used by Lt Russell

Maughan on 23 June 1924 in the first crossing of the USA between dawn and dusk. Later the third XPW-8 was rebuilt.

Above left: The PW-8 was the first military airplane to have the outstanding D-12 engine.

Above: This PW-8, Air Service 23-1201, was the original prototype, in August 1923.

Above: The PW-8 showed the way to streamlined engines. In this 6th PS aircraft the D-12 has no fewer than 24 exhaust stubs.

Below: In contrast, this PW-8 of the famed 17th Pursuit Squadron has a long exhaust pipe on each side.

Below: The second aircraft, Air Service 24-202, was one of the first aircraft with a turbosupercharger. It is seen in September 1925 at McCook Field.

Boeing PW-9/FB

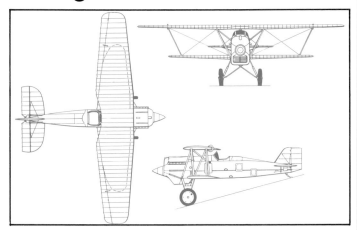

Origin: The Boeing Airplane Company, Seattle, Washington.
Type: Single-seat pursuit (FB, carrier-equipped).
Engine: (PW-9 and FB-1) one 435hp Curtiss V-1150 (D-12D) V-12 water-cooled, (FB-2/5) one 510hp Packard 1A-1500 V-12.
Dimensions: Span 32ft (9.75m); length (most) 23ft 5in (7.14m), (FB-5) 23ft 9in (7.24m); height (most) 8ft 2in (2.49m), (FB-5) 9ft 5in (2.87m); wing area (all) 260sq ft (24.15m²) gross, 241sq ft (22.39m²) net.
Weights: Empty (PW-9D) 2,328lb (1,056kg), (FB-5) 2,458lb (1,115kg); maximum (PW-9C) 3,170lb (1,438kg), (9D) 3,234lb (1,467kg), (FB-5) 3,249lb (1,474kg).
Performance: Maximum speed (9C) 163mph (262km/h), (9D) 155mph (249km/h), (FB-5) 176mph (283km/h); service ceiling (all) about 18,500ft (5,640m); range (most) 390 miles (628km), (FB-5) 420 miles (676km).
Armament: (PW-9) two forward-firing 0.3in guns; (FB) one 0.5in and one 0.3in.
History: First flight (Model 15) 2 June 1923, (FB-5) 7 October 1926.
Users: AS, AAC, Navy, Marine Corps.

Boeing built the Model 15 as a company venture, because its experience building Thomas-Morse scouts suggested that it should be possible to create an American pursuit far superior to foreign types still in service in the early 1920s. Like the Fokker D.VII, which still in-

Above: Many PW-9Cs had wire wheels, but all had upper/lower wings of almost 2:1 size ratio.

fluenced designers, the Model 15 had a welded steel-tube fuselage and wooden wings, all with fabric covering. After evaluating it at Mc-Cook Field the Army ordered XPW-9s (experimental pursuit, water-cooled), followed by 30 production PW-9s. In October 1925, just as deliveries began to AS squadrons in Hawaii and the Philippines, a batch of 25 PW-9As was ordered, these having duplicate bracing wires. Minor changes distinguished 40 PW-9Cs, but the 16 -9Ds had balanced rudders (retrofitted to earlier PW-9s), brakes and revised cowl and radiator shape. There were several experimental variants.

In 1925 the Navy ordered 16 FB-1s similar to the PW-9, but only ten were delivered, nine serving in China with the Marines. Two FB-2s had the Packard engine, but the 27 FB-5s had acute wing stagger, balanced rudder and other changes. They were loaded from the plant into barges and thence hoisted aboard *Langley*, from whose deck they made their maiden flights. All entered service in January 1927.

Below: This PW-9 was photographed at Mather Field, California, while taking part in exercises in April 1930. No squadron insignia can be seen.

Loening OA and OL

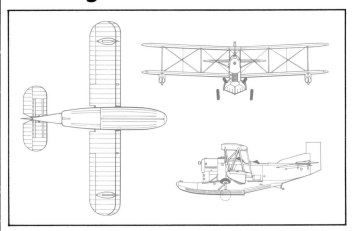

Origin: Loening Aeronautical Engineering Co, New York, NY.
Type: Observation amphibian.
Engine: See text.
Dimensions: Span 45ft (13.72m); length 34ft 7in (10.4m) (COA) to 35ft 1in (10.7m) (OL-3); height 12ft 9in (3.89m); wing area 504sq ft (46.82m²).
Weights: Empty from 3,440lb (1,560kg) (COA) to 3,766lb (1,708kg) (OA); maximum (COA) 5,010lb (2,273kg), (OL-3) 5,316lb (2,411kg), (OA-2) 5,325lb (2,415kg), (OL-9) 5,404lb (2,451kg).
Performance: Maximum speed 119-125mph (192-201km/h); service ceiling 12,000-14,300ft (3,660-4,360m); range typically 600 miles (966km).
Armament: Normally one fixed 0.30in Marlin or Browning firing ahead and two 0.30in Lewis aimed by observer.
History: First flight (XCOA) 1923; final delivery (OA-9) 1933.
Users: AS, AAC, Navy, Marine Corps.

Grover Loening, the world's first aero-engineering graduate, set up his factory on the East River in 1917. His most famous family were these innovative amphibians. He calculated that the inverted Liberty, which appeared in 1923, raised the propeller high enough for a new seaplane configuration to be possible with the central float attached direct to the fuselage and the stabilizing floats direct to the wings. Landing gears were attached to the central float and swung up into recesses for water operation. To offset the strangeness, Loening wisely used wings interchangeable with the DH-4, though of improved profile (many wing sets were retrofitted to DH-4 variants). First came the XCOA-1, COA

Above: The Loening OA-1C was a late member of the family, with inverted-V Wright engine.

meaning Corps Observation Amphibian. The fuselage and floats were all-metal, while the wings had wood spars, metal ribs and fabric covering. There followed ten of the production COA-1 and 15 OA-1s with redesigned tail. By 1929 Loening had delivered nine OA-1Bs, ten OA-1Cs and eight OA-2s, the latter having the inverted air-cooled Wright V-1460 of 480hp, and with the pilot's Browning moved outside the propeller disc in the upper left wing. They were called Keystone OA-2s because that company took over Loening in 1928, moving the operation to Bristol, Pennsylvania. The XO-10 had a single retractable wheel and skids on the outer floats.

Navy models began with two OL-1s with three cockpits, and the 440hp Packard 1A-1500. Five OL-2s were similar to the COA-1, three being Army COAs turned over in haste for a 1925 Arctic expedition. Four OL-3 three-seaters had the 475hp Packard 1A-2500, while six OL-4s had the inverted Liberty. Then came 28 OL-6s with the Packard 1A-2500, many being catapult ship-planes. The two OL-8s introduced the 450hp P&W Wasp R-1340-4, and the central propeller shaft of the radial meant that the engine had to be raised, spoiling forward vision. Otherwise the Wasp was great, and 20 OL-8As followed with carrier hooks, then 26 improved OL-9s and two XHL-1 ambulances with six seats inside the fuselage, the pilot remaining in an open cockpit.

Below: Taken on 19 January 1925, this shows a "Keystone" OA-2 at Bolling Field.

Keystone bombers

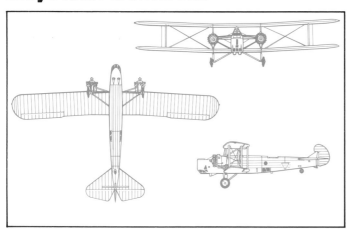

Origin: (1) Huff-Daland and Co, Ogdensburg, NY, (others) Keystone Aircraft Corp, Bristol, Pennsylvania.
Type: Bomber.
Engine(s): (LB-1) one 800hp Packard 2A-2540 V-12 water-cooled, (LB-5) two 420hp Liberty V-1650-3 V-12 water-cooled, (LB-6) two 525hp Wright Cyclone R-1750-1 nine-cylinder radials, (B-3A) two 525hp Pratt & Whitney Hornet R-1690-3 nine-cyinder radials, (B-4A) two 575hp P&W R-1860-7 nine-cylinder, (B-6A) two 575hp Wright Cyclone R-1820-1.
Dimensions: Span (LB-1) 66ft 6in, (LB-5) 67ft (20.4m), (LB-6) 75ft (22.8m), (B-3/4/6) 74ft 8in (22.76m); length (-1) 46ft 2in, (5) 44ft 8in, (6) 43ft 5in, (B-3/4/6) 48ft 10in (14.89m); height (B series) 15ft 9in (4.8m); wing area 1,137 to 1,148sq ft, (B series) 1,145sq ft (106.37m²).
Weights: Empty (1) 6,237lb (2,829kg), (5) 7,024lb (3,186kg), (6) 6,836lb (3,100kg), (B-3A) 7,705lb (3,495kg) , (4) 7,951lb (3,607kg), (6) 8,037lb (3,646kg); maximum (1) 12,415lb (5,631kg), (5) 12,155lb

Above: The B-4A was one of the final group with aircooled radial engines and single vertical tail surfaces. All had four ailerons.

(5,513kg), (6) 13,440lb (6,096kg), (B-3A) 12,952lb (5,875kg), (4) 13,209lb (5,992kg), (6) 13,374lb (6,066kg).
Performance: Maximum speed 107-121mph (172-195km/h); service ceiling 11,500-14,000ft (3,350-4,270m); range around 430 miles (692km) except B-3A/B-4A both 855-860 miles (1,380km).
Armament: (LB series) twin 0.30in Marlin or Lewis in nose (except LB-1 which had two in lower wing firing ahead), two more in rear cockpit and one in lower rear position, plus 2,000lb (907kg) bombload; (B series) single 0.30in in nose, upper rear and lower rear positions, plus 2,500lb (1,134kg) bombload.
History: First flight (XLB-1) late 1923, others see text.
Users: AS, AAC.

For ten years from 1923 this series

Above: B-4 combat and ground crews parade for inspection at March Field, Ca, 3 February 1934. Squadron unknown.

Below: This B-3A was serving late in its life in the Philippines, with the 28th Bomb Squadron (photo dated 8-16-35).

Curtiss CS (Martin SC)

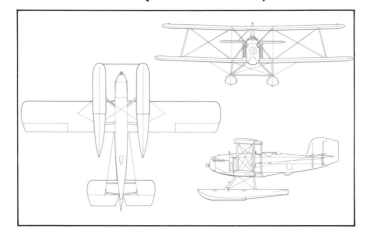

Origin: Design and CS prototypes by Curtiss Aeroplane and Motor Co, Buffalo, NY; production SC by Martin.
Type: 2/3-seat torpedo bomber.
Engine: One Wright V-12 water-cooled, (-1) 525hp T-2, (-2) 585hp T-3.
Dimensions: Span 56ft 7in (17.24m); length 37ft 8¾in (11.5m); height (landplane) 14ft 8in (4.47m);

Above: Shown in its usual float seaplane form, the Martin SC-2 had the more powerful T-3 engine.

wing area 856sq ft (79.53m²).
Weights: (SC-2 land) empty 5,007lb (2,271kg); maximum 8,422lb (3,820kg).
Performance: (SC-2 land) maximum speed 103mph

Above: A-6835 was the 35th and last Martin-built SC-1, seen as a landplane. Radiators were on the fuselage sides.

(166km/h); service ceiling 8,000ft (2,440m): range 1,018 miles (1,640km).
Armament: One 0.30in gun on Scarff ring in centre cockpit and one 1,618lb (734kg) torpedo.

History: First flight (CS-1) late 1923; service delivery (CS-1 and -2) April 1924.
User: Navy.

Curtiss had extensive torpedo dropping experience with the R series, but the company's first airplane designed for this duty was the CS-1. Necessarily large, it was slow and unwieldly despite its

of biplanes monopolized Army bomber procurement, apart from a dozen Curtiss B-2 Condors. Huff-Daland, a supplier of a few Army and Navy trainers, built the XLB-1 in 1923 as a conventional LB (light bomber) with steel-tube fuselage and tapered wooden wings. Bombs were carried in the fuselage and aimed by a sight in the belly. Army experience with ten LB-1 Pegasus, with an extra (fourth) seat and an improved Packard engine, suggested a twin-engine layout would be better, and ship 27-333 was planned as the XLB-3 with two Liberty V-1410-1 inverted air-cooled engines. It was actually completed as the XLB-3A with 410hp P&W Wasps, a fifth crew member being added in the nose with the bombsight beneath, and the tail having three fins. In parallel Huff-Daland built the XLB-5 with ordinary upright Liberty engines, as well as the bigger single-engine XHB-1 Cyclops in the Heavy category.

The first twins to be delivered were ten LB-5 Pirates. In March 1927 the company was reorganized as Keystone, and this name was used for the 25 LB-5A Pirates with twin fins and rudders in place of the original central fin/rudder plus two auxiliary fins. Ship 27-344, last of the original LB-5s, was then rebuilt with new wings which were untapered and slightly swept back, and with Cyclone radials raised well above the lower wing. This XLB-6 was followed by 17 LB-6 Panthers with reshaped vertical tails.

The next aircraft to come were 18 LB-7 Panthers (in addition to three re-engined LB-6s), all of which were fitted with R-1690-3 Hornet radial powerplants. The LB-6s and -7s were the equipment of the 2nd Bomb Group and the

5th Composite Group based in Hawaii.

A host of minor rebuilds, with different engines and tails, led to the LB-8 to -14, orders being placed for 73 new -10, -13 and -14. In 1930, however, the LB/HB distinction was abolished, and so the next batch comprised 63 B-3As (ex LB-10A), with Hornets and single-fin tail. Five of the seven LB-13s were completed as Y1B-4s with R-1860 engines, and 25 B-4As followed.

The three LB-14s were completed as Y1B-5s with Cyclones, and these were followed by 27 B-5As converted from B-3As. Five bombers ordered as LB-13s were completed as Y1B-6s with the new R-1820 Cyclone, and the 39 B-6As delivered in 1932 completed the Keystone production. They enabled the Air Corps to form two new Bomb Groups, the 7th and 19th, and re-equipped the 2nd BG and units in Hawaii, CZ and the Philippines.

Above: Rather bigger than the rest, the XB-1 (XHB) was a heavy bomber powered by two of the massive Packard 2A-1500 water-cooled engines (photo 2-13-28).

Below: Last of the line, the B-6As were certainly the most efficient. A few were still flying when World War II began in 1939, but none saw action.

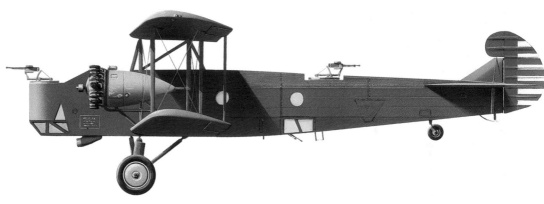

massive engine. Built mainly of wood, it had untapered wings, the upper having the shorter span and the interplane struts sloping inwards. There were three cockpits in a row, and provision was made for wheel or float gear, for photo reconnaissance and for high-level

visual bombing. Curtiss built six, followed by two CS-2s with the T-3 engine, extra tankage and an optional third float.

These airplanes were delivered to squadron VT-1 and proved good enough for the Navy to put out a tender for 35 production aircraft.

As commonly happened the original design firm was underbid, Martin delivering the airplanes as SC-1s. These entered service in early 1925, immediately followed by 40 SC-2s based on the CS-2. They had a fairly brief career, being replaced by Martin's own T3M.

Below: Seen here as a float seaplane, the SC-2 was powered by the more powerful T-3 engine. The original Curtiss CS-1 differed in having a propeller spinner faired into the nose. By mid-1927 the SCs had been withdrawn except from VT-2B.

Douglas O-2, O-25, O-38

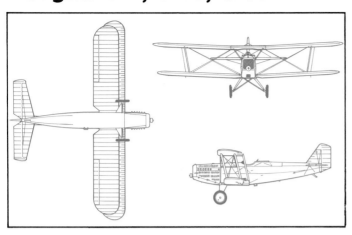

Origin: Douglas Aircraft Co, Santa Monica, California.
Type: Observation.
Engine: (2) one 420hp Liberty 12A, (25) 600hp Curtiss Conqueror V-1570-27, (38) 525-hp Pratt & Whitney Hornet R-1690-3 or -5 or 625hp R-1690-13.
Dimensions: Span (pre O-2H) 39ft 8in (12.09m), (rest) 40ft (12.19m); length 29ft 6in (8.99m) for O-2, up to 32ft (9.75m) for O-38B; height (O-38B) 10ft 8in (3.25m); wing area (O-2C) 411sq ft (38.18m²), (O-25, -38) 371sq ft (34.47m²).
Weights: Empty (O-2C) 3,100lb (1,406kg), (38B) 3,072lb (1,393kg); maximum (2C) 4,706lb (2,135kg), (38B) 4,458lb (2,022kg).
Performance: Maximum speed (2C) 126mph (203km/h), (38B) 153mph (246km/h); service ceiling (2C) 14,700ft (4,480m), (38B) 20,700ft (6,300m); range (typical) 300 miles (480km).

Above: A middle member of the family, this early O-2H has a smaller vertical tail than later O-2Hs and all subsequent variants.

Armament: Almost all had one fixed 0.30in (sometimes 0.50in) firing ahead through propeller disc, and twin 0.30in (Lewis, Marlin or Browning) in rear cockpit; (38) provision for four 100lb (45kg) bombs.
History: First flight (XO-2) early 1924; service delivery 1925; final delivery 1934; withdrawal from use January 1943.
Users: AAC, AAF, ANG, Coast Guard.

This little-known family of biplanes was the most diverse and numerous of all Army types between the World Wars. The XO-2 was derived from the Navy DT and submitted in two Army competitions for

Above: A.S.25-355 was one of the original O-2s. This carried its fuel in thickened inboard sections of the lower wings.

observation airplanes, one with the Liberty and the other with the 500hp Packard 1A-1500. It was offered with short and long wings, and had the usual steel-tube fuselage and wooden wings. The Army ordered 75 of the long-wing version, 70 with the Liberty as O-2s and five with the costly Packard. The latter received different designations. Only 46 O-2s were built, the rest of the 70 comprising 18 night-equipped O-2As and six dual O-2Bs. The 35 O-2Cs had the radiator moved from below to above the front of the engine, there being several variants plus two OD-1s for the Marines.

The O-2H introduced a new airframe with greater dimensions,

staggered wings (main gears being attached to the fuselage), fuel in the fuselage instead of the thickened lower wing roots, a new tail and other changes. The 143 saw wide use, followed by O-2J VIP conversions, 60 dual O-2Ks (40 became BT-1 trainers) and several other variants. The XO-25A had a new engine, with large left-hand propeller, followed by 49 O-25As, three dual O-25Bs and 30 streamlined O-25Cs using Prestone glycol cooling. Various radial prototypes led to 30 O-32As delivered as BT-2s, followed by 44 O-38s with the Hornet engine with the ring cowl, followed by 63 O-38Bs and a single Coast Guard O-38C. The O-38D introduced a new deep fuselage, new tail, long engine cowl, enclosed cockpits and single-strut gear, leading to 37 O-38Es and eight dual O-38Fs. In World War II many were converted as targets.

Curtiss P-1/P-6/F6C Hawk

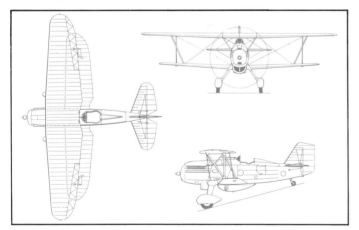

Origin: Curtiss Aeroplane and Motor Co, Garden City and Buffalo, NY.
Type: Single-seat pursuit (F6C, carrier equipped).
Engine: (P-1/-5/F6C-1) one 435hp Curtiss V-1150-1 (D-12) V-12 water-cooled, (P-6) 600hp Curtiss V-1570 Conqueror (various sub-types) V-12 water-cooled, (F6C-4) 410hp Pratt & Whitney Wasp R-1340-4 nine-cylinder radial.
Dimensions: Span (all) 31ft 6in (9.6m); length 22ft 6in (6.86m) (F6C-4, shortest) to 23ft 8in (7.21m) (P-5, longest); height 8ft 6in (2.59m)

Above: Last and best of the Hawks, the P-6E had a three-blade propeller and auxiliary drop tank under the fuselage.

(P-1C, lowest) to 10ft 11in (3.33m) (F6C-4, tallest); wing area (all) 252sq ft (23.41m²).
Weights: Empty (F6C-4, lightest) 1,980lb (898kg), (P-6E, heaviest) 2,699lb (1,224kg); maximum (P-1A, lightest) 2,866lb (1,300kg), (P-6E) 3,392lb (1,539kg), (F6C-4) 3,171lb (1,438kg).
Performance: Maximum speed at sea level (P-1A) 160mph

Above: A.C. 27-84 was a P-1B. It is shown with the insignia of the 43rd School Squadron at Kelly Field, Texas.

(257km—h), (P-5) 146mph (235km—h), (P-6E) 198mph (319km—h), (F6C-4) 155mph (249km/h); service ceiling typically 22,000ft (6,700m) except P-5 31,900ft (9,725m); range typically 300 miles (480km) or over 550 miles (890km) with auxiliary belly tank.
Armament: (all) two synchronized 0.30in guns above (P-6E, at sides of) cowling, (F6C only) plus wing

racks for bombload up to two 116lb (52.6kg).
History: First flight (P-1) May 1925, (P-6E) 1929.
Users: AS, AAC, Navy, Marine Corps.

The most diverse family of biplane pursuits stemmed from the XPW-8B (see PW-8), which among various refinements introduced tapered wings. On 7 March 1925 the Army ordered 15 XPW-8Bs under the new pursuit designation of P-1.

The major buy was 25 P-1As with

Curtiss Falcon

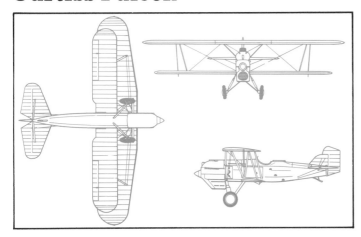

Origin: Curtiss Aeroplane and Motor Co, Garden City, NY.
Type: (O) Observation, (A) Attack.
Engine: One 435hp Curtiss V-1150-5 (D-12) V-12 water-cooled.
Dimensions: Span 38ft (11.58m); length (O-1E, A-3B) 27ft 2in (8.28m); height 10ft 6in (3.2m); wing area 353sq ft (32.79m²).
Weights: (A-3B) empty 2,875lb (1,304kg); maximum 4,476lb (2,030kg).
Performance: (A-3B) maximum speed 139mph (224km/h); service ceiling 14,100ft (4,300m); range 628 miles (1,010km).
Armament: (O series) two forward-firing 0.30in guns above nose and two aimed by observer; (A) two additional forward-firing underwing guns and 200lb (91kg) bombload.
History: First flight (37) August 1924, (O-1) late 1925.
Users: AS, AAC (variants, Navy and Marines).

Above: The A-3B was an attack O-1E, with Conqueror engine, six guns and 200lb (91kg) bombload under the wings.

In 1924 the Liberty-engined Model 37 Falcon (L-113) was evaluated as the XO-1 to find a replacement for the DH-4, but the Douglas O-2 was chosen. Re-engined with the Packard 1A-1500 it was accepted, but the D-12 engine was substituted for the first batch of ten, and this remained standard. Features included wooden wings with sweepback on the upper plane, and an unusual fuselage truss of aluminium tubing with bracing by steel ties, with fabric covering of the whole airframe. The 25 O-1Bs of 1927 introduced brakes and a jettisionable auxiliary tank. Four were converted as O-1C staff transports with a wide side-by-side rear cockpit without guns. In 1929 Curtiss built

Above: Though it has plain A-3 stencilled on the rudder, this is clearly an A-3A with bomb racks and lower-wing guns.

37 O-1Es with Frise ailerons, horn-balanced elevators and oleo shock struts. Among many conversions Curtiss went on to deliver 30 O-1Gs with better streamlining.

In 1927/28 Curtiss built 66 O-11 Falcons with the 420hp Liberty V-1650-3, and the last of the family comprised ten O-39s delivered in 1932 with O-1G airframes and Prestone (glycol)-cooled 600hp Curtiss Conqueror V-1570-25 engines. The front end resembled the P-6E, and most eventually received enclosed canopies over the pilot and spatted main gears.

The A-3 attack airplane was a modified O-1B with extra guns in the lower wings and twin Lewis on a rear-cockpit Scarff ring. Curtiss

delivered 76 in 1927-28, followed in 1930 by 78 A-3Bs incorporating O-1E improvements. Many Falcons ended their days in National Guard units, often converted as dual trainers.

One O-11 was fitted with a Wasp radial, becoming the XO-12. From this stemmed the F8C fighter for the Navy, leading to four OC-1 observation airplanes (delivered as F8C-1s) for the Marines. These were followed by 21 OC-2s (delivered as F8C-3s) which served as fighter, bomber (including dive-bombing) and observation aircraft with Marine squadrons VO-8M and -10M.

On page 46 appears a photo of an F8C-1 in an entry devoted to later F8Cs. A major difficulty in chronicling Curtiss biplanes is the way each design merged into others. The Hawk family below are a prime example of this.

slightly longer fuselage and extra equipment. A second batch of 25 were completed as P-1Bs with changes which included bigger wheels (all Hawks could have skis or floats). By 1929 Curtiss was delivering 33 P-1Cs with brakes. Another 71 P-1s were delivered by converting AT-4 and AT-5 advanced trainers. The nine Navy F6C-1s of late 1925 differed from the P-1 only in detail, but two of the nine were delivered as F6C-2s with hooks and stronger airframes, which in 1927 were features of 35 F6C-3s delivered to VF-5S "Red Rippers" and Marine VF-8M. After testing a Wasp conversion the Navy bought 31 F6C-4s with spreader-bar landing gear.

The Army bought five P-3As with Wasp engines, five P-5s with turbocharged V-1150-3s, and finished the series with 18 Conqueror-powered P-6s, all later modified as P-6Ds with turbochargers, and 46 of the best Hawk of all, the P-6E with a much better engine installation, single-strut gear with spats, and guns moved to the sides.

Right: In 1932 the 17th Pursuit Squadron, from Selfridge Field, Michigan, was one of the Air Corps' crack P-6E units.

Naval Aircraft Factory PN series

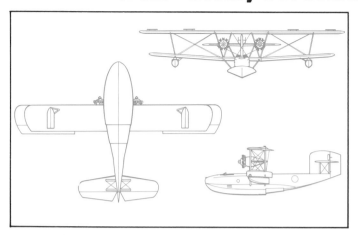

Origin: Naval Aircraft Factory, Philadelphia, Pennsylvania; PN-12 production by Douglas, Martin and Keystone, and PH developed by Hall, see text.
Type: Patrol flying boat.
Engines: (6) two 400hp Liberty, (7) two 525hp Wright T-2 V-12 water-cooled, (8) two 475hp Packard 1A-2500 V-12, (9, 10) as 8 but frontal radiators, (11, 12) two 525hp Wright Cyclone R-1750D nine-cylinder radials, (PD/PK/PM) see text, (PH) 620hp R-1820-86 or 875hp R-1820-F51.
Dimensions: Span 72ft 10in (22.2m); length 49ft 1in (14.95m)

Above: Apart from the modern engines the PN-12 might almost have been an F-5 of wartime origin. Tail shapes varied.

(PH, 51ft, 15.54m); height (12) 16ft 9in (5.1m); wing area 1,217sq ft (113.1m²).
Weights: Empty (7) 9,637lb (4,371kg), (12) 7,669lb (3,479kg); maximum (7) 14,203lb (6,442kg), (12) 14,122lb (6,406kg), (PH) 16,152lb (7,327kg).
Performance: Maximum speed 104-114mph (167-183km/h), (PH, 159mph, 256km/h); service ceiling typically 9,500ft (2,900m)

Above: The PN-7 combined the old wooden hull of the F-5L with new metal-framed wings. Engines were Wright T-2s.

(PH, 21,350ft, 6,500m); range (7) 655 miles (1,054km), (12) 1,310 miles (2,110km), (PH) 1,937 miles (3,120km).
Armament: (Most) one 0.30in Lewis in bow and dorsal cockpits, and four 230lb (104kg) bombs; (PH) two pairs of 0.30in and four 200lb or 250lb (113kg) depth charges.
History: See text.
Users: Navy, Coast Guard.

After World War I the standard patrol flying boat was the F-5L. Two modified F-6Ls led to a version with new metal-framed wings, with deep section profile enabling span to be reduced to a single bay outboard of the engines. This F-7L became the PN-7 under the new designation system of 1922. This was a step in the right direction, so next the PN-8 was built with better engines and an aluminum hull followed by a PN-9 with frontal radiators and a redesigned tail. This flew out of San Francisco on 31 August 1925, ran out of fuel over 350 miles short of Hawaii and, using

Martin T3M, T4M

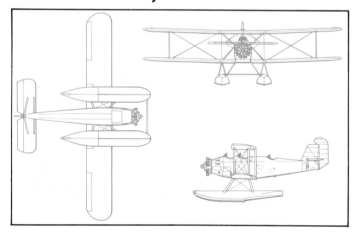

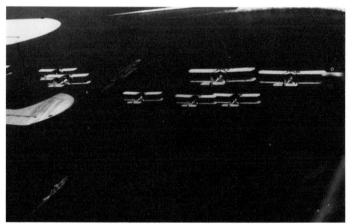

Origin: Glenn L. Martin Co, Cleveland, Ohio.
Type: Carrier-based torpedo bomber.
Engine: (3-1) one 575hp Wright T-3B V-12 water-cooled, (3-2) one 770hp Packard 3A-2500 V-12 water-cooled, (4) 525hp Pratt & Whitney Hornet R-1690-24 nine-cylinder radial, (TG) 620hp Wright Cyclone R-1820-86 nine-cylinder radial.
Dimensions: Span (3) 56ft 7in (17.25m), (rest) 53ft (16.15m); length (3) 41ft 4in (12.6m), (4, land) 35ft 7in (10.84m), (TG) 34ft 8in (10.57m); height (3) 15ft 1in, (4, land) 14ft 9in (4.5m), (TG) 14ft 10in; wing area (3) 883sq ft (82m²), (rest) 656sq ft (60.94m²).
Weights: Empty (3) 5,814lb (2,637kg), (4) 3,931lb (1,783kg), (TG) 4,670lb (2,118kg); maximum (3) 9,503lb (4,311kg), (4) 8,071lb

Above: Apart from the cockpit locations the T3M was almost an SC-2 (CS). Next came the Hornet-powered T4M-1 shown here.

(3,661kg), (TG) 9,236lb (4,189kg).
Performance: Maximum speed at sea level (3-2), 107mph (172km/h), (4) 114mph (183km/h), (TG) 127mph (204km/h); service ceiling (3) 7,900ft (2,400m), (4) 10,150ft (3,100m), (TG) 11,500ft (3,500m); range (3) 410 miles (660km), (4) 363 miles (585km), (TG) 330 miles (530km).
Armament: One 0.30 gun aimed by observer, one 1,835lb (832kg) torpedo.
History: First flight (3) June 1926, (4) April 1927.
User: Navy.

Having built Curtiss CS/SC airplanes in quantity Martin was well

Above: T4M-1s of Torpedo Squadron one fly over USS Lexington (CV-2) 26 February 1929. Note distant smoke screen.

placed to offer an improved design, and in October 1925 the Navy procured 24 T3M-1s. These retained the longer-span lower wings, folding for carrier stowage, and ability to have wheel or float gear, but differed in having a welded steel-tube fuselage with the pilot moved ahead of the wing, seated alongside the bombardier. A large radiator filled the space between the upper wing and fuselage behind them, cutting them off from the gunner. Deliveries began in September 1926, by which time Martin was producing the T3M-2 with equal-span wings with vertical struts, and the crew accommodated in three cockpits in

tandem. The more powerful Packard engine had a nose radiator. Martin built 100, used on wheels from Lexington and Langley and on floats.

By 1927 the Navy recognized the massive advantages of the new air-cooled radials, and the first T3M-2 (BuNo A-7224) was re-engined first with a Hornet and then with an R-1750 Cyclone. Next came the Martin 74, XT4M-1, with shorter wings and a taller rudder. Its Hornet installation weighed precisely half as much as the installed Packard, and soon the water-cooled aircraft were replaced by 102 T4M-1s aboard Lexington and Saratoga, all with wheels. In October 1928 Martin sold the Cleveland plant to Great Lakes, which continued with 18 TG-1s with minor changes, and finished the series with 32 TG-2s.

wing fabric, sailed the rest of the way! Four PN-10s with revised engine installations followed, the second pair being completed as PN-12s, one with Cyclones and the other with Hornets. All subsequent boats had air-cooled radials. Following the two NAF PN-12s came 25 built by Douglas as PD-1s with 575hp Cyclones in flat-tailed nacelles, 30 built by Martin as PM-1s with 525hp Cyclones with ring cowls and an enclosure over the side-by-side pilots, a further 25 Martin PM-2s with the bigger 575hp Cyclone and twin fins, and 18 Keystone PK-1s with 575hp Cyclones and twin fins.

All these retained the World War I hull shape with side sponsons. In the PN-11 the NAF introduced a modern full-width hull, built with twin fins as the Keystone PK and Martin PM with Hornets or Cyclones. In December 1927 Hall Aluminum developed the PN-11 into the XPH-1 with single fin and fully cowled Cyclones, leading to nine PH-2s and seven PH-3s for the Coast Guard in World War II.

Right: This PN-12 combined the new radial engines with the same hull and tail as the PN-9. The unit is the 1st Utility Squadron.

Vought Corsair O2U, O3U, SU

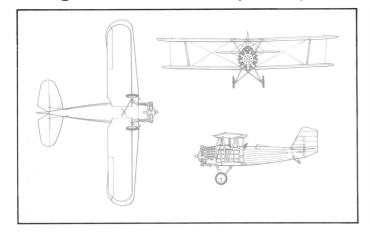

Origin: Chance Vought Corporation, (O2U) Long Island City, NY, (others) East Hartford, Connecticut.

Type: Observation and scout (landplanes carrier-based, seaplanes and amphibians on warships).

Engine: One Pratt & Whitney nine-cylinder radial, (O2U) 450hp Wasp R-1340, (O3U) 450hp R-1340 or 550hp R-1340 or 600hp R-1690 Hornet, (SU) 600hp R-1690.

Dimensions: Span (O2U -1) 34ft 6in (10.5m), (rest) 36ft (10.97m); length (O2U) 24ft 6in (7.47m), (rest, landplane) 27ft 5in (8.36m); height (O3U) 11ft 6in, (3.5m); wing area (O2U) 320sq ft (29.73m²)m, (rest) 337sq ft (31.3m²).

Weights: Empty (O2U) 2,342lb (1,062kg), (SU-4) 3,312lb (1,502kg); maximum (O2U) 3,893lb (1,766kg), (SU-4) 4,765lb (2,161kg).

Above: Last of the O2U Corsairs, the O2U-4 is shown here as a landplane; it could have a central-float seaplane configuration.

Performance: Maximum speed (O2U) 147mph (237km/h), (SU-4) 167mph (269km/h); service ceiling (all) 18,500-18,700ft (5,700m); range (O2U) 608 miles (980km), (rest) 680 miles (1,095km).

Armament: (All) one 0.30in fixed above engine, two 0.30in aimed by observer, and wing racks for light bombs.

History: First flight (O2U) 11 October 1926, (O3U) 1930; final delivery (O3U-6) 1936.

Users: Navy, Marine Corps, Coast Guard, Army.

One of the most famous families of US warplanes, the name Corsair was first applied to the O2U-1, the

Above: O2U-1s of a shipboard observation squadron drone past the newly commissioned CV-3 Saratoga on 3 May 1929.

first airplane ever designed to use a Pratt & Whitney engine. Seating two in tandem, it had a welded steel-tube fuselage with "cheek" fuel tanks let into the sides as in earlier Vought types. Able to act as fighters or bombers in addition to the primary mission, the Corsairs had wheel landing gear or were centre-float seaplanes, some having the Grumman amphibious central float with retractable wheels. There were 130 O2U-1s, 37 increased-span O2U-2s, 80 new-tail O2U-3s, 42 improved O2U-4s, 87 O3U-1s with wings of equal sweep and dihedral, 29 stronger Hornet-powered O3U-2s (delivered as SU-1s), 76 Wasp-engined O3U-3s, 65

ordered as O3U-4 but delivered as SU-2 and -3 scouts, 16 O3U-6 with long cowls, enclosed cockpits and spats, and 40 SU-4s.

Like the Curtiss Falcons and Hawks, the Vought Corsairs formed a gigantic and complex family, made more complicated by the succession of rebuilds and conversions during the 1930s. The later 03Us served aboard all the Navy's battleships and carriers and at many shore stations, while the Marines used their SU-1 and SU-4 scouts from all their shore bases and from the carrier *Lexington*.

The last of the conversions took place in 1939-40 when, in a program managed by Cdr D. S. Fahrney which included Curtiss N2C-2s and Stearman-Hammonds, 03U-6s were rebuilt as radio-controlled drones with tricycle gear.

Boeing F2B/F3B

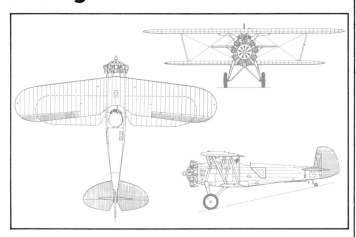

Origin: The Boeing Airplane Co, Seattle, Washington.
Type: Carrier-based fighter.
Engine: One 425hp Pratt & Whitney R-1340 Wasp nine-cylinder radial.
Dimensions: Span (F2B) 30ft 1in (9.17m), (F3B) 33ft (10.06m); length (2) 22ft 11in (6.99m), (3) 24ft 10in (7.57m); height (both) 9ft 2in, (2.79m); wing area (2) 243sq ft (22.58m²), (3) 275sq ft (25.55m).
Weights: Empty (2) 1,989lb (902kg), (3) 2,179lb (988kg); maximum (2) 2,805lb (1,272kg), (3) 2,945lb (1,336kg).
Performance: Maximum speed at sea level (2) 158mph (254km/h), (3) 157mph (253km/h); service ceiling (both) 21,500ft (6,553m); range (2) 317 miles (510km), (3) 340 miles (547km).
Armament: (Both) one fixed 0.5in and one 0.3in guns firing ahead, plus wing and fuselage racks for five 25lb (11.3kg) bombs.
History: First flight (2) 3 November 1926, (XF3B) 2 March' 1927, model 77, F3B-1 3 February 1928.
User: Navy.

Below: Three F2B-1s in full Navy service but without squadron designators. They are not the Three Sea Hawks aerobatic team.

Above: Whereas the F2B closely resembled a Wasp-engined FB or PW-9, the F3B-1 shown here had a completely new airframe. Tail and ailerons were metal.

Boeing's Model 54, built in 1924, was a neat seaplane fighter with a Wright P-1 engine, and when this was tested by the Navy as the FB-4 it showed major advantages over the heavy and unreliable water-cooled engines. Re-engined in 1926 with the brand-new Wasp it was even better, and Boeing then fitted a B-series Wasp to a fighter based on the one-off Army XP-8 (Model 66) which had flown with the inverted-V Packard 2A-1500 engine. The result was the Model 69 XF2B. This led to 32 production F2B-1s which equipped one fighter and one bomber squadron aboard *Saratoga*.

The three-float Model 74 (XF3B) showed little improvement, so the company redesigned the airframe with new wings and tail, longer fuselage and many other changes. The resulting Model 77 was better, despite the R-1340-80 having unchanged power. Orders were received for 74 F3B-1s to equip squadrons aboard carriers *Langley*, *Saratoga* and *Lexington*.

Douglas T2D and P2D

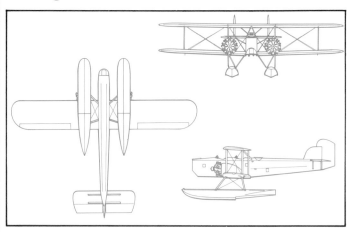

Origin: Douglas Aircraft Co, Santa Monica, California.
Type: (T) torpedo bomber, (P) patrol bomber.
Engines: Two Wright Cyclone nine-cylinder radials, (T) 525hp R-1750, (P) 575hp R-1820E.
Dimensions: Span 57ft (17.37m); length 44ft 11½in (13.7m) (landplane 42ft, 38.4m); height 14ft 7¾in (4.45m); wing area 886sq ft (82.3m²).
Weights: (T seaplane) empty 6,011lb (2,727kg); maximum 10,890lb (4940kg).
Performance: (Seaplane) maximum speed 124mph (200km/h); service ceiling 13,830ft (4,215m); range 422 miles (680km).
Armament: Two 0.30in Marlin guns aimed from bow and rear cockpits, plus one 1,618lb (734kg) torpedo or bombload.
History: First flight 27 January 1927; service delivery 25 May 1927.
User: Navy.

In 1925 the Navy BuAer designed a large twin-engine torpedo bomber

Below: A7051 was the first production T2D-1, seen here as originally built with wheel landing gear, silver/yellow.

Above: The first twin designed for carrier operation, the T2D-1 was operated on floats to avoid offending the Army!

intended to be faster than the DT or T3M and to have some ability to fly on one engine. The Naval Aircraft Factory built an XTN-1 to this design, but the production version (which appeared at the same time in 1927) was ordered from Douglas as the T2D-1. Fabric-covered, these had folding wings of equal span. Pilot and co-pilot sat in tandem cockpits, with two gunners at front and rear, the bow gunner also using the bomb/torpedo sight in the nose. VT-2 embarked in *Langley* in 1927, this being the first carrier operation of large twin-engine airplanes. Douglas delivered 12 T2D-1s, the last nine as seaplanes because of Army criticism of Navy landplane bombers. The 18 further aircraft ordered in 1930 were not only seaplanes but were redesignated in the patrol category for the same political reason. They differed only in having more powerful engines and twin fins. They served with patrol squadron VP-3 based at Coco Solo, Canal Zone, until replaced by PBY-2s in 1937-38.

Curtiss B-2 Condor

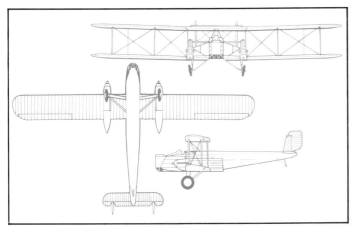

Origin: Curtiss Aeroplane and Motor Co, Garden City, N.Y.
Type: (B-2) heavy bomber, (C-30, R4C) transport.
Engines: (B-2) two 630hp Curtiss Conqueror GV-1570 -7 V-12 watercooled. (C-30, R4C) 710hp Wright Cyclone R-1820-F3 nine-cylinder radials.
Dimensions: Span (B) 90ft (27.43m), (C/R) 82ft (25m); length (B) 47ft 4½in (14.43m), (C/R) 49ft 6in (15.09m); height (both) 16ft 4in (4.98m); wing area (B) 1,496sq ft (138.97m²), (C/R) 1,276sq ft (118.54m).
Weights: Empty (B) 9,300lb (4,218kg), (C/R) 10,445lb (4,738kg) maximum (B) 16,591lb (7,526kg), (C/R) 17,500lb (7,938kg).
Performance: Maximum speed (B) 132mph (212km/h), (C/R) 182mph (293km/h); service ceiling (B) 17,500ft (5,210m), (C/R) 23,000ft (7,000m); range (B) 805 miles (1,295km), (C/R) 900 miles (1,450km).
Armament: (B only) six Lewis or Browning 0.30in in pairs in nose and rear of engine nacelles;

Below: B-2 Condors of the 11th Bombardment Squadron, from March Field, over Death Valley, California, in February 1932.

Above: The B-2 Condor had a biplane tail unit, and long nacelles with gunner cockpits at the back. The Army never bought the BT-32 Condor which came later.

bombload of 2,508lb (1,138kg).
History: First flight (XB-2) July 1927, (C/R) 1934.
Users: AAC, Navy, Marine Corps.

Curtiss built the Martin MB-2 (NBS-1) and developed this into the NBS-4 of 1924. This introduced a welded steel-tube fuselage and gunner cockpits in the tail of extended nacelles. This led to the XB-2 with Conqueror engines with radiators arranged vertically above each nacelle, and a biplane tail. Curtiss delivered 12 production B-2s as the only Air Corps heavy bombers, equipping the 11th BS from 1929. Curtiss developed the Condor as a transport with a much larger fuselage, single fin, radial engines and retractable mainwheels. The Army bought two of this T-32 family as the YC-30, one surviving into 1938. The Navy bought two R4C-1s which went to Marine squadron VJ-7M and were finally abandoned in the Antarctic in 1941.

Above: This B-2, with 96th BS insignia, was said to be "piloted by robot" in April 1930. The pilot is standing up almost completely out of the cockpit. The "robot", of course, was a Sperry autopilot.

Below: One of a series of fine formation shots taken during Army maneuvers in May 1931. Flight identification bands surround the fuselages, but there is no record of the unit.

Boeing F4B/P-12

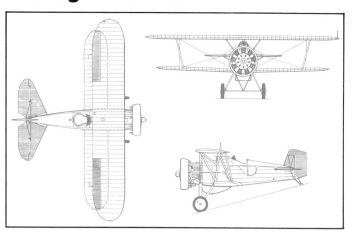

Origin: The Boeing Airplane Company, Seattle, Washington.
Type: Single-seat pursuit (day fighter); data for F4B-4/P-12E.
Engine: 500hp Pratt & Whitney SR-1340-16 or -17 direct-injection Wasp nine-cylinder radial.
Dimensions: Span 30ft (9.14m); length 20ft 1in-20ft 8in (6.1m-6.3m); height 9ft 3in (2.8m); wing area 227.5sq ft (21.14m²).
Weights: Empty about 2,100lb (952kg); loaded 2,557-2,750lb (1,160-1,240kg), (F4B-4, 3,611lb, 1,638kg).
Performance: Maximum speed 189mph (319km/h); cruising speed 150mph (241 km/h); service ceiling 27,000ft (8,230m); range 371 miles (F4B-4) to 520 miles (P-12E) (597-837km).
Armament: Two 0.30in Colt-Browning machine guns in top decking.
History: First flight (Model 83) 25 June 1928; (first production F4B-1) 6 May 1929; (first P-12E) 15 October 1931; last delivery (an

Above: The Army P-12D was very similar to the Navy F4B-2. Features including Townend-ring cowl, belly tank and corrugated tail and ailerons.

F4B-4) 28 February 1933.
Users: AAC (P-12), Navy (F4B).

Known in their commercial forms as the Boeing 100, these were extremely agile and widely used fighters. The prototype was built as a company venture, largely because Boeing could envisage a pursuit aircraft that was much better than anything at that time asked for by the Army or Navy (and also because the new Pratt & Whitney company had obviously scored a great success with their Wasp engine which Boeing had fitted to the F2B and F3B). Apart from an odd switch from welded steel tube to riveted and bolted square-section aluminum tube for the fuselage, the only major advantage of the new design was that it was

Above: The original P-12 (Boeing Model 102) was tested at Wright Field as the P-544, later becoming Army 29-353. It was virtually a repainted F4B-1.

Below: P-12B with merely the legend "Kelly Field" on the rudder. The fuselage has the 43rd School background but no insignia!

Curtiss F8C/O2C Helldiver

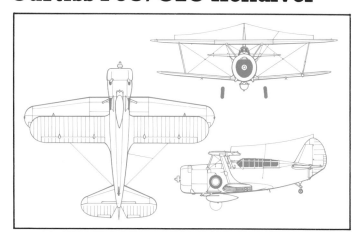

Origin: Curtiss Aeroplane and Motor Co, Buffalo, N.Y.
Type: Carrier-based dive bomber and observation.
Engine: One 450hp Pratt & Whitney R-1340-4 nine-cylinder radial.
Dimensions: Span 32ft (9.75m); length 25ft 8in (7.71m); height 10ft 3in (3.1m); wing area 308sq ft (28.6m²).
Weights: Empty 2,520lb (1,143kg); maximum 4,020lb (1,823kg).

Above: The F8C-4, 25 of which served aboard Saratoga, was almost identical to the O2C-1 Helldiver observation/scout (initially designated F8C-5s).

Performance: Maximum speed 153mph (246km/h); service ceiling 16,700ft (5,090m); range 720 miles (1,160km).
Armament: Two 0.30in Marlin guns in upper wing firing ahead, one or two 0.30in Lewis aimed by

Above: A7945 was the first F8C-1 (OC-2), a member of the earlier Falcon family. The later Helldiver family were smaller, and had Townend-ring engine cowls.

observer, plus one 500lb (227kg) or two 116lb (52.6kg) bombs.
History: First flight (XF8C-2) 1929, (F8C-5) late 1930.
Users: Navy, Marine Corps.

Following Marine Corps develop-

ment of dive bombing, Curtiss designed the first Helldiver in 1929, basing the aircraft on the F8C-1 Falcon but with shorter span, cowled engine, and "cheek" fuel tanks. Designated as fighters, the first 25 F8C-4s served with VF-1B aboard Saratoga before going to the Marines. Next came 63 designated O2C-1, followed by a further batch of 30. There were many sub-variants, plus publicity from the Gable/Beery movie Helldiver.

smaller and lighter than its predecessors. As a result its performance was higher.

The Navy tested two prototypes, the Model 83 with arrester gear and the Model 89 with split-axle gear and a rack for a 500lb (227kg) bomb. The initial order was for 27 F4B-1 fighter dive-bombers, with 450hp R-1340-8 engines and both arrester gear and bomb racks. In 1931 followed 46 F4B-2 with ring cowls, Frise ailerons, tailwheel, and a supercharged engine. Then came 21 F4B-3 with a completely new light-alloy monocoque fuselage, followed by 92 F4B-4s with a wider fin; a further 23 were added for Brazil.

Army buys started with ten P-12s, after which came 90 P-12B, 96 P-12C, 35 P-12D, 110 P-12E, 25 P-12F and a long string of specials. Differences were mostly minor, including better engine installations, night lighting, a large headrest, an enlarged vertical tail and, in the P-12F, a high-altitude supercharged 600hp engine.

Painted in glorious squadron markings the Navy and Army Boeings droned on until World War II and several are still in existence (one of them flying in the markings of VF-5B, the Navy "Red Rippers"). The P-12E was the chief Army fighter in 1932-35, while the F4B-4 was one of the chief Navy aircraft in 1932-37. Some survivors saw limited use as radio-controlled targets with Army and Navy in 1940-41.

Right: A P-12E of the 27th Pursuit Squadron, Selfridge Field, flying over nearby downtown Detroit in August 1932.

Below: Another 27th PS photo dating from 1932, this time showing the whole squadron.

Douglas O-31, O-43 and O-46

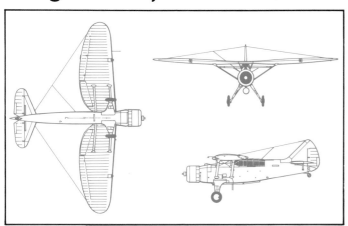

Origin: Douglas Aircraft Co, Santa Monica, California.
Type: Two-seat observation.
Engine: (31A) one 675hp Curtiss V-1570-53 V-12, (43A) 675hp V-1570-59, (46A) 725hp Pratt & Whitney Twin Wasp Junior R-1535-7 14-cylinder radial.
Dimensions: Span 45ft 9in (13.94m); length (31, 43) 33ft 11in (10.34m), (46) 34ft 6¾in (10.53m); height (46) 10ft 8in (3.25m); wing area 332sq ft (30.84m²).
Weights: Empty (31A) 3,751lb, (46A) 4,776lb (2,166kg); maximum (31) 4,635lb, (46) 6,639lb (3,011kg).
Performance: Maximum speed (31) 190mph (306km/h), (46A) 200mph (322km/h); service ceiling (31) 22,700ft (6,919m), (46A) 24,150ft (7,360m); range (46) 435 miles (700km).
Armament: One 0.30in Marlin (later Browning) in right wing firing ahead outside propeller arc, and one 0.30in aimed by observer.
History: First flight December 1930, (43) early 1933, (46A) late 1935.
Users: Army, ANG.

Above: The radial-engined O-46A was the last and most important of the family. The drawing shows the small split flaps, neat landing gears, and a direction-finding loop antenna under the fuselage.

Almost monopoly supplier of Army observation biplanes, Douglas proposed an all-metal monoplane in this category in 1929. In January 1930 it received a contract for two XO-31s, the second being completed as the YO-31 with a geared engine and revised fin. The gull wing was wire-braced to a cabane pylon above and to the bottom of the corrugated-skin fuselage, and the pilot and observer had open cockpits aft of the wing. Five YO-31As introduced smooth fuselages, elliptical wings, spats and enclosed cockpits, the latter being faired into the tail in the 31B. Next came five Y1O-43s with parasol wings and cantilever landing gear. Production began with 24 O-43As, the last of which had the R-1535 radial engine and became the XO-46. The definitive O-46A, of which 90 were built in 1936-37, had a new canopy

Above: Seen at Wright Field in July 1931, the YO-31 was a shapely machine despite its bracing wires and corrugated skin. The engine was a kind of Conqueror, a GIV-1570-C.

faired straight into the tail, much extra equipment and struts instead of wire bracing, the unsightly cabane being eliminated. The 2nd Observation Squadron was still flying these popular machines from Nicholas Field, Philippines, in December 1941.

Below: Still in natural metal finish, this O-46A was seen on 12 August 1940 — the day the Battle of Britain started — at Fort Dix, New Jersey, with the NJ Air National Guard.

Below: These three O-46As got to the Air National Guard when still in their youth, for this photograph was taken at Hartford, Connecticut, on 20 June 1937. They are painted in regulation blue and yellow, emphasizing their dragonfly-like appearance.

Non-rigid airships

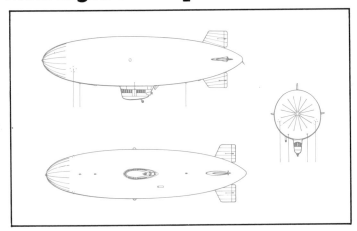

Origin: Numerous contractors notably Goodyear Aircraft (pre-1930, Goodyear-Zeppelin) Corporation, Akron, Ohio.
Type: Patrol, anti-submarine, trainer and other tasks; data for typical WWII Navy K-series.
Engines: Two Pratt & Whitney Wasp R-1340-AN2 or 425hp Wright Whirlwind R-975-28 nine-cylinder radials.
Dimensions: Length 251ft 8in, (76.72m); diameter 57ft 9in (17.6m) or 62ft 6in (19m); volume 425,000 or 456,000cu ft (12,025 or 12,912m³)
Weights: Loaded about 28,000lb (12,700kg), of which about 2,200lb (1,000kg) was useful load.
Performance: Maximum speed 75mph (121km/h); range 2,000 miles (3,220km) at 45mph (72km/h).
Armament: Several 0.30in guns and up to 750lb (340kg) of AS bombs or depth charges.
History: See text.
Users: (all types) AS, AAC, Navy.

Above: This drawing is typical of the major K-class, of which 134 were built with numerous small differences. Later Ks had a crew comprising three officers and nine ratings. Endurance was 48 hr.

Not including motorized balloons, more than 350 non-rigids served with the US armed forces, more than 200 being built for the Navy alone in World War II. There were dozens of different classes, early types being filled with hydrogen and having cars suspended well away from the envelope. The Navy C-7 of December 1921 used helium, and much later this led to the direct attachment of the car under the envelope. The Army devoted few funds to LTA (lighter than air) after 1930, and terminated operations in 1936. This cleared the way for a massive build-up in Navy strength in World War II, previously difficult because of political assignment to the Army of the

Above: Two Navy blimps of different wartime classes seen over an unidentified coastal town in about 1946. They differ only in detail from the various non-rigids flying today.

coastal patrol mission.

By far the most important series were the K. K-1 of 1931 — the date chosen for this entry — introduced the use of gaseous fuel but was much smaller than the true prototype K-2 of December 1938. Subsequently 134 of this class were delivered. It was said no ship was ever lost from a convoy with airship protection. On 18 July 1943 K-74 attacked a surfaced U-boat and was shot to ribbons by the submarine's flak. One crewman was killed by a shark before the rescue, but the U-boat was also destroyed.

After the war Goodyear delivered the biggest and most advanced non-rigids in history. Starting with the ZPN-1 (from 1954 ZPG-1) of

875,000cu ft (24,762m³), and a beautiful streamlined form, the Navy received 12 ZPG-2s of 1,011,000cu ft (28,611m³), with flight endurance up to a demonstrated 264 hours, five ZPG-2Ws with early-warning radars (as carried by EC-121s) above and within the envelope, and finally four ZPG-3Ws, the biggest ever (1,516,000cu ft, 42,903m³ length 403ft, 122.8m) with a speed of over 90mph (145km/h) on two 1,525hp Cyclones. The Navy terminated airship operations in June 1961, but in 1985 was discussing proposals for new non-rigids with Goodyear, Airship Industries (UK) and other possible contractors.

Though no decision on major procurement appeared imminent in mid-1986, it is interesting that this oldest of all aviation technologies looks to be making a comeback. The Navy has even studied the use of high-flying non-rigids as fixed stations.

Atlantic (Fokker) B-8/O-27

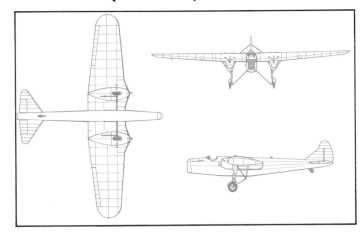

Origin: Atlantic Aircraft Corporation, New Jersey.
Type: Bomber/observation.
Engines: Two 600hp Curtiss Conqueror V-1570-23 or -29 V-12 water-cooled.
Dimensions: Span 64ft 3in (19.58m); length 47ft (14.33m); height 15ft (4.57m); wing area 619sq ft (57.50m²).
Weights: Empty (B-8) 6,861lb (3,112kg); maximum (O-27) 8,918lb (4,045kg), (B-8) 10,545lb (4,783kg).
Performance: Maximum speed

Above: The XO-27 had a curious wing/nacelle relationship. The later YO-27s and B-8s had normal engines which projected ahead of the wing, and other detail changes.

(all) 160mph (257km/h); service ceiling 20,000ft (6,100m); range (O-27) 950 miles (1,530km).
Armament: Two 0.30in Lewis or Marlin guns in nose and dorsal cockpits; (B-8) external bombload of 1,600lb (726kg).

Above: The XB-8 seen at Wright Field in July 1931. Powered by direct-drive Conqueror V-1570C engines, in odd stumpy cowls, it differed considerably from the later O-27 series.

History: First flight (XO-27) 1929, (YO-27) 1931.
User: AAC.

Atlantic Aircraft, the US Fokker company, built two XO-27s in 1929 to meet a requirement for a three-

seat observation aircraft. The design was typical Fokker, with an angular steel-tube fuselage and thick wooden cantilever wing, and fixed landing gears. The No 2 prototype was completed as the XB-8 with a longer nose for a bombardier, and bomb racks. Next came six YO-27s and six YB-8s with more shapely cowls over geared engines, enclosed pilot cockpit and revised tail. All were eventually used in the observation role as O-27s, not withdrawn until 1938.

Douglas B-7/O-35

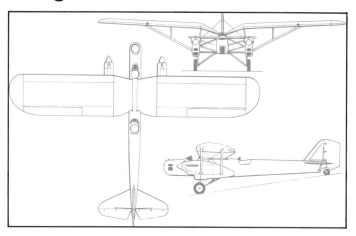

Origin: Douglas Aircraft Co, Santa Monica, California.
Type: (B) bomber, (O) observation.
Engines: Two 675hp Curtiss Conqueror V-1570-53 V-12 water-cooled.
Dimensions: Span 65ft 3in (19.89m); length 46ft 7in (14.2m); height 11ft 7in (3.54m); wing area 621.2sq ft (57.7m²).
Weights: (B-7) empty 5,519lb, (2,503kg); maximum 11,177lb (5,070kg).
Performance: Maximum speed 182mph (293km/h); service ceiling 20,400ft (6,220m); range with bombload 411 miles (660km).

Above: The Y1B-7 was one of the interim machines of the early 1930s. Though braced by struts and wires, it had a smooth metal skin, quite well-streamlined engine nacelles and retractable main landing gears.

Armament: Two 0.30in Marlin or Lewis aimed from cockpits in nose and aft of wing; external fuselage racks for 1,200lb (544kg) of bombs.
History: First flight March 1931; service delivery December 1932.
User: AAC.

Faced with competition from the

Above: Fully loaded with underfuselage bombs, the corrugated-skin XB-7 (formerly XO-36) is seen at Wright Field in December 1931. The main landing gears retracted into the nacelles of the V-1570C engines.

Fokker XO-27, in 1929 Douglas decided to design an even more advanced rival. In 1930 it secured orders for two prototypes, the XO-35 and XO-36, differing only in that the 35 had geared Conquerors and the 36 had direct drive. Structurally they were much more advanced than the XO-27, having an all-metal stressed-skin design with

retractable main gears. The gull wing gave them a distinctive grace, and their appearance created quite a stir. Maneuverability was excellent, and in fiscal 1932 the Army ordered seven Y1B-7s and five Y1O-35s, which after evaluation remained in front-line squadrons as the B-7 and O-35. These four-seaters were popular, and differed from the prototypes in having smooth instead of corrugated fuselages. Their use was intensive, and during the disastrous four months in 1934 when the Army carried the mails no fewer than four crashed in severe conditions. The last O-35 was not retired until 1939.

Rigid airships

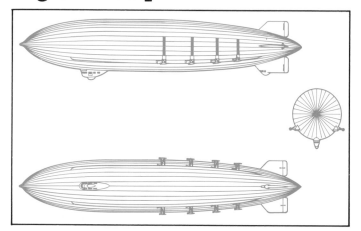

Origin: See text.
Type: Oceanic scouts; data for ZR-4 and -5.
Engines: Eight 560hp Maybach VL-11 V-12 water-cooled.
Dimensions: Length 785ft (239.3m); diameter 132ft 11in (40.50m); volume 6,500,000cu ft (184,084m³).
Weights: Empty 244,744lb (111,000kg), 95 per cent inflation gross lift 430,000lb (195,048kg); useful load (-4) 160,644lb (72,868kg), (-5) 182,000lb (82,555kg).
Performance: Maximum speed 87mph (140km/h); range (still air) 10,500 miles (16,900km); normal operational endurance 108h at 63mph (101km/h).
Armament: None normally.
History: First flight (-4) 23 September 1931, (-5) 21 April 1933.
Users: Navy.

Above: The giant ZRS-4 and ZRS-5 were almost identical externally. Lines up the side are condensers.

The Navy designed a rigid airship during World War I but this would have been outclassed by later Zeppelins. Technology used in the latter was then used in designing the ZR-1 *Shenandoah*, built by the Naval Aircraft Factory and flown from 4 September 1923. Basically a good ship, she was lost in a storm just two years later, probably because in trying to conserve helium most of the blow-off valves were removed (leading to rupture of cells).

ZR-2 was built in England but was destroyed on test before delivery. ZR-3 *Los Angeles* was built as war reparations by Luftschiffbau Zeppelin in Germany. A fine ship of

Above: The metal-clad ZMC-2 was strictly a non-rigid and is seen on test in 1929.

Below: ZRS-5 Macon riding at her mast, which ran on rails into the vast hangar in the rear.

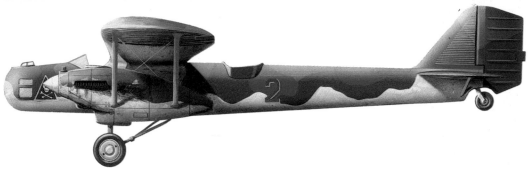

Above: A formal portrait of a B-7, with ground and combat crews, at March Field in June 1934. This was an era when the streamlined airplane was rapidly being perfected.

Right: A Y1B-7 of the 31st Bomb Squadron, specially painted in water-wash camouflage for the 1933 maneuvers between the Army Air Corps and the Army. Note unit insignia on the nose.

2,472,000cu ft (70,028m³), she was delivered across the Atlantic on 12-14 October 1924 and had a career as successful as her near-sister *Graf Zeppelin*, finally being broken up in 1939.

In 1926 the Navy received sanction for two gigantic airships for scouting with or ahead of the fleet. The design competition was won by Goodyear-Zeppelin Corporation, of Akron, Ohio. Designated as ZRS-4 *Akron* and ZRS-5 *Macon*, they were in almost every respect the most advanced ships up to that time. Designed for helium, they were in consequence able to have their engines inside the hull, driving through shafts to propellers which could be pivoted to thrust in any desired direction. To eliminate the need to valve-off the precious gas, the cooling water was passed through giant condensers (visible up the sides in line with the engines) and repeatedly reused. Among many other features was a large hangar for four Curtiss F9C-2 Sparrowhawk fighters (a neat little machine not included in this book because only six were delivered) which "took off" and were recaptured on a hook.

Early in her career *Akron* made a ten-hour cruise with 270 people on board. Sadly on 4 April 1933 she inadvisedly penetrated a storm over the Atlantic and was forced down by violent gusts into the raging sea, with only three survivors. Her sister, with a refined design 8,000lb (3,630kg) lighter, proved a

Above: ZRS-4 Akron set new standards in airship technology when she entered service in 1931.

splendid ship in service over the Pacific. By late 1934 severe storms had caused damage, but this was repaired during each mission, and on 11 February 1935 only the top fin joints needed replacement. Running into violent turbulence, she lost the top fin and most of her rear gas. Sinking to the sea, two crewman were lost out of 81. No further giant rigids joined the Navy.

Right: A March 1926 publicity sketch showing the proposed "G.Z.1" (later the ZRS-4) at right.

Boeing B-9

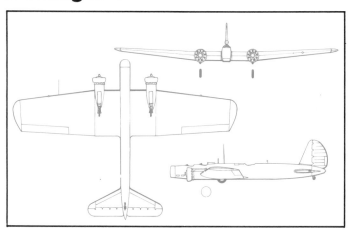

Origin: The Boeing Airplane Company, Seattle, Washington.
Type: Five-seat bomber.
Engines: (Model 215) two 575hp Pratt & Whitney R-1860-13 Hornet radials, (214) two 600hp Curtiss GIV-1570-29 Conqueror V-12, (246) 600hp R-1860-11 supercharged Hornets.
Dimensions: Span 76ft 10in (23.42m); length 51ft 9in (15.77m); height 12ft (3.66m); wing area 954sq ft (88.63m²).
Weights: (246) empty 8,941lb (4,056kg); maximum 14,320lb (6,496kg).
Performance: Maximum speed 188mph (303km/h); service ceiling 20,750ft (6,325m); range with bombload 540 miles (869km).
Armament: See text.
History: First flight (215) 13 April 1931, (214) 5 November 1931, (246) 14 July 1932.
User: AAC.

Above: The Y1B-9A came at the dawn of the transition period when fabric biplanes yielded to metal monoplanes.

In 1930 Boeing recognized that no Army bomber then planned was a cantilever all-metal stressed-skin aircraft. The company was already building the Monomail with smooth skin throughout, semi-monocoque fuselage and retractable main gears (the wheels partly protruding). As a private venture, Boeing built the Curtiss-engined 214 and Hornet-powered 215. They were excellent aircraft, with a bombload of 2,260lb (1,025kg) divided between an internal bay and underwing racks, and with the heavy defensive armament of twin 0.5in guns in the front and rearmost cockpits. The Army bought both aircraft as the Y1B-9 and YB-9 (originally XB-901) respectively. In

Above: The Hornet-engined YB-9 (Model 215) on test in 1931 with the Wright Field insignia on the fuselage.

Below: The Model 215 on delivery from Seattle, prior to receiving Army markings and then known as the XB-901.

August 1931 the Army bought five service-test Y1B-9As (Model 246), with curved rudders, intercommunicating cockpits and reduced

armament of just two 0.3in guns. By this time Martin was building the Model 123 which gained the expected production orders.

Grumman FF-1

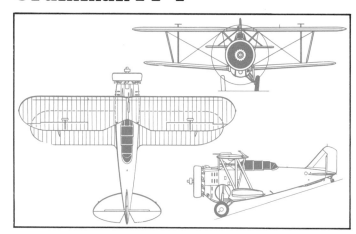

Origin: Grumman Aircraft Engineering Corporation, Bethpage, NY.
Type: Two-seat fighter.
Engine: One Wright R-1820 Cyclone nine cylinder radial, of following sub-types: (XFF-1) 575hp R-1820E, (FF-1 and FF-2) 750hp R-1820-78; (SF-1) 775hp R-1820-84.
Dimensions: Span 34ft 6in (10.51m); length 24ft 6in (7.47m); height 11ft 1in (3.4m); wing area 310sq ft (28.8m²).
Weights: Empty (typical) 3,300lb (1,500kg); loaded 4,828lb (2,190kg).

Above: The FF-1 was the first of the "barrels" (so-called from their portly bodies) which established Grumman in the front rank of fighter builders.

Performance: Maximum speed (typical) 207mph (333km/h); initial climb 1,600ft (488m)/min; service ceiling 21,100ft (6,430m); range 920 miles (1,480km).
Armament: Originally, standard armament was one 0.30in machine gun in top of forward fuselage firing ahead, and a pair aimed by observer from rear cockpit; some

Above: The prototype FF-1, A8878, on test by the Navy in early 1932. It had the first fully retractable gear in naval service.

aircraft unarmed, and later there were several variations.
History: First flight (XFF-1) December 1931.
User: Navy.

The Grumman Aircraft Engineering Corporation was incorporated in December 1929, and began operations at Bethpage, Long

Island, where it has been centered ever since. One of its first contracts was with the US Navy to build seaplane floats incorporating retracting land wheels. Out of this stemmed a contract, placed on 2 April 1931, for a prototype of the XFF-1.

This was the first fighter to be designed around Wright's powerful Cyclone engine and also the first in the US Navy to have retractable landing gear and all-light-alloy structure. The deep-bellied fuselage contained wheel-size depressions into which the main gears could be retracted by manually

Curtiss Shrike

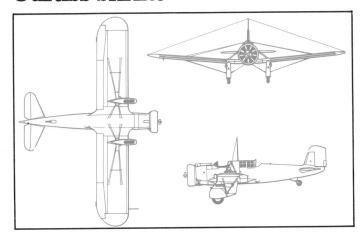

Origin: Curtiss Aeroplane and Motor Co, Garden City, NY.
Type: Two-seat attack bomber.
Engine: (A-8) one 600hp Curtiss Conqueror V-1570-57 V-12 liquid-cooled, (A-12) 690hp Wright Cyclone R-1820-21 nine cylinder radial.
Dimensions: Span 44ft (13.41m); length (12) 32ft 3in (9.83m); height 9ft 4in (2.84m); wing area 285sq ft (26.48m²).
Weights: (A-12) empty 3,898lb (1,768kg); max 5,900lb (2,676kg).
Performance: Maximum speed (8) 170mph (273km/h), (12) 177mph (285km/h); service ceiling (both) 15,200ft (4,633m); range 510 miles (820km).
Armament: Four 0.30in guns firing ahead outside propeller disc from gear trousers and one 0.30in aimed by gunner; four 100lb (45kg) or ten 30lb (13.6kg) bombs.

Above: Last of the Shrikes, the A-12 had a Hornet radial which proved decisively superior to Curtiss' own water-cooled V-12.

History: First flight (XA-8) June 1931; service entry April 1932.
User: AAC.

In 1929 the Army recognized a need for a high-speed monoplane attack bomber, and in preference to the Atlantic Fokker XA-7 the Army picked the XA-8. This had the same configuration and engine as its rival but was more modern, with a smooth stressed metal skin, full-span slats and wide flaps. The Pilot and gunner were far apart, each cockpit having a sliding canopy.

Orders were placed for five YA-8s and eight Y1A-8s, and when these entered service with the 3rd Attack Group at Fort Crockett they were by far the most advanced and

Above: Resplendent in chrome yellow and blue, an A-12 Shrike of the 3rd Attack Group cruises over Oahu in early 1936.

Below: This Conqueror-engined A-8 has the auxiliary fuel tank under its fuselage. Bombs went under the wings.

modern machines in the Air Corps. A further 46 production A-8Bs had been ordered, with open pilot cockpits, but tests with a Hornet-engined YA-10 showed the superiority of radial engines and the production machines accordingly became Cyclone-powered

A-12s, with the gunner's cockpit relocated nearer to that of the pilot. Many served with the 3rd Group at Hickam Field, Hawaii, named for the Group's CO Lt-Col Horace W. Hickam, who was killed in an A-12. Nine were still there on 7 December 1941.

---

operating long jackscrews. This was one of the tasks of the observer, because the XFF-1 had tandem seats, with both cockpits covered by sliding canopies.

Despite the penalty of the second man, the prototype outpaced every aircraft in the Navy at 195mph, and it exceeded 200mph (322km/h) with a more powerful Cyclone engine. The Navy bought a second example, designated XSF-1, equipped for scouting (reconnaissance) duties; later an XSF-2 was ordered with the R-1340 Wasp engine. In 1933 came an order for 27 FF-1 fighters for use from Navy carriers, notably the new *Lexington*. In service the FF-1 became the "Fifi", and later some were converted to FF-2 trainers by fitting dual pilot controls. Grumman also built 34 SF-1 scout fighters, with the rear-seat man occupied with overwater navigation and photography. By the end of 1936 all FFs and SFs had been transferred to the Reserves.

In 1934 Canadian Car & Foundry decided to enter aircraft manufacture, and acquired a license for the basic GE-23 design. In 1935-37 a total of 57 were built, 15 going to the RCAF as Goblin Is, one each to Japan and Nicaragua, the rest to Spanish Republican forces.

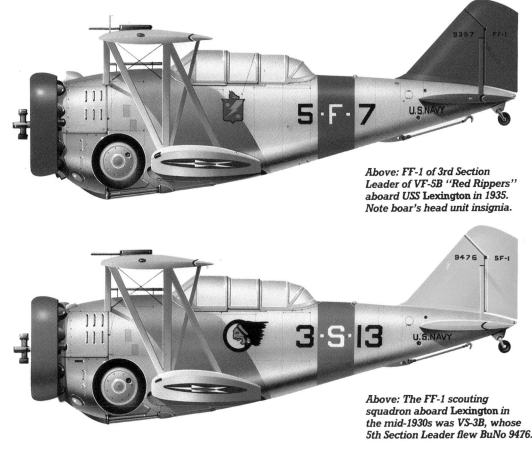

Above: FF-1 of 3rd Section Leader of VF-5B "Red Rippers" aboard USS Lexington in 1935. Note boar's head unit insignia.

Above: The FF-1 scouting squadron aboard Lexington in the mid-1930s was VS-3B, whose 5th Section Leader flew BuNo 9476.

Martin Bomber

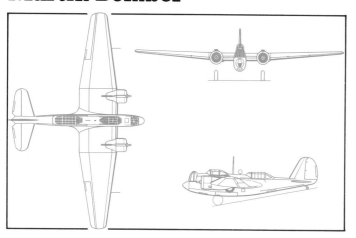

Origin: Glenn L. Martin Co, Cleveland, Ohio.

Type: 4/5-seat medium bomber.

Engines: (YB-10) two 775hp Wright R-1820-25 Cyclone nine-cylinder radials; (B-10B) 775hp R-1820-33; (YB-12) two 665hp Pratt & Whitney R-1690-11 Hornet nine-cylinder radials; (XB-14) two 850hp Pratt & Whitney R-1830-9 Twin Wasp 14-cylinder two-row radials.

Dimensions: Span 70ft 6in (21.48m); length 44ft 8¾in (13.63m); (XB-10) 45ft; (B-12A) 45ft 3in; height 11ft (3.35m); (XB-10) 10ft 4in (3.15m); (B-10B) 15ft 5in (4.7m); wing area (XB-10) 640sq ft (59.45m²), (B-10B) 678sq ft (62.99m²).

Weights: Empty (typical B-10, 139) 8,870lb-9,000lb (4,023-4,082kg), (166) 10,900lb (4,944kg); maximum loaded (XB-10) 12,560lb (5,697kg); (B-10B) 14,600lb (6,622kg); (B-12A) 14,200lb (6,441kg).

Performance: Maximum speed (all B-10, B-12) 207-213mph (340km/h); initial climb (all) 1,290-1,455ft (about 410m)/min; service ceiling (all) 24,200-25,200ft (about 7,500m); range with full

Above: The B-12A differed in small respects, such as the engine and cowls, from the main B-10B version.

bombload (typical) 700 miles (1,125km); maximum range with extra fuel (early models) 1,240 miles (1,995km).

Armament: (All) three rifle-calibre (usually 0.3in) machine guns manually aimed from nose turret, rear cockpit and rear ventral hatch; bomb load of 1,000lb (454kg) in internal bay beneath centre section in fuselage.

History: First flight (Model 123) January 1932; service delivery (123) 20 March 1932; (YB-10) June 1934; final delivery to AAC late 1936.

User: AAC.

The Glenn L. Martin Company was one of the earliest important suppliers of US Army and Navy aircraft. In 1931 Martin built the Model 123 as a company venture. Several observers have judged the "Martin Bomber" one of the most significant single advances in the history of

Above: The original "Martin Bomber", designated XB-907 by the Army, was one of the great technical advances in aviation.

Below: After much development the B-12 reached the squadrons. This one flew with the 11th BS from March Field, California.

Consolidated P2Y

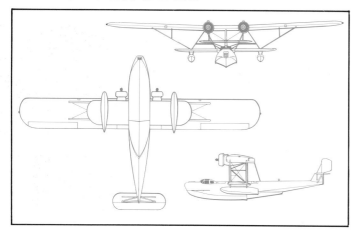

Origin: Consolidated Aircraft Company, Buffalo, NY.

Type: Long-range patrol flying boat.

Engines: Two Wright R-1820 Cyclone nine-cylinder radials, (-1) 575hp R-1820E, (-3) 750hp R-1820-90.

Dimensions: Span 100ft (30.48m); length 61ft 9in (18.82m); height 19ft

Above: Immediate predecessor of the famed PBY Catalina, the P2Y originally flew with a third engine above the upper wing.

1in (5.82m); wing area 1,514sq ft, (140.7m²).

Weights: (-3) empty 12,769lb (5,769kg); maximum 25,266lb (11,461kg).

Above: Not many photographs were taken of the original form of XP2Y-1, with three engines. This is dated 9 May 1932.

Performance: (-3) maximum speed 139mph (224km/h); range with full bombload 1,180 miles (1,900km).

Armament: Three 0.30in machine

guns in bow and two dorsal positions behind wings, plus bombload of 2,000lb (907kg).

History: First flight 26 March 1932; service delivery 1 February 1933.

User: Navy.

In 1927 Isaac M. "Mac" Laddon joined Consolidated and began designing the Navy's first mono-

Right: The first version in service was the B-10, seen here with the 9th Bombardment Group on 18 June 1934. By modern standards the structure and systems look prehistoric. The true yardstick is that export customers paid in 1937.

military aircraft. For the first time it introduced cantilever monoplane wings, flaps, all-metal stressed-skin construction, retractable landing gear, advanced engine cowls, variable-pitch propellers, fully-glazed cockpit and gun turret, and an internal bomb bay with power-driven doors.

Despite having only 600hp Cyclone engines, the prototype walked away from every pursuit (fighter) in the US Army, and the Model 139 went into production as the YB-10, followed by the -12 and -14, total delivery being 152 by 1936.

There were various experimental versions, including a YB-10A with turbocharged Cyclones giving a speed of 236mph (380km/h) at 25,000ft (7,620m). Some had skis or floats, and on several important long-range exercises the landing gears were changed in the field. In 1938 many Martins were converted for target towing as B-10Ms and B-12AMs.

Export sales were inevitable and once these were permitted, in 1935, a further 189 were built. By far the largest user was the Dutch East Indies, which bought 120 Martin 139W and 18 of the improved 166 with single "glasshouse" canopy. All the Netherlands Indies machines were in constant action from December 1941 as the only bombers available until late January 1942, fighting fiercely and with much success against Japanese sea and land forces.

Above: The badge on the nose of this B-12A is that of the 11th Bombardment Squadron, Hamilton Field, in 1935–38.

plane flying boat, the XPY-1. Powered by two Wasps, this also flew with a third engine above the wing during its first month. Martin underbid Consolidated for the nine production boats, which were delivered as three P3M-1s and six P3M-2s with R-1690 Hornet engines and a glazed enclosure over the pilots' cockpits.

In May 1931 Consolidated received a contract for a developed version, and this was a sesquiplane (biplane with a small lower wing). The prototype again flew with a third engine, the others being well below the upper wing. The lower wing replaced wide struts which in the P3M had carried the stabilizing floats. On 7 July 1931 the Navy ordered 23 twin-engined P2Y-1s, followed by a further 23 P2Y-3s with more powerful Cyclones mounted directly on the upper wing, reducing drag.

Right: Six P2Ys are visible in this classic picture taken in late 1933 — and two PN-12s.

Boeing P-26

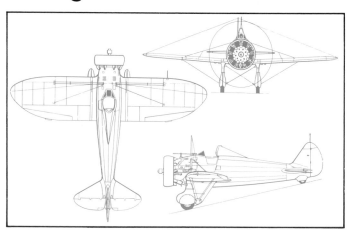

Origin: Boeing Airplane Company, Seattle, Washington.
Type: Single-seat pursuit (day fighter); data for P-26C.
Engine: 600hp Pratt & Whitney SR-1340-33 Wasp direct-injection nine-cylinder radial.
Dimensions: Span 27ft 11½in (8.82m); length 23ft 9in (7.28m); height 10ft 0½in (3.1m); wing area 149.5sq ft (13.89m²).
Weights: Empty about 2,200lb (998kg); loaded 3,075lb (1,395kg).
Performance: Maximum speed 235mph (378km/h); cruising speed 200mph (322km/h); initial climb 2,500ft (762m)/min; service ceiling over 28,000ft (8,530m); range 635 miles (1,100km).
Armament: Two synchronized

Above: The "Peashooter" has gained a fame that cannot be explained by its qualities, numbers or accomplishments. This is a regular P-26A.

Colt-Brownings (first batch both 0.30in, rest one 0.30in and one 0.5in); optional underwing racks for light bombs up to 200lb (91kg).
History: First flight (Model 248) 20 March 1932; (first production P-26A) 10 January 1934; (P-26C) late 1934.
User: AAC.

Having firmly switched from biplane to monoplane with the Monomail, the Model 247 airliner and the B-9 bomber, it was natural for Boe-

Above: This P-26A was at March Field, California, in July 1934, serving with the 95th Pursuit Squadron. Colors were OD (olive drab) with yellow wings and tail.

ing to design an all-metal (so-called stressed-skin) monoplane fighter. However, when the company-funded Model 248 first flew, care was taken not to make it too advanced for the conservative Army Air Corps. It had an open cockpit, wire-braced wing and fixed landing gear. Indeed the design was undertaken in partnership with the Air Corps, who provided such expensive hardware as engine, instruments and guns.

Three prototypes were built,

tested by the Army and — despite the landing speed of 73mph, which was extremely high for 1932 — adopted for production. In January 1933 the Air Corps ordered 111 P-26As, and these soon became known as "peashooters". In service they received radio, flotation gear and deeper headrest fairings. Boeing also built two P-26B with fuel-injection engines and split flaps on the wings, plus 23 P-26C with just the flaps.

P-26A deliveries began in late spring 1934, and from then until 1939 these distinctive snarling monoplanes were the main front-line pursuits of the Air Corps. They operated with seven famed PGs (pursuit groups), in the continental

Curtiss F11C/BF2C Goshawk

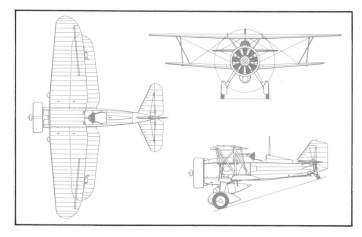

Origin: Curtiss Aeroplane Division, Buffalo, NY.
Type: Single-seat fighter-bomber; data for BF2C-1.
Engine: 750hp Wright R-1820F-53 Cyclone nine-cylinder radial.
Dimensions: Span 31ft 6in (9.59m); length 23ft 6in (7.16m); height 10ft (3.05m); wing area 262sq ft (24.34m²).
Weights: Empty 3,100lb (1,406kg); loaded (Hawk III) 4,317lb (1,958kg), (BF2C-1) 5,086lb (2,307kg).
Performance: Maximum speed (Hawk III) 240mph (386km/h); (BF2C-1) 228mph (368km/h); initial climb 2,200ft (671m)/min; service ceiling 27,000ft (823m); range (Hawk III) 575 miles (925km); (BF2C-1) 797 miles (1,282km).

Above: Originally delivered as F11C-2 Goshawks, these carrier-based fighter-bombers were later modified with a higher rear deck and hood as BFC-2s.

Above: This F11C-2 was photographed on manufacturer's flight test in early 1933, in plain silver finish. Soon it would be redesignated a BFC-2.

Below: Last of the Hawk biplane fighters, the BF2C-1 was the first Curtiss for the Navy with retractable landing gear. It served with VB-5 (USS Ranger).

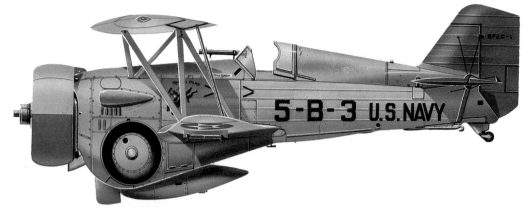

USA, in Hawaii and in the Canal Zone.

As the Model 281, eleven aircraft were exported, one to Spain and the rest to China. In the latter country the Boeings fought Japanese air power and in Philippine Army colors they did so again in 1941-42.

Above: On 17 February 1935 the entire 17th Pursuit Group was on parade at March Field for inspection by the Commanding General. The two nearest the camera bear the red and yellow bands of the HQ section; "OO" wears 1st Pursuit Wing badge.

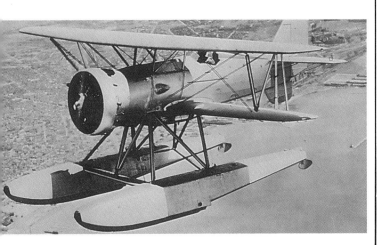

Armament: (basic) two 0.30in machine guns (usually Colt-Browning) in fuselage (often changed or increased locally); underwing racks for four 116lb (52.5kg) bombs, plus one 474lb (215kg) on centerline in place of extra fuel tank.
History: First flight (XF11C-2) June 1932; (XF11C-3) May 1933; final export delivery, after 1936.
User: Navy.

In 1931 the emergence of the dive bomber led to Navy studies of single-seat fighters able to operate in this role. In April 1932 Curtiss received an order for two Goshawks the XF11C-1 with the Wright R-1510 engine and the XF11C-2 with the single-row

Above: This was the only F11C flown on floats; Curtiss demonstrated this capability, but it was not used by the Navy. Note the rudders on the floats.

SR-1820 Cyclone. New features included metal wings and a large bomb swung down on crutches to clear the three-blade propeller. Curtiss then delivered 28 improved F11C-2s (later redesignated BFC-2) for Navy squadron VF-1B "Top Hatters" aboard USS *Saratoga*.

In 1933 appeared the XF11C-3 (later BF2C1) with a new fuselage and retractable main gear to compete with the Grumman FF. They were not adopted by the Army but found wide Navy acceptance.

Consolidated P-30 and PB-2A

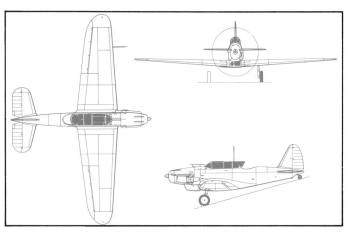

Origin: Consolidated Aircraft Corporation, San Diego, California.
Type: Two-seat pursuit.
Engine: One 700hp Curtiss Conqueror V-1570-61 V-12 water-cooled with turbocharger.
Dimensions: Span 43ft 11in (13.38m); length 30ft (9.14m); height 8ft 3in (2.51m); wing area 297sq ft (27.59m²).
Weights: (PB-2A) empty 4,306lb (1,953kg); maximum 5,643lb (2,560kg).
Performance: (PB-2A) maximum speed 274mph (441km/h) at 25,000ft (7,620m); service ceiling 28,000ft (8,535m); range 508 miles (820km).
Armament: Two forward-firing 0.30in guns above engine and one 0.30in aimed by gunner.
History: First flight (Y1P-25) late 1932, (P-30) mid-1934.
User: AAC.

In September 1931 the Army purchased eight fighter and attack prototypes derived from the speedy Lockheed Altair, but the original Lockheed went bankrupt. Designer Robert Wood (later of Bell) moved to Consolidated and produced an improved version, the Y1P-25. There followed four P-30s which had impressive performance.

Below: This Wright Field photo is undated but shows the original XP-30. This turbosupercharged monoplane knocked everything else for six, even though it was a large two-seater.

Above: The first stressed-skin, retractable-gear airplane to go into US military service, the PB-2A (originally P-30A) also had a turbosupercharger.

Members of a rare species, the modern stressed-skin two-seat pursuit, they were clean cantilever monoplanes, with one of the first examples of neat inward-retracting landing gear (inherited from the Altair). Other advanced features included a streamlined enclosure over the tandem cockpits, a ducted coolant radiator and split flaps, but the high performance stemmed mainly from the GE turbosupercharger on the left side, which was at last becoming sufficiently reliable for service use. With this fitted, the big two-seater gained 60mph (97km/h) in top speed from sea level up to over 20,000ft (6,096m).

Turbos were first used in production on the batch of 50 P-30A fighters ordered in December 1934. These were redesignated as the only production aircraft in the PB (pursuit biplace) category, becoming PB-2As. They bore serials 35-001/050, and were not withdrawn until 1941. Consolidated also delivered an XA-11 attack prototype with two extra guns (in the wings) and a 400lb (181kg) bombload, followed by four A-11s, one of which became the XA-11A testbed for the Allison V-1710 engine.

For more than three years these attractive machines were the fastest in the entire AAF, especially at high altitudes.

Curtiss SBC Helldiver

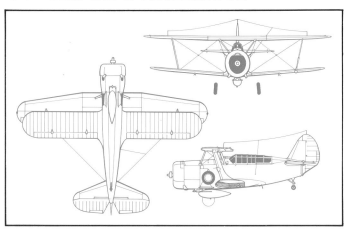

Origin: Curtiss-Wright Airplane Division, Buffalo, NY.
Type: Carrier-based scout/dive bomber.
Engine: (-3) one 715hp Pratt & Whitney Twin Wasp Junior R-1535-94 14-cylinder radial, (-4) one 950hp Wright Cyclone R-1820-34 nine-cylinder radial.
Dimensions: Span 34ft (10.36m); length (3) 28ft 11in (8.81), (4) 28ft 1in (8.56m); height 12ft 7in (3.83m); wing area 317sq ft (29.45m²).
Weights: (4) empty 4,841lb (2,196kg); maximum 7,632lb (3,462kg).
Performance: Maximum speed (4) 237mph (381km/h); range with 500lb (227kg) bomb 590 miles (950km).
Armament: One forward-firing 0.30in gun, one 0.30in aimed from rear cockpit, and bomb under fuselage of (3) 500lb (227kg) or (4) 1,000lb (454kg).
History: See text.
Users: Navy, Marine Corps.

Above: Final SBC model was this SBC-4, also final US combat biplane in production.

Few airplanes have had so uncertain a gestation as this rather pedestrian naval biplane (the last produced in the US). It began as the XF12C-1 pursuit, with parasol monoplane wing, flown in January 1933. Twice re-engined, it became the XS4C-1 scout in 1933 and the XSBC-1 scout bomber in January 1934, but crashed in June 1934. The

Above: SBC-4 BuNo 1813 was the lead aircraft of VB-8 (note all-red cowl) throughout 1941.

parasol wing was thought unsuited to dive bombing, and the same Navy number (9225) was transferred to the XSBC-2 biplane flown on

Below: SBC-3 BuNo 0563 was leader of Section 3 of scouting squadron VS-5 aboard USS Yorktown in 1937. Note Mk III telescope sight.

9 December 1934. In March 1936 it became the XSBC-3 with R-1535 engine, and in July 1937 delivery began to VS-5 of the first of 83 production SBC-3s. These were followed by 174 SBC-4s with the Cyclone and doubled bombload. Two units, VB-8 and VS-8, were aboard *Hornet* on 7 December 1941, but the SBCs saw little combat duty and were relegated to training and support tasks.

Grumman JF, J2F Duck

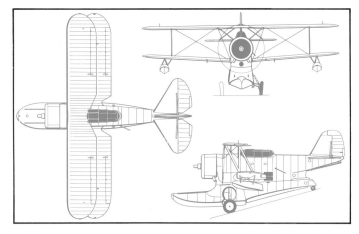

Origin: Grumman Aircraft Engineering Corp, Bethpage, NY; J2F-6 built by Columbia Aircraft, Valley Stream, NY.
Type: Multirole amphibian.
Engine: See text.
Dimensions: Span 39ft (11.89m); length 32ft 7in to 33ft 10in (10.3m); height on ground (most) 14ft 6in (4.4m); wing area 409sq ft, (38m²).
Weights: (JF-1) 4,113lb (1,866kg), (-6) 4,941lb (2,241kg); maximum (-1) 5,375lb (2,438kg), (-5) 6,696lb (3,037kg).

Above: Ultimate expression of the Loening-style amphibian, the Columbia-built J2F-6 ought strictly to have been the JL-1. Ducks were sluggish yet popular among aircrew.

Performance: Maximum speed (-1) 168mph (270km/h), (-6) 188mph (303km/h); service ceiling (-1) 18,000ft (5,490m), (-6) 27,000ft (8,320m); range (-6) 780 miles (1,255km).
Armament: One 0.30in Browning

Above: A pristine color photo of a JF-2 of the US Coast Guard. The airplane is probably V148, based at CG Air Station Port Angeles, Washington, in 1941. The USCG had 14 of these.

aimed by observer, and two 100lb (45kg) bombs, (-5 and -6) in addition, two 325lb (147kg) depth bombs.
History: First flight (XJF) 4 May 1933, (3) September 1935, (5) June 1941.

Users: Navy, Marine Corps, Coast Guard.

Grumman's first products were patented amphibian floats with neat landing gears retracting flush into the sides. The company was thus well placed to take over where Loening left off with single-engine amphibians. The XJF-1 was a conventional single-bay biplane with a 700hp Pratt & Whitney R-1535-62 Twin Wasp Junior and 9ft (2.74m) Hamilton three-blade propeller. It

Vought SBU

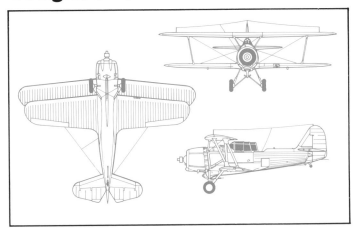

Origin: Chance Vought Division of United Aircraft, East Hartford, Connecticut.
Type: Scout bomber.
Engine: One 750hp Pratt & Whitney Twin Wasp Junior 14-cylinder radial, (-1) R-1535-80, (-2) -98.
Dimensions: Span 33ft 3in (10.13m); length 27ft 10in (8.50m); height 11ft 11in (3.63m); wing area 327sq ft, (30.38m²).
Weights: Empty 3,645lb (1,653kg); maximum 5,520lb (2,504kg).
Performance: Maximum speed 208mph (335km/h); service ceiling 23,700ft (7,225m); range 548 miles (880km).
Armament: One fixed 0.30in gun, one 0.30in aimed by observer, and swinging attachment for 500lb (227kg) bomb under fuselage, with light bombs under wings.
History: First flight May 1933; service delivery 20 November 1935.
User: Navy.

Above: The Navy's first 200mph airplane was Vought's two-seat fixed-gear SBU biplane.

Below: SBU-1 No 9812 was assigned to scouting squadron VS-2B. Note radio antenna wires.

Above: BuNo 9750 was the first production SBU-1, delivered to VS-3B. Note the gray fuselage.

This neat enclosed-cockpit biplane originated as the XF3U-1 two-seat carrier-based fighter, but in Nov-ember 1933 the Navy asked that it be modified as a scout bomber. Vought delivered 84 SBU-1s follow-ed by 40 SBU-2s. They were all just being withdrawn at the time of Pearl Harbor, after service with scouting and reserve squadrons.

Right: Last of the breed was the Columbia-built J2F-6. Many were unpainted, or finished silver, unlike this one.

started one of the most enduring and popular multirole airplanes ever used by the Navy.

Though in practice the were used mainly as catapult ship-planes and for shore links by carriers, the Duck (originally the name was unofficial) was armed for general patrol duties and equipped various combat units such as VMS-3 in the Virgin Isles. The JF-1 had the slim R-1535, the JF-2 the bulky 700hp Wright Cyclone R-1820-102, the -3 the 750hp R-1820-80, the J2F-1 the 750hp R-1820-20 and full carrier gear, the J2F-2 the 790hp R-1820-30, the J2F-3 had VIP furnishing, the -4 had minor changes, the -5 the 950hp R-1820-50 and tow-target gear, smoke tank and cameras, and the final 330 were made by Columbia as the J2F-6 with the 1,050hp R-1820-54. Most were three-seaters.

Right: BuNo 1651 was J2F-4, the last model with the short-chord cowl. Most were used to tow targets.

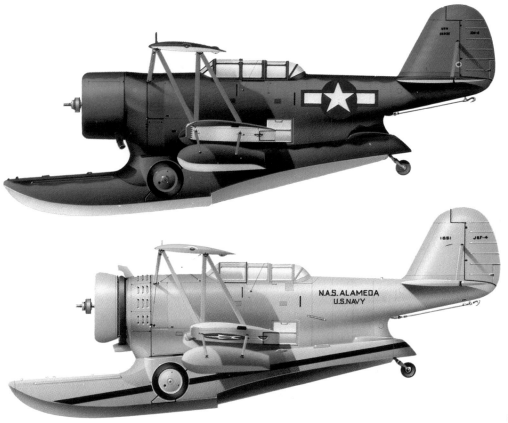

Northrop A-17

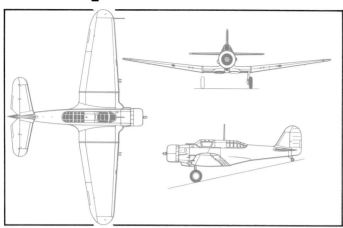

Origin: Northrop Corporation, El Segundo, California.
Type: Attack bomber.
Engine: One Pratt & Whitney Twin Wasp Junior 14-cyinder radial, (17) 750hp R-1535-11, (17A) 825hp R-1535-13.
Dimensions: Span 47ft 9in (14.55m); length 31ft 8in (9.65m); height 12ft (3.66m); wing area 362sq ft (33.63m²).

Above: Unlike the original A-17 shown in the photographs the A-17A had retractable landing gear. In its day it was the last word in Army airplanes.

Weights: (A) empty 5,106lb (2,316kg); maximum 7,543lb (3,422kg).
Performance: (A) maximum speed 220mph (354km/h); service

Above: An idyllic echelon of fixed-gear A-17s operated from Albrook Field, CZ (Panama) in November 1937. Two years later they were obsolete.

ceiling 19,400ft (5,900m); range 732 miles (1,180km).
Armament: Four 0.30in Brownings in outer wings firing ahead, one aimed by gunner, plus up to 900lb

(408kg) of bombs internally or 650lb (295kg) external.
History: See text.
User: AAC.

Northrop was one of the pioneers of all-metal stressed-skin construction. With his brilliant designer Ed Heinemann he turned the Gamma mailplane into the Model 2-C attack airplane, bought by the Army as

Grumman F2F and F3F

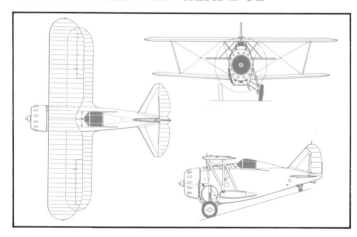

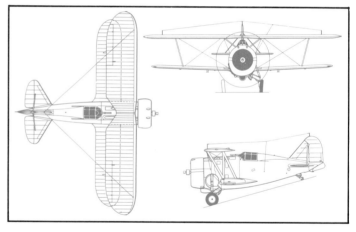

Origin: Grumman Aircraft Engineering Corporation, Bethpage, NY.
Type: Carrier-based fighter-bomber.
Engine: (F2F) one 650hp Pratt & Whitney Twin Wasp Junior R-1535-72 14-cylinder radial, (F3F-1) one R-1535-72, (F3F-2) one 850hp Wright Cyclone R-1820-22 nine-cylinder radial, (-3) same as (-2) uprated to 950hp.
Dimensions: Span (2) 28ft 6in (8.69m), (3) 32ft (9.75m); length (2) 21ft 5in (6.53m), (3) 23ft 2in (7.07m); height 9ft 4in (2.84m); wing area (2) 230sq ft (21.37m²), (3) 260sq ft (24.15m²).
Weights: Empty (2) 2,691lb (1,221kg), (3) 3,258lb (1,478kg); maximum (2) 3,782lb (1,716kg), (3) 4,502lb (2,042kg).
Performance: Maximum speed (2) 238mph (383km/h), (3) 264mph (425km/h); service ceiling (2) 27,500ft (8,382m), (3) 30,200ft (9,205m); range (2) 750 miles (1,200km), (3) 825 miles (1,328km).
Armament: (2) two 0.30in Browning guns above fuselage

Above: F2F-1 combined the company's patented landing gear with an enclosed cockpit and metal-skinned fuselage.

and two 116lb (52.6kg) bombs, (3) one 0.30in and one 0.50in, plus two 116lb (52.6kg) bombs.
History: First flight (2) 18 October 1933, (3) 20 March 1935.
Users: Navy, Marine Corps.

Following success with its FF-1, Grumman boldly schemed a single-seat fighter, the G-8, and submitted this to the Navy in June 1932. Five months later the XF2F-1 prototype was awarded. Naturally smaller than the FF it continued the policy of a metal-skinned fuselage and fabric-covered metal wings, with ailerons on the upper planes only. The slim R-1535, driving a 6ft 6in (1.98m) Smith R-3 propeller, was lost inside a forward fuselage made distinctively pot-bellied by the retractable landing gears. After fitting a bigger cockpit canopy and extending the span 6in, the type was accepted as the F2F-1, 54 be-

Above: Last of the Navy biplane fighters, the F3F-3 had a powerful Cyclone engine, longer fuselage and increased span.

Below: In Grumman's early years its trump card was its patented retractable landing gear, here on XF2F prototype.

the XA-13, with Cyclone engine. It proved outstanding, and from first flight in August 1933 set new standards despite fixed landing gear. In December 1934 the Army placed an unprecedented order for 100, but trials with a Twin Wasp as the XA-16 proved that this engine was overlarge. The slim R-1535 resulted in the A-17, and all 110 were delivered from August 1935.

In December 1935 new contracts were placed for the A-17A with inwards-retracting landing gear and more power. All were delivered, so that by 1939 the agile Northrop was the standard attack type. In June 1940 the Army returned 93 for sale to Britain (which passed them to the S African AF in North Africa). In 1936 two three-seat A-17AS command transports were delivered, with R-1340 Wasp engines of 600hp.

Right: Taken on 21 July 1936, this shows an A-17 operating from Barksdale Field, Louisiana. The stressed-skin Northrop equipped the 3rd and 17th Attack Groups.

ing delivered during 1935. They had a most successful career, VF-2B "Fighting Two" keeping the type until 30 September 1940.

In October 1934, before the start of F2F deliveries, the Navy ordered a prototype XF3F (G-11) with increased span and a longer fuselage to improve handling and especially stability. It crashed in a dive pull-out, and the replacement failed to recover from a spin. Despite this, 54 production F3F-1s were ordered, with Hamilton v-p propellers and small rear underfins, these being delivered in 1936. Carburetion problems delayed the Cyclone-engined F3F-2, distin-guished by its larger-diameter engine, but 81 were delivered in 1937-38. The Navy's last fighter biplanes were 27 F3F-3s with an uprated Cyclone and improved cowl and landing gear. The last of these famed Grummans was not struck off until November 1943.

Above: The national insignia near the nose of this F3F was worn by "Neutrality Patrol" aircraft in 1940. This VF-7 airplane flew from USS Wasp.

Below: The F2F flown by the CO of VF-2B renumbered VF-5.

Douglas TBD Devastator

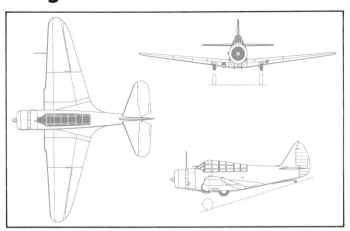

Origin: Douglas Aircraft Company, El Segundo, California.
Type: Three-seat carrier-based torpedo bomber.
Engine: One 850hp Pratt & Whitney R-1830-64 Twin Wasp 14-cylinder two-row radial.
Dimensions: Span 50ft (15.24m); length 35ft 6in (10.82m); height 15ft 1in (4.6m); wing area 422sq ft (39.20m²).
Weights: Empty 7,195lb (3,264kg);

Above: All TBDs were TBD-1s. They arrived in an era of rapid change and soon became obsolescent. Wing loading was a mere 24 lb/sq ft.

maximum loaded 10,141lb (4,622kg).
Performance: Maximum speed 206mph (332km/h); initial climb at maximum weight 900ft (274m)/min; service ceiling

Above: The TBD was one of the first aircraft to use the R-1830 Twin Wasp, though in the mid-1930s it was rated at only 850hp: not enough for 1942.

19,700ft (6,000m); range with full weapon load 435 miles (700km).
Armament: One 0.30in Colt-Browning fixed on right side of nose, one 0.5in manually aimed in rear cockpit, single 21in (1,000lb,

454kg) Bliss-Leavitt torpedo recessed into belly, light bomb racks under wings for total additional load of 500lb (227kg).
History: First flight (XTBD-1) January 1935; production delivery 25 June 1937.
User: Navy.

In the early 1930s the US Navy ordered new aircraft carriers, the *Ranger, Yorktown* and *Enterprise*.

Consolidated PBY Catalina

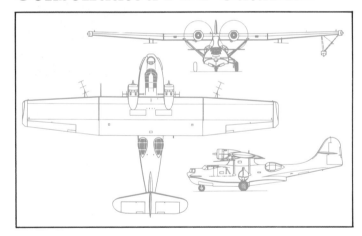

Origin: Consolidated Vultee Aircraft Corporation, San Diego, California; also made by Naval Aircraft Factory, Canadian Vickers and Boeing Canada.
Type: Maritime patrol flying boat with normal crew of seven; data for PBY-5.
Engines: Two 1,200hp Pratt & Whitney R-1830-92 Twin Wasp 14-cylinder two-row radials.
Dimensions: Span 104ft (31.72m); length 63ft 11in (19.5m); height 18ft 10in (5.65m); wing area 1,400sq ft (130.06m²).
Weights: Empty 17,465lb (7,974kg); loaded 34,000lb (15,436kg).
Performance: Maximum speed 196mph (314km/h); climb to 5,000ft (1,525m) in 4min 30sec; service ceiling 18,200ft (5,550m); range at 100mph (161km/h) 3,100 miles (4,960km).
Armament: US Navy, typically one 0.30in or 0.50in Browning in nose, one 0.50in in each waist blister and one in "tunnel" in underside behind hull step; wing

Above: The PBY-5A amphibian was an aircraft of tremendous versatility and value. Here it is seen with British ASV radar.

racks for 2,000lb or 4,000lb (907 or 1,814kg) of bombs and other stores including two torpedoes or four 325lb (147kg) depth charges.
History: First flight (XP3Y-1) 21 March 1935; first delivery (PBY-1) October 1936; (Model 28-5 Catalina) July 1939; final delivery, after December 1945.
Users: AAF, Navy, Marines.

Consolidated of Buffalo battled with Douglas of Santa Monica in 1933 to supply the US Navy with its first cantilever monoplane flying boat. Though the Douglas was good, its rival, designed by Isaac M. Laddon, was to be a classic aircraft and made in bigger numbers than any other flying boat before or since, by the new plant at San Diego, to which the company moved in October 1935. Its features included two 825hp Twin Wasps mounted close

Above: Equipped with British ASV (air to surface vessel) radar, a PBY-5 patrols at about 100ft altitude in 1942.

Below: It is fair to say the drone of the "Cat" covered the world. This US Navy PBY was somewhere in the US West Coast.

Among their complement were to be squadrons of torpedo bombers, and on 30 June 1934 orders were placed for two prototypes of rival designs. One was the Great Lakes XTBG-1 biplane, rather similar to the later British Swordfish. The other was the first cantilever monoplane designed for such a duty, the Douglas XTBD-1.

The monoplane started with the drawback of being radically new; though the wing was very thick, the retracted main wheels protruded far enough for safe landings, and the landing speed was only 59mph (95km/h). The large canopy over the pilot, radio operator and gunner opened into six sections for "open cockpit" vision, and the all-round performance of the monoplane was superior. Despite competition from another mono-

Left: Most TBDs were overall light gray in 1941; some were "sea green and gray" with tailstripes. This TBD began its life with a torpedo squadron but is seen after reassignment to Scouting Squadron 42 in 1942.

plane contender, on 3 February 1936 the Douglas won the production order for 110 aircraft, at that time the largest peacetime order for aircraft ever placed by the US Navy.

The production TBD had a taller canopy with crash pylon, power-folding wings and other changes. Altogether 129 were delivered, and over 100 were still the only carrier-based torpedo bombers in US service at the time of Pearl Harbor. Named Devastator, they immediately went into violent action, bombing and torpedoing almost on a round-the-clock basis. The middle crewmember aimed the torpedo, sighting through doors in the belly and from a not very comfortable prone-position.

In the Marshalls and Gilberts these aircraft proved formidable, but they were obsolescent and no match for Japanese fighters in 1942. In the summer of that year at the fateful Battle of Midway 35 were shot down by flak and Zeros in a single action. The Devastator was soon afterwards replaced by the TBF Avenger.

---

together on a wide clean wing, on the tips of which were to be found the retracted stabilizing floats. The Consolidated Model 28, or Navy XP3Y-1, clocked a speed of 184mph, which was high for a 1935 flying boat. The order for 60 was exceptional for those days, but within a decade the worldwide total had topped 4,000.

All versions were of all-metal stressed-skin construction. The wing was carried on a central pylon, and there were four small struts bracing the wide untapered center section. The hull was wide but shallow, with a round top. Wartime versions had a huge observation blister on each side which could be swung open in flight. Most PBY-6As had ASV radar in a blister on a pylon above the cockpit, earlier versions often having British-supplied ASV.II radar with external dipole arrays.

In 1938 three were bought by the Soviet Union, which urgently tooled up to build its own version, called GST, with M62 engines. In 1939 one was bought by the RAF, which soon placed large orders and called the boat Catalina, a name adopted in the USA in 1942. In December 1939 came the PBY-5A (OA-10) with retractable landing gear, which was named Canso by the RCAF. Many hundreds of both the boat and the amphibian were built by Canadian Vickers (as the PBV-1) and Boeing Canada (PB2B-1), and revised tall-fin versions were made

Right: After the end of World War II PBYs engaged on rescue missions became more colorful. This Canadian Vickers-built OA-10A of the USAAF, No 44-33924, has radar above the cockpit.

by a new Convair plant at New Orleans (PBY-6A) and by the Naval Aircraft Factory at Philadelphia (PBN-1 Nomad).

The "Cat's" exploits are legion. One found the *Bismarck* in mid-Atlantic; one attacked a Japanese carrier in daylight after radioing: "Please inform next of kin"; in 1942 Patrol Squadron 12 started the Black Cat tradition of stealthy night devastation; and one had both ailerons ripped off by a storm but crossed the Atlantic and landed safely. Hundreds served in many countries for long after World War II, some air/sea rescue versions carrying a lifeboat under one wing.

Below: A PBY-5 on Neutrality Patrol in 1941, serving with Patrol Squadron VP-44. Later variants had a taller fin.

Above: PBY-5s on patrol in early 1942. Unit designators have been obliterated, though the center PBY has individual "u".

North American T-6, SNJ

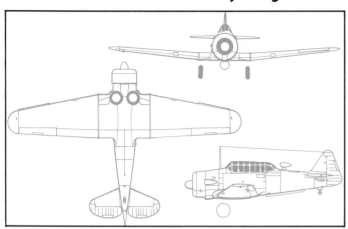

Origin: North American Aviation Inc, Inglewood, Downey and Dallas; built under licence by Noorduyn Aviation and (post-war) Canadian Car & Foundry, Canada.

Type: Two-seat (some, single-seat) basic or advanced trainer, FAC and attack.

Engine: Typically one 550hp Pratt & Whitney R-1340-AN1 nine-cylinder radial (see text).

Dimensions: 42ft ¼in (12.8m); length 29ft 6in (8.99m); height 11ft 8½in (3.56m); wing area 253.75sq ft (23.57m²).

Weights: (T-6G) empty 4,271lb (1,938kg); loaded 5,617lb (2,546kg).

Performance: (T-6G) maximum speed 212mph (341km/h); initial climb 1,640ft (500m)/min; service ceiling 24,750ft (7,338m); range 870 miles (1,400km).

Armament: Normally provision for machine gun in either or both wing roots and manually aimed in rear cockpit; light series wing bomb racks.

History: First flight (NA-16 prototype) April 1935; (production

Above: The final new-build version was the T-6G, produced for FAC duties in Korea. Some had canopies with frameless side windows for better view.

BT-9) April 1936; (NA-26) 1937.
Users: AAC, AAF, AF, Navy, Marine Corps.

Perhaps the most varied family of aircraft in history began as a little monoplane trainer, with fixed gear and two open cockpits but all-metal stressed-skin construction, flown as a US civil machine in 1935. Its first offspring was the BT-9 basic trainer, supplied to many countries and made in many more, powered by Wright R-975 Whirlwind, Pratt & Whitney Wasp Junior or Wasp engine. About 970 were built by North American. A second family were combat warplanes. Biggest family were the T-6 Texan (British name Harvard) trainers derived from the NA-26, of which 15,109 were made by NAA in 1938-45, 755 in Australia as CAC Wirraways, 2,610 by Noorduyn in Canada, 176 by Japan (even receiving an Allied

Above: Hoses, buckets and brooms scrub down a Navy SNJ (probably a flag officer's SNJ-3) at NAS Miami at about the time of Pearl Harbor.

Below: Thousands of USAAF and Navy gunners learned how to aim from the rear cockpit of an AT-6 or SNJ. The rear section of canopy folded up and over.

code-name: "Oak") and 136 by Saab in Sweden. By far the most important Allied training machine in World War II, thousands were refurbished or remanufactured (2,068 by the original maker) in 1946-59 for 54 nations. Cancar built 555 T-6G in 1951-54 to meet an urgent AF need for these aircraft in

FAC (forward air control) and general close-support duties in Korea.

Below: It was unfair to combine a T-6 instrument training school with an F-80 jet conversion unit at Williams AFB, Arizona, 1949. This is a Dallas-built AT-6D.

Curtiss P-36

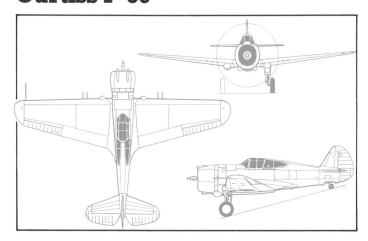

Origin: Curtiss-Wright Airplane Division, Buffalo, NY.

Type: Single-seat pursuit.

Engine: One Pratt & Whitney Twin Wasp 14-cylinder radial, (A) 1,050hp R-1830-13, (C) 1,200hp R-1830-17.

Dimensions: Span 37ft 4in (11.38m); length 28ft 6in (8.69m); height (excluding propeller) 9ft 6in (2.90m); wing area 236sq ft (21.92m²).

Weight: Empty (C) 4,620lb (2,096kg); maximum (A) 6,010lb (2,726kg), (C) 6,150lb (2,790kg).

Performance: Maximum speed (A) 300mph (482km/h), (C) 311mph (500km/h); service ceiling 33,000ft (10,000m); range 825 miles (1,328km).

Armament: (A) one 0.50in with 200 rounds and one 0.30in with 500 rounds, both above cowling, (C) as (A) plus two 0.30in wing guns each with 500 rounds.

History: First flight (Model 75) April 1935, (Y1P-36) February 1937.

Users: AAC, AAF.

In 1934 the Army planned to hold a pursuit competition in May 1935 to select a replacement for the P-26. Don Berlin quickly designed the first Curtiss to have a Type number from the outset — 75 — and this was ready on the due date, but absence of rivals resulted in postponements until August 1936. This was unfortunate because while the Curtiss design was good for 1934 it was one that would rapidly be overtaken by such foreign types as the Bf 109 and Spitfire.

Features included smooth stressed-skin construction, a multi-spar wing with no bracing wires, sliding cockpit canopy, variable-pitch Hamilton propeller and hydraulic split flaps and main gears folding backwards, the wheels rotating to lie flat inside the wing. The Model 75 had the 900hp Wright XR-1670 engine, but this was discontinued and replaced by an XR-1820. This gave much trouble and was partly responsible for the contest being won by Seversky's P-35. Nevertheless in August 1936 the Army ordered three Y1P-36s for evaluation, and these

Above: Called Hawk 81A2 by the maker, the P-36A was in many ways a good 1937 design, with toughness, agility and six guns. But by 1940 it was an also-ran.

proved so outstanding that on 7 July 1937 Curtiss received the biggest-ever peacetime pursuit contract, for 210 P-36As.

From No 178 on the line the designation changed to P-36C with wing guns and a more powerful engine. There were several one-offs and conversions. The production aircraft had a Curtiss constant-speed propeller, and prolonged troubles were overcome by 81 major and minor modifications which increased weight and reduced speed in service often to below 300mph. These difficulties delayed overseas deployment until 1941, but on 7 December 1941 the 46th and 47th PS were in Hawaii and the former unit, flying from Wheeler Field, scored two kills on that day. Designation P-36G was applied to 30 fighters intended for Norway and finally donated to Peru.

Above: Many of the first P-36 pursuits (members of the famed Hawk family) were retained at Wright Field for tests on engine, propeller, guns and radio.

Below: Another of the first P-36As to come off the line and sent to Wright Field. Early problems were terrible; the flight restrictions severe.

Above: P-36Cs, with wing guns (note collector box) in War Games camouflage in 1939. Unit was 27th PS.

Right: This P-36A flew with the 79th Pursuit Sqn of the 20th PG at Barksdale. At one time faults cut the group to six flyable P-36s.

Seversky P-35

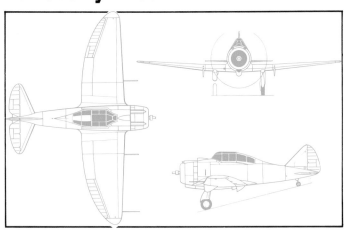

Origin: Seversky Aircraft (from 1939 Republic Aviation) Corporation, Farmingdale, NY.
Type: Single-seat fighter.
Engine: One Pratt & Whitney Twin Wasp 14-cylinder radial, (35) 950hp R-1830-9, (35A) 1,050hp -45.
Dimensions: Span 36ft (10.97m); length 26ft 10in (8.19m); height 9ft 9in (2.97m); wing area 220sq ft (20.44m²).
Weights: (35A) empty 4,575lb (2,075kg); maximum 6,723lb (3,050kg).
Performance: (35A) maximum speed 303mph (488km/h); service

Above: The P-35A was a frustrated export pursuit for Sweden. A good 1935 design, it was obsolete by Pearl Harbor.

ceiling 31,400ft (9,570m); range 950 miles (1,530km).
Armament: (35) one 0.50in and one 0.30in above engine plus 300lb (136kg) bombload under wings, (35A) two 0.50in above cowling and two 0.30in in outer wings, same bombload.
History: First flight (SEV-2XP) April 1935, (P-35) May 1937.
Users: AAC, AAF.

Above: The P-35A of Lt Body Wagner, CO of the 17th Pursuit Sqn, at Nichols Field, Philippines, just before Pearl Harbor.

Seversky's (later Republic's) famed designer Alexander Kartveli designed the SEV-2XP to participate in the Army pursuit competition of May 1935. It was a clean stressed-skin monoplane with a Cyclone engine and fixed gear. After two rebuilds it emerged as the AP-1 with a Twin Wasp, new tail and gears folding back into bathtub fairings under the horizontal center

section of the elliptical wings. The Army bought 77 but the last was completed as the XP-41 (see Republic P-43). Republic sold 120 similar EP-1s to Sweden, but on 18 October 1940 the US Government requisitioned the final 60 of these and the Army took them as P-35As. Of these 48 went to the Philippines, but their lack of armor and self-sealing tanks resulted in only eight being airworthy two days after the Japanese attack.

Right: An unusual air-to-air shot of an early P-35, without wing guns.

North American O-47

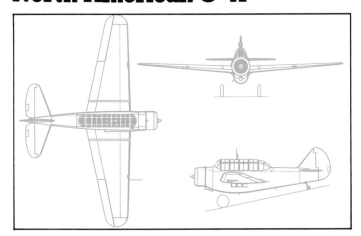

Above: A masive three-seater, the O-47A still had a fair speed, thanks to the growing power of the R-1820 engine.

Below: Many O-47s on coastal ASW patrol in 1942 were painted Midnight Blue, though they served with the Army Air Force.

Above: The observer/gunner had a "thirty-caliber" Browning, mounted on a traversing rail. Note the D/F loop antenna.

Origin: North American Aviation Inc, Inglewood, California.
Type: Observation.
Engine: One Wright Cyclone nine-cylinder radial, (A) 975hp R-1820-49, (B) 1,060hp R-1820-57.
Dimensions: Span 46ft 4in (14.12m); length 33ft 7in (10.23m); height 12ft 2in (3.7m); wing area 350sq ft (32.52m²).
Weights: Empty 5,980lb (2,713kg); maximum 7,636lb (3,464kg).
Performance: Maximum speed 221mph (356km/h); service ceiling 23,200ft (7,070m); range 400 miles (645km).
Armament: One 0.30in in right wing firing ahead, one 0.30in aimed from rear cockpit.
History: First flight (GA-15) June

1935; service delivery October 1937.
Users: AAC, AAF, ANG.

In 1934 General Aviation, successor to Atlantic (Fokker), of Dundalk, Maryland, designed a radically new observation airplane. All-metal, it was to parallel the new high-performance pursuits, with enclosed cockpits, variable-pitch propeller, flaps and retractable gear. The pot-bellied fuselage housed the observer/photographer under the wing, with all-round glazing. By the time the GA-15 had been built the company had become NAA, and in the new

Right: This O-47A (38-306) is probably olive drab, the blue color probably being due to the old film (see landscape). It has its AAF number in correct yellow, unlike the O-47 opposite.

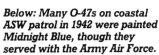

California plant 164 O-47As were built in 1937-38, 48 of them for the ANG. Most had a curved belly with little glazing. Production was completed with 74 O-47Bs with higher gross weight and increased fuel capacity. A few saw one-sided combat in the Pacific in December 1941, but most were used for anti-submarine patrol and target towing.

Right: A color photo of marvellous quality dating from long before World War II, showing an O-47B on test from Wright Field, bearing the arrow emblem used by that base from 1932 to 1941.

Douglas SBD/A-24 Dauntless

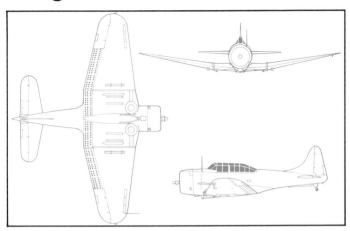

Origin: Douglas Aircraft Company, El Segundo, California.
Type: Two-seat carrier-based (SBD) or land-based (A-24) dive bomber.
Engine: One 1,000hp Wright R-1820-32 or -52, or (-5) 1,200hp R-1820-60 or (-6) 1,350hp R-1820-66 Cyclone nine-cylinder radial.
Dimensions: Span 41ft 6in (12.65m); length 33ft (10.06m); height 12ft 11in (3.94m); wing area 325sq ft (30.19m²).
Weights: Empty, typically 6,535lb (2,970kg); loaded 9,519-10,700lb (4,320-4,853kg).
Performance: (SBD-5): maximum speed 252mph (406km/h); initial climb, 1,500ft (457m)/min; service ceiling 24,300ft (7,400m): range (dive bomber) 456 miles (730km), (scout bomber) 773 miles (1,240km).

Above: The three-view is typical of the main production versions, such as the SBD-4 and SBD-5. Note the perforated flaps, used as dive brakes.

Armament: (SBD-1, -2) two 0.3in Browning machine guns fixed above nose, (-3, -4, -5, -6) two 0.5in Browning machine guns fixed in nose; one (later two) 0.30in Brownings manually aimed from rear cockpit; one bomb or other store of up to 1,000lb (454kg) or on SBD-5 and -6 up to 1,600lb (726kg) on swinging crutch under belly, outer-wing racks for two 100lb (45kg) bombs or, sometimes, two 250lb (113kg) bombs or depth charges.
History: First flight (XBT-1) July 1935; service delivery (XBT-1) 12 December 1935; (BT-1) 15

Above: This photograph was probably taken in early 1943, because while the aircraft are blue the marking is of the pre-July 1943 type. They are SBD-3s.

November 1937 to 19 October 1938; (XBT-2, Dauntless prototype) 23 July 1938; (SBD-1) 4 June 1940; termination of production 22 July 1944.
Users: AAF, Navy, Marine Corps.

In 1932 John K. Northrop set up his own company to specialize in the new technique of all-metal stressed-skin construction, though he retained close links with his former employer, Douglas Aircraft. His brilliant designer, Ed Heinemann, started in 1934 to develop a carrier-based dive-bomber for the new Navy carriers,

basing the design on the established Northrop A-17A. The resulting Northrop BT-1 was ordered in quantity (54) in February 1936. It featured an 825hp Pratt & Whitney R-1535 Twin Wasp Junior in a small-diameter cowl, perforated split flaps, and main gears folding backwards into large "bathtub" fairings. The last BT-1 was delivered in a greatly modified form, as the BT-2, with inward-retracting mainwheels, a 1,000hp Cyclone engine and many refinements.

By this time Northrop had become the El Segundo division of Douglas and in consequence the production BT-2 was redesignated

Below: All the first batches of SBD-1s went to the Marines. This echelon came from VMSB-132 (pre-Pearl Harbor VMB-1).

SBD-1. From June 1940 until four years later this was one of the most important US combat aircraft; indeed, in the first half of 1942 it saw more action than any other American type.

In comparison with the Northrop BT it had a better streamlined fuselage, and different canopy and tail, but it retained the very broad wing with a horizontal center section and sharply tapered outer panels with dihedral, with huge perforated split flaps opened fully for use as brakes in steep dive-bombing attacks. Main gears folded inwards into the center section, the main bomb could be swung round under the belly on a hinged crutch, and the observer could open up his cockpit and raise his twin guns into the firing position.

After the 57 SBD-1s came 87 SBD-2s with greater fuel capacity, 584 SBD-3s with armor and self-sealing tanks (and 168 more for the Army with pneumatic tailwheel tire and no hook), 780 SBD-4s (24V electrics) plus 170 for the Army, 3,024 SBD-5s with 1,200hp engine (including 615 as Army A-24Bs) and 451 SBD-6s (1,350hp), to make the total 5,936.

The SBD Dauntless sank more Japanese shipping than any other Allied weapon, stopped the Imperial Fleet at Midway and played a major role at the Coral Sea and Solomons actions. It was extremely popular and generally greatly preferred to the more powerful SB2C planned to replace it.

Right, upper: This SBD-3 flew with VSB-6 aboard USS **Enterprise** *in February 1942.*

Right: Bearing the short-lived red-border insignia, this SBD-4 operated from Munda, New Georgia, with VMSB-243.

Below: Bombed-up SBD-3s ranged on a carrier deck in 1942. The photograph might have been taken during Operation Torch.

Above: A fabulous color picture of one of the first SBD-1s to reach the Marine Corps, serving with the renumbered VMSB-132 in early 1942. The gray paint, called "sea green", shows hard use.

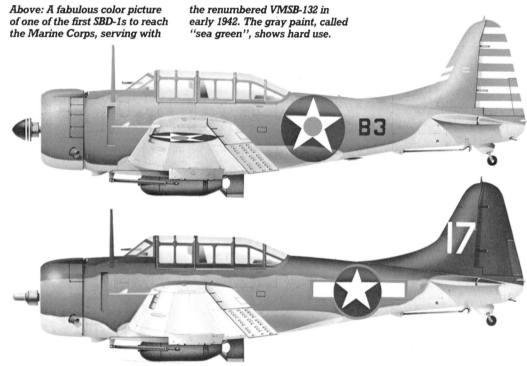

Boeing B-17 Fortress

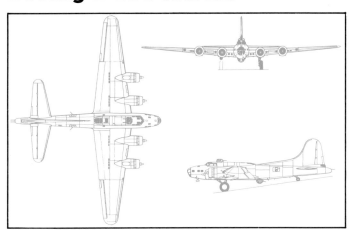

Origin: Boeing Airplane Co, Seattle, Washington; also built by Vega Aircraft Corporation, Burbank, California and Douglas Aircraft Company, Tulsa, Oklahoma.
Type: High-altitude bomber, with crew of six to ten; data for B-17G.
Engines: Four 1,200hp Wright Cyclone R-1820-97 (B-17C to E, R-1820-65) nine-cylinder radials with exhaust-driven turbochargers.
Dimensions: Span 103ft 9in (31.6m); length 74ft 9in (22.8m); (B-17B, C, D) 67ft 11in; (B-17E) 73ft 10in; height 19ft 1in (5.8m); (B-17B, C, D) 15ft 5in; wing area 1,420sq ft (131.92m²).
Weights: Empty 32,720-35,800lb (14,855-16,200kg); (B-17B, C, D) typically 27,650lb; maximum loaded 65,500lb (29,700kg); (B-17B, C, D) 44,200-46,650lb (20,049-21,160kg); (B-17E) 53,000lb (24,040kg).
Performance: Maximum speed

Above: The B-17E was the first of the grossly redesigned versions (formerly Model 299O) which helped win World War II. Oil coolers had leading-edge inlets and upper-surface exits.

287mph (462km/h); (B-17C, D) 323mph (520km/h); (B-17E) 317mph (510km/h); cruising speed 182mph (293km/h); (B-17C, D) 250mph (402km/h); (B-17E) 210mph (338km/h); service ceiling 35,000ft (10,670m); range 1,100 miles (1,760km) with maximum bomb load (other versions up to 3,160 miles -5,084km with reduced weapon load).
Armament: Twin 0.50in Browning guns in chin, dorsal, ball and tail turrets, plus two in nose sockets, one in radio compartment and one in each waist position. Normal internal bombload 6,000lb (2,724kg), but maximum 12,800lb (5,800kg).
History: First flight (299) 28 July

Above: One of the 13 Y1B-17s near Mt Rainier, Washington, in May 1937. This had five 0.30in guns and could fly 1,377 miles (2,216km) with maximum bombload of 10,496lb (4,761kg).

1935, (Y1B-17) January 1937; first delivery (B-17B) June 1939; final delivery April 1945.
Users: AAC/AAF, Navy.

In May 1934 the Army Air Corps issued a specification for a multi-engined anti-shipping bomber to defend the nation against enemy fleets. The answer was expected to be similar to the Martin B-10, but Boeing proposed four engines in order to carry the same bombload faster and higher. It was a huge

Below: The B-17 will forever be associated with "The Mighty Eighth" Air Force. Here in the 8th's early days B-17Fs of 322BS, 91BG, depart Bassingbourn.

financial risk for the Seattle company, but the resulting Model 299 was a giant among combat airplanes, with four 750hp Pratt & Whitney Hornet engines, a crew of eight and stowage for eight 600lb (272kg) bombs internally. Tragically this aircraft crashed because it took off with controls locked, but by this time the AAC had no doubt of the worth of what a newsman dubbed "The Flying Fortress".

The service-test batch of 13 Y1B-17s adopted the Wright Cyclone engine, later versions all being turbocharged for good high-altitude performance. The production B-17B introduced a new nose and bigger rudder and flaps, though the wing loading was conservative, and an enduring characteristic of every "Fort" was sedate flying which helped many wounded pilots bring back badly damaged B-17s.

Despite this stately progress the introduction of the 1,200hp Cyclone

in the B-17C, first flown in July 1940, brought a level of performance similar to the best Army fighters, top speed going up to 323mph (520km/h) at 25,000ft (7,620m). The latter was a normal cruising altitude, and the turbocharged B-17s established a wholly new concept in bombing, in which massed formations flying at what was by previous standards high speed at very high altitude protected each other by their combined gunfire and made life difficult for intercepting fighters as well as for outranged AA gunners far below. The crews perfected their long-range navigation and learned to use the Norden bomb-sight.

At the same time there was much to learn. In return for combat data 20 C-models were supplied to the RAF, and 90 Sqn soon found its fast and high-flying bombers being shot to ribbons. A few survivors were passed to Coastal Command, and for the rest of the war the RAF harbored the feeling that formations of "heavies" in daylight was suicide — over northwest Europe at least. Undeterred the Army brought in the B-17D with extra armor and self-sealing tanks, but with hand-aimed "fifties" above, below and in the flush waist positions, and twin 0.30in in the sides of the nose. Boeing carefully studied the RAF reports and brought out a completely revised Model 299O, which by December 1941 was entering service as the B-17E. Its enlarged tail improved bombing accuracy, and new twin 0.50in turrets appeared above and below, the ventral turret soon giving way to a spherical "ball turret" that need-

ed small gunners. Another pair of 0.50in appeared in the extended tail, with an extra gunner. Gross weight climbed and reduced the speed, but the E was the first model really to go to war in large numbers (512). It was followed by the F (2,000 by Seattle, 500 by Vega and 605 by Douglas), with still more weight and external bomb racks, as well as a longer nosecap of molded Plexiglas.

Though B-17s served in all theaters it was the British-based 8th Air Force that had the hardest time, with the most airplanes. In 1942-43 losses were often unacceptably high, and by the end of 1942 the definitive B-17G was in massive production. Seattle built 4,035,

Vega 2,250 and Douglas 2,395 (to bring the grand B-17 total to 12,731). Most were unpainted, and they had a valued chin turret which brought the number of 0.50in up to 13, as well as improved staggered waist positions. Better turbos increased high-altitude power, but weight and drag brought down mission speed, and until the decline of the Luftwaffe in the final six months of the European war there were often desperate battles, with the giant 8th AF armadas facing rocket and jet fighters and a host of new weapons.

At least 25 war-weary B-17s were turned into BQ-7 Aphrodite radio-controlled missiles loaded with 12,000lb (5,443kg) of high explosive for use against U-boat shelters.

Above: Catholic chaplain Capt Michael Ragan holds mass for the crew of a veteran B-17G prior to a mission in the closing months of the war.

Many F and G models were fitted with H_2X radar with the scanner retracting into the nose or rear fuselage, while other versions included the F-9 reconnaissance, XC-108 executive transport, CB-17 utility transport, PB-1W radar early-warning, PB-1G lifeboat-carrying air/sea rescue and QB-17 target drone. After the war came other photo, training, drone-director, search/rescue and research versions, including many used as engine and equipment testbeds.

Curtiss A-18 Shrike II

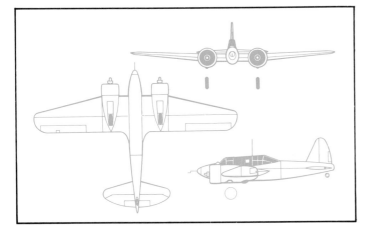

Origin: Curtiss Division of Curtiss-Wright, Buffalo, NY.
Type: Attack.
Engines: Two 800hp Wright Cyclone R-1820-47 nine-cylinder radials.
Dimensions: Span 59ft 6in (18.14m); length 41ft (12.5m); height 11ft 6in (3.5m); wing area 526sq ft (48.87m²).
Weights: Empty 9,410lb (4,268kg); maximum 13,170lb (5,974kg).
Performance: Maximum speed 247mph (398km/h); service ceiling

Above: The A-14 Shrike sadly had underpowered engines delivering only 600hp.

28,650ft (8,733m); range 651 miles (1,048km).
Armament: Four 0.30in Browning guns fixed in nose and one aimed by observer; bombload of 400lb (181kg) inside wings plus 200lb (91kg) under wings.
History; First flight (76) September 1935, (18) January 1937.
User: AAC.

Above: The original XA-14, after being re-engined with SGR-1670s, seen as civil X15315 in 1935.

Curtiss built the Model 76 to meet a requirement for an Army twin-engine attack aircraft. Submitted for evaluation, it was a modern stressed-skin machine of excellent aerodynamic form, with 765hp Wright R-1510 twin-row engines. Re-engined with 735hp R-1670-5 Cyclones it received designation XA-14, and was good enough for a

service trials order of 13 of a more powerful model to be ordered as the Y1A-18. With wing bomb cells and provision for spraying smoke or gas, these served intensively with the 8th Attack Squadron, being redesignated A-18 on attaining full service status. Their Army numbers were 37-52 to -64 inclusive, and they were at once popular and frightening, because of their advanced high-speed design. A few survived on various duties until 1943.

Douglas B-18 Bolo

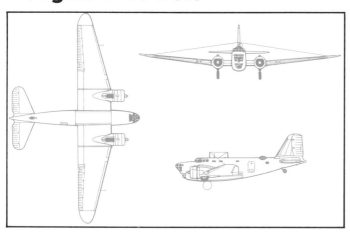

Origin: Douglas Aircraft Company, Santa Monica, California.
Type: Heavy bomber (later maritime patrol) aircraft, with normal crew of six; data for B-18A.
Engines: Two 930hp Wright R-1820-45 or -53 Cyclone nine-cylinder radials.
Dimensions: Span 89ft (27.3m); length 57ft 10in (17.63m); height 15ft 2in (4.62m); wing area 965sq ft (89.65m²).
Weights: Empty 19,700lb (8,936kg); loaded 27,673lb (12,550kg).
Performance: Maximum speed 215mph (349km/h); service ceiling 23,900ft (7,285m); range with maximum bombload 1,180 miles (1,900km).
Armament: Normally one 0.30in Browning machine gun in nose, dorsal and retractable ventral positions, all aimed manually;

Above: Three-view of Douglas B-18A as originally built, shown without armament and with dorsal turret retracted.

internal bombload of up to 4,000lb (1,814kg), or overload of 6,500lb (2,948kg).
History: First flight (DB-1) October 1935; service delivery (B-18) 1937, (B-18A) 1939.
Users: AAC/AAF.

In 1934 the Army issued a requirement for a new bomber to replace the Martin B-10. Martin entered an improved B-10, Boeing the four-engined Model 299 and Douglas the DB-1 (Douglas Bomber 1). It was the last-named which won and nobody at the time expected that, whereas the Douglas would have a short career and soon be forgotten, the controversial Boeing giant would become perhaps the most

Above: Detail of the nose of a B-18A on the flight line at March Field, California, in the spring of 1939.

famous bomber in history.
Douglas were awarded an immediate contract for the unprecedented number (since 1918, at least) of 133 aircraft, designated B-18. Based on the DC-2 transport, the B-18 had an all-metal stressed-skin structure, with a fat body bulged under the wing to accommodate an internal bomb bay. Orders were later placed, in 1937-38, for a further 217 modified aircraft designated B-18A, plus another 20 called Digby for the Royal Canadian Air Force. These had more powerful R-1820 engines and a revised nose with the bombardier station sloping forwards above the front gun.
In 1937-40 this family was the most important heavy warplane in North

America, but after that it faded rapidly. No big orders were placed by France or Britain, as was the case with all the newer American bombers, and the B-17 gradually replaced the B-18 in US Army bombardment squadrons.
In December 1941 most of the 33 aircraft on Hawaiian airfields were destroyed, and B-18s saw little action. In 1942 a total of 76 B-18As were converted as anti-submarine patrol aircraft, with a large nose radome and the first MAD installation projecting behind the tail, for use in the Caribbean and off the east coast of the United States. The rebuilds were designated as B-18Bs or B-18Cs. Many other B-18s were converted as transports, the designation C-58 being allotted but seldom used. The Digbys were also used for maritime duties until 1943. A few B-18s were later converted for use as business aircraft.

Douglas C-47 Skytrain

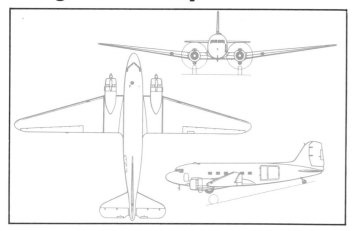

Origin: Douglas Aircraft Company, Santa Monica, California.
Type: Utility transport (formerly also paratroop/glider tug): AC-47 air/ground weapon platform.
Engines: Usually two 1,200hp Pratt & Whitney R-1830-90D or -92 Twin Wasp 14-cylinder two-row radials; (C-117D and R4D-8) two 1,535hp Wright R-1820-80 Cyclone nine-cylinder radials.
Dimensions: Span 95ft (28.96m); length 64ft 5½in (19.64m); height 16ft 11in (5.16m); wing area 987sq ft (96.69m²).

Above: Three-view of a standard C-47/47A/47B, with the tailcone replaced by glider tow cleat.

Weights: Empty, about 16,970lb (7,700lb); loaded, about 25,200lb (11,432kg); overload limit 33,000lb (14,969kg).
Performance: Maximum speed about 230mph (370km/h); initial climb, about 1,200ft (366m)/min; service ceiling 23,000ft (7,000m); maximum range 2,125 miles (3,420km).
Armament: Usually none; (AC-47) usually three 7.62mm Miniguns;

Above: An EC-47 of the USAF 360th Tactical Electronic Warfare Squadron over Vietnam in 1970.

many other types of armament in other special versions.
History: First flight (DST) 17 December 1935; first service delivery (C-41) October 1938.
Users: AAC, AAF, AF, Navy, Marines.

When, in 1935, Douglas designer Arthur E. Raymond planned the Douglas Sleeper Transport (DST) as an enlarged and improved

DC-2, he little thought that, as well as becoming the worldwide standard airliner of its day, it would be by far the most widely used military transport in history. Basic features included a modern all-metal stressed-skin structure, efficiently cowled engines, wide-span split flaps, retractable landing gears and constant-speed three-blade propellers.
During World War II there were numerous versions, some civil aircraft impressed into military use, some paratroopers and tugs and the vast majority utility C-47 ver-

Vought SB2U Vindicator

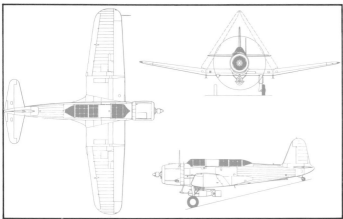

Origin: Vought-Sikorsky Division of United Aircraft, East Hartford, Connecticut.
Type: Carrier-based scout/dive bomber.
Engine: One 825hp Pratt & Whitney Twin Wasp Junior R-1535-96 or (-3) -102 14-cylinder radial.
Dimensions: Span 41ft 11in (12.78m); length 33ft 11¾in (10.36m); height 14ft 3in (4.34m); wing area 305.3sq ft (28.36m²).
Weights: Empty 5,634lb (2,556kg); maximum 9,763lb (4,428kg).
Performance: Maximum speed 250mph (402km/h), (at max weight, 215mph, 346km/h); service ceiling 16,400ft (5,000m); range (with bombload) 1,170 miles (1,885km).
Armament: (-1) one 0.30in gun in right wing and one aimed from rear cockpit, plus bombload up to 1,500lb (680kg), (-3) same but both

Above: Three-view of SB2U.

Below: SB2U-2 No 1337 of squadron VB-2 (USS Lexington).

Above: Probably taken in 1942, this SB2U was operating in the Pacific theater, almost certainly with the Marines.

guns 0.50in.
History: First flight 4 January 1936; service delivery 20 December 1937.
Users: Navy, Marine Corps.

An immediate successor to the SBU, the SB2U had all-metal upward-folding wings but retained the traditional fabric-covered steel-tube fuselage. Main gears, however, retracted backwards, the wheels turning to lie inside the wing ahead of the small split flaps. Good

when it was designed, the SB2U swiftly become obsolescent, though Vought delivered 54 SB2U-1s, 58 Dash-2s and 57 long-range Dash-3s to the Marines. The latter saw brief courageous action in the first Battle of Midway.

---

sions with a strong cargo floor and large double doors. Most had cleats for towing gliders. Impressed aircraft usually had R-1820 Cyclone engines, but the standard engine of the wartime versions was the R-1830. Oddities included a glider and a twin-float amphibian.

US military production totaled 10,048 by June 1945, followed by small batches of redesigned Super DC-3 versions including the Navy R4D-8 and USAF C-117.

Many hundreds of these aircraft, most of them C-47s, remain in daily use in numerous air forces. Many serve as platforms for research projects and countermeasures, and in Vietnam the AC-47 — called ''Puff the Magic Dragon'' — was developed in several versions to deliver suppressive fire against ground targets. Other important variants were the EC-47 series used for multi-spectral sensing, electronic systems training and electronic reconnaissance. Other major versions were VIP-furnished VC-47s, trainer TC-47s and air/sea warfare SC-47s.

Right: Loading a C-47A at Patterson Field, Ohio, in 1944. Note the serial number (43-15972) repeated above the wing.

Grumman F4F/FM Wildcat

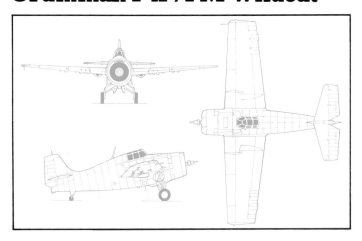

Origin: Grumman Aircraft Engineering Corporation, Bethpage, NY; also built by Eastern Aircraft.

Type: Single-seat naval fighter.

Engine: (XF4F-2) one 1,050hp Pratt & Whitney R-1830-66 Twin Wasp 14-cylinder two-row radial; (G-36A) one 1,200hp Wright R-1820-G205A Cyclone nine-cylinder radial; (F4F-3) 1,200hp R-1830-76; (F4F-4 and FM-1) R-1830-86; (FM-2) 1,350hp R-1820-56.

Dimensions: Span 38ft (11.6m); length 28ft 9in to 28ft 11in (FM-2, 28ft 10in, 8.5m); height 11ft 11in (3.6m); wing area 260sq ft (24.15m²).

Weights: Empty (F4F-3) 4,425lb, (F4F-4) 4,649lb, (FM-2) 4,900lb (2,226kg); loaded (F4F-3) 5,876lb, (F4F-4) 6,100lb (2,767kg), rising to 7,952lb (3,607kg) with final FM-1s; (FM-2) 7,412lb (3,362kg).

Performance: Maximum speed

Above: Twin-Wasp-engined F4F-4. Note the complex junction between the root and skew-hinged wing.

(F4F-3) 325mph (523km/h), (F4F-4, FM-1) 318mph (509km/h), (FM-2) 332mph (534km/h); initial climb, typically 2,000ft (610m)/min (3,300ft/min in early versions, 1,920ft (585m/min in main production and over 2,000ft (610m)/min for FM-2); service ceiling, typically 35,000ft (10,670m) (more in light early versions); range, typically 900 miles (1,448km).

Armament: (XF4F-2) two 0.5in Colt-Brownings in fuselage; (F4F-3) four 0.5in in outer wings;. (F4F-4 and subsequent) six 0.5in in outer wings; (F4F-4, FM-1 and FM-2) underwing racks for two 250lb (113kg) bombs.

History: First flight (XF4F-2) 2 September 1937; (XF4F-3)

Above: F4F-3As of fighter squadron VF-5 from USS Saratoga saw action against the Japanese armadas from the start of 1942.

12 February 1939; production (G-36 and F4F-3) February 1940; (FM-2) March 1943; final delivery August 1945.

Users: Navy, Marines.

Designed as a biplane to continue Grumman's very successful F3F series of single-seat carrier fighters, the XF4F-1 was replanned on the drawing board in the summer of 1936 as a mid-wing monoplane. Though this machine, the XF4F-2, lost out to the Brewster F2A Buffalo, Grumman continued with the XF4F-3 with a more powerful engine and in early 1939 received a French Aéronavale order for 100 designated G-36A, the US Navy following with 54 in August. The French aircraft were diverted to

Britain and named Martlet I.

Though always limited by having rather small engines, the F4F made up for its lack of performance by having large square-cut wings which made it extremely agile in combat. It was also very tough and could survive battle damage that would destroy typical Japanese aircraft. The pilot had an outstanding view from the cockpit high above the wing; there were also small windows giving downwards vision.

Production built up with both Twin Wasp and Cyclone engines, manually folding wings being introduced with the F4F-4, of which Grumman delivered 1,169 plus 220 Martlet IVs for the Fleet Air Arm. Eastern Aircraft Division of General Motors very quickly tool-

Below: F4F-3As of Marine Corps squadron VMF-111 acting as "Red Force" in 1941 maneuvers with the Army in Louisiana.

ed up and delivered 839 FM-1s and 311 Martlet Vs, the British name then being changed to the US name of Wildcat.

Grumman switched to the Avenger, Hellcat and other types, but made F4F-7 reconnaissance versions, weighing 10,328lb (4,685kg) and having a 24-hour endurance, as well as a single F4F-3S floatplane version. Eastern took over the final mark, the powerful and effective FM-2, delivering 4,467 of this type (including 340 Wildcat VI) in 13 months. By 1945 the FM-2 was standard fighter on almost all the Navy's 114 escort carriers.

A Martlet I shot down a Ju 88 on Christmas Day 1940, and an F4F-3 of VMF-211 destroyed a Japanese bomber at Wake Island on 9 December 1941. Each event was the first of thousands of furious actions from which this rather slow but tough fighter emerged with a splen-

Above: XF4F-3 BuNo 0383, was the prototype of the only Navy fighter to face the Zero until August 1943.

did reputation. Wildcats were especially valuable for their ability to operate from small escort carriers, the pioneer work having been done with British Martlets based in November 1940 on the 5,000 ton captured German vessel *Audacity* on which a flat deck had been built.

Noted for their strength and maneuverability, Wildcats even sank Japanese submarines and a cruiser. They were virtually the only Navy and Marines fighters facing the massive onslaught of the Japanese from Pearl Harbor until the arrival of the F6F at the end of August 1943.

Right: Another "Red Force" F4F in the 1941 maneuvers.

Piper L-4 Grasshopper

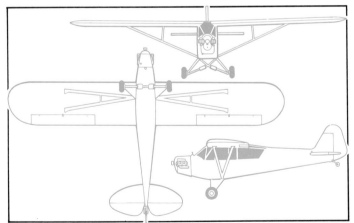

Above: The mass-produced wartime Grasshoppers all looked like this, though the actual model shown is an L-4B. The first L-4 mission was from a carrier!

Above: The giant 1941 Army maneuvers (see caption above) also saw evaluation of the first YO-59s, which were merely drab-painted Cub J3Cs. Note gas pump!

Origin: Piper Aircraft Corporation, Lock Haven, Pennsylvania.
Type: Observation and liaison.
Engine: (L-4) one 65hp Continental O-170-3 flat-four aircooled.
Dimensions: Span 35ft 3in (10.74m); length 22ft 4½in (6.83m); height 6ft 8in (2.03m); wing area 179sq ft (16.63m²).
Weights: (Typical) empty 695lb (315kg), (740lb with radio); maximum 1,220lb (553kg).
Performance: Maximum speed 87mph (140km/h); service ceiling

9,500ft (2,900m), (11,500ft solo); range 260 miles (420km).
Armament: None.
History: First flight (J-3 Cub Trainer) 1937, (YO-59) 1941.
Users: AAF, Navy.

Along with similar machines by Aeronca, Interstate, Stinson and

Taylorcraft, the popular Piper Cub was evaluated as an Army observation machine, four YO-59s being procured in 1941. After Pearl Harbor hundreds of Cubs, Coupes and Cruisers were impressed as the L-4C to -4G, others becoming UC-83s. New production began on a version revised for Army use with

extensive rear cabin glazing, two-way radio and many detail changes. After delivering 140 O-59s and 671 O-59As the designation changed to L-4, main wartime models including 980 L-4B, 1,801 L-4H and 1,680 L-4J with controllable-pitch propeller, plus 230 NE-1 dual trainers for the Navy. From 1943 L-4s used Brodie cable/harness gear for operations without the wheels ever touching the ground. Post-war versions were the 90hp L-18 series and 125hp L-21 family.

Bell YFM-1 Airacuda

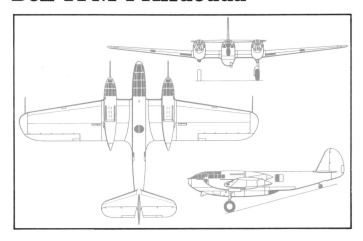

Origin: Bell Aircraft Corporation, Buffalo, NY.
Type: Multi-seat fighter.
Engines: Two 1,150hp Allison V-1710-13, -23 or -41 V-12 liquid-cooled.
Dimensions: Span 70ft (21.34m); length 45ft 11½in (14.01m); height 12ft 5in (3.78m); wing area 600sq ft (55.74m²).
Weights: Empty equipped 13,674lb (6,202kg); maximum 19,000lb (8,618kg).
Performance: Maximum speed 270mph (435km/h); service ceiling 29,900ft (9,115m); range 1,670 miles (2,690km).

Above: Bell's design team had the nerve to launch their new company with the novel YFM-1; note the bomb sight.

Armament: Two AAC T9 37mm cannon on pivoted mounts, dorsal and ventral mounts for 0.3in guns and beam windows for 0.5in guns; underwing racks for 20 bombs of 30lb (13.6kg).
History: First flight 1 September 1937; final delivery October 1940.
User: AAC.

When Consolidated moved from Buffalo to California in 1935 many of

Above: This may well be the only surviving color photograph of an Airacuda. It shows a YFM-1A on test without armament.

its top management and engineers stayed behind and formed a new company. Designers Robert J. Woods and Harland M. Poyer conceived two Army fighters of the most radical and advanced form possible. First to fly was the XFM-1, the only example of the "fighter, multiplace" category. Intended as a "destroyer" in the same class as the German Bf 110, it was far more heavily armed, and all its five guns

were aimed by gunners. Powered by special versions of the new Allison engine driving pusher propellers via short extension shafts, the Airacuda proved sufficiently promising for the prototype to be followed by 12 further service-test aircraft, completed as nine YFM-1s with the full armament and three -1As with tricycle gear. The crew numbered five, there being crawlways from the fuselage to the nacelles where the 37mm cannon were mounted. These remarkable machines never became operational with a regular Army squadron but launched the Bell company.

Consolidated PB2Y Coronado

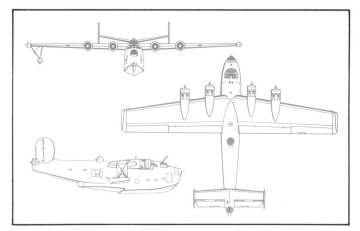

Origin: Consolidated Aircraft (Consolidated Vultee, or Convair, from March 1943), San Diego, California.
Type: Ocean patrol, transport and ambulance flying boat.
Engines: Four 1,200hp Pratt & Whitney R-1830 Twin Wasp 14-cylinder radials (see text).
Dimensions: Span (floats up) 115ft (35.05m); length (all, within 4in) 79ft 3in (24.16m); height 27ft 6in (8.38m); wing area 1,780sq ft (165.37m²).
Weights: Empty (-3) 40,935lb (18,568kg), (-3R) about 33,000lb (14,970kg); maximum (all) 68,000lb (30,845kg).
Performance: Maximum speed (typical) 223mph (359km/h); econ cruise 141mph (227km/h); range with max weapons (-3) 1,370 miles (2,204km), (-5) 1,640 miles (2,640km); max range (-3) 2,370

Above: The main production model was the PB2Y-3, seen here without either of the two types of radar installation. Some -3s were converted to transports (suffix -3R) with low-rated engines.

miles (3,813km), (-5) 3,900 miles (6,275km).
Armament: (Except transports) eight 0.5in guns in three power turrets and two manual beam windows; offensive load of up to 8,000lb (3,629kg) internal plus 4,000lb (1,814kg) external, including torpedoes.
History: First flight 17 December 1937; service delivery 31 December 1940; final delivery October 1943.
User: Navy.

In July 1936 the Navy ordered a prototype of the Model 29 as the

Above: Coronado No 7092 was one of a batch converted as unarmed PB2Y-3R transports by Rohr at Chula Vista. Note the national flag and PanAm badge. It had wheeled beaching chassis.

XPB2Y-1, and this flew in 1937. Its huge hull was high enough to carry the wing without a pylon, and there were no bracing struts. Retractable wingtip floats resembled those of the PBY, and there was a single fin and rudder. Engines were early Twin Wasps, but production PB2Ys had R-1830-78 or -88 with two-stage superchargers.

Few aircraft have been more extensively modified than the Consolidated Model 29, XPB2Y-1, in 1937-39, and the production PB2Y-2 of 1940 was again totally different with a vast new hull and twin-fin tail which nevertheless did

not stop it reaching 255mph (410km/h). The main production run of 210 boats was designated PB2Y-3, though it saw little service in its basic patrol version. The -3B served with RAF Transport Command, the -3R was stripped of military gear and had low-rated R-1830-92 engines giving better low-level performance carrying 44 passengers or 16,000lb (7,258kg) cargo, the -5 had more than 60 per cent more fuel and -92 engines, and the -5H was an unarmed ambulance.

The Coronado was trusty but rather sluggish, and often needed the takeoff rockets which it pioneered. Most combat-equipped -3 and -5 had ASV radar above the flight deck, which was retained on a few of the transport versions. Almost all PB2Ys were withdrawn from Navy use prior to 1946.

Brewster F2A Buffalo

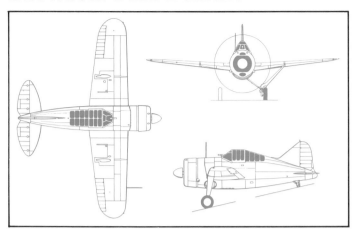

Origin: Brewster Aircraft Company, Long Island City, NY.
Type: Single-seat carrier-based fighter; data for F2A-2.
Engine: 1,100hp Wright R-1820-40 (G-205A) Cyclone nine-cylinder radial.
Dimensions: Span 35ft (10.67m); length 26ft 4in (8m); height 12ft 1in (3.7m); wing area 209sq ft. (19.4m^2).
Weights: Empty 4,630lb (2,100kg); loaded 7,055lb (3,200kg) (varied from 6,848-7,159lb, 3,106-3,247kg).
Performance: Maximum speed 300mph (483km/h); initial climb 3,070ft (935m)/min; service ceiling 30,500ft (9,300m); range 650-950 miles (1,045-1,530km).
Armament: Four machine guns, two in fuselage and two in wing, calibre of each pair being 0.30in, or, mostly commonly, 0.50in.
History: First flight (XF2A-1) December 1937; first service delivery April 1939; termination of production 1942.
Users: Navy, Marines.

The Brewster company was established in 1810 to build carriages. In 1935 it plunged into planemaking and secured an order for a US Navy scout-bomber. It also entered a competition for a carrier-based monoplane fighter and won. Not surprisingly, it took almost two years — a long time in those days — to fly the first prototype Model 139 XF2A-1. Yet one must give the team

Below: Navy No 1393 was one of the 11 F2A-1s actually to reach the Navy, and it was photographed before reaching squadron VF-3 (probably while still on Bureau testing).

Above: The F2A-3 shown here had four 0.5in guns. Main gears were pulled in and up by their diagonal bracing struts.

their due, for the F2A-1 was confirmed as the Navy's choice for its first monoplane fighter even after Grumman had flown the G36 (Wildcat).

Features included all-metal construction, a cantilever wing in the mid-position fitted with split flaps, a cockpit covered by very large fixed and sliding transparent canopies, and main gears pivoted to the wings but pulled inwards so that the retracted wheels were housed in the flanks of the forward fuselage. Maneuverability was excellent, and performance well above the level of previous Navy fighters.

In June 1938 a contract was placed for 54 of these tubby mid-wingers, then armed with one 0.50in and one 0.30in machine guns. Only 11 reached USS *Saratoga;* the rest went to Finland, where from February 1940 until the end of World War II they did extremely well. The Navy bought 43 more powerful and more heavily armed F2A-2 (Model 339), and then 108 F2A-3 with armor and self-sealing tanks. Of these, 21 in the hands of the Marine Corps (VMF-221) put up a heroic struggle in the first Battle of Midway.

In 1939 bulk orders were placed by Belgium and Britain, and the RAF operated 170 delivered in 1941 to Singapore. Another 72 were bought by the Netherlands. All were decimated during the Japanese advance in 1942, providing no match for the "Zero".

Republic P-43 Lancer

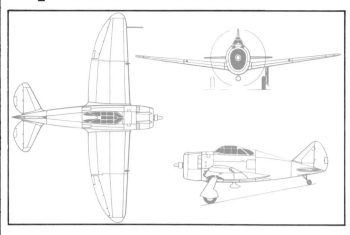

Origin: Republic Aviation Corporation, Farmingdale, NY.
Type: Single-seat fighter.
Engine: One 1,200hp Pratt & Whitney Twin Wasp 14-cylinder radial, (43) R-1830-35, (43A) -49, (43A-1) -57.
Dimensions: Span 36ft (10.97m); length 28ft 6in (8.69m); height 14ft (4.27m); wing area 223sq ft (20.72m^2).
Weights: Empty (43) 5,654lb (2,565kg), (A-1) 5,996lb (2,720kg); maximum (43) 7,935lb (3,599kg), (A-1) 8,480lb (3,847kg).
Performance: Maximum speed (43) 349mph, (A-1) 356mph (573km/h); service ceiling 38,000ft (11,580m); range (A-1) 650 miles (1,050km) with bomb or 1,450 miles (2,335km) with drop tank.
Armament: (43) two 0.50in guns above engine and two 0.30in in wings, (43A-1) wing guns changed to 0.50in and provision under fuselage for one 200lb (90kg) bomb in lieu of tank, or six 20lb (9kg) under wings.
History: First flight (AP-4) 1938, (YP-43) mid-1940; service delivery (P-43) May 1941.
Users: AAC, AAF.

The last Seversky P-35 was delivered in an improved form designated AP-4 (Army XP-41), with uprated R-1830 with a turbosupercharger in the rear fuselage fed via ducting passing under the wing from an inlet in the bottom of a deeper cowl. Other changes inclu-

Above: The P-43 formed the link between the P-35 and the P-47, and just missed being an important type in its own right.

ded main gears which retracted inwards into a wing having dihedral from the roots. From this was developed the YP-43 with the turbo ducting moved to the bottom of the deep oval cowl, revised canopy and two wing guns added.

It performed well, though it was soon clear that fighter development in Europe was making even this impressive machine obsolete, so that the planned P-44 development was terminated in favour of the much bigger P-47, the P-43 was accepted as a major interim Army pursuit. Republic delivered 13 YPs, 54 P-43s, 80 P-43As (both versions differing from the YPs in sub-type of engine) and finally 125 P-43A-1s with bigger wing guns and provision for bombs. In 1942 most Lancers (150) were converted as P-43Bs with a reconnaissance camera installation in the rear fuselage; there were also small numbers of P-43C, D and E with different camera installations. Many Lancers were handed over to China.

Below: A North American BT-9 basic trainer is framed by the landing gear of this P-43 in 1941. The pilot has a seat-pack chute and headset, but no oxygen mask or hand mike.

Douglas C-54 Skymaster

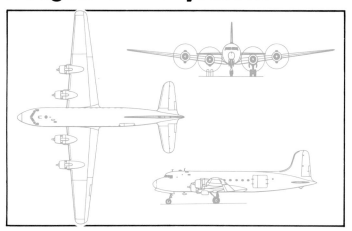

Origin: Douglas Aircraft Company, Santa Monica, California, and Chicago, Illinois.
Type: Strategic transport.
Engines: Four 1,350hp Pratt & Whitney R-2000-7 Twin Wasp 14-cylinder radials, (from late batches C-54D/R5D-3) R-2000-11 with better altitude performance.
Dimensions: Span 117ft 6in (35.81m); length 93ft 11in (28.63m); height 27ft 6¼in (8.39m); wing area 1,460sq ft (135.64m²).
Weights: (C-54B) empty 38,200lb (17,328kg); maximum 73,000lb (33,113kg).
Performance: Max cruise at optimum height 239mph (385km/h); max range with max useful load 1,500 miles (2,414km); max range with max fuel 3,900 miles (6,276km) at 190mph (306km/h).
History: First flight (prototype) 21 June 1938, (production C-54) 14

Above: The main production models, such as the C-54B, D and G, all had large rear cargo doors. Leading edges have deicer boots.

February 1942; final delivery (civil) post-war.
Users: AAF, AF, Navy.

The pre-war DC-4 did not prove a success, and eventually was sold to Japan, but in 1940 Douglas cut the DC-4 down in size and simplified it to produce a much better transport. In 1941 the production batch was taken over by the Army, and again altered for military use as the C-54. Thus the first off the production line (there was no prototype of the new design) flew in olive drab.

Of all-metal stressed-skin construction, the C-54 had an efficient tubular fuselage with a constant circular cross-section throughout the cabin, with oval windows,

Above: The 17th C-54, newly arrived from Santa Monica, is seen in 1942 at Westover Field, Massachussetts.

though the interior was unpressurized. The fully retractable tricycle landing gears had twin mainwheels and a steerable nosewheel, and though it kept the floor high off the ground it held the fuselage level. By previous standards the wing was highly loaded, but powerful slotted flaps brought the field length down to match wartime runways. Early versions were basic 26-passenger civil conversions, but once the new assembly line at Chicago was operating, improved C-54s with full cargo provisions and up to 50 seats began to appear in numbers.

Ultimately 1,242 of these excellent machines were built, all having large freight doors and strong

Right: Built as a wartime C-54E, No 44-9130 is pictured during the Korean war when she was a casevac MC-54M with MATS.

floors, about 44 removable seats, glider tow cleats and military gear throughout. The B had integral outer-wing tanks, the C was a VIP machine with an electric hoist for President Roosevelt's wheelchair, and later marks (made mainly at Chicago) were convertible to several roles.

Post-war military versions took model sub-types up to C-54T, all rebuilds. Navy versions were all designated as R5Ds. Many basic trucking versions played a central role in the Berlin Airlift in 1948-49, and served in Korea in 1950-53. Special MC-54Ms ferried wounded from Japan to the US. In the 1950s SC-54Ds served the Air Rescue Service, with radar.

Vought OS2U Kingfisher

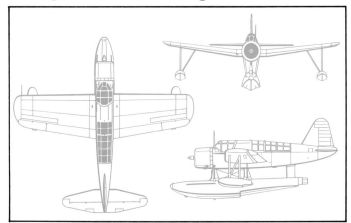

Origin: Vought-Sikorsky Division of United Aircraft, East Hartford, Connecticut.
Type: Observation scout.
Engine: One 450hp Pratt & Whitney Wasp Junior R-985 nine-cylinder radial.
Dimensions: Span 35ft 10¹¹⁄₁₆in (10.94m); length (land) 30ft 4in (9.24m), (sea) 33ft 10in (10.33m); height (land) 8ft 8in (2.64m), (sea) 15ft 1in (4.6m); wing area 262sq ft (24.34m²).
Weights: Empty (-3 land) 3,749lb (1,700kg), (sea) 4,123lb (1,870kg); maximum 6,000lb (2,722kg).

Above: Hallmark of a sound design, all OS2Us and OS2Ns looked almost identical, though all could have wheels or floats. The main model was the OS2U-3.

Performance: Maximum speed (-3 land) 172mph (277km/h), (sea) 164mph (264km/h); service ceiling (land) 15,500ft (4,725m), (sea) 13,000ft (3,960m). range (land) 1,480 miles (2,380km).
Armament: One synchronized 0.30in gun, one 0.30in aimed by observer, two bombs of 100lb (45kg) or 325lb (147kg) under wings.

Above: These OS2U-3s were parked at the Army Air Base, Richmond, in October 1942. Landplane versions predominated, though not overwhelmingly so.

History: First flight 20 July 1938; service delivery 16 August 1940.
User: Navy.

Seemingly a pedestrian aircraft, the OS2U was worth all the other wartime Navy observation aircraft put together — and that includes its intended replacements. With an all-metal framework, its wings

were fabric-skinned aft of the spar, but the fuselage was a metal-skinned semi-monocoque. Both crew members had a superb view, and with full-span flaps and drooping ailerons it could fly for hours at under 70mph (113km/h), using spoilers for sprightly aileron control even at this low speed.

Vought built 54 OS2U-1s, 158 Dash-2s with small changes and finally 1,006 Dash-3s with armor and self-sealing tanks, the Naval Aircraft Factory adding a further 300 OS2Ns similar to the -3. They served in every kind of mission

from every kind of ship (as a center-float seaplane), carrier and land base. They dive-bombed the Aleutians with 150 per cent of the permitted bombload, while another taxied through 40 miles (64km) of stormy sea bringing back Capt Eddie Rickenbacker and his crew. Meanwhile the much later Curtiss SO3C was withdrawn in 1944.

Above: An OS2U-3 about to be catapulted from the newly commissioned battleship Iowa *in early 1943.*

Right: An echelon of three early OS2U-1s newly assigned to shore-based VO-3 in 1940. Vertical tail color was used to identify the unit, ship or station.

Curtiss P-40 Warhawk family

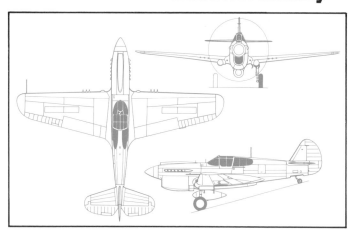

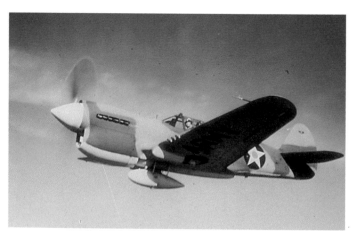

Origin: Curtiss-Wright Airplane Division, Buffalo, NY.

Type: Single-seat fighter and ground attack, also reconnaissance and as advanced trainer.

Engine: One liquid-cooled V-12 piston engine, (P-40/B/C) 1,040hp Allison V-1710-33, (P-40E) 1,150hp V-1710-39, (P-40F/L) 1,300hp Packard V-1650-1 (Merlin), (P-40K) 1,325hp V-1710-73, (P-40N) 1,200hp V-1710-81/-99/-115, (P-40Q) 1,425hp V-1710-121.

Dimensions: Span 37ft 3½in (11.36m); length (early) 31ft 9in (9.68m), (E) 31ft 2in (9.5m), (F/L/K/N) 33ft 4in (10.16m), (Q) 35ft 4in (10.77m); height (typical) 12ft 4in (3.75m); wing area 236sq ft (21.92m²).

Weights: Empty (40) 5,376lb (2,439kg), (B) 5,590lb (2,536kg), (C) 5,812lb (2,636kg), (E) 6,350lb (2,880kg), (F/L) 6,590lb (2,989kg), (K) 6,400lb (2,903kg), (N) 6,000/6,200lb (2,722/2,903kg), (Q) typically 6,600lb (2,994kg); maximum (40) 7,215lb (3,273kg), (B) 7,600lb (3,447kg), (C) 8,058lb (3,655kg), (E) 9,200lb (4,173kg), (F/L) 9,350lb (4,241kg), (K) 10,000lb (4,536kg), (N) 11,500lb (5,216kg), (Q) 9,000lb (4,082kg).

Performance: Maximum speed (40) 357mph (575km/h), (B) 352mph, (C) 364mph, (E) 362mph, (F/L) 364mph, (K) 363mph, (N) varied from 379mph (610km/h) in early blocks to 343mph (552km/h) later at full weight, (Q) 422mph (679km/h); range (clean) varied from 730 miles (1,175km) in early versions to 650 (E), 700 (F/L/K)

Above: The P-40E was Allison-powered and the first variant to have the definitive armament of six 0.5in guns in the wings.

and 750 miles (1,045, 1,126 and 1,207km) (N-15).

Armament: (40) two 0.5in guns above cowling, (B) two 0.5in above cowling plus two 0.3in in wings, (C) as B but four 0.3in in wings, (E) six 0.5in in wings plus one 500lb (227kg) and two 100lb (45kg) bombs, (N) six 0.5in plus three 500lb bombs, (Q) proposed four 20mm or six 0.5in.

History: First flight (XP-40) 14 October 1938, (P-40) 4 April 1940, (F) 25 November 1941, (N) March 1944.

Users: AAC, AAF.

At the start of World War II Curtiss was undisputed leader of US pursuit (fighter) builders. The classic Hawk 75 (P-36) airframe had been used in 1936 to fit the Allison V-1710 engine, a conventional V-12 which had been under development from 1931 and was ready for production. The resulting YP-37 also had a turbosupercharger, and its flashing performance convinced the Army the Allison was the way to go. The P-37 had a poor view from a rear-mounted cockpit, so the new engine was put in the tenth P-36A.

The result was the Hawk 81,

Below: The 11th P-40 seen in spring 1940 flying with the Materiel Division at Wright Field. First unit was 8th PG.

Above; The P-40E saw more action than any other variant, with 2,320 delivered from 1941. Note the British style camouflage.

Army XP-40, flown in October 1938. It was the first of nearly 14,000 progressively improved P-40s which served on every front and with virtually all the Allied air forces in World War II. Unfortunately, at the start of production in 1940 the basic P-40 had been surpassed in performance and firepower by such foreign types as the Bf 109E and Spitfire. Later versions never caught up, but their toughness and frontline serviceability proved of great value and they served as tactical attack fighter bombers with great success.

The initial order, gigantic for its day, was for 524 P-40s, later reduced to 200. In 1941 European feedback led to the P-40B and C, with armor, self-sealing tanks and heavier armaments. Many hundreds of P-40Bs and Cs were supplied to the Soviet Union, China and Turkey, and perhaps the most famous were those of Gen Claire Chennault's American Volunteer Group fighting the Japanese in China, which between December 1941 and 4 July 1942 was credited with 286 Japanese kills for the loss of 23 US pilots.

With the P-40D a new series of Allison engines allowed the nose to be shortened and the radiator was deepened, changing the appearance of the aircraft. The fuselage guns were finally thrown out and

the standard armament in the P-40E became the much better one of six "fifties" in the wings. The RAF had ordered 560 of the improved fighters in 1940, and they were called Kittyhawk I. When the US Army bought it the name Warhawk was given to subsequent P-40 versions.

The Merlin engine went into production in the USA in 1941 and gave rise to the P-40F, some being supplied to the Soviet Union and Free French. Most Fs introduced a longer fuselage to improve directional stability. Subsequent K and M models had a dorsal fin as well and reverted to the Allison engine.

Great efforts were made to reduce weight and improve performance, because the whole family was fundamentally outclassed by the other front-line fighters on both sides; but, predictably, weight kept rising. It reached its peak in the capable and well-equipped P-40N, of which no fewer than 4,219 were built. Some of the early Ns had all the weight-savings and only four guns, and could reach 378mph (608km/h), but they were exceptions.

Altogether deliveries of P-40 versions to the US government amounted to 13,738. In April 1944 USAAF units had 2,500 late-model P-40s, but this fell to a single combat group before VJ-day. Though it was foolhardy to tangle with a crack enemy fighter in close combat, the Hawk family were tough, nimble and extremely useful weapons, especially in close support of armies.

Douglas A-20 Havoc

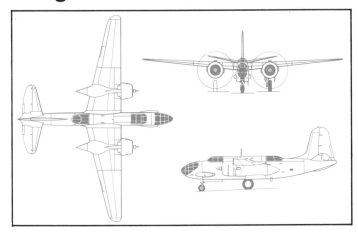

Origin: Douglas Aircraft Company and Boeing Airplane Company.

Type: Two-seat fighter and intruder, three-seat bomber or two-seat reconnaissance aircraft.

Engines: Early DB-7 versions, two 1,200hp Pratt & Whitney R-1830-S3C4-G Twin Wasp 14-cylinder two-row radials; all later versions, two 1,500, 1,600 or 1,700hp Wright GR-2600-A5B, -11, -23 or -29 Cyclone 14-cylinder two-row radials.

Dimensions: Span 61ft 4in (18.69m); length varied from 45ft 11in (13.99m) to 48ft 10in (14.88m) (A-20G, 48ft 4in, 14.74m); height 17ft 7in (5.36m); wing area 464sq ft (43.10m²).

Weights: Early A-20, typically, empty 11,400lb (5,171kg), loaded 16,700lb (7,574kg); (A-20G, typical of main production) empty 12,950lb (5,874kg), loaded 27,200lb (12,340kg).

Performance: Maximum speed, slowest early versions 295mph (475km/h); fastest versions 351mph (565km/h); (A-20G) 342mph (549km/h); initial climb, 1,200-2,000ft (366-610m)/min; service ceiling typically 25,300ft (7,720m); range with maximum weapon load typically 1,000 miles (1,610km).

Armament: (A-20B) two fixed 0.5in Brownings on sides of nose, one 0.5in manually aimed dorsal, one 0.30in manually aimed ventral, 2,000lb (907kg) bombload; (A-20G) four 20mm and two 0.5in or six 0.5in in nose, dorsal turret with two 0.5in, manually aimed 0.5in ventral, 4,000lb (1,814kg) bombload or two torpedoes. Many other schemes, early A-20s having fixed rearward-firing 0.30in in each nacelle.

History: First flight (Douglas 7B) 26 October 1938; (production DB-7) 17 August 1939; service delivery (France) 2 January 1940; termination of production September 1944.

Users: AAC/AAF and Navy.

Designed by Jack Northrop and Ed Heinemann, the DB-7 family was one of the great combat aircraft of all time. Originally planned to meet a US Army Air Corps attack specification of 1938, it was dramatically altered and given more powerful Twin Wasp engines and a nose-

Above: Most important of the "first generation", the A-20C had R-2600 engines and a broad vertical tail.

wheel-type landing gear (for the first time in a military aircraft).

All versions had smooth stressed-skin construction and a mid-high wing which by previous standards was very heavily loaded. The initial production model was the A-20, the first aircraft to be powered by the new 14-cylinder Cyclone R-2600. These engines were turbocharged, and the A-20 reached 390mph (628km/h), but the turbos gave so much trouble they were removed, and the A-20s finally entered service as F-3 photo-reconnaissance aircraft and P-70 night fighters.

In February 1939 the French government ordered 100 of a further modified type, with deeper but narrower fuselage and other gross changes. This model, the DB-7, went into production at El Segundo and Santa Monica, with 1,764lb (800kg) bombload, beginning operations on 31 May 1940.

Much faster than other bombers, the DB-7 was judged "hot", because it was a modern aircraft in an environment of small unpaved airfields and because it was very different from, and more complex, than contemporary European machines. One unusual feature was the emergency control column in the rear gunner's cockpit for use if the

Above: Seen here with a P-61, 39-753 was one of 60 A-20s rebuilt as a P-70 with four 20mm in the belly and British radar.

pilot should be killed. A few DB-7s escaped to Britain, which used very large numbers of Boston bomber versions and Havoc night fighters.

The first US Army model in action was the A-20C, similar to the RAF Boston III (in fact the latter was flown for the first few missions by the initial AAF combat units, the 15th BS in England in July 1942). By this time

production had begun of the most important model, the A-20G, with heavier bombload, dorsal turret and devastating nose armament.

Among other important US Army versions were the transparent-nosed A-20J and K, often used as bombing lead ships by the 9th and 15th Air Forces (respectively in Northwest Europe and Italy). The RAF counterparts of the J and K were the Boston IV and V, of the 2nd Tactical Air Force and Desert AF (Italy). Total production was 7,385, of which 3,125 were supplied feeely to the Soviet Union.

Above: The first A-20Cs took part in the big 1941 Army maneuvers. These bear the white crosses of White Force.

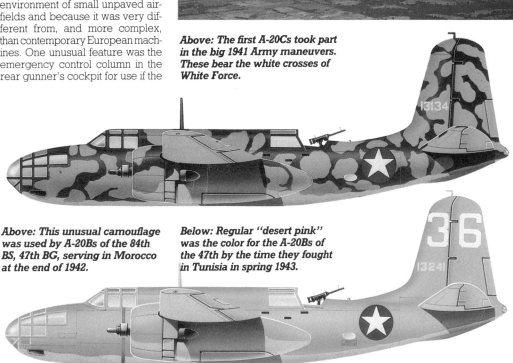

Above: This unusual camouflage was used by A-20Bs of the 84th BS, 47th BG, serving in Morocco at the end of 1942.

Below: Regular "desert pink" was the color for the A-20Bs of the 47th by the time they fought in Tunisia in spring 1943.

North American B-25 Mitchell

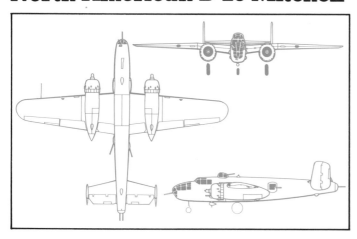

Origin: North American Aviation Inc, Inglewood, California, and Kansas City, Missouri.
Type: Medium bomber and attack with crew from four to six (see text).
Engines: (B-25, A, B) two 1,700hp Wright R-2600-9 Cyclone 14-cylinder two-row radials; (C, D, G) two 1,700hp R-2600-13; (H, J, F-10), two 1,850hp (emergency rating) R-2600-29.
Dimensions: Span 67ft 7in (20.6m); length (B-25, A) 54ft 1in (16.71m); (B, C, J) 52ft 11in (16.1m); (G, H) 51ft (15.54m); height (typical) 15ft 9in (4.80m); wing area 610sq ft (56.67m²).
Weights: Empty (J, typical) 21,100lb (9,580kg); maximum loaded (A) 27,100lb (12,293kg); (B)

Above: The B-25J was the most important model. The four "package guns" improved pilot morale in low attacks.

28,640lb (12,991kg); (C) 34,000lb (15,422kg); (G) 35,000lb (15,876kg); (H) 36,047lb (16,350kg); (J) normal 35,000lb, overload 41,800lb (18,960kg).
Performance: Maximum speed (A) 315mph (507km/h); (B) 300mph (483km/h); (C, G) 284mph (459km/h); (H, J) 275mph (443km/h); initial climb (A, typical) 1,500ft (460m)/min; (late models typical) 1,100ft (338m)/min; service ceiling (A) 27,000ft (8,230m); (late models, typical) 24,000ft (7,315m); range (all, typical) 1,500 miles (2,414m).

Above: This B-25C was painted Desert Sand, commonly called Desert Pink. Its unit was possibly the 340th Bomb Group.

Armament: See text.
History: First flight (NA-40 prototype) January 1939; (NA-62, the first production B-25) 19 August 1940; (B-25G) August 1942.
Users: AAC/AAF, Navy.

Named in honor of the fearless US Army Air Corps officer who was court-martialed in 1924 for his uncompromisingly outspoken belief in air power, the B-25 — designed by a company with no previous experience of twins, of bombers or of high-performance warplanes — was made in larger quantities than

any other American twin-engine combat aircraft, and has often been described as the best aircraft in its class in World War II.

Led by Lee Atwood and Ray Rice, the design team first created the Twin Wasp-powered NA-40, but had to start again and build a better-engineered and more powerful machine to meet revised Army specifications demanding twice the bombload (2,400lb, 1,089kg). The resulting stressed-skin NA-62 had a wider fuselage with a side-by-side cockpit, tricycle landing gear, twin-finned tail and a wing mounted above the mid position with a large bomb bay beneath.

The Army ordered 184 off the drawing board, the first 24 being B-25s and the rest B-25A with armor

Lockheed P-38 Lightning

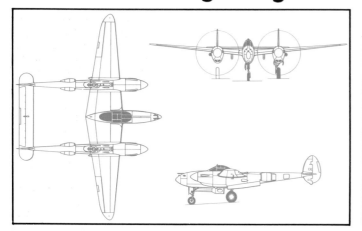

Origin: Lockheed Aircraft Corporation, Burbank, California.
Type: Single-seat long-range fighter (see text for variations)
Engines: Two Allison V-1710 vee-12 liquid-cooled turbocharged piston engines; (YP-38) 1,150hp V-1710-27/29 (all P-38 engines handed with opposite propeller rotation, hence pairs of engine sub-type numbers); (P-38E to G) 1,325hp V-1710-49/52 or 51/55; (P-38H and J) 1,425hp V-1710-89/91; (P-38L and M) 1,600hp V-1710-111/113.
Dimensions: Span 52ft (15.86m); length 37ft 10in (11.53m); (F-5G, P-38M and certain "droop-snoot" conversions fractionally longer); height 12ft 10in (3.9m); wing area

Above: This configuration is illustrative of the P-38F, G and H, with original engine cowls and with tank or bomb pylons under the inner wings.

327.5sq ft (30.43m²).
Weights: Empty, varied from 11,000lb (4,990kg) in YP to average of 12,700lb (5,766kg), with heaviest sub-types close to 14,000lb (6,350kg); maximum loaded, (YP) 14,348lb (6,508kg); (D) 15,500lb (7,030kg); (E) 15,482lb (7,022kg); (F) 18,000lb (8,165kg); (G) 19,800lb (8,918kg); (H) 20,300lb (9,208kg); (L, M) 21,600lb (9,798kg).
Performance: Maximum speed (all) 391-414mph (630-666km/h); initial climb (all) about 2,850ft

Above: Marshall Headle flying the first of the 13 YP-38s on 16 (also reported as 17) September 1940. Guns have yet to be installed.

(870m)/min; service ceiling (up to G) 38,000-40,000ft (11,580-12,190m); (H, J, L) 44,000ft (13,410m); range on internal fuel 350-460 miles (563-740km); range at 30,000ft with maximum fuel (late models) 2,260 miles (3,650km).
Armament: See text.
History: First flight (XP-38) 27 January 1939; (YP-38) 16 September 1940; service delivery (USAAC P-38) 8 June 1941; (F-4) March 1942; (P-38F) September 1942; final delivery

September 1945.
Users: AAC/AAF.

In February 1937 the US Army Air Corps issued a specification for a long-range interceptor (pursuit) and escort fighter, calling for a speed of 360mph at 20,000ft and endurance at this speed of one hour. Lockheed, which had never built a purely military design, jumped in with both feet and created a revolutionary fighter bristling with innovations and posing considerable technical risks.

Powered by two untried Allison liquid (glycol)-cooled engines, with GEC turbochargers recessed into the tops of the tail booms, it had a tricycle landing gear, small central

and self-sealing tanks. After the first nine original B-25s directional stability was improved by eliminating wing dihedral outboard of the engine nacelles, giving a distinctive gull-wing appearance. The defensive armament was a 0.5in manually aimed in the cramped tail and single 0.3in manually aimed from waist windows and the nose; bombload was 3,000lb (1,361kg).

The B had twin 0.5in in an electrically driven dorsal turret and a retractable ventral turret, the tail gun being removed. On 18 April 1942 16 B-25Bs led by Lt-Col Jimmy Doolittle made the daring and morale-raising raid on Tokyo and several other Japanese cities, having made free take-offs at maximum gross weight from the carrier *Hornet* 800 miles distant. Extra fuel, external bomb racks and other additions led to the C, supplied to the RAF, China and Soviet Union, and as the PBJ-1C to the US Navy.

The D was similar, but built at the new plant at Kansas City. In 1942 came the G, with solid nose fitted with a 75mm M-4 gun, loaded manually with 21 rounds. At first two 0.5in were also fixed in the nose, for flak suppression and sighting, but in July 1943 tests against Japanese ships showed that more was needed and the answer

Left: Most of the 14 heavy machine guns can be seen on this B-25H, but not the 75mm.

was four 0.5in "package guns" on the sides of the nose. Next came the B-25H with the fearsome armament of a 75mm gun of improved type, 14 0.5in guns (eight firing ahead, two in waist bulges and four in dorsal and tail turrets) and a 2,000lb (907kg) torpedo or 3,200lb (1,451kg) of bombs.

Biggest production of all was the J, with glazed nose, normal bomb load of 4,000lb (1,814kg) and no fewer than 13 0.5in guns supplied with 5,000 rounds. The corresponding attack version had a solid nose with five additional 0.5in guns. Total J output was 4,318, and the last delivery in August 1945 brought total output to 9,816.

The F-10 was an unarmed multi-camera reconnaissance version, and the CB-25 was a post-war transport model. The wartime AT-24 trainers were redesignated TB-25 after 1947, supplemented by more than 900 bombers rebuilt as the TB-25J, K, L and M. The 117 TB-25Ks and 40 TB-25Ms were converted by Hughes to train operators on the E-1 and E-5 interceptor fire-control systems, while the 90 Ls and 47 Ns were rebuilt by Hayes Aircraft as pilot trainers for large multi-engine airplanes. The last were retired from Reese AFB in January 1959, and some ended their days as research hacks or target tugs, and one carried the cameras for the early Cinerama films.

nacelle mounting a 23mm Madsen cannon and four 0.5in Brownings firing parallel directly ahead of the pilot, twin fins, Fowler flaps, cooling radiators on the flanks of the booms and induction intercoolers in the wing leading edges. This box of tricks ran into a ditch on its first taxi test, and two weeks after first flight undershot at Mitchell Field, NY, and was demolished. What made headlines, however, was that it had flown to New York in 7hr 2min, with two refueling stops, demonstrating a performance which in 1939 seemed beyond belief.

The enthusiasm of the Air Corps overcame the doubts and high cost, and by 1941 the first YP-38 was being tested, with a 37mm Oldsmobile cannon, two 0.5s and two Colt 0.3s. Thirteen YPs were followed on the Burbank line by 20 P-38s, with one 37mm and four 0.5, plus armor and, in the 36 D models, self-sealing tanks. In March 1940 the British Purchasing Commission had ordered 143 of this type, with the 37mm replaced by a 20mm Hispano and far greater ammunition capacity. The State Department prohibited export of the F2 Allison engine, so RAF aircraft, called Lightning I, had early C15 engines without turbochargers, both having right-hand rotation (P-38s had propellers turning outward). The result was poor and the RAF rejected these machines, which were later

Above: This "smoke curtain" installation was tested in late 1942, and it became a standard optional fitment on the P-38F as an alternative to 2,000lb of bombs, torpedoes or tanks.

brought up to US standard, designated as P-322s and used as trainers.

The E model adopted the British name Lightning and the RAF Hispano gun. Within minutes of the US declaration of war, on 7 December 1941, an E shot down an Fw 200C Condor near Iceland, and the P-38 was subsequently in the thick of fighting in North Africa, Northwest Europe and the Pacific.

The F was the first to have inner-wing pylons for 1,000lb bombs, torpedoes, tanks or other stores. Later P-38Fs introduced a special 8° combat setting of the Fowler flaps to enhance dogfight maneuverability. By late 1943 new G models with internal equipment changes were being flown to

Europe across the North Atlantic, while in the Pacific 16 aircraft of the 339th Fighter Squadron destroyed Admiral Yamamoto's G4M aircraft 550 miles from their base at Guadalcanal.

The J had the intercoolers moved under the engines, changing the appearance, providing room for 55 extra gallons of fuel in the outer wings. Later J models had hydraulically boosted ailerons, but retained the wheel-type lateral control instead of a stick.

The L, with higher war emergency power, could carry 4,000lb of bombs or ten rockets, and often formations would bomb under the direction of a leadship converted to droop-snoot configuration with a bombardier in the nose. The P-38L version came off the line in floods in 1944, Lockheed building 3,810 in a few months and Vultee a further 113 at Nashville before that contract was canceled.

Hundreds were built as F-4 or F-5 photographic aircraft, and the M was a two-seat night fighter with ASH radar pod under the nose. Lightnings towed gliders, operated on skis, acted as fast ambulances (carrying two litter cases) and were used for many special ECM missions. Total production was 9,942, and the P-38 made up for slightly inferior maneuverability by its range, reliability and multi-role effectiveness.

Martin PBM Mariner

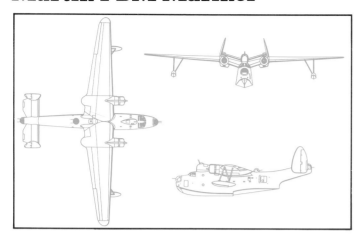

Origin: The Glenn L. Martin Company, Baltimore, Maryland.
Type: Maritime patrol and anti-submarine flying boat with typical crew of nine.
Engines: (PBM-1) two 1,600hp Wright R-2600-6 Cyclone 14-cylinder two-row radials; (3C, 3S, 3R) 1,700hp R-2600-12; (3D) 1,900hp R-2600-22, (5, 5A) 2,100hp Pratt & Whitney R-2800-34 Double Wasp 18-cylinder two-row radials.
Dimensions: Span 118ft (36m); length (-1, 3S) 77ft 2in (23.5m); (3C) 80ft (24.38m); (5, 5A) 79ft 10in; height (-1) 24ft 6in; (remainder) 27ft 6in (8.4m); wing area 1,408sq ft (130.81m²).
Weights: Empty (-1) 26,000lb (11,790kg); (-3, typical) 32,328lb (14,690kg); (-5A) 34,000lb

Above: The PBM-3D is shown with the then-novel search radar installation above the cockpit where it "saw" everything ahead.

(15,422kg); maximum loaded (-1) 41,139lb (18,660kg); (3S) 56,000lb (25,400kg); (5) 60,000lb (27,216kg).
Performance: Maximum speed (all) about 205mph (330km/h); initial climb (typical) 800ft (244m)/min; service ceiling (-1) 22,400ft (6,830m); (3S) 16,900ft (5,150m); (5) 20,200ft (6,160m); maximum range with military load (-1) 3,450 miles (5,550km); (3C) 2,137 miles (3,439km); (3S) 3,000 miles (4,828km); (5) 2,700 miles (4,345km).
Armament: (-1) one 0.5in Browning in nose turret, two in

Above: One of the 20 PBM-1s, seen serving with VP-74 a few weeks after Pearl Harbor. The stabilizing floats are retracted.

dorsal turret and two manually aimed from waist windows, one 0.30in in extreme tail (manually aimed over small cone of fire); (3B, 3C) twin 0.5in dorsal, nose and tail turrets; (3S) four manually aimed 0.5in in nose, tail and two waist windows; (5) eight 0.5in in three power turrets and two waist windows; weapon bays in engine nacelles with capacity of 2,000lb (907kg) in (-1), 4,000lb (1,814kg) in all later versions (with provision for two externally hung torpedoes).
History: First flight (XPBM-1)

18 February 1939; service delivery, (-1) September 1940; first flight (-5) May 1943; final delivery (5A) April 1949.
Users: Navy, Coast Guard.

Had it not been for the Catalina the PBM would have been by far the most important Allied patrol flying boat of World War II. It was designed in 1936 and proved by flying a quarter-scale model (Martin 162A). The full-size Model 162 prototype was ordered on 3 June 1937, followed by 20 production -1 in December 1937. These were advanced and challenging boats, with high wing and power loading and stabilizing floats which retracted inwards into the wing.

They were made possible by

Bell P-39 Airacobra

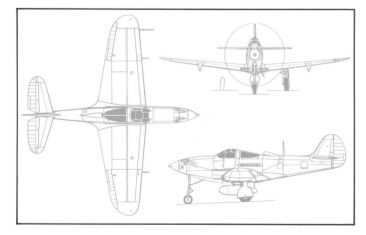

Origin: Bell Aircraft Corporation, Buffalo, NY.
Type: Single-seat fighter, data for P-39L version.
Engine: 1,325hp Allison V-1710-63 vee-12 liquid-cooled.
Dimensions: Span 34ft (10.37m); length 30ft 2in (9.2m); height (one prop-blade vertical) 11ft 10in (3.63m); wing area 213sq ft (19.79m²).
Weights: Empty 5,600lb (2,540kg); loaded 8,400lb (3,811kg).
Performance: Maximum speed 380mph (612km/h); initial climb 4,000ft (1,220m)/min; service ceiling 35,000ft (10,670m); ferry range with drop tank at 160mph (256km/h) 1,475 miles (2,360km).
Armament: One 37mm cannon

Above: Distinguished by its underwing 0.5 in guns, the P-39Q was the last production model, most going to the Soviet Union.

with 30 rounds (twice as many as in first sub-types), two synchronized 0.5in Colt-Brownings and two or four 0.30in in outer wings; one 500lb (227kg) bomb.
History: First flight of XP-39 6 April 1939; (P-39F to M-sub-types, 1942); final batch (P-39Q) May 1944.
User: AAF.

First flown as a company prototype in the early spring of 1939, this design by R. J. Woods and O. L. Woodson was unique in having a

Above: Some of the very first YP-39s seen on test at the Bell plant in the winter 1940-41. Note the back-pack parachute.

nosewheel-type landing gear and the engine behind the pilot. The propeller was driven by a long shaft under the pilot's seat and a reduction gearbox in the nose, the latter also containing a big T-9 cannon firing through the propeller hub. Other guns were also fitted in the nose, the first production aircraft, the P-39C of 1941, having two 0.30in and two 0.5in all synchronized to fire past the propeller.

Britain ordered the unconventional fighter in 1940, but RAF No 601 Sqn did poorly with it and failed

to keep the unusual aircraft serviceable. The rest of the British contract, with the cannon of only 20mm caliber, went to the AAF and Soviet Union, some serving as P-400s with the 347th FG at Guadalcanal.

The US Army Air Force used the P-39 in big numbers. Altogether 9,588 were built and used with fair success in the Mediterranean and Far East, some 5,000 being supplied to the Soviet Union, mainly through Iran. In Northwest Europe the P-39 was outclassed, mainly because of its poor climb and high-altitude performance, but in the Tunisian campaign it did well, as it did in Soviet hands.

Its agility, toughness, armor and big cannon endeared it to many

Wright's development of the powerful 14-cylinder Cyclone engine. These turned large propellers which in most PBMs had four blades, and the gull-wing layout put the propellers well above most waves and spray. A unique feature at the time was that the nacelles incorporated large weapon bays, and another was the inward tilt of the fins and rudders, set at right angles on the tips of a dihedralled tailplane.

Only one XPBM-2 was built, with long-range tanks and stressed for catapulting. Hundreds followed of the -3, -3C (which sank the U-boat which sank *Ark Royal*), -3R transport and -3S long-range anti-submarine versions, followed by the turreted -3D used throughout the South West Pacific. All -3 and subsequent versions had fixed stabilizing floats, and larger nacelles.

The more powerful -5 had improved dorsal ASV radar (usually APS-15), the -5A was an amphibian and the post-war 5E had later equipment. Total deliveries were 1,235 and over 500 were in front-line service in the Korean war in 1950-53. The Coast Guard replaced the PBM-5G with the -5A amphibian, using these in the air/sea rescue role until 1959.

Right: One of the very first Mariners, a PBM-1 of VP-56 in September 1940.

ground-attack operators, but it cannot be said that putting the engine above the wing, on the center of gravity, resulted in a superior fighter. It did achieve the lowest loss rate per 1,000 sorties of any AAF fighter in the ETO, but this was largely because it operated in circumstances where 109s and 190s were rare. Biggest production version was the P-39Q, of which over 4,900 were built. The P-39 was succeeded in production in 1944 by the P-63 Kingcobra, described on a later page.

Above: Two of the first Airacobra pursuits to reach the Army were these early P-39Ds, seen with special markings as part of Red Force during the big 1941 maneuvers. They were assigned to the 8th Pursuit Group.

Right: Freelance test pilot Jimmy Taylor gets aboard the XP-39 prototype in April 1939. At this time a Curtiss Electric propeller was fitted (with no cannon through the hub), and air inlets were in the fuselage.

Consolidated Vultee B-24 Liberator

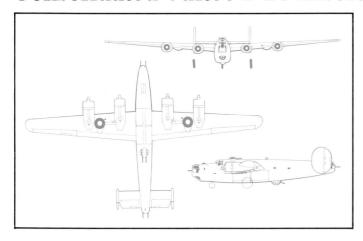

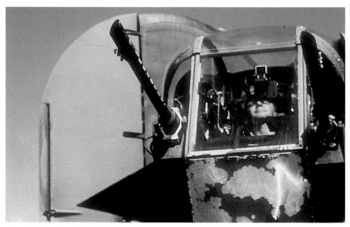

Origin: Consolidated Vultee Aircraft Corporation, San Diego, California; also built by Douglas, Ford and North American Aviation.
Type: Long-range bomber with normal crew of ten, data for B-24J.
Engines: Four 1,200hp Pratt & Whitney Twin Wasp R-1830-65 14-cylinder two-row radials.
Dimensions: Span 110ft (33.5m); length 67ft 2in (20.47m); height 18ft (5.49m); wing area 1,048sq ft (97.36m²).
Weights: Empty 37,000lb (16,783kg); loaded 65,000lb (29,484kg).
Performance: Maximum speed 290mph (467km/h); initial climb 900ft (274m)/min; service ceiling 28,000ft (8,534m); range at 190mph (306km/h) with 5,000lb (2,268kg) bombload 2,200 miles (3,540km).
Armament: Ten 0.5in Brownings

Above: B-24G, H and J (shown here) were similar apart from turrets. Note oval cowlings and "roll up" bomb doors.

arranged in four electrically operated turrets (Consolidated or Emerson in nose, Martin dorsal, Briggs-Sperry retractable ventral "ball" and Consolidated or Motor Products tail) with two guns each plus two singles in manual waist positions; two bomb bays with roll-up doors with vertical racks on each side of central catwalk for up to 8,000lb (3,629kg); two 4,000lb (1,814kg) bombs could be hung externally on inner-wing racks instead of internal load.
History: First flight (XB-24) 29 December 1939; first delivery (LB-30A) March 1941; first combat service (Liberator I) June 1941; first combat service with US Army

Above: Six companies supplied B-24 turrets. The most common tail turret was by Consolidated, here fitted to a painted B-24J.

(B-24C) November 1941; termination of production 31 May 1945; withdrawal from service (various smaller air forces) 1955-56.
Users: AAF, Navy, Marine Corps.

This distinctive aircraft was one of the most important in the history of aviation. Conceived as the Consolidated Model 32 five years after the B-17 it did not, in fact, notably improve on the older bomber's performance, and in respect of engine-out performance and general stability and control it was inferior, being a handful for the average pilot. It was also by far the most complicated and expensive

combat aircraft the world had seen — though in this it merely showed the way things were going to be in future.

Yet it was built in bigger numbers than any other American aircraft in history, in more versions for more purposes than any other aircraft in history, and served on every front in World War II and with 15 Allied nations. In terms of industrial effort it transcended anything seen previously in any sphere of endeavor.

It had a curious layout, dictated by the slender Davis wing placed above the tall bomb bays. This wing was efficient in cruising flight, which combined with great fuel capacity to give the "Lib" longer range than any other landplane of its day. But it meant that the main gears were long, and they were retracted outwards into the wing by electric motors, nearly everything

Curtiss C-46 Commando

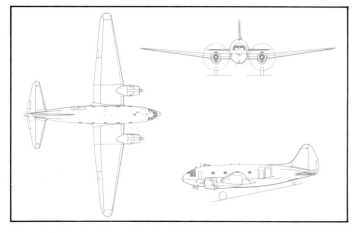

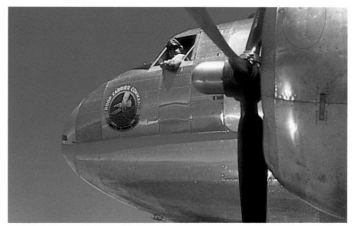

Origin: Curtiss-Wright Corporation, Buffalo, NY; production at St Louis, Missouri, and Louisville, Kentucky.
Type: Troop and cargo transport.
Engines: (A, D) two 2,000hp Pratt & Whitney R-2800-51 Double Wasp 18-cylinder radials, (E, F) 2,200hp R-2800-75.
Dimensions: Span 108ft 1in (32.92m); length 76ft 4in (23.27m); height 21ft 9in (6.63m); wing area 1,360sq ft (126.35m²).
Weights: Empty (A) 29,483lb (13,373kg); maximum (A) 56,000lb (25,400kg).
Performance: Cruising speed (67

Above: Apart from the rare C-46E with stepped windscreen, all C-46s looked almost identical. The aircraft adapted to tow gliders (CG-4s) had a blunt tailcone.

per cent) 227mph (365km/h), (econ) 193mph (311km/h); service ceiling 27,600ft (8,410m); max range (no fuselage tanks) 1,600 miles (2,575km), (max payload) 890 miles (1,432km).
History: First flight 26 March 1940; service delivery (C-46) October 1941; final delivery 1945.
Users: AAF, Navy.

Above: The badge of the AAF Troop Carrier Command adorns the nose of this C-46E. Only 17 were made of this model, which was the only one to feature a stepped windscreen.

In 1936 Curtiss-Wright planned an exceptionally large and capable twin-engined airliner, of modern stressed-skin type, to try to recover its airline sales that had been swept away by the new monoplanes from Boeing, Lockheed and Douglas. In 1940 the CW-20 impressed not only airlines but also the US Army, and it was totally redesigned as a military

transport.
The sumptuous pressurized fuselage was replaced by an unpressurized one with large doors and strong floor, and with ports in the windows for firing infantry weapons; twin fins became one, the R-2600 engines became more powerful R-2800s and the whole machine was tailored to quick production and troublefree service. By 1945 about 3,330 of these extremely useful aircraft had been delivered, almost all as various C-46 models but 160 were taken into service as Navy transports designated R5C-1.
Carrying up to 50 passengers, or

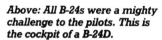

Left: A radar-equipped PB4Y-1 of the US Navy operating in 1943 from Dunkeswell, England.

Above: All B-24s were a mighty challenge to the pilots. This is the cockpit of a B-24D.

on board being electric. A perilous catwalk traversed the length of the two wide and deep bomb bays under the wing, which were covered by "roll-top desk" doors driven by sprockets to open up the sides of the fuselage.

Early versions supplied to the RAF were judged not combat-ready, and they began the Atlantic Return Ferry Service as LB-30A transports, but led to the RAF Liberator I, used by Coastal Command with ASV radar and a battery of fixed 20mm cannon. The B-24C introduced power-driven dorsal and tail turrets and served as a bomber with the stateside AAF and with the RAF in the Middle East.

The first mass-produced version was the B-24D, with turbocharged engines in oval cowls, more fuel and armament and many detail changes; 2,738 served US Bomb

Groups in Europe and the Pacific, and PB4Y-1s of the Navy and RAF Coastal Command closed the mid-Atlantic gap, previously beyond aircraft range, where U-boat packs lurked. War-weary PB4Ys were packed with 25,000lb (11,340kg) of Torpex/RDX explosives and rigged up with TV and radio guidance to destroy hardened land targets in Northern Europe in the Aphrodite program.

Biggest production of all centered on the B-24G, H and J (Navy PB4Y), of which 10,208 were built. These all had four turrets, and were made by Convair, North American, Ford and Douglas. Other variants included the L and M with different tail turrets, the N with single fin, the luridly painted CB-24 lead ships, the TB-24 trainer, F-7 photo-reconnaissance, C-109 fuel tanker which supplied the

B-29s in China, and QB-24 drone. There was also a complete family of Liberator Transport versions, known as C-87 Liberator Express to the Army, RY-3 to the Navy and

Below: Line service for a B-24J somewhere in the Pacific theater late in World War II.

C.VII and C.IX to the RAF, many having the huge single fin also seen on the PB4Y-2 Privateer described separately. Excluding one-offs such as the redesigned R2Y transport and 1,800 equivalent aircraft delivered as spares, total production of all versions was a staggering 19,203.

33 litter casualties and four attendants, or about 12,000lb (5,440kg) of cargo, they were the mainliners of the "Hump" airlift to China, and by late 1944 were also numerous in Europe, where they towed up to two CG-4 gliders each, taking part in the Rhine crossing. Though Curtiss never did achieve the civil sales it sought, the ex-wartime C-46 was destined to play a major role in outback nations right up to the present day, about 140 still being in daily use in Latin America.

American military service also did not stop in 1945, but the A, D and F versions, differing mainly in details, saw extensive use in Korea. A few TC-46D crew trainers were converted for Air Training Command, and the last survivors of these big twins served with TAC's 1st Air Commando Group on Co-In operations in the early years of the Vietnam War.

Right: Army airplane 43-47313 was a C-46A built by Curtiss-Wright at Louisville, Kentucky. The beautiful fuselage shape was designed for pressurization, and in fact a more box-like one might have been more useful for the harsh wartime trucking job. What nobody could foresee was that C-46s would fly 40 years.

Sikorsky R-4, HNS

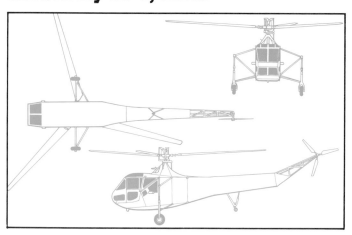

Origin: Sikorsky Aircraft Division of United Aircraft Corporation, Bridgeport, Connecticut.
Type: Light utility helicopter.
Engine: One Warner Super-Scarab seven-cylinder radial: (XR-4) 165hp R-500-3, (YR) 180hp R-550-1, (R-4B) 200hp R-550-3.
Dimensions: Diameter of three-blade rotor (XR) 36ft (10.97m); (rest) 38ft (11.58m); overall length

Above: The VS-316A became the R-4B in its main production form, but 25 went to the Navy as HNS-1 trainers. Variants looked similar.

(rotors turning) 48ft 11in (14.91m); length of fuselage 35ft 5in (10.8m); height overall (R-4B) 12ft 5in (3.78m); main-rotor disc area 1,018sq ft (94.56m²).
Weights: (R-4B) empty 2,020lb

Above: Nearly half the YR-4Bs and R-4Bs spent most of their time on pontoon floats. This one has rescue litters.

(916kg); maximum loaded 2,535lb (1,150kg).
Performance: (R-4B) Maximum speed 77mph (124km/h); cruising speed 70mph (113km/h); range 220 miles (322km).

Armament: None.
History: First flight (VS-300) see text, (VS-316A) 14 January 1942.
Users: AAF, Navy, Coast Guard.

The R-4 series were the first production helicopters outside Germany, and among the first in the world. They stemmed directly from the pioneer VS-300 research machine first gingerly lifted off the

Vought F4U Corsair

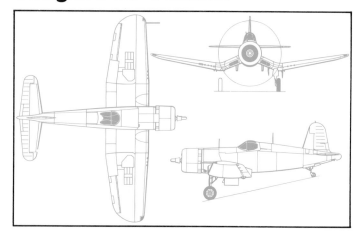

Origin: Chance Vought Division of United Aircraft Corporation, Stratford, Connecticut; also built by Brewster and Goodyear.
Type: Single-seat carrier-based fighter-bomber (sub-variants, see text).
Engine: (F4U-1) 2,000hp Pratt & Whitney R-2800-8 (B) Double Wasp 18-cylinder two-row radial; (-1A) 2,250hp R-2800-8 (W) with water injection; (-4) 2,450hp R-2800-18W with water-methanol; (-5) 2,850hp R-2800-32 (E) with water-methanol; (F2G) 3,000hp Pratt & Whitney R-4360 Wasp Major 28-cylinder four-row radial.
Dimensions: Span 40ft 11¾in (12.48m); length 33ft 8¼in (10.27m); (-1, -3) 33ft 4in (10.15m); (-5N and -7) 34ft 6in (10.5m); height (late models) 14ft 9¼in (4.49m); (-1, -2) 16ft 1in (4.8m); wing area 314sq ft (29.17m²).
Weights: Empty (-1A) 8,873lb (4,025kg); (-5, typical) 9,900lb (4,490kg); maximum loaded (-1A) 14,000lb (6,350kg); (-5) 15,079lb (6,840kg); (AU-1) 19,398lb (8,798kg).

Above: This major variant, the F4U-1D, looked very much like the others. The F4U-1 had a flat framed canopy.

Performance: Maximum speed (-1A) 395mph (635km/h); (-5) 462mph (744km/h); initial climb (-1A) 2,890ft (880m)/min; (-5) 4,800ft (1,463m)/min; service ceiling (-1A) 37,000ft (11,280m); (-5) 44,000ft (13,400m); range on internal fuel, typically 1,000 miles (1,609km).
Armament: See text.
History: First flight (XF4U) 29 May 1940; (production -1) June 1942; combat delivery July 1942; final delivery (-7) December 1952.
Users: Navy, Marine Corps.

Designed by Rex Beisel and Igor Sikorsky, the inverted-gull-wing Corsair was one of the greatest combat aircraft in history. Planned to use the most powerful engine and biggest propeller ever fitted to a fighter, the V-166 design got its bent-wing look from the need to keep the propeller clear of the ground or deck and still retract relatively short landing gears

Above: Early F4U-1 Corsairs, such as this, went to the Marines at Cherry Point. This very early example lacks a rear-view mirror.

backwards inside the wings. The down-sloping center-sections housed ducts to the oil radiators and engine supercharger. The XF4U-1 prototype was the first US warplane to exceed 400mph and outperformed all other American aircraft of its day. Originally fitted with two fuselage and two wing guns, it was replanned with six 0.5in Browning MG 53-2 in the folding outer wings, each with about 390 rounds.

This seemingly simple change caused a major redesign. Fuel had to be moved from the wing leading edges to the fuselage, resulting in the cockpit being moved further back, and internal bomb racks in the wings were eliminated. The aft cockpit adversely affected view ahead, and moreover the carrier landing qualities were at first considered unacceptable (except by Britain's Fleet Air Arm), so all early deliveries went to the Marines,

notably to "Pappy" Boyington's Black Sheep, alias VMF-124.

Action with land-based Marine squadrons began in the Solomons in February 1943; from then on the Corsair swiftly gained air supremacy over the previously untroubled Japanese. The -1C had four 20mm cannon, and the -1D and most subsequent types carried a 175gal drop tank and two 1,000lb (907kg) bombs or eight rockets. Many hundreds of P versions carried cameras, and N variants had an APS-4 or -6 radar in a wing pod for night interceptions.

Brewster made 735 F3A, and Goodyear 4,008 FG versions, but only ten of the fearsome F2G. Fabric-skinned wings became metal in the post-war -5, most of which had cannon, while the 110 AU-1 attack bombers carried a 4,000lb (1,814kg) load in Korea at speeds seldom exceeding 240mph! In December 1952 the last of 12,571 Corsairs came off the line after a longer production run (in terms of time) than any US fighter prior to the Phantom.

ground (but tethered to a heavy plate) by Igor Sikorsky on 14 September 1939. After many modifications, including the addition of a long truss fuselage with a tail carrying three rotors, two of them with axes vertical to provide positive lateral control, Sikorsky began free flight trials on 13 May 1940. Power was increased from 90 to 150hp, and as the VS-300A it reached a definitive stage with operative cyclic pitch and only one (antitorque) tail rotor by mid-1941. This set the configuration for the classic helicopter with one lifting rotor which has been followed by most rotorcraft ever since.

In early 1941 Vought-Sikorsky (as the division was then styled) began development of a military helicopter derived from the 300A to meet a requirement issued by the AAF. The resulting VS-316A had a larger rotor, driven by a radial engine via a 90° angle gearbox, fabric-covered fuselage of welded steel tube, fixed tailwheel landing gear (or two inflated rubber pontoons) and side-by-side seats in a nose cabin, with side doors. Dual controls were optional, and one of the many fashions set was that the pilot in command sat on the right, with cyclic stick in front and twist-grip throttle on a collective stick low down beside his seat on the left side. The USAAF applied designation XR-4 to the first VS-316A, which in May 1942 flew by easy stages the 761 miles (1,225km) from Connecticut to Wright Field in a total time in the air of just over 16 hours.

By early 1943 three YR-4As and 27 YR-4Bs were conducting Arctic and tropical trials and flights from a platform on a tanker at sea. Three YRs went to the Coast Guard. By 1944 a batch of 100 R-4Bs were being built, 22 going to the Navy as HNS-1 and 45 to the British RAF. Used mainly for pilot training and

Above: Like the R-4B opposite this example bears no Army or Navy titles, nor any kind of serial or unit number, and thus is still in the maker's hands at Bridgeport. Olive drab indicates eventual Army service.

trials purposes, survivors in the USAF in 1948 were redesignated H-4B. Total production was 131.

Right: Perhaps the best day fighter version was the F4U-4C, here seen with orange Reserve band serving at NAS Glenview, Illinois, in 1947-54.

Below: At full load the AU-1 attack version had a top speed half that of other Corsairs! This very heavy attack version saw much action in Korea.

North American P-51 Mustang

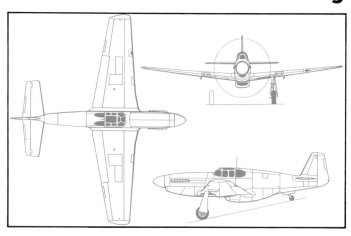

Origin: North American Aviation Inc, Inglewood, California; also built at Dallas, Texas.

Type: (P-51) single-seat fighter; (A-36) attack bomber; (F-6) reconnaissance; (Cavalier and Piper models) Co-In.

Engine: (P-51, A-36, F-6A) one 1,150hp Allison V-1710-F3R or (P-51A) 1,200hp V-1710-81 vee-12 liquid-cooled; (P-51B, C, D and K, F-6C) one Packard V-1650 (licence-built R-R Merlin 61-series), originally 1,520hp V-1650-3 followed during P-51D run by 1,590hp V-1650-7; (P-51H) 2,218hp V-1650-9; (Cavalier) mainly V-1650-7; (Turbo-Mustang III) 1,740hp Rolls-Royce Dart 510 turboprop; (Enforcer) 2,535hp Lycoming T55-9 turboprop.

Dimensions: Span 37ft 0½in (11.29m); (tip-tanked Cavalier models, 40ft 1in (12.1m); length 32ft 2½in (9.81m); (P-51H) 33ft 4in; (Turbo-Mustang and Enforcer) 38ft 6in; height (P-51, A, A-36, F-6) 12ft 2in (3.72m); (other P-51) 13ft 8in (4.1m); wing area 233sq ft (21.65m²).

Weights: Empty (P-51 early V-1710 models, typical) 6,300lb (2,858kg); (P-51D) 7,125lb (3,230kg); (Cavalier 2500) 7,500lb (3,402kg); (Turbo-Mustang/ Enforcer) 6,696lb (3,037kg); maximum loaded (P-51 early) 8,600lb (3,901kg); (P-51D) 11,600lb (5,260kg); (Cavalier) 10,500lb (4,763kg); (Turbo) 14,000lb (6,350kg).

Performance: Maximum speed (early P-51) 390mph (628km/h); (P-51D) 437mph (703km/h); (Cavalier, typical) 457mph (735km/h); initial climb (early) 2,600ft (792m)/min, (P-51D) 3,475ft (1,060m)/min; service ceiling (early) 30,000ft (9,144m); (P-51D 41,900ft (12,770m), (also typical for Cavaliers); range with maximum fuel (early) 450 miles (724km); (P-51D) combat range 950 miles (1,530km), operational range 1,300 miles (0,000km) with drop tanks and absolute range to dry tanks of 2,080 miles, (3,350km) (Cavaliers) 750-2,500 miles (1,250-4,025km) depending on customer choice; (Turbo) 2,300 miles (3,700km).

Armament: P-51 four 20mm Hispano cannon in wings; (P-51A and B) four 0.5in in wings; (A-36A) two 0.5in in cowling and four in wings, and wing racks for two

Above: First of the "Merlin" models, the P-51B scored its first victories in January 1944. Until then the Allison-engined P-51s had held the line.

500lb (227kg) bombs; (all subsequent P-51 production models) six 0.5in Browning MG53-2 with 270 or 400 rounds each, and wing racks for tanks or two 1,000lb (454kg) bombs; (Cavalier or Turbo, typical) six 0.5in with 2,000 rounds, two hardpoints each 1,000lb, and four more each 750lb.

History: First flight (NA-73X) 26 October 1940; (production RAF Mustang I) 1 May 1941; service delivery (RAF) October 1941; first flight (AAF A-36A) September 1942, (Merlin conversion) 13 October 1942; (P-51B) December 1942; final delivery (P-51H) November 1945.

In April 1940 the British Air Purchasing Commission concluded with "Dutch" Kindelberger, chairman of North American Aviation, an agreement for the design and development of a completely new fighter for the RAF. Completed in 117 days (and then held up six weeks by failure of Allison to deliver the engine) this silver prototype was the start of the most successful fighter program in history.

NAA had never before designed a pursuit (fighter), but its design was a masterpiece. Structurally and aerodynamically it was clean and simple, and it combined every known form of drag reduction including a so-called laminar profile wing and a coolant radiator in a long profiled duct under the rear fuselage so that in most flight regimes the radiator gave net forward thrust. The wide-track main

Above: This section from the 375FS, 361FG, operating from Bottisham, England, in 1944, is made up of a B, a C and two Ds, one with a dorsal fin.

Below: An A-36A attack model of the 86th Fighter Bomber Group in Sicily in summer 1943. Note the yellow insignia ring, and bombs.

gears retracted straight in and up as in the T-6, the wheels lying ahead of the front spar in a slightly extended wing root. Immediately to the rear was a big self-sealing fuel tank on each side giving total capacity of 184gal (697lit). The tailwheel was fully retractable, and the rudder and elevators were fabric-covered though the ailerons were metal-skinned. The well arranged and comfortable cockpit had a rather heavily framed hood which opened up by hinging to each side. The heavy armament comprised two 0.5in guns in the lower part of the cowling, two more in the wings plus a further four 0.3in

Below: 190 small bombs each denote a combat mission by this A-36A of the 27th FB Group, based in Corsica in July 1944.

in the wings.

The V-1710 engine's power fell away so rapidly with increasing altitude, so the N.A.73, called Mustang I by the RAF, was not used as a fighter but for low-level reconnaissance and ground attack. The USSAF had asked NAA to furnish, without charge, two examples of the N.A. 73 for evaluation. The Nos 4 and 10 off the line were duly delivered to Wright Field, but though considered excellent aircraft there was no move to procure the N.A.73 for the inventory until after Pearl Harbor. then some British Mustangs were impressed as P-51s and orders were placed

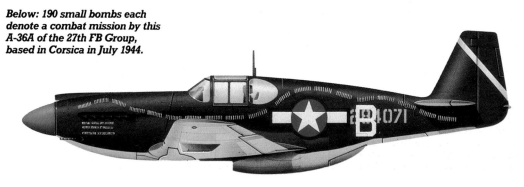

Above: 44-13357 was an Inglewood-built P-51D-5 assigned to the 374FS of the 361FG. It later had a dorsal fin added.

for 500 of an attack model designated A-36A, with revised armament, racks for two bombs and hydraulically opened dive brakes above and below the wings. These saw action in the Sicilian and Italian theaters, with dive brakes locked inoperative.

Next came the P-51 armed with four 20mm cannon, shared with the RAF as the Mustang IA, one example (41-37426) being transferred to the Navy and 57 being converted as F-6 photo-recon aircraft. These were followed by 310 slightly more powerful P-51As with only the wing guns, but with wing racks for bombs or tanks; 50 became RAF Mustang IIs and 35 F-6A photo aircraft. But the performance of the Mustang was transformed by fitting the Packard V-1650 Merlin engine. NAA carried out a major revision at the same time, fitting the intercooler along with the original radiator in a reprofiled duct, relocating the carb-air inlet below the spinner, modifying the ailerons and fitting a new HamStan propeller with four "paddle" blades. Colossal production built up at Inglewood, duplicated by a plant at Dallas which built the P-51C. An 85gal (322lit)

tank was added behind the cockpit, and some aircraft had six wing-mounted 0.5in guns. The folding hood was replaced first by the sliding bulged Malcolm hood and finally the rear fuselage was cut down and a new teardrop hood was fitted. Directional stability, already marginal with the big propeller and rear-fuselage tank, was improved by adding a dorsal fin. The resulting P-51D outnumbered all other versions combined, the P-51K differing only in having an Aeroproducts propeller. Special lightweight versions with high-power Packard or Allison engines led to the final production model, the 487mph (784km/h) P-51H, yet curiously the worldwide post-war model was the earlier P-51D. Total Mustang production was 15,586.

Mustang and P-51 variants served mainly in Europe, their prime mission being the almost incredible one of flying all the way from British bases to targets of the 8th AF deep in Germany — to Berlin or beyond

— escorting heavies and gradually establishing Allied air superiority over the heart of Germany.

The longer Twin Mustang (with two fuselages) is the subject of another entry.

After the war the Mustang proved popular with at least 55 nations. In 1945-48 Commonwealth Aircraft of Australia made under licence 200 Mustangs of four versions. In 1967 the P-51 was put back into production by Cavalier for the US Air Force and other customers, and the turboprop Turbo III and Enforcer versions were developed for the Pave Coin program for Forward Air Control and light attack missions. Many of the new or remanufactured models of 1968-75 are two-seaters.

Below: 42-106950 was an Inglewood P-51B assigned to the 354FS, 355FG and refitted with the bulged sliding Malcolm canopy.

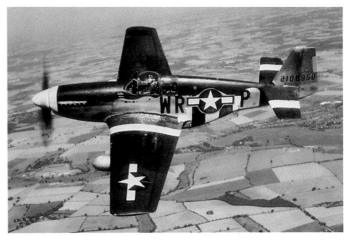

Martin B-26 Marauder

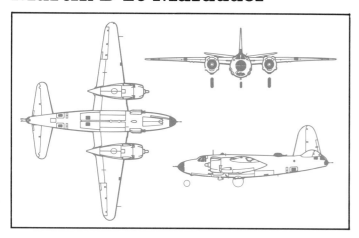

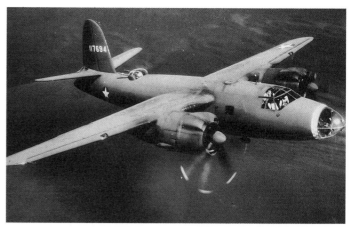

Origin: Glenn L. Martin Co, Baltimore, Maryland, and Omaha, Nebraska.

Type: Five- to seven-seat medium bomber.

Engines: Two Pratt & Whitney Double Wasp 18-cylinder two-row radials; (B-26) 1,850hp R-2800-5; (A) 2,000hp R-2800-39; (B, C, D, E, F, G) 2,000hp R-2800-43.

Dimensions: Span (B-26, A and first 641 B-26B) 65ft (19.8m); (remainder) 71ft (21.64m); length (B-26) 56ft (17m); (A, B) 58ft 3in (17.75m); (F, G) 56ft 6in (17.23m); height (up to E) 19ft 10in (6.04in); (remainder) 21ft 6in (6.55m); wing area (65ft) 602sq ft (55.93m²), (71ft) 658sq ft (61.13m²).

Weights: Empty (early, typical) 23,000lb (10,433kg); (F, G) 25,300lb (11,490kg); maximum loaded (B-26) 32,000lb (14,515kg); (A) 33,022lb

Above: From the B-26B-10 most Marauders had approximately this appearance.

(14,980kg); (first 641 B) 34,000lb (15,420kg), then 37,000lb (16,783kg); (F) 38,000lb (17,235kg); (G) 38,200lb (17,340kg).

Performance: Maximum speed (up to E, typical) 310mph (500km/h); (F, G) 280mph (451 km/h); initial climb 1,000ft (305m)/min; service ceiling (up to E) 23,000ft (7,000m); (F, G) 19,800ft (6,040m); range with 3,000lb (1,361kg) bomb load (typical) 1,150 miles (1,850km).

Armament: (B-26, A) five 0.30in or 0.50in Browning in nose (1 or 2), power dorsal turret (2), tail (1, manual) and optional manual ventral hatch; (B to E) one 0.5in manually aimed in nose, twin-gun turret, two manually aimed 0.5in

Above: 41-17694 was a B-26B-1, with short span, small tail, old tail guns and no package guns.

waist guns, one "tunnel gun" (usually 0.5in), two 0.5in in power tail turret and four 0.5in fixed as "package guns" on sides of forward fuselage; (F, G) same but without tunnel gun; some variations and trainer and Navy versions unarmed. Internal bomb load of 5,200lb (2,359kg) up to 641st B, after which rear bay was disused (eliminated in F, G) to give maximum load of 4,000lb (1,814kg). Early versions could carry a 21.7in torpedo hung beneath the bomb doors.

History: First flight 25 November 1940; service delivery 25 February 1941; final delivery March 1945.

Users: AAF, Navy.

With its background of leadership in bomber design Martin pulled out all the stops to win the 1939 Medium Bomber competition of the US Army, and boldly chose a wing optimized for high-speed cruise efficiency rather than for landing. Though the Model 179 won the competition — 201 being ordered "off the drawing board" on 5 July 1939 — the actual hardware proved too much for inexperienced pilots to handle, with unprecedented high wing loading. In fact there were no real problems, but the newness of the first B-26 versions, coupled with their reputation of being a "widow maker", created a vicious circle of high casualties.

The relatively huge fuselage had a circular section but was unpressurized, and it was beautifully streamlined. The powerful new

Curtiss SB2C/A-25 Helldiver

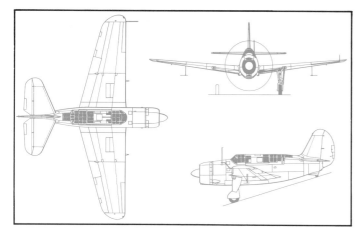

Origin: Curtiss-Wright Corporation; also built by Fairchild and Canadian Car & Foundry (CanCar).

Type: Two-seat carrier-based dive bomber; data for SB2C-1.

Engine: 1,700hp Wright R-2600-8 Cyclone 14-cylinder two-row radial.

Dimensions: Span 49ft 9in (15.2m); length 36ft 8in (11.2m); height 16ft 11in (5.1m); wing area 422sq ft (39.20m²).

Weights: Empty 11,000lb (4,990kg); loaded 16,607lb (7,550kg).

Performance: Maximum speed 281mph (452km/h); service ceiling

Above: This SB2C-1 is shown with underwing ASB radar. Apart from omission of the spinner, later versions looked similar.

24,700ft (7,530m); range 1,110 miles (1,786km).

Armament: Two 20mm or four 0.50in guns in wings and two 0.30in or one 0.50in in rear cockpit; provision for 1,000lb (454kg) bombload internally (later versions added wing racks).

History: First flight (XSB2C-1) 18 December 1940; (production SB2C-1) June 1942; termination of production 1945.

Users: Navy, Marines, AAF.

Above: Typical of the ultimate Helldiver was SB2C-5 No 83520, seen here on routine production flight test in 1944.

During World War II the most numerous Allied dive bomber was the Helldiver, which perpetuated the name established with the biplane SBC. The new monoplane was a totally different design, with very powerful engine, large folding wing and internal bomb bay. Yet development took a long time, partly because the prototype crashed but mainly because the US services asked for 880 further major design changes after the

SB2C-1 had been frozen for production in November 1941. This was partly for Army/Navy/Marine Corps standardization, the Army/Marines aircraft being called A-25 Shrike or SB2C-1A.

Eventually production rolled ahead at Curtiss, at Fairchild (who built SBFs) and Canadian Car & Foundry (who made SBWs). Altogether 7,200 Helldivers were delivered, roughly equally divided between the -1, -3, -4 and -5 subtypes. The -2 was a twin-float seaplane.

From Rabaul in November 1943 Helldivers fought hard and effectively in every major action of the

engines drove large four-blade propellers and were neatly cowled in giant nacelles which projected well aft of the trailing edge, dividing the flaps into four small sections. The nacelles housed the large single wheels of the tricycle landing gear, all three units of which had single-strut legs. The wing was mounted shoulder-high, leaving almost the whole mid-fuselage as a bomb bay.

Production B-26A models, with torpedo shackles between the bomb doors, were deployed to Australia the day after Pearl Harbor (8 December 1941). Later B models saw extensive Southwest Pacific service with the rear bomb bay used as a fuel tank (maximum bombload 2,000lb). The accident rate remained high and Martin decided to extend the wing span.

From the 641st B the wing and vertical tail were extended, and on 14 May 1943 the Marauder began its career as the chief medium bomber of the 9th AF in the ETO (European Theater of Operations). Quickly the crews found a new confidence, and by VE-day the B-26 had set a record for the lowest loss-rate of any US Army bomber in Europe.

About 522 also served with the RAF and South African AF in Italy. Total production amounted to 5,157 for the US Army (including Allied forces) plus a few dozen JM-1 and -2 target tug, reconnaissance and utility versions for the US Navy, and about 200 AT-23 (later called TB-26) trainers.

In 1948 the Marauder was withdrawn, and the B-26 designation passed to the Douglas Invader.

Above: Possibly at Wright Field, next to a P-38, the B-26A was in action by April 1942.

Below: Twin "fifties" arrived in the tail with the B-10 version — one of six tail-gun variations.

Pacific war, but despite their countless great accomplishments the SB2C was never popular (the designation was said to mean "Son of a Bitch, 2nd Class"). Its basic handling and stability were poor, and most Navy crews far preferred the old SBD, which was never replaced by the SB2C but remained in full production alongside the troubled Curtiss product.

Above: BuNo 1758 was the original XSB2C-1 prototype of 1940. It was destroyed less than a week after first flight, and nearly 1,000 improvements were to be needed to get a usable SB2C.

Right: Nobody could stop the production lines but at least by 1945 SB2Cs (like this Dash-4) could be converted to target tugs.

Republic P-47 Thunderbolt

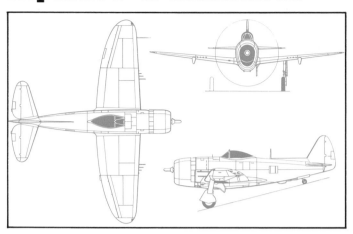

Origin: Republic Aviation Corporation, Farmingdale, NY; P-47G made by Curtiss.
Type: Single-seat fighter; (D and N) fighter-bomber.
Engine: One Pratt & Whitney R-2800 Double Wasp 18-cylinder two-row radial; (B) 2,000hp R-2800-21; (C, most D) 2,300hp R-2800-59; (M, N) 2,800hp R-2800-57 or -77 (emergency wet rating).
Dimensions: Span (except N) 40ft 9¼in (12.4m); (N) 42ft 7in (12.98m); length (B) 34ft 10in (10.6m); (C, D, M, N) 36ft 1¼in (11.03m); height (B) 12ft 8in (3.8m); (C, D) 14ft 2in (4.3m); (M, N) 14ft 8in (4.5m); wing area (except N) 300sq ft (27.87m²), (N) 322sq ft (29.9m²).
Weights: Empty (B) 9,010lb (4,087kg); (D) 10,700lb (4,853kg); maximum loaded (B) 12,700lb (5,760kg); (C) 14,925lb (6,770kg); (D) 19,400lb (8,800kg); (M) 14,700lb; (N) 21,200lb (9,616kg).
Performance: Maximum speed (B) 412mph; (C) 433mph; (D) 428mph (690km/h); (M) 470mph; (N) 467mph (751km/h); initial climb (typical) 2,800ft (855m)/min; service ceiling (B) 38,000ft; (C-N) 42,000-43,000ft (12,800-13,000m); range on internal fuel (B) 575 miles (952km); (D) 1,000 miles (1,600km); ultimate range (drop tanks) (D) 1,900 miles (3,060km); (N) 2,350 miles (3,800km).
Armament: (Except M) eight 0.5in Colt-Browning M-2 in wings, each with 267, 350 or 425 rounds; (M) six 0.5in; (D and N) three to five racks for external load of tanks, bombs or rockets to maximum of 2,500lb (1,134kg).
History: First flight (XP-47B) 6 May 1941; production delivery (B) 18 March 1942; final delivery (N) September 1945.
Users: AAF, ANG, AF.

Before the United States entered World War II it was eagerly digesting the results of air combats in Europe. In 1940, existing plans for the AP-4 pursuit by Republic's chief designer Alexander Kartveli were urgently replaced by sketches for a much bigger fighter with the new R-2800 engine. This appeared to be the only way to meet the Army Air Corps' new targets for fighter performance. Kartveli began by designing the best installation of the big engine and its

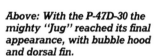

Above: With the P-47D-30 the mighty "Jug" reached its final appearance, with bubble hood and dorsal fin.

turbocharger, placed under the rear fuselage. The air duct had to pass under the elliptical wing, and there were problems in achieving ground clearance for the big propeller (12ft, 3.66m diameter, even though it had the exceptional total of four blades) with landing gear able to retract inwards and still leave room in the wing for the formidable armament of eight 0.5in guns. Kartveli submitted the design in June 1940.

After severe and protracted technical difficulties the P-47B was cleared for production in early 1942, and at the beginning of 1943 two fighter groups equipped with the giant new fighter (one the famed 56th, to become top scorers in Europe, and the other the black/white checkered 78th) joined the 8th AF in Britain to begin escorting B-17 and B-24 heavies. Their value was dramatically increased when they began to carry 200gal (757lit) drop tanks and fly all the way to the target.

Despite the development difficulties the production P-47B looked almost the same as the prototype XP-47B, apart from the fact production machines were painted

Above: The massive "Jug" caused much controversy when it arrived in England to replace Spitfires in the famed 4th Fighter Group.

olive drab and had a forward-raked antenna mast. Less obvious differences were a sliding cockpit hood and metal-skinned control surfaces. Republic delivered only 170 production Bs before switching to the C model in which the combat maneuverability was improved by moving the engine 8in (203mm) further forward. This model also introduced the belly shackles and plumbing for a drop tank. Four blocks totalling 602 of the C model were followed by what proved to be the definitive model, the P-47D. These introduced wing pylons for extra tanks or bombs, paddle-blade propeller, new turbo, more armor and, like most C-series, a more powerful R-2800 with water injection. This model was made at Farmingdale (6,510), a new plant at Evansville, Indiana (6,093), and by Curtiss-Wright at Buffalo (354 P-47G). From Block-25 the original "razorback" model, the only kind made by Curtiss, was replaced by a bubble hood and cut-down rear fuselage; Block 27 introduced a dorsal fin and Block 35 zero-length rocket launchers. Two Curtiss aircraft were converted to TP-47G2, modifications including a new for-

ward cockpit instead of fuel.

The P-47 was known as "The Jug", from its being something of a juggernaut. Despite its size and weight it was no mean dogfighter, as well as being a much-feared bomber and, with devastating firepower, vast numbers of P-47Ds strafed and bombed throughout the European and Pacific theaters until the end of World War II. Republic's output of D models (12,603) is the largest total of one fighter sub-type by one builder, total production of the "Jug" amounting to 15,660. The lightweight M sprint model was too late for its role of chasing flying bombs, but scored successes against the Me 262 and Ar 234 jets. The long-range P-47N matched the M fuselage with a bigger wing giving exceptional range for the Pacific war. There were numerous experimental versions, one of which reached 504mph.

After World War II "The Jug" was popular with many air forces until well into the 1950s. The D and N models served until after the formation of the USAF, and as the F-47 continued in ANG squadrons until 1955.

Below: Two years later 42-27995, a P-47D-23, was blasting the Japs from the sky and land on the Luzon, Philippines, front.

Waco CG-4A Haig

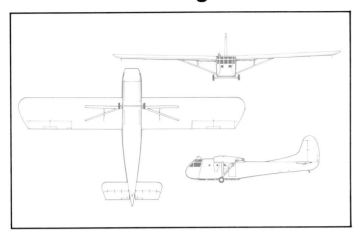

Origin: The Waco Aircraft Company; also built by 14 other companies.

Type: Unpowered assault glider.

Dimensions: Span 83ft 8in (25.5m); length 48ft 3¾in (14.7m); height 12ft 7½in (3.84m); wing area 852sq ft (79.15m²).

Weights: Empty 3,790lb (1,721kg); normal loaded 7,500lb (3,405kg); overload 9,000lb (4,086kg).

Performance: Normal towing speed 125mph (200km/h); typical speed off tow 65mph (105km/h); minimum speed 38mph (61km/h).

Armament: None.

History: First flight, early 1941; (production CG-4A) May or June

Above: All CG-4As looked about the same despite being made in vast numbers by 16 companies! A thin cable on the triangular bracket pulled the nose open.

1942; final delivery, December 1944.

User: AAF.

Though the vast US aircraft industry developed many types of military glider during World War II, the entire production effort was concentrated upon this one type, which was the only US glider to see combat service. In sharp contrast to Britain's larger, all-wood Horsa, the CG-4A fuselage was constructed of

Above: To get a Jeep in you cranked the nose up. With special tackle on board the Jeep could then pull the nose up after landing in order to drive out.

welded steel tube with fabric covering. The entire nose was arranged to hinge upwards for loading/unloading vehicles up to Jeep size, or light artillery. The side-by-side pilot stations hinged with the nose, the two control wheels being suspended from the roof.

In the main fuselage were benches for up to 15 fully armed troops or cargo up to 3,710lb (1,683kg), or 5,210lb (2,363kg) as overload. The

wing loading was very low; there were no flaps, but spoilers above the wing to steepen the glide. No fewer than 15 companies collaborated to build the CG-4A, and in two years more than 12,393 were delivered.

The commonest tug was the C-47/C-53. In 1943 an RAF Hadrian (British name) was towed in stages from Montreal to Britain in a flight time of 28 hours. A few weeks later hundreds were used in the invasion of Sicily. Several thousand were used in 1944 in Normandy and the Rhine crossing, while large numbers went to the Far East for the planned invasion of Japan.

Vultee A-31 Vengeance

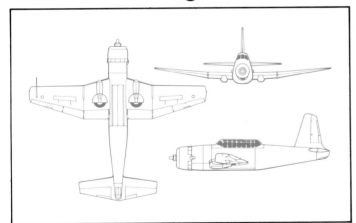

Origin: Consolidated Vultee Aircraft Corporation, Nashville Division, Tennessee; also built by Northrop Aircraft, Hawthorne, California.

Type: Two-seat dive bomber.

Engine: One Wright R-2600 Cyclone 14-cylinder two-row radial; (A-31) 1,600hp R-2600-19; (A-35) 1,700hp R-2600-13.

Dimensions: Span 48ft (14.63m); length 39ft 9in (12.12m); height 14ft 6in (4.40m); wing area 332sq ft (30.84m²).

Weights: Empty (typical) 9,900lb (4,490kg); maximum loaded (A-31) 14,300lb (6,486kg); (A-35) 15,600lb; (A-35B) 17,100lb (7,756kg).

Performance: Maximum speed (all) 273-279mph (440-450km/h); initial climb, typically 1,200ft (366m)/min; service ceiling (typical) 22,000ft (6,700m); range

Above: The Vengeance was hardly used by the USAAF, except as a lowly target tug.

(typical) 600 miles (966km).

Armament: (A-31, Vengeance I to III) four 0.303in Brownings in wings, and two manually aimed from rear cockpit; internal bomb load of up to 2,000lb (907kg); (A-35A, Vengeance IV) four 0.5in in wings, one manually aimed from rear, same bombload; (A-35B) same but six 0.5in in wings.

History; First flight July 1941; service delivery (RAF) November 1942; end of production Sept. 1944.

Users: AAF, Navy.

Designed by a team led by Richard Palmer to a British specification passed to Vultee in July 1940, the Vengeance eventually became

Above: This Northrop-built RAF Vengeance II retained British serial AF769 in US service.

combat-ready in a different world. No longer was the dive bomber the unstoppable agent of destruction; by 1943 it was recognized to have value only in conditions of local air superiority, and even then to need fighter cover. Eventually 1,528 of all types were built, of which 1,205 were passed to the RAF (some purchased in 1940, others on Lend-Lease). Many served with the RAF, RAAF and Indian AF in Burma and

Southeast Asia, where they at least saw considerable active duty. In 1940 it had been thought vast numbers would be needed, and a second production line was opened at Northrop, while the US Army adopted the type as the A-31. In 1942 the Americanized A-35 was in production at Convair's Nashville plant, but the Army soon dropped even this version and the US versions saw no action.

Below: AN838 was the very first RAF Vengeance I made by Vultee. Official US Army tag was V-72.

Lockheed PV B-34 and Ventura/Harpoon

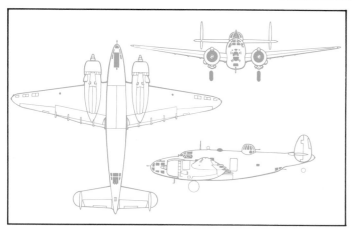

Origin: Vega Aircraft Corporation, Burbank, California.
Type: Bomber and reconnaissance aircraft.
Engines: Two 2,000hp Pratt & Whitney R-2800-31 Double Wasp 18-cylinder radials.
Dimensions: Span (V) 65ft 6in (19.96m); (H) 75ft (22.86m); length 51ft 5in to 51ft 9in (15.77m); height 13ft 2in (3.9m) to 14ft 1in (4.29m); wing area (V) 551sq ft (51.19m²), (H) 686sq ft (63.73m²).

Above: Lockheed Vega Ventura was originally built for the British, with a turret.

Weights: Empty (V) 19,373lb (8,788kg), (H) about 24,000lb (10,886kg); maximum (V) 31,077lb (14,097kg), (H) 40,000lb (18,144kg).
Performance: Maximum speed (V) 300mph (483km/h), (H) 282mph (454km/h); maximum range with max bombload (all) about 900 miles (1,448km).

Above: Still retaining RAF serial AJ364, this B-34 Lexington was in May 1943 at Hondo, Texas.

Armament: See text.
History: First flight (RAF) 31 July 1941; service delivery (RAF) June 1942, (Navy) December 1942; final delivery (H) 1945.
Users: AAF, Navy.

Vega Aircraft, a 1940 subsidiary of Lockheed, was awarded a contract

by the British Purchasing Commission in June 1940 for 875 of a new design of bomber derived from the Lockheed 18 Lodestar airliner. Called Lockheed V-146, or Vega 37, it resembled a more powerful Hudson, with longer fuselage provided with a rear ventral position with two 0.303in Brownings. Two (later four) more were in the dorsal turret, and the nose had two fixed 0.5in and two manually aimed 0.303in. Bombload was 2,500lb

Grumman TBF/TBM Avenger

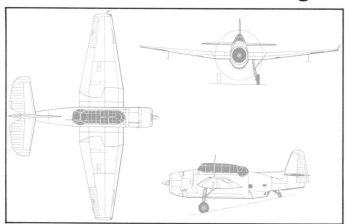

Origin: Grumman Aircraft Engineering Corporation, Bethpage, NY; also built by Eastern Aircraft.
Type: Originally, three-seat torpedo bomber; later ASW (anti-submarine warfare) aircraft and AEW (airborne early warning) aircraft.
Engine: One 1,700hp Wright R-2600-8 or -20 Cyclone 14-cylinder two-row radial.
Dimensions: Span 54ft 2in (16.5m); length (to TBM-3) 40ft (12.2m); (TBM-3E) 40ft 11½in (12.48m); height 16ft 5in (5m); wing area 490sq ft (45.52m²).
Weights: Empty (TBF-1) 10,100lb (4,580kg); (TBM-3) 10,545lb (4,787kg); loaded (TBF-1) 15,905lb (7,214kg); (TBM-3) 18,250lb (8,278kg); (TBM-3E) 17,895lb (8,117kg).
Performance: Maximum speed (TBF-1) 278mph (445km/h); (TBM-3) 267mph (430km/h); initial climb (TBF-1) 1,075ft (376m)/min; service ceiling (TBF, TBM-1 to -3)

Above: Wartime Avengers were more or less identical, the only distinguishing feature of this TBF-1C being the two 0.5in wing guns.

about 23,400ft (7,132m); (TBM-3E) 30,100ft (9,175m); range with full weapon load, 1,010-1,215 miles (1,600-1,950km); ferry range, 2,530 miles (4,072km).
Armament: (TBF-1, TBM-1) one 0.30in Browning in upper forward fuselage, one 0.5in in dorsal power turret and one 0.30in manually aimed in rear ventral position; internal bay for one 22in torpedo or 2,000lb (907kg) of bombs; (TBF-1C, TBM-1C, TBM-3) as above plus one 0.5in in each outer wing and underwing racks for eight 60lb (27kg) rockets. Most subsequent versions unarmed, or fitted for ASW weapons only.
History: First flight (XTBF-1) 1 August 1941; service delivery 30 January 1942; final delivery from new production,

Above: Almost certainly being collected from the maker's plant by a Navy ferry pilot, this appears to be TBF-1C BuNo 24344. Note ASB underwing radar.

September 1945; final delivery of rebuild, August 1954.
Users: Navy, Marines.

Grumman's outstanding design and engineering staff, under W. T. (Bill) Schwendler, designed and developed this big and extremely useful torpedo bomber very quickly and it became one of the key aircraft in the Pacific war. Two prototypes were ordered on 8 April 1940 and large numbers into action at the Battle of Midway just over two years later. From the start the TBF was robust and well equipped and one could not help comparing it with the British Barracuda which lacked power, self-defence and a weapon bay. Fortunately a proportion of deliveries went to the Fleet Air Arm, which originally con-

sidered the name Tarpon before adopting the US Navy name.

Like all products of the so-called "Grumman Iron Works" the TBF was well-engineered and almost unbreakable. The fuselage was inevitably bulky and lumpy because it accommodated a pilot at the front, where he had a fine view, a gunner in an electrically controlled spherical turret, a capacious internal bay for torpedoes or bombs under the mid-mounted wing, and a radio operator who manned a lower rear "tunnel gun". The vast wings had inbuilt slots ahead of the ailerons, and were neatly folded on diagonal hinges to lie alongside the rear fuselage. Unlike earlier Grummans, the main gears retracted outwards into the wings.

The first six TBF's came off the line inside a giant new plant that had not itself been finished. Their crews from VT-8 flew them all the way from NAS Norfolk, Virginia, to Midway island to join the *Hornet*. On 4 June 1942 on their first mission five

(1,134kg). In October 1942 Bomber Command's No 21 Sqn swept into action with a gallant daylight attack on the Philips works at Eindhoven, Holland, but the Ventura proved a mediocre bomber and deliveries stopped at about 300.

The B-34 Lexington absorbed many of the unwanted machines, though the Army Air Force never used them operationally in the planned role of coastal patrol aircraft. The B-34B was a navigation trainer. Eighteen R-2600-powered reconnaissance models (originally O-56) were delivered as B-37s, but the bulk of the 1,600 Venturas were Navy PV-1 patrol bombers.

These retained all features of the original machine, with tapered pointed wings with Fowler flaps, glazed nose and rear lower gun near the tail. The weapon bay under the wing could accommodate six 500lb (227kg) bombs, two mines or a torpedo, and two 1,000lb (454kg) bombs could be attached to wing racks. Typical armament comprised two 0.5in guns firing ahead, two in the dorsal turret and twin 0.3in in the lower rear position.

The PV-2 Harpoon was redesign-

ed as a much better Navy bomber, with larger wings, new tail and up to ten 0.5in guns, rockets and 4,000lb (1,814kg) of bombs or torpedoes internally, plus two 1,000lb (454kg) under the wings. The 535 built saw brief service before being passed to Allies, one problem being fuel leakage from the integral wing tanks.

Above: Lexingtons in color are rare, especially showing the AAF serial (4527), that on the facing page being 4602, special "reverse Lend/Lease" numbers.

Right: A famous color photo of either the first or second production TBF-1 on flight test in January 1942. Six months later 145 had been delivered.

were shot down and No 6 returned as a flying wreck, with one gunner dead and the other wounded. This was very far from being typical of the thousands of missions that followed, when the TBF sustained a brilliant career that, with the SBD, destroyed Japan's sea power.

Of 2,293 Grumman-built aircraft delivered by December 1943, 402 went to the RN and 63 to the RNZAF. Eastern Aircraft, the second source, delivered 2,882 of the TBM-1 and -1C type, before switching to the slightly modified -3 in April 1944. Many -3s had no turret, all had strengthened wings for rockets or a radar pod, and no fewer than 4,664 were delivered by Eastern in 14 months.

After 1945 development suddenly blossomed out into new versions, produced as conversions. The TBM-3E was packed with ASW search equipment, the TBM-3W and -3W2 were grotesque "guppy" type early-warners with huge belly radar, the -3U was a target-towing tug and the -3R a COD (carrier on-board delivery) transport with seven passenger seats. The -3Q was an ECM platform, the -3S had ASW weapons and partnered the -3E, the -3N was a special night attack version, and there were several other rebuilds which went on in Navy service until about 1960.

Right: One of the gallant five of VT-8 shot down in the TBF's first combat mission (see text).

Below: Eastern Aircraft TBM-3 serving with Task Force 58 in the Pacific aboard USS Randolph.

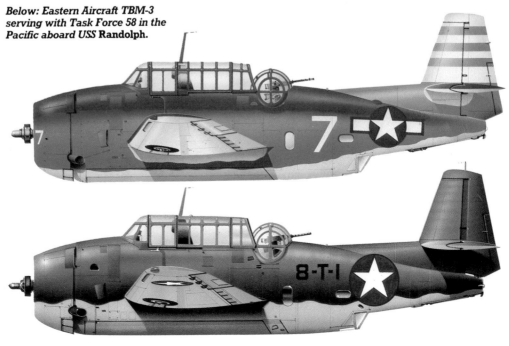

Northrop P-61 Black Widow

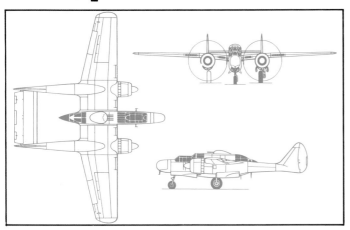

Origin: Northrop Aircraft Inc, Hawthorne, California.
Type: (P-61) three-seat night fighter; (F-15) two-seat strategic reconnaissance.
Engines: Two Pratt & Whitney R-2800 Double Wasp 18-cylinder two-row radials; (P-61A) 2,000hp R-2800-10; (B) 2,000hp R-2800-65; (C and F-15) 2,800hp (wet rating) R-2800-73.
Dimensions: Span 66ft (20.12m); length (A) 48ft 11in (14.92in); (B, C) 49ft 7in (15.1m); (F-15) 50ft 3in (15.3m); height (typical) 14ft 8in (4.49m); wing area 664sq ft (61.69m²).

Above: The drawing shows a P-61B-20, but the first 37 P-61As looked the same and the P-61C differed only in having under-wing pylons and more power.

Weights: Empty (typical P-61) 24,000lb (10,886kg); (F-15) 22,000lb (9,979kg); maximum loaded (A) 32,400lb (14,696kg); (B) 38,000lb (17,237kg); (C) 40,300lb (18,280kg); (F-15, clean) 28,000lb (12,700kg).
Performance: Maximum speed (A, B) 366mph (590km/h); (C) 430mph (692km/h); (F-15) 440mph (708km/h); initial climb (A, B) 2,200ft (670m)/min; (C, F-15) 3,000ft

Above: 42-5507 was one of the first batch of P-61A-1s, which were olive drab and had the dorsal turret; photographed over California in January 1944.

(914m)/min; service ceiling (A, B) 33,000ft (10,060m); (C, F-15) 41,000ft (12,500m); range with maximum fuel (A) 500 miles; (B, C) 2,800 miles (4,500km); (F-15) 4,000 miles (6,440km).
Armament: Four fixed 20mm M-2 cannon in belly, firing ahead, plus (in first 37 A, last 250 B and all C) electric dorsal turret with four 0.5in remotely controlled from

front or rear sight station and fired by pilot; (B and C) underwing racks for 6,400lb (2,900kg) bomb or tank load; (F-15A) no armament;
History: First flight (XP-61) 21 May 1942; service delivery (A) May 1944; first flight (F-15A) 1946.
User: AAF.

The first aircraft ever designed from the start as a radar-equipped night fighter, the XP-61 prototypes were ordered in January 1941 on the basis of combat reports from the early radar-equipped fighters of the RAF. A very big aircraft, the P-61 had the new SCR-720 airborne

Grumman F6F Hellcat

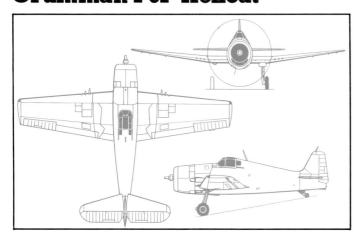

Origin: Grumman Aircraft Engineering Corporation, Bethpage, NY.
Type: Single-seat naval fighter; later versions, fighter-bombers and night fighters.
Engine: Early production, one 2,000hp Pratt & Whitney R-2800-10 Double Wasp 18-cylinder two-row radial; from January 1944 (final F6F-3 batch) two-thirds equipped with 2,200hp (water-injection rating) R-2800-10W.
Dimensions: Span 42ft 10in (13.05m); length 33ft 7in (10.2m); height 13ft 1in (3.99m); wing area 334sq ft (31.0m²).
Weights: Empty (F6F-3) 9,042lb (4,101kg); loaded (F6F-3) 12,186lb (5,528kg) clean, 13,228lb (6,000kg) maximum, (F6F-5N) 14,250lb (6,443kg).
Performance: Maximum speed (F6F-3, -5, clean) 376mph

Above: The production F6F-3 and F6F-5 looked almost identical. This is a Dash-3.

(605km/h); (-5N) 366mph (590km/h); initial climb (typical) 3,240ft (990m)/min; service ceiling (-3) 37,500ft (11,430m); (-5N) 36,700ft (11,185m); range on internal fuel (typical) 1,090 miles (1,755km).
Armament: Standard, six 0.5in Brownings in outer wings with 400 rounds each; a few -5N and -5 Hellcats had two 20mm and four 0.5in. Underwing attachments for six rockets, and centre-section pylons for 2,000lb of bombs.
History: First flight (R-2600) 26 June 1942; (same aircraft, R-2800) 30 July 1942; (production F6F-3) 4 October 1942; production delivery (F6F-3) 16 January 1943; final delivery November 1945.
Users: Navy, Marine Corps.

Above: Two early production F6F-3s, photographed in summer 1943 at the time the Hellcat first saw action (on 31 August 1943, with VF-5 from Yorktown, in an attack on Marcus Island).

interception radar in the nose, the armament being mounted well back above and below the rather lumpy nacelle housing pilot, radar operator and gunner with front and rear sighting stations. The broad wing had almost full-span double-slotted flaps, very small ailerons and lateral-control spoilers in an arrangement years ahead of its time.

The tail was carried on large booms behind the powerful R-2800 engines which turned large four-blade propellers. Single-leg tricycle landing gears were fitted, and the oil coolers were in ducts fed from inlets in the leading edge of the wing. Altogether the P-61 was one of the largest, most powerful and most complex fighters of the World War II era.

Black-painted (hence the name), the P-61A entered service with the 18th Fighter Group in the South Pacific and soon gained successes there and in Europe. The P-61's massive fuel capacity and superb agility (for its size) proved very valuable. Buffet from the turret led to this soon being deleted, but it was later restored and the B and C also had pylons for the very heavy load of four 250gal (946 litre) drop tanks or four 1,600lb (726kg) bombs.

Right: Unusual view of 42-5570, serving at Scorton, England, with the 422nd Night Fighter Squadron, 9th Air Force.

Total production was 941, followed by 35 slim F-15 Reporter photo-reconnaissance versions which had no armament and seated the crew of two in tandem under a giant molded plastics canopy.

Below: 42-39468 was a P-61B-1 (note drop tanks) with the 550th NFS on Morotai Island, SW Pacific.

Bottom: 42-5528, a P-61A-1, was "Jap Batty", 6th NFS, Saipan.

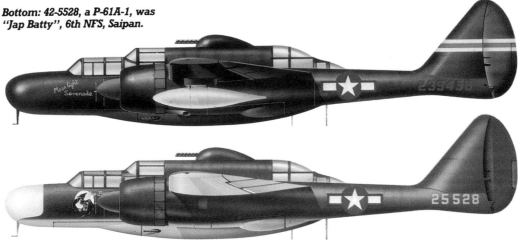

Though pugnacious rather than elegant, the Hellcat was a truly war-winning aircraft. It was designed and developed with great speed, mass-produced at a rate seldom equalled by any other single aircraft factory and used to such good effect that, from the very day of its appearance, the Allies were winning the air war in the Pacific.

It began as the XF6F-1, a natural development of the F4F Wildcat with R-2600 14-cylinder Cyclone engine. The wing folded like an F4F but was mounted lower on the redesigned fuselage, and the main landing gears folded backwards with the wheels rotating 90° to be housed inside the horizontal center-section aft of the rear spar.

Within a month the more powerful Double Wasp had been substituted and in the autumn of 1942 the production line took shape inside a completely new plant that was less advanced in construction than the Hellcats inside it! This line flowed at an extraordinary rate, helped by the essential rightness of the Hellcat, and lack of major engineering changes during subsequent sub-types. Deliveries in the years 1942-45 inclusive were 10, 2,545, 6,139 and 3,578, a total of 12,272 (excluding two prototypes) of which 11,000 were delivered in exactly two years.

Left: Fire crews hustle to save Lt (jg) A.W. Magee Jr, USNR, after an emergency landing on USS Cowpens (CVL-25) on 24 November 1943. The F6F was saved, too.

These swarms of big, beefy fighters absolutely mastered the Japanese, destroying more than 6,000 hostile aircraft (4,947 by USN carrier squadrons, 209 by land-based USMC units and the rest by Allied Hellcat squadrons).

The F6F-3N and -5N were night fighters with APS-6 radar on a wing pod, the -5K was a drone and the -5P a photographic reconnaissance version. After VJ-Day hundreds of late models were sold to many nations.

Right: The first F6F-3 Hellcats to be delivered were painted in early 1943 style with upper surfaces sea blue merging to a white underside, and with unbordered markings.

Below; After the war hundreds of nearly new F6F-5s and 5Ns, such as 94267, wore the orange band of the Reserve squadrons.

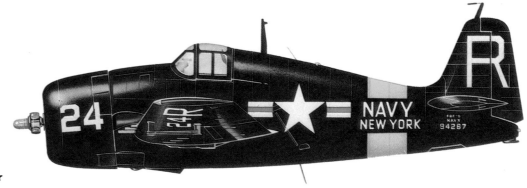

Douglas A-26 Invader

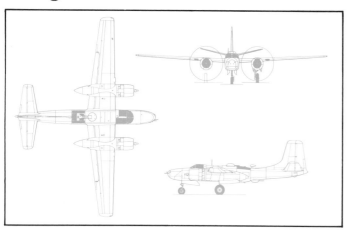

Origin: Douglas Aircraft Company, El Segundo and Long Beach, California, and Tulsa, Oklahoma; (post-war B-26K) On Mark Engineering.
Type: Three-seat attack bomber; FA-26 reconnaissance, JD (Navy) target tug.
Engines: Two 2,000hp Pratt & Whitney R-2800-27, -71 or -79 Double Wasp 18-cylinder two-row radials; On Mark B-26K, 2,500hp R-2800-103W.
Dimensions: Span 70ft (21.43m) (B-26K, 75ft, 22.86m, over tip tanks); length 50ft (15.24m); height 18ft 6in (5.64m); wing area 540sq ft (50.17m²).
Weights: Empty, typically 22,370lb (10,145kg); loaded, originally 27,000lb (12,247kg) with 32,000lb (14,515kg) maximum overload, later increased to 35,000lb (15,876kg) with 38,500lb (17,460kg) maximum overload.
Performance: Maximum speed 355mph (571km/h); initial climb

Above: The A-26B was the standard wartime attack version, with gun-packed nose. Like the contemporary B-29 and B-32 it had remotely aimed power turrets.

2,000ft (610m)/min; service ceiling 22,100ft (6,736m); range with maximum bombload 1,400 miles (2,253km).
Armament: (A-26B) ten 0.5in Brownings, six fixed in nose and two each in dorsal and ventral turrets; internal bombload of 4,000lb (1,814kg), later supplemented by underwing load of up to 2,000lb (907kg); (A-26C) similar but only two 0.5in in nose; (B-26K, A-26A) various nose configurations with up to eight 0.5in or four 20mm, plus six 0.30in guns in wings and total ordnance load of 8,000lb (3,628kg) in bomb bay and on eight outerwing pylons.
History: First flight (XA-26) 10 July 1942; service delivery

Above: 41-39136 was an A-26B-10, one of the first Invaders built. It served in England with the 553rd BS, 386th BG, from August 1944, and survived the war.

December 1943; final delivery 2 January 1946; first flight of B-26K, February 1963.
Users: AAF, AF, Navy.

The Douglas Invader has a unique history. It was one of very few aircraft to be entirely conceived, designed, developed, produced in quantity and used in large numbers all during World War II. The whole program was terminated after VJ-Day and anyone might have judged the aircraft finished. With new jets under development, Douglas made no effort to retain any design team on Invader development, neither did the Army Air Force show any interest.

Yet this aircraft proved to be of vital importance in the Korean war

and again in Vietnam and, by 1963, was urgently being re-manufactured for arduous front-line service. Some were in combat units 33 years after they were first delivered, a record no other kind of aircraft can equal.

The design was prepared by Ed Heinemann at El Segundo as a natural successor to the DB-7 family, using the powerful new R-2800 engine. The Army Air Corps ordered three prototypes in May 1941, one with 75mm gun, one with four 20mm forward-firing cannon and four 0.5in guns in an upper turret, with radar nose, and the third as an attack bomber with optical sighting station in the nose and two defensive turrets.

In the event it was the bomber that was bought first, designated A-26B. Much faster than other tactical bombers with the exception of the Mosquito, it was 700lb lighter than estimate, and capable of carrying twice the specified bomb

Consolidated Vultee B-32 Dominator

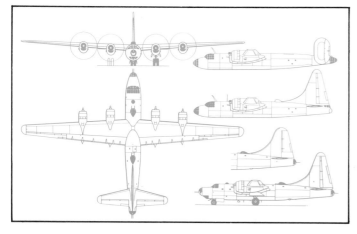

Origin: Consolidated Vultee Aircraft Corporation (Convair), Fort Worth, Texas; second-source production by Convair, San Diego, California.
Type: Long-range strategic bomber; (TB) crew trainer.
Engines: Four 2,300hp Wright R-3350-23 Duplex Cyclone 18-cylinder radials, with turbosuperchargers.
Dimensions: Span 135ft (41.15m); length 83ft 1in (25.33m); height 32ft 9in (9.98m); wing area 1,422sq ft

Above: Production B-32 with (upper) 2nd XB-32, (middle) 3rd XB, and pre-production tail.

(132.1m²).
Weights: Empty 60,272lb (27,340kg); loaded 111,500lb (50,576kg); maximum 120,000lb (54,432kg).
Performance: Maximum speed 365mph (587km/h); service ceiling at normal loaded weight 35,000ft (10,670m); range (max bomb load) 800 miles (1,287km), (max fuel)

Above: This B-32-CF was 42-108476, only the sixth production aircraft to be built.

3,800 miles (6,115km).
Armament: (XB) two 20mm and 14 0.50in guns in seven remote-controlled turrets; (B) ten 0.50in in nose, two dorsal, ventral and tail turrets; max bombload 20,000lb (9,072kg) in tandem fuselage bays.
History: First flight (XB) 7 September 1942; service delivery (B) 1 November 1944.

User: AAF.

Ordered in September 1940, a month after the XB-29, the Consolidated Vultee Model 33, XB-32, was designed to the same Hemisphere Defense Weapon specification and followed similar advanced principles with pressurized cabins and remote-controlled turrets. Obviously related to the smaller B-24, the XB-32 had a slender wing passing above the capacious bomb bays, but the twin-load. It was the first bomber to use a NACA laminar-flow airfoil, double-slotted flaps and remote-control turrets (also a feature of the B-29). Combat missions with the 9th AF began on 19 November 1944, and these aircraft dropped over 18,000 tons of bombs on European targets.

A total of 1,355 A-26Bs were delivered, the last 535 having -79 engines boosted by water injection. The A-26C, in service in January 1945, had a transparent nose, lead-ship navigational equipment and was often fitted with H_2S panoramic radar; production of this model was 1,091. In 1948 Martin's B-26 Marauder was retired from duty and the A-26 was redesignated as the B-26.

In the Korean War (1950-53) over 450 were used intensively, and at the same time the French used all the B-26B, B-26C and RB-26C Invaders they could get hold of to fight the Viet Minh in what was then Indo-China. A decade later the Invader returned to the same area, which had become South Vietnam, this time with the US Air Force. Large numbers fought mainly by night until late in 1970.

The ultimate version was On Mark's B-26K, later restyled A-26A, and these fine aircraft were one of the most favored platforms for night attack on the Ho Chi Minh trail and in other interdiction areas. Though top speed was depressed to about 350mph, the A-26A (as the rebuilt B-26K was called) could carry up to 11,000lb (4,990kg) of armament and deliver it accurately and, with 2hr over target, over a wide radius.

Eventually it was replaced by the special AC-119K or AC-130.

Above: Start of another night mission by an On Mark B-26K of 609 Special Missions Sqn at Nakhon Phanom.

Below: 43-22369 was an A-26B-15 built at Tulsa. It too went to the 386th BG in England but served in the 552nd BS.

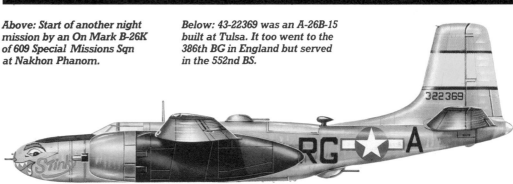

wheel main gears folded into the large inner nacelles. There was a smoothly streamlined nose, like the XB-29, and twin fins. The second aircraft introduced a stepped pilot windscreen and the third a vast single fin like the final B-24 versions.

Eventually the heavy and complex armament system was scrapped and replaced by simpler manned turrets, while in late 1943 the decision was taken to eliminate the troublesome pressurization and operate at 30,000ft or below. The B-32 was late and disappointing, though still a great performer. Large orders were placed at Fort Worth and San Diego, but only 115 had been delivered by VJ-Day and a single squadron in the Marianas, the 386th BS, made two combat missions. Most Dominators had a brief AAF career as TB-32 trainers concerned mainly with navigation and R-3350 cruise control techniques.

Right: Two TB-32 Dominators setting out on a long simulated bombing mission. The B-32 is perhaps the biggest and most complicated aircraft ever to have gone to war and then vanished into the limbo of history

Boeing B-29 Superfortress

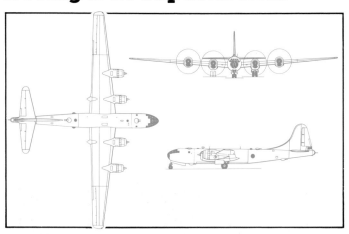

Above 42-24473 was a B-29-30 from Boeing Wichita, photographed on flight test.

Origin: Boeing Airplane Co, Seattle and Renton, Washington and Wichita, Kansas; also built by Bell Aircraft, Marietta, Georgia, and Glenn L. Martin Co, Omaha, Nebraska.
Type: High-altitude heavy bomber, with crew of 10-14.
Engines: Four 2,200hp Wright R-3350-23 Duplex Cyclone 18-cylinder radials each with two exhaust-driven turbochargers.
Dimensions: Span 141ft 3in (43.05m); length 99ft (30.2m); height 29ft 7in (9.02m); wing area 1,739sq ft (161.56m²).
Weights: Empty 74,500lb (33,795kg); loaded 135,000lb (61,240kg).
Performance: Maximum speed 357mph (575km/h) at 30,000ft (9,144m); cruising speed 290mph (467km/h); climb to 25,000ft (7,620m) in 43 min; service ceiling

Above: The standard B-29. In contrast to the B-32 it hardly changed from XB to production.

31,850ft (9,708m); range with 10,000lb (4,540kg) bombs 3,250 miles (5,230km).
Armament: Four GE twin-0.50in turrets above and below, sighted from nose or three waist sighting stations; Bell tail turret, with own gunner, with one 20mm cannon and twin 0.5in or three 0.5in; internal bombload up to 20,000lb (9,072kg). Carried first two nuclear bombs. With modification, carried two 22,000lb British bombs externally under inner wings.
History: First flight 21 September 1942; (pre-production YB-29) 26 June 1943, squadron delivery June 1943; last delivery May 1946.
Users: AAF, AF, Navy.

Development and mass production of the B-29, the Boeing Model 345, was one of the biggest tasks in the history of aviation. It began with a March 1938 study for a new bomber with pressurized cabin and tricycle landing gear. This evolved into the 345 and in August 1940 money was voted for two prototypes. By January 1942 the Army Air Force had ordered 14 YB-29s and 500 production aircraft. In February, while Boeing engineers worked night and day on the huge technical problems, a production organization was set up involving Boeing, Bell, North American and Fisher (General Motors). Martin came in later and by VJ-Day more than 3,000 Superforts had been

delivered. This was a fantastic achievement because each represented five or six times the technical effort of any earlier bomber. In engine power, gross weight, wing loading, pressurization, armament, airborne systems and even basic structure the B-29 set a wholly new standard.

The basic design had a fuselage of circular section, to suit the pressurized cabins occupying the nose and a section aft of the wing for gunners, the two cabins being linked by a tube above the wing just large enough for a crewman to crawl through. The tail gunner had a pressurized rear compartment. The fuselage ring between the two vast bomb bays incorporated the wing centre section, the wing being stronger than any previously built. The wing loading, fantastic by earlier standards, was made possi-

Bell P-59 Airacomet

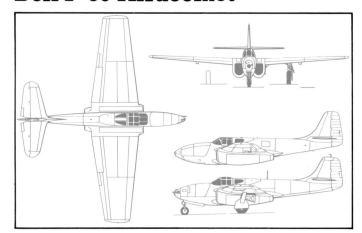

Above: America's very first jet aircraft, photographed at Muroc just before first flight. Later this XP-59A (42-108784) had an open nose cockpit added.

Origin: Bell Aircraft Corporation, Buffalo, NY.
Type: Single-seat jet fighter trainer, data for P-59B.
Engines: Two 2,000lb (907kg) thrust General Electric J31-GE-3 turbojets.
Dimensions: Span 45ft 6in (13.87m); length 38ft 1½in (11.63m); height 12ft (3.66m); wing area 385sq ft (35.77m²).
Weights: Empty 7,950lb (3,610kg); loaded 13,700lb (6,214kg).
Performance: Maximum speed 413mph (671km/h); service ceiling 46,200ft (14,080m); maximum range with two drop tanks 520

Above: The upper side view shows the original XP-59A. The other views show a typical P-59A, with short span and cropped vertical tail.

miles (837km) at 289mph (465km/h) at 20,000ft (6,096m).
Armament: Usually fitted with nose guns (eg one 37mm cannon and three 0.5in) and one rack under each wing for bomb as alternative to drop tank.
History: First flight (XP-59A) 1 October 1942; (production P-59A) 7 August 1944.
Users: AAF, Navy.

In June 1941 the US government and General "Hap" Arnold of the Army Air Corps were told of Britain's development of the turbojet engine. On 5 September 1941 Bell Aircraft was requested to design a jet fighter, and in the following month a Whittle turbojet, complete engineering drawings and a team from Power Jets Ltd arrived from Britain to hasten proceedings. The

result was that Bell flew the first American jet in one year from the start of work. The Whittle-type centrifugal engines, Americanized and made by General Electric as the 1,100lb (500kg) thrust I-A, were installed under the wing roots, close to the centerline and easily accessible (two were needed to fly an aircraft of useful size). Flight development went extremely smoothly, and 12 YP-59As for service trials were delivered in 1944.

Total procurement amounted to 66 only, including three XF2L-1s for the US Navy, and the P-59A was classed as a fighter-trainer be-ble by enormous electrically driven Fowler flaps. The giant engine nacelles, made by Fisher, carried a turbo on each side, and the engines drove large four-blade propellers.

Deliveries began in June 1943 to the 58th BW (VH), VH meaning very heavy. For more than a year crews struggled with their superb but challenging equipment, which suffered engine fires and many other problems. At first crews could get only half the expected range, but after the four BGs of the 58th moved to India in spring 1944 the distance flown per gallon had been almost doubled.

First combat mission was flown by the 58th BW on 5 June 1944, and by 1945 20 groups from the Marianas were sending 500 B-29s at a time to flatten and burn Japan's cities. (Three aircraft made emergency landings in Soviet territory. They were never returned; instead the design was pirated and put into production as the Tu-4 bomber and Tu-70 transport.) Hundreds of B-29s had all guns except those in the tail removed, increasing speed and altitude.

After the war there were 19 variants of B-29, not including the Washington B.1 supplied to help the RAF in 1950-58. Variants included the F-13A (from 1948 redesignated RB-29A) strategic reconnaissance aircraft, the SB-29A rescue aircraft with airborne lifeboat, WB-29 series for weather reconnaissance and a series of KB-29 air refueling tankers, some

with the British probe/drogue system and others with the newly developed Boeing Flying Boom. In 1950-53 five B-29 Bomb Groups raided Korea, often dropping giant Razon radio-guided bombs and occasionally suffering losses to MiG-15s. The four P2B-1s were Navy aircraft for launching D-558-II supersonic reseach aircraft.

Above: The B-29 cockpit was a new experience in every way. The Russians liked it so much they used similar cockpits even on early jet airliners!

Right: 44-22640 was one of the 30 P-59Bs, which like the P-59As had clipped wings, shorter fins and sliding hoods. The B also had a long ventral fin.

cause it was clear it would not make an effective front-line fighter. Most P-59As and very similar P-59Bs had the much more powerful J31 engine and were distinguished by clipped wings and fin. The P-59s sat low on the ground and were pleasant to fly, but the large airframe and modest power precluded the attainment of high performance. But in comparison with the fast timescale it was a remarkable achievement, performance being very similar to that attained with the early British Meteors. Some examples were equipped as RPV drone directors with an open cockpit in the nose. The first two-seater flew on 30 October 1942.

Center right: Reluctant Robot was a drone controlled by all-black YP-59A 42-108783, and survives on a plinth at Edwards.

Right: YP-59A No 42-108778 (an earlier number than the XPs) went to the Navy and became 63960. Most flying at Pax River was in glossy sea blue and gray.

Bell P-63 Kingcobra

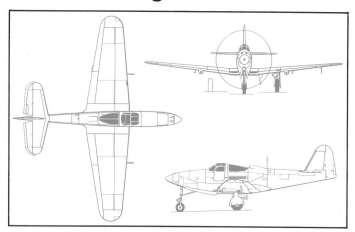

Origin: Bell Aircraft Corporation, Buffalo, NY.
Type: Single-seat fighter-bomber.
Engine: One Allison V-1710 vee-12 liquid-cooled, (A) 1,500hp (war emergency rating) V-1710-93, (C) 1,800hp V-1710-117.
Dimensions: Span 38ft 4in (11.68m); length 32ft 8in (9.96m); height 12ft 7in (3.84m); wing area 248sq ft (23.04m²).

Above: This P-63A-1 has broken lines showing the enlarged horizontal tail and wing bomb racks of later versions.

Weights: Empty (A) 6,375lb (2,892kg); maximum (A) 10,500lb (4,763kg).
Performance: Maximum speed (all) 410mph (660km/h); typical range with three bombs 340 miles

Above: 42-69432, a P-63A-9, was pictured over Niagara Falls near its birthplace. This block introduced additional armor.

(547km); ferry range with three tanks 2,575 miles (4,143km).
Armament: Usually one 37mm and four 0.5in (two in nose, two below wings), plus up to three 500lb (227kg) bombs.

History: First flight 7 December 1942; service delivery October 1943; final delivery early 1945.
User: AAF.

Though it looked like a P-39 with a different tail, in fact the P-63 was a completely different design, greatly improved in the light of painful combat experience. It fully met a February 1941 Army require-

Lockheed C-69 to EC-121 Warning Star

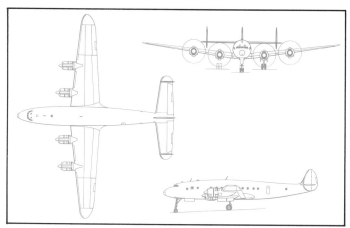

Origin: Lockheed Aircraft Corporation, Burbank, California.
Type: Transport (C-69, C-121), radar warning and fighter control aircraft (EC-121D, T), sensor relay aircraft (EC-121R), airborne television transmitter (C-121J).
Engines: (Early) four 2,200hp Wright R-3350-35 18-cylinder radials, (most) four 3,250hp Wright R-3350-34 or -91 Turbo-Compound radials.
Dimensions: Span 123ft (37.49m), (tip tank versions) 126ft 2in (37.95m); length (C-69) 95ft 2in (29m), (C-121) 116ft 2in (35.41m); height 27ft (8.1m); wing area 1,650sq ft (153.29m²).
Weight: (C-69A) empty 50,500lb (22,907kg), maximum 72,000lb (32,659kg); (EC-121D) empty 80,611lb (36,275kg); gross weight 143,600lb (64,620kg).
Performance: (EC-121D) maximum speed 321mph (517km/h) at 20,000ft (6,100m); range 4,600 miles (7,405km).
Armament: None.
History: First flight (C-69) 9 January 1943, (RC-121) 1953.

Above: General arrangement of the original EC-121C and WV-2 Warning Stars. All used the Super Connie basic airframe.

Users: AAF, AF, ANG, Navy.

The first Constellations, developed for Howard Hughes' TWA, were requisitioned before completion, so that the first flight was by an olive-drab C-69, of which the AAF received 22. More advanced than any previous transport, the "Connie" was pressurized and had turbocharged engines giving unprecedented performance. Enormous Fowler flaps, power boosted flight controls and twin-wheel landing gears were other impressive features.

The C-69s were mostly 64-seaters, but there were many VIP versions in the heavier, longer-range C-121 series delivered from 1948, Navy examples being R7Os. Lockheed's letter changed to V, and the R7V-1 was, with the AF's C-121C, similar to the stretched L-1049 Super Constellation, seating

Above: 141292 was an EC-121P packed with receivers, pulse analysers and libraries, serving with VAQ-33 at Norfolk NAS.

Below: Though it looks like an ordinary C-121, the "farm" of ventral antennas shows this is an EC-121R Igloo White station.

ment, but the air war developed so fast that — though Bell did a competent job to a fast schedule — the P-63 was outclassed before it reached the squadrons. It never fought with the US forces, but 2,421 of the 3,303 built went to the Soviet Union where their tough airframes and good close-support capability made them popular. At least 300 went to the Free French, in both A and C variants (both of which had a wealth of sub-types). The D had a sliding bubble canopy and larger wing, and the E extra fuel.

Apart from a handful of P-63As the only USAAF Kingcobras were 332 completed or modified as heavily armored RP-63A or C manned target aircraft, shot at by live "frangible" (easily shattered) bullets. Each hit illuminated a powerful lamp at the tip of the spinner. After the war P-63s were modified to test V-type "butterfly" tails and (for the Navy) swept wings.

Right: Most of the Kingcobras went to the Soviet Union, including these P-63A-10s.

about 88, or 72 equipped troops. The new 3,250hp Turbo-Compound engine was first used on the R7V-1, and all subsequent versions had this engine, often rated at 3,400hp, which allowed a large increase in weight. In 1954 manufacture began of RC-121 and R7V Warning Star AEW and Elint aircraft with enormous radar and avionics installations and crews of 22-26. Eventually under EC-121 designations there were 20 distinct sub-types.

In the mid-1960s the AF sent the EC-121D Warning Star — an official name that never supplanted Constellation or "Connie" among those who flew the type — to Southeast Asia to maintain radar surveillance over North Vietnam and sound the alarm if Il-28 light bombers based there should launch an air attack against the South. The mission of the EC-121s changed, however, and airborne radar operators began warning of MiG attacks and alerting American pilots who were straying over Chinese territory. The EC-121D and the improved EC-121H/J/Q undertook still other missions, directing fighters into position to down MiGs, guiding fighters low on fuel to rendezvous with tankers, and plotting the positions of downed aircraft.

Many EC-121Ds were rebuilt as EC-121T Elint and EW recon platforms. Shortly before the Rolling Thunder bombing of North Vietnam ended in 1968, the Tactical Air Command tried another version, the EC-121H, as an airborne command and control center. There were also 30 EC-121Rs which served as airborne relay stations for the Igloo White electronic surveillance net emplaced in southern Laos to detect truck traffic on the Ho Chi

Above: USAF No 55-139 was the last of the 72 RC-121Ds (later EC-121D) with a medal ribbon signifying its NORAD service.

Right: With 19 men aboard an EC-121K of VQ-1 thunders out of Guam on a mission that may last 18 hours.

Minh Trail. Sensors planted along roads were triggered by sound or movement and broadcast a radio signal relayed by the Constellation to a surveillance center at Nakhon Phanom, Thailand.

Meanwhile, AF Reserve and Military Airlift Command crews flew passengers across the Pacific in EC-121Cs and Gs. Navy airmen operated the C-121J, which served as an airborne radio and TV transmitter for the armed forces network in South Vietnam. Taped or live broadcasts could originate on board the "Blue Eagle", or it could function as a relay station. Navy EC-121K early warners were among seven other variants which soldiered on into the 1970s.

Sikorsky S-51, R-5, HO2S

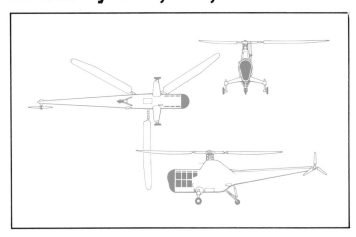

Origin: Sikorsky Aircraft Divison of United Aircraft, Bridgeport, Connecticut.
Type: Light helicopter for observation, training, casevac and liaison.
Engine: One 450hp Pratt & Whitney R-985-4B Wasp Junior nine-cylinder radial.
Dimensions: Diameter of three blade rotor (R-5A, HO2S-1) 48ft (14.6m), (rest) 49ft (14.94m); length overall (rotors turning) 57ft 1in (17.4m); (fuselage) 40ft 11in

Above: The original R-5 had what might be called "tailwheel landing gear". Production variants had tricycle gear.

(12.47m); height overall 12ft 11in (3.94m); main-rotor disc area (49ft) 1,886sq ft (175m²).
Weights: Empty (R-5A) 3,770lb (1,710kg), maximum loaded (R-5A) 5,000lb (2,268kg).
Performance: Maximum speed (R-5A) 90mph (144km/h), cruising speed, about 82mph (132km/h);

Above: The silhouette shows this helicopter to be an early HO2S, seen winching up "rescuees" in 1946 exercises.

range (typical) 300 miles (482km).
Armament: Normally none.
History: First flight (R-5A) 18 August 1943; service delivery 1945.
Users: AAF, AF, Army, Navy.

The R-5 was developed in 1942 to meet a need for a military observa-

tion helicopter which, though still seating only two, would be much more powerful than the rather marginal R-4. The rotor was increased in size, and driven by a radial engine installed with its crankshaft vertical, via a clutch and cooling fan. The center fuselage, mainly comprising the engine compartment, remained a welded steel-tube structure, though instead of fabric the covering was resin-bonded moulded plywood panels. The tubular tail boom was a

Consolidated Vultee PB4Y-2 (P4Y) Privateer

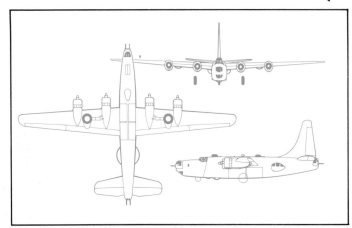

Above: The second of the three B-24Ds which were totally rebuilt into Navy XPB4Y-2s in 1943. The wing, landing gear and weapon bay were retained.

Below: Another view of the same aircraft, which differed in many details — for example, in having B-24 type turrets at nose and tail — from the production PB4Y-2.

Origin: Consolidated Vultee Aircraft Corporation, San Diego, California.
Type: Maritime patrol bomber with normal crew of 11; later Elint aircraft.
Engines: Four 1,200hp Pratt & Whitney R-1830-94 Twin Wasp 14-cylinder two-row radials.
Dimensions: Span 110ft (33.5m); length 74ft (22.6m); height 26ft 1in (7.9m); wing area 1,048sq ft (97.36m²).
Weights: Empty 41,000lb (18,600kg); loaded 65,000lb (29,484kg).
Performance: Maximum speed 247mph (399km/h); initial climb 800ft (244m)/min; service ceiling 19,500ft (5,970m); range with maximum ordnance load 2,630 miles (4,230km).
Armament: Consolidated nose and tail turrets, two Martin dorsal turrets and two Erco blister-type waist turrets each armed with two 0.50in Brownings; internal bomb

Above: A veritable oceanic battleship, the PB4Y-2 had the same tail as some B-24s, but the engine air ducts were above and below instead of on each side.

bay accommodating up to 6,000lb (2,722kg) bombs, depth charges and other stores. In PB4Y-2B provision to launch and control two ASM-N-2 Bat missiles.
History: First flight (XPB4Y-2) 20 September 1943; first production delivery 1944; final delivery September 1945.
Users: Navy, Coast Guard.

In May 1943 the US Navy placed a contract with Convair (Consolidated Vultee Aircraft) for a long-range oversea patrol bomber derived from the B-24 Liberator. Three B-24Ds were taken off the San Diego line and largely rebuilt, with fuselages 7ft (2.14m) longer, with completely different interior arrangements, radically altered

Right: 43-28237 was the second XR-5 built for the Army in 1943. The main new feature of the production R-5 (later H-5) was tricycle landing gear. Britain's Westland took a license.

wooden monocoque, while the forward fuselage was a light-alloy monocoque with a large glazed cabin. This seated the crew in tandem, the observer ahead of the pilot. The fixed landing gear included a stalky tailwheel at the joint between the body and the tail boom.

Five XR-5 prototypes were followed by 26 YR-5As with provision for a litter on each side of the fuselage; five were later converted as R-5E dual trainers and the rest to R-5D standard with a tricycle landing gear, third seat and rescue hoist. The Navy HO2S-1 was likewise followed by the HO3S family to the same revised formula, many of the 90 built being four-seaters.

Later USAAF and USAF versions were the R-5F, H-5G and H-5H, all to the new layout and the two last models having hydraulic boosted controls and untapered metal blades. Total production was 379.

Above: HO3S-1 No 123120 served with a Marine maintenance unit during the Korean War. Compare with the old XR-5 above.

Right: A production Privateer seen in combat service in 1945. Many were converted to launch ASM-N-2 Bat anti-ship missiles.

defensive armament and many airframe changes, such as hot-air de-icing, and engine cowlings in the form of vertical ovals instead of flattened horizontal ones. The distinctive vertical tail was similar to that adopted on the final Liberator transport versions (C-87C, RY-3 and RAF C.IX) and much taller than that of the Liberator B-24N.

The Navy bought a straight run of 739, of which 286 were delivered in 1944 and 453 in 1945. From the start performance was lower than that of Liberators of equal power because of the bigger and heavier airframe, extra equipment and emphasis on low-level missions. PB4Y-2s saw little active service during World War II, though patrol squadron VP-24 did become operational with the Bat anti-ship cruise missile, two of which were carried under the wings of the PB4Y-2B.

Over the ten years of service the Privateer — called P4Y from 1951 — grew more and more radar and secret countermeasures, and finally made long Elint electronic probing flights round (and probably over) the edges of the Soviet Union, at least four being shot down in the process. Variants included the P4Y-2S with ASW radar and weapons, the P4Y-2G of the Coast Guard and P4Y-2K target RPV redesignated QP-4B in 1962.

Right: Seen off Miami in 1948, this PB4Y-2 began a new and dangerous Elint career.

Grumman F7F Tigercat

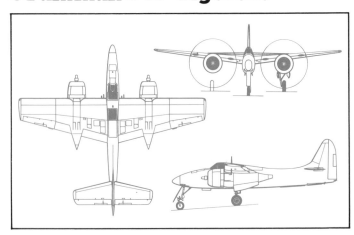

Origin: Grumman Aircraft Engineering Corporation, Bethpage, NY.

Type: Single-seat or two-seat fighter bomber or night fighter (-4N for carrier operation).

Engines: Two Pratt & Whitney R-2800-22W or -34W Double Wasp 18-cylinder two-row radials each rated at 2,100hp (dry) or 2,400hp (water injection).

Dimensions: Span 51ft 6in (15.7m); length (most) 45ft 4in or 45ft 4½in (13.8m), (-3N, -4N) 46ft 10in (14.32m); height (-1, -2) 15ft 2in (4.6m), (-3, -4) 16ft 7in (5.06m); wing area 455sq ft (42.27m²).

Weights: Empty (-1) 13,100lb (5,943kg), (-3N, -4N) 16,270lb (7,379kg); loaded (-1) 22,560lb (10,235kg), (-2N) 26,194lb (11,880kg), (-3) 25,720lb (11,667kg), (-4N) 26,167lb (11,869kg).

Performance: Maximum speed (-1) 427mph (689km/h), (-2N) 421mph, (-3) 435mph, (-4N) 430mph; initial climb (-1) 4,530ft (1,380m)/min; service ceiling (-1) 36,200ft (11,033m), (-2N) 39,800ft (12,131m), (-3) 40,700ft (12,405m),

(-4N) 40,450ft (12,329m); range on internal fuel (-1) 1,170 miles (1,885km), (-2N) 960 miles (1,588km), (-3) 1,200 miles (1,930km), (-4N) 810 miles (1,303km).

Armament: Basic (-1) four 0.5in Browning each with 300 rounds in the nose and four 20mm M-2 cannon each with 200 rounds in the wing roots; outer-wing pylons for six rockets or two 1,000lb (454kg) bombs; alternatively, one 21in torpedo on fuselage centerline, (-3), nose guns only; (-2N, -3N, -4N) wing guns only.

History: First flight (XF7F-1) December 1943; first service delivery October 1944; final delivery December 1946.

Users: Navy, Marines.

Ordered on the same day as the F6F Hellcat prototypes in June 1941, the F7F was one of the boldest designs in the history of combat air-

Above: The F7F saw little carrier service. This F7F-2N night fighter retained its nose guns, absent from the -3N.

Above: Marine F7F-single seaters (which retained nose guns) in the Pacific just after VJ-Day. They went on to China.

craft. During the preceding two years the US Navy had keenly studied air war in Europe and noted that the things that appeared to count were the obvious ones; engine power, armament, and protective armor and self-sealing tanks. At a time when the average US Navy fighter had 1,000hp and two machine guns, the Bureau of Aeronautics asked Grumman to build a fighter with more than 4,000hp and a weight of fire more than 100 times as great.

The company had embarked on a venture along these lines in 1938 with the XF5F, which remained a one-off prototype that was judged not worth the cost, and incompatible with Navy carriers. In contrast the F6F, though dramatically heavier and faster than any previous carrier aircraft, was matched with the deck of the large Midway class carriers under con-

struction.

Most, however, were ordered for the Marine Corps for use from land. The F7F-1, of which 34 were built, were single-seaters with APS-6 radar in a wing pod. The 66 F7F-2Ns followed, with nose radar in place of guns and the observer in place of the rear fuel tank. The -3 introduced the -34W engine and so had a larger tail; most of the 250 built were -3N night fighters or -3P photographic aircraft. The final models were strengthened -4s, cleared for carrier use, the whole batch being -4Ns.

Tigercats arrived at a time when emphasis was rapidly switching to the jet. Various delays kept them out of action in World War II, but in the immediate post-war era they played an important role with Marine squadrons based in the United States the Pacific theater and China.

Below: The chief production model was the Dash-3, here in Marine service in 1946. BuNo "last three" appeared boldly.

Lockheed F-80 Shooting Star and T-33

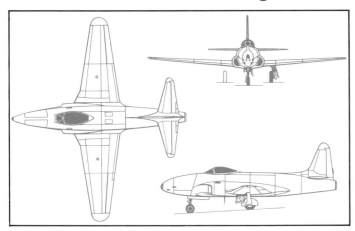

Origin: Lockheed Aircraft Corporation, Burbank, California.

Type: (F-80) single-seat fighter-bomber, (T-33) dual-control trainer.

Engine: (P-80A and B) one 4,600lb (2,087kg) thrust Allison J33-9 or -19 single-shaft centrifugal turbojet; (P-80C or F-80C) one 5,400lb (2,450kg) thrust J33-23; (T-33A) one 5,200lb (2,360kg) Allison J33-35; (CL-30) one 5,100lb (2,313kg) Rolls-Royce Nene 10 centrifugal turbojet; (T2V-1, T-1A) one 6,100lb (2,767kg) J33-24.

Dimensions: Span (basic) 38ft 10½in (11.85m); (F-94C) 42ft 5in (12.9m); length (F-80) 34ft 6in (10.51m), (T-33) 37ft 9in (11.48m); height (F-80, T-33) 11ft 8in (3.55m); wing area (all) 238sq ft (22.11m²).

Weights: Empty (F-80C) 8,240lb (3,741kg); (T-33A) 8,084lb (3,667kg); (T-1A) 11,965lb (5,428kg); maximum loaded (F-80C) 15,336lb (6,963kg); (T-33A) 14,442lb (6,551kg) (T-1A) 15,800lb (7,167kg).

Performance: Maximum speed (all) 590-606mph (950-975km/h); initial climb (all) about 5,000ft (1,524m)/min; service ceiling (all) about 48,000ft (14,630m); range (all) 1,100-1,250 miles (1,770-2,000km).

Armament: See text.

History: First flight (XP-80) 8 January 1944; service delivery (YP-80A) October 1944; first flight (TF-80C) 22 March 1948; final delivery (Lockheed) August 1959, (Canada) 1958, (Japan) 1959.

Users: AAF, AF, ANG, Navy, Marine Corps.

Lockheed sketched a jet fighter in 1941, but dropped it for lack of a suitable engine. In June 1943 Wright Field, excited by the imported Whittle engine but depressed by the obvious unsuitability of the P-59 Airacomet for combat duty, sent Col M. S. Roth to talk over the prospect of a Lockheed jet fighter with chief engineer Clarence L. "Kelly" Johnson. The latter decided to go ahead within a time limit of 180 days and fly a fighter designed around the British Halford H.1 (Goblin).

The schedule was beaten easily and ground running began in December 1943. Unfortunately Lockheed had not heeded the warning of a resident British engineer that the skin of the inlet

Above: The original YP-80A was larger than the prototype and had six nose guns. The P-80A had underwing tanks and bomb racks.

ducts was too thin, and these collapsed and were sucked into the engine at full throttle. Generously, de Havilland sent Lockheed the engine that was being installed in the second prototype Vampire. With this fitted behind stronger inlets, test pilot Milo Burcham took off on a maiden flight which was such sheer joy he turned it into a breathtaking display of low-level aerobatics!

The delicately curved inlets were a feature of all subsequent variants, though the prototype was rather smaller than its successors. The wing had a thin laminar profile, ailerons were hydraulically boosted, fuel tanks were hung under the tips, combat-maneuver flaps (airbrakes) were under the center-section, and the neat tricycle landing gears had main units retracting inwards. Nose armament comprised six 0.5in, and the P-80C (F-80C from 1948) introduced wing racks for two 1,000lb (454kg) bombs or ten 5in rockets.

By January 1945 two Shooting Stars were serving under combat conditions in Italy and more soon came to Britain, but the type did not reach squadrons until after VJ-day. In the Korean War the F-80C bore

Above: The original Navy trainer version was the TV-2, similar to the T-33A. From it was developed the T-1A SeaStar.

Below: The T-33 was an excellent "hack" for research and trials. This one flew with a research pod from Edwards in 1959.

the brunt of the initial fighting, flying 15,000 sorties in the first four months and shooting down the first MiG-15 on 8 November 1950 in what is thought to have been the first jet-v-jet combat.

Total Shooting Star production was 1,718, many being converted into FP-80 (later called RF-80) reconnaissance and QF-80 drone versions.

The T-33 has for 20 years been the world's most widely used jet trainer, the whole program stemming from an F-80C taken from the production line and given an extra section of fuselage with a second seat, covered by a long clamshell

canopy, and known as the TF-80C. Normal "T-bird" armament is two 0.5in guns. Lockheed delivered approximately 5,820, including 217 of an improved T2V (T-1A) SeaStar model for the Navy with a new airframe having a raised instructor seat and slatted wing.

Canadair built 656 CL-30 Silver Star T-birds with the Nene engine, and Kawasaki built 210 in Japan. More than 2,000 T-33s were converted into RT (photo), WT (weather), DT (drone director), QT (drone or RPV) or AT (close-support attack) versions. Small numbers of these very popular aircraft survived into the 1980s.

Below: 47-547, an F-80C, saw action in Korea with the 36th FB Sqn, 8th FB Wing.

Bottom: Modified with Fletcher tip tanks, this early P-80A became an ANG transition trainer.

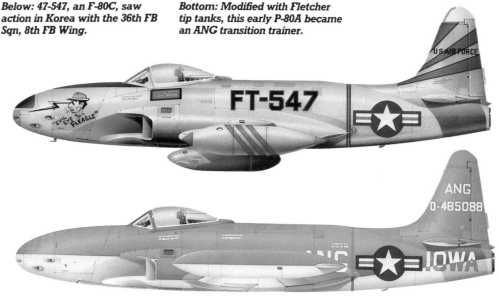

Ryan FR-1 Fireball

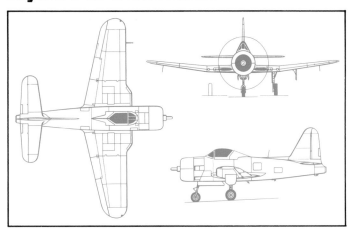

Origin: Ryan Aeronautical Corporation, San Diego, California.
Type: Carrier-based fighter.
Engines: One 1,425hp Wright Cyclone R-1820-72W nine-cylinder radial and one 1,600lb (726kg) General Electric J31-2 turbojet.
Dimensions: Span 40ft (12.19m); length 32ft 4in (9.85m); height 13ft 11in (4.24m); wing area 275sq ft (25.55m²).
Weights: Empty 7,915lb (3,590kg); maximum 11,652lb (5,285kg).
Performance: Maximum speed (R-1820 only) 295mph (475km/h), (both) 426mph (686km/h); service ceiling 43,100ft (13,140m); range (R-1820 cruise, no drop tank) 1,030 miles (1,660km).
Armament: Four 0.5in guns plus one 1,000lb (454kg) bomb or eight 5in (127mm) rockets.
History: First flight 25 June 1944; service delivery January 1945.

Above: There was just one batch of production FR-1s, all looking the same apart from the fact some had bomb/tank pylons inboard of the main gears.

User: Navy.

This novel fighter combined the docile carrier compatibility and fuel economy of traditional fighters with the greater performance possible with a jet. Produced as the Model 28 under a Letter of Intent issued in February 1943, the FR-1 was one of the first Navy aircraft flush-riveted throughout. Features included a Whittle-derived jet in the tail (which was in consequence removable) fed from inlets in the wing roots, tricycle landing gear, laminar-profile wings which power-folded upwards, and guns in the horizontal center section outboard of the propeller disc. Ryan developed the Fireball quickly, but

Above: The Fireballs first served with VF-66 with numbers from B1 upwards. Here the piston engine is stopped, which was a pure "party trick".

it just failed to see combat duty and most were canceled. Production totaled three XFRs, and 66 for in-ventory, one being retrofitted with a 3,400lb (1,542kg) J34 fed by flush side inlets. The turboprop/jet XF2R Dark Shark remained a single conversion.

Below: The first XFR-1 prototype, possibly on first takeoff in the hands of Ryan's Al Conover.

Grumman F8F Bearcat

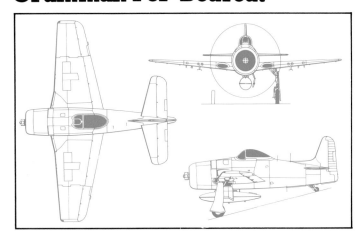

Origin: Grumman Aircraft Engineering Corporation, Bethpage, NY.
Type: Single-seat carrier-based fighter-bomber or night fighter.
Engine: One Pratt & Whitney R-2800-34W Double Wasp 18-cylinder radial rated at 2,400hp (wet) for take-off, with emergency combat rating of 2,800hp.
Dimensions: Span (-1) 35ft 10in, (-2) 35ft 6in (10.7m); length (-1) 28ft 3in, (-2) 27ft 8in (8.43m); height 13ft 10in (4.2m); wing area 244sq ft (22.67m²).

Above: The F8F-1 sacrificed much for rate of climb and agility. In the -1B the guns became 20mm.

Weights: Empty (-1) 7,070lb (3,206kg); loaded (-1) 12,947lb (5,873kg), (-2) 13,494lb (6,120kg).
Performance: Maximum speed (-1) 421mph (680km/h), (-2) 447mph (720km/h); initial climb 5,000ft (1,520m)/min; sevice ceiling 40,000ft (12,190m); range on internal fuel (-1) 1,105 miles (1,775km), (-2) 865 miles (1,400km).

Above: Marine pilot making a textbook three-pointer at Quantico, Virginia, in a tall-fin, cannon-armed Dash-2.

Armament: (-1) four 0.5in Brownings in inboard wings beyond propeller disc; pylons under inboard wing for two 1,000lb (454kg) bombs, drop tanks or rockets, (-1B, -2) four 20mm M-2 cannon and same stores load, (-2P) only two 20mm.
History: First flight (XF8F-1) 21 August 1944, (production

F8F-1) November 1944; final delivery May 1949.
User: Navy.

As a contrast to the big Hellcat and Corsair, the Navy decided in 1943 to buy a lightweight fighter designed to the smallest size that would accommodate the R-2800 engine and specified fuel. The philosophy ran in parallel with that which produced the XP-51F and H Mustangs, except that the Navy bought a completely fresh design.

It was a requirement that the new

Boeing C-97 Stratofreighter/Stratotanker

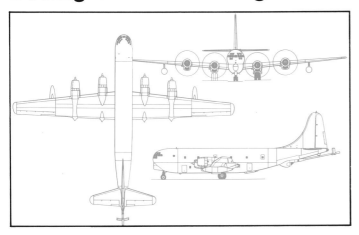

Origin: Boeing Airplane Company, Seattle and Renton, Washington.
Type: Air refueling tanker and logistic transport with crew of six or seven; data for KC-97G.
Engine: Four 3,500hp Pratt & Whitney R-4360-59B Wasp Major 28-cylinder four-row radials; (KC-97L) in addition two 5,200lb (2,359kg) thrust GE J47 turbojets.
Dimensions: Span 141ft 3in (43.05m); length 117ft 5in (35.8m); height 38ft 3in (11.75m); wing area 1,720sq ft (159.8m²).
Weights: Empty 85,000lb (38,560kg); loaded 175,000lb (78,980kg).
Performance: Maximum speed 370mph (595km/h); service ceiling 30,000ft (9,144m); range at 300 mph (482km/h) without using transfer fuel, 4,300 miles (6,920km).
Armament: Normally none.
History: First flight (XC-97) 15 November 1944, (production

Above: Final model was the KC-97G, of which 592 were built. Note nose radar, underwing tanks and Flying Boom. A few were fitted with J47 jet pods.

C-97A) 28 January 1949, (KC-97G) 1953; final delivery July 1956.
Users: AF, ANG.

Big as the B-29 Superfortress was, it was dwarfed by the transport derived by adding on top of the existing fuselage a second fuselage of much greater diameter so that the final whale-like body had a section like a figure 8 (called a "double bubble"). The Army Air Force had ordered three of these monster XC-97s in January 1942 when it first bought the B-29, but their development took second place behind the vital bomber programs. But when the first did fly it soon startled everyone; on 9 January 1945 it flew non-stop from Seattle to Washing-

Above: 48-399 was the third production Stratofreighter, a C-97A with APS-42 nose radar and HamStan propellers, seen with MATS Pacific Division.

ton in 6hr 4min, at an average of 383mph (616km/h), whilst carrying a payload of ten tons. Only a few years earlier the transcontinental journey had required three days (air by day, rail by night).

The YC-97A was even more capable, for it had the Wasp Major engine. Eventually 50 C-97As were built, with nose radar and extra outer-wing tankage, plus 14 aeromedical C-97Cs for casualty evacuation from Korea. Distinguished from the civil Stratocruiser by having only seven windows on each side of the main cabin, the C-97A could carry a payload of 53,000lb (24,041kg) or 134 equipped troops. The VC-97D was a special airborne command post which led the way to

later EC-135 special versions.

Nevertheless, it was Strategic Air Command's need for an air refueling tanker that made the C-97 a giant program. By July 1956 Boeing had delivered 60 KC-97Es, carrying nearly double the original fuel load, plus 159 KC-97F and no fewer than 592 KC-97G with underwing tanks and the capability of serving as a heavy cargo aircraft without removing the refueling gear.

The latter was standardized as the Boeing Flying Boom system, which was considered preferable for SAC bombers because of its high flow rate. Many Gs were converted to C-97G cargo aircraft, or C-97K SAC mission-support passenger carriers, or HC-97G sea/air rescue aircraft (pending delivery of the NC-130H), or rebuilt by Hayes as KC-97L tankers with GE J47 jet booster pods (removed from KB-50s) for Air National Guard service.

---

fighter should be able to fly from small CVE carriers, and this resulted in a large wing with high-lift slotted flaps, and wide-track inwards-retracting landing gears. The cockpit was high amidships, and altogether the F8F emerged as a very simple and effective design with outstanding dogfight performance. An odd feature, later abandoned, was that the folding wingtips were originally designed to break off in flight, should the airplane be overstressed in violent maneuvers.

Prototypes were ordered on 27 November 1943, and it took Grumman ten months to fly the first. In October 1944 Grumman were awarded a contract for 2,023, with Eastern Aircraft receiving an order for 1,876 designated F3M-1. Deliveries began on 1 December 1944 and VP-19 was almost combat-ready when the war ended. The F3M contract was canceled, but Grumman retained a considerable order that was modified to introduce new versions.

After delivering 765 F8F-1s Grumman built 100 -1B and 36 -1Ns with APS-6 radar, followed by 293 -2s with a taller fin and 60 -2P photographic aircraft. US Navy

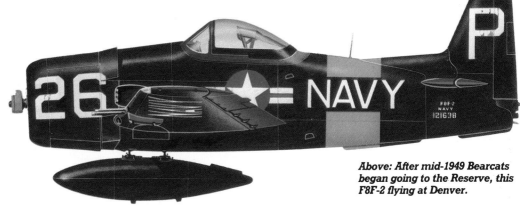

front-line service petered out in 1951-52, but the Bearcat was one of the fastest and most maneuverable piston-engined aircraft ever built and attracted overseas interest.

More than 250 rebuilt versions, most of them F8F-1Ds with revised fuel system, served with the Armée de l'Air in Indo-China, the survivors being taken over by the Vietnamese Air Force (both North and South). Another big operator was Thailand, which received 29 -1Bs and 100 -1Ds. Several were modified for civilian racing in the United States, the hotted-up aircraft of Darryl Greenamyer setting a new world speed record for non-jet air-

craft at 482.5mph (776.3km/h) in August 1969.

Above: After mid-1949 Bearcats began going to the Reserve, this F8F-2 flying at Denver.

Below: The four-20mm guns arrived with the F8F-1B.

McDonnell FH-1 Phantom

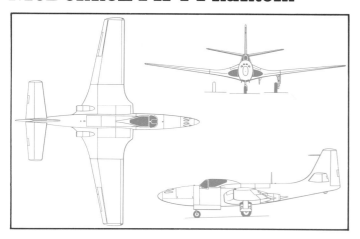

Origin: McDonnell Aircraft Company, St Louis, Missouri.
Type: Carrier-based fighter.
Engines: Two 1,600lb (726kg) Westinghouse J30-2 turbojets.
Dimensions: Span 40ft 9in (12.42m); length 37ft 3in (11.35m); height 14ft 2in (4.32m); wing area 276sq ft, (25.64m²).
Weights: Empty 6,683lb (3,031kg); maximum 12,035lb (5,459kg).
Performance: Maximum speed at sea level 479mph (771km/h); service ceiling 41,100ft (12,530m); range 980 miles (1,580km).

Above: Like the FR-1 the FH-1 comprised a single production block, all looking alike. Docile in deck operation, it lacked thrust and firepower.

Armament: Four 0.50in guns in the nose.
History: First flight 26 January 1945; service delivery 23 July 1947.
Users: Navy, Marine Corps.

One of the most significant US military contractual documents was

Above: VF-17A goes aboard USS Randolph to become the world's first jet squadron at sea. But technology was moving fast and the FH-1 was withdrawn in 1950.

a Bureau of Aeronautics letter of intent of 30 August 1943 inviting the infant McDonnell company to design a naval jet fighter. Westinghouse was developing a series of slim axial turbojets for the Navy and the first studies used six of the 9.5in size, three in each wing root. By late 1943 the mock-up was appearing

with a single 19in-diameter engine in each root. The rest was clean and conservative, the pressurized cockpit being ahead of the upward-folding wings, with short but wide-track gears folding inwards. The prototype first flew on a single 1,165lb (528kg) 19XB engine, the second still being awaited! The Navy ordered 60 FD-1s, later redesignated as FH-1s to avoid confusion with Douglas. Easy to fly, the Phantom served with VF-17A (in May 1948 the world's first embarked jet unit) and VMF-122 and -311.

Douglas A-1 (AD) Skyraider

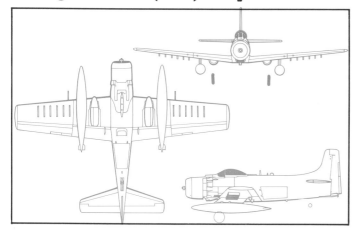

Origin: Douglas Aircraft Company, El Segundo Division, California.
Type: Initially, naval torpedo and dive bomber; later, many roles (see text).
Engine: One 3,020hp Wright R-3350-26W or 3,050hp R-3350-26WB Cyclone 18-cylinder two-row radial.
Dimensions: Span 50ft (15.24m); (A-1J) 50ft 9in, (15.49m); length 38ft 2in to 40ft 1in (11.63m to 12.22m); (A-1J) 38ft 10in (11.84m); height 15ft 5in to 15ft 10in (4.7m to 4.83m); (A-1J) 15ft 8¼in (4.77m); wing area 400sq ft (37.16m²).
Weights: Empty 10,090-12,900lb (4,577-5,851kg); (A-1J) 12,313lb (5,585kg); maximum loaded 18,030lb-25,000lb (8,178-11,340kg); (A-1J) 25,000lb (11,340kg).
Performance: Maximum speed 298-366mph (497-589km/h); (A-1J) 318mph (512km/h); initial climb (typical) 2,300ft (700m)/min;

Above: The A-1J was the final production model, looking much like the first. In between came wide-body multi-seaters.

service ceiling (typical) 32,000ft (9,753m); range from 900 miles (1,448km) with maximum ordnance to 3,000 miles (4,828km) with maximum external fuel.
Armament: Varied with sub-type, but attack variants generally four 20mm cannon in outer wings and 15 pylons for total ordnance/fuel load of 8,000lb (3,629kg).
History: First flight (XBT2D-1) 18 March 1945; service delivery (AD-1) November 1946; termination of production February 1957.
Users: Navy, Marines, AF.

Like so many of Ed Heinemann's designs the Skyraider simply refused to grow obsolete. Planned in 1944 as the first combined torpedo/dive bomber to be a

Above: BuNo 124006 flew on 17 August 1951 rebuilt as the first of the wide-body AD-5s — a big advance in versatility.

single-seater, the XBT2D competed against three rival designs and, due to Martin's protracted detailed development of the more powerful AM-1 Mauler, soon became the favored type. Its obvious versatility led to modifications for additional missions, explored in 1946 with prototypes fitted with various kinds of radar, searchlights and countermeasures.

Of 242 AD-1s, 35 were AD-1Q ECM aircraft with a counter-measures operator in the rear fuselage. The AD-2 was strengthened and given greater fuel capacity, and several were equipped for drone control and target towing. The AD-3 branched out into anti-submarine detection/strike and, equipped with a vast belly radome,

airborne early-warning duties.

The further refined AD-4 was built in the largest number (1,032), also used by the Royal Navy and the French Armée de l'Air. In the AD-5 (later redesignated A-1E) the wider fuselage allowed some versions to have side-by-side seating, with a rear cabin for 12 seats or four litters. None of the A-1E variants were single-seaters, but the A-1H (AD-6) reverted to the single seat and 713 were built for multi-role operations. The final A-1J (AD-7) single-seat version had strengthened wings for low-level tactical attack.

Altogether 3,180 of this amazingly versatile aircraft were built. Whereas it was almost terminated in 1946, by 1962 the Skyraider was fast becoming one of the most important weapon platforms in the US inventory with the renewed outbreak of warfare in Vietnam. Eventually more than 1,000 Skyraiders

Piasecki HRP Rescuer

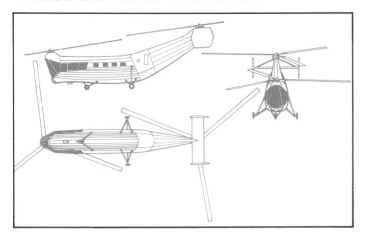

Origin: Piasecki Helicopter Corp, Morton, Pennsylvania.
Type: Transport helicopter.
Engine: One 600hp Pratt & Whitney Wasp R-1340 nine-cylinder radial.
Dimensions: Diameter of each main rotor 41ft (12.5m); length of fuselage 48ft 2in (14.69m); height 12ft 6in (3.81m); total rotor-disc area 2,640sq ft (245.3m²).
Weights: Empty 5,150lb (2,336kg); loaded 7,225lb (3,227kg), (overload) 8,000lb (3,629kg).
Performance: Maximum speed

Above: Aerodynamically the HRP-1 was little different from the more powerful HRP-2, but it was a tube/fabric design which saw limited combat duty.

105mph (170km/h); crusing speed 85mph (137km/h); normal range 300 miles (482km).
Armament: None.
History: First flight (XHRP-1) March 1945, (HRP-1) 15 August 1947.
Users: Navy, Marine Corps, Coast Guard.

Above: Flying Bananas clatter aloft from Marine Corps Air Station Quantico, Virginia, on Christmas Eve, 1948. The unit was styled HMX-1.

Frank N. Piasecki was one of the American pioneers of the helicopter. His PV-2 was the second US helicopter to fly publicly, on 11 April 1943. In February 1944 the infant company received a Navy contract for a large tandem-rotor transport helicopter, and this, the PV-3, became the XHRP-1.

Nick-named The Flying Banana, it had a metal-framed fabric-covered fuselage seating a crew of two and eight passengers, or six litter casualties or cargo. In the rescue role at overload weight it could pick up eight rescuees at a radius of 300 miles (482km). Subsequently 35 production HRP-1s were delivered to the Navy, three being diverted to the USCG.

The HRP-2 version introduced a new metal-skinned fuselage, as described under the H-21 entry on page 133.

---

were sent to Vietnam, operated not only by the Navy and Marines but also by the US Air Force and the air force of the Republic of Vietnam (ARVN). It proved one of the most effective combat types, as it had done earlier in Korea, with huge weight-lifting ability, ten-hour endurance and ability to survive severe flak damage. Universally called the "Spad", it bore a heavy burden of combat in Southeast Asia until 1973.

Besides serving the US Navy, the A-1E was adopted by the US Air Force's Tactical Air Command. This command acquired 50 Navy A-1s to equip the first Air Commando group engaged in Counter-insurgency (Co-in) operations supporting the South Vietnamese forces. The US Navy used several types of the A-1 in Vietnam, including specialized electronic

counter-measure versions.
In 1967 the Navy pulled its remaining A-1s out of Vietnam leaving the US Air Force and the South Vietnamese Air Force as the prime users of the Spad. At the time of the January 1973 truce, about 100 A-1s were turned over to the South Vietnamese and several squadrons were still operational at the time of the fall of South Vietnam in 1975. The US Air Force had disbanded the last of its Spad units in the fall of 1974.

The A-1 had a varied role in Vietnam, such as flying rescue, close air support and forward air control (FAC) missions. The aircraft was credited with many achievements

Below: These A-1H Skyraiders were being flown by US pilots immediately prior to formal handover to the VNAF.

in its combat role in Southeast Asia. For example, in December 1964, VNAF A-1Hs and USAF A-1Es inflicted more than 400 casualties and were credited with averting the destruction of a regional force company near Long My after that unit's resupply convoy had been ambushed.

In August 1965 Air Force A-1Es began escorting rescue units. During a typical recovery operation, two A-1Es flew directly to the general search area and looked for some sign of the downed crewmen while two other A-1Es escorted the helicopter to the area. If it was determined that the pilot was in a hostile area, the A-1Es would com-

Below: Lovely study of an A-1H of VA-25 recovering to USS Midway. VA-25 bagged two MiG-17s in air combat!

mence attacking with bombs, rockets and 20mm cannon fire suppressing the defenses so the helicopter could land.

In March 1966 A-1Es of the First Air Commando Squadron braved bad weather to go to the aid of a Special Forces Camp in the A Shau Valley which was under attack by a force of 2,000 North Vietnamese regulars. In the midst of the battle the A-1E pilots found a hole in the thick overcast that blanketed the mountainous area and flew 210 strikes that slowed the enemy advance.

The A-1Es received credit for killing some 500 of the enemy, and General Westmoreland, commander of US forces in Southeast Asia at that time, later called the air support on this occasion one of the most courageous displays of airmanship in aviation history.

North American F-82 Twin Mustang

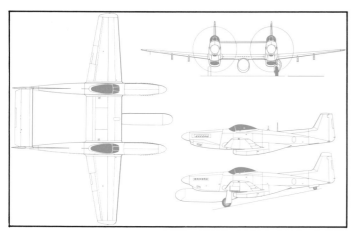

Origin: North American Aviation Inc, Inglewood, California.
Type: Escort and night fighter.
Engines: (E,F,G) two 1,900hp Allison V-1710-143/145 V-12 liquid cooled.
Dimensions: Span 51ft 3in (15.62m); length (E) 39ft 1in (11.9m), (G) 42ft 5in (12.93m); height 13ft 10in (4.23m); wing area 408sq ft (37.9m²).
Weights: Empty (G) 15,997lb (7,256kg); maximum (E) 24,864lb

Above: The upper side view shows the XP-82, with V-1650 Merlin engine and lower fins. The main drawing shows the F-82G night fighter with SCR-720 radar pod — 50 delivered.

(11,278kg), (G) 25,591lb (11,608kg).
Performance: Maximum speed (E) 469mph (755km/h), (G) 461mph (742km/h); service ceiling (G) 38,900ft (11,860m); range (E) 2,500 miles (4,200km), (G) 2,240 miles

Above: One of the first F-82E day escorts to reach the 27th Fighter Group at McChord Field, Washington, in January 1948. This group converted to the F-84E in July 1950.

(3,600km).
Armament: Six 0.50in in wing center section; (E) same but in detachable tray, plus 4,000lb (1,814kg) bombload or 24 5in rockets.

History: First flight 15 April 1945; inventory service (E,F,G) 1947.
Users: AAF, AF, ANG.

This brilliant design was created to provide a superior long-range escort for the Pacific war. Many parts of the fuselage, outer wings and vertical tail were similar to the P-51, though length was greater. The two fuselages were joined by rectangular center wings and tailplane, and one main gear was

Lockheed P2V (P-2) Neptune

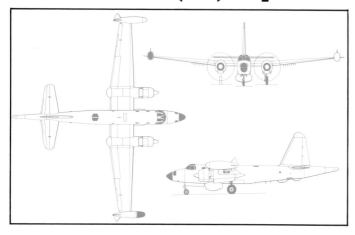

Origin: Lockheed-California Company, Burbank, California.
Type: Maritime patrol and ASW aircraft.
Engines: (P2V-1) two 2,300hp Wright R-3350-8 Cyclone 18-cylinder two-row radials, (-2) 2,800hp R-3350-24W, (later batches of -4) 3,080hp R-3350-26W, (-3) 3,250hp R-3350-30W Turbo-Compound, (-5F, P-2E) same plus two 3,400lb (1,540kg) thrust Westinghouse J34-36 turbojets, (-7, P-2H) same jets but 3,700hp R-3350-32W Turbo-Compound.
Dimensions: Span (early versions) 100ft (30.48m), (H) 103ft 10in (31.65m); length (-1) 75ft 4in (22.96m), (-2 to -4/D) 77ft 10in (23.7m), (E) 81ft 7in (24.87m), (H) 91ft 8in (27.94m); height 28ft 1in (8.58m), (H) 29ft 4in, (8.94m); wing area 1,000sq ft (92.9m²).
Weights: Empty (-1) 31,000lb (14,061kg), (-3) 34,875lb (15,833kg), (H) 49,935lb (22,650kg); maximum loaded (-1) 61,153lb (27,740kg), (-3) 64,100lb (29,075kg), (H) 79,895lb

Above: Built as a P2V-5, this model (SP-2E) eliminated nose and tail turrets and added new ASW gear. Some (not this one) also had jet booster pods.

(36,240kg).
Performance: Maximum speed (-1) 303mph (489km/h), (H) 356mph (573km/h), 403mph, 648km/h with jets); initial climb (all) about 1,200ft (366m)/min, (H 1,800ft/min with jets); service ceiling 25,000-30,000ft (7,620-9,144m) depending on sub-type; range (early models, typical) 4,000 miles (6,440km), (H) about 2,500 miles (4,000km).
Armament: See text.
History: First flight (XP2V-1) 17 May 1945; service delivery (-1) March 1947, (-7, H) 26 April 1954.
Users: Navy, AF, Army.

On 1 October 1946 the P2V leapt into prominence. Three days earlier the third production P2V-1

Above: VO-67 flew the rebuilt OP-2E from Nakhon Phanom to detect traffic on the Ho Chi Minh trail. It used radars and special acoustic sensor buoys.

had taken off from Perth, Western Australia, at 85,000lb with fuel weighing 1½ times its empty weight. By flying non-stop 11,235 miles (18,077km) to Columbus, Ohio, it set a world distance record for piston-engined aircraft that has never been broken.

Lockheed's Vega subsidiary had begun the design in 1941, studies of the Lockheed Model 26 by Mac Short (who later designed the T-bird) showing that with two R-3350 engines this could be heavier than wartime four-engine heavy bombers, and have much longer range. Work had low priority, but eventually the prototype flew near the war's end. The mid-high wing was very efficient with high aspect ratio but large Fowler flaps for good field performance.

The large weapons bay could carry two or four torpedoes or 12 depth charges. There was ample room for a crew of seven, with two turret gunners, masses of mission electronics and much special equipment. The P2V-1 had three pairs of 0.5in guns and 16 underwing rockets. The P2V-2 had six 20mm cannon firing ahead, two more in a power tail turet and two 0.5in in the dorsal turret.

Gradually defensive or offensive gun armament was removed, later models having instead many tons of extra anti-submarine sensing systems, as well as retaining the 8,000lb (3,629kg) weapon bay.

The P2V-4 of 1949 introduced the powerful Turbo-Compound engine, and like some P2V-3s had a giant belly radome for APS-20 surveillance radar. Another new feature was wingtip auxiliary tanks, one also housing a searchlight. In the P2V-5 these tanks were enlarged, and a twin-20mm turret was added in the nose. The P2V-5F (P-2E

pivoted under each fuselage. Two NA-120 (XP-82) had Packard Merlins and an XP-82A had Allisons. The AAF ordered 500 P-82Bs but 480 were canceled. One B was converted into the P-82C night fighter with large SCR-720 radar in a massive pod under the centerline, while another became the P-82D with APS-4 centimetric radar in a very small pod.

In 1946 the AAF managed to procure 250 Allison-powered P-82s, all with opposite-rotation engines and normally flown from the left cockpit (designations given are post-1948); 100 dual-control P-82E day escorts with heavy attack load; 100 F-82F with APS-4; and 50 F-82G with SCR-720. The main user was Air Defense Command, and almost all saw action in Korea, Lt Hudson of the 68th Sqn scoring the very first victory of that conflict (and the first of the AF). Nine F's and five Gs were converted as F-82H winterized interceptors for Alaska.

Right: 44-65168 was one of the 20 P-82Bs, which never became operational. They were the last to retain the V-1650 Merlin.

from 1962) added the J34 booster jets to improve takeoff and add extra combat speed. Later a MAD "stinger" was added at the tail, and in the P2V-6 (P-2F) and -7 (P-2H) guns were eliminated.

These final versions had a pointed glazed nose, raised cockpit roof, smaller tip tanks and much special equipment. The SP-2H had Julie/Jezebel ASW detection gear, and the weapon bay could carry a much wider range of stores. Altogether Lockheed delivered 838 Neptunes to the Navy.

In Vietnam the OP-2E dropped electronic sensors to detect trucks moving along the supply route through southern Laos. The Neptune received the sensor planting mission because it had precise navigational equipment and accurate optical bombsight. Planners believed it could place the seismic or acoustic device within a few yards of the desired point. To do so, however, the OP-2E had to fly low and level, making it an easy target for the enemy's 37mm guns.

The AF and Army also used many modified Neptunes in Southeast Asia. The AP-2H derivatives of the P2V-7 were used for night and bad-weather attack, especially against truck convoys. A small number of earlier AP-2Es were also used. The first AF Neptunes had been seven ex-Navy P2V-5Us in 1954 used to train ECM operators and redesignated as RB-69s. Army OP-2s were used for special electronic recon missions.

Right: A fine picture of one of the last Neptunes, P2V-7 No 147949. It is seen new, painted Midnight Blue.

Douglas C-74 and C-124 Globemaster

Origin: Douglas Aircraft Company, Long Beach, California.
Type: Strategic transport.
Engines: (C-74) four 3,000hp Pratt & Whitney R-4360-49 Wasp Major 28-cylinder four-row radials; (C-124A) four 3,500hp R-4360-20WA; (C-124C) four 3,800hp R-4360-63A.
Dimensions: Span 173ft 3in (52.78m), (C-124A and C) over tip heater pods 174ft 1½in (53.08m); length (C-74) 124ft 1½in (37.83m), (C-124) 130ft 5in (39.75m); height (C-74) 43ft 8in (13.31m), (C-124) 48ft 3½in (14.7m); wing area 2,506sq ft, (232.8m²).
Weights: (C-74) empty 92,000lb (41,731kg), loaded 165,000lb (74,910kg); (C-124) empty 101,165lb (45,887kg); maximum loaded 194,500lb (88,223kg).
Performance: Maximum speed (C-74) 325mph (523km/h), (C-124) 304mph (489km/h); initial climb 760ft (232m)/min; service ceiling 21,800ft (6,645m); range with maximum fuel (C-74) 7,800 miles

Above: The C-124C was easily identified by its tip pods housing combustion heaters. Note the fairings for the low-mounted flap and aileron hinges.

(12,553km), (C-124) 6,820 miles (10,975km); range with maximum 56,000lb (25,400kg) payload (both) about 1,200 miles (1,931km).
History: First flight (XC-74) 5 September 1945, (YC-124) 27 November 1949; service delivery (C-74) 11 October 1945, (C-124A) May 1950; last delivery May 1955.
Users: AAF (C-74 only), AF.

The Douglas Long Beach division drew up plans during World War II for a giant transport resembling a scaled-up DC-4 and secured a military (Army Air Force) order for a prototype in 1942. The main emphasis was placed on post-war civil transoceanic use and Pan American ordered 26, with the designation DC-7, in 1945. The first

Above: AAF No 42-65402 was one of the C-74s to have its bug-eye canopies replaced by a normal flight deck. It was No 1 of 14.

(military) prototype flew in that year, but PanAm canceled its order and the planned Army Air Force contract was cut back to 14.

These were delivered in 1946-47, the C-74 having curious twin bug-eye pilot canopies above the two cockpits in the nose, full-span Fowler flaps and an almost circular-section fuselage. The civil C-74 was to have been pressurized, but the large doors and freight hoists in the C-74 made this impractical with 1945 technology. The C-74 had enormous integral fuel tanks in the wings, an electric cargo hoist which lifted a large platform up to the rear of the hold, and an advanced Sperry A-12 autopilot. These monsters served on the Berlin Airlift in 1948–49, and later were rebuilt with conventional airline

type flight decks. Advantage was taken of deletion of pressurization to redesign the C-74 with a huge fuselage offering twice the volume and capable of being fitted with two passenger decks. The vast nose had a normal flight deck above and large left and right clamshell doors for loading vehicles and heavy freight. This aircraft was the C-124A Globemaster II, flown as a prototype by converting the fifth C-74.

Ultimately 204 C-124As were delivered plus one turboprop C-124B and 243 C-124Cs. The C-124C introduced higher gross weight, with more fuel and payload, as well as two features retroactively added to C-124As, APS-124 weather radar in a nose "thimble" and wingtip combustion heaters to deice the wings and tail and heat the cabin.

Below: By later standards the C-124 was a lumbering brute, needing a calendar on the flight deck. No 52-1035 was a C-124C.

Bell H-13 Sioux, Model 47

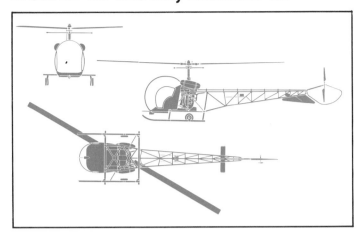

Origin: Bell Helicopter Co (now Bell Helicopter Textron), Fort Worth, Texas.

Type: Three-seat utility and training helicopter.

Engines: Flat-six piston engine with crankshaft vertical, usually 178/200hp Franklin (early models), 240hp Lycoming VO-435 or (late) 270hp TVO-435.

Dimensions: (Typical of late models) diameter of two-blade main rotor 37ft 1½in (11.32m); length overall (rotors turning) 43ft 4¾in (13.20m); height overall 9ft 3½in (2.83m); main-rotor disc area 1,082.5sq ft (100.5m²).

Weights: (47J-3) empty 1,819lb (825kg); maximum loaded 2,950lb (1,340kg).

Performance: (Typical late model) maximum speed 105mph (169km/h); crusing speed 86mph (138km/h); range at low level, no reserve, 210 miles (338km).

Armament: Many equipped with fixed forward-firing gun (LMG, GPMG or Minigun), rocket pods

Above: This Bell 47 is typical of many models such as the H-13H and HTL-6. Other variants had a longer cabin and covered rear fuselage structure.

or early anti-tank wire-guided missiles.

History: First flight (prototype) 8 December 1945; service delivery of first YH-13 and HTL-1, 1946.

User: AF, Army, Navy, Marines.

Larry Bell flew his first experimental helicopter in mid-1943, and in 1946 a derived machine became the first Model 47, the first helicopter in the world to be certificated for general use. Over 5,000 were built by Bell and by Kawasaki (designation KH-4 series) and more than 1,200 were built by Agusta between 1954–76, Italian parts being supplied to Westland to support production in Britain of the 47G-3B for the British Army as the Sioux, the

Above: Straight out of "M.A.S.H." comes this H-13E, seen in Korea on casevac duty watched by US and British and Australian troops. Note litter carriers.

name chosen by the US Army. The TV series "MASH" has brought fame to the H-13s used for casualty

evacuation missions in Korea in 1950-53.

Most surviving military Model 47s are of the 47G family though numerous 47J series are also in use with uprated transmission and other changes. Some J models are four-seaters, while trainers, such as the Navy HTL, were usually two-seat with dual control.

Above: This OH-13S was seen well into the 1970s at a NATO Allied Mobile Force (Land) HQ "somewhere in Turkey".

Below: This H-13D, 51-2527, was used in a training role in 1952 with the 4th Medium Tank Battalion, 1st Armored Division.

Republic F-84 Thunderjet family

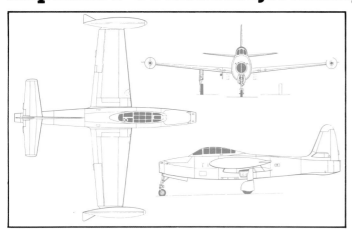

Origin: Republic Aviation Corporation, Farmingdale, NY.
Type: Single-seat fighter-bomber (RF-84F, photo-reconnaissance).
Engine: One single-shaft axial turbojet: (A) 3,750lb (1,701kg) Allison J35-15; (B, C) 4,000lb (1,814kg) J35-15C or -13; (D, E) 5,000lb (2,268kg) J35-17D; (G) 5,600lb (2,540kg) J35-29; (F) 7,220lb (3,275kg) Wright J65-3 (US Sapphire); (RF-84F) 7,800lb (3,538kg) J65-7.
Dimensions: Span (not including tip tanks) 36ft 5in (11.09m), F/RF-84F) 33ft 7¼in (10.24m); length (B, C, D) 37ft 5in, (E, G) 38ft 1in (11.61m), (F-84F) 43ft 4¾in (13.22m), (RF-84F) 47ft 7¾in (14.51m); heigl. .(B, C, D) 12ft 10in (3.91m), (G) 12ft 7in (3.84m), (F-84F) 14ft 4¾in (4.38m), (RF-84F) 15ft (4.57m); wing area (except F, RF) 260sq ft (24.15m²), (F) 325sq ft (30.19m²), (RF) 361sq ft (33.54m²).
Weights: Empty (B) 9,540lb (4,325kg), (G) 11,095lb (5,030kg), (F) 13,800lb (6,260kg); maximum loaded (B) 15,800lb (7,167kg), (C) 19,798lb (8,980kg), (D) 20,076lb (9,106kg), (E) 22,463lb (10,189kg), (G) 23,525lb (10,670kg), (F) 28,000lb (12,700kg), (RF) 26,790lb (12,152kg).
Performance: Maximum speed (B) 587mph (944km/h), (G) 622mph (1,000km/h), (F) 695mph (1,118km/h), (RF) 679mph (1,093km/h); initial climb (B) 5,800ft (1,768m)/min, (G) 5,000ft (1,524m)/min, (F) 8,200ft

Above: Most numerous variant, the F-84G had a multi-framed canopy. Triangular doors in the left wing leading edge cover the boom receptacle.

(2,500m)/min; service ceiling (B, C, D, G) 41,000ft (12,500m), (F, RF) 46,000ft (14,000m); range (hi, clean) all models, about 870 miles (1,400km); maximum range with maximum fuel (all) 2,000–2,200 miles (3,500km).
Armament: Six 0.5in Colt-Browning M-3, four in nose and two in wing roots (RF-84F, four, in wing above inlet ducts); underwing pylons for rockets (B, C) or two 375gal drop tanks (RF) or variety of tanks, nuclear and/or conventional bombs or other stores to total load of (C, D, E) 2,000lb (907kg), (G) 4,000lb (1,814kg), (F) 6,000lb (2,722kg).
History: First flight (XP-84) 28 February 1946, (production F-84B) May 1947, (production F-84F) 22 November 1952; final delivery (G) July 1953, (F/RF) March 1958.
Users: AAF, AF, ANG.

After studying derivatives of the P-47 with an axial turbojet, the P-84 was begun in November 1944 as a completely new design. It had a slender fuselage, nose intake to ducts which split each side of the nosewheel bay and cockpit, and unswept 12 per cent wing of the fashionable "laminar" profile. The

Above: Testing one of the standard USAF runway arrester barriers in 1956. The aircraft is an RF-84F-26, with long nose full of cameras, and wing-root inlets.

wing was mounted well above the low position, but the inlet ducts passed above it to merge and feed the slim axial engine. The latter was bolted to the rear spar and Republic claimed the engine could be changed in 50min by disconnecting the entire rear fuselage and tail, as Lockheed had done with the P-80. The fixed tailplane (horizontal stabilizer) was mounted on the fin above the fuselage, and had 5° dihedral. Compared with the P-80 the landing gears were remarkably long. Except for the prototypes the Thunderjets had drop tanks mounted centrally on the broad wingtips.

Following generally excellent performance by three XP-84 prototypes, Republic delivered 15 service-test YPs with the first Allison-built J35s (designed by GE, which built the TG-180/J35-7 used in the prototypes) and carried guns. Then followed 226 P-84Bs for the AAF inventory, with a little more thrust, ejection seat, fast-firing M-3 (instead of (M-2) guns and, in the final 140, zero-length attachments

Below: AAF No 45-59488 was the seventh YP-84A development prototype, though it looked very like a production F-84.

for up to 32 rockets. Three Bs were lost during wing-tip towing trials in an endeavour to develop "parasite fighters" to escort B-29s over Korea. The 191 C-models, called F-84C from 1948, had better fuel/electric/hydraulic systems and pylons under the inner wings for 1,000lb (454kg) bombs ahead of the main gears. Then came 154 F-84Ds with thicker skins over wings and ailerons, more power, JP-4 fuel system and mechanical shortening of the gears during retraction.

By December 1950 the 27th Fighter Escort Wing was in action with the D in Korea, where the "plank-wing" (ie, unswept) F-84 soon became the No 1 AF fighter/bomber. Operating at maximum weight on hot days many T-jets ran out of runway and all full-load takeoffs were marginal. A further problem was that the jarring ride over front-line airstrips caused trouble with the intentionally loose blading in the Dash-17D engine. The addition of two 1,000lb-thrust JATO assisted-takeoff rockets in the 843 E-models was welcome, as was the greater legroom in a longer fuselage. Other additions included a radar ranging sight and more varied ordnance load. Last of the plank-wingers, no fewer than 3,025 F-84Gs were built, with a multi-framed canopy, more power, auto-pilot, boom receptacle in the left wing, and two outboard pylons for a doubled bombload. From November 1950 TAC pioneered tactical

Above: 45-59515 was a production Thunderjet, actually a P-84B-3. The Buzz Number for the T-jet was PS only until 1948; then it became FS with the change in designation to F-84.

nuclear delivery by F-84, and three years later came the LABS (low-altitude bombing system) for upward tossing of nuclear bombs from low level. Though by this time the F-84 had come to be known unofficially as "The Hog" or "Ground Hog" because of its reluctance to become airborne, G models made impressive global deployments to Japan, England and Morocco in SAC wing strength, refueled by KB-29Ps.

In 1949 Republic flew the amazing XF-91 Thunderceptor, a total redesign with swept wings and tail and outward-retracting tandem-wheel main gears. This remained experimental, but the YF-96A flown in June 1950 was a direct conversion of the F-84E with swept wings. It was redesignated YF-84F, but with the Korean war funding became easier, and the swept F model was totally redesigned with a deeper fuselage accommodating the J65 engine and deeper duct. The canopy was arranged to swing up on four parallel arms and was faired by a spine into the tall swept fin.

Geometry of the main gears was such that the track was increased to over 20ft (6m), incidentally making most of the wing box unavailable for fuel. The wing retained a hard leading edge, slotted flaps and outboard ailerons. Perforated lift dumpers were added above the wing ahead of the flaps, and per-

forated door airbrakes were added on the sides of the fuselage. All controls were fully powered, and later F-84Fs had a one-piece "slab" stabilator (horizontal tail). Another plus was a drag chute, but the big minus was lack of an afterburner. Republic built 2,476, and 237 came from a second-source line by General Motors at Kansas City.

The F-84F served with practically every friendly air force, as did the RF-84F Thunderflash which had a long camera-filled nose which displaced the air inlets to large extended wing roots. Republic built 715, 25 of which were converted as RF-84K in the FICON (Fighter Conveyor) project at Malmstrom AFB in which photo aircraft were launched from GRB-36 carrier aircraft and (hopefully) retrieved after overflying the distant target.

Above: Ingestion research with a later "plank-wing" F-84, an F-84E-30. This was the last model with a frameless canopy.

Above: Though having a G canopy, this is actually an F-84E-39 (49th FB Wing). Bombs hang ahead of main gears.

Below: In the mid-1950s it was not thought at all provocative to use "nuclear" emblems, as on this F-84F-50 Thunderstreak.

Convair B-36 Peacemaker

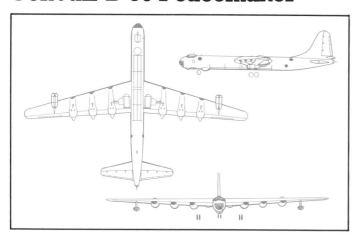

Origin: Convair Division of General Dynamics, Fort Worth, Texas.
Type: Heavy bomber, reconnaissance and weapon platform.
Engines: (B-36B) six 3,500hp Pratt & Whitney R-4360-41 Wasp Major 28-cylinder four-row radials driving pusher propellers, (B-36D) six R-4360-41 and four 5,200lb (2,360kg) thrust General Electric J47-19 single-shaft turbojets, (B-36F H and J) six 3,800hp R-4360-53 and four J47-19.
Dimensions: Span 230ft (70.14m); length 162ft (49.4m); height 46ft 9in (14.26m); wing area 4,772sq ft (443.3m^2).
Weights: Empty (B-36B) 140,640lb (63,794kg), (B-36D, J) 179,000lb (81,200kg); maximum loaded (B-26B) 278,000lb (126,000kg), (B-36D) 357,500lb (162,200kg), (B-36J) 410,000lb (185,970kg).
Performance: Maximum speed (B-36B) 381mph (613km/h), (B-36D) 439mph (707km/h), (B-36J) 411mph (662km/); service ceiling (B-36B) 42,500ft (12,955m), (B-36D) 45,200ft

Above: All jet-boosted B-36 bombers were broadly similar, though this shows a B-36J (III), so-called Featherweight, with only the tail turret for defense.

(13,780m), (B-36J) 39,900ft (12,162m); typical range with bomb load (B-36B) 8,175 miles (13,160km), (B-36D) 7,500 miles (12,070km), (B-36J) 6,800 miles (10,945km).
Armament: Normally sixteen 20mm M24A1 cannon with 9,200 rounds in eight remotely controlled turrets, in nose and tail and in six retractable installations along the fuselage, covered by sliding doors except when extended for use; internal bomb load up to 84,000lb (38,140kg).
History: First flight (XB-36) 8 August 1946, (production B-36A) 28 August 1947, (YB-36) 4 December 1947, (B-36B) 8 July 1948, (B-36D) 10 March 1949; delivery of last B-36J 14 August 1954; withdrawal from service February 1959.
User: AF.

Above: Nose of a B-36H engaged in the Continental nuclear test program at Indian Springs AFB, Nevada, in March 1953, with the 4925th Test Group (Atomic).

To meet the possible need to continue World War II after the collapse of Britain, the B-36 was planned to operate against Nazi-held Europe from bases in the United States or Canada. The specification called for a bombload of 10,000lb delivered to a target 5,000 miles from its 5,000ft runway. This was challenge enough, but the prototype program was crippled by shortages due to its low priority and need to devote all efforts to wartime production.

Only at the end of World War II did the work gather momentum, and when the XB-36 flew it was the largest and most powerful aircraft to take to the air anywhere in the world. The unarmed B-36A was used for training crews of the newly formed USAF Strategic Air Command (SAC), which included the controversial monster as its central

item of equipment. Production aircraft had bogie main gears, pressurized front and rear crew compartments linked by an 80ft trolley tunnel, comprehensive radar bombing and navigation system and automatic defensive guns with five sighting stations.

The RB-36 models had 14 cameras in place of two of the four weapon bays and a crew increased from 15 to 22. To increase over-target height and speed the B-36D was boosted by two twin-jet pods with inlet shutters which were closed in cruising flight. Main propulsion remained six Wasp Majors inside the vast wing, driving 19ft (5.79m) pusher Curtiss Electric propellers, each engine having two exhaust turbos. Technical problems were severe, and until 1951 reliability was poor.

In 1944–49 it was planned to carry the tiny egg-shaped McDonnell F-85 Goblin jet fighter inside the forward bomb bay for added defence. In 1953 FICON trials were held with 12 GRB-36Fs being used to carry and launch RF-84K man-

Martin P4M Mercator

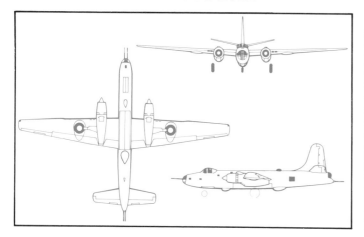

Origin: Glenn L. Martin Co, Baltimore, Maryland.
Type: Ocean patrol, (Q) ECM/Elint.
Engines: Two 3,250hp Pratt & Whitney Wasp Major R-4360-20A 28-cylinder radials, plus two 4,600lb (2,087kg) Allison J-33-10A or -12 turbojets.
Dimensions: Span 114ft (34.75m); length 85ft 3in (25.98m); height 29ft

Above: The P4M-1 had unusual engine nacelles with large piston engines in front and a jet at the back, the latter fed by inlets with doors.

9in (9.07m); wing area 1,311sq ft (121.8m^2).
Weights: Empty 43,420lb (19,695kg); maximum 83,378lb (37,820kg).

Above: This is how the Mercators looked after partial conversion to P4M-1Q standard for long-range "Ferret" (Elint) missions with squadron VQ-1.

Performance: Maximum speed (all engines) 411mph (661km/h); service ceiling 36,000ft (11,000m); range (no jet use) 3,100 miles (5,000km).

Armament: Four 20mm cannon in twin turrets at nose and tail, two 0.5in in mid-upper turret, two 0.5in aimed from beam hatches and internal bay for up to 16,000lb (7,258kg) of bombs, mines and other stores.
History: First flight 20 September 1946; service delivery (VP-21) 28 June 1950.
User: Navy.

ned reconnaissance fighters.

Some of the final examples of the 385 B-36s built were stripped of most armament and used for very long range high-altitude recon-naissance carrying large quantities of ECM and other special sensing systems. The reverberating snarl of these high-flying monsters per-vaded much of the globe during the Cold War of the 1950s. An NB-36H flew with a working nuclear reactor on board, but Convair's swept-wing all-jet YB-60 derivative was re-jected in favour of the B-52.

Above: 44-92033 was eighth of 73 B-36Bs, seen here in Arctic paint. Most of the majestic Bs were brought up to D standard, with underwing jet pods.

Designed towards the end of World War II, the P4M was one of many US types which sought to add jet speed without losing range. The centrifugal turbojets were installed in the large engine nacelles under the long-span wings; the single-wheel main gears resembled those of the B-24 and retracted outwards, the wheels being faired by blisters in the wing underside. Radar was carried aft of the weapon bay. The P4M was a big and complex air-craft, and after long development with two prototypes the 19 ap-propriated in 1947 finally entered service. Their importance lay in their conversion as P4M-1Q aircraft and subsequent ten years of dangerous Elint (electronic in-telligence) missions. On 22 August 1956 an aircraft of VQ-1 was shot down near Wenchow, the crew of 16 (six flight crew and ten mission specialists) being killed; on 16 June 1959 another was attacked by MiGs but made it back to Japan.

Right: First takeoff by the XP4M-1 prototype.

North American F-86 Sabre and FJ Fury

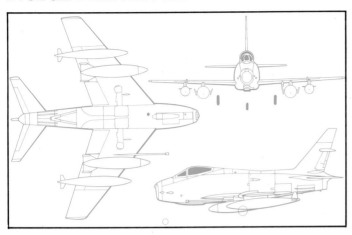

Origin: North American Aviation Inc, Inglewood, California, and (FJ) Columbus, Ohio.

Type: Basically single-seat fighter-bomber; certain versions, all-weather interceptor or (FJ) carrier-based fighter-bomber.

Engine: (FJ-1) one 4,000lb (1,814kg) thrust Allison J35-2 single-shaft axial turbojet, (F-86A) one 4,850lb (2,200kg) General Electric J47-1 of same layout, (F-86D) one J47-17 or -33 rated at 7,650lb (3,470kg) with afterburner, (F-86E) one 5,200lb (2,358kg) J47-13, (F-86F) one 5,970lb (2,710kg) J47-27, (F-86H) one 8,920lb (4,046kg) GE J73-3E of same layout, (F-86K) one J47-17B rated at 7,500lb (3,402kg) with afterburner, (FJ-2) one 6,100lb (2,767kg) J47-27A, (FJ-3, F-1C) one 7,200lb (3,266kg) Wright J65-2 (Sapphire) single-shaft turbojet, (FJ-4, F-1E) one 7,800lb (3,538kg) J65-4, (FJ-4B, AF-1E) one 7,700lb J65-16A.

Dimensions: Span (most) 37ft 1½in (11.31m) (F-86F-40 and later blocks, F-86H, K, L, F-1E, AF-1E) all 39ft 1in or 39ft 1½in (11.9m);

Above: Virtually nothing of the F-86A was left in the final model, the FJ-4B, which after 1962 became the AF-1E. Note the two pairs of airbrakes.

length (most) 37ft 6in (11.43m), (D) 40ft 3¼in (12.27m), (H) 38ft 10in (11.84m), (K) 40ft 11in (12.47m), (F-1C) 37ft 7½in (11.47m), (F-1E, AF-1E) 36ft 4in (11.07m), height (typical) 14ft 8¾in (4.47m); wing area (most) 288sq ft (26.76m²), (H, K, L) 313sq ft (29.08m²), (F/AF-1E) 339sq ft (31.49m²).

Weights: Empty (A) 10,606lb (4,620kg), (F) 11,125lb (5,045kg), (H) 13,836lb (6,276kg), (D) 13,498lb (6,123kg), (K) 13,367lb (6,063kg),(AF-1E) 13,990lb (6,346kg), maximum loaded (A) 16,223lb (7,359kg), (F) 20,611lb (9,350kg), (H) 24,296lb (11,021kg), (D) 18,483lb (8,384kg), (K) 20,171lb (9,150kg), (AF-1E) 26,000lb (11,794kg).

Performance: Maximum speed (A) 675mph, (F) 678mph (1,091km/h), (H, D, K) 692mph (1,113km/h), (AF-E) 680mph (1,094km/h), (peak Mach of all

Above: A totally redesigned all-weather interceptor, the F-86D had masses of avionics conferring automatic "collision course" aiming of a battery of rockets.

versions, usually 0.92); initial climb (clean) typically 8,000ft (2,440m)/min, (D, H, K) 12,000ft (3,658m)/min; service ceiling (clean) typically 50,000ft (15,240m); range, with external fuel, high, typically 850 miles (1,368km), except (F-1E) 2,020 miles (3,250km/h) and (AF-1E) 2,700 miles (4,344km/h).

Armament: (A, E, F) six 0.5in Colt-Browning M-3, usually with 267 rounds per gun, underwing hardpoints for two tanks or two stores of 1,000lb (454kg) each, plus eight rockets or two Sidewinders, (D, L) retractable pack of 24 2.75in folding-fin aircraft rockets, (H) four 20mm M-39 each with 150 rounds plus 1,200lb (544kg) tac-nuke or 3,000lb (1,360kg) of external stores or tanks, (K) four 20mm M-24 cannon each with 132 rounds and two Sidewinders, (FJ-2, F-1C, F-1E)

four 20mm M/24, (AF-1E) four 20mm and four tanks, six Sidewinders, five Bullpups or 5,500lb (2,495kg) of other stores.

History: First flight (XFJ-1) 27 November 1946, (XP-86) 1 October 1947; service delivery (F-86A) December 1948; first flight (YF-86D) 22 December 1949, (XFJ-2) 27 December 1951, (FJ-3) 3 July 1953, (FJ-4) 28 October 1954; final delivery (FJ-4B) October 1958.

Certainly the most famed aircraft of its day, if not of the whole period since World War II, the Sabre story began with the award of Army and Navy contracts for jet fighters in 1944. The land-based program moved fastest, with prototype contracts for the NA-140 (XP-86) signed on 18 May 1944; but by 1945 the plans were boldly discarded and replaced by a design with swept-back wings and tail.

The three Navy prototypes, ordered on 1 January 1945, were continued and flown as conventional straight-wing aircraft. The order for 100 Furies was cut to 30,

Grumman AF Guardian

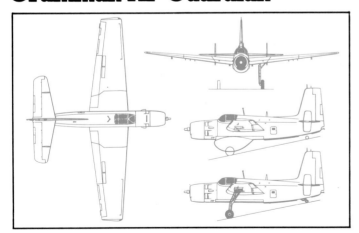

Origin: Grumman Aircraft Engineering Corporation, Bethpage, NY.

Type: Carrier-based ASW search (W) or strike (S).

Engine: One 2,400hp Pratt & Whitney Double Wasp R-2800-48W 18-cylinder radial.

Dimensions: Span 60ft 8in (18.49m); length 43ft 4in (13.2m);

Above: The AF-2W (upper side view) detected the targets while the AF-2S (remaining views) did the killing.

height 16ft 2in (4.93m); wing area 560sq ft (52m²).

Weights: (S) empty 14,580lb (6,613kg); maximum 25,500lb (11,567kg).

Above: After being replaced by the S2F-1 the Guardians went to the USN Reserve. These AF-2Ss date from 1955.

Performance: (S) maximum speed 317mph (510km/h) at altitude (about 260mph, 418·km/h at sea level); service ceiling 32,500ft (9,900m); range 1,500 miles (2,415km).

Armament: (W) none (S) two 20mm guns, one 2,000lb (907kg) torpedo, two 2,000lb or five 1,000lb (454kg) bombs, or two 1,600lb (725kg) depth charges in weapon bay.

History: First flight 19 December 1946, (AF) 17 November 1949; service delivery 18 October 1950.

User: Navy.

but VF-5A (later VF-51) operated it at sea and this otherwise undistinguished fighter was the first jet to complete an operational tour at sea.

The more dramatic XP-86 set a speed of 618mph (994km/h) even with its primitive 3,750lb (1,701kg) Chevrolet-built GE TG-180 engine and, with the 5,000lb (2,268kg) TG-190 (J47) in 1949, soon broke the world speed record at 671mph (1,080km/h) without being in any way modified from the standard fighter.

Like the P-51 before it, the F-86 was a classic design, but it entered a new realm of structural and aerodynamic technology. The two-spar wings had a thickness/chord ratio of 11 per cent at the root, thinned off to 10 per cent at the tip. Upper and lower skins were two-layer aluminum sandwiches, with integral tanks inboard. Aft of the rear spar the short main gears folded inwards to stow the multi-ply wheels with disc brakes in the fuselage. Along the leading edge were full-span slats, while on the trailing edge were hydraulically boosted ailerons and slotted flaps. The fuselage broke in two aft of the wing, the entire tail being removed for access to the slim axial engine, fed by a single duct from the fish-like nose inlet. The duct curved under the pressurized nose cockpit, with three guns each side and the nose gear lying flat beneath it. There were additional tanks under the duct and engine, large door-type speed brakes on the sides of the rear fuselage, and hydraulically boosted elevators.

In Korea the main model was the F-86E with a so-called all-flying tail, the elevators being hinged to a fully powered movable surface. This was succeeded in production by the F-86F with extra power. Almost

all Fs had a new "6-3" wing, with slats removed and the leading edge extended by 6in (159mm) at the root and 3in at the tip. At the cost of poorer low-speed handling and faster landing this gave enhanced dogfight maneuverability against the MiG-15. Last of the regular fighter/bomber Sabres was the largely redesigned F-86H with a bigger engine, deeper fuselage, larger wing and tailplane (without dihedral) and four 20mm guns.

The most numerous of all Sabres (2,504) was the totally revised F-86D "Dogship", a gunless all-weather interceptor. The forward fuselage was packed with complex avionics (which caused severe problems and delayed the program), the main feature being a large radome for the APG-36 search radar above a chin inlet. To handle the greater weight the engine was a C-series J47 with afterburner, the horizontal tail had no dihedral and armament comprised a tray of rockets in the belly which was extended into the airstream and fired automatically at the appropriate moment by the radar fire control. From 1954 the Europeans led by Fiat built the F-86K which was a D with a more primitive export-cleared radar and cannon armament. From 1956 NAA rebuilt 827 Ds into F-86L interceptors with the long-span wing, new slats, upgraded avionics and other changes.

Naturally the Navy watched the F-86 closely, and in October 1952 deliveries began of the FJ-2, used by the Marines. This was almost a hooked F-86E with four cannon. Next came the more powerful J65-engined FJ-3 with power-folding wings, extra internal fuel, an extended unslatted leading edge with fence and, in the FJ-3M, Sidewinder AAMs. The NA-208

prototype of 28 October 1954 was a total redesign leading to the FJ-4, with a wing only 6 per cent thick, forming integral tanks out as far as folding tips and with mid-span ailerons. The cockpit was raised and joined by a dorsal spine to a tall fin and small rudder reminiscent of the F-100. This model was followed by the further redesigned FJ-4B

Above: An October 1951 photo of an F-86A (then being replaced by the E-model in the squadrons) letting go a Zuni attack rocket.

with a stronger wing with six pylons and inflight-refueling probe, and many other changes. These survived after 1962 to be redesignated as AF-1E attack aircraft.

Right: The prototypes of the AF-2W (nearer camera) and AF-2S hunter/killer team.

Grumman's first attempt to replace the TBF was the XTB2F, a tremendous battle-wagon with two Double Wasps, ten 0.50in guns and a 75mm cannon! Next came XTB3F-1, with a Double Wasp and Westinghouse turbojet. The jet was removed, reducing dash speed but increasing space for crew and weapons. After much further development the same G-70 design entered production as the AF-2W (153 built) and AF-2S (193). Operating in "hunter/killer" pairs, the W with a four main crew searched for submarines with APS-20 radar and other sensors, the three-seat S then making the attack, using its own underwing APS-31 radar, AVQ-2 searchlight and sonobuoys. Production was completed in 1953 with 40 AF-3S with extra sensors including a MAD boom on the right side of the fuselage. Several units flew FFs in Korean waters.

McDonnell F2H (F-2) Banshee

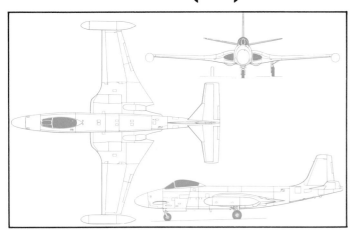

Origin: McDonnell Aircraft Company, St Louis, Missouri.
Type: Carrier-based fighter, later all weather fighter-bomber.
Engines: Two Westinghouse J34 single-shaft axial turbojets: (F2H-1) 3,000lb (1,361kg) thrust J34-22, (F-2B [F2H-2 family]) and F-2C[F2H-3)] 3,250lb (1,474kg) J34-34, (F-2D [F2H-4]) 3,600lb (1,633kg) J34-38..

Above: The F2H-4 (later F-2D) was distinguished by its extended inboard horizontal tail.

Dimensions: Span (F2-H) 41ft 6in (12.65m), (F2H-2, -3) 44ft 10in (13.67m), (F-2D) 44ft 11in; length (-1) 39ft (11.89m), (-2) 40ft 2in (12.24m), (F-2C and D) 47ft 6in (14.48m); height (-1) 14ft 2in

Above: 123318 was a regular F2H-2, seen on test from St Louis. Later a probe was fitted.

(4.32m), (other variants) 14ft 6in (4.4m); wing area 294sq ft. (27.31m²).
Weights: Empty (-1) 10,600lb (4,808kg), (F-2C, D) 12,790lb (5,800kg); maximum loaded (-1)

17,000lb (7,711kg), (-2) 22,312lb (10,270kg), (F-2C, D, clean) 19,000lb (8,618kg).
Performance: Maximum speed (-1) 587mph (944km/h), (-2, maximum weapons) 523mph (842km/h), (F-2C, D) 610mph (982km/h); initial climb (all, clean) 9,000ft (2,743m)/min; service ceiling (-1) 48,500ft (14,783m), (-2,

North American B-45 Tornado

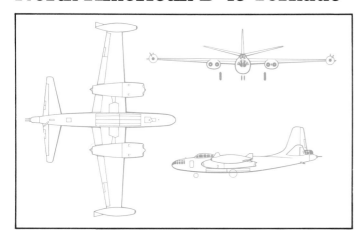

Origin: North American Aviation Inc, Inglewood, California.
Type: (B) tactical bomber, (RB) photo-reconnaissance and Elint.
Engines: (XB) four 4,000lb (1,184kg) General Electric J35-4 axial turbojets, (A) 4,000lb Allison J35-11, later retrofitted as (C), (C) General Electric J45-13/15 rated at 5,200lb (2,359kg) or 6,000lb (2,722kg) with water injection.
Dimensions: Span (A) 89ft (27.13m), (C, over tanks) 96ft (29.26m); length 75ft 4in (22.96m), (RB) 75ft 11in (23.14m); height 25ft 2in (7.67m); wing area 1,175sq ft (109.16m²).
Weights: Empty (C) 48,903lb (22,182kg); maximum (A) 95,558lb (43,345kg), (C) 112,952lb (51,235kg), (RB) 110,721lb (50,223kg).
Performance: Maximum speed 575-580mph (933km/h) at low level; service ceiling (C) 43,250ft (13,180m); range (C, max bombload) 1,910 miles (3,075km), (RB) 2,530 miles (4,070km).
Armament: Two 0.5in in tail turret, plus up to 22,000lb (9,979kg) of various bombs including nuclear,

Above: Something approaching today's winglets were fitted to the large tip tanks of the B-45C.

(RB) no bombs.
History: First flight 17 March 1947; inventory service (A) November 1948, (RB) June 1950.
User: AF.

NAA designed the Model 130 before German swept-wing data became available, but it was produced so quickly it was bought for the inventory. Features included a so-called laminar-profile wing mounted shoulder-high above a large weapon bay, twin-engine pods at a convenient height, single-wheel main gears retracting inwards into the wing, and a crew comprising two pilots in tandem under a large fixed canopy (entry by a side door), bombardier in the nose and a tail gunner. Inglewood delivered 96 B-45As, which were progressively updated, many to the standard of the ten B-45Cs with strengthened airframe, large 1,200gal (4,542lit) tip tanks, single-point fueling and water injection

Above: A B-45A-5 on bombing tests. Radar-directed bombing was quite a new technique.

engines. The most significant buy was 44 RB-45Cs with 12 cameras and, later, various sensors for the Elint intelligence mission. At first allotted to the 91st SRW, they often crossed hostile frontiers, and some

flew from England with British insignia. Later in the 1950s some Tornados were converted as target tugs, drone directors, trainers and testbeds.

Below: 48-001 was the first of the heavier and more powerful B-45Cs. Black paint on the tanks and nacelles reduced glare.

maximum weapons) 44,800ft (13,655m), (F-2C, D, clean) 56,000ft (17,000m); range (-1, -2) 1,400 miles (2,250km), (F-2C, D) 2,000 miles (3,220km).
Armament: Four 20mm M-2 cannon, each with 160 rounds; F2H-2 had four underwing racks for total load of 3,000lb (1,361kg) and F-2C and D had eight pylons for total load of 4,000lb (1,814kg); many C and D were wired for two or four Sidewinder air-to-air missiles.
History: First flight 11 January 1947; service delivery March 1949; final delivery (F2H-4) October 1953.
Users: Navy, Marine Corps.

The infant McDonnell Company's FD-1 (later FH-1) Phantom proved entirely satisfactory. From this was derived the outstanding Banshee, originally designated F2D, later F2H and finally F-2.

The design team under vice-president G. C. Covington kept to the unswept formula with two

Westinghouse axial engines inside the fattened wing roots, but with the Banshee engine thrust was adequate for a formidable multi-role machine.

The F2H was made possible by the early development by Westinghouse of an engine of 24in (0.61m) diameter, the Model 24C, which matured swiftly as the J34. The contract for two prototypes was placed on 2 March 1945, and the more powerful fighter closely followed the lines of its predecessor, with very short main gears (retracting outwards instead of inwards, the wheels being housed in the upward-folding outer wings), pressurized cockpit ahead of the wings and a fairly high tailplane (horizontal stabilizer) with dihedral. This dihedral was removed from production aircraft.

An order for 56 F2H-1 fighters was placed in May 1947, followed by one for 188 F2H-2s, with a longer fuselage for extra fuel, and 200 US gal fixed tip tanks. A further 176 -2s followed, plus 14 -2N radar night

fighter and 58 -2P photo versions. Almost all were hard-worked in Korea in carrier attack missions, usually against heavily defended point targets.

The 250 F2H-3s (F-2C) were longer still, with further increased fuel capacity and Westinghouse APQ-41 radar, this large item being accommodated by moving the guns back in the sides of the fuselage, plus a flight refueling probe. The 150 F2H-4s (F-2D) had more

powerful engines and extended-chord delta-shape tailplanes. All Banshees had laminar wings, high-gloss finish, and electric flaps, gear and wing folding. Altogether 892 were built, 60 F-2Cs being passed in 1955 to what was then the Royal Canadian Navy.

Below: 126344 was an F2H-3, which combined true all-weather capability with greatly enhanced range and endurance.

Boeing B-50 Superfortress

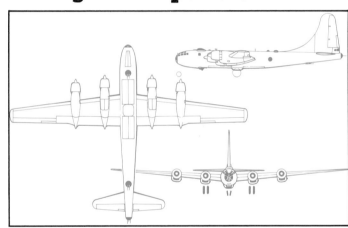

Origin: Boeing Airplane Company, Seattle, Washington.
Type: Strategic bomber with crew of 11; data for B-50D.
Engines: Four 3,500hp Pratt & Whitney R-4360-35 Wasp Major 28-cylinder four-row radials each with one CH-7A turbocharger.
Dimensions: Span 141ft 3in (43.05m); length 100ft (30.48m); height 34ft 7in (10.5m); wing area 1,720sq ft (159.8m²).
Weights: Empty 81,000lb (36,741kg); loaded 173,000lb (78,471kg).
Performance: Maximum speed 400mph (640km/h); cruising speed 277mph (445km/h); service ceiling 38,000ft (11,580m); range with maximum bombload 4,900 miles (7,886km).
Armament: Four remote-control turrets above and below, forward upper with four 0.50in guns and remainder with two; tail gunner in turret with three 0.50in; maximum internal bombload 28,000lb (12,701kg); exceptionally, could substitute bombs for drop tanks.
History: First flight 25 June 1947; last delivery (a TB-50H unarmed

Above: The B-50A retained the nose of the B-29, but the later B-50D introduced a longer nose.

bomb/nav trainer) March 1953.
User: AF.

When Japan surrendered in 1945, 5,092 B-29 bombers were canceled at the stroke of a pen. However, one batch of 200 B-29Ds was merely cut back to 60. The D model was to be powered by a completely new and very powerful engine, the Wasp Major, then giving 3,250hp and expected ultimately to yield 4,000hp in a turbo-compound version. The new bomber was also to have an airframe in lighter yet stronger alloy and many other detail changes, including a taller fin and hydraulically boosted rudder for better stability with the longer engines and paddle-blade propellers. Redesignated B-50A, this became the standard front-line aircraft of Strategic Air Command.

All of the 371 B-50s were built by Boeing, there being 80 A models, 48 Bs (increased gross weight and probe/drogue flight refueling), 222

Above: Demilitarized TB-50s trained crews for the SAC fleet of B-36 bombers.

Ds (molded nose, Flying Boom inflight-refueling receptacle and 4,000lb (1,814kg) outer-wing attachments for bombs or 700gal drop tanks), and 24 dual-control TB-50H trainers without flight-refueling provisions or armament.

These were very soon being rebuilt in a score of variants, major families being RB reconnaissance versions, WB weather reconnaissance, and KB tanker conversions using either the British hose-reel system or the Boeing Flying Boom. The KB-50J of which 112 were converted by Hayes Aircraft

for Tactical Air Command, had triple hose-reels and under-wing J47 turbojet pods to boost speed and height to improve contacts with high-performance tactical aircraft.

Airframes were strengthened, extra crew stations added, tankage increased and systems altered, armament being removed and long tailcones added. The weather aircraft were packed with special atmospheric instrumentation. The final WB-50D, WB-50H and KB-50J aircraft were not withdrawn until 1968, after seeing valued service in Vietnam.

Below: 49-360 was a B-50D-125, serving at Davis-Monthan with the 15th AF's 43rd BW.

Grumman Albatross

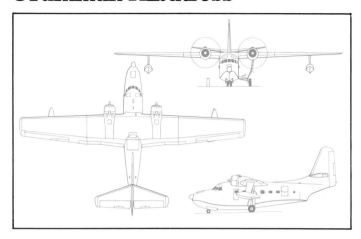

Origin: Grumman Aircraft Engineering Corporation, Bethpage, NY.
Type: Rescue and utility amphibian.
Engines: Two 1,425hp Wright R-1820-76A or -76B radials.
Dimensions: Span 96ft 8in (29.46m); length 62ft 10in (19.18m); height 25ft 10in (7.87m); wing area 1,035sq ft (96.15m²).
Weight: Empty 22,883lb (10,380kg); normal loaded weight 30,353lb (13,768kg); maximum loaded weight 37,500lb (17,010kg).
Performance: Maximum speed 236mph (379km/h); maximum cruising speed 224mph (362km/h); range with maximum fuel 2,850 miles (4,587km).
Armament: None.
History: Prototype first flight 24 October 1947; first production model entered military service July 1949; first flight HU-16B

Above: With the SA-16B (Navy UF-2) Grumman effected a complete aerodynamic redesign, with longer span and larger tail.

16 January 1956.
Users: AF, ANG, CG, Navy, Marine Corps.

Grumman was famed for its small twin-engine amphibians, such as the JRF Goose. In 1944 the company began designing a successor with more than three times the power, but with the same all-metal construction, cantilever high wing and main gears retracting into the sides of the hull. The new G-64 had a much wider and deeper hull, able to seat 20 passengers in comfort or carry 12 litter casualties.

The prototype proved so good that it was bought not only by the Navy but also the USAF. Basic missions were utility transport and

Above: 51-7169 was an SA-16A completed as a long-span SA-16B and photographed with the MATS ARS in February 1955.

air/sea rescue, but the Albatross was also used for training and many other duties. At first the Navy designation was JR2F-1 and then UF-1, while the AF called it the SA-16. In 1955 Grumman introduced the UF-2/SA-16B with new long-span wing, fixed camber instead of slats and a taller fin. Existing aircraft were rebuilt to this standard, and all were given U-16 series designations in 1962.

The Navy also operated the UF-2S anti-submarine version, with nose radar, MAD, searchlight and four wing stations for depth charges, torpedoes or rockets.

In June 1964, the first HU-16Bs arrived at Da Nang, South Vietnam, to begin flying rescue missions over

the Gulf of Tonkin. At the time, the only other rescue craft serving in Southeast Asia was the short-range HH-43 helicopter. By the end of 1965, the Albatross had landed at sea to rescue 60 downed airmen. Besides recovering crews from coastal waters, sometimes racing North Vietnamese junks to the life raft that was keeping an aviator afloat, the HU-16B functioned as a radio relay station during rescues.

Development of the HH-3E helicopter, which could refuel from the HC-130 rescue control aircraft, signaled the end of the Albatross. This helicopter could remain on station as long as the Grumman amphibian and recover a downed flier while hovering above him, without risking a landing and takeoff in the open sea. The last of these popular machines in service were Coast Guard HU-16Es and ANG transports for Army Special Forces.

Grumman F9F Panther and Cougar

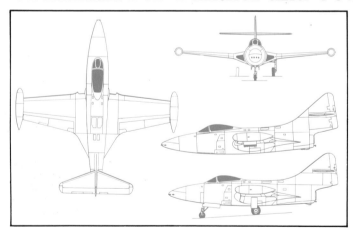

Origin: Grumman Aircraft Engineering Corporation, Bethpage, NY.
Type: Single-seat carrier-based fighter bomber; -P sub-types, photo reconnaissance; -8T, trainer.
Engine: One single-shaft centrifugal turbojet of following types: (F9F-2) Pratt & Whitney J42-2 or -6 of 5,000lb (2,270kg) or J42-8 of 5,750lb (2,608kg), (-5) Pratt & Whitney J48-2, -6 or -8 of 7,000lb (3,175kg) wet, (-6 and -8) J48-8 later uprated to 7,200lb (3,266kg) wet, (-7) Allison J33-16A of 7,000lb (3,175kg) wet.

Above: The chief difference between the F9F-2 and the F9F-5 (upper side view) was the latter's taller vertical tail. Later F9Fs were swept.

Dimensions: Span (-2, -5 excluding tip tanks) 38ft (11.58m), (-6, -8) 36ft 4in (11.1m); length (-2) 37ft 3in (11.4m), (-5) 38ft 10in (11.8m), (-6, -8) 42ft 7in (13m), (-8T) 45ft 5in (13.95m); height (-2) 11ft 4in, (-5) 12ft 3in (3.72m), (-8) 15ft (4.57m); wing area (-2 / -5) 250sq ft (23.23m²), (-6) 294sq ft (27.31m²), (-8) 337sq ft (31.31m²).

Above: A beautiful picture of one of the last of the F9F family, a Dash-8P (after 1962 redesignated an RF-9J). Grumman built 110 of this sub-variant.

Weights: Empty (-2) about 11,000lb (4,990kg), (-5) 10,147lb (4,607kg), (-8) about 13,000lb (4,897kg); loaded (-2) 19,494lb (8,840kg), (-5) 18,721lb (8,490kg), (-8) 20,000lb (9,072kg).
Performance: Maximum speed (-2) 526mph (849km/h), (-5) 579mph (931 km/h), (-8) 690mph (1,110km/h); initial climb (-2)

5,000ft (1,524m)/min, (-8) 6,100ft (1,860m)/min; service ceiling (-2) 44,600ft (13,600m), (-5) 42,800ft (13,060m), (-8) 50,000ft (15,240m); range with external fuel (-2) 1,353 miles, (-5) 1,300 miles (2,092km), (-8) 1,000 miles (1,610km).
Armament: All versions except -P photo and -8T trainer, four 20mm M-2 cannon; underwing pylons for up to 2,000lb (907kg) external load, (-8) 4,000lb.
History: First flight (XF9F-2) 24 November 1947, production (-2), 24 November 1948; (XF9F-6 Cougar) 20 September

Fairchild C-119 Flying Boxcar

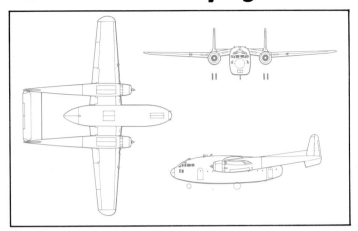

Above: This shows a C-119G, though (apart from YC-119H) all looked similar until jet pods and armament arrived.

Above: Air Force 0-52-5927 was an AC-119G Shadow gunship, which without jet pods had a ceiling below Vietnam's peaks.

Origin: Fairchild Aircraft Division, Hagerstown, Maryland; during Korean War C-119C also built by Kaiser at Willow Run, Detroit, Michigan.

Type: C-119 tactical transport; AC-119 multi-sensor armed interdiction.

Engines: In most variants two 3,350hp Wright R-3350-85WA or 3,700hp R-3350-89B Turbo-Compound 18-cylinder two-row radials (older versions, two 3,250hp Pratt & Whitney R-4360-20WA Wasp Major 28-cylinder four-row radials); (AC-119K) two additional underwing booster pods each containing a 2,850lb (1,293kg) thrust General Electric J85-17 turbojet.

Dimensions: Span 109ft 3in (34.3m); length 86ft 6in (26.36m); height 26ft 6in (8.07m); wing area 1,447sq ft (134.4m^2).

Weights: Empty (C-119B) 37,691lb (15,981kg), (C-119K) 44,747lb (20,300kg), (AC-119K) 60,955lb (27,649kg); maximum loaded (C-119B) 74,000lb (33,600kg), (C-119K) 77,000lb (34,925kg), (AC-119K) 80,400lb (36,468kg).

Performance: Maximum speed (all versions) 243-250mph (391-402km/h); initial climb (all) 1,100-1,300ft (335-396m)/min; service ceiling, typically 24,000ft (7,315m); range with maximum payload 990-1,900 miles (1,595-3,060km).

Armament: Transport versions, none; (AC-119K) two 20mm and four 7.62mm multi-barrel rapid-fire guns firing laterally, with over 100,000 rounds total ammunition. For sensors, see text.

History: First flight (C-119A) November 1947; service delivery (C-119B) December 1949, (AC-119) 1967.

Users: AF, ANG, Marine Corps.

Fairchild began the design of an improved C-82 cargo and troop transport in 1947. The C-119 introduced a new nose, with the flight deck ahead of the cargo compartment instead of on top. Fuselage width was increased, engine power was greatly increased, and the wings were strengthened for operation at higher weights.

By 1955, when production of new aircraft ceased, 946 C-119s had been delivered to US forces, plus 141 supplied to Italy, Belgium and India under assistance programs. Subsequently many ex-USAF C-119s were sold to allies.

Many earlier 119s were converted to the C-119J configuration with a rear beaver-tail openable in flight, instead of a hinged rear end that could be opened only on the ground. The AC-119G Shadow and jet-boosted AC-119K Stinger were extremely heavily armed interdiction aircraft formerly used by night in Southeast Asia. Fitted with batteries of Gatling guns, 26 AC-119Gs were delivered with night illumination systems, image intensifiers, computer fire-control, various gunsights, flare launchers, crew armor and other gear. The 26 AC-119Ks, with underwing jets, added 20mm Gatlings, forward looking infra-red (FLIR), forward and side-looking radar (SLAR) and precision nav/com equipment.

1951, (-8T) 4 April 1956; final delivery from new, October 1959.
Users: Navy, Marine Corps.

Grumman's first venture into jet propulsion was the G-70 anti-submarine aircraft with a 1,600lb (726kg) Westinghouse 19XB (J30) in the tail helping the Double Wasp in the nose. A few months later, in January 1945, work began on the G-79 night fighter, powered by four of the same small axial engines buried in the inner wing. The design was well advanced when it was ordered on 22 April 1946 as the XF9F-1 Panther.

But the US Navy had noticed the promise of the British 5,000lb (2,270kg) Rolls-Royce Nene, and imported two for testing at the Naval Air Materiel Center in Philadelphia. So well did the British engine perform that it was quickly adopted for many American aircraft, and in May 1947 Pratt & Whitney took a license and tooled up to make an Americanized version designated J42. This was substituted for the four J30s in the Grumman F9F-2, which first flew with one of the imported Nenes.

The whole design was straightforward and efficient, and no attempt was made to introduce swept-wing aerodynamics in this carrier-based fighter. The straight wings had power folding straight upwards until the permanently installed tip tanks almost met overhead. The leading edge could hinge downwards, while the trailing edge had plain flaps, with split flaps under the fuselage and giant root fillets. The engine was fed via wing-root inlets, and the nozzle was well forward under the tail, which had a high tailplane (horizontal stabilizer) with separate rudders above and below. Guns were under the nose, and main units of the tricycle landing gear folded inwards into the wing roots and fuselage.

Performance maneuverability, handling and pilot view were excellent, and service entry with VF-51 in May 1949 was painless. Grumman built 567 of the -2, as well as 54 more converted from the -3, which was ordered with the Allison J33 as insurance against failure of the J42. The J33 was also to have powered the -4, but these were completed as J48-powered -5s with a longer fuselage and taller fin. About 100 of the 761 -5s were -5P reconnaissance machines.

Panthers were the first Navy jets in action in Korea, on 6 August 1950.

Thereafter F9Fs flew nearly half the Navy and Marines combat missions, mainly for ground attack.

The -6 Cougar (G-93) introduced a swept wing of quite different profile, deliveries beginning in December 1951. Sweep angle was 35°, and the wing was fitted with slats, enlarged flaps, spoilers instead of ailerons, and fences, but lost the tip tanks. The tailplane was swept and there were many other changes. The -6 and -6P had the J48 but the -7 finally used the J33 engine. The -8 had a broader cambered wing and a longer fuselage and greater fuel capacity. Many were -8P photo and -8T dual trainer versions.

Total Cougar production was 1,985, bringing total Panther/Cougar numbers up to 3,367. After 1955 an increasing number of these fine fighters were converted as drones and for research, and in 1962 all surviving examples were given new designations in the F-9F to TF-9J series.

Below: The last version of all was the TAF-9J, former -8B close-support single-seater. Cadet Gene Porter is on the approach to CVS-16 Lexington in 1968.

Boeing B-47 Stratojet

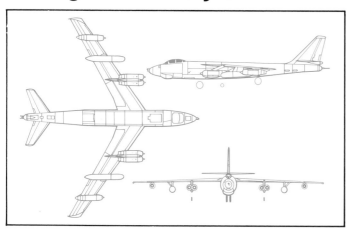

Origin: Boeing Airplane Company, Seattle, Washington.
Type: Three-seat medium bomber; data for B-47E.
Engines: Six 5,970lb (2,707kg) thrust (7,200lb/3,266kg with water injection for takeoff) General Electric J47-25A single-shaft turbojets.
Dimensions: Span 116ft (35.36m); length 109ft 10in (33.5m); height 27ft 11in (8.52m); wing area

Above: The B-47E-II was one of the USAF's most graceful airplanes, as well as one of the very first importance. Underwing tanks were usual.

1,428sq ft (132.67m²).
Weights: Empty 78,200lb (36,281kg); loaded 206,700lb (93,760kg); maximum permissible 220,000lb (99,790kg).
Performance: Maximum speed

Above: To describe the prototype XB-47 as futuristic would be an understatement. Nothing remotely like it had ever been seen before December 1947.

606mph (980km/h); combat speed 557mph (994km/h); cruise Mach number 0.75 (early in mission) to 0.82 (later); service ceiling 32,000ft (9,754m) (early) to 38,000ft (11,582m) (later), difference, as

with Mach, due to burnoff of fuel; range with maximum bombload 3,600 miles (5,794km).
Armament: Remotely controlled tail turret with twin 20mm M24A1 cannon. Internal bombload of up to 22,000lb (9,979kg), all free-fall.
History: First flight (XB-47) 17 December 1947, (B-47A) 25 June 1950, (B-47E) 30 January 1953; final delivery February 1957.
Users: AF, Navy.

Hiller UH-12 Raven

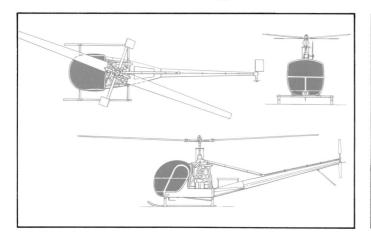

Origin: Hiller Helicopters, Palo Alto, California.
Type: Three-seat training, observation and utility helicopter.
Engine: (360) 178hp Franklin 6V4-B33 flat-six; (HTE, YH-23) 178hp Franklin O-335-4; (H-23B) 200hp O-335-6; (H-23D onwards) 250hp Lycoming O-540-23B flat-six.
Dimensions: Diameter of two-blade rotor 35ft (10.67m) or 35ft 6in (10.82m); length of fuselage (typical) 27ft 9½in (8.45m); height (typical) 9ft 9½in (2.98m); main-rotor disc area 962sq ft (89.4m²).
Weights: (H-23D) empty 1,816lb (824kg); maximum loaded 2,700lb (1,225kg).
Performance: (H-23D) maximum speed 95mph (153km/h); cruising speed 82mph (132km/h); initial climb 1,050ft (320m)/min; range without reserves 205 miles (330km).
Armament: Not usually fitted.
History: First flight (360) January 1948, (UH-12) October 1948; service delivery (H-23A) February 1950.

Above: This UH-12E (company designation) is typical of later H-23 Ravens, the most numerous (793) being the H-23G trainer.

Users: Army, Navy, AF.

Young Stanley Hiller Jr flew his first helicopter, the coaxial-rotor XH-44, in August 1944. He then made a completely fresh start, with single main rotor with hanging control column, and, by way of UH-5 Commuter prototypes, perfected a patented Rotor-Matic control system with the cyclic stick connected not to the main blades but to short auxiliary blades set at 90° and rotating as part of the main rotor. The production development was designated Model 360, and this was simplified into the open-cockpit UH-12A which was evaluated in early 1950 by the Army as the YH-23 (later given family name Raven) and by the Navy as the HTE-2.

Adopted as standard observation helicopter, the Army bought

Above: Well into the 1970s this H-23D was flying intensively at White Sands Missile Range, New Mexico.

100 H-23s with optional dual control and with equipment for carrying two litter casualties in external panniers. Five H-23As were sold to the AF, while the Navy bought 16 HTE-1 trainers followed immediately by large batches of HTE-2s with quad landing gear or skids. A batch of 273 H-23B for the Army had wheeled skids instead of tricycle gear, most going to the

school at Ft Wolters. The H-23C (145 built) had three seats side-by-side, one-piece canopy, metal blades and a new hub. The Army then took 483 H-23Ds with more power and overhaul life increased from 600 to 1,000 hours. A batch of 22 H-23Fs were four-seaters, and the last model was the OH-23G with autostabilizer and a new rotor, bringing production to over 2,000.

Below: Built 14 years earlier, the H-23A served in Korea as a casevac transport with neat enclosed litter panniers.

Boeing began studies of jet bombers in 1943 but it was the discovery of swept wings in Germany that spurred the Model 450, which the Army Air Force rather dubiously bought in prototype form in 1945. As flight test results with this dramatically futuristic design began to come in it was clear that it was an unprecedented technical success. Drag was 25 per cent lower than estimate and, though it could not fly the very long missions Strategic Air Command wanted, the B-47A was ordered in quantity in 1949. It introduced the new all-American axial turbojets, though six were needed for adequate performance and even then rocket boost was provided for maximum-weight takeoff with early versions. The podded engine installation was novel in 1947, and swept wings and tail, a remote-control tail turret (initially with twin 0.5in guns) and bicycle landing gear were other advanced features.

The whole aircraft posed gigantic technical problems. Eventually it was decided to house the fuel in the fuselage, above and at each end of the weapon bay. In turn this left the relatively very small and slender wing with very thick skins of immense strength but no room for the engines, which were mounted in what was then a novel way (which later became common). This arrangement precluded the installation of a normal landing gear, and the bicycle arrangement made it necessary to land very accurately at a speed determined according to the weight, so that the fuselage arrived nose-high with the front and rear trucks hitting the runway simultaneously. A large braking parachute was another innovation, on later versions deployed in the air. Most versions were equipped with rocket-assisted takeoff, and normal bombers seated two pilots in tandem under a giant fighter-type canopy, while the bombardier/radar navigator sat in the opaque nose, the very heavy B-47B introducing 1,500 US gal (5,680 litre) drop tanks and Flying Boom flight refueling, and the B-47E adding ejection seats and water-injection engines.

The first major service version was the B-47B, which the Korean War pitchforked into a vast production program involving Boeing-Wichita, Lockheed-Georgia and Douglas-Tulsa. In 1951 production switched to the more powerful B-47E, with 20mm guns, new radar bombing system, and a jettisonable rocket pack as well as features listed earlier. Despite a very high wing-loading the B-47E was a delight to fly. Throughout the perilous 1950s it equipped 28 SAC Bomb Wings, each with 45 combat-ready aircraft, and there were also over 300 RB-47E and RB-47K reconnaissance aircraft and ERB-47H Elint "Ferret" aircraft, some of which were shot down over international waters. More than 19 other test, weather, electronic and drone versions existed, two EB-47Es of the Navy remaining in support of Aegis system testing until late 1976.

Below: 53-4280 was the first of 32 aircraft built as RB-47H Elint platforms, packed with receivers and analysers and with three men in the bomb bay.

Douglas F3D (F-10) Skyknight

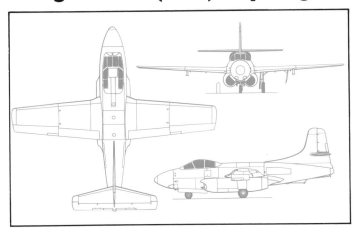

Origin: Douglas Aircraft Company, El Segundo Division, California.
Type: Carrier-based night and all-weather interceptor; later see text.
Engines: Two Westinghouse J34 axial turbojets, (1) 3,100lb (1,406kg) J34-24, (2) 3,400lb (1,542kg) J34-36 or -38.
Dimensions: Span 50ft (15.24m); length 45ft 6in (13.87m); height 16ft 1in (4.92m); wing area 400sq ft (37.16m²).
Weights: Empty (1) 14,313lb (6,492kg), (2) 18,160lb (8,237kg); maximum (1) 21,500lb (9,752kg), (2) 27,681lb (12,556kg).
Performance: Maximum speed (1) 535mph (860km/h) at medium heights, (2) 565mph (910km/h) at medium heights; service ceiling (typical) 33,000ft (10,000m); range (1) 1,297 miles (2,090km).
Armament: Four 20mm M2 cannon under nose, (1M, 2M) four AAM-N-7 Sparrow I missiles; also provision for large and varied attack loads.
History: First flight 23 March 1948,

Above: The 237 F3D-2 (F-10B) Skynights carried fuel tanks or jammer pods on wing pylons.

(2) 14 February 1951.
Users: Navy, Marine Corps.

Like most aircraft designed by Ed Heinemann the Skyknight was compact, tractable and eminently useful, and many times the users wished there were more. Had it not been chronically short of engine thrust it would have been one of the truly great US warplanes.

It was designed at the end of World War II, the order for three XF3D-1 prototypes being awarded on 3 April 1946. Westinghouse supplied the slim J34 engines hung on the flanks of the fuselage, the cumbersome APQ-35 radar, secondary avionics including the tail-warning APS-28 system, and the electric generation system. The giant nose was filled by the APQ-35 with its 300 vacuum tubes which (like other early radars) gave per-

Above: A Midnight Blue F3D-2 (later rebuilt as an EF-10B) making practise carrier landings in the mid-1950s.

petual trouble. Behind came the pilot and radar operator seated side-by-side behind flat windshields giving both a good view ahead. The pressurized cockpit, with 349 switches and circuit breakers, contained a crew escape chute leading down to a cartridge-actuated belly door serving as a windbreak. For fairly obvious reasons the F3D was soon known as Willy the Whale.

The 28 F3D-1s entered service in early 1951. They were soon augmented by the 237 F3D-2s which had to stick with the small J34 because of failure of the more powerful J46 to mature sufficiently. At first these fine airplanes went to Marine units, and on 3 November 1952 a crew from VMF(N)-513 shot down a Yak-15 in the first night jet combat. This squadron gained five more night victories, and without

publicity Willy the Whale downed more enemies than any other Navy or Marines type in the Korean War. In 1955 selected aircraft were being updated, 16 becoming -2Ms with Sparrow missiles and CW guidance antennas, others becoming -2B close-support fighters with Tiny Tim rockets and similar stores, while 55 became -2T and -2T2 trainers for radar operators and interceptor pilots.

From 1962 survivors were redesignated as F-10s, trainers becoming TF-10Bs, missile carriers MF-10Bs and a growing fleet of ECM jamming and dispensing aircraft being designated EF-10B. Not forgetting the EB-66 it is fair to describe the EF-10B as the only fully suitable and available EW platform in Vietnam, and the average flight time per aircraft of the VMCJ squadrons set new records. These aircraft had previously obtained the first signatures of Soviet surveillance and SAM radars in China and Cuba, without any interest by the media.

Piasecki (Vertol) HUP/H-25

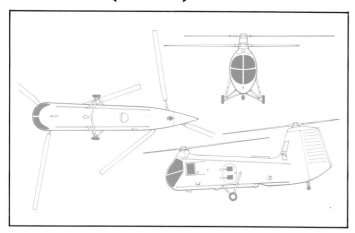

Origin: Piasecki Helicopter (after March 1956 Vertol Aircraft) Corporation , Morton, Pennsylvania.
Type: Utility, support, casevac and rescue helicopter.
Engine: One Continental R-975 seven-cylinder radial: (HUP-1) 525hp R-975-34, (rest) 550hp R-975-42 or -46A.
Dimensions: Diameter of each three-blade rotor 35ft (10.67m); length (fuselage) 31ft 10in (9.7m); height overall 13ft 2in (4.01m); total area of rotor discs 1,924sq ft (178.8m²).
Weights: (H-25A) empty 3,928lb (1,782kg); maximum loaded 6,100lb (2,767kg), (HUP) 5,750lb (2,608kg).
Performance: Maximum speed 108mph (174km/h); cruising speed 80mph (129km/h); typical range 340 miles (547km).
Armament: None (except two depth bombs under HUP-2S).
History: First flight (XHJP) March 1948; service delivery (HUP-1) February 1949.
Users: Army, Navy.

Above: The HUP-2 introduced a new tail without auxiliary fins. The H-25 Army Mule was almost identical.

In late 1945 Piasecki responded to a Navy BuAer request for a helicopter designed specifically for operation from ships, compact in design yet capable enough to fly planeguard, rescue, casevac and vertical replenishment missions. Naturally the company offered a tandem-rotor machine, compact in layout and with folding blades. Of stressed-skin construction, the PV-14 prototype was given Navy designation XHJP-1 on its acceptance in February 1946, and in 1948 an order was placed for 22 (later 32) HUP-1 Retrievers based on the refined PV-18 design with minor changes including endplate fins in the tailplane.

The cockpit housed a crew of two, and the main cabin five passengers, or three litters. Trials with a Sperry autopilot led to the more powerful autopilot-equipped HUP-

Above: A HUP-1 returns students to dry land after a water survival training exercise in Pearl Harbor in July 1963.

2, with no tail apart from the integral giant fin. This type had a rescue hoist working through a floor hatch, and a proportion of the 165 delivered had dunking sonar and were HUP-2S anti-submarine machines (possibly the first ever delivered).

In 1951 work began on the H-25A Army Mule with hydraulically boosted flight controls, strong cargo floor and provision for casualties. Piasecki built 70,

alongside the last Navy batch of 50 HUP-3s, of which three went to Canada. Both could carry a slung load, and the Navy model had a 400lb (181kg) hoist and autopilot. These helicopters were fully successful in their limited way, but the substantial uprating in capability that would have followed the switch to the R-1300 engine was finally rejected. By 1962 only the HUP-2 and -3 were still in the inventory, being redesignated UH-25B and -25C.

Below: HUP-3 No 147595, flying with NC-1 "Angels" on planeguard and SAR duty aboard Midway.

Martin P-5 Marlin

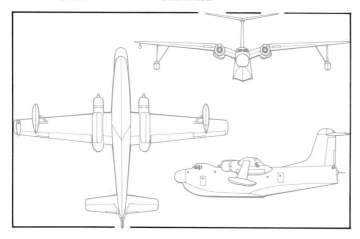

Origin: The Martin Company, Baltimore, Maryland.
Type: Maritime patrol and anti-submarine flying boat (boat seaplane) with normal crew of eight, with sub-types described in text.
Engines: (P-5A family) two 3,250hp Wright R-3350-30WA Turbo-Compound 18-cylinder two-row compound radials, (B) 3,700hp (wet rating) R-3350-32W.

Above: P5M-2 is distinguished from its predecessor by T-tail. The small wing-tip pod houses a searchlight.

Dimensions: Span (A) 118ft (36m), (B family) 118ft 2in; length (A, typical) 90ft 8in (27.69m), (B, typical) 101ft 1in (30.9m); height (A) 37ft 3in (11.35m), (B) 32ft 8in (9.95m); wing area 1,406sq ft (130.62m²).

Above: Among the last flying boats in service, the SP-5Bs of VP-40 operated on ASW patrol from Cam Ranh Bay in 1967.

Weights: Empty (A, typical) 47,200lb (21,400kg), (B, typical) 50,485lb (22,900kg); maximum loaded (A) 72,837lb (33,040kg), (B) 85,000lb (38,555kg).
Performance: Maximum speed (A) 262mph (421km/h); (B) 251mph

(403km/h); initial climb 1,200ft (366m)/min; service ceiling (A) 22,400ft (6,827m), (B) 24,000ft (7,315m); range with full combat ordnance load (A) 3,600 miles (5,800km), (SP-5B) 2,050 miles (3,300km).
Armament: (A) two 20mm M-2 cannon in radar-directed tail turret; four 2,000lb (907kg) bombs or two torpedoes in nacelles or eight 1,000lb (454kg) bombs on

North American AJ Savage

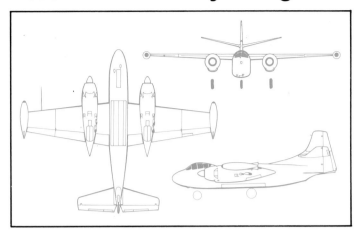

Origin: North American Aviation Inc, Inglewood and Downey, California, and (2) Columbus, Ohio.
Type: Carrier-based attack bomber, (2P) photo reconnaissance, (KA) flight-refueling tanker.
Engines: (XAJ) Two 2,300hp Pratt & Whitney Double Wasp R-2800-44 and one 4,000lb (1,814kg) Allison J33-19 turbojet, (1) 2,400hp R-2800-44W and 4,600lb (2,087kg) J33-10, (2, 2P) 2,500hp R-2800-48 plus J33-10.
Dimensions: Span (over tip tanks) 75ft 2in (22.9m); length 63ft 10in (19.46m) (2P slightly longer); height 20ft 5in (6,23m); wing area 835.5sq ft (77.62m²).
Weights: Empty (1) 29,203lb (13,246kg); maximum (1) 52,862lb (23,978kg), (2) 59,750lb (27,103kg).
Performance: Maximum speed (1) 472mph (760km/h) at 35,000ft (10,670m), (piston engines alone) 401mph (645km/h); service ceiling 45,000ft (13,720m); range (max bombload) 1,670 miles (2,690km).

Above: Even from three angles the original AJ-1 gave few hints of having a jet in its rear fuselage. Most became tankers.

Armament: Internal bay for nuclear weapon or 10,500lb (4,763kg) of conventional bombs.
History: First flight 3 July 1948; service delivery September 1949.
User: Navy.

Ordered on 24 June 1946, the NA-147 prototype (XAJ-1) was intended to combine nuclear attack capability with strategic range, jet speed and the ability to fly from a carrier. The crew of three occu-

Above: The AJ-2P photo version became the RA-2 in 1962 and was not finally replaced by the RA-3B until 1964.

pied a pressurized cockpit, and the booster turbojet was fed from a flush inlet in the top of the rear fuselage. Despite problems with the jet and need for two different fuel systems, the Savage proved an outstanding machine and the Downey plant delivered 55 AJ-1s, the first unit being VC-5. The Columbus plant (ex-Curtiss) then delivered 70 AJ-2s with increased fuel capacity and a horizontal tail without dihedral, plus 30 camera-

equipped AJ-2P. Redesignated A-2A and -2B from 1962, many became hosereel-equipped KA-2s.

Below: 134072 was the very last AJ-2 built, after 1962 still flying from Midway as a KA-2B air-refueling tanker. A common misapprehension is the belief that the J33 turbojets were removed at this time.

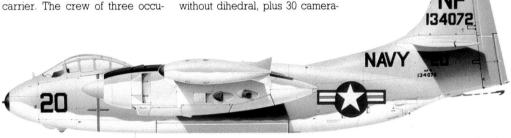

underwing racks, with wide range of other stores; (B) no guns, but same offensive weapon load.
History: First flight (XP5M-1) 30 April 1948, (production P5M-1) 22 June 1951; service delivery December 1951; first flight (P-5B) 29 April 1954; final delivery 20 December 1960.
Users: Navy, CG.

Designed as a logical successor to the PBM, the Marlin turned out to be both the final type of Martin aircraft to go into service and the final operational flying boat outside the Soviet Union and Japan.

Its main advances were much more powerful and efficient engines and a new hull of greater length/beam ratio and improved hydrodynamic form. Another major advance was replacing the bow turret with the search radar, the large and powerful APS-80 occupying a huge radome and giving outstanding power and, for its day, good discrimination. The US Navy received 160 P5M-1s by 1954, most seeing active service at Iwakuni, Japan, and other bases in support of

activities in the Korean War.
Under the 1962 designation system these boats became the P-5A, the specialized anti-submarine version with the Julie/Jezebel underwater detection system and an ASQ-8 MAD "stinger" projecting from the top of the tail being designated SP-5A. In 1951 the Marlin was revised with a

T-tail and lowered bow chine, and 103 of the new P5M-2 model were delivered by 1957, followed by 12 for the French Aéronavale.
Redesignated SP-5B these continued in first-line service until 1968, the last squadron being VP-47. In Vietnam they patrolled the Gulf of Tonkin round the clock, and in 1964 one SP-5B was evaluated with a

booster turbojet in the rear fuselage. Sub-types included the P5M-1G rescue aircraft of the Coast Guard and the TP-5A anti-submarine trainers.

Below: Early P5M-1s of a Navy patrol squadron in transit across the Pacific to Iwakuni, Japan, during the Korean War.

Northrop F-89 Scorpion

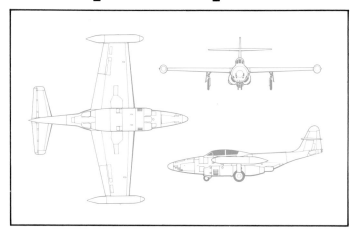

Origin: Northrop Aircraft Inc., Hawthorne, California.
Type: Two-seat all-weather and night interceptor.
Engines: Two Allison J35 single-shaft axial turbojets with simple afterburners (augmented ratings

Above: The F-89C had six 20mm guns, and internally balanced elevators. Later the tip tanks were given fins.

given): (XF-89) 3,750lb (1,701kg) J34-13, (F-89A) 6,800lb (3,084kg),

Above: F-89D-30 No 51-11416 ripples its 104 rockets. The rocket flames escaped around apertures ahead of the tip fuel.

J35-21; (B) 7,000lb (3,175kg) J35-33, (C) 7,500lb (3,402kg) J35-35,

(D, H, J) 7,500lb J35-47.
Dimensions: Span (A) 56ft (17.07m), (remainder, over pods) 59ft 8in (18.18m); length (A) 53ft 6in (16.33m), (remainder) 53ft 10in (16.4m); height (typical) 17ft 7in (5.36m); wing area 562sq ft (52.21m²).

Vought F7U Cutlass

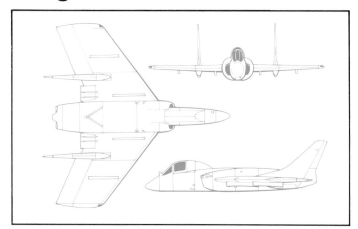

Origin: Chance Vought Aircraft, Dallas, Texas.
Type: Carrier-based fighter-bomber; (P) reconnaissance.
Engines: (-1) two Westinghouse J34-32 single-shaft turbojets each rated at 4,200lb (1,905kg) with Solar afterburner; (-3) two Westinghouse J46-8B each rated at 6,000lb (2,722kg) with afterburner.
Dimensions: Span 39ft 8in (12.02m); length (-1) 39ft 7in, (-3, -3M) 44ft 3in (13.48m), (-3P) 46ft 4in; height (-1) 9ft 10in (3m), (-3) 14ft 7in (4.45m); wing area 496sq ft (46.08m²).
Weights: Empty (-1) 11,870lb (5,385kg), (-3M) 15,900lb (7,212kg); maximum loaded (-1) 16,840lb (7,640kg), (-3) 31,642lb, (-3M) 32,954lb (16,950kg).
Performance: Maximum speed (-1) 665mph (1,070km/h), (-3M) clean 696mph (1,120km/h), with missiles 648mph (1,043km/h); initial climb (-1) 11,280ft (3,438m)/min, (-3, clean) 17,600ft (5,380m)/min service ceiling (all) about 41,000ft (12,500m); range with maximum fuel (-1) 600 miles (966km), (-3M, -3P) 1,400 miles (2,250km).
Armament: (-1) four 20mm M-2

Above: Though the F7U-3M is shown, the regular Dash-3 was closely similar apart from provision for Sparrows.

cannon under cockpit floor, (-3) four 20mm M-2 above inlet ducts, plus four wing pylons for up to 5,500lb (2,495kg) weapons, (-3M) as -3 but equipped to carry up to four Sparrow I air-to-air missiles; (-3P) none.
History: First flight (XFU-1) 29 September 1948, (production -1) March 1950, (prototype -3) 12 December 1951; combat delivery (-3) June 1954.
Users: Navy, Marines.

Designed in 1946, when fighter aerodynamics were in turmoil, the unique Cutlass had a 38° swept wing carrying powered elevons and twin vertical stabilizers. The usual rear fuselage and tail were absent! After building three prototypes and 14 production F7U-1 day fighters — used only as trainers at Corpus Christi — the whole aircraft was redesigned as the V-346A with more powerful engines.
Westinghouse suffered severe

Above: BuNo 128454 was the fourth F7U-3, and first to look like the production model. Span was increased 12in (0.3m).

Below: No 128475 was a regular F7U-3, seen here on the deck of USS Coral Sea in 1955. Behind is a Cougar from Pax River.

engine problems, and the first 16 F7U-3 had non-afterburning Allison J35-29 engines. Finally, by December 1955, Vought delivered 288 of the far more capable -3 series which equipped 13 Navy and Marine squadrons ashore and afloat. The last 98 were missile-armed F7U-3Ms, the first fighters to carry the Sparrow I missile. Vought also

delivered 12 F7U-3P photo-reconnaissance versions.
Despite a poor accident record and excessive maintenance needs, the Cutlass was popular, being unbreakable in alleged 16g maneuvers, exciting to fly, and an excellent aerobatic machine. But the program was stopped sharply once the Crusader flew.

Weights: Empty (A) 19,800lb (8,981kg), (H) 26,100lb (11,840kg); loaded (A) 32,500lb (14,740kg), (D) 41,000lb (18,600kg), (H, J) 46,000lb (20,865kg).
Performance: Maximum speed (A) 570mph (917km/h), (D) 610mph (982km/h), (H, J) 595mph (958km/h); initial climb (typical) 5,250ft (1,600m)/min; service ceiling (typical) 36,000ft (10,980m); range (A) 1,300 miles, (remainder, typical) 1,000 miles (1,610km).
Armament: (A, B, C) six 20mm M-24 cannon each with 200 rounds, (D) 104 Mighty Mouse 2.75in FFAR (folding-fin aircraft rockets) in wing-tip pods, all guns being removed, (H) six GAR-1D or -2A (later AIM-4C or -4D) Falcon semi-submerged around tip pods, plus two MB-1 (AIR-2A or -2B) Genie on wing pylons, plus 42 FFAR inside tip pods, (J) two AIR-2A or -2B Genie on wing pylons, plus four AIM-4C or -4D on wing pylons (tip pods fuel only).
History: First flight (XF-89) 16 August 1948, (YF-89A) 27 June 1950, (YF-89D, converted from B) June 1952; final delivery from new (H) 1956.
Users: AF, ANG.

Having cut their teeth with the P-61, Northrop naturally responded to an Army Air Force request dated September 1945 for a jet night fighter. The N-24 (XP-89) prototype, painted black, was first flown at Edwards AFB in mid-1948, but subsequent development was rather slow, partly because improved versions kept emerging.

It was a large but slim machine, with a thin but very broad unswept wing passing below the crew but above the two rather primitive engines. To fit inside the wing the main wheels were very thin and so were of extraordinary diameter (crews said they came from old steam locomotives). All controls were powered, and the large ailerons could open into upper and lower halves to serve as "decelerons" (ailerons/air brakes) to assist the pilot in getting into firing position behind his quarry. The observer in the back seat managed the SCR-720 radar, carried ahead of the six cannon.

After delivering 30 F-89As, from July 1950, production was switched to the F-89B with APG-33 radar, a Lear autopilot, and ILS with Zero Reader cross-pointer instrument. These were followed by 164 F-89Cs with progressively more powerful engines, internal elevator balance weights and finned tip tanks to try to overcome severe flutter problems.

Then came 682 of the dramatically different F-89D with an autopilot linked to a big new Hughes radar to fly the aircraft automatically on a collision course.

The D naturally had a longer reprofiled nose, and the collision-course attack was made with new armament of 104 rockets in giant tip-mounted pods which also housed fuel. Engine power was again increased.

Final batches added up to 156 of the H model (bringing the total to 1,050) armed with guided missiles, 350 of the D-type being similarly updated and restyled F-89J. After arduous service all over the world the Scorpion passed to the Air National Guard from 1958 and out of service in 1963. In many ways popular and forgiving aircraft, the F-89 never had really adequate engine power, and its service career was marred by a few inflight structural failures from various causes.

Northrop built only a mock-up of the F-89F, with giant mid-span pods housing landing gears, extra fuel and advanced AAMs.

Piasecki (Vertol) H-21 Shawnee/Work Horse

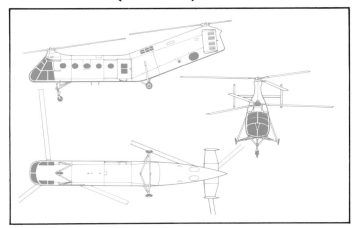

Above: USAF Work Horses were unpainted except for Arctic Red as on this H-21B (O-53-4323) from Elmendorf.

Below: In contrast Army Shawnees were olive drab. These from the 121st Aviation Co. were at Bac Lieu with Viet Marines.

Origin: Piasecki Helicopter Corporation (from March 1956 Vertol Aircraft), Morton, Pennsylvania.
Type: Transport, assault and rescue helicopter; data for H-21C
Engine: One 1,425hp Wright Cyclone R-1820-103 nine-cylinder radial.
Dimensions: Diameter of each main rotor 44ft 6in (13.56m); length of fuselage 52ft 4in (15.98m); height 15ft 1in (4.6m); total rotor-disc area 3,111sq ft (289m²).
Weights: Empty (HRP-2) 5,054lb (2,295kg), (H-21C) 8,700lb (3,946kg); loaded (HRP-2) 6,978lb (3,168kg), (H-21C) 13,500lb (6,124kg).
Performance: Maximum speed (H-21) 130mph (209km/h); cruising speed 98mph (158km/h); normal range 300 miles (482km).
Armament: In US service, none.
History: First flight (HRP-2) 1949, (YH-21) 11 April 1952, (production H-21A) October 1953.
Users: AF, Army, Marine Corps, Coast Guard.

In June 1948 Piasecki received a

Above: Originating with the HRP-2, the H-21 Work Horse (AF) and Shawnee (Army) had more powerful R-1820 engine.

Navy contract for an improved version of the HRP-1 with an all-metal fuselage. The resulting HRP-2, or PD-22, in fact also introduced a completely redesigned fuselage seating the two crew side-by-side instead of in tandem, and providing a rear cabin measuring 20ft (6.1m) long, 68in (1.72m) wide and 66in (1.67m) high. The better surface profile improved flight performance compared with the HRP-1, but otherwise the HRP-2 resembled the earlier machine. Five went via the Marines to the USCG.

Evaluation by the AF led to an order for an uprated Arctic rescue version, the H-21, with R-1820 engine and all-terrain tricycle landing gear comprising three inflated pontoons each housing a wheel. The 18 initial YH-21 service test helicopters and 38 H-21A Work Horses for inventory had R-1820-103 engines flat-rated at 1,150shp, but the main batch of 163 H-21Bs had the fully rated engine, as well as an

autopilot, armor and provision for external tanks. In the rescue role, with 400lb (182kg) hydraulic hoist, all versions were limited on volumetric grounds to 12 litters, but the H-21B could carry 20 armed troops compared with the previous 14. The Army bought a

further 334 H-21C Shawnees (CH-21C from 1962), with the side winch replaced by a ventral winch and cargo sling of 4,000lb (1,814kg) capacity. In Vietnam many carried light armament. Two became T58 turbine-engined H-21Ds.

Martin/GD B-57 Canberra

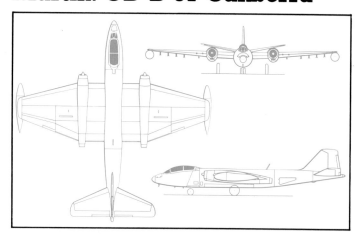

Origin: Basic design English Electric Co; B-57 produced by The Martin Company, Baltimore, Maryland; (RB-57F) General Dynamics, Fort Worth, Texas.
Type: Two-seat tactical attack and reconnaissance, (RB versions, strategic reconnaissance at extreme altitude).
Engines: (A, B, C, E, G) two 7,220lb (3,275kg) thrust Wright J65-5 (US Sapphire) single-shaft turbojets, (D) two 11,000lb (4,990kg) Pratt & Whitney J57-37A two-shaft turbojets, (F) two 18,000lb (8,165kg) Pratt & Whitney TF33-11A two-shaft turbofans and two 3,300lb (1,500kg) Pratt & Whitney J60-9 single-shaft turbojets.
Dimensions: Span (A, B, C, E, G) 64ft (19.51m), (D) 106ft (32.3m), (F) 122ft 5in (37.32m); length (A, B, C, D, E) 65ft 6in (19.96m), (G) 67ft (20.42m), (F) 69ft (21.03m); height (A, B, C, E, G) 15ft 7in (4.75m), (D) 14ft 10in (4.52m), (F) 19ft (5.79m); wing area (most) 960sq ft (89.19m^2), (F) 2,000sq ft (185.8m^2).

Above: This B-57B is typical of derived versions including the B-57C and E series.

Weights: Empty (A, B, C, E, typical) 26,800lb (12,200kg), (G) about 28,000lb (12,700kg), (D) 33,000lb (14,970kg), (F) about 36,000lb (16,330kg); maximum loaded (A) 51,000lb (23,133kg), (B, C, E, G) 55,000lb (24,950kg), (D) not disclosed, (F) 63,000lb (28,576kg).
Performance: Maximum speed (A, B, C, E, G) 582mph (937km/h), (D, F) over 500mph (800km/h); initial climb (A, B, C, E, G) 3,500ft (1,070m)/min, (D, F) about 4,000ft (1,220m)/min; service ceiling (A, B, C, E, G) 48,000ft (14,630m), (D) 65,000ft (19,800m), (F) 75,000ft (22,860m); maximum range with combat load (high altitude) (A, B, C, E, G) 2,100 miles (3,380km), (D) about 3,000 miles (4,828km), (F) about 3,700 miles (5,955km).
Armament: (A and all RB versions) none, (B, C, E, G) provision for four 20mm or eight

Above: This B-57E tug was over Edwards on 6 September 1956. It later became an EB-57E (EW).

0.5in guns fixed in outer wings (very rarely, other guns fixed in forward fuselage); internal bomb load of 5,000lb (2,268kg) on rotary bomb door plus eight rockets, two 500lb (227kg) bombs or other stores on underwing pylons (while retaining tip tanks).
History: First flight (Canberra in UK) 13 May 1949, (production B-57A) 20 July 1953, (B) 28 June 1954.
Users: AF, ANG.
In October 1949 Martin flew the extremely advanced XB-51 trijet attack bomber; but this proved to be inflexible and operationally unattractive. The seemingly less advanced British Canberra, on the other hand, proved to have precisely the qualities the Air Force was seeking, with near-perfect operational flexibility, versatility, outstanding maneuverability, long range and endurance and a good weapon load.

The decision to adopt this foreign combat aircraft — a step unprecedented in the US since 1918 — was swiftly followed by choice of Martin and development of the B-57A as a version built to US standards with many small modifications. The main batch comprised B-57B tandemseaters, with dual C trainers and multi-role (tactical bomber/recce/trainer/tug) E models.

Martin also made 20 grossly redesigned RB-57D reconnaissance aircraft with J57 engines on greatly extended wings. Though incapable of Canberra-style maneuvers, or of high speed at low levels, the D flew many valuable multi-sensor missions over a great deal of Communist territory with the USAF and Nationalist Chinese. There were at least three D subtypes, some having countermeasures and sensing pods on the wing tips and/or tail and one version having large radomes at each end of the fuselage for strategic electronic reconnaissance. Another B-57D task was to work

Lockheed F-94 Starfire

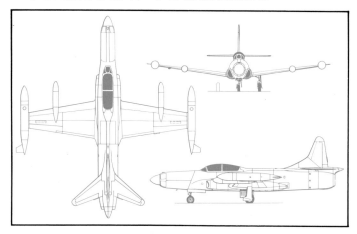

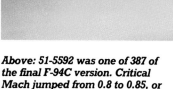

Origin: Lockheed Aircraft Corporation, Burbank, California.
Type: Two-seat night and all-weather fighters.
Engine: (F-94A and B) one 6,000lb (2,722kg) thrust J33-33 single-shaft centrifugal turbojet with Solar afterburner, (F-94C) one 8,750lb (3,970kg) thrust Pratt & Whitney J48-5 Turbo-Wasp

Above: The F-94C entered service with this pointed radome and extra pods of FFAR rockets on the redesigned thin wings.

(R-R Tay derived) centrifugal turbojet with afterburner.
Dimensions: Span (basic) 38ft 10½in (11.85m), (F-94C) 42ft 5in (12.9m); length (F-94A) 40ft 1in (12.2m), (F-94C) 44ft 6in (13.57m);

Above: 51-5592 was one of 387 of the final F-94C version. Critical Mach jumped from 0.8 to 0.85, or Mach 1 in a dive!

height (F-94A) 12ft 8in (3.89m), (F-94C) 14ft 11in (4.56m); wing area 238sq ft (22.11m^2).
Weights: Empty (F-94A) 11,090lb (5,030kg), (F-94C) 13,450lb (6,100kg); maximum loaded

(F-94A) 15,710lb (7,125kg), (F-94B) 16,500lb (7,484kg), (F-94C) 24,200lb (10,980kg).
Performance: Maximum speed (A) 606mph (975km/h), (C) 646mph (1,040km/h); initial climb (A) 3,300ft (1,000m)/min, (C) 7,980ft (2,432m)/min; service ceiling (all) about 48,000ft (14,630m); range (all) 1,100-1,250 miles (1,770-2,000km).

Left: This WB-57F (new serial 63-13288) was pictured over Death Valley, California, in February 1968, collecting air samples after an underground nuclear explosion.

On 3 April 1965 a C-130 equipped with flares and accompanied by two B-57s flew a night mission over routes 12, 23 and 121 in the southern panhandle of Laos. The mission marked the beginning of Operation Steel Tiger, an interdiction campaign against enemy troop and supply movements. The B models departed Southeast Asia in 1969, leaving behind the squadron of Gs.

The B-57G could find the enemy at night and attack him. Faced with serious problems regarding night strike operations, the AF decided to equip three B-57Bs with an infrared sensor. The aircraft with the modification, known as Tropic Moon II, arrived at Phan Rang on 12 December 1967. Another infrared modification became known as Tropic Moon III. This involved considerable equipment at great cost and eventually included new weapons, computers and navigational system, additional armor plating, new ejection seats, and self-sealing tanks. A total of 16 B-57Gs served as night intruders until the spring of 1972.

Reconnaissance variants of the B-57 flew missions in Southeast Asia employing cameras and infrared sensors. Use of the latter device, which proved valuable against an enemy which moved by night, was pioneered by the RB-57E. The last B-57s served as EW targets and tugs with the ANG until 1982.

with U-2Ds in upper-atmospheric sampling, but all of this type were grounded in 1963 as a result of structural fatigue.

It was partly because of the interim nature of the D that, in 1960, General Dynamics was entrusted with the task of designing and building an even more dramatic high-altitude B-57 version, the F. Though the 21 of this type were not new aircraft, little of the old was evident. The wing was entirely new, with more than double the area of the original Canberra wing and a new fatigue-resistant multi-spar structure. Most of the fuselage was new, as was the vertical tail. There were four underwing hard points for pylons, two of which were often occupied by the J60 boost engine pods supplementing the large turbofans. The nose was packed with electronics, and multi-sensor equipment could be seen all over the fuselage. Various F models operated from the United States (notably from Kirtland AFB), Europe, Middle East, Japan, Alaska, Panama, Argentina and possibly other countries.

Meanwhile many of the B, C and E models were updated by the fitment of modern night and all-weather systems.

Right: Four of the 110 of the original A-model, with F-80 type tip tanks. Delivery to 319FS(AW) began in June 1950.

Armament: See text.
History: First flight (F-94A) 16 April 1949, (C) 19 January 1950; final delivery May 1954.
Users: AF, ANG.

In 1949 development of the Northrop F-89 night fighter appeared to be slow, and the AF accepted Lockheed's proposal to provide a low-risk and relatively cheap interim night interceptor based on the lately flown T-33 two seater.

No attempt was made to use automatic radar control of trajectory to salvo rockets, and the F-94A was a fairly basic aircraft. It required an afterburner to lift it off with 940lb (426kg) of added radar even though the nose armament was cut from six 0.5in to four.

The interim F-94B had much bigger Fletcher tanks centered on the wing tips instead of hung beneath, and improved all-weather instruments. This proved a useful aircraft, despite slightly marginal performance at full load, an in 1951-52 Lockheed delivered 357, compared with only 110 of the A model.

The redesigned F-94C Starfire had much more thrust, a thinner wing, swept tailplane and much longer fuselage with Hughes E-5 radar. Gross weight jumped by 50 per cent, and handling characteristics changed completely. Surrounding the radar were arranged 24 Mighty Mouse rockets, and a further 24 were salvoed from pods projecting ahead of the wing. Despite its straight wing and centrifugal engine the F-94C could go supersonic in a dive, and it had no flight limitations.

Altogether 853 F-94s were delivered, the A and B models being used in Korea on various very difficult night missions.

North American T-28 Nomad

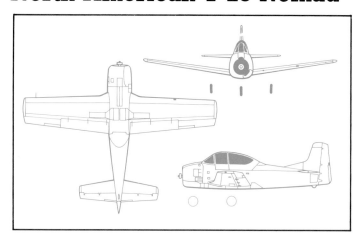

Origin: North American Aviation Inc, Inglewood, California; data for T-28D.
Type: Two-place armed counter-insurgence aircraft.
Engine: One 1,425hp Wright R-1820-86 nine-cylinder radial.
Dimensions: Span 40ft (12.19m) to 40ft 7½in (12.35m); length 32ft 10in (10.0m) to 33ft 8in (10.26m); height 12ft 8in (3,86m); wing area 272.1sq ft (25.3m²).
Weights: Empty 7,750lb 3,515kg); normal takeoff weight 15,600lb (7,075kg).
Performance: Maximum level speed 360mph (580km/h); cruising speed 207mph (333km/h); rate of climb at sea level 5,130ft (1,560m)/min; maximum ferrying range 2,760 miles (4,440km).
Armament: Two 0.50in guns, 1,800lb (816kg) of rockets and bombs.

Above: The T-28A was powered by the small seven-cylinder version of the Cyclone. Later models had the nine-cylinder.

History: First flight 26 September 1949, (T-28D) July 1961.
Users: AF, Navy.

NAA produced the T-28A to meet an AAF (later AF) need for a more modern successor to the T-6 with a large frameless canopy and tricycle landing gear. Powered by an 800hp Wright R-1300-1A seven-cylinder engine, it proved most successful and 1,194 were delivered. The Navy adopted the same basic design, but for its T-28B Trojan specified the 1,425hp nine-cylinder Cyclone, giving much higher performance; 489 were delivered, followed by 299 carrier-equipped T-28Cs.

Above: One of the first T-28D conversions looking for Viet Cong as early as 1962. Rebuilds were done by NAA and Fairchild.

Many of these early trainer versions were converted as DT-28 drone control aircraft.

After 1960 strong interest in Co-In type aircraft resulted in conversion of large numbers of AF T-28s for attack and close-support missions. They first went to South Vietnam in the Farm Gate assistance program in 1962, at that time still with the smaller engine. Later all became T-28D Nomads.

The T-28s normally flew in two-plane formations for day strikes against previously selected targets or for armed escort of A-26 or helicopter operations. During daylight, the Nomad usually attacked in a shallow

dive, releasing its bombs and recovering at 2,000ft (618m) to avoid small arms fire, for shock effect on the enemy, as well as to lighten the aircraft and increase its maneuverability. Night operations usually consisted of armed reconnaissance by single T-28s. At night pilots could dive below 2,000ft.

One of the most successful uses of the T-28 was on hunter-killer missions teamed with a Forward Air Control (FAC) O-1F that mounted a starlight scope. Circling 1,000ft (309m) above the O-1F, the T-28 pilot waited for the Forward Air Control aircraft to detect trucks with his scope, then dived to the attack according to instructions. The T-28 could also perform the same mission with any aircraft equipped with a night vision scope, such as the C-123 or C-130.

Sikorsky S-55, H-19

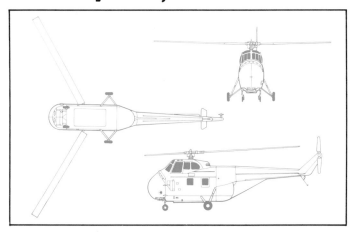

Origin: Sikorsky Aircraft Division of United Aircraft, Bridgeport, Connecticut.
Type: Multi-role helicopter (see text).
Engine: (Initial versions) one 600hp Pratt & Whitney R-1340-40 or -57 Wasp nine-cylinder radial, (S-55A family) 700hp Wright R-1300-3 Cyclone seven-cylinder radial, (S-55T) Garrett TSE331-3U turboshaft flat-rated at 650shp.
Dimensions: Diameter of three-blade rotor (S-55) 49ft (14.94m), (S-55A) 53ft (16.15m); length overall (rotors turning) typically

Above: S-55 with developed tail boom and fin-like rear-rotor pylon which became standard.

59ft 11in (18.26m); length of fuselage (most) 41ft 8½in (12.71m) to 42ft 3in (12.88m); overall height (typical) 13ft 4in (4.06m); main-rotor disc area (53ft) 2,206sq ft (20.5m²).
Weights: empty (YH-19) 3,992lb (1,811kg), (typical simple H-19 or Whirlwind) 4,395lb (1,994kg), (H-19D) 5,250lb (2,381kg); maximum loaded (YH) 6,500lb (2,948kg); (most R-1340 types)

Above: A Navy HRS-3 from USS Glacier (AGB-4) during Deep Freeze Four in October 1958.

6,800lb (3,084kg), (R-1300, usually) 7,200lb (3,266kg).
Performance: Maximum speed (all, typical) 105mph (169km/h); cruising speed (piston engined, typical) 85mph (137km/h); range with max payload, no reserves (typical) 350 miles (563km).
Armament: See text.
History: First flight (YH-19) 10 November 1949; service delivery (Navy) 27 December 1950.

Users: AF, Army, Navy, Marine Corps, Coast Guard.

The S-55 was one of the greatest single advances in helicopter design, though it adopted a configuration now obsolete. In order to carry a substantial payload in a cabin under the rotor, so that varying load would have minimal effect on center of gravity position, the engine had to be placed either behind (as in the Kaman HOK) or in the nose. The latter arrangement was chosen, the engine being accessible via

Cessna O-1 Bird Dog

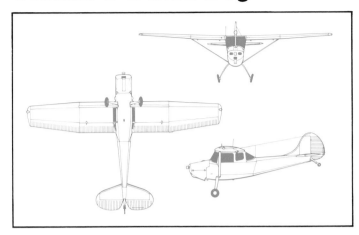

Origin: Cessna Aircraft Company, Wichita, Kansas.
Type: Two-place observation aircraft.
Engine: One 213hp Continental O-470-11 air-cooled flat-6 piston engine.
Dimensions: Span 36ft (10.9m); length 25ft 10in (7.89m); height 7ft 1in (2.23m); wing area 174sq ft (16.16m²).
Weight: Empty 1,614lb (680kg); loaded 2,400-2,430lb (1,090-1,103kg); (F) 2,800lb (1,273kg).
Performance: Maximum speed 115mph (184km/h); cruising speed at 5,000ft (1,525m) 104mph (166km/h); cruising range 530 miles (848km).
Armament: Target marking rockets.
History: First contract placed by US Army June 1950; deliveries from December 1950.

Above: Like some old biplane pursuits, Bird Dog variants had corrugated-metal control surfaces (and, in this case, flaps).

Users: Army, AF, Marines.

Cessna won an Army competition in June 1950 for a two-seat observation and liaison machine with the Model 305, derived from the civil 170. A typical high-wing Cessna, it had all-metal structure, braced wings, cantilever spring-leaf main gears, large slotted flaps on the untapered center section, and all-round visibility. Whereas the wartime L-4 had had 65hp the Cessna had 213, showing influence of the German Storch.

Designated L-19A (changed to O-1 in 1962), deliveries began in 1950. Later there were many variants including TL-19

Above: Bearing an O (obsolete) prefix, this O-1E was operating round the clock on FAC duty from Pleiku AB in May 1967.

instrument-flight trainers and 60 OE-1s for the Marines. Deliveries reached 2,486 by late 1954, and Bird Dogs were then built intermittently until 1962 when 3,431 had been produced. Later versions (O-1D, E, F) had constant-speed propellers and extra equipment.

As late as 1968, the Bird Dog served a majority of the forward air controllers in South-East Asia. Either flying alone or carrying a second crewman, these pilots searched out targets, marked them, determined the location of friendly troops, and directed air strikes. The presence of a Bird Dog could mean survival for embattled American or South Vietna-

mese units. Smoke from carefully placed rockets brought swift destruction upon the enemy and also prevented accidental bombing of friendly trooops. The very presence of O-1s often deterred the enemy from opening fire.

At the same time, although the simple liaison and observation requirement seemed the easiest of all military airplane specifications to meet, in practice it was one of the most difficult. One company better known for bigger stuff, Convair, tried to compete from 1945 with the angular L-13. Bigger than the Cessna, and powered by a 245hp Franklin engine, it did essentially the same job at greater cost, its one advantage being that in emergency it could carry six people. Convair sold the USAF 300 L-13As and 28 Arctic L-13Bs, but Cessna's design prevailed in the longer term.

Left: BuNo 129032 was an HRS-2, another of the variants with the original airframe.

clamshell doors to engineers standing on the ground. A diagonal shaft took the drive to the gearbox under the hub, which was essentially an enlarged R-5 hub with an offset flapping hinge to allow greater freedom in center of gravity position. The only place for the cockpit was on top, the crew of two climbing up the stressed-skin side of the helicopter and taking their places on each side of the drive shaft.

The USAF was impressed by five YH-19s (all but the first having a triangular fillet fairing the body

into the tail boom) and soon all US services were using the S-55 as the H-19 (USAF, utility), H-19C Chickasaw (USA, transport), HRS (USMC, assault with eight troops), HO4S (USN, transport), and HO4S-2G (USCG, rescue, with power winch which became common on many variants).

The first production versions were the Navy HO4S-1 used for ASW observation and the AF H-19A, many of which became SH-19A rescue machines with MATS (Military Air Transport Service). Before really large

numbers were delivered the tail boom was angled downwards to prevent its being hit by the main rotor, the designation changing to H-19B. This also replaced the sharply anhedralled tail stabilizers by a horizontal surface on each side, and the tail-rotor pylon was turned into a swept fin. All Army Chickasaws had this improved airframe, and the AF's H-19B and Army H-19D had the powerful Wright engine, which also became standard on the Navy HO4S-3 and Marines HRS-3. A few Wasp-powered helicopters

were re-engined, especially by the Marines, and a larger number of H-19A type machines were given the improved airframe.

In Korea many hundreds of these helicopters pioneered airborne assault, rapid battlefront resupply and speedy relocation of mortars and light artillery, often within yards of hostile troops. Rescue of downed aircrew became standard, and on occasion SH-19s brought back downed Cessnas and light helicopters. Field experiments with weapons led to official trials at Ft Rucker in 1956 with 5in (127mm) rocket tubes, 0.5in guns and various other weapons which later included fitting the French S.S.10 anti-tank missile. Navy ASW models experimented with sonobuoys but never carried weapons. One of the lesser known variants was a black YH-19 prototype with special avionics and hoist which flew clandestine missions for the CIA. Sikorsky built 1,281 S-55s, the military models becoming CH-19s, HH-19s and UH-19s after 1962.

Douglas F4D (F-6) Skyray

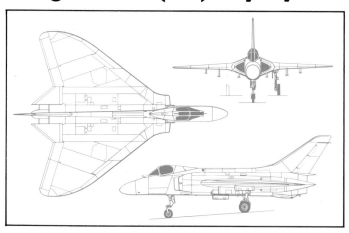

Origin: Douglas Aircraft Company, El Segundo, California.
Type: Carrier-based interceptor and attack aircraft.
Engine: One 16,000lb (7,257kg) thrust Pratt & Whitney J57-8 two-shaft turbojet with afterburner.
Dimensions: Span 33ft 6in (10.2m); length 45ft 8in (13.9m); height 13ft (3.96m); wing area 557sq ft (51.75m²).
Weights: Empty 16,030lb (7,250kg); loaded 27,000lb (12,250kg).
Performance: Maximum speed 725mph (1,167km/h); initial climb 18,000ft (5,300m)/min; service ceiling 55,000ft (16,760m); typical range 950 miles (1,530km).
Armament: Four 20mm cannon in wings, with muzzles above leading edge; six pylon attachments for total external load of 4,000lb (1,814kg).
History: First flight (XF4D-1) 23 January 1951; service delivery 16 April 1956; last delivery December 1958.
Users: Navy, Marine Corps.

Based in part on the wartime projects of Alex Lippisch, this unusual fighter was planned by

Above: All "Fords" looked the same, once El Segundo got the right engine.

Ed Heinemann to have a large wing, for good combat maneuverability, with minimum structure weight. There was no horizontal tail, the elevators and outboard ailerons all being on the trailing edge of the broad rounded wing. From the start it was planned for possible supersonic performance, and when the XF4D first flew it was much more advanced in concept than any other naval fighter.

One of its features was powered flying controls with manual reversion, the stick being unclipped and extended by the pilot to give more leverage. Another was the double skin, with a very light outer sheet stiffened

Above: Sidewinder-equipped Skyrays at NAS Chincoteague, Virginia. Note radar exposed.

by an inner "waffle plate"; this was not wholly successful, because it was prone to being dented, with degraded flight performance. On 3 October 1953 a prototype gained the world speed record at 753mph (1,212km/h) — a great shock to the Air Force — but the program was severely hurt by the technical failure of the Westinghouse J40 engine which was the original powerplant.

After a delay of three years the J57 was adopted instead, and then the Skyray never looked back. A straight run of 419 was delivered to Navy and Marine Corps squadrons for use from carriers and NAS Alameda, with

equipment for "buddy" refueling. A service Skyray took world time-to-height records, reaching 50,000ft (15,240m) in 2.6 minutes from a standing start.

A development, the highly supersonic F5D Skylancer with thicker skin, was canceled after four had flown very successfully. In 1962 the F4D-1 was redesignated F-6A, squadrons progressively re-equipping with the Phantom. It was an agile and generally popular fighter, universally known from its original designation as the Ford,

Below: BuNo 139084 served with the Marines throughout its life. Probed Buddy packs were optional.

McDonnell F3H (F-3) Demon

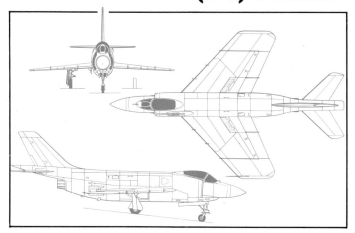

Origin: McDonnell Aircraft Company, St Louis, Missouri.
Type: Carrier-based interceptor, later all-weather fighter.
Engine: Originally one 11,600lb (5,262kg) thrust Westinghouse J40-22 single-shaft turbojet with

afterburner; finally one 14,250lb (6,463kg) Allison J71-2 of same layout.
Dimensions: Span 35ft 4in (10.76m); length (F3H-1) 58ft 4in, (others) 58ft 11in (17.95m); height (F3H-1) 13ft 11in (4.24m), (others)

14ft 7in (4.45m); wing area 519sq ft (48.2m²).
Weights: Empty (F3H-1) 14,990lb (6,799kg), (others, typical) 22,300lb (10,115kg); maximum loaded (F3H-1) 23,400lb (10,614kg), (others, typical)

Above left: The basic F3H-2 (later F-3B) was really a very fine aircraft, but several years late.

Above: An F3H-2N, with retractable FR probe, in full 'burner near Mt Fuji in April 1958.

Kaman H-43 Huskie

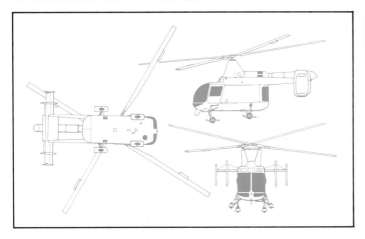

Origin: Kaman Aircraft Corporation, Bloomfield, Connecticut.
Type: Crash rescue helicopter.
Engines: (HH-43B) One 860shp Lycoming T53-L-1B turboshaft.
Dimensions: (HH-43B) Main rotor diameter 47ft (14.33m); fuselage length 25ft 2in (7.67m); height 12ft 7in (3.84m); main-rotor disc area (total) 3,470sq ft (322.1m^2).
Weight: (HH-43B) empty 4,469lb (2,027kg); normal takeoff 5,969lb (2,708kg); maximum takeoff 9,150lb (4,150kg).
Performance: (HH-43B) maximum level speed at sea level 120mph (193km/h); range at 5,000ft (1,525m), no allowances, 277 miles (445km).
Armament: None.
History: First flight (HOK) early 1951, (HH-43B) December 1958; service delivery June 1959.
Users: AF.

In 1959-79 the HH-43B was the only crash rescue helicopter in the AF inventory. Local base rescue units throughout the United States and overseas commands operated the Huskie on a 30-second alert basis, with another 30 seconds needed to

clip on a spherical container of fire-suppressant to the external sling.

After World War II Kaman was formed to build helicopters with "eggbeater" type intermeshing rotors. In 1950 the Model 600, larger than previous models, won a Navy competition for an observation and utility helicopter for the Marines. An all-metal machine, it had a roomy five/six-place cabin with a fully transparent front cockpit. At the rear was a 600hp Pratt & Whitney R-1340 Wasp engine, driving the left/right two-blade rotors mounted on inclined pylons. Twin booms carried the triple-fin tail, and the helicopter rested on four separate landing gears.

In the mid-1950s the Marines received 81 HOK-1s (OH-43D after 1962). From 1958 the Navy received 24 HUK-1 utility transports (UH-43C from 1962). Gross weight of these piston-engined machines was 6,800lb (3,085kg). Another 18 were bought by the AF as H-43As,

Above: HH-43B had blade control flaps, four fins, wheel/ski gear and a giant jetpipe discharging at tail.

Above: An HH-43B (58-1854) still without camouflage in 1967 with the 48th ARRS at Eglin.

Below: 62-4518, a later HH-43B, about to depart on a night rescue mission in May 1967.

followed by 193 of the more powerful H-43B version with a long exhaust pipe, four fins and up to ten seats.

In March 1964 three HH-43 units were transferred to Southeast Asia from the Philippines and Okinawa, followed by others. Their HH-43Fs possessed heavy armor plating to protect the crews from hostile fire, and a 250ft

(76.2m) cable to facilitate rescues in the high rain forest. The air rescue groups also installed extra fuel tanks in the helicopters and caried either 150 gal (682 litre) containers, or 55 gal (250 litre) drums. They could land en route to the objective and top off the fuel supply. Huskies were generally replaced from the late 1970s.

33,900lb (15,376kg).
Performance: Maximum speed (F3H-1, intended) 758mph (1,219km/h), (production F-3, typical) 647mph (1,040km/h); initial climb 12,000ft (3,660m)/min; service ceiling (F-3) 42,650ft (13,000m); maximum combat range 1,370 miles (2,200km).
Armament: Four 20mm M-2 cannon; (F-3 versions) four underwing pylons for various ordnance.
History: First flight (XF3H-1) 7 August 1951, (F3H-2) 23 April 1955; service delivery (-2N) 7 March 1956; final delivery November 1959.

"Mr Mac's" prowess as a producer of extremely advanced jet combat aircraft was unsurpassed from the very first XFD-1 Phantom, and the severe challenge of the XF3H Demon found that the

company measured up to it. Ordered in September 1949, the Demon was to equal in performance the fastest land-based fighters, and a completely new all-swept layout was chosen with a single powerful afterburning engine and an exceedingly advanced airframe.

The big Westinghouse engine occupied the rear fuselage, fed by fixed sharp-lipped lateral inlets and with the afterburner nozzle well forward under the long overhanging "beaver tail" of flat rectangular cross-section. This cantilevered rear fuselage carried the swept vertical stabilizer and a slab tailplane (horizontal stabilizer) forming a one-piece powered control surface with no separate elevators. The thin but broad wings had full-span drooped leading-edge flaps, large ailerons, and spoiler/air-brakes inboard of the

diagonal hinges. Door-type airbrakes extended on each side of the fuselage aft of the wing. The cockpit was well ahead of the wing, and the Demon could claim to have been the most advanced and promising fighter in the world flying in 1951.

Unfortunately the J40 engine proved totally unacceptable, with poor reliability and inadequate thrust, while ever-greater demands caused aircraft weight to grow. After catastrophic failures and inability to deliver the required power, the J40 was abandoned, and in June 1953 the J71 was adopted instead. Orders for 529 F3H-1Ns were cut. Temco's second-source line was canceled, and of the 60 completed -1s, 21 were used as ground trainers and 29 converted to J71-powered F3H-2s (F-3Bs after 1962).

Even the F3H-1 had already had

a fuselage redesigned to house 40 per cent more fuel, and it was then redesigned again to take the J71. The wing was made 40in (1.02m) broader and given four pylons, while two body pylons were plumbed for large tanks.

McDonnell's hard work rescued the Demon as a fine fighter which joined the Navy carrier squadrons and served in intensive operations in many theaters. The basic F-3B was a strike fighter with 6,600lb (2,994kg) weapon load; the F-3C had Hughes APG-51A radar, four Sidewinder missiles and limited all-weather capability; and the MF-3B had APG-51A and four AIM-7C Sparrow III missiles, the first aircraft ever to carry these formidable all-weather air-to-air weapons. Total Dash-2 Demon production was 519, and the last F-3Bs were not replaced by F-4s until 1965.

Boeing B-52 Stratofortress

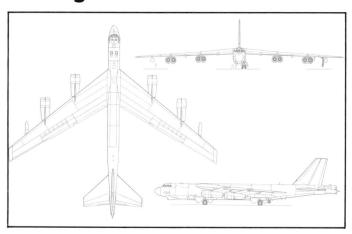

Origin: Boeing Airplane Company (from May 1961 The Boeing Company), Seattle, Washington, and Wichita, Kansas.
Type: Heavy bomber and missile platform.
Engines: (D) Eight 12,100lb (5,489kg) thrust Pratt & Whitney J57-19W or -29W turbojets, (G) eight 13,750lb (6,237kg) thrust Pratt & Whitney J57-43W or -43WB turbojets, (H) eight 17,000lb (7,711kg) thrust Pratt & Whitney TF33-1 or -3 turbofans.
Dimensions: Span 185ft (56.39m); length (D, and G/H as built) 157ft 7in (48.0m), (G/H modified) 160ft 11in (49.05m); height (D) 48ft 4½in (14.7m), (G/H) 40ft 8in (12.4m); wing area 4,000sq ft (371.6m²).
Weights: Empty (D) about 175,000lb (79,380kg), (G/H) about 195,000lb (88,450kg); loaded (D) about 470,000lb (213,200kg), (G) 505,000lb (229,000kg), (H) 505,000lb at takeoff, inflight refuel to 566,000lb (256,738kg).
Performance: Max speed (true airspeed, clean), (D) 575mph (925km/h), (G/H) 595mph (957km/h); penetration speed at low altitude (all) about 405mph (652km/h), Mach 0.53; service ceiling (D) 45,000ft (13.7km), (G) 46,000ft (14.000m), (H) 47,000ft (14.300m); range (max fuel, no external bombs/missiles, optimum hi-alt cruise), (D) 7,370 miles (11,861km), (G) 8,406 miles (13,528km), (H) 10,130 miles (16,303km); takeoff run, (D) 11,100ft (3,383m), (G) 10,000ft (3,050m), (H) 9,500ft (2,895m).
Armament: (D) Four 0.5in guns in occupied tail turret, MD-9 system, plus 84 bombs of nominal 500lb (227kg) in bomb bay plus 24 of nominal 750lb (340kg) on wing pylons, total 60,000lb (27,215kg), (G) four 0.5in guns in remote-control tail turret, ASG-15 system, plus eight nuclear bombs, or up to 20 SRAM (eight on internal dispenser plus 12 on wing pylons), or 12 AGM-86B ALCMs on wing pylons, (H) single 20mm six-barrel gun in remote-control tail turret, ASG-21 system, plus bombload as G (later to have AGM-86B internal dispenser). B-52G Maritime Support, see text.

Above: The 102 B-52H bombers have fan engines and a six-barrel tail gun. This shows all add-ons except OAS and CMI.

History: First flight 15 April 1952; later, see text.
User: AF.

A legend in its own time, the B-52 was designed to the very limits of the state of the art in 1948-49 to meet the demands of SAC for a long-range bomber and yet achieve the high performance possible with jet propulsion. The two prototypes had tandem pilot positions and were notable for their great size and fuel capacity, four double engine pods and four twin-wheel landing trucks which could be slewed to crab the aircraft on to the runway in a crosswind landing. The B-52A changed to a side-by-side pilot cockpit in the nose and entered service in August 1954, becoming operational in June 1955. Subsequently 744 aircraft were built in eight major types, all of which have been withdrawn except the B-52D, G and H.

The B-52D fleet numbered 170 (55-068/–117, 56-580/-630 built at Seattle and 55-049/-067, 55-673/-680 and 56-657/-698 built at Wichita) delivered at 20 per month alongside the same rate for KC-135 tankers in support. The B-52G was the most numerous variant, 193 being delivered from early 1959 (57-6468/-6520, 58-158/-258 and 59-2564/-2602, all from Wichita), introducing a wet (integral tank) wing which increased internal fuel from 35,550 to 46,575 US gal and also featured shaft-driven generators, roll control by spoilers only, powered tail controls, injection water in the leading edge, a short vertical tail, rear gunner moved to the main pressurized crew compartment, and an inner wing stressed for a large pylon on each side of the fuselage. The final model, the B-52H, numbered 102 (60-001/-062 and 61-001/-040), and was essentially a G with the TF33 fan engine and a new tail gun.

During the Vietnam War the B-52D was structurally rebuilt for HDB (high-density bombing) with conventional bombs, never considered in the original design.

Above: Much-revised noses of these H-models show new radar, EVS, ALT-28 ECM (above) and ALQ-117 radar warning (side).

Below: The other end of the H-model terminates in a T171 six-barrel gun, last of five different tail gun arrangements.

The wings were given inboard pylons of great length for four tandem triplets of bombs on each side, and as noted in the data 108 bombs could be carried in all with a true weight not the "book value" given but closer to 89,100lb (40,400kg). Another far-reaching and costly series of structural modifications was needed on all models to permit sustained operations at low level, to keep as far as possible under hostile radars, again not previously considered.

The newest models, the G and H, were given a stability augmentation system from 1969 to improve comfort and airframe life in turbulent dense air. From 1972 these aircraft were outfitted to carry the SRAM (Short-Range Attack Missile), some 1,300 of which are still with the SAC Bomb Wings. Next came the EVS (Electro-optical Viewing System) which added twin chin bulges. The Phase VI ECM (electronic countermeasures) cost $362.5 million, fitted from 1973. Quick Start added cartridge engine starters to the G and H for a quick getaway to escape missile attack. Next came a new threat-warning system, a satellite link and "smart noise" jammers to thwart enemy radars. From 1980 the venerable D-force was updated by a $126.3

million digital nav/bombing system. Further major changes to the G and H include the OAS (offensive avionics system) which is now in progress costing $1,662 million.

The equally big CMI (cruise missile interface) will eventually fit the G-force for 12 AGM-86B missiles on the pylons in tandem triplets, the internal bay being the wrong size and remaining available for a SRAM dispenser.

Under current plans 99 B-52Gs are being modified for cruise missiles, each also having a curved wing root fairing to identify it to recon satellites as a missile carrier (to comply with the SALT II

treaty articles, even though these were never ratified). The 416th BW at Griffiiss AFB became fully operational with AGM-86B in December 1982, and other wings have converted, or are doing so, at Blytheville, Grand Forks, Fairchild and Barksdale AFBs. Some of these have the B-52H, 96 of which are also being converted, and later in the 1980s the H will be more radically modified to accommodate the newly developed AGM-86B rotary launcher in the internal bay.

As 168 B-52Gs were rebuilt with OAS, 69 are left over from the CMI conversion, and these are replacing Ds in the non-nuclear

Above: Two B-52Hs were used for the secret CIA-sponsored missions of Lockheed GTD-21B unmanned Mach 4 vehicles. Base unit was 4200 Test Wing, Beale.

maritime support role. Here one of their new weapons is the AGM-84 Harpoon cruise missile, clusters of which can be carried in the long-range anti-ship role. In 1983 one of the numerous test launches was from 30,000ft (9,144m), but all were successful and two squadrons of Harpoon-Gs were operational by early 1985.

Yet another new weapons is the GD AGM-109H MRASM (medium-

Top: Takeoff from Boeing (Kansas) of a fully upgraded B-52G, with the CMI and OAS both integrated. Age at retirement will be about 32 to 34 years.

range ASM), a variant of the Tomahawk cruise missile. With a range of 285 miles (459km), this dispenses large conventional submunitions, the usual design being for cratering runways. Four missiles are carried on each wing pylon. Another cruise-type weapon used by the maritime B-52s is the GBU-15(V) stand-off precision-guided conventional weapon for use against ships and other clearly defined targets.

Douglas A3D (A-3) Skywarrior

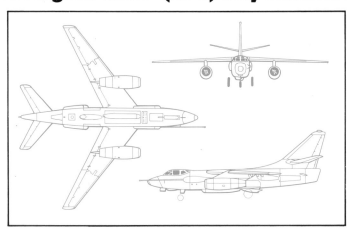

Origin: Douglas Aircraft Co., El Segundo, California.
Type: Originally carrier-based strategic bomber; later, different roles (see text).
Engines: Two 12,400lb (5,625kg) thrust Pratt & Whitney J57-10 two-shaft turbojets.
Dimensions: Span 72ft 6in (22.1m); length, typical (EA-3B) 76ft 4in (23.3m); height 23ft 6in (7.16m); wing area 812sq ft (75.44m^2).
Weights: Empty (A-3B) 39,409lb (17,875kg); maximum loaded (A-3B) 82,000lb (37,195kg).
Performance: Maximum speed (typical) 610mph (982km/h); initial climb 3,600ft (1,100m)/min;

Above: Virtually all remaining Skywarriors are EKA-3Bs with capability in electronic warfare and inflight refueling.

service ceiling 43,000ft (13,110m); range with maximum fuel 2,000 miles (3,220km).
Armament: Normally none; as built, most bomber A-3s had two remotely controlled 20mm cannon in a tail turret and internal provision for 12,000lb (5,443kg) of bombs including nuclear weapons.
History: First flight (XA3D-1) 28 October 1952; service delivery (A3D-1) December 1954 (first squadron, March 1956); last

Above: An EA-3B, with pressurized fuselage, serving with VQ-1 World Watchers at Agana, Guam.

delivery of new aircraft (A3D-2Q) January 1961.
User: Navy.

The Douglas El Segundo design team under Heinemann produced the A3D as the world's first carrier-based strategic bomber, matching the design both to the predicted size and mass of future thermonuclear bombs and to the deck length and strength of the super-carriers of the Forrestal class in 1948.

The large bomb bay dictated a high wing, which in turn meant the landing gears had to retract into the fuselage. The crew of three occupied a pressurized cockpit glazed all over, with emergency escape via a large chute leading to a ventral hatch. Outer wings and vertical tail folded hydraulically, and the nose was filled with an advanced blind-bombing radar. Unfortunately Westinghouse, supplier of the J40 engines and the radar, succeeded in delivering only the Aero-21B tail turret.

Redesigned with the J57 engine, the A3D-1 finally equipped VAH-1 (Heavy Attack

Grumman S-2 Tracker family

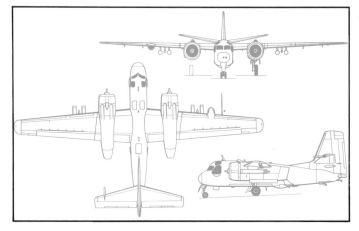

Origin: Grumman Aircraft Engineering Corporation, Bethpage, NY.
Type: (S-2) carrier ASW aircraft; (C-1) COD transport; (E-1) AEW aircraft.
Engines: Two 1,525hp Wright R-1820-82WA (early versions, -82) Cyclone nine-cylinder radials.
Dimensions: Span (S-2A to -2C, C-1 and E-1) 69ft 8in (21.23m), (S-2D to -2G) 72ft 7in (22.13m); length (S-2A to -2C) 42ft 3in (12.88m), (S-2D to -2G) 43ft 6in (13.26m); height (S-2A to -2C) 16ft 3½in (4.96m), (S-2D to -2G) 16ft 7in (5.06m); wing area (D, G) 499sq ft (46.36m^2).
Weights: Empty (S-2A) 17,357lb (7,873kg), (S-2E) 18,750lb (8,505kg); loaded (S-2A) 26,300lb

Above: This S2F-3 (S-2D) is typical of subsequent models with the enlarged airframe. Radar and MAD boom are shown retracted.

(11,929kg), (S-2E) 29,150lb (13,222kg), (C-1A, E-1B) 27,000lb (12,247kg).
Performance: Maximum speed (S-2A) 287mph (462km/h), (S-2E) 267mph (430km/h), (C-1A) 290mph (467km/h); initial climb (S-2A) 1,920ft (586m)/min, (S-2E) 1,390ft (425m)/min; service ceiling (S-2A) 23,000ft (7,010m), (S-2E) 21,000ft (6,400m); range (S-2A) 900 miles (1,448km), (S-2E) 1,300 miles (2,095km).
Armament: Weapon bay accommodates two Mk 44 or 46 electric acoustic-homing torpedoes, two Mk 101 depth

Above: A new S2F-1, not yet assigned to a unit, with radar and MAD extended in the mid-1950s. Note black deicer boots.

bombs (some versions, one) or four 385lb (175kg) depth charges; six underwing pylons for 5in rockets, Zuni rockets or 250lb (113kg) bombs, or for ferrying torpedoes (two on each wing); (S-2E) as above, with provision for Betty nuclear depth charge, AS.12 or other guided missiles and 7.62mm Miniguns; (C-1 and E-1) no armament.
History: First flight (XS2F-1) 4 December 1952; production S2F-1 (S-2A) 30 April 1953; combat service February 1954; final delivery February 1968.
User: Navy.

This very ordinary-looking piston aircraft entered a world of advanced gas-turbine machines and has outlasted nearly all of them. It stemmed from the belief that an aircraft compatible with carrier operation could be made to combine the two roles of anti-submarine warfare (ASW) search and strike, previously accomplished by one aircraft equipped with sensors and another equipped with weapons.

Grumman developed the G-89 Tracker extremely rapidly, despite the need to package an extraordinary diversity of equipment into a small space. Its low-speed handling stemmed from the long span, with almost full-span slotted flaps and fixed slots on the outer folding wings. In the

Squadron 1) in 1956. Soon the Skywarriors on the catapults of giant carriers of the 6th Fleet in the Mediterranean and the 7th Fleet in the Pacific were playing a central role in the balance of power in the Cold War, and giving a new global dimension to naval air power.

Eventually, though only 280 Skywarriors were built (not enough, as it turned out), the changing scene called for numerous completely different versions mainly achieved by rebuilding bombers. Major production was of the A3D-2 bomber, restyled A-3B. From this evolved the A3D-2P (RA-3B) reconnaissance, A3D-2Q (EA-3B) electronic countermeasures and A3D-2T (TA-3B) radar/nav trainer, followed by rebuilds for the KA-3B tanker, EKA-3B ECM/tanker and various special-mission and test versions. As this book went to press small numbers of EKA-3Bs were still in active carrier service, mainly as tankers.

Right: A fabulous portrait of EKA-3B TACOS (Tanker Aircraft, Countermeasures Or Strike) which served with VAQ-135 Detachment 1. The Skywarrior is likely to remain the biggest aircraft ever to be regularly operated from aircraft carriers.

Right: This S2F-3 (from 1962 S-2D) was every inch on combat duty, serving with VS-26 aboard USS Randolph (CV-15). Free (non-catapult) takeoffs were possible.

nose were seats for pilot, co-pilot/navigator and two radar plotters. In the S-2A (formerly S2F-1) the radar was the APS-38, in a retractable ventral bin. A magnetic anomaly detector (MAD) boom extended behind the tail, an upper search radar had its scanner above the cockpit, a 70 million candle-power searchlight was hung under the right wing and the engine nacelles each housed eight sonobuoys ejected through tubes to the rear. The TS-2A was an ASW trainer and the CS2F-1 and -2 were built by de Havilland Canada.

The S-2B was equipped with the Julie acoustic (explosive) echo-ranger and associated Jezebel passive acoustic sensor. The S-2C had a bulged asymmetric weapon bay and larger tail, most being converted into US-2C utility or RS-2C photo aircraft. The S-2D, ordered in 1958, was physically larger, with improved accommodation in a bigger forward fuselage, extended wingspan, larger tail, extra fuel, 16 sonobuoys per nacelle and much enhanced equipment. The S-2E was a D with Julie/Jezebel equipment, and the S-2F had this

as well as AQA-7 Difar sonic processors giving target direction and range equipment.

The total of these versions was 1,281, including 100 Canadian-built, and several hundred have been modified to the S-2F and G versions for service until late 1976 with the Navy, and serving to this day with many of the 12 countries that have used Trackers.

The C-1A Trader (G-96) is a nine-passenger COD (carrier on board delivery) transport, and the 87 built included four EC-1A used for ECM missions. The E-1B Tracer (G-117) is an airborne early warning machine with a huge teardrop-shaped radome above a C-1 size fuselage, with a three-finned tail. The radar antenna revolves inside the fixed radome of aerofoil profile, which is attached at the tail to the central fin. Originally, in 1957, the Tracer was called the WF-1, which resulted in the popular name Willy Fudd. Production totalled 88.

North American F-100 Super Sabre

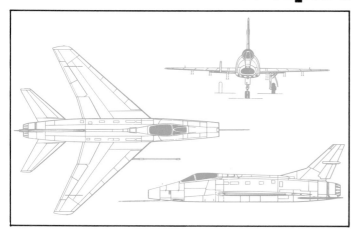

Origin: North American Aviation Inc, Inglewood, California, and Columbus, Ohio.
Type: Single-seat fighter-bomber, (F-100F) two-seat operational trainer, (DF) missile or RPV director aircraft.
Engine: One Pratt & Whitney J57 two-shaft turbojet with afterburner, (most blocks of A) 14,500lb (6,576kg) J57-7, (late A, all C) 16,000lb (7,257kg) J57-39, (D, F) 16,950lb (7,690kg) J57-21A (all ratings with afterburner).
Dimensions: Span (original A) 36ft 7in (11.15m), (remainder) 38ft 9½in (11.81m); length (except F, excluding pilot boom) 49ft 6in (15.09m) (fuselage, 47ft exactly), (F) 52ft 6in (16.0m), (boom adds about 6ft to all models); height (original A) 13ft 4in (4.06m), (remainder) 16ft 2¾in (4.96m); wing area (except early A) 385sq ft (35.77m²).

Above: Last and most important of the single-seaters, the F-100D was a versatile fighter/bomber distinguished by its kinked trailing edge and flaps.

Weights: Empty (original A) 19,700lb (8,935kg); (C) 20,450lb (9,276kg); (D) 21,000lb (9,525kg); (F) 22,300lb (10,115kg); maximum loaded (original A) 28,935lb (13,125kg), (C, D) 34,832lb (15,800kg), (F, two tanks but no weapons) 30,700lb (13,925kg).
Performance: Maximum speed (typical of all) 864mph at height (1,390km/h, Mach 1.31); initial climb (clean) 16,000ft (4,900m)/min; service ceiling (typical) 45,000ft (13,720m); range (high, two 375gal tanks) 1,500 miles (2,415km).
Armament: Usually four (F, only two) 20mm M-39E cannon each with 200 rounds; (A) pylons for

Above: An F-100C-20, with "O" prefix denoting over ten years old, flying near Holloman AFB, New Mexico, while with Air Defense Command in 1967.

two 375 gal (1,419 litre) supersonic tanks and four additional hardpoints (seldom used) for 4,000lb (1,814kg) ordnance; (C, D) two tanks and six pylons for 7,500lb (3,402kg) ordnance; (F) two tanks and maximum of 6,000lb (2,722kg) ordnance.
History: First flight (YF-100) 25 May 1953, production (A) 29 October 1953; final delivery October 1959.
Users: AF, ANG.

The success of the Sabre made it natural to attempt a successor, and in February 1949 this was planned as a larger and much more powerful machine able to

exceed the speed of sound in level flight (had it been started two years later it might have been smaller, in view of the Korean pressure for simple fighters with the highest possible climb and performance at extreme altitudes).

When the NA-180 basic design was being planned very little was known about how to create a supersonic fighter. Fortunately NAA rejected unconventional layouts and adhered to the F-86 configuration; in fact the new fighter was at first known as the Sabre 45, because the sweepback of the wing was increased to 45°. The thickness ratio of the

Below: An F-100D, with serial rearranged to look like 53-658, seen in dive-bombing action in the early years of the Southeast Asia war.

wing was reduced to 6 per cent, and despite extremely strong and stiff structure, with multiple spars and heavy machined skin, aeroelastic twisting of the wing was feared under aileron forces. Accordingly the ailerons were placed inboard, flaps being omitted and the only high-lift feature being full-span leading-edge slats. The tailplane (horizontal stabilizer) was made in the form of left and right powered slabs mounted right at the bottom of the rear fuselage. A very large door-type airbrake was fitted in the belly, ahead of the wheel bays, making fuselage stores pylons impractical.

At first the NAA-180 was a company venture, but in November 1951 the AF placed an order for two YF-100 prototypes and 110 production aircraft. Level supersonic speed was achieved, but after very rapid development, with the first (479th) Tac Fighter Wing fully equipped, the F-100A was grounded in November 1954. Trouble due to the inertia coupling between the roll and yaw axes necessitated urgent modification, the wings and fin being lengthened. Subsequently the career of the "Hun" was wholly successful.

Inglewood delivered 203 F-100As, all eventually with extended wings and fin and the final 39 with a more powerful engine. They had provision for six pylons, but seldom carried more than two 275gal (1,040 lit) drop tanks of unusual banana profile with four fins which could remain attached at supersonic speed. Next came the F-100B which matured as the J75-powered F-107A. This despite being a superb airplane, lost out to the rival Republic F-105. The F-100C was a fighter/bomber with eight pylons on a stronger wing with increased internal fuel and an inflight-refueling probe. This gave way to the F-100D with a kinked trailing edge with outboard ailerons and broad inboard flaps, as well as an autopilot programmed for LABS (low-altitude bombing system) toss maneuvers with nuclear weapons. The final model was the tandem dual F-100F with a longer fuselage. All versions were substantially updated.

Above: In its youth the "Hun" (from Hundred) was regarded as the hottest thing in the Air Force. This C-model was snapped on 25 June 1956.

Total production was lower than expected at 2,294, many being built by NAA's newly occupied factory at Columbus, Ohio. In their early years the later versions pioneered global deployment of tactical aircraft by means of probe/drogue refueling, and in Vietnam they proved outstandingly good at both low attack and top cover, flying more missions than over 15,000 Mustangs flew in World War II.

Seven two-place F-100Fs were rebuilt as Wild Weasel I aircraft. These had the APR-25 vector radar homing and warning (RHAW) receiver. Four aircraft were deployed to Korat,

Above: This F-100D-90 was toting a GAM-83 (later AGM-12) Bullpup air/surface missile round the Philippines on 22 April 1963. Camouflage and war were near.

Thailand, on 21 November 1965 and assigned to the 388th Tactical Fighter Wing. Three more Wild Weasel Is were deployed to the theater in February 1966 to participate in Iron Hand anti-SAM missions. In 1966 some Wild Weasel F-100Fs began using AGM-45 Shrike missiles, designed to home on radar transmitters.

Because of the F-100's ability to carry a heavy load of munitions, the Air Force examined the wings for signs of corrosion. The prime contractor also examined the lower wing skin in order to redesign it for further use. Finally, in late 1967 the Air Force developed a complete structural

modification plan for the wing and, by 1969, center wing sections of 682 F-100Ds had been modified. Other modifications included a Motorola SST-181 X-band radar, which provided a ground-directed bombing capability for night and bad weather missions. In addition, the weapon release and firing systems were improved, and new guns and a more accurate target-marking system were added.

The only F-100Cs to serve in South Vietnam arrived in the spring of 1968 and remained about a year. The aircraft belonged to Air National Guard squadrons mobilized as a result of North Korea's capture of the American intelligence ship *Pueblo*.

In the 1970s "Huns" flew with the Air National Guard, Armée de l'Air, Denmark, Turkey and Nationalist China.

Below: This colorful F-100D-25 is illustrated early in its career, in natural metal and with an FW "buzz number".

Below: Shark teeth were favored by the 127th TFS of the Kansas ANG. Note the outline of Kansas on the tail band.

Below: Jeanne Kay was an F-100D-6 (originally 56-2910) which served at Tuy Hoa AB with the 308th TFS, 31st Tac Fighter Wing, in 1970.

145

Convair F-102 Delta Dagger

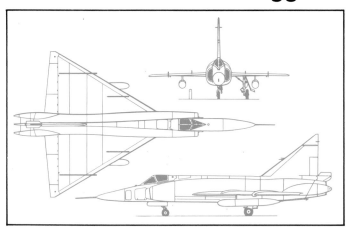

Origin: Convair Division of General Dynamics, San Diego, California.
Type: (F) single-seat all-weather interceptor, (TF) trainer, (QF) manned RPV (remotely piloted vehicle), (PQM) drone target.
Engine: One 17,200lb (7,802kg) thrust Pratt & Whitney J57-23 two-shaft afterburning turbojet.
Dimensions: Span 28ft 1½in (11.6m); length (F-102A) 68ft 5in (20.83m), (TF-102A) 63ft 4½in (19.3m); height (F-102A) 21ft 2½in (6.45m), (TF-102A) 20ft 7in (6.27m); wing area 661.5sq ft (61.46m^2).
Weights: Empty (F-102A) 19,050lb (8,630kg); loaded (F-102A, clean) 27,700lb (12,564kg), (maximum) 31,500lb (14,288kg).
Performance: Maximum speed (F-102A) 825mph (1,328km/h, Mach 1.25), (TF-102A) 646mph (1,040km/h); initial climb (F-102A) 13,000ft (3,962m)/min; service ceiling 54,000ft (16,460m); range 1,350 miles (2,172km).
Armament: Air-to-air guided missiles carried in internal bay, typical full load comprising three

Above: All production F-102As were almost identical, and this shows the final configuration with supersonic tanks and an IR sensor ahead of the windshield.

Hughes AIM-4E Falcon beam-riders with semi-active homing and three AIM-4F with infrared homing. No armament in TF, QF, or PQM.
History: First flight (YF-102) 24 October 1953, (YF-102A) 20 December 1954, (TF) 8 November 1955, (QF) mid-1974, (PQM) early 1975.
User: AF.

In 1948 Convair flew the world's first delta-wing aircraft, the XF-92A, which was part of a program intended to lead to a supersonic fighter. This was terminated, but the US Air Force later issued a specification for an extremely advanced all-weather interceptor to carry the Hughes MX-1179 system which included radar, computer and guided missiles.

For the first time the carrier aircraft became subordinate to its avionics, as a mere portion of a

Above: An F-102A-41 on test from San Diego. From this angle another subtle aerodynamic feature can be seen: "conical camber" of outer leading edges.

weapon system. The whole weapon system represented a major challenge in 1951-52 and it did not help when early flight trials in the winter of 1953-54 showed that the specified supersonic speed could not be reached. In an urgent "crash program" the whole aircraft had to be redesigned to a modified shape complying with the lately discovered Area Rule, making it much longer, and fatter at the back.

Once the design had been got right, 875 were delivered in 21 months, together with 63 of the subsonic side-by-side TF version. In 1957, when the F-102s were still new, Convair put the whole force through an update program. This redelivered all to a common standard, with a taller fin, MG-10 instead of MG-3 radar fire control system and launch tubes for 2.75in FFARs (folding-fin aircraft

rockets) in the large missile-bay doors. In the 1960s a further update deleted the rockets and added an IR sensor ahead of the knife-edge windshield.

The Delta Dagger was big and impressive, painted a glossy pale gray, and had a small but comfortable cockpit· where the pilot flew with two control columns, that on the left being used to adjust the sweep angle and range gate of the MG-10 radar. In the search mode the pilot flew with one hand on each stick and his eyes pressed into the viewing hood of the radar display screen. In the semi-automatic mode missiles could be extended automatically into the airstream and fired at the correct moment.

By 1974 surviving F-102s — called "Deuces" — had been assigned to the US Air National Guard and to the air forces of Greece and Turkey. Sperry converted surviving US Deuces into remotely piloted QF and unmanned PQM versions for use in threat evaluation, F-15 Eagle pilot combat training and other aerial research.

Lockheed F-104 Starfighter

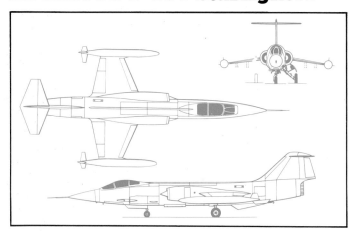

Origin: Lockheed-California Company, Burbank, California.
Type: (A, C) single-seat day interceptor, (B, D) dual trainer, (QF) drone RPV.
Engine: One General Electric J79 single-shaft turbojet with afterburner, (A, B) 14,800lb (6,713kg) J79-3B, (C, D) 15,800lb

Above: All single-seat Starfighters looked superficially similar. This is an F-104G, used in USAF markings to train Luftwaffe pilots. Underwing pylons dotted.

(7,165kg) J79-7A.
Dimensions: Span (without tip tanks) 21ft 11in (6.68m); length

Above: Nobody could deny that the Starfighter, in this case a new F-104A-20, was striking to look at. Whether it was a good fighter was another matter.

54ft 9in (16.69m); height 13ft 6in (4.11m); wing area 179sq ft (16.64m^2).

Weights: Empty (A) 12,562lb (5,698kg); maximum loaded 19,600lb (8,891kg).
Performance: Maximum speed 1,450mph (2,330km/h, Mach 2.2); initial climb 50,000ft (15,250m)/min; service ceiling 58,000ft (17,680m) (zoom ceiling óver 90,000ft, 27,400m); range

Sikorsky S-56, H-37 Mojave

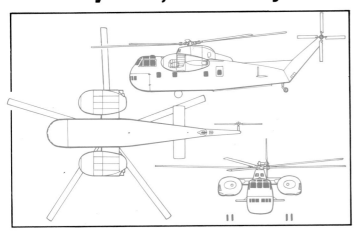

Origin: Sikorsky Aircraft Division of United Aircraft, Bridgeport, Connecticut.
Type: HR2S, heavy assault transport, HR2S-1W, radar picket/AEW, H-37, heavy transport.
Engines: Two 1,900hp Pratt & Whitney Double Wasp R-2800-50 or -54 18-cylinder two-row radials.
Dimensions: Diameter of five-blade rotor 72ft (21.95m); length overall (rotors turning) 82ft 10in (25.25m), (fuselage only) 64ft 3in (19.58m); height overall 22ft (6.71m); main-rotor disc area 4,072sq ft (378.2m^2).
Weights: (H-37A) empty 20,831lb (9,449kg); maximum loaded 31,000lb (14,062kg).
Performance: Maximum speed 130mph (209km/h); cruising speed 115mph (185km/h); range with max payload (typical) 145 miles (233km).
Armament: None.
History: First flight (XHR2S) 18 December 1953; (HR2S-1) 25 October 1955; service delivery July 1956; final delivery May 1960.

Above: The HR2S and derived H-37 Mojave were almost the same apart from equipment details. Engines had open-side cowls and twin exhausts.

Users: Navy, Marine Corps.

Designed to meet a 1950 requirement for a large assault helicopter for the US Marine Corps, the S-56 was unfortunate in that it missed by a few year being able to use turbine engines. It thus was a heavy and rather cumbersome machine, with its big fan-cooled piston engines housed in nacelles carried outboard on stub wings, and also accommodating the long legs of the retractable twin-wheel main gears. A cockpit rather like that of an S-55 was mounted above full-width clamshell nose doors admitting 26 troops, 24 litters, three Jeeps, a 105mm howitzer and crew, or similar loads, equipment including a 2,000lb (907kg) winch on an overhead rail. An Honest John rocket or light armor could be carried as a slung load, the record being 13,250lb (6,010kg)

Above: A Marine Corps HR2S-1 pictured landing on the escort/-ASW carrier Boxer (CVS-21) in November 1959. The speck overhead is a Sikorsky HRS (S-55).

lifted to 7,000ft (2,134m).

The Marines took 55 HR2S-1s (CH-37C after 1962), while the Army bought 94 H-37As, all eventually fitted with autostabilization, crashproof tanks and other changes to bring them up to CH-37B standard. The Navy attempted to use the S-56 as a radar picket, today called an AEW (airborne early-warning) platform.

Two HR2S-1W helicopters were tested, fitted with the APS-25E surveillance radar in a grotesque chin installation occupying the entire space under the cockpit and with operators in the rear fuselage, but ceiling and endurance were unimpressive. A major result of the S-56 was dynamic parts suitable for the later families of twin-turbine helicopters.

Below: One of the two swollen-chin HR2S-1W radar picket (AEW) rebuilds. The US today has no AEW-AWACS helicopter.

---

with maximum weapons, about 300 miles (483km); range with two drop tanks (high altitude, subsonic) 1,000 miles (1,610km).
Armament: Two underwing pylons each rated at 1,000lb (454kg); additional racks for small missiles (eg Sidewinder) on under wings or on tips; certain versions have reduced fuel and one 20mm M61 Vulcan multi-barrel gun in fuselage.
History: First flight (XF-104) 7 February 1954, (F-104A) 17 February 1956.
Users: AF, ANG.

Clarence L. ("Kelly") Johnson planned the Model 83 after talking with fighter pilots in Korea in 1951. The apparent need was for superior flight performance, even at the expense of reduced equipment and other penalties. When the XF-104 flew, powered by a 10,500lb 4,763kg) J65 Sapphire with afterburner, it appeared to have hardly any wing; another

odd feature was the downward-ejecting seat.

The F-104 was one of the biggest paradoxes in the history of fighters. It was created by a brilliant team very experienced in fighters, and had the benefit of two world-beating new products of US industry: the J79 engine, with a multi-variable-stator compressor giving tremendous performance, and the M61 "Vulcan" multi-barrel gun (incidentally a product of the same company) which enabled a single gun to provide devastating firepower, yet the overall result proved disappointing. Largely because of the concentration on sheer flight performance, the F-104 proved to be a very "hot" and unforgiving aircraft to fly, and the small wing area restricted mission flexibility, weapon load and combat maneuverability.

In fact the wing was not only incredibly small but also almost "razor thin", with a thickness/

chord ratio of only 3.6 per cent. This made it difficult to accommodate the aileron power units, which had to fit into a depth of one inch. The entire leading edge hinged down for takeoff and landing, and it was planned to boost low-speed lift by using powerful blown flaps, using high-pressure air from the engine, but this was not ready for the develpoment prototypes. Very neat main gears folding forward into the fuselage used Liquid Spring shock struts by Dowty. In the pointed nose was an MA-10 gunsight system with small ASG-14 ranging radar, but the airplane was intended strictly for visual daytime air combat.

The production F-104A had a more powerful engine and blown flaps, and after lengthy development entered limited service with Air Defense Command in 1958. Only 153 were built and after a spell with the Air National Guard, survivors again saw ADC service

with the powerful GE-19 engine. Three were modified as Astronaut trainers with rocket boost, one gaining a world height record at nearly 119,000ft (36,271m) in 1963.

The B was a dual tandem trainer, the C a fighter-bomber for Tactical Air Command with refueling probe, and the D a trainer version of the C. Apart from the 77 F-104Cs which equipped the 479th TFW at George AFB in 1958-65, the F-104 saw little combat duty. In camouflage surviving C models saw brief use in Vietnam, but by the late 1960s most A/B/C/D models were being used up as QF-104 targets.

From 1960 Lockheed sold the strengthened and totally re-equipped F-104G and its sub-variants to many countries. The only examples of this later generation to bear AF insignia were Luftwaffe F-104G and TF-104G airplanes used as conversion trainers at Luke AFB.

Sikorsky S-58, H-34 Choctaw/Seahorse

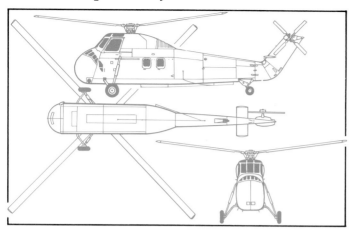

Above: Apart from details, mainly along the underside, this Army Choctaw could be a Navy Seabat or Marine Seahorse. All versions had the folding tail section.

Above: 148073, a regular HUS-1 Seahorse seen in action with Marine Aircraft Group 26, HMH-362. Today this squadron flies the Super Stallion, which is just ten times as powerful.

Origin: Sikorsky Aircraft Division of United Aircraft Corporation, Bridgeport, Connecticut.
Type: ASW or transport helicopter.
Engine: One 1,525hp Wright R-1820-84C piston radial engine.
Dimensions: Main (4-bladed) rotor diameter 56ft (17.07m); fuselage length 46ft 9in (14.25m); height 14ft 3½in (4.36m).
Weights: Empty 7,650lb (3,515kg); gross 13,000lb (5,900kg).
Performance: Maximum speed at sea level 122mph (196km/h);

cruising speed 97mph (156km/h); service ceiling 9,500ft (2,900m); range with maximum fuel plus 10 per cent reserve 247 miles (400km).
Armament: None.
History: First flight 8 March 1954; deliveries to US Army began April 1955.
Users: Army (H-34A), Marines

(UH-34D Seahorse), Navy (SH-34).

This useful helicopter was designed by Sikorsky to meet the needs of the US Navy for a helicopter able to do a much more complete ASW role than the S-55 versions (the planned dedicated ASW helicopter, the HSL-1, having pro-

ved unsatisfactory). With the designation HSS-1 Seabat, it followed the layout of the SS-55 but was larger and had a conventional fuselage, without a pod-and-boom configuration. Another difference was that instead of having "a wheel at each corner" there was a traditional tailwheel-type landing gear. For shipboard stowage the main rotor and the entire tail could be folded. Service started in August 1955.

The HSS-1 (from 1962 redesignated SH-34G) soon showed that with its doppler radar, automatic hover coupler and ad-

Douglas A-4 Skyhawk

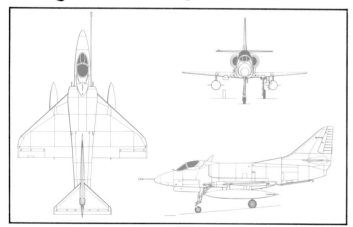

Above: The second production model, and first to have an inflight-refueling probe, the A4D-2 became the A-4B.

Above: Near Nellis, two Air Force Eagles lead two TA-4J attack trainers of VA-127 Royal Blues, from NAS Lemoore.

Origin: Douglas Aircraft Company, El Segundo, California, later moved to McDonnell Douglas, Long Beach, California.
Type: Single-seat attack bomber; TA, dual-control trainer.
Engine: (B, C) one 7,700lb (3,493kg) thrust Wright J65-16A single-shaft turbojet (US Sapphire); (E, J) 8,500lb (3,856kg) Pratt & Whitney J52-6 two-shaft turbojet; (F) 9,300lb (4,218kg) J52-8A; (M, N) 11,200lb (5,080kg) J52-408A.
Dimensions: Span 27ft 6in (8.38m); length (A) 39ft 1in (11.91m), (B) 39ft 6in (12.04m) (42ft 10¾in 13.07m) over FR probe), (E, F) 40ft 1½in (12.22m), (M, N) 40ft 3¼in (12.27m), (TA series, excluding probe) 42ft 7¼in (12.98m); height 15ft (4.57m), (early single-seaters 15ft 2in, TA

series 15ft 3in); wing area 260sq ft (24.15m²).
Weights: Empty (A) 7,700lb (3,493kg), (E) 9,284lb (4,211kg), (typical modern single-seat, eg M) 10,465lb (4,747kg), (TA-4F) 10,602lb (4,809kg); maximum loaded (A) 17,000lb (7,711kg), (B) 22,000lb (9,979kg), (all others, shipboard) 24,500lb (11,113kg), (land-based) 27,420lb (12,437kg).
Performance: Maximum speed (clean) (B) 676mph (1,088km/h), (E) 685mph (1,102km/h),(M) 670mph (1,078km/h), (TA-4F) 675mph; maximum speed (4,000lb-1,814kg bombload) (F) 593mph (954km/h), (M) 645mph (1,038km/h); initial climb (F)

5,620ft (1,713m)/min, (M) 8,440ft (2,572m)/min; service ceiling (all, clean) about 49,000ft (14,935m); range (clean, or with 4,000lb/1,814kg weapons and maximum fuel, all late versions) about 920 miles (1,480km); maximum range (M) 2,055 miles (3,307km).
Armament: Standard on most versions, two 20mm Mk 12 cannon, each with 200 rounds; pylons under fuselage and wings for total ordnance load of (A, B, C) 5,000lb (2,268kg), (E, F) 8,200lb (3,720kg), (M, N) 9,155lb (4,153kg).
History: First flight (XA4D-1) 22 June 1954, (A-4A) 14 August

1954, squadron delivery October 1956, (A-4C) August 1959, (A-4E) July 1961, (A-4F) August 1966; (A-4M) April 1970, (A-4N) June 1972, first of TA series (TA-4E) June 1965.
Users: Navy, Marine Corps.

Most expert opinion in the US Navy refused to believe the claim of Ed Heinemann, chief engineer of what was then Douglas El Segundo, that he could build a jet attack bomber weighing half the 30,000lb (13,600kg) specified by the Navy. The first Skyhawk, nicknamed "Heinemann's Hot Rod", not only flew but gained a world record by flying a 311 miles (500km) circuit at over 695mph (1,118km/h). Today over 30 years later, greatly developed versions are still in use. These late versions do weigh close to

vanced stabilization system it could do a really useful job even at night or in bad weather, but it could not carry dipping sonar or other ASW sensors as well as torpedoes, so helicopters either worked in pairs or called up surface ships to do the killing.

Soon the Army and Marines realized what a useful trucking system the S-58 could make, and respectively bought the H-34 Choctaw and HUS-1 Seahorse. After 1962 the latter became the UH-34D. These transport versions could seat 16, or carry eight litters or 5,000lb (2,268) of cargo including Jeeps or artillery slung underneath.

Seven VH-34Ds were assigned in 1960 to the joint Army/Marines Executive Flight Detachment in Washington, and there were various versions bringing Sikorsky's production total to 1,821, which was until recently a record for any Sikorsky type. These helicopters served all over the world, including the Arctic, but saw peak employment in Vietnam.

Right: It is not possible to read the unit on this Navy S-58, which is probably HUS-1 BuNo 149323. Finish is Midnight Blue.

30,000lb, but only because the basic design has been improved with more powerful engines, increased fuel capacity and much heavier weapon load. The wing was made in a single unit, forming an integral fuel tank and so small it did not need to fold. The tall main gears fold forwards, the legs lying under the main wing box and the wheels ahead of it. The rudder has a single skin down the centre, with ribs on each side.

Hundreds of Skyhawks have served aboard carriers, but in the US involvement in SE Asia "The Scooter" (as it was affectionately known) flew many kinds of mission from land bases. In early versions the emphasis was on improving range and load and the addition of all-weather avionics. The F model introduced the dorsal hump containing additional avionics, and the M, the so-called Skyhawk II, marked a major increase in mission effectiveness. Most of the TA-4 trainers closely resembled the corresponding single-seater, but the TA-4J and certain other models have simplified avionics and are used not only for advanced pilot training but also by the "Top Gun" and similar fighter-pilot training units for dissimilar aircraft combat training.

In the Vietnam War hundreds of A-4s saw intensive action from the summer of 1964. The types involved were the A-4C, D, E, F, M and TA-4F, operated by many squadrons of the Navy and

Left: An A-4M Skyhawk II, with a two-seat TA-4F in attendance, serving with Marine light attack squadron VMAT-102 Hawks, from MCAS Yuma, Arizona.

Marine Corps. In August 1965, during the 37-month Rolling Thunder bombing campaign against North Vietnam, two A-4Es became the first Navy aircraft, and almost the first in history, to be brought down by SAMs. Vast amounts of ordnance were delivered, usually with great accuracy, the Marines aircraft operating chiefly from Bien Hoa AB. Among missions flown by the two-seaters was spotting for the guns of the 7th Fleet offshore.

Though production was completed in 1979 after 26 unbroken years, with deliveries amounting to 2,405 attack models and 555 two-seaters, updating programs continue to improve survivors in Navy and Marine Corps service. There is also a major rebuild program which since 1980 has given the Marines 23 two-seat TA-4F trainers rebuilt as OA-4M FAC (Forward Air Control) platforms with avionics basically as in the A-4M and rear canopy sections faired into the "camel hump". Many versions, both new and ex-US service, have been exported.

Left: A Zuni, the biggest unguided rocket in regular use, blasts earthward from A-4M Skyhawk II BuNo 158158, with VMA-324 at Beaufort, Maryland.

Douglas B-66 Destroyer

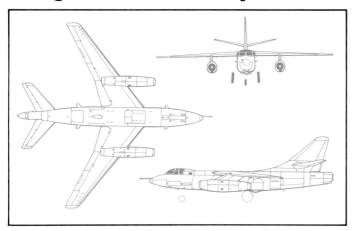

Above: 53-506 was photographed in January 1957 when newly built at Tulsa as a B-66B. Paint and add-ons had yet to come.

Origin: Douglas Aircraft Company, Long Beach, California, and Tulsa, Oklahoma.
Type: Originally tactical attack bomber; later, different roles (see text).
Engines: Two 10,000lb (4,536kg) thrust Allison J71-13 single-shaft turbojets.
Dimensions: Span 72ft 6in (22.1m); length depending on sub-type, 75ft 2in - 78ft 9in (22.9 -24m); height 23ft 6in (7.16m); wing area 780sq ft (72.46m²).

Above: One of the rebuilds for electronic warfare in Vietnam was the EB-66E, with multiple antennas but no guns.

Weights: Empty (B-66B) 42,369lb (19,218kg); maximum loaded (B-66B) 83,000lb (37,648kg).
Performance: Maximum speed (typical) 610mph (982km/h); initial climb 3,600ft (1,100m)/min; service ceiling 43,000ft (13,110m); range with maximum fuel 2,000 miles (3,220km).

Armament: Normally none; as built, most bomber B-66s had two remotely controlled 20mm cannon in a tail turret and internal provision for 15,000lb (6,804kg) bombload.
History: First flight (RB-66A) 28 June 1954, service delivery (RB-66B) March 1956; last

delivery of new aircraft (WB-66D) September 1958.
User: AF.

The B-66 Destroyer was produced by the Long Beach plant to meet the needs of the US Air Force. What had begun as a minimum modification of the Skywarrior turned into a totally different aircraft. Though it looked similar, apart from the changed wing plan, hardly a single airframe part or item of equipment

Grumman F11F Tiger

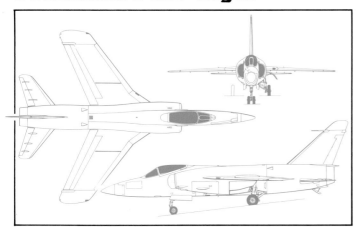

Above: BuNo 138620 was a regular F11F-1 (later F-11A), with long nose and inflight-refueling probe. Probably the Tiger was unlucky to run into such a rival as the Vought F-8.

Origin: Grumman Aircraft Engineering Corporation, Bethpage, NY.
Type: Single-seat carrier-based fighter bomber.
Engine: (F-11A) one 11,000lb (4,990kg) thrust Wright J65-4 single-shaft turbojet with afterburner; (F11F-1F) one 15,000lb (6,804kg) thrust General Electric J79-3A single-shaft turbojet with afterburner.
Dimensions: Span 31ft 7½in (9.63m); length 44ft 11in (13.7m); height 13ft 3in (4.05m); wing area 250sq ft (23.23m²).
Weights: Empty (F-11A) 13,428lb (6,092kg); loaded (F-11A) 22,160lb (10,052kg).
Performance: Maximum speed (F-11A) 890mph (1,432km/h), (F11F-1F) about 1,350mph (2,170km/h, Mach 2.05); initial climb (F-11A) 18,000ft (5,500m)/min, (F11F-1F) over 25,000ft (7,620m)/min; service ceiling (F-11A) 50,500ft (15,400m);

Above: F11F-1 Tigers of the second batch had a longer nose with provision for radar which was never fitted. Only the tips of the wings folded outboard of leading- and trailing-edge flaps.

range (F-11A) 700 miles (1,130km).
Armament: Four 20mm cannon and four AIM-9C or similar Sidewinder air-to-air missiles.
History: First flight 30 July 1954; service delivery March 1957; final delivery December 1958.
User: Navy.

Originally designated F9F-9, the Tiger was intended to be a further development of the Panther/Cougar family, but with the agreement of the Navy Bureau of Aeronautics the attempt was changed into a totally new design. One of the insistent cries heard during the Korean War was for fighters having higher combat

performance to beat the MiG-15 and this exerted a major influence on American designers. Ed Heinemann produced the A-4 Skyhawk, Kelly Johnson the F-104 Starfighter and the Grumman fighter team the G-98.

It was an outstandingly attractive little design and it took shape very fast. The Navy contract for six development aircraft was placed on 27 April 1953, and first flight followed 15 months later. The timing was exactly right for the Tiger to incorporate the NACA Area Rule for minimum transonic and supersonic drag and as a result the body was waisted to allow for the volume of the wing. The latter was only 6.5

per cent thick, with full-span slats and flaps, long spoilers and skins made from single slabs of light-alloy machined to shape. The nose gear had twin wheels and was steerable, and main gears retracted into the fuselage. With the thrust of the J65 engine — the British Armstrong Siddeley Sapphire in an Americanized version — the Tiger was easily supersonic.

It was also a delight to fly and together 201 production examples were delivered, including 12 of the tandem dual trainer version. The superseded F9F-9 Navy designation was changed to F11F-1, the trainer being F11F-1T. In 1962 the designation was changed again to F-11A. Tigers served in fighter/attack squadrons and also equipped the Navy Blue Angels aerobatic team. Though very popular these small fighters had various limitations, and were transferred from front-line

was common, and the B-66 proved difficult and expensive.

After building five RB-66s for indoctrination, Long Beach and a re-opened wartime plant at Tulsa built 145 RB-66B reconnaissance aircraft as well as 72 B-66B bombers. There followed 36 RB-66C electronic reconnaissance aircraft with a four-man crew, and 36 WB-66Ds for weather reconnaissance. Modified further over the years for many clandestine special ferreting missions, a number of EB-66E aircraft served throughout the Vietnam War.

Unarmed, these aircraft were packed with special electronics for Elint and tactical ECM jamming, and until the EF-111A Raven entered service in 1982 the EB-66B, C and E were the Air Force's only dedicated EW platforms. One unit, the 39th TEWS, flew EBs in West Germany from 1969 until 1982.

Below: Climbing out of Takhli AB an EB-66E has on board a pilot, navigator and four EWOs (electronic-warfare officers).

Below: Looking down on a B-66B during toss-bombing tests with dummy nuclear weapons near Edwards in fall 1957.

squadrons to Advanced Training Command in 1959.

The much more powerful F11F-1F Super Tiger did not go into production, but one of the two built achieved fame by colliding from behind with 20mm shells it had fired about a minute previously!

Right: A fine line of F11F-1s of an Atlantic Fleet squadron in 1959, the year this fighter began to be replaced.

Below: The Tiger was one of the more popular mounts of the famed Blue Angels Navy Aerobatic team here seen in 1968.

Lockheed C-130 Hercules

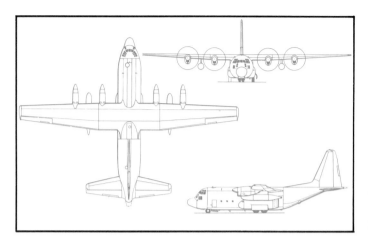

Origin: Lockheed-Georgia Company, Marietta, Georgia.
Type: Multirole airlift transport; special variants, see text.
Engines: Four Allison T56 turboprops, (B and E families) 4,050ehp T56-7, (H family) 4,910ehp T56-15 flat-rated at 4508ehp; (J) Allison AE 2100D3 flat-rated at 4,591ehp.
Dimensions: Span 132ft 7in (40.41m); length (basic) 97ft 9in (29.79m), (HC-130H, arms spread) 106ft 4in (32.41m), (C-130H-30) 112ft 9in (34.37m); height overall wing area 1,745sq ft (162.12m²).
Weights: Empty (basic E, H) 72,892lb (33,063kg); operating weight (H) 75,832lb (34,397kg); loaded (E, H) 155,000lb (70,310kg), max overload (H, J) 175,000lb (79,380kg).
Performance: Max speed at 175,000lb (E, H), also max cruising speed 386mph (621km/h), (J) 400mph; economical cruise 345mph (556km/h); initial SL

Above: Most standard-length "Herky birds" look similar. This C-130E has tanks but no pillbox-like SKE (station-keeping equipment) antenna above the forward fuselage, now standard.

climb (E) 1,830ft (558m)/min, (H) 1,900ft (579m)/min; service ceiling at 155,000lb, (E) 23,000ft (7,010m), (H) 26,500ft (8,075m); range with max payload (H) 2,407 miles (4,002km), (J) 3,262 miles (5,250km); ferry range with reserves (H) 4,606 miles (7,412km); takeoff to 50ft (15m) (H at 175,000lb) 5,160ft (1,573m), (J at 175,000lb) 4,700ft (1,433m); landing from 50ft (15m) (H at 100,000lb/45,360kg) 2,700ft (823m).
Armament: Normally none.
History: First flight (YC-130A) 23 August 1954, (production C-130A) 7 April 1955; service delivery December 1956.
Users: AF, ANG, Coast Guard, Navy, Marine Corps.

Above: Greatest cloak 'n dagger experts of any Western air force, the MC-130Es "insert" and recover agents, grab special cargo from enemy territory and lead a James Bond style existence.

Certainly the greatest military transport aircraft in history, the C-130 was originally designed for USAF Tactical Air Command in 1951. At that time all military transports were piston engined, and almost all had tailwheel landing gears giving a sloping floor accessed by side doors. In contrast the C-130 had a high wing, unobstructed interior 10ft 3in (3.13m) wide and 9ft 2.7in (2.8m) high, with a flat level floor at truck-bed height, pressurization and air-conditioning, full-section rear door and vehicle ramp, turboprop propulsion for high performance, a modern flight deck, and retractable landing gear with "high flotation" tires for use from unprepared airstrips.

All were incorporated in the Lockheed Model 82 which in June 1951 won an Air Force requirement for a new and versatile transport for TAC. The Allison turboprop matured at the right time, together with a new species of advanced propeller and other new-technology items including high-strength 2024 aluminum alloy, machined skin planks for the wing and cargo floor, metal/metal bonding and titanium alloys for the nacelles and flap skins. Another new feature was a miniature APU (auxiliary power unit) in one of the landing-gear blisters to provide ground power for air-conditioning and main-engine pneumatic starting. In the air the C-130 handled almost like a fighter, with a wholly new level of capability.

The most numerous variant is the C-130H of 1975, with new engines flat-rated to give high power under hot/high conditions and with numerous small updates

Fairchild C-123 Provider

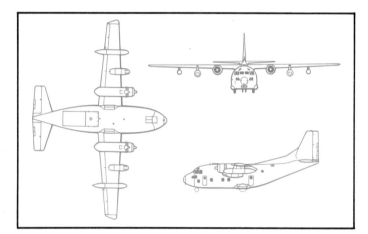

Origin: Fairchild Hiller, previously Fairchild Aircraft Division, Hagerstown, Maryland.
Type: Transport, night attack system and special operations.
Engines: Two 2,300hp Pratt & Whitney R-2800-99W radials; (C-123K) the two piston engines plus two 2,850lb (1,293kg) thrust General Electric J85-GE-17 auxiliary turbojets mounted in underwing pods.
Dimensions: Span 110ft (33.35m); length 75ft 3in

Above: The final version, used intensively in Vietnam, was the C-123K. These were rebuilds with auxiliary jet pods.

(23.25m); height 34ft 1in (10.38m); wing area 1,223sq ft (113.62m²).
Weights: Empty (B) 31,058lb (14,000kg), (K) 35,336lb (16,042kg); maximum takeoff weight (all) 60,000lb (27,240kg).
Performance: (B) maximum speed 245mph (329km/h);

Above: A C-123B-17 on a routine paratroop exercise in the pre-camouflaged 1950s. The left MLG door is missing.

cruising speed 190mph (304km/h); (K) maximum speed at 10,000ft (3,050m) 228mph (367km/h); cruising speed at 10,000ft (3,050m) 173mph (278km/h); range (B) 1,470 miles (2,365km).
Armament: (AC-123B) bomb canister dispenser.

History: First flight (C-123B prototype) 1 September 1954; (K) 27 May 1966.
Users: AF, ANG.

In 1949 Chase Aircraft produced the XG-20 all-metal cargo glider, with a cantilever high wing and large box-like cargo compartment with full-section rear ramp door. This was then fitted with R-2800 Double Wasp engines, becoming the XC-123 Avitruc; another had four J47 turbojets in

throughout the airframe (so that, in the Lockheed advertising, the "Herky bird keeps acting newer and newer"). Certainly it is remarkable how supposed replacements or successors to the C-130 have come and gone while customers continue to queue up for Brand X. Current versions are listed below.

EC-130E is the USAF ABCCC (Airborne Battlefield Command and Control Center) carrying a giant 40ft (12.2m) windowless capsule filled with special communications and a battle staff of 12. Another EC-130E variant is the Coronet Solo II model for Elint, packed with trailing-wire antennas each at least a mile (1.6km) long as well as a mass of new blade and blister antennas of which the largest are under the outer wings and ahead of the fin.

MC-130E is the Combat Talon black-painted model used by the USAF 1, 7 and 8 Special Ops Sqns

Above: LAPES (low-altitude parachute extraction system) pulls an M551 Sheridan from a MAC C-130 in 1976.

for clandestine missions at treetop level, with a mass of special gear (including a STAR retrieval yoke for snatching agents off the ground), FLIR, TFR, ECM and crew of 9 to 11.

C-130H-CAML is a cargo-aircraft minelayer, with large sea mines pushed out with any desired time-spacing on hydraulically powered pallets. C-130H-MP is a maritime patrol model for surveillance and SAR, with very complete navaids and communications, forward-looking and side-looking radars. FLIR, passive image intensifier, airdrop rescue kit, loudspeaker, cameras and crew stations matched to patrol times up to 17h on station.

C-130H-30 has a stretched fuselage (see data). EC-130H is a spe-

Above: Not listed below, but still very much in use, the armed models include this AC-130A, seen flying from Eglin in 1977.

cial Compass Call aircraft with high-powered jammers interlinked with friendly surface systems to interfere with enemy command, control and communications. HC-130H is an extended-range model for mid-air recovery of spacecraft, RPVs and other objects. JHC-130H is a special space-capsule recovery version. KC-130H is a standard long-range tanker/transport model for probe/drogue air refuelling. C-130J is the latest variant, privately funded by Lockheed Martin initially for the RAF. Every part of the structure, systems, engines and the avionics is up-graded, yet the only part that shows is the new six-blade propeller.

HC-130N is an SAR version for USAF with augmented navaids

and space-retrieval gear. HC-130P is as HC-130N with added hose drum for refueling helicopters. EC-130Q is the latest US Navy Tacamo communications platform with special VLF system for contact with submerged submarines. It orbits around a vertically hanging wire antenna 26,000ft (8km) long.

KC-130R is the Marine Corps tanker/transport, able to offload 52,000lb (23,587kg) at a radius of 1,150 miles (1,850km). LC-130R is a wheel/ski Navy version for polar missions. KC-130T is an improved KC-130R with new avionics (R can only top up fighters). AC-130U Spectre is a third-generation gunship with new avionics and weapons. EC-130V is a Coast Guard AWACS version with Hawkeye radar.

Total Hercules orders exceed 2,200, and the order book has been revitalised by the C-130J version. Sales have been made to 60 air forces and 30 civil customers.

---

underwing pods! The basic design was obviously good, and in 1953 Kaiser-Frazer was awarded a contract for 300 C-123Bs. Difficulties at the Willow run, Michigan, plant led to a new contract with Fairchild.

Fairchild delivered 302 on AF contracts, plus 24 for friendly nations. There were many experimental and one-off variants, and production Providers underwent various modifications. A wider undercarriage on the C-123H, for instance, helped correct a sensitivity to crosswinds during landings. Also, ten of the B models each received wingtip auxiliary Fairchild J44 turbojets for service in the Arctic as C-123Js.

In the hands of a group known as The Mule Train, the C-123B became the first transport to see service in South Vietnam.

The Providers flown by The Mule Train were joined by the UC-123Bs of Project Ranch Hand, which sprayed pesticides for malaria prevention and herbicides that destroyed both the forest that concealed the Viet Cong and the rice and manioc plants that fed them.

One C-123B served as a personal transport for General William C. Westmoreland. Two others, unofficially called AC-123s, mounted a sensor capable of detecting enemy trucks. Upon locating a convoy, the night attack model dropped canisters that opened to scatter small, spherical bomblets. The C-123 also dispensed flares to illuminate targets

for fighters or bombers. These Candlestick C-123s proved effective against truck traffic in Laos.

The addition of jet engines improved performance. The C-123K could climb at 1,220ft (372m)/min with one piston engine shut down, and in that same condition maintain level flight at 21,000ft (6,430m). It could clear a 50ft (15m) obstacle after a

takeoff run of 1,809ft (551m). A few wheel/ski C-123Js were still flying with the Alaska ANG until 1979.

Below: A C-123B-9 still hard at it on a rescue training mission out of Fort Benning, Georgia, in June 1975. By this time most Providers, including 54-669, had gone to AFRES.

McDonnell F-101 Voodoo

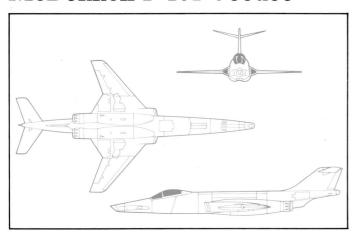

Origin: McDonnell Aircraft Company, St Louis, Missouri.
Type: (A, C) day fighter-bomber; (B) all-weather interceptor; (RF) all-weather reconnaissance.
Engines: Two Pratt & Whitney J57 two-shaft turbojets with afterburner; (F-101B) 14,990lb (6,800kg) J57-53 or -55; (others) 14,880lb (6,750kg) J57-13.
Dimensions: Span 39ft 8in (12.09m); length 67ft 4¾in (20.55m), (RF) 69ft 3in; height 18ft (5.49m); wing area 368sq ft (34.19m²).
Weights: Empty (typical of all) 28,000lb (12,700kg); maximum loaded (B) 46,700lb (21,180kg); (all versions, overload 51,000lb (23,133kg).
Performance: Maximum speed

Above: The most valuable model in Vietnam was the RF-101C, the long-nosed reconnaissance version. Many were later rebuilt into the ANG's RF-101G and H.

(B) 1,220mph (1,963km/h, Mach 1.85), (others, typical) 1,100mph (1,770km/h); initial climb (B) 17,000ft (5,180m)/min; service ceiling 52,000ft (15,850m); range on internal fuel (B) 1,550 miles (2,500km), (others) 1,700 miles (2,736km).
Armament: (A) four 20mm M-39 cannon in nose plus three AIM-4 Falcon AAMs or 12 HVAR rockets on rotary weapon-bay doors; (B) three Falcon (usually AIM-4D) air-to-air missiles semi-submerged in underside,

Above: An F-101B all-weather interceptor of the 49th FIS (oddly devoid of external stores or unit markings) during a gunnery meet at Tyndall AFB in 1967.

sometimes supplemented by two AIR-2A Genie nuclear rockets on fuselage pylons; (C) three 20mm M-39 cannon (provision for four, with Tacan removed) in fuselage; (RF) none. As built, all C and derivatives were fitted with a centerline crutch for a 1 MT tactical nuclear store and wing pylons for two 2,000lb (907kg) bombs, four 680lb (310kg) mines or other ordnance.
History: First flight 29 September 1954; service delivery (A) May 1957; final

delivery (B) March 1961.
Users: AF, ANG.

By far the most powerful fighter of its day, the Voodoo was based on the XF-88 Voodoo prototype flown on 20 October 1948. This was an outstanding all-swept aircraft packed with new technology which exceeded Mach 1 in dives. On the limited power of two Westinghouse J34 engines it could not have the range needed for its role of escort for SAC bombers.

The concept was resurrected in 1951, and with more than three times the engine power and an extra fuel tank section in the fuselage the F-101A prototype was much heavier and twice as powerful as any previous US

Cessna T-37 Tweet and A-37 Dragonfly

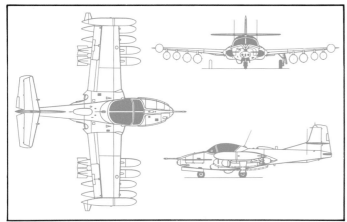

Origin: Cessna Aircraft Company, Wichita, Kansas.
Type: T-37, primary trainer; A-37, light attack.
Engines: (T) two 1,025lb (465kg) thrust Teledyne CAE J69-25 turbojets, (A) two 2,850lb (1,293kg) thrust General Electric J85-17A turbojets.
Dimensions: Span (T) 33ft 9¼in (10.3m), (A, over tanks) 35ft 10.5in (10.93m); length (T) 29ft 2in (8.92m), (A, excl refueling probe) 28ft 3in (8.62m); height 9ft 2in (2.79m); wing area 183.9sq ft (17.09m²).
Weights: Empty (T) 3,870lb (1,755kg), (A) 6,211lb (2,817kg); loaded (T) 6,600lb (2,993kg), (A) 14,000lb (6,350kg).

Above: This A-37B is shown with the maximum load of external stores (dotted in side view). The earlier T-37B will not now be replaced by the new T-46A.

Performance: Maximum speed (T) 426mph (685km/h), (A) 507mph (816km/h); normal cruising speed (T) 380mph (612km/h), (A, clean) 489mph (787km/h); initial climb (T) 3,020ft (920m)/min, (A) 6,990ft (2,130m)/min; service ceiling (T) 35,100ft (10,700m), (A) 41,765ft (12,730m); range (T, 5 per cent reserves, 25,000ft/7,620m cruise) 604 miles (972km), (A, maximum fuel, four drop tanks), 1,012 miles (1,628km), (A, maximum

Above: Today the Dragonflies are painted in low-contrast gray colors, with toned-down markings. This example took part in "Team Spirit '85".

payload including 4,100lb/1,860kg ordnance) 460 miles (740km).
Armament: (T) none, (A) GAU-2B/A 7.62mm Minigun in fuselage, eight underwing pylons (four inners 870lb/394kg each, next 600lb/272kg and outers 500lb/227kg) for large number of weapons, pods, dispensers, clusters, launchers or recon/EW equipment.
History: First flight (T) 12 October 1954, (A)

22 October 1963.
Users: AF, ANG.

After prolonged study the Air Force decided in 1952 to adopt a jet primary pilot trainer, and after a design competition the Cessna Model 318 was selected. Features included all-metal stressed-skin construction, side-by-side seats and a single broad clam-shell canopy, two small engines in the wing roots with nozzles at the trailing edge, fixed tailplane half-way up the fin, manual controls with electric trim, hydraulic slotted flaps and hydraulic tricycle landing gear of exceptional track but short length, placing the parked aircraft low on the ground.

fighter. In the nose was a search radar, behind which was the cockpit far ahead of the relatively tiny wing, with sharp-lipped fixed root inlets. The engines were behind the wing spars, with short afterburners under the rear fuselage. The slab horizontal tail had dihedral and was mounted near the top of the broad fin.

Originally a long-range escort for Strategic Air Command, the F-101A became a tactical attack machine; 77 were followed by 47 improved C models with nuclear-bomb pylons, all of which set records for accident-free operation and were converted to unarmed RF-101G and H for the Air National Guard, augmenting 35 RF-101A and 166 RF-101C built earlier with long camera-filled noses and used intensively at all levels in Vietnam.

The B interceptor sacrificed fuel for a radar operator to work the MG-13 radar fire-control. It had more powerful afterburners, and altogether 478 were built and converted to F-101F or dual-control TF-101F for Air Defense Command, later passing to the Air National Guard.

In 1961 66 ex-ADC aircraft were transferred to the RCAF as CF-101s; in 1970 the CAF exchanged the 58 survivors for 66 improved F and TF versions which were the last Voodoos in service.

Below: Supersonic shock-diamonds glow in the jet from a massive nuclear-head AIR-2A Genie missile fired by an F-101B of USAF 2nd FIS of ADC (Adcom).

Above: The F-101Bs, the last of the many versions in service, ended their time with the ANG, in this case the 179th FIS based at Duluth AFB, Minnesota.

Below: The F-101B version had larger afterburners than the others. Here they slam to full 'burn on takeoff from Malmstrom AFB (HQ of a Minuteman wing).

The introduction was delayed by numerous trivial modifications and even when service use began in 1957 pupils were first trained on the T-34. Altogether 534 T-37As were built, but all were brought up to standard of the T-37B of 1959, which had more powerful J69 engines, improved radio, navaids and revised instrument panel. After 41 had been converted to A-37As further T-37Bs were brought in 1957 to bring the total of this model to 447. They serve in roughly equal numbers with the advanced T-38A at all the USAF's pilot schools: 12th Flying Training Wing at Randolph; 14th at Columbus (Miss); 47th at Laughlin; 64th at Reese; 71st at Vance; 80th at Sheppard and 82nd at Williams.

The A-37 was derived to meet a need in the early 1960s for a light attack aircraft to fly Co-In (counter-insurgent) missions. Cessna had previously produced two T-37C armed trainers (many of this model were later supplied to Foreign Aid recipients, including South Vietnam in the 1960s, and later these aircraft were then rebuilt as AT-37 prototypes (designation YAT-37D) with much more powerful engines and airframes restressed for increased weights which, in stages, were raised to 14,000lb (6,350kg). No fewer than eight

underwing pylons plus wingtip tanks were added, giving a great weapon-carrying capability whilst increasing performance.

Redesignated A-37A, a squadron converted from T-37B on the production line was evaluated in Vietnam in 1967. Altogether 39 A-37As were built by converting T-37Bs on the line, followed by 511 of the regular USAF production model with full-rated J85 engines, 6g structure, flight-refueling probe, greater internal tankage and other changes. The A-37 Dragonfly proved valuable in Southeast Asia, where many were left in South Vietnamese hands after the US withdrawal.

After the end of the US involvement, the A-37B was withdrawn from regular USAF service except in South Korea, but it continues to equip a Reserve wing and two Air National Guard groups. All surviving Dragonflies in the ANG have been equipped for FAC (Forward Air Control) duty. The AFR's 434th TFW flies the A-37B at Grissom AFB, Bunker Hill, Indiana, and the ANG units are the 174th TFG (Syracuse, NY) and the 175th (Baltimore, Md).

Right: Chocks away under a camouflaged hide as an A-37B starts a 1985 combat exercise.

Vought F8U (F-8) Crusader

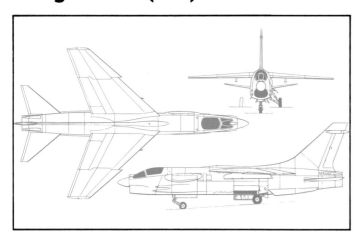

Origin: Chance Vought Aircraft, Dallas, Texas.
Type: Carrier-based day fighter and fighter-bomber, (RF) photo reconnaissance.
Engine: One Pratt & Whitney J57 two-shaft turbojet with afterburner; (A, B, F, L) 16,200lb (7,327kg) J57-12; (C, K) 16,900lb (7,665kg) J57-J16; (D, E, H, J) 18,000lb (8,165kg) J57-20A. About 100 F-8J re-engined with 19,600lb (8,890kg) J57-420.
Dimensions: Span 35ft 8in (10.87m), (E, J) 35ft 2in; length

Above: The F-8J was a remake of the F-8E (F8U-2NE), the final new-build variant for the US Navy. Note FR probe blister.

54ft 3in (16.54m), (E, J) 54ft 6in; height 15ft 9in (4.8m); wing area 350sq ft (32.5m^2).
Weights: Empty (C) about 17,000lb (7,710kg), (J) 19,700lb (8,935kg); maximum loaded (C) 27,550lb (12,500kg), (J) 34,000lb (15,420kg).
Performance: Maximum speed, clean, at altitude (A, B, L, H)

Above: F8U-2NE No 143710 was rebuilt into the unique TF-8A trainer, which had a long career with the Naval Test Pilot School.

1,013mph (1,630km/h); (RF-8A) 982mph (1,580km/h), (RF-8G) 1,002mph (1,612km/h), (C, K, J) 1,105mph (1,780km/h, Mach 1.68), (E) 1,135mph (1,826km/h), (D) 1,230mph (1,979km/h); initial climb (typical) 21,000ft (6,400m)/min; service ceiling, from 38,400ft (11,704m) for J to 42,900ft (13,100m) for D; combat

radius, from 368 miles (592km) for C, K to 440 miles (708km) for J and 455 miles (732km) for D.
Armament: (A, B, C) four 20mm Colt Mk 12 cannon each with 84 rounds; one sidewinder on each side and 32 folding-fin rockets in belly pack; (D) four 20mm plus four Sidewinder; (E, H, J) four 20mm plus four Sidewinder plus 12 Mk 81 bombs, or two Bullpups or eight Zuni rockets; (K, L) as J but 144 rounds per gun; RF versions, none.
History: First flight (XF8U-1) 25

Lockheed TR-1 and TR-2

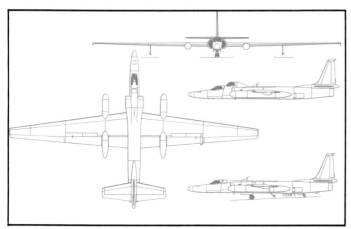

Origin: Lockheed-California Company, Burbank, California.
Type: High-altitude photo-reconnaissance, multisensor reconnaissance and special reconnaissance aircraft; (CT) dual trainer; (WU) weather research aircraft.
Engine: (U-2A), one 11,200lb (5,080kg) thrust Pratt & Whitney J57-37A turbojet; (U-2R, TR-1) one 17,000lb (7,711kg) thrust Pratt & Whitney J75-13B turbojet; (36 of 37 survivors, from 1997) one 17,000lb (7,711kg) thrust General Electric F118-101 turbofan.
Dimensions: Span (A, B, C, CT, D) 80ft (24.38m), (R, WU-2CV, TR-1) 103ft (31.89m); length (typical of early versions) 49ft 7in (15.1m), (R, TR) 62ft 9in (19.13m); height (R, TR) 16ft 1in (4.9m) wing area (early) 565sq ft (52.49m^2), (R, TR) 1,000sq ft (92.9m^2).
Weights: Empty (A) 9,920lb (4,500kg), (B, C, CT, D) typically

Above: The TR-1A is very like the U2R. The upper side view shows the two-seat TR-1B (these are painted white, not black).

11,700lb (5,350kg), (R) 14,990lb (6,800kg), (TR-1A) 15,500lb (7,031kg), (TR-1B) 15,750lb (7,144kg); loaded (A) 14,800lb (6,713kg), (B, C, CT, D, clean) typically 16,000lb (7,258kg), (with 89 US gal wing tanks) 17,270lb (7,833kg), (R) 41,000lb (18,598kg), (TR-1A) 41,300lb (18,734kg), (TR-1B) 41,550lb (18,847kg).
Performance: Maximum speed (A) 494mph (795km/h), (B, C, CT, D) 528mph (850km/h), (R) about 510mph (821km/h), (TR) probably about 495mph (797km/h), max cruising speed (most) 460mph (740km/h), (TR) 430mph (692km/h); operational ceiling (A) 70,000ft (21,340m), (B, C, CT, D) 85,000ft (25,908m), (R, TR) about 90,000ft (27,432m);

Above: 80-10329 was the first of the giant U-2Rs, serving as an Elint sleuth with the 100th SRW from about 1972.

max range (A) 2,200 miles (3,540km), (B, C, CT, D) 3,000 miles (4,830km), (R) about 3,500 miles (5,833km), (TR) about 4,000 miles (6,437km); endurance on internal fuel (A) 5$\frac{1}{2}$hr, (B, C, CT, D). 6$\frac{1}{2}$hr, (R) 7$\frac{1}{2}$hr, (TR) 12hr.
Armament: None.
History: First flight (U-2) 1 August 1955, (TR-1A) September 1981.
Users: AF, NAVY, NASA.

How the original U-2A was secretly built in the Lockheed Skunk Works, under the direction of Clarence L. "Kelly" Johnson, for the CIA has become part of history. So too has the thrilling tale of the clandestine overflights by unmarked U-2Bs, suddenly halted when F. G. Powers' aircraft was

shot down over Sverdlovsk on May Day 1960. But this was by no means the end of the program.

Lockheed built 104 aircraft of this graceful long-span family, and there are almost as many different versions. At least 40 of the original variants are still flying, but the only models currently operational in the USAF inventory are the U-2R and TR-1, the latter being in production as recently as 1984.

All are of the enlarged family created in the mid-1960s, except for USAF No 56-6953, one of the U-2CT pilot trainers which did an important job teaching pilots how to cope with the trickiest airplane to fly – and the most difficult to land – in any modern air force.

The original mission was direct overflights of hostile territory at the greatest possible height. The original J57 engine was soon replaced by the bigger and more powerful J75, which has remained

March 1955; (production F-8A) November 1956; service delivery 25 March 1957; final delivery 1965. **Users:** Navy, Marine Corps.

This outstanding carrier-based fighter, notable for its variable-incidence wing, outperformed the F-100 on the same engine, besides having 1,400gal (6,365 litres) internal fuel! Exceeding Mach 1 on the level on the first flight, the F8U (as it then was) was rapidly developed for carrier service, and for 12 years was a popular combat aircraft of the US Navy and Marines. Its most unusual feature was that the wing was mounted on top of the fuselage and arranged to pivot under pilot control. For takeoff or landing the incidence could be increased to give greater lift whilst holding the fuselage in a level attitude. This gave the pilot an excellent view ahead and enabled short landing gears to be used, retracting into the fuselage. The belly rocket pack was actually hinged down to enable the rockets to be fired straight ahead, and in turn it carried the large door-type airbrake. Most of the fuel was housed in integral tanks occupying almost the entire wing out as far as the hinges of the upward-folding outer panels, which had extended-chord leading edges with dog teeth.

Altogether 1,259 were built, plus two prototypes, and in 1966-71 446 were rebuilt to a later standard (B to L, C to K, E to J and D to H). The continual process of improvement added all-weather radar, improved autopilot and weapon-delivery systems, air/ground weapons, and completely rebuilt structures for continued first-line duty in the updated versions. Variants include RF reconnaissance, DF Drone RPV and QF RPV-control aircraft; a single dual trainer was also built.

The F-8 Crusader represented over half of the carrier fighters in the Gulf of Tonkin in the first four years of the Vietnam War. The Navy's Crusader under Cdr Jim Stockdale made first use of 2,000lb (907kg) bombs on the F-8. His innovation required a catapult launch with minimum fuel; the air-craft then refueled from an aerial tanker. F-8s often played the role of decoy against SAMs,

above and ahead of the strike force. This was done to get the radar-controlled SAM battery to concentrate on the first and clearest target, thereby allowing the attacking divisions to reach their targets at little or no risk.

Photo escort missions generally involved one fighter covering an RF-8. On these missions the reconnaissance aircraft usually flew at 4,000ft (1,220m). This mission was the most dangerous and most costly, because the RF-8 had to fly straight and constant courses.

Above: Cleaning the windshield of an F-8E of VF-111 Sundowners prior to a mission over Vietnam from CVA-34 Oriskany in 1967.

Twenty RF-8Gs were lost during the war, nearly a quarter of the total Crusader losses.

The Crusader is credited with downing 19 MiGs in Vietnam, the majority with the AIM-9 missile. For the period 1965-68 the Crusader dominated the carriers' air combat statistics, claiming 63 per cent of the total MiG kills.

---

basically unchanged ever since (though the engines in all current aircraft are Dash-13Bs originally built with afterburners to power supersonic F-105s).

After the Cuban crisis of 1962 the overflights were mainly replaced by stand-off surveillance without actually violating frontiers, and in any case at this time Compass Cope and other RPVs were expected to handle the overflight missions. The requirement thus changed to demand a much heavier payload of reconnaissance sensors, while improving hostile defenses increasingly called for much more comprehensive ECM and other defense systems. Combined with the often critically marginal nature of the original U-2 sub-types the opportunity was taken to produce a new aircraft, with a much larger airframe, though still called a U-2.

All current machines, as noted, are of this bigger species, and though they were originally designated U-2R or TR-1, depending on when they were built, they are broadly the same aircraft (differences almost always being confined to equipment carried). Span was increased by 23ft (7m), and the increase in fuselage volume was no less than 100 per cent; other basic changes included a new and enlarged tail and stronger landing gears, the front and rear units being closer together, and the removable or jettisonable outriggers under the wings being of improved design.

The external oil coolers on each side of earlier models were eliminated, greatly reducing drag and improving lift/drag ratio to 27. Four integral tanks in the wings were supplemented by stainless sump tanks, internal capacity being raised from 1,100 to 1,562gal (5,000 to 7,100lit), eliminating the need for slipper external tanks. A zero/zero seat was fitted, and the sensor and equipment payload was more than doubled, with ample room in the fuselage "Q-bay" and in two giant "superpods" which can be attached to the wing. Handling was improved, especially at great heights, while the tricky landing was made easier by adding roll and lift spoilers above the wings, and an arrester hook.

Only 12 U-2Rs are known (68-10329/10340), though the assigned numbers go up to 10353. Most are matt black, but a few are in Europe 1 camouflage. Nearly all are distinguished by special sensors or antennas. A few began life with plain wingtip skids, but almost all today have tip pods housing a RHAWS with flat oblique ends covering the internal spiral receiver. Aircraft assigned to Elint (Sigint and Comint) data-gathering missions sprout a "farm" of ventral antennas, most of them straight or curved blades.

Total production comprised 55 of the original U-2A version in 1955-60, 12 U-2Rs in 1967-68, and a final upgraded batch in 1980-89 comprising seven U-2Rs, a U-2RT trainer, 25 TR-1As, two TR-1B trainers and two ER-2s for NASA. Over the years the U-2Rs and TR-1s have been brought approximately to the same standard, and since 1994 all survivors have been called U-2Rs, the trainers being U-2RTs. A total of 37 are in service, and 36 are in 1996-98 being re-engined with the General Electric F118-101 turbofan, which is much lighter and offers greatly increased aircraft range and improved reliability. The re-engined aircraft are designated U-2S.

The F118 helps to counter the increasing weight of sensors, and it notably includes ASARS (which stands for advanced synthetic-aperture radar system) in either or both superpods, with a flat face for the directional aerial array. Known as UPD-X, this radar provides a finegrain printout of everything within 35 miles (55km) to one side of the flight path (U-2/TR-1 optical cameras can give even better definition out to 100 miles, 161km, but may be thwarted by cloud or other obscurity).

The most striking modification is the C-Span III, which adds a giant dome on a pylon above the fuselage for real-time communication of reconnaissance information via satellite. Another sensor is the PLSS (originally PELSS, precision emitter location strike system), which derived from Pave Nickel and Pave Onyx tested on U-2Rs over many years. This DME-type system enables two (preferably three) aircraft to pinpoint the location of every emitter on the ground to within an accuracy of 3ft (1m).

Below: The U-2R is only slightly less difficult to fly than earlier models. Both the centerline gears retract forward; outriggers are off.

Republic F-105 Thunderchief

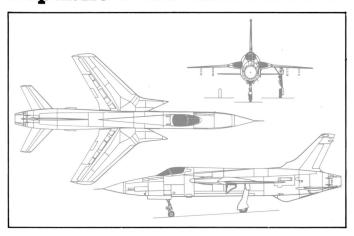

Origin: Republic Aviation Corporation, Farmingdale, NY.
Type: Single-seat all-weather fighter-bomber; (F-105F) two-seat operational trainer; (G) two-seat ECM.
Engine: One Pratt & Whitney J75 two-shaft afterburning turbojet; (B) 23,500lb (10,660kg) J75-5, (D, F, G) 24,500lb (11,113kg) J75-19W.
Dimensions: Span 34ft 11¼in (10.65m); length (B, D) 64ft 3in (19.58m), (F, G) 69ft 7½in (21.21m); height (B, D) 19ft 8in (5.99m), (F, G) 20ft 2in (6.15m); wing area 385sq ft (35.77m²).
Weights: Empty (B) 23,905lb, (10,843kg), (D) 27,500lb (12,474kg), (F, G) 28,393lb (12,879kg); maximum loaded (B) 44,598lb (20,230kg), (D) 52,546lb (23,834kg), (F, G) 54,027lb (24,507kg).
Performance: Maximum speed (B) 1,254mph (2,818km/h), (D, F,

Above: As originally delivered the F-105D did not have a full-length dorsal spine fairing.

G) 1,480mph (2,382km/h, Mach 2.25), initial climb (B, D, typical) 34,500ft (10,500m)/min, (F, G) 32,000ft (9,750m)/min; service ceiling (typical) 52,000ft (15,850m); tactical radius with 16 750lb (340kg) bombs (D) 230 miles (370km); ferry range with maximum fuel (typical) 2,390 miles (3,846km).
Armament: One 20mm M-61 gun with 1,029 rounds in left side of fuselage; internal bay for ordnance load of up to 8,000lb (3,629kg), and five external pylons for additional load of 6,000lb (2,722kg). From 1960 the internal bay was usually occupied by a fuel tank, and bombs up to 3,000lb (1,361kg) and other stores were hung externally.

Above: F-105Ds of the 34th TFS, 388th TFW, toting 750-pounders during Combat Sky Spot in 1968.

History: First flight (YF-105A) 22 October 1955, (production B) 26 May 1956, (D) 9 June 1959; (F) 11 June 1963; final delivery 1964.
Users: AF, ANG.

The AP-63 project was a private venture by Republic Aviation to follow the F-84. Its primary mission was delivery of nuclear or conventional weapons in all-weathers, with very high speed and long range. Though it had only the stop-gap J57 engine, the first YF-105A Thunderchief exceeded the speed of sound on its maiden flight, and the B model was soon in production for Tactical Air Command.

Apart from being the biggest single-seat, single-engine combat aircraft in history, the 105 was

Right 58-1173, an F-105D-5, was used for armament tests (such as 16 GP bombs).

notable for its large internal bomb bay and unique swept-forward engine inlets in the wing roots, which were so high off the ground that only a tall athletic pilot could jump up to inspect them on preflight walkround. Another odd feature was that going into afterburner partly opened the airbrakes, these four large petal doors surrounding the engine nozzle!

Only 75 F-105Bs were delivered, but 610 of the advanced D model were built, with Nasarr R-14A monopulse radar and doppler navigation. Production was completed with 143 tandem-seat F-105Fs with full operational equipment and dual controls.

Known as "the Thud", this

Douglas C-133 Cargomaster

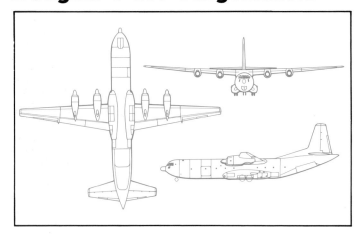

Origin: Douglas Aircraft Company, Long Beach, California.
Type: Heavy logistic freighter.
Engines: (C-133A) four 7,000ehp Pratt & Whitney T34-7 single-shaft axial turboprops; (C-133B) 7,500ehp T34-9W.
Dimensions: Span 179ft 8in (54.75m); length 157ft 6½in (48.02m); height 48ft 3in (14.7m); wing area 2,673sq ft (248.33m²).
Weights: Empty 120,263lb (54,550kg); maximum loaded (early 133A) 275,000lb (124,740kg), (133B) 286,000lb (129,727kg).

Above: There were only 68 C-133s. This C-133A had a different rear ramp door from that fitted to the C-133B.

Performance: Maximum speed 359mph (578km/h); initial climb 1,280ft (389m)/min; service ceiling at gross weight 29,950ft (9,129m); range with 44,000lb (19,960kg) payload 4,300 miles (6,920km).
Armament: None.
History: First flight (first production C-133A) 23 April 1956; service delivery 29 August 1957;

Above: This C-133A (56-2007) visited Santa Monica for the compatibility test with the SM-65 Atlas on 19 September 1958.

first flight of C-133B 31 October 1959.
Users: AF, ANG.

Designed to meet an Air Force requirement for a logistic transport capable of carrying indivisible bulky loads which could not easily be loaded into the C-124, the C-133 was a bold, clean design with four

Right: A famous shot of a C-133B of MATS heading in over San Francisco, 50 miles (80km) southwest of Travis.

of the powerful single-shaft turboprops developed at Pratt & Whitney since 1944. These engines had powered C-97, R7V-2 (Navy Super Constellation) and YC-124B aircraft, and were fully developed in time for the C-133.

The C-133 owed little to the C-124 but was a totally new design following the logical layout of the C-130,

emissions. Thirteen of these modified Fs were sent to South-East Asia in 1966, and 10 others soon followed. Of the 86, 14 were modified to launch another anti-radiation missile, the AGM-78 Standard ARM.

The F-105G was a modified Wild Weasel F-105F which could protect itself by jamming enemy radar. This model used the Standard ARM rather than the older, shorter range Shrike, and it carried ALQ-105 ECM pods scabbed on flush against the fuselage sides.

Right: Typifying the Wild Weasel conversions for Vietnam, 63-8265 was a two-seat F-105G with ECM pods, three tanks and two Shrike ARM missiles.

greatest of all single-engined combat jets bore a huge burden throughout the Vietnam War. It was in early 1965 that F-105Ds first struck north of the 17th parallel. Thunderchiefs also performed tactical air strikes in South Vietnam and Laos. The D made more strikes against North Vietnam than any other US aircraft, and also suffered more losses. They were continually being modified to meet changing South-East Asia combat needs. By 1971 F-105Ds were equipped with armor plate, a secondary flight control system,

an improved ejection seat, ECM pods for the wings, and a suite of new radar homing and warning systems, chaff dispensers and other self-defense items.

Various avionics contractors developed the Thunderstick improved navigation and fire-control system. By 1970 a batch of 30 F-105Ds had received the T-stick II installation giving a blind-bombing capability. This was distinguished by a large saddleback fairing from cockpit to fin.

Since it had the same basic failings as the D, the F underwent similar modifications to reduce vulnerability. Because it carried a second crewman, the F model seemed well suited to the role of suppressing North Vietnam's missile defenses. Eighty-six F-105s fitted with radar homing and warning gear formed the backbone of the Wild Weasel program, initiated in 1965 to improve the AF's electronic warfare capability. Upon pinpointing the radar at a missile site, the Wild Weasel attacked with Shrike missiles that homed on radar

As the war losses continued, the aircraft was gradually phased out until by mid-1973 only 17 F-105Fs still flew, five with the AF and 12 with the ANG. From 1965 to 1972 the aircraft performed yeoman service on many diversified missions in South-East Asia. They had dropped bombs by day and occasionally by night from high or low altitude and, in Wild Weasel guise, attacked SAM sites with their radar tracking air-to-ground missiles. During the war the versatile Thud was also credited with 25 MiG kills.

with the cantilever wing placed above a large pressurized fuselage of circular section with full width rear doors. The latter allowed the giant new Atlas and Titan ICBMs to be carried. Two tandem pairs of large main wheels retracted into an unpressurized fairing on each side of the fuselage. Flight controls were powered, the wing had large track-mounted flaps, and a nose "thimble" housed weather radar.

No prototype was ordered, a

contract for 35 being signed in 1954. While these aircraft were being delivered from the Long Beach plant, changes were made in the shape of the rear fuselage and freight door arrangement, and the final three introduced clamshell rear doors which extended the usable interior length, enabling Titan to be conveyed with both stages mated. A further 15 more powerful aircraft were then ordered as the C-133B, delivery

being completed in 1961.

These B-models were specially adapted to the carriage of the Thor, Jupiter, Atlas, Titan and Minuteman ballistic missiles, which they delivered to operational sites throughout the United States and to Europe. An A-model set a world record by lifting a load of 117,900lb, (53,479kg), and approximately 96 per cent of all US military equipment could be carried by these capable machines.

During the build-up in Vietnam in 1965, the Military Airlift Command became hard-pressed for cargo aircraft. The C-141A was just entering service, the C-135 was better suited to carrying passengers, and the C-130Es remained basically tactical, rather than long-range, transports. The Douglas C-124A boasted a cavernous cargo hold, but the lumbering aircraft required some 95 hours' flying time for a round trip between Travis AFB and Tan Son Nhut airfield at Saigon. Almost by default, the three squadrons of C-133As and Bs emerged as the best of the trans-Pacific cargo carriers, even though they suffered recurring and sometimes fatal problems with their engines.

Throughout the Southeast Asia conflict, Military Airlift Command faced shortages of crews and aircraft like those that had arisen during the 1965 deployments. Members of the Air Force Reserve flew as crew members on transport missions to Southeast Asia even though their units were not called to active duty. The C-133 saw the conflict out but was progressively retired from MAC duty in 1977-79. Three survive as civil aircraft.

Boeing KC-135 Stratotanker

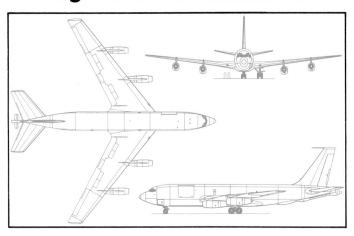

Origin: Boeing Airplane Company (from May 1961 The Boeing Company,), Seattle/Renton, Washington.
Type: Tankers, transports, EW, Elint, command-post and research aircraft.
Engines: (A and derivatives) four 13,750lb (6,273kg) thrust Pratt & Whitney J57-59W or -43WB turbojets, (B and derivatives) four 18,000lb (8,165kg) thrust Pratt & Whitney TF33-3 turbofans, (R) four 22,000lb (9,979kg) thrust F108-CF-100 turbofans; (18 special-role C-135 and 88 KC-135) retrofitted with 18,000lb (8,165kg) JT3D-3B ex-airline turbofans.
Dimensions: Span (basic) 130ft

Above: Apart from early models with short fin, all of the original run of KC-135As looked like this. Some are now being given F108 engines.

10in (39.88m); length (basic) 134ft 6in (40.99m); height (basic) 38ft 4in (11.68m), (tall fin) 41ft 8in (12.69m); wing area 2,433sq ft (226m²).
Performance: Max speed (all) about 580mph (933km/h); typical high-speed cruise 532mph (856km/h) at 35,000ft (10.700m); initial climb (J57, typical) 1,290ft (393m)/min, (TF33) 4,900ft (1,494m)/min; service ceiling (KC, full load) 36,000ft (10.975m), (C-135B) 44,000ft (13.410m);

Above: Typical of the numerous "funny" rebuilds, the RC-135V has enormous hamster-like SLAR cheeks, new chin sensor, and antennas on wingtips and tail.

mission radius (KC) 3,450 miles (5,552km) to offload 24,000lb (10,886kg) transfer fuel; 1,150 miles (1,950km) to offload 120,000lb (54,432kg); field length (KC, ISA + 17°C) 13,700ft (4,176m).
Armament: None.
History: First flight 31 August 1956, variants see text.
Users: AF, National Command Authorities.

In 1954 what was then the Boeing

Airplane Company risked more than its net worth to build a prototype jetliner, first flown in July 1954. An important factor behind the gamble was the belief the USAF would buy a jet tanker/ transport to replace the Boeing KC-97 family, and this belief was justified by the announcement of an initial order for 29 only three weeks after the company prototype flew, and before it had done any inflight refueling tests.

The KC-135A Stratotanker differed only in minor respects from the original prototype, whereas the civil 707 developed in a parallel program was a totally fresh design with a wider fuselage, airframe of

Bell UH-1 (Huey) Iroquois

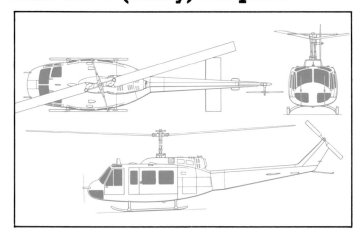

Origin: Bell Helicopter Textron, Fort Worth, Texas.
Type: Multirole utility helicopter.
Engines: (204) One Avco Lycoming T53 turboshaft rated at 770, 825 or 930shp, (205) usually one T53-13B flat-rated at 1,100shp, (212) Pratt & Whitney Canada PT6T-3 twin turboshaft flat-rated at 1,250shp but with each engine section able in emergency to delivery 900shp, (412) PT6T-3B-1 flat-rated at 1,308shp and with each engine able to supply 1,025shp in emergency.
Dimensions: Diameter of main rotor (two blades except 412) (204, UH-1B, -1C) 44ft (13.41m), (205, 212) 48ft (14.63m), (212 tracking tips) 48ft 2in (14.69m), (412, four-blades) 46ft (14.02m); overall length (rotors turning) (early) 53ft

Above: This drawing is typical of Iroquois versions based on the Model 205 and powered by the T53 engine. UH-1N versions have a visibly different engine, the T400 coupled unit.

(16.15m), (virtually all modern versions) 57ft 3in (17.46m); height overall (modern, typical) 14ft 5in (4.39m); main-rotor disc area (UH-1D/H/V) 1,809.57sq ft (168.11m²).
Weights: Empty (XH-40) about 4,000lb (1,814kg), (typical 205) 4,667lb (2,116kg), (typical 212) 5,549lb (2,517kg); maximum loaded (XH-40) 5,800lb (2,631kg), (typical 205) 9,500lb (4,309kg), (212/UH-1N) 10,500lb (4,762kg), (412) 11,500lb (5,212kg).
Performance: Maximum speed (all) typically 127mph (204km/h);

Above: This Navy UH-1N is typical of the Model 212 variants, powered by the PT6T (military designation T400) engine which with twin power sections adds safety.

econ cruise speed, usually same; max range with useful payload, typically 248 miles (400km).
Armament: See below.
History: First flight (XH-40) 22 October 1956, (production UH-1) 1958, (205) August 1961, (212) 1969.
Users: Army, AF, Marines, Navy.

Used by more air forces, and built in greater numbers, than any other military aircraft since World War II, the "Huey" family of helicopters grew from a single prototype, the XH-40, for the US Army. Over 20

years the gross weight has been almost multiplied by three, though the size has changed only slightly.

Early versions seat eight to ten, carried the occasional machine-gun, and included the TH-1L Seawolf trainer for the US Navy. Prior to 1962 the Army/Navy designation was basically HU-1, which gave rise to the name Huey, though the (rarely used) official name is Iroquois. Since 1962 the basic designation has been UH-1 (utility helicopter type 1). In August 1961 Bell flew the first Model 205 with many changes, of which the greatest was a longer fuselage giving room for up to 14 passengers or troops, or six litters and an attendant, r up to 3,880lb (1,759kg) of cargo.

All versions have blind-flying in-

2024 alloy designed on fail-safe principles, and totally revised systems. The KC-135A was thus a rapid program and deliveries began on 30 April 1957, building up to a frantic 20 per month, reaching 732 by January 1965.

The basic KC-135A has a windowless main fuselage with 80 tip-up troop or ground-crew seats and a cargo floor with tiedown fittings. Fuel is carried in 12 wing tanks and nine in the fuselage, only one of the latter being above the main floor (at the extreme tail). All but 1,000US gal (3,785lit) may be used as transfer fuel, pumped out via a Boeing high-speed extensible boom steered by a boom operator lying prone in the bottom of the rear fuselage.

The original short fin was later superseded by a tall fin and powered rudder, and many tankers were given an ARR (air refueling receiver) boom receptacle. The KC force numbers 615 active aircraft in 35 squadrons, including 80 aircraft in Reserve units. The 100th ARW (Air Refueling Wing) at Beale AFB exclusively uses the KC-135Q with special avionics and JP-7 fuel for the SR-71 aircraft. Many have been completely updated as KC-135Rs with the new-technology F108 engine, while 88 KC-135Es of the Air National Guard have ex-airline JT3Ds (TF33s).

MATS, now MAC, bought 15 C-135A and 30 C-135B Stratolifter transports, the Bs having fan engines with reversers and much sprightlier performance with less noise and smoke. These remained windowless but had the refueling boom removed (though retaining the operator's blister) and were equipped for 126 troops or 89,000lb (40,370kg) cargo loaded through a large door forward on the left side. In MATS these aircraft were soon replaced by the C-141. The final new-build versions were the four RC-135A survey/mapping aircraft for MATS and ten RC-135B for strategic reconnaissance. Thus, total C-135 production for the USAF numbered 808, completed in February 1965.

Since then the family has swelled by modification to become perhaps the most diverse in aviation history, the following all being USAF variants: EC-135A, radio link (SAC post-attack command control system); EC-135B, AF Systems Command, ex-RIA (Range Instru-

mented Aircraft) mainly twice-rebuilt; EC-135C, SAC command posts; EC-135G, ICBM launch and radio link (with boom); EC-135H, airborne command posts; EC-135J, airborne command posts (Pacaf); EC-135K, airborne command posts (TAC); EC-135L, special SAC relay platforms; EC-135N, now C-135N, Apollo range, four with A-LOTS pod tracker; EC-135P, communications/command posts; KC-135A, original designation retained for SAC relay links; KC-135R, also RC-135R, special recon/EW rebuilds; NC-135A, USAF, NASA and AEC above-ground nuclear-test and other radiation studies; NKC-135A, Systems Command (and Navy) for ECM/ECCM, laser, ionosphere, missile vulnerability, icing, comsat, weightless, boom and other research; RC-135B and C, recon aircraft with SLAR cheeks and other sensors; RC-35D, different SLARs and thimble noses; RC-135E, glassfiber forward fuselage and inboard wing pods; RC-135M, numerous electronic installations,

fan engines; RC-135S, most M installations plus many others; RC-135T, single special SAC aircraft; RC-135U, special sensors and aerials cover almost entire airframe, including SLAR cheeks, extended tailcone and various chin, dorsal, ventral and fin aerials; RC-135V, rebuild of seven Cs and one U with nose thimble, wire aerials and ventral blades; RC-135W, latest recon model mostly rebuilt from M with SLAR cheeks added; WC-135B, standard MAC weather platforms.

Today few of these rebuilds remain in service, and many have been reconverted as tankers.

Below: USAF No 61-2663 was the fourth of the sprightly C-135B Stratolifters powered by the then-new TF33 fan engine. It retained the boom operator's station, but not the boom, had a long-span tailplane, and is shown in its original MATS livery.

struments, night lighting, FM/-VHF/UHF radios, IFF transponder, DF/VOR, powered controls and searchlight. Options include a hook for a slung load, rescue hoist and various fits of simple weapons or armor. Most important of the Model 205 helicopters in US military service is the UH-1H, which remained in production until 1980. Ten have been converted as EH-1H Quick Fix EW (electronic-warfare) machines, but this role will be taken over by the more powerful EH-60A. About 220 were given augmented avionics and special equipment as UH-1V medevac transports.

The US Army plans to retain at least 2,700 improved UH-1Hs beyond the year 2000 for a wide range of duties, and apart from fitting glassfiber composite blades they will be completely upgraded with over 220 new items or improvements including a radar-warning receiver, chaff/flare dispenser, IR jammer, exhaust IR suppressor, radar altimeter, DME and secure communications even in NOE (nap of the Earth) flying. The Model 212 twin-engine helicopter is used by the US Navy, Marines and Air Force (total of 300) with designation UH-1N.

US services do not use the Bell Model 412, made by Agusta in Italy as the AB412 Griffon, which has a four-blade main rotor. By 1986 Bell had also not managed to sell to US military customers the bigger and much more powerful Model 214

family. Initially built for Iran, with a 2,930shp Lycoming T55, it is today produced as the further stretched 214ST with two 1,625shp GE T700s, and with a weight of 17,500lb (7,938kg).

Right: Most important of the early models was the UH-1D, still only powered by the 1,100shp T53 engine but with the bigger cabin of the Model 205. More than 1,000 were delivered from 1963 to serve as troop carriers with the Army in South Vietnam.

Below: Seldom seen today, the original model was the HU-1A, later restyled UH-1A, Army No 59-1695 being one of the 182 delivered. Compare the sliding cabin door with that of the stretched UH-1D in the picture above: The UH-1N is even longer.

Convair B-58 Hustler

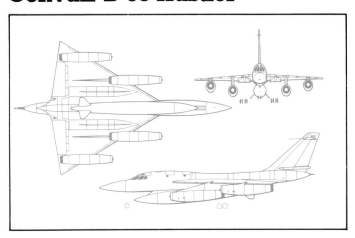

Origin: General Dynamics, Fort Worth, Texas.
Type: Three-seat supersonic bomber.
Engines: Four 15,600lb (7,076kg) thrust General Electric J79-5B or -5C single-shaft afterburning turbojets.
Dimensions: Span 56ft 10in (17.31m); length 96ft 9in (29.5m); height 31ft 5in (9.6m); wing area 1,542sq ft (143.26m²).
Weights: Empty (without pod)

Above: Extremely expensive to operate, the B-58 nevertheless was in many ways a staggering achievement. It almost always flew with a bomb/fuel pod.

55,560lb (25,200kg); maximum (take-off) 163,000lb (73,930kg); maximum (after air refueling) 177,0090lb (80,485kg).
Performance: Maximum speed 1,385mph (2,215km/h, Mach 2.1); initial climb at gross weight

Above: B-58A No 61-2066 pictured on 20 April 1964 on special Cat.2 stability and control tests without the bomb/fuel pod at Edwards, California.

17,400ft (5,310m)/min: service ceiling 64,000ft (19,500m); range on internal fuel 5,125 miles (8,248km).
Armament: One 20mm T-171 multi-barrel gun in tail with remote aiming; droppable pods of various

kinds, some having their own propulsion, containing thermonuclear bombs; additionally, underwing racks for four smaller nuclear or conventional bombs to total of 7,000lb (3,175kg). Normal payload drop weight 19,450lb (8,820kg).
History: First flight 11 November 1956; (production B-58A) September 1959; (TB-58) 10 May 1960; withdrawal January 1970.
User: AF.

Convair F-106 Delta Dart

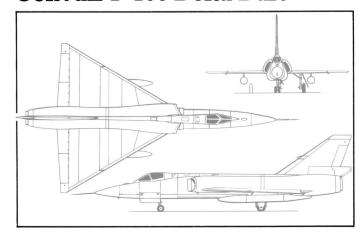

Origin: General Dynamics Convair Division, San Diego, California.
Type: All-weather interceptor, (B) operational trainer.
Engine: One 24,500lb (11,113kg) thrust Pratt & Whitney J75-17 afterburning turbojet.
Dimensions: Span 38ft 3in (11.67m); length (both) 70ft 8¾in (21.55m); height 20ft 3¼in (6.18m); wing area 661.5sq ft (61.52m²).
Weights: Empty (A) about 24,420lb (11,077kg); loaded (normal) 34,510lb (15,668kg).
Performance: Maximum speed (both) 1,525mph (2,455km/h) or Mach 2.3 at 36,000ft (10,973m); initial climb about 29,000ft (8,839m)/min; service ceiling 57,000ft (17,374m); range with drop tanks 1,800 miles (2,897km).
Armament: One 20mm M61A-1 gun, two AIM-4F plus two AIM-4G Falcons, plus one AIR-2A or -2G Genie nuclear rocket.
History: First flight (aerodynamic prototype) 26 December 1956, (B)

Above: The head-on view especially shows the total redesign of the F-106A compared with the F-102A.

9 April 1958; squadron delivery June 1959.
User: AF, ANG.

Derived from the earlier F-102 Delta Dagger, and originally designated F-102B, the F-106 completely met the requirements of Air (later Aerospace) Defense Command (Adcom) for a manned interceptor to defend the continental United States. The 106 was a natural development of the F-102A with new engine and avionics. By redesigning from scratch to the supersonic Area Rule, the fuselage was made much neater and more efficient than that of the earlier aircraft, with a slimmer profile, rear-mounted fully variable inlets and new internal bay for different weapons. The landing gears were new, the twin-wheel nose gear be-

Above: Firing a Genie nuclear-warhead rocket from an F-106A of the Air National Guard 144th Fighter Interceptor Sqn, Fresno.

ing steerable. The vertical tail was redesigned, and the more powerful engine resulted in a peak speed approximately twice as fast.

The Hughes MA-1 fire control, though no bulkier or heavier than that of the 102, was far more capable and integrated via a digital data-link with the SAGE (Semi-Automatic Ground Environment) defense system covering the continental United States in an automatic manner.

Though bought in only modest numbers, the 106 has had an exceptionally long life-span in the USAF Aerospace Defense Command front-line inventory. Indeed, it served much longer than intended, and in fact never did see a successor, despite the continued threat of the manned bomber. However, there were numerous

engineering improvements and some substantial updates, including the addition of the gun as well as improved avionics, an infra-red sensor of great sensitivity facing ahead for detecting heat from hostile aircraft and assisting the lock-on of AAMs, and a flight-refueling boom receptacle. Convair completed many other studies including an improved electric power system, solid-state computer, the AIMS (aircraft identification monitoring system) and an enhanced-capability variant for Awacs control.

The last of 277 F-106As and 63 tandem-seat F-106B armed trainers were delivered in 1961. Adcom was disbanded in 1980 and the F-106 ended its days flown only by fighter interceptor units in the ANG, assigned to TAC. It never did receive look-down shoot-down radar and missiles. Even in 1986 planned conversion of the last F-106 squadron to the F-15 has been put off for budgetary reasons.

The B-58 was an historic aircraft on many counts. It was the first supersonic bomber to go into production, and the first to reach Mach 2. It was the first aircraft constructed mainly from stainless-steel honeycomb sandwich; the first to have a slim body and fat payload pod so that, after dropping the payload (bomb plus empty fuel tank) it became a significantly smaller aircraft; the first to have stella-inertial navigation; and the first weapon system to be procured as a single package from a prime contractor responsible for every part of the system (of which the air vehicle was only a portion).

Technical difficulties were gigantic, yet the B-58 was developed with amazing speed and success. A tailless delta configuration was adopted, with flight control by a rudder and enormous wing elevons driven by hydraulic power units of unprecedented output. Almost the entire aircraft was sealed to form integral tankage. The entire airplane, with its pod, was area ruled for minimum drag. The stalky landing gear had main bogies each with eight very small wheels on

gatefold legs, all folding into thicker boxes in the very thin wings.

Pilot, navigator and defense-systems operator sat in tandem in encapsulated cockpits each capable of being ejected in emergency. The TB-58 crew trainers (eight converted B-58As) had stepped dual pilot cockpits, and no bomb/nav and ECM systems. In the tailcone was a 20mm "Gatling gun".

Only 116 B-58s were built, 30 for

development and 86 for combat duty, and in their decade in the inventory they set more world records than any other type of combat aircraft. The 43rd and 305th Bomb Wings frequently flew air-refueled missions lasting 12 to 20 hours, and set highly supersonic timings on such routes as New York to Paris and Tokyo to London. Despite its lack of high-lift devices, the B-58 was pleasant to fly and straightforward to land. It was also

Above: As B-58A No 60-1124 gets airborne its 16 main tires rotate faster than those of any other airplane. Note the payload pod.

exceptionally good at low-level.

The withdrawal from active operations in 1970 stemmed mainly from high costs. There were many proposals for improved B-58s, for fighter versions and for ECM, special-mission and missile-launch versions, but none was accepted.

Boeing Vertol H-46 Sea Knight

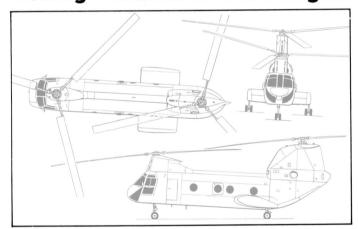

Origin: Boeing Vertol, Morton, Pennsylvania.
Type: Transport, search/rescue, and minesweeping helicopter.
Engines: Two 1,250-1,870shp General Electric T58 turboshafts.
Dimensions: Diameter of each three-blade main rotor 50ft (15.24m); fuselage length 44ft 10in (13.66m); height 16ft 8½in (5.09m); total area of rotor discs 4,086sq ft (379.6m²).
Weights: Empty (CH-46D) 10,732lb (4,868kg),(CH-46E) 11,585lb (5,240kg); max loaded (D) 23,000lb (10,432kg), (E) 21,400lb (9,706kg).
Performance: Typical cruise 120mph (193km/h); range with 30min reserve (6,600lb, 3,000kg payload) 109 miles (175km), (2,400lb, 1,088kg payload) 633 miles (1,020km).
Armament: Normally none.
History: First flight (107) April 1958, (prototype CH-46A) 27 August 1959.
Users: Marine Corps, Navy.

Above: All CH-46s and UH-46s look similar; early (CH-46A) versions had a smaller side door and there are small tail differences.

In the mid-1950s Vertol (later Boeing Vertol) developed the twin-turbine Model 107. From this the H-46 series, named Sea Knight in US service, was developed as a Marine Corps assault transport carrying 25 equipped troops or cargo payloads up to 7,000lb (3,175kg), with water landing and takeoff capability.

Of all-metal construction, the H-46 has the engines installed on each side of the large fin-like rear rotor pylon, a large unobstructed rectangular cabin, integrated cargo loading systems, full all-weather navaids, fixed twin-wheel tricycle landing gears and power-folding blades on the tandem rotors. Total deliveries amounted to 624, completed in 1970.

The basic CH-46 fleet is being updated with approximately 3,000

Above: CH-46Ds ferry Marines ashore from USS Tripoli in 1976.

Below: Unidentified Navy UH-46s.

glassfiber rotor blades, uprated T58-16 engines of 1,870shp, crash-attenuating crew seats, combat-resistant fuel system and improved rescue gear. The new helicopter is

designated CH-46E. Conversions are being done "in house" by Naval Air Systems Command with the aid of 345 update kits being supplied during 1985-88. A dedicated SAR (search and rescue) model is HH-46, while the US Navy uses the UH-46 for ship replenishment. Small numbers were delivered of the RH-46A for MCM (mine countermeasures).

McDonnell Douglas F-4 Phantom II

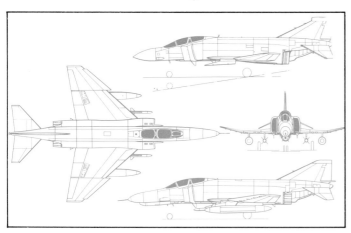

Origin: McDonnell Aircraft Company, division of McDonnell Douglas, St Louis, Missouri.
Type: Originally carrier-based all-weather interceptor, later all-weather multi-role fighter for ship or land operation, (RF) all-weather multisensor reconnaissance, (QF) RPV, (F-4G) defense-suppression aircraft.
Engines: (B) two 17,000lb (7,711kg) thrust General Electric J79-8 single-shaft turbojets with afterburner; (C, D) 17,000lb J79-15; (E, G) 17,900lb (8,120kg) J79-17; (J, N, S) 17,900lb J79-10.
Dimensions: Span 38ft 5in (11.7m); length (B, C, D, J, N, S) 58ft 3in (17.76m), (E and all RF versions) 62ft 11in or 63ft (19.2m); height (all) 16ft 3in (4.96m); wing area 530sq ft (49.24m²).
Weights: Empty (B) 28,000lb (12,700kg), (C, D, J) 28,200lb (12,792kg), (RF) 29,300lb (13,290kg), (E) 30,328lb (13,757kg), (G) 30,900lb (14,016kg); maximum (B) 54,600lb (24,767kg), (C, D, J, RF) 58,000lb (26,309kg), (E, G) 60,360lb (27,379kg).

Above: Main three-view shows the long-lived F-4E armed with Sparrow AAMs, while side view at top is of the F-4M.

Performance: Maximum speed with Sparrow missiles only (low) 910mph (1,464km/h, Mach 1.19), (high) 1,500mph (2,414km/h, Mach 2.27); initial climb, typically 28,000ft (8,534m)/min; service ceiling over 60,000ft (19,685m); range on internal fuel (no weapons) about 1,750 miles (2,817km); ferry range with external fuel, typically 2,300 miles (3,700km), (E and variants) 2,600 miles (4,184km).
Armament: (All versions except RF, QF which have no armament) four AIM-7 Sparrow air-to-air missiles recessed under fuselage; inner wing pylons can carry more AIM-7 or four AIM-9 Sidewinder missiles; in addition all E versions except RF have internal 20mm M-61 multi-barrel gun, and virtually all versions can carry the same gun in external centerline pod; all except RF, QF have centerline and four wing

Above: Toting AGM-45 Shrike anti-radar missiles, an F-4G screeches over Spangdahlem AB, West Germany.

pylons for tanks or stores to total weight of 16,000lb (7,257kg).
History: First flight (XF4H-1) 27 May 1958; service delivery (F-4A) February 1960 (carrier trials), February 1961 (inventory); first flight (Air Force F-4C) 27 May 1963, (F-4E) 30 June 1967, (EF-4E, later redesignated F-4G) 1976; final delivery March 1979.
Users: AF, ANG, Navy, Marine Corps.

McDonnell designed the greatest postwar fighter as a company venture to anticipate future needs. Planned as an attack aircraft with four 20mm guns, it was changed into an advanced gunless all-weather interceptor with advanced radar and missile armament.

A crucial factor behind the excellence of what first flew as the XF4H-1 was the choice of two of the slim and powerful J79 engines. Each was installed in a beautifully

tailored duct system with fully variable ramp-type lateral inlets and variable nozzles. The latter were close together under the rear fuselage, well forward of the tail as in the F3H. The overall layout resembled the F3H, but the bigger success was area ruled and had enormous blown flaps and blown drooping leading edges. Unusual features were the sharp dihedral on the folding outer wings and even sharper anhedral on the slab tailplanes (powered horizontal stabilizers). There was room for more fuel than in any previous Navy fighter, as well as a crew of two in tandem Martin-Baker seats. There were no guns, but in the broad flat underside of the fuselage were recesses for four Sparrows.

In this form it entered service as the F-4A, soon followed by the F-4B used in large numbers (635) by the US Navy and Marine Corps,

Below: With ALQ-119 ECM pods on board, F-4Es of 3TFW, from Clark AB, Philippines, fly in Exercise Team Spirit '85.

with Westinghouse APQ-72 radar, IR detector in a small fairing under the nose, and many weapon options. Pilot and radar intercept officer sit in tandem under canopies which in the F-4B were raised above the top line of the fuselage, and the aircraft had comprehensive combat equipment.

A level Mach number of 2.6 was achieved and many world records were set for speed, altitude and rate of climb. Not replaced by the abandoned F-111B, the carrier-based Phantom continued in production for 19 years through the F-4G with digital communications, F-4J with AWG-10 pulse-doppler radar, drooping ailerons, slatted tail and increased power, and the N (rebuilt B). In 1973-75 Navy facilities delivered 178 F-4Ns with completely revised avionics and strengthened airframe, as well as conversions of the original F-4A to TF-4A trainers and F-4Bs to QF-4B remotely piloted drones, since used in large numbers as missile targets and for other purposes.

The F-4Gs were returned to normal (N) standard and the designation was later used for a totally different USAF model. The final Navy/Marines variant is the F-4S, 265 of which were produced in-house by rebuilding F-4Js with improved avionics, strengthened structure (including completely new outer wings with very powerful slats) and a total rewiring.

These outstanding aircraft outperformed and outnumbered all other US combat aircraft of the 1960s. Vastly increased production, rising to a remarkable 75 per month in 1967, stemmed not only from the Vietnam war but also because the Air Force recognized that the F-4 beat even the specialist land-based types at their own missions, and after prolonged study decided to buy the basic F-4B version with minimal changes. The original Air Force designation of F-110 Spectre was changed to F-4C Phantom II under the unified 1962 system, the F-4C being a minimum-change version of the Navy B and preceded (from 24 January 1962) by the loan to TAC of 30 B models ex-Navy.

After buying 583 F-4Cs with dual controls, a boom receptacle, Dash-15 engines with cartridge starters, larger tires and increased-capacity brakes, inertial navigation and improved weapon aiming, the Air Force produced 793 of the F-4D model which was tailored to its own land-based missions, with APQ-109 radar, ASG-22 servoed sight, ASQ-91 weapon-release computer for nuclear LABS maneuvers, improved inertial system and 30kVA alternators. Visually, many Ds could be distinguished by removal of the AAA-4 IR detector in a pod under the radar, always on the C.

Next came the sophisticated RF-4C multi-sensor reconnaissance aircraft, a major rebuild in a program which preceded the D by two years and was the first Air Force variant to be authorized. Designed to supplement and then replace the RF-101 family, the RF-4C was unarmed but was modified to carry a battery of forward-looking and oblique cameras, IR linescan, SLAR (side-looking airborne radar) and a forward oblique mapping radar, as well as over 20 auxiliary fits including photo flash/flare cartridges in the top of the rear fuselage, and special ECM and HF shunt antennas built into the fin behind the leading edge on each side. TAC bought 505 of this model in 1964-73 and the Marines took 46 similar RF-4Bs.

All these variants were very heavily engaged in the war in SE Asia in 1966-73, where political rules combined with other problems to reduce the air-combat performance. Prolonged calls for an internal gun resulted in the F-4E, which had the most powerful J79 engine to permit the flight performance to be maintained despite adding weight at both ends. In the nose was the new solid-state APQ-120 radar and the M61 gun, slanting down on the ventral centerline with the 6 o'clock firing barrel near-horizontal, and at the rear was a new (No 7) fuel cell giving enhanced ranges. The first E was delivered to TAC on 3 October 1967, about three months after

first flight, and a total of 949 were supplied to maintain the F-4 as leading TAC aircraft with an average of 16 wings equipped throughout the period 1967-77. From 1972 all Es were rebuilt with a slatted leading edge, replacing the previous blown droop which permitted much tighter accelerative maneuvers to be made, especially at high weights, without stall/spin accidents which had caused many losses in Vietnam.

The final Air Force variant was the F-4G, the standard Advanced Wild Weasel platform replacing the F-105F and G which pioneered Wild Weasel missions in the late 1960s. The name covers all dedicated EW and anti-SAM missions in which specially equipped electronic aircraft hunt down hostile SAM installations (using radar for lock-on, tracking or missile guidance) and destroy them before or during an attack by other friendly aircraft on nearby targets. The F-4G (the same designation was used previously for modified F-4Bs of the Navy) is a rebuild of late-model F-4E (F-4E-42 through -45) fighters, and has almost the same airframe. It is the successor to the EF-4C, two squadrons of which were fielded by TAC from 1968 and which showed excellent performance with a simpler system.

In the F-4G the main EW system is the AN/APR-38, which provides very comprehensive radar homing

and warning and uses no fewer than 52 special antennas, of which the most obvious are pods facing forward under the nose (replacing the gun) and facing to the rear at the top of the vertical tail. The system is governed by a Texas Instruments reprogrammable software routine which thus keeps up to date on all known hostile emitters. Offensive weapons normally comprise triple AGM-65 EO-guided Mavericks on each inboard pylon plus a Shrike on each outer pylon; alternatively weapons can include the big Standard ARM (Anti-Radiation Missile), AGM-88 HARM (High-speed ARM) or various other precision air/ground weapons. A Westinghouse ALQ-119 jammer pod is fitted in the left front missile recess. The other three recesses carry Sparrow AAMs for self-protection. Another change is to fit the F-15 type centerline tank which can take 5g when full with 600gal (2,271lit). The G total was 116 aircraft.

The F-4F is to be retired from the USAF and ANG in 1997. By 1998 the only Phantoms with US forces are likely to be the QF-4E and QRF-4C remotely piloted drones and targets.

Below: An F-4C of the 171st FIS, Michigan ANG, based at historic Selfridge, seen before application of low-visibility markings.

Right: An F-4J (rebuilt as F-4S) of VF-32 blasts away from the John F. Kennedy (CVA-67) in 1969.

Lockheed P-3 Orion

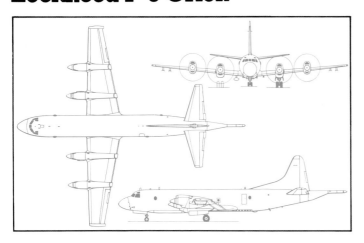

Origin: Lockheed-California Company, Burbank, California.
Type: Maritime patrol and ASW aircraft, (EP) EW platform; data are for P-3C Update.
Engines: Four 4,910ehp (4,510shp) Allison T56-14 turboprops.
Dimensions: Span 99ft 8in (30.37m); length 116ft 10in (35.61m); height overall 33ft 8½in (10.27m); wing area 1,300sq ft (120.77m²).
Weights: Empty 61,491lb (27,890kg); normal loaded 135,000lb (61,235kg); max 142,000lb (64,410kg).

Above: This basic P-3C has a plain nose with neither the camera gondola nor FLIR turret, but the LLTV pod is fitted.

Performance: Max speed (15,000ft/4,570m at 105,000lb/47,625kg) 473mph (761km/h); patrol speed 237mph (381km/h); takeoff over 50ft (15m) 5,490ft (1,673m); mission radius (3h on station at low level) 1,550 miles (2,494km), (no time on station) 2,383 miles (3,853km).
Armament: Internal bay can accommodate eight AS torpedoes,

Above: A P-3C Update development airplane gives a clear view of sonobuoy tubes, nose FLIR turret and external ALQ-78 pod.

or two Mk 101 nuclear depth bombs plus four torpedoes or a variety of mines and other stores; ten underwing pylons carry mines, depth bombs, torpedoes, Harpoon anti-ship missiles or other stores. Total expendable load 20,000lb (9,072kg).
History: First flight (aerodynamic prototype YP3V, converted Electra) 19 August 1958; (YP-3A)

November 1959, (P-3A) 15 April 1961, (P-3C) 18 September 1968; service delivery (A) August 1962, (C Update) April 1974, (Update II) August 1977, (Update III) August 1983.
Users: Navy, Navy Reserve.

Derived from the L-188 Electra passenger airliner, the P-3 Orion was specifically ordered as an off-the-shelf type, for operation in the ocean patrol and ASW role from shore bases. Nobody expected it to have a production run of over 30 years; moreover, it has become vir-

Sikorsky S-61, H-3 Sea King

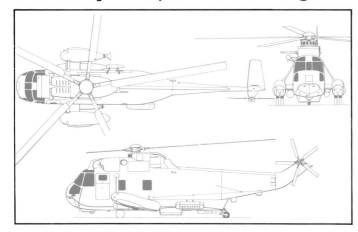

Origin: Sikorsky Aircraft, Division of United Technologies Corporation, Stratford, Connecticut.
Type: See text.
Engines: Two General Electric T58 free-turbine turboshaft; (SH-3A and derivatives) 1,250shp T58-8B; (SH-3D and derivatives) 1,400shp T58-10, (S-61R versions) 1,500hp T58-5.
Dimensions: Diameter of main rotor 62ft (18.9m); length overall 72ft 8in (22.15m); (61R) 73ft (22.25m); height overall 16ft 10in (5.13m); main-rotor disc area 3,019sq ft (280.5m²).
Weights: Empty (simple transport versions, typical) 9,763lb (4,428kg), (ASW, typical) 11,865lb (5,382kg), (armed CH-3E) 13,255lb (6,010kg); maximum loaded (ASW) about 18,626lb (8,449kg), (transport) usually 21,500lb (9,750kg), (CH-3E) 22,050lb (10,000kg).
Performance: Maximum speed

Above: The sophisticated SH-3H, uprated ASW version of the most versatile Sea King range which also includes transport (including Presidential), MCM and rescue types.

(typical, maximum weight) 166mph (267km/h); initial climb (not vertical but maximum) varies from 2,200 to 1,310ft (670-400m)/min, depending on weight; service ceiling typically 14,700ft (4,480m); range with maximum fuel typically 625 miles (1,005km).
Armament: See below.
History: First flight (HSS-2) 11 March 1959, (CH-3) 17 June 1963.
Users: AF, Navy, Marine Corps, Coast Guard.

One of the most famous families of helicopters in the world, the S-61 stemmed from a Navy requirement

Above: The SH-3H is used everywhere the Navy goes except Antarctica. This one was with VC-5 (Composite squadron) based at Subic Bay in the Philippines in October 1981.

of 1957 for a more powerful machine than the HSS-1 Seabat. Though the latter was a fine helicopter it was incapable of flying the hunter/killer ASW mission. Modern turbine engines promised a quantum jump in capability. Britain's Royal Navy merely put turbine engines in the HSS-1, but the US Navy got Sikorsky to create an entirely new helicopter, the S-61. This was procured as the HSS-2, inevitably called "Hiss 2". It virtually made all previous helicopters obsolete.

As had been done in 1955 by Mil in the USSR, it had its two turbine engines mounted close beneath

the rotor, above the fuselage, driving direct into the main gearbox. This got the engines and transmission completely away from the cockpit and cabin, and left the interior completely unobstructed. For the first time the fuselage was made in the form of a flying boat hull, with a watertight planing bottom. Struts at the sides carried stabilizing floats accommodating the retracted twin-wheel main landing gears, the tailwheel being at the stern. Streamlining was excellent, there being no trace of any pod/boom configuration, and the complete tail and five-blade main rotor could be folded to stow the big helicopter in small warship hangars. Twin T58 engines offered not only unprecedented power from a small weight and bulk, whilst eliminating cooling problems, but also freed the Navy from the need to have stocks of high-octane

tually the standard aircraft in its class and in the Netherlands has now even replaced the Atlantic which was a "clean sheet of paper" design.

The P-3 inherited from the L-188 good short-field performance, outstanding handling even with three of the broad-bladed propellers feathered, thermal de-icing (bleed air on the wings, electric on the tail) and a pressurized fuselage with a circular section giving a maximum cabin width of 10ft 10in (3.3m).

Instead of adding a giant weapon bay, as was done with the Nimrod, Lockheed merely put in a shallow bay under the floor and made up the required payload with external pylons. Typically the P-3 is flown by a flight crew of five, with the centre fuselage occupied by the tactical crew, also numbering five. There is the usual dinette and two folding bunks at the extreme rear.

Early P-3A and B versions are still serving with some export customers, though all have had some updating and a few in the USA have been converted for other roles. US Navy squadrons VQ-1 and -2 replaced their EC-121 Warning Stars with the EP-3E, gross rebuilds of early P-3s to serve in the Elint role. Distinguished by their

giant "doghouse" radomes and other antennas above and below the fuselage, the EP-3Es are equipped for detecting, fixing and recording emissions from unfriendly ships, their main sensors being passive receivers, direction finders and signal analysers.

The US Navy and Lear Siegler developed a modification kit to update early P-3s, especially the P-3B, with new navaids and sensors; the RNZAF aircraft have been thus modified. The only current P-3A operator is Spain, whose aircraft are ex-USN and replaced leased examples. Even the improved P-3B in the US Navy serves only with Reserve squadrons.

Standard model today is the P-3C Update III. This has APS-115 radar, ASA-64 MAD in the tail boom, a battery of sonobuoys and other sonics installations in the rear fuselage, and launchers for A- and B-size buoys immediately aft of the wing.

In many Orions, including P-3Cs of early vintage, the chin position is occupied by a glass-paned gondola housing a KA-74A gimbal-mounted surveillance camera; today, this is replaced by a retractable FLIR. Another variable feature is the choice of pods on the two inboard pylons under the wing

roots. It is common to find the ALQ-78 ESM (passive receiver, with what look like anhedralled delta wings) on the left pylon and the AXR-13 LLLTV on the right. Today the latter is usually replaced by the nose FLIR, and the ESM will eventually be replaced by a completely new AIL system in wingtip pods which will also provide targeting data for the Harpoon missiles, provision for which was incorporated at the Update II stage.

The three Update stages have dramatically multiplied processor speed and memory, added

Above: The EP-3E of Navy squadron VQ-2 is for the most demanding oceanic Elint missions.

navaids such as VLF/Omega to the original INS and mix of doppler and Loran, and completely new sub-systems for managing and processing the sonics, including a new receiver and the IBM Proteus acoustic processor.

Lockheed is also flying a demonstrator of an AEW&C (airborne early warning and control) P-3 aimed at export customers.

gasoline and for the first time almost removed the threat of engine failure. The boat hull was an extra; operations from the sea were not normally intended.

The HSS-2, called SH-3 from 1962, was the first fully equipped ASW helicopter. It had a full spectrum of sensors including radar, dunking sonar, dispensed sonobuoys and MAD (magnetic-anomaly detection) "bird" towed on a cable. These all fed information to the tactical compartment amidships manned by two sensor operators. Along the sides could be carried up to 840lb (381kg) of weapons including a homing torpedo or depth bombs.

Deliveries continued with SH-3Ds with greater power, SH-3G and 3H with later equipment, RH-3As for MCM (mine countermeasures) and VH-3As for the DC-based Executive Flight Detachment to carry the President and other VIPs. The HH-3A was a special combat rescue model operated mainly by HC-7 in Vietnam. It had high-speed refueling and fuel dumping, armor, uprated engines and twin TAT-102

Below: Largely redesigned for the transport role, the USAF's CH-3C has retractable tricycle landing gear and a full-width rear cargo door.

turrets each with a 7.62mm Minigun.

In 1962 the AF borrowed three Sea Kings and decided to get a special version to meet its own long-range transport requirements. The result was the CH-3C (S-61R), a major redesign with an ordinary land fuselage and a full-width rear ramp door. The landing gear was changed to tricycle type with all units retractable, the twin-

Below: The definitive S-61 variant was the specially equipped HH-3E "Jolly Green" of Vietnam fame. Note the refueling probe.

wheel nose gear being raised into an open nose compartment and the twin-wheel main gears folding into large rear sponsons. The fuselage was made watertight for emergency sea descents. Provision was made for firing 0.50in guns from the cabin windows, and in the special HH-3E Jolly Green Giant version for Vietnam new equipment included two or four Miniguns, extra armor, an inflight refueling probe and jettisonable external tanks. These did a tremendous job rescuing downed aviators and even bringing back crashed aircraft in Vietnam, while others stood by during space launchings.

North American (Rockwell International) A3J/A-5 Vigilante

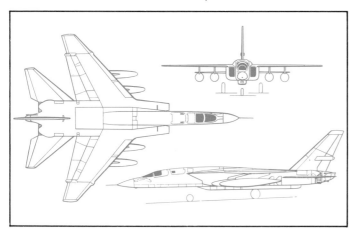

Origin: North American Aviation Inc, Columbus, Ohio.
Type: (A, B) carried-based attack; (C) carrier-based reconnaissance, with crew of two.
Engines: Two General Electric J79 single-shaft afterburning turbojets; (A, B) as originally built 16,150lb (7,325kg) J79-2 or -4, (RA-5C, pre-1969) 17,000lb (7,710kg) J79-8, (post-1996) 17,860lb (8,118kg) J79-10.
Dimensions: Span 53ft (16.15m); length 75ft 10in (23.11m) (folds to 68ft); height 19ft 5in (5.92m); wing area 754sq ft (70.05m^2).
Weights: Empty (C) about 38,000lb (17,240kg); maximum loaded 80,00lb (36,285kg).
Performance: Maximum speed at height 1,385mph (2,230km/h, Mach 2.1); service ceiling (C) 67,000ft (20,400m); range with external fuel about 3,200 miles (5,150km).
Armament: None (A, see text).
History: First flight (YA3J-1) 31

Above: The last and most important version was the RA-5C. The biggest sensor was the SLAR under the fuselage centreline.

August 1958, (A-5A) January 1960, (A-5B) 29 April 1962, (RA-5C) 30 June 1962; final delivery of new aircraft 1971.
User: Navy.

No aircraft in history introduced more technology than the first Vigilante, planned in 1956 as a carrier-based general-purpose attack aircraft. Among its features were automatically scheduled engine inlets and nozzles, single-surface vertical tail, differential slab tailplanes (horizontal stabilizers), a unique linear bomb bay between the engines (with two emptied fuel tanks and a nuclear weapon ejected rearwards in the form of a long tube) and a comprehensive radar-inertial navigation system.

The basic configuration also set

Above: This RA-5C BuNo 156608 was the first of the final batch of 46. It is seen with RVAH-7 over the Philippines in 1979.

a trend still seen in fighters today, with a broad high wing, long engine installations on each side of a wide box-like fuselage, with a relatively narrow forward fuselage projecting forwards from between the inlets. All three landing gears had to fold into the fuselage. Another feature was flap-blowing, and in the A-5B full-span leading-edge droop blowing was added to allow a 15,000lb (6,800kg) weight increase from saddle tanks in the new hump-backed fuselage.

When carriers gave up a strategic nuclear role, the 57 A-5A bombers were followed by the RA-5C, the airborne element of an integrated intelligence system serving the whole fleet and other forces. The RA-5C was extremely comprehensively equipped with multiple sensors including a side-looking

radar under the fuselage.

They also carried a complete set of vertical, oblique and split-image cameras, as well as ECM receivers and jammers for survival in contested airspace.

These valuable aircraft have been hard-worked in many theaters; 63 were built in 1962-66, 53 A-5A and the 6 A-5B were converted to RA-5C standard, and in 1966-71 the production line at Columbus was reopened for 46 Phase II aircraft with GE-10 engines and improved intakes and wing/body fillets. Throughout the southeast Asia conflict the Navy's RVAH squadrons operated around the clock from carriers in the Gulf of Tonkin, gathering intelligence on the most heavily defended areas of North Vietnam. The RA-5C proved specially effective in photographing missile sites, others acted as tankers. Today, high costs have resulted in withdrawal of the RA-5Cs, and there is no comparable successor.

Kaman SH-2 Seasprite

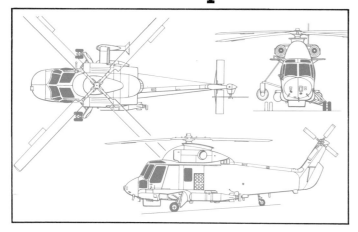

Origin: Kaman Aerospace Corporation, Bloomfield, Connecticut.
Type: Ship-based multirole helicopter (ASW, anti-missile defense, observation, search/rescue and utility).
Engine(s): (UH-2A/B) one 1,050 or 1,250hp General Electric T58 turboshaft, (SH-2C/D/F) two 1,350hp T58-8F, (SH-2G) 1,723hp General Electric T700-401.
Dimensions: Main-rotor diameter 44ft (13.41m), overall

Above: The SH-2F is in wide use with the LAMPS configuration shown, but may later be further upgraded with T700 engines.

length (blades turning) 52ft 7in (16m); fuselage length 40ft 6in (12.3m); height 13ft 7in (4.14m); main-rotor disc area 1,520sq ft (141.2m^2).
Weights: Empty 6,953lb (3,153kg); max 13,300lb (6,033kg), (1985 on) 13,500lb (6,124kg).

Above: Navy stencilling says it all on SH-2F No 151321, with special art supplied by the squadron's Detachment Seven.

Performance: Max speed 168mph (270km/h); max rate of climb (not vertical) 2,440ft (744m)/min; service ceiling 22,500ft (6,858m); range 422 miles (679km).
Armament: See below.
History: First flight (XHU2K-1) 2

July 1959; service delivery (HU2K-1, later called UH-2A) 18 December 1962; final delivery (new) 1972, (conversion) 1975, (rebuild) 1982.
User: Navy.

Originally designated HU2K-1 and named Seasprite, this neat helicopter was at first powered by a single T58 turbine engine mounted close under the rotor hub and was able to carry a wide range of loads,

Grumman OV-1 Mohawk

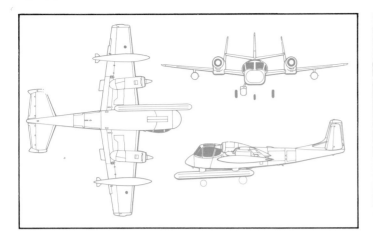

Origin: Grumman Aerospace Corporation, Bethpage, NY.
Type: (OV) Observation, (RV) Elint aircraft.
Engines: Two 1,160shp Lycoming T53-701 turboprops.
Dimensions: Span (A, C) 42ft (12.8m), (B, D) 48ft (14.63m); length 41ft (12.5m), (D with SLAR) 44ft 11in (13.69m); height overall 12ft 8in (3.86m); wing area 360sq ft (33.45m²).
Weights: Empty (A) 9,937lb (4,507kg), (B) 11,067lb (5,020kg), (C) 10,400lb (4,717kg), (D) 12,054lb (5,467kg); max (A) 15.031lb (6,818kg), (B, C) 19,230lb (8,722kg) (D) 18,109lb (8,214kg).
Performance: Max speed (all variants) 297-310mph (480-500km/h); initial climb (A) 2,950ft (900m)/min, (B) 2,250ft (716m)/min, (C) 2,670ft (814m)/min, (D) 3,618ft (1,100m)/min; service ceiling (all) 28,000-31,000ft (8,535-9,450m); range with external fuel

Above: The Army refurbished its Mohawks to RV-1D standard. The large offset pod is the SLAR sensor, carried by the OV-1D.

(A) 1,410 miles (2,270km), (B) 1,230 miles (1,980km), (C) 1,330 miles (2,140km), (D) 1,011 miles (1,627km)
Armament: Not normally fitted, but can include a wide variety of air-to-ground weapons such as grenade launchers, Minigun pods and small guided missiles.
History: First flight (YOV-1A) 14 April 1959, service delivery (OV-1A) February 1961.
User: Army.

Unique in concept, the OV-1 family were planned as battlefield observation platforms, normally without weapons but with STOL capability for operation from austere front-line strips, and with enough armor, redundancy and other protection to survive hostile small-arms fire. The resulting machine has modest

Above: This fully updated OV-1D, in now standard gray livery, was photographed investigating fallout around Mt St Helens.

performance but great agility, good ability to carry special payloads (during the Vietnam War they carried bombs, rocket launchers and gun pods) and excellent avionics for all-weather operations.

Twin turboprops were used, swinging large propellers, which combine with stubby high-lift wings to give amazing STOL performance. Long-stroke landing gears, retracting into the fuselage, give rough-field capability. De-icer boots are fitted to the wings and triple-finned tail, and large door-type airbrakes are fitted on each side of the rear fuselage.

The pilot on the left and observer or sensor operator on the right sit in Martin-Baker ejection seats and have a commanding field of view through the bulged "bug eye" canopy except to the rear. Among

discontinued versions was the JOV-1A with four extra weapon pylons, used by the 11th Air Assault Division. Early models mainly had dual pilot controls, unlike most current Mohawk versions. Total deliveries amounted to 375, completed in December 1970.

The standard current model is the OV-1D which, apart from the optical cameras and, in some cases, Elint receivers, can be quickly converted to carry either UAS-4 IR linescan surveillance equipment or an APS-94 SLAR (Side-Looking Aircraft Radar) slung externally under the fuselage.

The US Army is maintaining a force of 35 RV-1Ds equipped solely for Elint missions. Israel has four OV-1Ds with local modifications. In mid-1983 a small number of OV-1Ds were refurbished for supply to Pakistan for surveillance along the frontier with India. They have new cameras, IRLS and SLAR for surveillance up to 93 miles (150km).

---

including nine passengers, in its unobstructed central cabin, with two crew in the nose. The main units of the tail-wheel-type landing gear retract fully. About 190 were delivered and all were later converted to have two T58 engines in nacelles on each side.

For over 20 years the Seasprite has been standard equipment on US Navy frigates, in various versions including the HH-2C rescue/utility with armor and various armament including chin Minigun turret and waist-mounted machine guns or cannon; others are unarmed HH-2D. One has been used

in missile firing (Sparrow II and Sidewinder) trials in the missile-defense role. All Seasprites have since 1970 been converted to serve in the LAMPS (light airborne multi-purpose system) for anti-submarine and anti-missile defense.

The SH-2D has more than two tons of special equipment including powerful chin radar, sonobuoys, MAD gear, ECM, new navigation

Below: Ten different radars have been flown in SH-2s, the most startling being this giant surveillance set with extending radome. 152191 is now an SH-2F.

and communications systems and Mk 44 and/or Mk 46 torpedoes. All have been brought up to SH-2F standard with improved rotor, higher gross weight and improved sensors and weapons.

Though only the interim LAMPS platform, the SH-2 is a substantial program. The first of 88 new SH-2F Seasprites became operational in 1973, and by 1982 Kaman had

Below: Like most of today's SH-2Fs, BuNo 149780 was built in the 1960s as a single-engined UH-2A. Here it is setting up a pattern of ASW sonobouys.

delivered 88, plus 16 rebuilt SH-2Ds. Despite the existence of the bigger and more costly SH-60B LAMPS III the decision was taken to keep production alive by ordering a major upgrade, the SH-2G Super Seasprite. This has fuel-efficient T700 engines which give more than three times the power of the first SH-2s. A new suite of sensors forms part of a digital avionics fit, and the main rotor has composite blades with a life of 10,000 hours. Six new Supers were ordered in 1987, the last coming off the line in 1993. A further 18 have been produced by rebuilding SH-2Fs.

Northrop F-5 Freedom Fighter, Tiger II

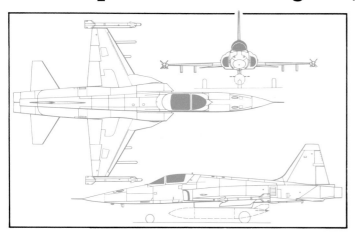

Origin: Northrop Corporation, Hawthorne, California
Type: (F-5A, E) light tactical fighter, (B/F) two-seat dual trainer.
Engines: Two General Electric J85 afterburning turbojets, (A/B) 4,080lb (1,850kg) thrust J85-13 or -13A, (E/F) 5,000lb (2,270kg) thrust -21A.
Dimensions: Span (A/B) 25ft 3in (7.7m), (A/B over tip tanks) 25ft 10in (7.87m), (E/F) 26ft 8in (8.13m), (E/F over AAMs) 27ft 11in (8.53m); length (A) 47ft 2in (14.38m), (B) 46ft 4in (14.12m), (E) 48ft 2in (14.68m), (F) 51ft 7in (15.72m); wing area (A/B) 170sq ft (15.79m²), (E/F) 186sq ft (17.3m²).
Weights: Empty (A) 8,085lb (3,667kg), (B) 8,360lb (3,792kg), (E) 9,683lb (4,392kg), (F) 10,567lb (4,793kg), max loaded (A) 20,576lb (9,333kg), (B)

Above: Though nearly 3,000 F-5s have been sold abroad, only the F-5E Tiger II shown in this drawing has found sustained employment in the US armed forces.

20,116lb (9,124kg), (E) 24,676lb (11,192kg), (F) 25,225lb (11,442kg).
Performance: Maximum speed at 36,000ft (10,793m), (A) 925mph (1,489km/h, Mach 1.4), (B) 886mph (1,425km/h, Mach 1.34), (E) 1,077mph (1,734km/h, Mach 1.63), (F) 1,011mph (1,628km/h, Mach 1.53); typical cruising speed 562mph (904km/h, Mach 0.85); initial climb (A/B) 28,700ft (8,750m)/min, (E) 34,500ft (10,516m)/min, (F) 32,890ft (1,025m)/min; service ceiling (all) about 51,000ft (15,545m); combat radius with max weapon

Above: New features of the F-5E Tiger II show clearly in this picture of an example from the 425th TFTS, 405th TFW, at Luke AFB, Arizona, in 1979.

load and allowances (A, hi-lo-hi) 215 miles (346km), (E, lo-lo-lo) 138 miles (222km); range with max fuel (all hi, tanks dropped, with reserves) (A) 1,565 miles (2,518km), (E) 1,779 miles (2,863km).
Armament: (A/B) total military load 6,200lb (2,812kg) including two 20mm M-39 guns and wide variety of underwing stores, plus AIM-9 AAMs for air combat; (E/F) very wide range of ordnance to total of 7,000lb (3,175kg) not including two (F-5F, one) M-39 A2 guns each with 280 rounds and two AIM-9 missiles on tip rails.
History: First flight (N-156F) 30

July 1959, (F-5A) 19 May 1964, (F-5E) 11 August 1972, (F-5F) 25 September 1974.
Users: AF, Navy.

The Air Force showed almost no interest in Northrop's N-156C Freedom Fighter, which was built with company funds and rolled out in 1959 without US markings. Derived from the T-38 trainer, it was a most attractive machine, with an area-ruled fuselage, side-by-side engines fed by fixed sharp-lipped inlets above the wing roots and with afterburner nozzles right at the back, a low tapered square-tipped wing with power drooping leading-edge flaps, short-span flaps and ailerons, and powered tailplanes (horizontal stabilizers) mounted low and Basic armament is two single-barrel cannon above the nose with Sidewinder AAMs as

Boeing C-137, EC-18

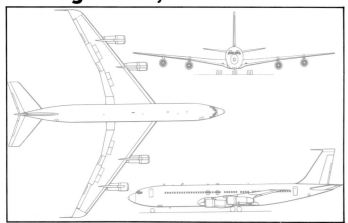

Origin: Boeing Commercial Airplane Co (707), Boeing Military Airplane Co (KE-3A and 707T/T) or Boeing Aerospace Co.
Type: See text.
Engines: Four 18,000lb (8,165kg) thrust Pratt & Whitney JT3D-3 (TF33) turbofans.
Dimensions: Span (most) 145ft 9in (44.42m), (VC-137B) 130ft 10in (39.87m); length (most) 152ft 11in (46.61m), (VC-137B) 144ft 6in (44.04m); height (most) 41ft 9in (12.73m); wing area (most) 3.010 sq ft (279m²), (VC-137B) 2.433sq ft (236m²).

Above: Based on the standard commercial 707-320C, the VC-137C (the type used for "Presidential" Air Force One) has HF probe antennas on the wingtips.

Weights: Empty (VC-137B) 124,200lb (56,337kg), (VC-137C) 140,550lb (63,730kg), max (VC-137B) 258,000lb (117,025kg), (VC-137C) 322,000lb (146,059kg).
Performance: Max speed (VC) 620mph (998km/h), service ceiling (VC) 38,500ft (11,730m); range with max payload (VC-

Above: The first VC-137C was 62-6000, seen here climbing out of Washington in 1964. Its replacement, 72-7000, had a predominantly blue livery. The next generation is based on the 747.

137B) 4,235 miles (6,820km) (VC-137C) 6,160 miles (9,915km).
Armament: None.
History: First flight (VC-137) October 1959, (civil-320B) 31 January 1962, (E-6) due early 1987.
Users: (EC, VC) AFT (E) Navy.

Though the commercial 707 began life superficially similar to the KC-135, in fact it had a new airframe with different dimensions and a wider fuselage. In May 1958 three 707-120s were ordered by the AF for high-priority passenger and cargo transport, receiving designation VC-173A. In 1963 they were re-engined with TF33 turbofans, becoming VC-137Bs. They are the only US military examples of the "small" 707. They have 22 VIP seats and special command communications.
In 1958 Boeing flew the first 707-320, with an enlarged air-

an alternative to area-ruled tanks on the wingtips.

Eventually Northrop secured orders for over 1,000 F-5A and B fighters for foreign customers, and 12 of the MAP (Mutual Assistance Program) F-5As were evaluated by the Air Force in Vietnam in a project called Skoshi Tiger, which demonstrated the rather limited capability of this light tactical machine, as well as its economy and strong pilot appeal. When the USAF withdrew from SE Asia it left behind many F-5As and Bs, most having been formally transferred to South Vietnam, and few of these remain in the US inventory.

In contrast the more powerful and updated F-5E Tiger II succeeded in winning Air Force support from the start, and the training of foreign recipients was handled mainly by TAC, with ATC assistance. The first service delivery of this version was to TAC's 425th TFS in April 1973. This unit at Williams AFB, Arizona (a detached part of the 58th TTW at Luke), proved the training and combat procedures and also later introduced the longer F which retains both the fire-control system and most fuselage fuel despite the second seat.

Ultimately the Air Force bought 112 F-5Es, both as tactical fighters and (over half the total) as Aggressor aircraft simulating potential enemy aircraft in DACT (Dissimilar Air Combat Training). About 60 F-5Es and a small number of Fs continue in Air Force service in the development of air-combat

techniques, in Aggressor roles, in the monitoring of fighter weapons meets and various hack duties. The F-5Es come in at least eight color schemes, three of which reproduce Warsaw Pact camouflage colors while others are low-visibility.

The F-5Fs at Williams are silver, with broad yellow bands and vertical tails. User units include the 58th TTW (425th TFS, as described),

57th TTW at Nellis (a major tactical and air combat center for the entire Air Force), 3rd TFW, Clark AFB, Philippines (Pacaf), 527th Aggressor TFS, attached to the 10th TRW at RAF Alconbury, England, and various Systems Command establishments. Eight F-5Es are also used by the Navy for Top Gun fighterpilot training at the Naval Fighter Weapons School at NAS Miramar,

California. The more powerful and updated F-20A Tigershark was never ordered into production.

Below: If you want to act well you must also dress for the part. These USAF F-5Es from the 527th TFTS (Aggressor) from RAF Alconbury, England, are painted in known Warsaw Pact camouflage schemes.

Left: The letters ASD on the tail signify the Aeronautical Systems Division at Wright-Patterson AFB, Ohio. One of the Division's largest tools is the first EC-18B (rebuilt 707-323Cs), seen in early 1986 flying with ASD's 4950th Test Wing. Their role is described in the text.

frame and greatly increased weights for longer-range missions. A single 707-353B was acquired as the VC-137C (62-6000) for use by the 89th MAW, becoming Air Force One when the President was aboard. In 1972 it was replaced by updated VC-137C 72-7000, and later by the two VC-25A aircraft based on the 747.

In 1982 AF Aeronautical Systems Division purchased six American Airlines 707-323Cs for conversion as replacements for the smaller EC-135N ARIA (advanced range instrumentation

aircraft) fleet operated by the 4950th Test Wing. The first of the rebuilt airplanes, designated as EC-18Bs, was completed in 1985. They have completely new cockpits and interiors, probe antennas on the wingtips and the world's largest steerable airborne antenna in the bulbous nose. They have weight/volume payload capability fitting them to a heavy workload in connection with many Shuttle and missile programmes.

Two 707-320s were built as EC-137D AWACS evaluation aircraft; these led to the E-3 Sentry described on pages 192-193.

Another Boeing company – Boeing Aerospace, of Kent, Washington – now merged into the Defense & Space Group – was the prime contractor for the E-6 TACAMO platforms for the Navy. In contrast, the prime contractor for the remarkable E-8 JointSTARS is Northrop Grumman. Both these derivatives of the 707-320 are described later.

BMAC (Boeing Military Airplane Co), at Wichita, Kansas, is rebuilding 707-320s as 707T/T tanker transports, the KE-3As of the Royal Saudi AF having CFM56 engines. So far none has been

bought by the US military.

Boeing Aerospace Co. of Kent, Washington, is prime contractor for the new E-6 Tacamo (take charge and move out) radio relay platforms which provide the global link between the US National Command Authorities and the US Navy's submerged Trident missile submarines, replacing the EC-130Q. A total of some $1,600 million will be needed to fund the required force of 15 aircraft, which use the E-3 airframe but without the rotodome pylon and AWACS features. Instead extremely comprehensive AVLF (airborne very low frequency) communications are installed, together with special generating plant for radiated powers averaging 200kW, and with a wire reel from which 2.5 miles of trailing aerial (antenna) can be unwound, as in some previous aircraft in the smaller C-135 family.

Grumman A-6 Intruder and EA-6 Prowler

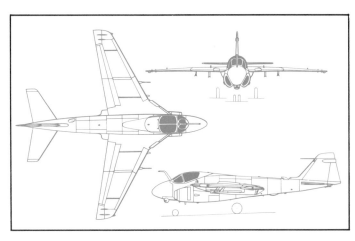

Origin: Grumman Aerospace Corporation, Bethpage, NY.
Type: (A-6A, B, C, E) two-seat carrier-based all-weather attack; (EA-6A) two-seat ECM/attack; (EA-6B) two-seat ECM; (KA-6D) two-seat air-refueling tanker.
Engines: (A-6A to E) two 9,300lb (4,218kg) thrust Pratt & Whitney J52-8A turbojets; (EA-6B) two 11,200lb (5,080kg) J52-408, (EA-6B ADVCAP) 12,000lb (5,443kg) J52-409.
Dimensions: Span 53ft (16.5m); length (except EA-6B) 54ft 7in (16.64m); (EA-6B) 59ft 5in (18.11m); height (A-6A, A-6C, A-6C, KA-6D) 15ft 7in (4.75m); (A-6E, EA-6A and B) 16ft 3in (4.95m); wing area 528.9sq ft (49.1m²).
Weights: Empty (A-6A) 25,684lb (11,650kg); (EA-6A) 27,769lb (12,596kg); (EA-6B) 34,581lb (15,686kg); (A-6E) 25,630lb (11,625kg); max loaded (A-6A

Above: The standard attack variant is at present the A-6E (with TRAM turret). Production is switching to the upgraded A-6F.

and E) 60,400lb (27,379kg); (EA-6B) 58,500lb (26,535kg).
Performance: Max speed (clean A-6A) 684mph (1,102km/h) at sea level or 625mph (1,006km/h, Mach 0.94) at height, (EA-6A) over 630mph (10,131km/h), (EA-6B) 599mph (964km/h) at sea level, (A-6E) 648mph (1,043km/h) at sea level; initial climb (A-6E, clean) 8,600ft (2,621m)/min; service ceiling (A-6A) 41,660ft (12,700m), (A-6E) 44,600ft (13,595m), (EA-6B) 39,000ft (11,582m); range with full combat load (A-6E) 1,077 miles (1,733km); ferry range with external fuel (all) about 3,100 miles (4,890km).
Armament: All attack versions including EA-6A, five stores

Above: Two A-6A Intruders of VA-52 with Mk 82 "slick" bombs. Their ship is CV-63 Kitty Hawk.

locations each rated at 3,600lb (1,633kg) with max total load of 15,000lb (6,804kg); typical load thirty 500lb (227kg) bombs; (EA-6B, KA-6D) none.
History: First flight (YA2F-1) 10 April 1960; service acceptance of A-6A 1 February 1963; first flight (EA-6A) 1963, (KA-6D) 23 May 1966 (EA-6B) 25 May 1968, (A-6E) 27 February 1970; final delivery (A-6E) after 1987.
Users: Navy, Marine Corps.

Despite its seemingly outdated concept, the A-6 Intruder will remain in low-rate production throughout the foreseeable future as the standard equipment of all the heavy attack squadrons of the US

Navy and Marine Corps. The design was formulated in the later part of the Korean War, in 1953, when the need for a truly all-weather attack aircraft was first recognized. After refinement of the requirement an industry competition was held in 1957, Grumman's G-128 design being chosen late in that year. The YA2F-1 prototype was notable for its downward-tilting engine jet-pipes, meant to give STOL performance, but these were not featured in the production machine.

Basic characteristics of all aircraft of the family include a conventional long-span wing with almost full-span flaps on both the leading and trailing edges. Ahead of the trailing-edge flaps are "flaperons" used as lift spoilers and ailerons, while the tips contain split airbrakes which are fully opened on each carrier landing. Plain turbojets were used, and these remained in all succes-

Grumman E-2C Hawkeye

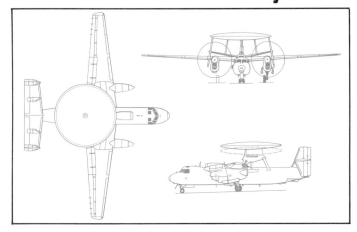

Origin: Grumman Aerospace Corporation, Bethpage, NY.
Type: Carrier- and land-based airborne early warning and control (AWACS) platform.
Engines: Two 4,910ehp Allison T56-A-425 turboprops (from 1986 two 5,250ehp T56-A-427).
Dimensions: Span 80ft 7in (24.56m); length 57ft 6.75in (17.54m); height 18ft 3.8in (5.58m); wing area 700sq ft (65.03m²).
Weights: Empty 37,945lb (17,211kg); max take-off 51,817lb (23,503kg).

Above: Below decks the E-2C retracts its rotodome (broken outline). Dash-427 engine does not alter the appearance.

Performance: Max speed 374mph (602km/h); cruising speed 310mph (500km/h); service ceiling 30,800ft (9,390m); endurance (max fuel) 6.1h.
Armament: None.
History: First flight (E-2) 21 October 1960, (E-2C) 20 January 1971; first delivery (E-2A) 19 January 1964, (E-2C) November 1973.
User: Navy

Above: An E-2C is cat-shot from CV-60 Saratoga in the Med on 28 January 1986. The bank angle is deliberate.

Unique in offering a valuable and comprehensive AEW package in an aircraft of compact dimensions and moderate operating cost, the Hawkeye has managed to make the transition from being a highly specialized aircraft for US Navy carrier air wings to become a major contender for sales in the world market for operation from land airfields.

Together with some EC-121 variants, the original E-2A of 1961 was the first aircraft to have the new style of rotodome in which the antenna itself is given a streamlined fairing instead of being housed inside a radome. The size of airframe needed to house the APS-96 radar was such that considerable ingenuity was needed; for example, four fins and rudders are used, all mounted at 90° to the dihedral tailplane and all well below the wake of the rotodome. The rotodome itself is set at a positive incidence to lift at least its own

sive production versions but are not being replaced (see later text). The nose is occupied by a giant radar array, with a fixed inflight-refueling probe above the centerline in front of the side-by-side cockpit with Martin-Baker seats (slightly inclined and staggered) which can be tilted back to reduce fatigue.

Grumman delivered 482 of the original A-6A model, ending in December 1969, and 62 of these were converted into KA-6D air-refueling tankers which can transfer over 21,000lb (9,526kg) of fuel through the hosereel. This remains the standard tanker of the 14 carrier air wings, with limited attack capability and equipment for use as an air/sea rescue control platform. The A-6A, B and C are no longer in use, the standard attack model being the A-6E. This has been equipped with totally new radar, the Norden APQ-148 replacing two radars in earlier versions, as well as an IBM/Fairchild computer-based attack and weapon-delivery system.

In 1974 an A-6E was fitted with the TRAM (target recognition and attack multisensor) package, comprising a stabilized chin turret containing a FLIR and a laser interlinked with the radar for detection, identification and weapon-guidance at greater ranges in adverse conditions. Other updates with TRAM include the Litton ASN-92 CAINS (carrier aircraft inertial navigation system), a new CNI suite and automatic carrier landing. A total of 240 A-6E Intruders was produced by upgrading A-6As. A further 205 were funded as new-build aircraft,

the final 21 having composite wings of graphite/epoxy construction built by Boeing Military Airplanes.

Meanwhile a major update program has fitted TRAM to all the 250 A-6Es in frontline carrier air wings, and to the similar aircraft equipping the five all-weather VMA (AW) attack squadrons of the Marines. Since 1981 all new and updated A-6Es have also been equipped to launch the Harpoon stand-off attack and anti-ship missile.

Further upgrades were studied and in part funded. The SWIP (Systems Weapon Integration Program) was to apply to all aircraft, both metal and composite-winged, and totally transform the outdated avionics and match the new systems with Harpoon, Maverick and HARM missiles. A comprehensive improvement programme resulted in testing four A-6F Intruder IIs which, among other upgrades, had General Electric F404 engines giving greater power for less weight and reduced fuel burn. Unfortunately for Grumman the decision was taken to replace the A-6 by the F/A-18E and JSF, and the SWIP has been cut back and the A-6F cancelled.

The EA-6B Prowler is the standard electronic warfare platform of the Navy carrier air wings and Marine Corps. Through it is based on the airframe of the A-6E, with local reinforcement to cater for the increased weights, fatigue life and 5.5g load factor, it is gutted of attack avionics and instead houses the AIL ALQ-99 tactical jamming system, which covers all anticipated hostile emitter frequency bands. Surveill-

ance receivers are grouped in the fairing on the fin and the active jammers are mounted in up to five external pods, each energized by a nose windmill generator and containing two (fore/aft) transmitters covering one of seven frequencies. To manage the equipment a crew of four is carried, comprising pilot (left front), an ECM officer in the right front seat to manage navigation, communications, defensive ECM and chaff/flare dispensing, and two more ECMOs in the rear seats who can each detect, assign, adjust and monitor the jammers.

All VAQ (fixed-wing EW) squadrons of the Navy fly the EA-6B, as do the three Marine EW squadrons. All in service have been updated with new avionics in two stages of ICAP

Above: Positioning a crewed-up EA-6B Prowler aboard CV-43 Coral Sea during Sixth Fleet operations on 29 January 1986.

(increased capability), and Norden is supplying about 100 advanced APS-130 navigation radars for retrofit to existing Prowlers.

Altogether Grumman delivered 170 Prowlers, all to the US Navy. Current aircraft comprise a few Standard, 25 Excap (expanded capability), 66 ICAP-1 and 72 ICAP-2, and a growing number of major upgrades called ADVCAP (advanced capability). A proposed Block 2000 for year 2000 had not been funded by 1997, and the EA-6B is expected to be replaced by a dedicated version of the F/A-18E/F.

weight, while on a carrier it is retracted a short distance to enable it to clear the hangar roof.

The dome rotates once every 10 seconds when in operation, and the radar gives surveillance from a height of 30,000ft (9,144m) within a radius of 300 miles (480km). Ten years into the program, the APS-96 was replaced by the APS-125 with an Advanced Radar Processing System (ARPS) which gives a much improved discrimination and detection capability over both land and water. With this new radar the aircraft designation changed to E-2C; it entered service as such in 1973 and remains the standard "eyes" of the US Navy at sea, with updates in the subsequent years.

The two pilots occupy a wide flight deck. Behind them, amidst a mass of radar racking and the high-capacity vapor-cycle cooling system (the radiator for which is housed in a large duct above the fuselage), is the pressurized Airborne Tactical Data System (ATDS) compartment. This is the nerve-centre of the aircraft, manned by the combat information officer, air control officer and radar operator. They are presented with displays and outputs not only from the main radar but also from some

30 other electronic devices, including passive detectors and communication systems. These combine to give a picture of targets, tracks and trajectories, and signal emissions, all processed and, where appropriate, with IFF interrogation replies. Passive Detection System (PDS) receivers are located on the nose and tail, and on the tips of the tailplane (horizontal stabilizer) for the lateral coverage.

An E-2C mission can last six hours, and at a radius of 200 miles (322km) time on station at 30,000ft (9,144m) can be 4 hours. This is shorter than the 10 hours at this radius of the E-3A and Nimrod, but Grumman claims a 2:1 price differential in acquisition and operating costs (the E-2C costs $58 million).

Production of the E-2C is slow but steady, with the 95th airframe delivered in 1987. The E-2C can detect airborne targets anywhere in a 3,000,000 cubic mile surveillance envelope, and it is claimed that a target as small as a cruise missile can be detected at ranges over 115 miles (185km), fighters at ranges up to 230 miles (370km), and larger aircraft at 289 miles (465km). All friendly and enemy maritime movements can also be monitored. The AN/ALR-59 PDS

can detect the presence of electronic emitters at ranges up to twice that of the radar system. High speed data processing enables the E-2C automatically to track more than 250 targets at the same time, and to control more than 30 airborne intercepts. A new Total Radiation Aperture Control Antenna (TRAC-A) is now under development, and this will enable the range to be increased, reduce the sidelobes and enhance the ECCM capability.

Grumman has for many years had a team working on improved Hawkeyes, some with turbofan

propulsion, and even on a completely new replacement (E-7). In 1994 production was transferred to Northrop Grumman's facility at St Augustine, Florida. Here 12 E-2Cs are being upgraded for the Navy, but the main effort is now centred on exports. Already Hawkeyes are serving with a remarkable six export customers, and others are in prospect.

Below: BuNo 150530 was one of the first W2F-1s (later E-2A). Here it is accompanied by its predecessor in RVAW-120, a piston-engined WF-2 Tracer.

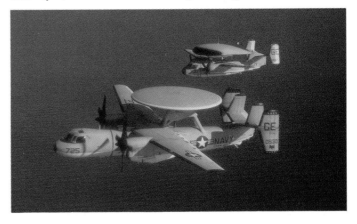

Cessna O-2

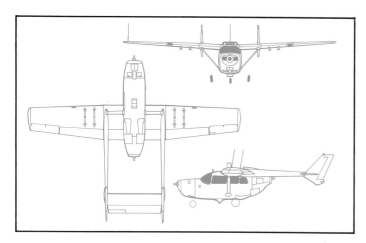

Origin: Cessna Aircraft Company, Wichita, Kansas.
Type: Two-place observation, forward air control and psywar aircraft.
Engines: Two 210hp Continental IO-360-C flat-six air-cooled piston engines in tractor pusher arrangement.
Dimensions: Span 38ft 2in (11.58m); length 29ft 9in (9.07m); height 9ft 4in (2.84m); wing area 201sq ft (18.67m²).
Weights: Empty 2,848lb (1,292kg); loaded 5,400lb (2,449kg).
Performance: Maximum speed 199mph (320km/h) at sea level; cruising speed 144mph (232km/h) at 1,000ft (305m); range 1,060 miles (1,706km).
Armament: (A) normally marking rockets only, though each of the four underwing hardpoints could accommodate a 7.62mm Minigun pack.
History: First flight 28 February 1961; ordered by the US Air Force 29 December 1966.
User: AF.

Above: A standard O-2A. The psywar O-2B did not have the wing pylons, but did have spinners on the propellers.

Involvement in Vietnam highlighted the urgent need for a more capable FAC aircraft, and the choice fell on a specially equipped version of the Cessna 337 Skymaster. New features on this all-metal push/pull retractable gear machine included extra windows for downward vision by the observer in the right seat, military radio, and four hardpoints under the wings.
Over 350 O-2A FAC aircraft were quickly delivered, plus O-2B psywar platforms which began with 31 conversions of off-the-shelf Skymasters. The latter were camouflaged, but O-2As were all gray with a white tip-to-tip band above the wing for enhanced visibility from above.
In Vietnam the O-2A, with greater range and double the number of target-marking rock-

Above: USAF 67-21465 was a civil Cessna converted as an O-2B psywar aircraft. These had a relatively short service career.

ets, served as stopgap replacement for the O-1 until the North American OV-10A arrived on the scene. At least one of the Bird Dog's shortcomings had not been corrected, for the new Cessna also lacked adequate armor.
The O-2B flew psychological warfare missions using a broadcasting set with three 600-watt

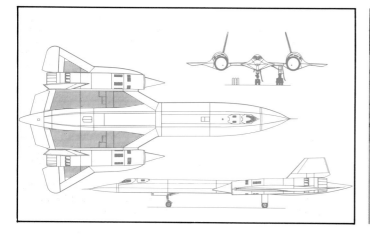

amplifiers and a leaflet dispenser. They urged the Viet Cong to surrender, offered messages of encouragement to those loyal to the Saigon government, and gave villagers under South Vietnamese control warning of impending air or ground attack by government forces.

Below: Seen in November 1982 with low-vis markings, an O-2A is guided out at Travis Field, Savannah, Georgia, during Exercise Quick Thrust 83-1.

Lockheed SR-71 Blackbird

Origin: Lockheed-California Company, Burbank, California.
Type: (A) strategic reconnaissance aircraft; (B, C) trainer.
Engines: Two 32,500lb (14,772kg) thrust Pratt & Whitney J58-1 (JT-11D-20B) continuous-bleed afterburning turbojets.
Dimensions: Span 55ft 7in (16.94m); length 107ft 5in

Above: All SR-71As have this configuration, for stealth and speed. The -71B and C models have raised rear cockpits.

(32.74m); height overall 18ft 6in (5.64m); wing area 1,800sq ft (167.2m²).
Weights: Empty not disclosed, but about 65,000lb (29,500kg); max 170,000lb (77,112kg).
Performance: Max speed

Above: One of the 9th SRW's fantastic birds returns to RAF Mildenhall, England, after a sleuthing mission up the Baltic.

(also max cruising speed) about 2,100mph (3,380km/h) at over 60,000ft (18,290m); world record speed over 15-mile (25km) course 2,193mph (3,350km/h, Mach 3.31); max sustained height (also world

record) 85,069ft (25,900m); range at 78,740ft (24,000m) at 1,983mph (3,191km/h, Mach 3) on internal fuel 2,982 miles (4,800km); corresponding endurance 1h 30min; endurance at loiter speed up to 7h.
Armament: None.
History: First flight (A-12) 26 April 1962, (SR) 22 December 1964.
User: AF

Boeing Vertol CH-47 Chinook

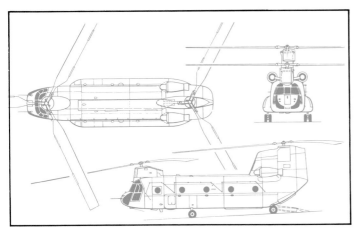

Origin: Boeing Vertol Company, Morton, Pennsylvania.
Type: Medium transport helicopter with normal crew of two/three – data for CH-47C.
Engines: Two 3,750shp Lycoming T55-L-11A free-turbine turboshafts.
Dimensions: Diameter of main rotors 60ft (18.29m); length, rotors turning, 99ft (30.2m²); length of fuselage 41ft (15.54m); height 18ft 7in (4.67m); total area of rotor discs 5,655sq ft (526m²).
Weights: Empty 20,616lb (9,351kg); loaded (condition I) 33,000lb (14,969kg); (overload condition II) 46,000lb (20,865kg); gross weight of CH-47D 50,000lb (22,680kg).
Performance: Max speed (condition I) 189mph (304km/h), (II) 142mph (229km/h); initial climb (I) 2,880ft (878m)/min, (II) 1,320ft (402m)/min; service ceiling (I) 15,000ft (4,570m), (II) 8,000ft (2,440m); mission radius, cruising speed and payload (I) 115 miles (185km) at 158mph

Above: Though similar to earlier models, the CH-47D differs in small details. Cargo ramp door is shown open in broken lines.

(254km/h) with 7,262lb (3,294kg), (II) 23 miles (37km) at 131mph (211km/h) with 23,212lb (10,528kg).
Armament: Normally none.
History: First flight (YCH-47A) 21 September 1961, (CH-47C) 14 October 1967, (D) 11 May 1979.
User: Army

Vertol (later Boeing Vertol) began developing the Vertol 114 in 1956, to meet the need of the US Army for a turbine-engined all-weather cargo helicopter able to operate in the most adverse conditions of altitude and temperature.

Retaining the tandem-rotor configuration, the first YCH-47A flew on the power of two 2,200shp Lycoming T55 turboshaft engines and led directly to the production CH-47A. With an unobstructed cabin 7½ft (2.29m) wide, 6½ft (1.98m) high and over 30ft (9.2m)

Above: A CH-47D of the 147th Aviation Company, which can lift roughly twice the load of the original CH-47A.

long, the Chinook proved a valuable vehicle, soon standardized as US Army medium helicopter and deployed all over the world.

By 1972 more than 550 had served in Vietnam, mainly in the battlefield airlift of troops and weapons but also rescuing civilians (on one occasion 147 refugees and their belongings were carried to safety in one Chinook) and lifting back for salvage or repair 11,500 disabled aircraft valued at more than $3,000 million. The A model gave way to the CH-47B, with 2,860hp engines and numerous improvements.

Since 1967 the standard basic version has been the CH-47C, with much greater power and increased internal fuel capacity. Most exports are of this model, which in 1973 began to receive a crashworthy fuel system and an

integral spar inspection system. Most US Army machines (210 so far) have been retrofitted with glassfiber blades.

From 1979 Boeing Vertol has been rebuilding all A, B and C models to CH-47D standard with 3,750shp L-712 long-life engines, 7,500shp transmission, redundant and uprated electrics, glassfiber blades, modular hydraulics, triple cargo hook, advanced flight control system, new avionics, single-point fueling, survivability gear and T62 APU. The result is a planned fleet of 436 upgraded helicopters. Useful load of the CH-47D is 22,783lb (10,334kg), compared with 11,000lb (4,990kg) for the original CH-47A. Using the external hook the D is permitted to lift the D5 bulldozer (24,750lb, 11,225kg).

By 1997 production was 1,124, comprising 940 by Boeing and the remainder by Agusta (Italy) and Kawasaki (Japan). The latest version is the MH-47E for US Special Forces, with a unique fit of avionics and weapons.

Fastest aeroplane in the world, the SR-71A is possibly also the most costly to operate, and each flight is planned like a space mission. Derived from the smaller single-seat A-12 (previously mis-reported by President Johnson as the A-11) via the YF-12A long-range interceptor, neither of which saw AF inventory service, the SR-71A is crewed by a pilot and RSO (recon systems officer) in separate tandem cockpits with roof hatches containing windows of heat-resistant glass. Most of the airframe is of aged B-120 titanium, and special refrigeration systems keep down local temperatures, though even then almost all materials and fluids are non-standard. The kerosene fuel is J-7, supplied by a fleet of KC-135Q tankers which, like the SR/s operating unit, the USAF 9th SRW, has Beale AFB, as home base. This unique fuel is used as the heat sink which absorbs all the colossal surplus heat loads throughout the aircraft.

These aircraft, popularly called Blackbirds on account of their special heat-emitting paint, are

often detached to distant temporary operating locations for over-flights of territory which cannot be reached from Beale. All SR missions are clandestine, very minutely planned and subject to special procedures. In flight the crew wear astronaut suits and fly for maximum range and minimal radar and IR signature. Radar cross-section is reduced partly by the stealth-type shaping of the aircraft and partly by the external paint whose surface incorporates billions of microscopic iron balls to give a conductive film to reduce radar effectively.

Two A-12(M) versions carried the Lockheed GTD-21 reconnaissance RPV in a pick-a-back mount, releasing it for overflights of the most sensitive or potentially dangerous targets. The SR subsequently acted as a data-link platform for the digitized pictures and Elint signals. So far as is known these Mach 3-plus vehicles were later carried only by the B-52, but are no longer in use.

Details of the SR-71A's sensors remain classified, but clearly include the largest and most

revealing kinds of spacecraft optical camera and, probably, variable palletized fits of SLARs and IR lines-can. It is possible to cover 80,000sq miles (207,000km²) per hour.

Originally designated RS-71 (again mis-reported by President Johnson), the SR-71 program comprised 31 aircraft, two of which were converted into SR-71B tandem dual pilot trainers, the raised instructor cockpit reducing maximum speed. The SR-71C replaced a crashed B, and was rebuilt from a YF-12A. Thus, the total Blackbird production amounted to 49 aircraft.

Nearly all the 30 SR-71As served

with the 9th SRW at Beale, detachments also operating from overseas bases, notably Kadena (Okinawa) and Mildenhall (England). Mainly on account of cost they were withdrawn from service in December 1989, 14 going to museums and three being transferred to NASA. Three were stored at Palmdale, and in a change of policy (because nothing else could do the job) were returned to service from June 1995. They operate from Edwards AFB.

Below: For most of their life the SR-71s operated from Beale AFB, California.

Sikorsky S-64, CH-54 Tarhe

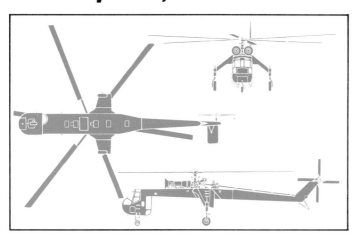

Origin: Sikorsky Aircraft, Division of United Technologies Corporation, Stratford, Connecticut.
Type: Heavy crane helicopter.
Engines: Two Pratt & Whitney turboshafts, (CH-54A) 4,500shp T73-1, (CH-54B) 4,800shp T73-700
Dimensions: Main rotor diameter 72ft (21.95m); fuselage length 70ft 3in (21.41m); height 25ft 5in (7.75m); main-rotor disc area 4,070sq ft (378.1m²).
Weights: Empty 19,234lb (8,724kg); maximum takeoff 42,000lb (19,050kg).
Performance: (At normal take-off weight of 38,000lb, 17,235kg) maximum speed at sea level 126mph (203km/h); cruising speed 105mph (169km/h); range with maximum fuel plus 10 per cent reserve 230 miles (370km).
Armament: None.
History: First flight 9 May 1962; first delivery late 1964. On 28 June 1968 the Army accepted the Universal Military Pod for the CH-54.
User: Army.

Above: The first Tarhes were CH-54As with single main wheels. Twin-wheel CH-54Bs also had more powerful T73 engines.

In the late 1950s Sikorsky began designing a new type of crane helicopter with the fuselage replaced by a slim beam carrying the two turbine engines and rotors, the cockpit being hung from the front and the main gears very tall and widely separated to leave plenty of room for bulky loads carried under the beam. The cockpit accommodated a regular crew of three, plus jump seats for two loader/technicians. At all times at least one crew member would face aft to watch the load and control the hooks and winches. Five of the six YCH-54As were evaluated at Fort Benning. Sikorsky delivered 54 CH-54A Tarhes plus 37 more powerful CH-54Bs with twin-wheel gears. Sikorsky designed containers for many purposes, as well as a Universal Military Pod for carriage of 45 troops or 24 litters, a command post, communications cen-

Above: This CH-54A, No 68-18437, was bringing back a drowned C-123 fuselage at Ben Tre, Vietnam, 9 April 1969.

ter or surgical hospital.

The CH-54 was assigned to the US Army's 478th Aviation Company and performed outstanding service in support of the First Cavalry Division (Airmobile) in Southeast Asia. The Tarhe's use in airmobile operations included the transportation of heavy artillery and recover of downed aircraft. On 29 April

1965 a CH-54 lifted 90 persons, including 87 combat equipped troops. Others transported bulldozers and road traders weighing up to 17,500lb (7,937kg) each and vehicles of 20,000lb (9,072kg), and other heavy hardware. They retrieved more than 380 damaged aircraft valued at $210 million.

Below: The first YCH-54 prototype (64-14202) during Army evaluation. It was toting an M114 howitzer (too much for earlier helicopters).

Bell OH-58 Kiowa

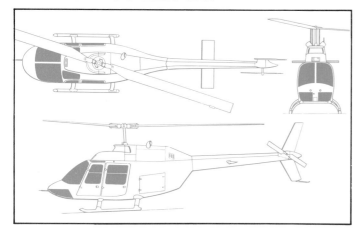

Origin: Bell Helicopter Textron, Fort Worth, Texas.
Type: Light multirole helicopter.
Engine: One 317shp Allison T63-700 or 250-C18 turboshaft; (206B models) 420shp Allison 250-C-20B or 400shp C20; (L and OH-58D) 650shp C30P.
Dimensions: Diameter of two-blade main rotor 35ft 4in (10.77m), (OH-58D) 35ft

Above: This Model 206 is a JetRanger III. The OH-58A Kiowa has increased main-rotor diameter and the OH-58C a flat-panel canopy. OH-58D has an MMS.

(10.67m); (206B) 33ft 4in (10.16m), (206L) 37ft (11.28m); length overall (rotors turning) 40ft 11¾in (12.49m), (206B) 38ft 9½in (11.82m); height 9ft 6½in (2.91m); main rotor disc

Above: Nap-of-the-Earth flying by a regular OH-58C Kiowa in 1980. Note the Allison's twin upward-pointing exhausts, and yellow cable cutter at the nose.

area (OH-58D) 926sq ft (89.38m²).
Weights: Empty 1,464lb (664kg), (206B slightly less), (206L) 1,962lb (809kg); maximum loaded 3,000lb (1,361kg), (206B) 3,200lb

(1,451kg), (206L) 4,000lb (1,814kg).
Performance: Economical cruise (Kiowa S/L) 117mph (188km/h), (206B, 5,000ft, 1,525m) 138mph (222km/h); max range S/L no reserve with max useful load, 305 miles (490km), (206B and L) 345 miles (555km).
Armament: Usually none (see text).

Hughes OH-6 Cayuse

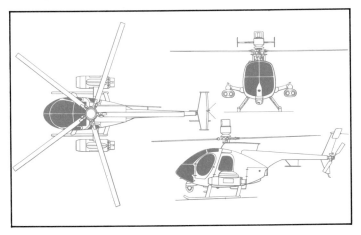

Origin: Hughes Helicopters, Division of McDonnell Douglas, Culver City, California.
Type: (OH-6A) Observation (500) light multi-role helicopter; (Defender) variants for close support, reconnaissance, ASW or dedicated anti-armor warfare.
Engine: One Allison turboshaft; (OH-6A) T63-5A flat rated at 252.5shp (500M) 250-C18A Flat-rated at 278shp, (Defender) 420shp 250-C20B.
Dimensions: Diameter of four-blade main rotor 26ft 4in (8.03m); length overall (rotors turning) 30ft 3¾in (9.24m); height overall 8ft 1½in (2.48m); main-rotor disc area 548sq ft (50.9m²).
Weights: Empty (OH) 1,229lb (557kg), (500M) 1,130lb (512kg); max loaded (OH) 2,700lb (1,225kg), (500M) 3,000lb (1,361kg).
Performance: Max cruise at S/L 150mph (241km/h); typical range on normal fuel 380 miles (611km).
Armament: See below.
History: First flight (OH-6A) 27 February 1963, (500M) early 1968.
User: Army.

Above: The Model 530MG is the most comprehensively equipped of the Defender family, with TOWs and a mast-mounted sight.

Original winner of the controversial LOH (Light Observation Helicopter) competition of the US Army in 1961, the OH-6A Cayuse is one of the most compact flying machines in history, relative to its capability. Amazingly light weights were achieved by the pod-and-boom airframe, with a streamlined glazed cabin and curious three-part tail. A novel feature is the high-speed rotor with four metal blades retained by multi-laminate straps to an articulated hub.

The LOH competition was large and protracted, but Hughes was named winner on 26 May 1965, receiving an immediate award for 714 OH-6 Cayuse helicopters. The controversy arose from political factors, exacerbated by subsequent cost-escalation and delays in delivery. Eventually the Army reopened the competition and awarded further contracts to Bell for the OH-58.

Above: 65-12931 was one of the first block of OH-6A Cayuse helicopters built on the original LOH contract of 1965.

The standard machine carries two crew and four equipped troops, or up to 1,000lb (454kg) of electronics and weapons including the XM-27 gun or XM-75 grenade launcher plus a wide range of other infantry weapons. The US Army bought 1,434, and several hundred other military or paramilitary examples have been built by Hughes or its licensees. The Loach (the name arose from "LOH") was worked intensively in

Vietnam, packed with special gear and weapons, and with courageous crews laden with sidearms and equipment. An indication of their operations is the fact that one Loach pilot was shot down 14 times.

By 1997 McDonnell Douglas had redelivered to the Army more than 140 OH-6As converted as the AH-6C/F/J, EH-6B/E and MH-6B/C/E/H/J. Later versions are NOTAR (no tail rotor), with air blown through slots at the tip of the tail boom.

Below: Last of the first block of 88 was 13003, seen here at Tan Son Nhut AB, South Vietnam, on 28 October 1967.

History: First flight (OH-4A) 8 December 1962; (206A) 10 January 1966, (206B) 1970.
Users: Army, AF, Marines, Navy.

In 1962 Bell's OH-4A was a loser in the US Army's LOH (light observation helicopter) competition. Bell accordingly marketed the same basic design as the Model 206 JetRanger, this family growing to encompass the more powerful 206B and more capacious 206L Long Ranger. In 1968 the US Army reopened the LOH competition, naming Bell the new winner and buying 2,200 OH-58A Kiowas similar to the 206A but with a larger main rotor. US Navy trainers are TH-57A Sea Rangers. Larger numbers have been exported and license-built abroad, notably by Agusta in Italy.

Sales of all versions exceed 5,500, most being five-seaters (206L, seven) and US Army Kiowas having the XM27 kit with 7.62mm Minigun and various other weapons. Bell has rebuilt 275 US Army OH-58As to OH-58C stan-

dard with many changes including an angular canopy with flat glass panels, the T63-720 (C20B) engine with IR suppression, new avionics and instruments and a day optical system. Some have the M27 armament kit, with a 7.62mm Minigun firing straight ahead.

Bell has produced a military version of the 206L LongRanger known as TexasRanger. Able to seat seven, it can fly many missions but is marketed in the attack role with uprated C30P engines, four TOW missiles, roof sight, FLIR (forward-looking infra-red) and laser rangefinder/designator.In 1981 Bell's Model 406 was named winner of the US Army AHIP (Army Helicopter Improvement Program), for a near-term scout, with designation OH-58D. New features include a much more powerful engine, an MMS (mast-mounted sight) and new avionics and cockpit displays, most of the latter by Sperry. The ball-type MMS contains a TV and a FLIR, and with equipment including inertial navigation, night vision goggles and an airborne-target hand-off system.

The Army received 382 upgrades in 1983-97, deliveries from No 202 onwards being to OH-58D(I) Kiowa Warrior standard, with additions including a pair of launch tubes for Stinger missiles on each side. The Quick Reaction Forces of XVIII and 82nd Airborne Divisions are receiving 81 to a Multi-Purpose Light Helo

Below: Newest of the Kiowas, the OH-58D is vastly uprated, with mast-mounted sight. Compare with the OH-58C opposite.

standard, able to fly 10 minutes after unloading from a C-130, fitted for six troops or four litters and able to carry a 2,000lb (907kg) slung load.

Lockheed C-141 StarLifter

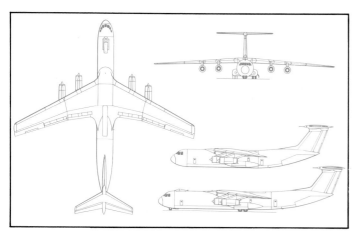

Origin: Lockheed-Georgia Company, Marietta, Georgia.
Type: Strategic airlift and aeromedical transport.
Engines: Four 21,000 (9,525kg) thrust P&W TF33-7 turbofans.

Above: All MAC StarLifters have been converted from C-141A (upper side view) to C-141B configuration.

Dimensions: Span 159ft 11in (48.74m); length 168ft 3in

Above: With rear cargo doors open, a MAC C-141B comes in low during an airlift exercise.

(51.29m) (originally 145ft, 44.2m); height overall 39ft 3in

(11.96m); wing area 3,228sq ft (299.9m²).
Weights: Empty 148,120lb (67,186kg) (originally 133,773lb, 60,678kg); max 343,000lb (155,585kg) (originally

Sikorsky S-65/S-80, H-53 Stallion family

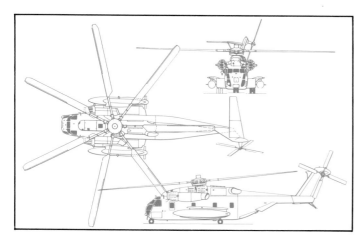

Origin: Sikorsky Aircraft, Division of United Technologies, Stratford, Connecticut.
Type: (C) assault transport helicopter, (M) mine countermeasures.
Engines: (Early versions) two 2,850shp General Electric T64-6 turboshafts; (CH-53D and G) 3,925shp T64-413; (RH-53D) 4,380shp T64-415; (CH-53E) three 4,380ship T64-415.
Dimensions: Diameter of main rotor (most, six blades) 72ft 3in (22.02m), (CH-53E, seven blades) 69ft (24.08m); length overall (rotors turning) 88ft 2in (26.9m); (CH-53E) 99ft 1in (30.2m); length of fuselage 67ft 2in (20.47m), (E) 73ft 4in (22.35m); height overall 24ft 11in (7.6m), (E) 28ft 5in (8.66m); main-rotor disc area (small) 4,070sq ft (378.1m²), (large) 4,902sq ft (455.37m²).
Weights: Empty (CH-53D) 23,485lb (10,653kg), (E) 33,226lb (15,071kg); max loaded (most) 42,000lb (19,050kg), (RH-53D) 50,000lb (22,680kg), (E) 73,500lb (33,339kg).
Performance: Max speed 196mph (315km/h); typical cruising speed 173mph (278km/h); initial climb (most) 2,180ft (664m)/min, (E) 2,750ft (838m)/min; range (with payload, optimum cruise) (most)

Above: Impressive by any standard the CH-53E is a different airlifter from the CH-53A, though dimensions are similar.

540 miles (869km), (E) 1,290 miles (2,075km).
Armament: (HH-53B only) three 7.62mm Miniguns, plus optional 20mm cannon and grenade launchers.
History: First flight 14 October 1964, (E) 1 March 1974; service delivery (CH-53A) May 1966, (E) March 1981, (MH) 1 September 1983.
Users: AF, Navy, Marine Corps.

Designed as a heavy assault transport helicopter for the US Marine Corps, the initial Sea Stallion CH-53A version of the S-65 was basically an enlarged version of the S-61, but with a conventional fuselage instead of a boat hull. The dynamic parts – gearboxes, transmission and rotors – were based on those of the CH-54 (S-64) but with the main rotor having a titanium hub and folding blades.
Other features include an unobstructed cabin 7ft 6in (2.29m) wide and 6ft 6in (1.98m) high, with full-width rear ramp doors for

Above: The MH-53E Sea Dragon has combined great power and fuel capacity with the ability to handle minesweeping gear.

loading vehicles or air dropping; tricycle landing gear with twin-wheel units, the main gears retracting forwards into large sponsons which contain the four fuel tanks; and in some versions fixed streamlined external tanks which carry the navigation lights.
The Marine requirement was to carry 38 equipped troops; other loads can include 8,000lb (3,629kg) or cargo, or 24 litters and four attendants. The initial buy was for 139, named Sea Stallion, and they quickly established a high reputation for good performance; despite their size, one was put through a test program involving prolonged looping and rolling. A group of 15 CH-53As were modified for Navy use as RH-53A minesweepers (MCM, mine countermeasures).
Sikorsky then secured orders from the USAF, initially for the HH-53B for the Aerospace Rescue & Recovery Service, with engines uprated to 3,080shp; six-man crew, retractable inflight-refueling probes, jettisonable external

tanks and with armament and armor for operations in Vietnam. The HH-53C Super Jolly, built in greater numbers, had 3,435shp engines, and changes including the ability to hoist the Apollo capsules from the ocean, with the external hoist rated at 20,000lb (9,072kg).
The CH-53C Super Jolly was a simple transport version of the HH-53C, while the Marines returned in 1969 with a big order for 126 CH-53Ds, with engines at first of 3,695shp and finally 3,925shp, automatic blade folding and the ability to carry 55 troops (though in an unchanged fuselage). Eight HH-53Cs plus the prototype were converted into HH-53H (Pave Low) night and all-weather search and rescue Super Jollies with IR sensors, B-52 type inertial navigation and terrain-following radar. This sub-family ended with 20 RH-53D Sea Stallions for the Navy, for MCM duties; they have refueling probes and external tanks. Several were lost in the abortive Iran rescue operation of 24 April 1980.
After long delays Sikorsky got a go-ahead in 1978 for the CH-53E, which is so greatly uprated it has a different maker's designation of S-80E, and is named SuperStallion.

316,600lb, 143,600kg).

Performance: Max speed (also max cruising speed) 566mph (910km/h); long-range cruising speed 495mph (796km/h); initial climb 2,920ft (890m)/min; service ceiling 41,600ft (12,680m); range (max payload) 2,935 miles (4,725km); takeoff to 50ft (15m) 5,800ft (1,768m).

Armament: None.

History: First flight 17 December 1963; service delivery 19 October 1964; first flight (C-141B) 24 March 1977.

User: AF.

Ordered in March 1961, the C-141 was the world's first purpose-designed military airlifter with jet propulsion. Compared with the contemporary fan-engined 707, then also in production for the USAF, the C-141 has a high wing with less sweep, matching the air-craft to shorter runways at the expense of slower cruising speeds. The only questionable decision was to stick to the same rather small (10ft x 9ft, 3m x 2.74m) cargo hold cross-section as was specified for another Lockheed aircraft, the C-130.

Other features included a full-section ramp/door, side paratroop doors, upper-surface roll/airbrake spoilers, four reversers, tape instruments, an all-weather landing system and advanced loading and positioning systems for pallets. Lockheed built 284.

Several of the first block were structurally modified to improve the ability of the floor to support the skids of a containerized Minuteman ICBM, a weight of 86,207lb (30,103kg). One of these aircraft set a world record in parachuting a single mass of 70,195lb (31,840kg). Standard loads included 10 regular 463L cargo pallets, 154 troops, 123 paratroops or 80 litter patients plus 16 medical attendants. Usable volume was 5,290cu ft (150m^3), not including the ramp. Service experience proved exemplary, and in the Vietnam War C-141s maintained essentially a daily schedule on a 10,000-mile (16,000km) trip with full loads both ways.

It was this full-load experience which finally drove home the lesson that the C-141 could use more cubic capacity. It was found in practice that the average load carried on ten pallets was only 46,000lb (20,866kg). Lockheed devised a cost/effective stretch which adds "plugs" ahead of and behind the wing to extend the usable length by 23ft 4in (7.11m), increasing the usable volume (including the ramp) to 11,399cu ft (322.7m^3).

The extended aircraft, desig-nated C-141B, carries 13 pallets of cargo, the payload rising to 94,508lb (42,869kg). There was no requirement to change the number of seats or litters carried, and the environmental system capacity was not increased. It also incorporates an improved wing/ body fairing which reduces drag and fuel burn per unit distance flown, while among other modifications the most prominent is a dorsal bulge aft of the flight deck housing a universal (boom or drogue) flight refueling receptacle. The first conversion, the TC-141B, was so successful that the Air Force decided to have Lockheed rework all the surviving aircraft to give in effect the airlift ability of 90 additional aircraft with no extra fuel consumption.

Lockheed-Georgia rebuilt 270 StarLifters, re-delivering the last in June 1982. All have been repainted in Europe 1 camouflage.

Seldom has a helicopter been so improved in capability as the Stallion, because from an original total of 5,700hp the CH-53E has no less than 13,140hp, from three of the most powerful T64 engines, the extra unit being at the rear of the others just to the left of the center-line. The power is absorbed by a new rotor with seven lengthened and redesigned blades the entire drive train being redesigned to handle the increased power.

The fuselage is longer and better streamlined, the tail is completely redesigned (eventually maturing with a large fin inclined to the left and carrying a kinked gull tail-plane on the right, opposite the enlarged tail rotor), and largely redesigned structure and systems bring them into line with the latest state of the art. Only 55 seats are fitted still, but the external cargo load can be 32,000lb (14,515kg). Sikorsky is delivering two a month, and by mid-1986 had supplied the Marines with 100 of the 200+ total scheduled for the 1990s.

The newest version is the MH-53E AMCM (airborne MCM) Sea Dragon, for the US Navy. The major change in this model is the 1,000gal (3,785lit) increase in internal fuel, housed in giant sponsons, but the hydraulics and electrical systems are also improved, and new avionics are fitted.

By 1997 over 750 S-65/S-80 helicopters had been delivered, including 172 CH-53Es and 56 MH-53Es. Production of the CH-

Above: Marine Corps CH-53D Sea Stallions raise the dust at Salines Airport during the US invasion of Grenada in October 1983. Guns project from windows.

53E is continuing at about three per year, and virtually all helicopters in service are the subject of upgrade programs. These include uprated engines, composite main and tail rotor blades and new avionics. Trials have been conducted with self-defence Sidewinders.

Grumman C-2A Greyhound

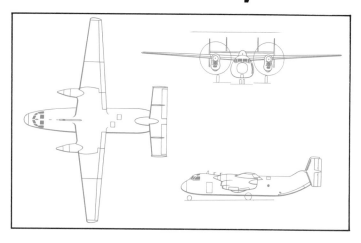

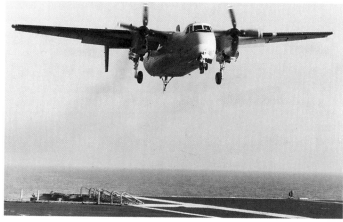

Origin: Grumman Aerospace Corporation, Bethpage, NY.
Type: COD transport (see text).
Engines: Two Allison T56 turboprops, (through 1985) 4,910ehp T56-425, (from 1986), 5,250shp (about 5,700ehp) T56-427.
Dimensions: Span 80ft 7in (24.56m); length 56ft 10in (17.32m); height 15ft 10¾in (4.83m); wing area 700sq ft (65.03m²).

Above: The C2A differs from the E-2C in its fuselage and tail. Note the broad rear fuselage to ease loading problems.

Weights: Empty about 32,000lb (14,500kg); maximum 54,354lb (24,655kg).
Performance: Maximum speed 357mph (574km/h); service ceiling 33,500ft (10,210m); range

Above: A C-2A of the original Dash-10 batch coming aboard with another load of people and stores in 1982.

(10,000lb, 4,536kg, cargo) 1,200 miles (1,930km).
Armament: None.
History: First flight (YC-2A converted from E-2A) 18 November 1964; service delivery

August 1966.
User: Navy.

Since World War II the navy has acquired ever better transports to fly its COD (carrier on-board delivery) mission. COD aircraft shuttle between carriers at sea and the nearest appropriate land base, bringing urgent cargo, personnel, spare parts, ammunition

General Dynamics F-111

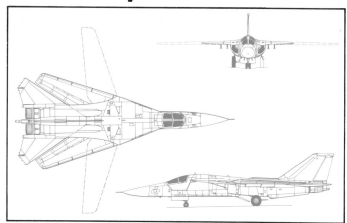

Origin: General Dynamics Corporation, Fort Worth, Texas.
Type: A, D, E, F, all-weather attack; FB, strategic attack.
Engines: Two Pratt & Whitney TF0 afterburning turbofans, (A) 18,500lb (8,390kg) TF30-3, (D, E) 19,600lb (8,891kg) TF30-9, (FB) 20,350lb (9,231kg) TF30-7, (F) 25,100lb (11,385kg) TF30-100.
Dimensions: Span (fully spread, 16° sweep) (A, D, E, F) 63ft (19.2m), (FB) 70ft (21.34m), (fully swept) (A, D, E, F) 31ft 11½in (9.74m), (FB) 33ft 11in (10.34m); length 73ft 6in (22.4m); wing area (A, D, E, F, gross, 16°) 525sq ft (48.77m²).
Weights: Empty (A) 46,172lb (20,943kg), (D) 49,090lb (22,267kg), (E) about 47,000lb (21,319kg), (F) 47,418lb (21,537kg), (FB) close to 50,000lb (22,680kg); loaded (A) 91,500lb (41,500kg), (D, E) 92,500lb (41,954kg), (F) 100,000lb (45,360kg), (FB) 114,300lb (51,846kg).
Performance: Max speed at 36,000ft (11,000m), clean and

Above: The F-111E retained the F-111A's small inlets but was otherwise much improved.

with max afterburner, (A, D, E) 1,450mph (2,335km/h Mach 2.2), (FB) 1,320mph (2,124km/h Mach 2), (F) 1,653mph (2,660km/h Mach 2.5); cruising speed, penetration, 571mph (191km/h); service ceiling at combat weight, max afterburner, (A) 51,000ft (15,500m), (F) 60,000ft (18,290m); range with max internal fuel (A, D) 3,165 miles (5,039km), (F) 2,925 miles (4,707km); takeoff run (A) 4,000ft (1,219m), (F) under 3,000ft (914m), (FB) 4,700ft (1,433m).
Armament: Internal weapon bay for two B43 bombs or (D, F) one B43 and one M61 gun; three pylons under each wing (four inboard swivelling with wing, outers being fixed and usable only at 16°, otherwise being jettisoned) for max external load 31,500lb (14,288kg), (FB only) provision for up to six SRAM, two internal, or heavy conventional

Above: An FB-111A of SAC's 509th BW gets away from Pease AFB during Global Shield 79.

loads (see text).
History: First flight 21 December 1964; service delivery (A) June 1967.
User: AF.

In 1960 the Department of Defense masterminded the TFX (tactical fighter experimental) as a gigantic program to meet all the fighter and attack needs of the Air Force, Navy and Marine Corps, despite the disparate requirements of these services, and expected the resultant aircraft to be bought throughout the non-Communist world. In fact, so severe were the demands for weapon load and mission range that on the lower power available the aircraft had inadequate air-combat capability and in fact it was destined never to serve in this role, though it is still loosely described as a 'tactical fighter'.

After prolonged technical problems involving escalation in

Right: Spearhead of NATO, the British-based F-111Fs of 48 TFW had Pave Tack and GBU-15s.

weight, severe aerodynamic drag, engine/inlet mismatch and, extending into the early 1970s, structural failures, the F-111 eventually matured as the world's best long-range interdiction attack aircraft which in the hands of dedicated and courageous Air Force crews pioneered the new art of 'skiing' – riding the ski-toe locus of a TFR (terrain-following radar) over hills, mountains and steep-sided valleys in blind conditions, in blizzards or by night, holding a steady 200ft (91m) distance from the ground by high-subsonic speed, finally to plant a bomb automatically within a few metres of a previously computed target.

Basic features of the F-111 include a variable-sweep "swing wing" (the first in production in the world) with limits of 16° and 72.5°, with exceptional high-lift devices, side-by-side seating for the pilot and right-seat navigator

and other stores, and also ferrying casualties or seriously sick ship crews. the mission is demanding because while a large cabin accessed by a large vehicle-size ramp door is a basic requirement, so too is full carrier compatibility. Thus the C-2A uses wing, engine, rear fuselage and tail parts of the E-2C, and likewise can make cat takeoffs and arrested landings, and fold to be struck below decks. Two pilots and a loadmaster look after up to 32 passengers or 12 litter patients in the pressurized cabin, or palletized cargo. Grumman delivered 19 C-2As in the 1960s, and worked on 39 new improved models (still called C-2A) for delivery in 1985-89. Most are powered by the uprated T56-A-427 turboprop, which may be retrofitted to earlier Greyhounds.

Right: The first C-2A to be built under the $678 million contract for 39 more aircraft. They will serve at Sigonella, Sicily, and Cubi point, Philippines.

(usually also a pilot), large main gears with low-pressure tires for no-flare landings on soft strips (these prevent the carriage of ordnance on fuselage pylons), a small internal weapon bay, very great internal fuel capacity (typically 5,022 US gal, 19,010lit), and emergency escape by jettisoning the entire crew compartment, which has its own parachutes and can serve as a survival shelter or boat.

General Dynamics cleared the original aircraft for service in 2½ years, and built 141 of this F-111A version, which equips 366TFW at Mountain Home AFB, Idaho (others have been converted into the Grumman EF-111A described

Right: This FB-111A of the 509th bombardment Wing of SAC, at Pease AFB, New Hampshire, at one time wore the winged 2 emblem of the 2nd Air Force, which has now been disbanded.

later). It is planned to update the A by fitting a digital, computer to the original analog-type AJQ-20A nav/bomb system, together with the Air Force standard INS and a new control/display set.

The F-111E is similar but has greater power; 94 were delivered and survivors equipped the 20th TFW at Upper Heyford, England.

Next came the F-111D, which at great cost was fitted with an almost completely different avionic system of a basically digital nature including the APQ-30 attack radar, APN-189 doppler and HUDs for both crew-members. This aircraft had great potential but caused severe technical

and manpower problems in service and never fully realized its capabilities, though it remained a major advance on the A and E. The 96 built equipped the 27th TFW at Canon AFB, New Mexico.

The F-111F was by far the best of all tactical F-111 versions, partly because Pratt & Whitney at last produced a really powerful TF30 which incorporates many other advanced features giving enhanced life with fewer problems. With much greater performance than any other model, the F could if necessary double in an air-control (fighter) role though it had no weapons for this role except the gun and if necessary the AIM-9. The 106 of this model served at Mountain Home until transfer to the 48th TFW in England at Lakenheath and finally to replace the F-111D in the 27th FW. They did well in the Gulf War but were retired in January 1996.

The most important of all F-111 post-delivery modifications has been the conversion of the F force to use the Pave Tack pod, normally stowed in the weapon bay but rotated out on a cradle for use. This complex package provides a day/night all-weather capability to acquire, tack, designate and hit surface targets using EO, IR or laser guided weapons. The first squadron to convert was the 48th TFW's 494th TFS, in September 1981. Their operations officer, Maj Bob Rudiger, has said: "Important targets that once required several

aircraft can now be disabled with a single Pave Tack aircraft; the radar tells the pod where to look and the laser allows us to put the weapon precisely on target."

The long-span FB-111A was bought to replace the B-58 and early models of B-52 in SAC, though the rising price resulted in a cut in procurement from 210 to 76, entering service in October 1969. it has so-called Mk-11B avionics, derived from those of the D but configured for SAC missions using nuclear bombs or SRAMs. With strengthened structure and landing gear, the FB had a capability of carrying 41,250lb (18,711kg) of bombs, made up of 50 bombs of 825lb (nominal 750lb size) each. This was not normally used, and the outer pylons associated with this load were not normally installed.

The FB equipped SAC's 380th BW at Plattsburgh AFB, NY, and the 509th at Pease, New Hampshire. From 1990 the force (by then down to 62) was dispersed, 30 being reconfigured as multirole strategic/tactical F-111Gs and the rest stored or sold to Australia as attrition replacements for the RAAF F-111C. The F-111Gs served briefly alongside the F-111F with the 27th FW at Cannon AFB before being replaced by the F-16C.

Grumman (General Dynamics) EF-111 Raven

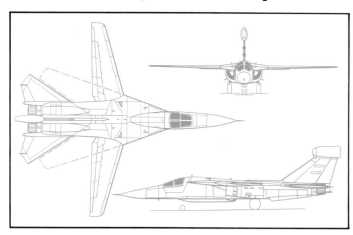

Origin: First built by General Dynamics Corporation, Fort Worth, Texas; rebuild by Grumman Aerospace Corporation, Bethpage, NY.
Type: EW aircraft.
Engines: Two 18,500lb (8,390kg) thrust Pratt & Whitney TF30-3 afterburning turbofans.
Dimensions: Span (fully spread) 63ft (19.2m), (fully swept) 31ft 11½in (9.74m); length 77ft 1½in (23.51m); wing area (gross, 16°) 525sq ft (48.77m²).
Weights: Empty 53.418lb (24,340kg); loaded 87,478lb (39,680kg).

Above: Grumman's expertise gave the USAF the EF-111, with 72.5° sweep shown dotted.

Performance: Maximum speed 1,160mph (1,865km/h, Mach 1.75) at 36,000ft (10,972m); cruising speed (penetration) 571mph (191km/h); initial climb 3,592ft (1,095m)/min; service ceiling (combat weight, max afterburner) 54,700ft (16,673m); range (max internal fuel) 2,484 miles (3,998km); take-off distance 3,250ft (991m).
Armament: None.
History: First flight (EF) 17 May

Above: First unit to become fully operational on the EF was Mountain Home's 390th ECS.

1977, (equipped second prototype) 17 May 1977, (first production EF) 26 June 1981.
User: AF.

Having become aware of the urgent need for a dedicated EW aircraft in the late 1960s, the AF first studied a modified EB-66 for what was known as the Interim Tac Early Warning System (ITEWS). This proved to be a costly and, in the end, impractica-

Right: In Europe the EF flew from RAF Upper Heyford with the 42nd EC Squadron.

ble solution. The next study, in 1968-70, concentrated on a buy of navy EA-6B Prowlers, which were faulted because they do not have a supersonic capability, although it is arguable how often such a performance would be needed on operations. Second, criticism focused on a lack of range, and again this is arguable. Third, the EA-6B was said to be too expensive, but it is difficult to compare a new airframe with a conversion.

McDonnell Douglas C-9

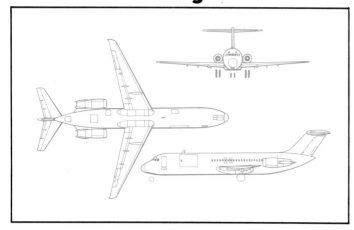

Origin: Douglas Aircraft Company, Long Beach, California.
Type: (C-9A) Aeromedical airlift transport, (VC-9C) special executive transport, (C-9B) passenger/cargo transport.
Engines: Two 14,500lb (6,575kg) Pratt & Whitney JT8D-9 turbofans.
Dimensions: Span 93ft 5in (28.47m); length 119ft 3½in (37.36m); height overall 27ft 6in (8.38m); wing area 934.3sq ft (86.77m²).
Weights: Empty (VC) about 57,190lb (25,940kg), (C-9A, C-9B in passenger configuration) about 65,283lb (29,612kg); max (C-9A, VC-9C) 121,000lb (54,884kg), (C-9B) 110,000lb (49,900kg).
Performance: Max cruise 564mph (907km/h); typical long-range cruise 510mph (821km/h); range with full payload and

Above: The USAF C-9A has passenger windows only along the rear part of the cabin.

reserves (C-9A, VC) about 1,923 miles (3,095km), (C-9B with 10,000lb, 4,535kg) 2,923 miles (4,704km).
History: First flight (DC-9) 25 February 1965; service delivery (C-9A) 10 August 1968, (C-9B) 8 May 1973, (VC) 1975.
Users: AF, Navy and Marine Corps.

The military variants of the DC-9 airliner are distinct from the standard commercial DC-9s bought

Above: The C-9A Nightingales of MAC fly with the 375th Aeromedical Airlift Wing, Scott AFB.

by several air forces, usually as VIP aircraft. The USAF C-9A Nightingale is the standard aeromedical transport, equipped for 40 litter patients and 40 seated, plus up to five nurses or technicians. It has three entrances, two with stairways, provision for hoisting wheelchairs, and a special care cabin.

The Navy/Marines C-9B Skytrain II is the longest-ranged of all DC-9 variants, a regular route

with full load being NAS Alameda to Hawaii. They seat up to 107, or 45 plus three pallets loaded through the large cargo door, and have INS and VLF/Omega. The three VC-9Cs are almost standard DC 9-30s used by the Special Air Missions Wing at Andrews AFB, near Washington.

Below: This C-9B Skytrain II flies with VR-1 based at NAS Norfolk, Virginia.

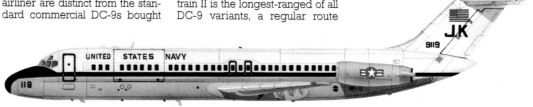

The main changes are the fin receivers and the installation of the jamming equipment pallet. Canadair supplies the fin, which is reinforced to carry 370lb (168kg) of pod structure loaded with 583lb (264kg) of electronic equipment. Grumman assembles the main jammer installation which, mounted on its pallet, weighs 4,274lb (1,939kg), while the canoe radome and door add a further 464lb (210kg). the EF-111A, therefore, flies like an F-111A with a 6,000lb (2,700kg) bombload, and on "Red Flag" and other exercises the aircraft has demonstrated its ability to fly in formation with F-111As on high-speed attack runs.

Grumman delivered a total of 42 Ravens from the Calverton plant. The operating units were the 42nd ECS (Electronic Combat Squadron) at RAF Upper Heyford, moving to Incirlik in Turkey for the Gulf War, and the 290th ECS at Mountain Home AFB, moving to Taif in Saudi Arabia for the Gulf War. In that conflict the EF-111A played a major role, being effective in its combination of high speed at low level and deep-penetration capability. By 1996 40 aircraft were still active, and Northrop Grumman was leader of a team engaged in a comprehensive avionics and systems update.

Perhaps the real reason was that the AF did not want to accept another aircraft designed under Navy control.

It was partly a matter of chance that it was found possible to convert the F-111 into an EW platform, even though it was said at the time that this would be not only the most cost-effective but also the lowest-risk solution Grumman, the Navy's prime contractor for the EA-6B, was not certain that the conversion was possible, a particular problem being the need for two extra seats with neither unacceptable aerodynamic penalties nor severe effects on the aircraft's range.

Improvements in the electronic suite, however, not only made the ALQ-99 able to handle hostile threats more quickly but also, by means of increased automation, enabled the operating crew to be reduced to one man. This system, the ALQ-99E, features inflight adaptable antennas, digital jamming, and the complete isolation of active and passive systems: the ALQ-99E jamming subsystem detects, identifies, locates, records and can jam every kind of hostile emitter using computer control over direction and time. It is generally thought to be the best EW system in the world at present.

Turning an F-111A into an EF-111A is a major rebuild operation.

Rockwell International OV-10 Bronco

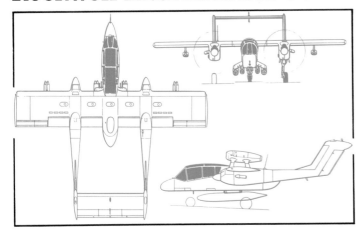

Above: This OV10A has four guns and 20 large Zuni rockets. Note long-stroke legs.

Above: With centerline tank, this OV-10A was with the 51st Composite Wing, Osan AB.

Origin: Rockwell International, Columbus, Ohio, Division of North American Aircraft Operations.
Type: Forward air control.
Engines: Two 715ehp Garrett T76-416/417 turboprops.
Dimensions: Span 40ft (12.19m); length 41ft 7in (12.67m); height 15ft 2in (4.62m); wing area 291sq ft (27.03m²).
Weights: Empty 6,893lb (3,127kg); loaded 9,908lb (4,494kg); overload 14,444lb (6,552kg).
Performance: Maximum speed (sea level, clean) 281mph (452km/h); initial climb (normal weight) 2,600ft (790m)/min; service ceiling 24,000ft (7,315m); takeoff run (normal weight) 740ft (226m); landing run, same; combat radius (max weapon load, low level, no loiter) 228 miles (367km); ferry range 1,382 miles (224km).

Armament: Carried on five external attachments, one on centerline rated at 1,200lb (544kg) and four rated at 600lb (272kg) on sponsons which also house four 7.62mm M60 with 500 rounds each.
History: First flight 16 July 1965, (production OV-10A) 6 August 1967; USAF combat duty June 1968.
Users: AF, ANG, Marine Corps.

This unique warplane was the chief tangible outcome of prolonged DoD studies in 1959-65 of Co-In (Counter-Insurgency) aircraft. The marines issued a LARA (Light Armed Recon Aircraft) specification, which was won by NAA's NA-300 in August 1965.

Features include superb all-round views for the pilot and observer seated in tandem ejection seats, STOL rough-strip performance and a rear cargo compartment usable by five paratroops or two casualties plus attendant.

Of the initial batch of 271 the Air Force took 157 for use in the FAC role, deploying them in Southeast Asia. Their ability to respond immediately with light fire against surface targets proved valuable.

In 1970 LTV Electrosystems modified 11 for night-FAC duty with sensors for detecting surface targets and directing accompanying attack aircraft, but most OV-10s in USAF use were of the original model. Units included TAC's 1st SOW at Hurlburt Field, Florida; the 602nd TACW, Bergstrom AFB, Texas; the 601st TCW, Sembach AB, West Germany; and Pacaf's 51st CW, Osan, South Korea.

The Marine Corps received 114 OV-10As to a standard differing only in detail (such as radio equipment) from the USAF model. They have served with VMO (observation) squadrons, duties including helicopter escort, FAC and armed recon. Since 1978 Rockwell has converted 17 to OV-10D standard for the NOS (night observation surveillance) role with a FLIR (forward-looking infrared) and laser designator in a nose ball turret and an M97 three-barrel 20mm gun in a chin turret. Other equipment included the APR-39 RHAWS (radar homing and warning system).

Bell AH-1 HueyCobra

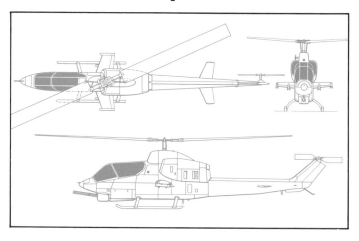

Origin: Bell Helicopter Textron, Forth Worth, Texas.
Type: Close-support and attack helicopter.
Engines: (AH-1G) one 1,400shp Lycoming T53-13 derated to 1,100shp for continuous operation, (-1J) 1,800shp Pratt & Whitney Canada T400 Twin Pac with transmission flat-rated at 1,100 shp, (-1R, -1S) 1,800shp T53-703, (-1T) 2,050shp T400-WV-402, (-1W) two 1,625shp General Electric T700-401 turboshafts.
Dimensions: Diameter of two-blade main rotor 44ft (13.41m), (1T) 48ft (14.63m), (Model 249) four blades, diam as original; overall length (rotors running) (G, Q, R, S) 52ft 11½in (16.14m), (J) 53ft 4in (16.26m), (T) 58ft (17.68m); length of fuselage/fin

Above: AH-1T SeaCobra with T400 power unit, M197 gun but original rounded canopy.

(most) 44ft 7in (13.59m) (T) 48ft 2in (14.68m); height (typical) 13ft 6¼in (4.12m); main-rotor disc area 1,520sq ft (141.26m²).
Weights: Empty (G) 6,073lb (2,754kg), (J) 7,2461lb (3,294kg), (S) 6,479lb (2,939kg), (T) 8,608lb (3,904kg); maximum (G, Q, R) 9,500lb (4,309kg), (J, S) 10,000lb (4,535kg), (T) 14,000lb (6,350kg).
Performance: Maximum speed (G, Q) 172mph (277km/h), (J) 207mph (333km/h), (S, with TOW) 141mph (227km/h); max rate of climb, varies from 1,090ft (332m)/min for J to 1,620ft (494m)/min for S; range with max fuel, typically 357 miles (574km).

Above: Latest, and most capable Cobra, the Marines' AH-1W Super-Cobra has T700 engines.

Armament: Typically one 7.62mm multibarrel Minigun, one 40mm grenade launcher, both in remote-control turrets, or GE Universal Turret for 20mm six-barrel or 30mm three-barrel cannon, plus four stores pylons for 76 rockets of 2.75in caliber or Minigun pods or 20mm gun pod, or (TOWCobra) eight TOW missiles in tandem tube launchers on two outer pylons, inners being available for other stores.
History: First flight 7 September 1965; combat service June 1967 (TOWCobra January 1973).
Users: Army, Marine Corps, National Guard.

Right: An Army AH-1S, with upturned jetpipe but still lacking the angular flat-plate canopy.

Bell was a pioneer of the concept of the armed battlefield helicopter, in initially using the small Model 47 as the basis for the Sioux Scout. In 1965, the Model 209 HueyCobra emerged as a combat development of the UH-1 Iroquois family. It combines the dynamic parts of the original Huey with a new streamlined fuselage providing for a gunner in the front and pilot above and behind him, and for a wide range of fixed and power-aimed armament systems.
The first version was the US Army AH-1G, with 1,100hp T53 engine, of which 1,124 were deliv-

Vought A-7 Corsair II

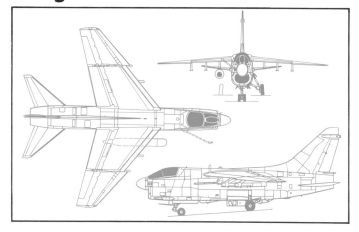

Origin: Vought Systems Division of LTV, later Vought Corporation, Dallas, Texas.
Type: Tactical attack (A, B, E, carrier-based); (K) combat trainer.
Engine: (A) one 11,350lb (5,150kg) thrust Pratt & Whitney TF30-6 two-shaft turbofan; (D, K) 14,250lb (6,465kg) Allison TF41-1 (Rolls-Royce Spey derivative) of same layout; (E) 15,000lb (6,804kg) TF41-2.
Dimensions: Wing span 38ft 9in (11.08m); length 46ft 1½in (14.06m), (K), 48ft 11½in (14.92m); height 16ft 0¾in (4.9m); wing area 375sq ft (34.83m²).
Weights: Empty (A) 15,943lb (7,214kg), (D) 19,781lb (8,972kg);

maximum loaded (A) 32,500lb (14,750kg), (D) 42,000lb (19,050kg).
Performance: Maximum level speed at sea level 698mph (1,123km/h); maximum level speed at 5,000ft (1,525m) with 12 Mk 82 bombs 646mph (1,040km/h); tactical radius with weapon load typically 715 miles (1,150km); ferry range with four external tanks approximately 4,100 miles (6,600km).
Armament: (A) two 20mm Colt Mk 12 in nose; six wing and two fuselage pylons for weapon load of 15,000lb (6,804kg); (D, E) one 20mm M61 Vulcan cannon on left side of fuselage with 1,000-round

Above left: Most single-seat Corsair IIs look alike, but this is a Navy A-7E with the FLIR pod on the right innermost wing pylon.

drum; external load up to theoretical 20,000lb (9,072kg). Weapons carried include air-to-air and air-to-ground missiles, general purpose bombs, rockets, gun pods, and auxiliary fuel tanks.
History: First flight (A) 27 September 1965, (D) 5 April 1968, (E) 25 November 1968, (K) January 1981; first deliveries to user squadrons (A) 14 October 1966; first combat (A) 3 December 1967.
Users: AF, ANG, Navy.

Above: Last of all the new-build Corsairs, the A-7K two-seater was supplied only to the ANG. It has combat capability.

In the early 1960s the Navy began searching for a subsonic attack aircraft able to carry a greater load of non-nuclear weapons than the A-4E Skyhawk. Ling Temco Vought entered the VAX competition, and to keep costs low based its entry on the F-8 Crusader. The strategy worked, for in 1964 the Navy selected LTV Aerospace the winner. The design and development phases took less than a year. The Navy's A-7A saw its first action during December 1967,

ered, including eight to the Spanish Navy for anti-ship strike and 38 as trainers to the US Marine Corps. The AH-1Q is an anti-armor version of ten called TOWCobra because it carries eight TOW missile pods as well as the appropriate sighting system. The AH-1J SeaCobra of the Marine Corps and Iranian Army has twin engines, the 1,800hp Twin Pac having two T400 power sections driving one shaft. Latest versions are the -1Q, -1R, -1S, 1T and 1W, with more power and new equipment. All Cobras can have a great variety of armament.

The standard single-engined HueyCobras, as used by the Army and some export customers, are all designated as AH-1S versions. Most Army Cobras are rebuilt AH-1Gs, but some are being newly built. There are five versions. The Mod AH-1S is an AH-1G fitted with the TOW missile, Dash-703 engine and other improvements including the rotor of the Production S. The TH-1S trainer has a PNVS (pilot's night vision sensor) and blue cockpit lighting compatible with NVGs (night vision goggles). The Production AH-1S has a non-glint flat-plate canopy, new rotor with Kaman composite blades, NOE

(nap of the Earth) instrumentation, radar altimeter, Conus navaid, improved communications and other changes. The Up-gun AH-1S has a GE Universal Turret, M138 wing stores management system, extra electric power and auto compensation for off-axis gun firing. The 1985 standard helicopter is the Modernised AH-1S which combines all previous improvements with an upgrade in avionics and defenses including doppler navigation, laser ranger/tracker, low-speed sensor, ballistic computer, HUD, IFF, IR jammer and hot-metal and plume IR suppressors.

The first Fuji-assembled AH-1S

for the JGSDF flew in Japan in June 1979. Dornier of West Germany is rebuilding US Army AH-1Gs to -1S standard. The company-financed Model 249 is an advanced Cobra with the four-blade Model 412 rotor, reduced in diameter.

The final development is the US Marine Corps' AH-1W, previously called the 1T+, by far the most powerful of all Cobras with two GE T700 engines. First flown on 16 November 1983, this combines enhanced weapon load with sparkling performance, even with one engine out. The Marines are buying 154 (140 delivered by 1997) plus 42 AH-1T conversions.

Left: An A-7E of VA-56 formerly operated over Vietnam from USS Midway. In 1986 Vought was trying to launch up-engined models.

after being launched from carriers on the Gulf of Tonkin. Delivery of 199 A-7As was completed the following spring, the more powerful B joining in March 1969.

One of the most cost-effective attack aircraft ever built, the A-7 demonstrated the ability to carry such heavy loads and deliver them so accurately that in 1966 it was selected as a major USAF type, and 457 were delivered of the uprated A-7D version with the TF41 engine and a new avionic suite providing

for continuous solution of nav/attack problems for precision weapon delivery in all weather. This version introduced the M61 gun and a flight-refueling boom receptacle, preceding Navy models (now retired from front-line units) having probes.

Like earlier models, the D had landing gears retracting into the fuselage, a large door-type airbrake, folding wings and triplex power for the flight controls. The pylons on the cliff-like sides of the fuselage are usually used by

Sidewinder self-defense AAMs. Most A-7 pilots have a high opinion of their air-combat capability, and agility (at least rate of roll) is good even with a heavy load of bombs. The A-7D was in combat in Vietnam from October 1972, flown by the 354th TFW, and on 15 August 1973 Capt. Ratley flew the last strike of the war.

In turn the USAF A-7D, 375 of which formerly equipped most of the attack squadrons of the Air National Guard, was the basis of the

ultimate single-seat version, the A-7E. This aircraft incorporated new avionics for all-weather and night attack, with EW capability. It had a more powerful engine, a retractable FR probe and other upgrades.

A total of 596 of this type were delivered, of which 222 were equipped to carry the Texas Instruments FLIR pod on the inboard pylon on the right side, linked to a new Marconi raster-type HUD for improved night attack capability. Budget limitations have held actual supply of these pods to 110.

Newest of all the US variants is the two-seat A-7K, 42 of which have been distributed in pairs to 11 of the 13 ANG combat-ready A-7D units plus a further 16 to the 162nd Tac Fighter Training Group at Tucson. A direct-view tube provides for Walleye and similar TV ASM guidance, and Pave Penny pods are carried for laser-guided stores, but even with "iron bombs" accuracy is under 10ft (3m).

Vought/LTV delivered 1,545 A-7s, the last in 1983. Many upgrade proposals came to nothing, though ANG A-7D and A-7K Corsairs did receive automatic terrain following and a wide-angle HUD.

Lockheed YO-3A, Q-Star

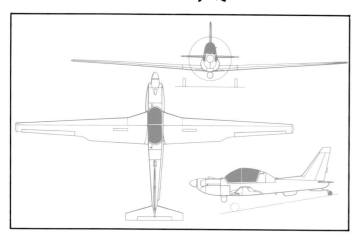

Lockheed C-5 Galaxy

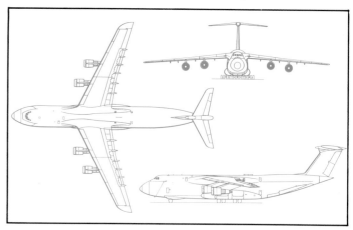

Origin: Lockheed Missiles & Space Company, Sunnyvale, California.
Type: Two-place special reconnaissance craft.
Engine: (YO-3A) one modified 210hp Continental air-cooled; (Q-Star) 100hp Continental O-200-A, replaced by a 185hp Wankel rotary combustion type.
Dimensions: (Q-Star, YO-3A) span 57ft (17.37m); length 30ft (9.14m).
Weights: (Q-Star) 2,166lb (983kg).
Performance: Operating speed range (all) 50 to 120kt (58-138mph, 93-222km/h); quietest speed around 71mph (114km/h); endurance (QT-2) 4h, (Q-Star, YO-3A) 6h.
Armament: None.
History: First flight (QT-2) 1967, (Q-Star) 1968; (YO-3A) prototype contract let July 1968; combat duty (Q-2PC) January 1968, (YO-3A) 1970.
User: Army.

By 1966 the Army had come to realize the value of an airplane that could fly quietly at low altitude, patrolling stealthily and using sensors capable of detecting the Viet Cong and North Vietnamese in

Below: The YO-3A was a completely fresh design, not derived from the Q-Star. It can be regarded as one of the first "stealth" aircraft to see combat duty.

Above: The YO-3As looked unchanged in flight when the original six-blade propeller was replaced by a three-blader. Note the mission sensor on the underside.

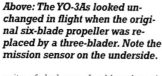

spite of darkness. Lockheed engineers attempted to modify a Schweizer two-place glider for this purpose, strengthening the wings, installing a muffled engine, and adding the necessary sensors. Called the QT-2 (standing for quiet thruster, two-place), two prototypes saw action in South Vietnam during February 1968, reportedly flying at an altitude of 100ft (30m) without alerting the enemy.

This success inspired further modifications that resulted in the Lockheed Q-Star. Its airframe further strengthened, this version finally was fitted out with a Wankel rotary engine, enclosed in a pylon behind the cockpit and attached by means of a long drive shaft to a slowly-turning six-blade propeller.

A combat evaluation in South Vietnam led to changes that were incorporated in the YO-3A. Instead of the earlier mid-wing design engineers chose a low-wing arrangement, with a more powerful engine enclosed in the forward fuselage rather than in a dorsal mount. The fixed landing gear gave way to a retractable type, a three-blade propeller was installed, but the principal sensor remained an infrared detector.

Origin: Lockheed-Georgia Company, Marietta, Georgia.
Type: Heavy airlift transport.
Engines: Four General Electric TF39 turbofans, (A) 41,000lb (18,598kg) thrust TF-39-1, (B) 43,000lb (19,505kg) TF39-1C.
Dimensions: Span 222ft 8½in (67.88m); length 247ft 10in (75.54m); height overall 65ft 1½in (19.85m); wing area 6,200sq ft (576m²).
Weights: Empty (A) 337,937lb (152,285kg), (B) 370,300lb (167,965kg); max (A) 769,000lb (348,810kg), (B) 840,000lb (381,025kg).
Performance: Max speed 571mph (919km/h); max cruising speed 564mph (908km/h); econ cruising speed 518mph (833km/h); takeoff over 50ft (15m) 9,800ft (2,987m); landing over 50ft (15m) f3,820ft (1,164m); range with 30min reserve (max payload) 2,729 miles (4,391km), (max fuel) 6,850 miles (11,024km).
Armament: None.
History: First flight (A) 30 June 1968; service delivery (A) 17 December 1969, (B) December 1985.
User: AF.

Growing appreciation of the need for an extremely large logistics transport to permit deployment of the heaviest hardware items on a global basis led in 1963 to the CX-HLS (Heavy Logistic System) specification calling for a payload of 250,000lb (113,400kg) over a coast-to-coast range, and half this load over the challenging unrefueled range of 8,000 miles (12,785km); it also demanded the ability to fly such loads into a 4,000ft (1,220m) rough forward airstrip.

Such performance was theoretically possible using a new species of turbofan, of high bypass ratio, much more powerful than existing engines. In August 1965 GE won the engine contract, and two months later Lockheed won the C-5A aircraft. Design was undertaken under extreme pressure, the wing being assigned to CDI, a group of British engineers from canceled programs. About half the value of each airframe was subcontracted to suppliers in the US and Canada, and construction of the first aircraft (66-8303) began as early as August 1966.

Meeting the requirements

Above: Today's C-5B has important structure and systems differences from those in the original C-5A.

Right: Externally, the C-5B is hard to tell from a C-5A. This one has just crossed the Golden Gate Bridge.

Right: One C-5 "cargo" could be 365 troops, plus the five flight crew and other personnel.

proved impossible, and cost-inflation reduced the total buy from 115 (six squadrons) to 81 (four squadrons), of which 30 were delivered by the end of 1970. As a cargo airlifter the C-5A proved in a class of its own, with main-deck width of 19ft (5.79m) and full-section access at front and rear. Features include high-lift slats and flaps, an air-refueling receptacle, advanced forward-looking radars and a unique landing gear with 28 wheels offering the required 'high flotation' for unpaved surfaces, as well as free castoring to facilitate ground maneuvering, an offset (20° to left or right) swivelling capability for use in crosswinds, fully modulating anti-skid brakes and the ability to kneel to bring the main deck close to the ground.

Avionics include triple INS, two nose radars and a MADAR (malfunction detection, analysis and recording) system which monitors 800 items throughout the aircraft.

Typical loads can weight up to 220,967lb (100,228kg) for the C-5A or 291,000lb (132,000kg) for the C-5B, and can include two M1 tanks, 16 trucks of ¾-ton size, five M113s, 36 Size 463L cargo pallets or 270 troops plus another 75 on the rear upper deck, in all cases with a flight crew of five and 15 others (relief crew, technicians or couriers) on the forward upper deck.

Despite highly publicized faults, most of which were quickly rectified, the C-5A was soon giving invaluable service; but a deep-rooted difficulty was that the wing accrued fatigue damage more rapidly than had been predicted. Several modification programs provided incomplete solutions, and in 1978 Lockheed's proposal for the introduction of a new wing was accepted. The wing uses a different detail design in new materials,

and though the moving surfaces are largely unchanged even these are to be manufactured again, the slats, ailerons and flap tracks for the second time being assigned to Canadair. Between 1982-87 all 77 surviving aircraft were re-winged. This was done with minimal reduction in airlift capability by MAC's 60th MAW at Travis, California, 436th at Dover, Delaware, and 443rd at Altus AFB, Oklahoma.

To meet a need for additional heavy airlift capability for USAF Military Airlift Command, Congress accepted a 1982 Lockheed proposal to build a minimum-change Galaxy from new. Then known as the C-5N, these airplanes are now designated C-5B. As well as the new wing the C-5Bs have an improved engine, also being retrofitted to the C-5As, which has a "bump rating" of 43,000lb (19,505kg) for maximum-weight takeoffs as well as a full normal rating maintained to 32°C (89.5°F), and other new features including on-condition maintenance instead of a fixed 5,000 hour overhaul life.

The C-5B also has MADAR II (an

Above: Test pilot Bernie Dvorscak and his crew lift off on the first flight of the C-5B on 10 December 1985.

updated system), color radar needing only a small nose radome, carbon brakes instead of beryllium, simpler landing gear door drives (with the number of gearboxes reduced from 48 to two!) and many other changes all aimed at prolonging troublefree life and reducing cost. Like the refurbished C-5As, the C-5Bs will all be painted Europe 1 camouflage.

The first C-5B was rolled out in July 1985. The Marietta plant delivered 50, the last on 17 April 1979. They have performed impressively in conflicts in the Gulf, Bosnia and elsewhere, and Lockheed Martin pushed an upgraded C-5D as an alternative to the C-17. Retrofitting the entire fleet with new engines remains a possibility.

Below: A C-5A lands, displaying multi-segment flaps and the 28 landing wheels needed to confer "flotation" for soft fields.

Boeing E-4B, VC-25A

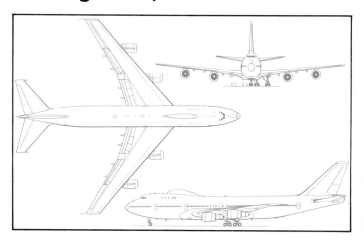

Origin: Boeing Aerospace Company, Kent, Washington.
Type: (E-4B) national command post, (VC-25) VIP transport.
Engines: Four General Electric turbofans, (E-4B) 52,500lb (23,814kg) F103-100, (VC-25A) 56,750lb (25,742kg) F103-102.
Dimensions: Span 195ft 8in (59.64m); length 231ft 4in (70.51m); height overall 63ft 5in (19.33m); wing area 5,500sq ft (511m^2).
Weights: Empty about 460,000lb (208,656kg); max 800,000lb (362,875kg); (VC-25A) 803,700lb (364,552kg).
Performance: Operating height about 40,000ft (12,192m); takeoff endurance on internal fuel over 12; normal mission duration 72h.
Armament: None.
History: First flight (747) 9 February 1969, (E-4A) 13 June 1973, (VC-25A) 26 January 1990.
Users: US National Command Authorities (AF crews).

Around 1970 the USAF began to cast covetous eyes on the giant 747, which in comparison with the

Above: World's most powerful airplane (though rivaled in size and weight by C-5B and An-124), the E-4B has F103 engines.

C-135 series offered much greater mission endurance with five times the payload and more than five times the internal volume. In February 1973 the USAF placed a contract for two 747-200Bs to be adapted as the AABNCP (Advanced AirBorne National Command Post); later two more were added.

The first E-4B (75-0125), the fourth in the E-4 series, was delivered on 21 December 1979. The E-4B has accommodation for an operating crew of 94, including a larger battle staff of 30 on its 4,620sq ft (429.2m^2) main deck, which is divided into six operating areas; the National Command Authorities area, conference room, briefing room, battle staff, communications control center and rest area. The flight deck includes a special navigation station (not in 747s) and crew rest area, essential for air-refueled

Above: 73-1676 was the first of the original three E-4As, subsequently re-engined with F103s and given a "doghouse".

missions lasting up to 72 hours.

The E-4B was designed for unique capabilities. Its extraordinary avionics, mainly communications but with many other types of system, were created by a team including Electrospace Systems, Collins, Rockwell, RCA and Burroughs, co-ordinated by E-systems and Boeing. Each engine drives two 150kVA alternators, and a large air-conditioning system (separate from that for the main cabin) is provided to cool the avionics compartments. Nuclear thermal shielding is extensive, and among the communications are an LF/VLF wire antenna trailed 5 miles (8km) behind the aircraft, and an SHF (super high frequency) system whose antennas are housed in the dorsal blister.

The idea of an AABNCP grew from the fear of all-out nuclear war. In such a situation it was considered necessary to provide an

airborne platform capable of acting as the nation's seat of executive authority in time of crisis or all-out war, secure against EMP (electromagnetic pulse), radiation and other nuclear effects and able to command the USAF and USN strategic retaliatory forces.

The main home base of the AABNCP force is Offutt AFB, Nebraska, HQ of SAC, but a stop would be made at Andrews AFB near the capital, Washington DC, should it be felt necessary for the US President to be on board.

In contrast, the two VC-25A aircraft are luxurious transports which have replaced VC-137Cs as conveyances for the President and other officials. When the President is aboard they used the callsign "Air Force One". Both aircraft are equipped for self-contained operation anywhere in the world, with special furnishings, avionics, inflight refuelling and powered airstairs.

Below: 75-125 was the first aircraft originally ordered as an E-4B. It is perhaps the most amazing HQ ever built.

McDonnell Douglas KC-10A Extender

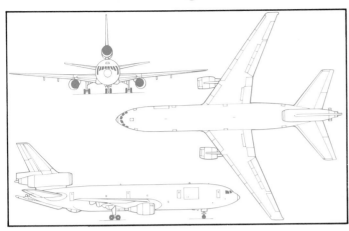

Origin: Douglas Aircraft Company, Long Beach, California.
Type: Air-refueling tanker and heavy cargo transport.
Engines: Three 52,500lb (23,814kg) thrust General Electric F103 (CF6-50C2) turbofans.
Dimensions: Span 165ft 4½in (50.41m); length 181ft 7in (55.35m); height 58ft 1in (17.7m); wing area 3,958sq ft (367.7m²).
Weights: Empty (tanker role) 241,027lb (109,328kg); maximum loaded 590,000lb (267,620kg).
Performance: Max speed (max weight, at 25,000ft/7,620m) about 600mph (966km/h); max cruising speed (30,000ft/9,144m) 555mph (893km/h); takeoff field length 10,400ft (3,170m); max range (with max cargo load) 4,370 miles (7,032km).
Armament: None.
History: First flight (DC-10) 29 August 1970, (KC-10A) 12 July 1980.
Users: AF.

Selected in December 1977 as the USAF's future ATCA (Advanced Tanker/Cargo Aircraft), the KC-10

Above: Though it can only refuel airplanes one at a time, the Extender has both a boom and a hose with drogue.

(the A is often omitted from the designation) is in production under a single multi-year contract which delivered a total of 60, the last in September 1988. The first entered service with the 32nd Air Refueling Sqn at Barksdale AFB in March 1981, followed by deliveries to the 9th ARS at March and the 911th ARS at Seymour Johnson in 1984. Associate AF Reserve squadrons share the new aircraft at each base.

Basically the KC-10 is a commercial DC-10-30CF convertible passenger/freighter, with military avionics and equipment, and with a major revision to the fuselage. Above the floor the area is equipped for cargo, with a main cargo door and five passenger doors, but no windows other than four to add natural light. Under the floor are seven Goodyear flexible fuel cells with capacity of 117,829lb (53,446kg, 18,125gal, 68,610lit) of

Above: KC-10s are painted dark green (not Europe 1) with sparse low-observables stencils and insignia.

fuel. At the rear is a boom operator station with an extra-large high-speed refueling boom with FBW control, able to transfer fuel at 1,500gal (5,678lit)/min.

The KC-10 is also equipped with two Flight Refuelling Mk 32B hose-drum pods under the outer wings. This enables it to refuel airplanes of the Navy, Marines and friendly air forces which are probe-equipped.

The entire on-board fuel capacity, comprising the underfloor cells plus the basic tankage of 238,236lb (108, 062kg), can be used as transfer fuel. It is possible to transfer 200,000lb (90,718kg) of fuel to receiver aircraft at a distance of 2,200 miles (3,540km) from the KC-10's base and return. The KC-10 also has an air-refueling receptacle.

The above-floor area is equipped with portable winches and power rollers, and can accom-

modate 27 USAF Type 463L pallets, or 25 with access along both sides. Max cargo payload is 169,370lb (76,825kg). At the forward end of the cabin is seating for essential support personnel (14), and six crew, as well as four rest bunks.

In service KC-10s act as "lead ship" on overseas fighter deployments. They are supported by the manufacturer under a separate contract, and the operational reliability rate exceeded 99 per cent overall, with several months at 100 per cent.

A fleet of 17 KC-10s can fully support the transatlantic deployment of an F-15 wing, instead of the 40 KC-135s formerly needed. As an additional bonus, their longer range reduces the need for foreign landing rights.

Below: During trials with the prototype KC-10 in 1980 a hook-up was made with a C-5A Galaxy over the Sierra Nevada mountains, resulting in a memorable photo. Today the C-5A and C-5B are routine recipients of KC-10 fuel.

Grumman F-14 Tomcat

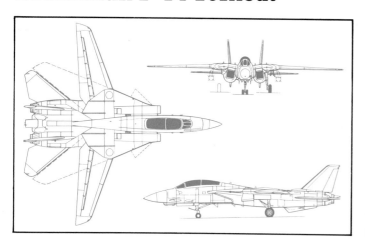

Origin: Grumman Aerospace Corporation, Bethpage, NY.
Type: Two-seat carrier-based multi-role fighter.
Engines: (F-14A) two 20,900lb (9,480kg) thrust Pratt & Whitney TF30-412A two-shaft afterburning turbofans, being replaced by TF30-414A, same rating, (B+, D) 26,800lb (12,156kg) General Electric F110-400 augmented turbofans.
Dimensions: Span (68° sweep) 38ft 2in (11.63m), (20° sweep) 64ft 1½in (19.54m); length 62ft 8in (19.1m); height 16ft (4.88m); wing area 565sq ft (52.49m^2).
Weights: Empty 40,104lb (18,191kg); loaded (normal) 58,539lb (26,553kg), (max) 74,348lb (33,724kg).
Performance: Maximum speed 1,544mph (2,485km/h, Mach 2.34) at height, 910mph (1,470km/h, Mach 1.2) at sea level; initial climb at normal gross weight, over

Above: Apart from the engine nozzles this F-14A looks similar to tomorrow's F-14B and F-14D.

30,000ft (9,144m)/min; service ceiling over 56,000ft (17,070m); range (fighter with external fuel) about 2,000 miles (3,200km) (F-14D, over 3,000 miles, 4,828km).
Armament: One 20mm M61-A1 multi-barrel cannon in fuselage; four AIM-7 Sparrow and four or eight AIM-9 Sidewinder air-to-air missiles, or up to six AIM-54 Phoenix and two AIM-9; maximum external weapon load in surface attack role 14,500lb (6,577kg).
History: First flight 21 December 1970; initial deployment with Navy carriers October 1972; first flight (F-14B) 12 September 1973, (F-14D) 1987.
User: Navy.

When Congress finally halted development of the compromised

Above: F-14s on deck with wings "overswept" beyond the airborne limit of 68°.

F-111B version of the TFX in mid 1968, Grumman was already well advanced with the project design of a replacement. After a competition for the VFX requirement Grumman was awarded a contract for the F-14 in January 1969. The company had to produce a detailed mock-up by May and build 12 development aircraft. Despite sudden loss of the first aircraft on its second flight, due to total hydraulic failure, the program has been a technical success and produced one of the world's outstanding combat aircraft.

Basic features include use of an automatically scheduled variable-sweep swing, to match the aircraft to the conflicting needs of carrier compatibility, dog-fighting and attack on surface targets at low

Right: Today F-14s are gray, but here a bright-stripe Tomcat from VF-2 picks up a wire.

level; pilot and naval flight officer (observer) in tandem; an extremely advanced airframe, with tailplane skins of boron-epoxy composite and similar novel construction methods, and one canted vertical tail above each engine; and the extremely powerful Hughes AWG-9 radar which, used in conjunction with the Phoenix missile (carried by no other combat aircraft), can pick out and destroy a chosen aircraft from a formation over 100 miles (160km) away.

For close-in fighting the gun is used in conjunction with snap-shoot missiles, with the tremendous advantage that, as a launch platform, the Tomcat is unsurpassed. Grumman claim it to be unrivalled, and to be able – by

Lockheed S-3 Viking

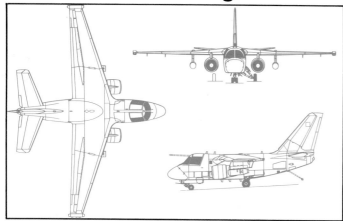

Origin: Lockheed-California Company, Burbank, California.
Type: Four-seat carrier-based anti-submarine aircraft.
Engines: Two 9,275lb (4,207kg) General Electric TF34-2 or TF34-400 two-shaft turbofans.
Dimensions: Span 68ft 8in (20.93m); length 53ft 4in (16.26m); height 22ft 9in (6.93m); wing area 598sq ft (55.56m^2).
Weights: Empty 26,600lb (12,056kg); normal loaded for carrier operation 42,500lb (19,277kg); maximum loaded

Above: S-3B, with retractable FLIR, flight-refueling probe and arrester hook depicted in broken lines.

47,000lb (21,319kg).
Performance: Maximum speed 506mph (814km/h); initial climb, over 4,200ft (1,280m)/min; service ceiling, above 35,000ft (19,670m); combat range, more than 2,303 miles (3,705km); ferry range, more than 3,454 miles (5,558km).
Armament: Split internal weapon bays can house for Mk 46 torpedoes, four Mk 82 bombs,

Above: MAD boom extended, an S-3A from VS-22 (CV-60 Saratoga) over the Atlantic.

four various depth bombs or four mines; two wing pylons can carry single or triple ejectors for bombs, rocket pods, missiles, tanks or other stores, the S-3B carrying two AGM-84A Harpoon missiles.
History: First flight 21 January 1972; service delivery October 1973; operational use (VS-41) 20 February 1974; final delivery 1980.
User: Navy.

Designed to replace the Grumman S-2, the S-3 is the most remarkable exercise in packaging in the history of aviation. It is also an example of an aircraft in which the operational equipment costs considerably more than the aircraft itself.

Lockheed-California won the Navy competition in partnership with LTV (Vought) which makes the wing, engine pods, tail and F-8-type landing gear. The long-span wings have high-lift flaps and spoilers, ESM receiver pods

new threat-warning and internal self-protection jammer system. In 1980-81, as a replacement for the FA-5C and RF-8G, 49 F-14As were fitted with Tarps (tac air recon pod system), containing optical cameras and an infra-red sensor.

Endemic problems with the engine resulted in a switch to the F110. This solved the safety problems and also improved flight performance. The F-14B can take off without using afterburner, and can climb to high altitude in 61 per cent less time and has 62 per cent greater mission range. Grumman built 38 F-15Bs, and converted 32 F-14As. The final version, the F-14D Super Tomcat, has new avionics and AMRAAM missiles. Grumman had delivered 37 of a planned 127 when the program was cancelled in 1989, but A/B versions have been upgraded. By 1993 there were nine kids of further upgrade proposed, a few of which are being incorporated in a core force of 251 aircraft, with the remainder stored.

automatic variation of wing sweep – to out-maneuver all previous combat aircraft. Introduction to the US Navy was smooth and enthusiastic, with VF-1 and -2 serving aboard Enterprise in 1974. But costs escalated beyond prediction, Grumman refusing at one time to continue the program and claiming its existing contracts would result in a loss of $105 million. For the same reason the re-engined F-14B, with the later-technology and much more powerful F401 engine, was held to a single prototype. In 1975 ongoing production agreements were concluded and F-14A deliveries were

completed in April 1987 at a total of 557, excluding 80 supplied to Iran.

The basic aircraft has remained virtually unchanged, though prolonged trouble with the engines has led to the P-414A version of the TF30 which it was hoped would improve safety and reliability. This engine arrived in late

1983 together with a new radar, programmable signal processor, a new target identification system, embodying Northrop's TCS (TV camera set) which has been slowly retrofitted to existing Tomcats since 1981, a laser-gyro inertial system, completely new cockpit displays and completely

Below: Another former bright paint scheme was worn by VF-32 from CVW-1. the same F-14A leads the box of four opposite.

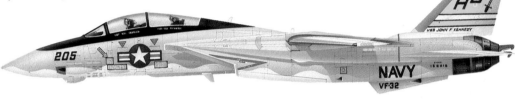

on the tips, and formal integral tanks inboard of the fold hinges. The latter are skewed so that the folded wings can overlap each other. The vertical tail also folds to lie flat.

Lockheed built eight development prototypes plus 179 inventory aircraft. In 1984 conversion began to S-3B standard, with updated equipment and avionics and provision to launch Harpoon anti-ship cruise missiles.

Developed versions, including a COD transport, tanker, ECM and AEW versions are also possible, for both carrier and land operation. The US-3A transport carries most of its payload in large underwing pods, but the Navy has decided to stick with the C-2S Greyhound (though four US-3As are in service in the Philippines). The KS-3A air-refueling tanker proved satisfactory on test, but none has been procured to augment the small fleet of KA-6D tankers, mainly because of the high cost of reopening the production line.

Right: The mighty deck of CV-69 Dwight D. Eisenhower will receive Vikings from VS-31.

Boeing E-3 Sentry

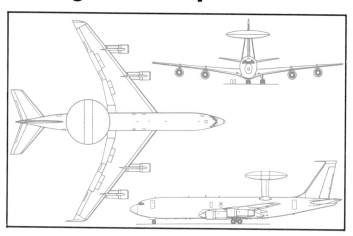

Origin: Boeing Aerospace
Company, Kent, Washington.
Type: Airborne Warning and
Control System (AWACS) platform.
Engines: Four 21,000lb
(9,526kg) thrust Pratt & Whitney
TF33-100/100A turbofans.
Dimensions: Span 145ft 9in
(44.42m); length 152ft 11in
(46.61m); height 41ft 4in (12.6m)
(over fin); wing area 3,050sq ft
(283.4m²).
Weights: Empty, not disclosed
but about 162,000lb (73,480kg),
loaded 325,000lb (147,400kg).
Performance: Maximum speed
530mph (853km/h); normal
operating speed, about 350mph
(563km/h); service ceiling, over
29,000ft (8.85km); endurance on
station 1,000 miles (1,609km)
from base, 6h.
Armament: None

*Above: All Sentries look similar
(apart from the Saudi KE-3A),
except that USAF E-3B and C have
HF antennas on both wingtips.*

History: First flight (EC-137D) 5
February 1972, (E-3A)
31 October 1975; service
delivery (E-3A) 24 March 1977.
User: AF

Back in the early 1950s the USAF
pioneered the concept of the overland radar surveillance platform,
mainly using EC-121 Warning Stars
(based on the Super Constellation,
and continuing in unpublicized
service until almost 1980). During
the 1960s radar technology had
reached the point at which, with
greater power and rapid digital
processing, an OTH (over the hori-
zon) capability could be achieved,

*Above: Tank boomer's view of an
E-3A as it noses in with
refueling doors open. The rotodome rotates throughout flight.*

plus clear vision looking almost
straight down to detect and follow
high-speed aircraft flying only just
above the Earth's surface.

One vital ingredient was the
pulse-doppler kind of radar, in
which the "doppler shift" in
received frequency caused by relative motion between the target
and the radar can be used to separate out all reflections except those
from genuine moving targets. Very
clever signal processing is needed
to eliminate returns from such false
"moving targets" as leaves vio-
lently distributed by wind, and the
most difficult of all is the motion of
the sea surface and blown spray

*Right: Kit strews an Egyptian
hardstand as a Sentry arrives
for joint exercise Bright Star in
1983. Results were valuable.*

in an ocean gale. For this reason
even more clever radars are needed
for the overwater mission, and the
USAF did not attempt to accomplish
it until well into the 1980s.

While Hughes and Westing-
house fought to develop the new
ODR (overland downlook radar),
Boeing was awarded a prime
contract on 8th July 1970 for the
AWACS (airborne warning and
control system). Their proposal
was based on the commercial
707-320; to give enhanced onsta-
tion endurance it was to be powered by eight TF34 engines, but to
cut costs this was abandoned and
the original engines retained

Fairchild Republic A-10A Thunderbolt II

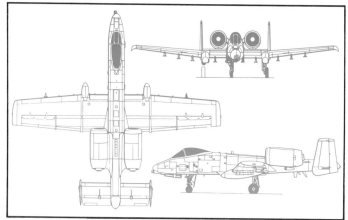

Origin: Fairchild Republic
Company, Farmingdale, NY.
Type: Close-support attack
aircraft.
Engines: Two 9,065lb (4,112kg)
thrust General Electric TF34-100
turbofans.
Dimensions: Span 57ft 6in
(17.53m); length 53ft 4in
(16.26m); height (regular) 14ft 8in
(4.47m), (NAW) 15ft 4in (4.67m);
wing area 506sq ft (47m²).
Weights: Empty 21,519lb
(9,761kg); forward airstrip weight
(no fuel but four Mk 82 bombs
and 750 rounds) 32,730lb
(14,846kg); max 50,000lb
(22,680kg).

*Above: Most A-10As have Pave
Penny laser pod under the right
side of the nose.*

Performance: Max speed (max
weight, A-10A) 423mph (681
km/h), (NAW) 420mph
(676km/h); cruising speed at sea
level (both) 345mph (555km/h);
stabilized speed below 8,000ft
(2,440m) in 45° dive at weight
35,125lb (15,932kg), 299mph
(481km/h); max climb at basic
design weight of 31,790lb
(14,420kg), 6,000ft (1,828m)/min;
service ceiling not stated; takeoff
run to 50ft (15m) at max weight
4,000ft (1,220m); operating

*Above: Lt-Col Dennis Myrick
(355TTW from Davis-Monthan)
comes in over Gila Bend range.*

radius in CAS mission with 1.8h
loiter and reserves 288 miles
(463km); radius for single deep
strike penetration 620 miles
(1,000km); ferry range with
allowances 2,542 miles
(4,091km).
Armament: One GAU-8/A
Avenger 30mm seven-barrel gun
with 1,174 rounds, total external
ordnance load of 16,000lb
(7,257kg) hung on 11 pylons,
three side-by-side on body and
four under each wing, several

hundred combinations of stores
up to individual weight of 5,000lb
(2,268kg) with max total weight
14,638lb (6,640kg) with full
internal fuel.
History: First flight (YA-10A) 10
May 1972, (production A-10A) 21
October 1975, (NAW) 4 May 1979.
Users: AF, ANG.

The concept of a relatively slow
tactical weapons platform, able to
survive over a battlefield by flying
very low and carrying special
armor and duplicated systems,
has always been a matter for prolonged argument. What has never
been in doubt is the devastating

cated; when on-station it rotates at 6rpm (once every 10 seconds) and the searchlight-like beam is electronically scanned under computer control to sweep from the ground up to the sky and space, picking out every kind of moving target and processing the signals at the rate of 710,000 complete "words" per second. The rival radars were flown in two EC-137D aircraft built from existing 707s, and the winning Westinghouse APY-1 radar was built into the first E-3A in 1975.

The first E-3A force was built up in TAC, to support quick-reaction deployment and tactical operation by all TAC units. The 552nd AWAC Wing received its first E-3A at Tinker AFB, Oklahoma, on 24 March 1977, and went on operational duty a year later. It was augmented from 1979 by NORAD (North American Air Defense) personnel whose mission is the surveillance of all North American airspace and the control of NORAD forces over the USA.

Production Sentries have been delivered to five standards. The so-called Core E-3A identifies the first 24 aircraft delivered to the USAF, with limited capability except against aerial targets. They had nine SDCs (situation display consoles) two ADUs (auxiliary display units) and 13 available communications channels.

The E-3B designation applies to the E-3A after complete updating with JTIDS (joint tactical information distribution system), the CC-2 computer, more radios and Have Quick anti-jamming, five more SDCs, a teletypewriter and an "austere" (limited) maritime surveillance capability

The US/NATO E-3A applies to 18 aircraft paid for by NATO nations and operated in NATO markings with crews of 15 men drawn in rotation from the 11 nations participating. They are based at Geilenkirchen, with FOBs (forward operating bases) at Preveza (Greece), Trapani (Italy) and Konya (Turkey), plus an FOL (location) at Oerland (Norway). This was also the original standard of the USAF aircraft Nos 25-34, which in fact are being updated to E-3C standard with five more SDCs, five more UHF radios and Have Quick anti-jamming. The modifications to both Core and USAF Standard aircraft are being made with Boeing kits being delivered by April 1987.

Perhaps the best Sentries are the E-3A/Saudis, five of which were delivered as part of a $4,660 million package in 1986. They have the quiet fuel-efficient CFM56 engine. Retrofit of this engine in USAF Sentries has been studied.

While the USAF Sentries are being progressively upgraded, Boeing has also sold the E-3D to the British RAF and the E-3F to France. Both these versions have the CFM F108 turbofan engine, which has been studied as a possible upgrade on the USAF fleet. The Saudi KE-3A is a tanker/transport, not an AWACS aircraft.

though driving high-power electric generators.

The antenna for the main radar, back-to-back with an IFF (identification friend or foe) and main communications antennas, is mounted on a pylon above the rear fuselage and streamlined by adding two D-shaped radomes of glass-fiber sandwich which turn the girder-like antenna beam into a deep circular rotodome of 30ft (9.14m) diameter. This turns very slowly to keep the bearings lubri-

punch that the A-10A can deliver, at least in conditions of reasonable visibility. Lingering doubts about the cost/effectiveness of this unique aircraft may have been dispelled by the appearance of the Soviet Su25, which is an exact counterpart (but modeled more on the A-10's unsuccessful rival, the Northrop A-9A).

Until 1967 the USAF had never bothered to procure a close-support aircraft, instead flying CAS missions with fighters and attack machines. With the A-10, emphasis was placed on the ability to operate from short unpaved front-line airstrips, to carry an exceptional

Above: A-10A in Europe. The name "Warthog" seems to have stuck, though totally unofficial.

load of weapons – in particular a very powerful high velocity gun – and to withstand prolonged exposure to gunfire from the ground. Avionics were left to a minimum, the official description for the fit being "austere", but a few extra items are now being added.

The original A-10A was a basically simple single-seater, larger than most tactical attack aircraft and carefully designed as a compromise between capability and low cost. As an example of the lat-

ter many of the major parts, including flaps, main landing gears and movable tail surfaces, are interchangeable left/right, and systems and engineering features were designed with duplication and redundancy to survive parts being shot away. The unusual engine location minimizes infrared signature and makes it almost simple to fly with one engine inoperative or even shot off.

Weapon pylons were added from tip to tip, but the chief tank-killing ordnance is the gun, the most powerful (in terms of muzzle horsepower) ever mounted in an aircraft, firing milk-bottle-size rounds at rates hydraulically controlled at 2,100 or 4,200 shots/min. The gun is mounted 2° nose-down and offset to the left so that the firing barrel is always on the centerline (the nose landing gear being offset to the right). The basic aircraft has a HUD (head-up display), good communications fit and both Tacan and inertial navigation. RHAWS and ECM have been internal from the start, but jammer pods are hung externally.

In 1979 Fairchild flew a company-funded NAW (night/adverse weather) demonstrator with augmented avionics and a rear-cockpit for a WSO seated at a higher level and with good forward view.

Both the regular and NAW aircraft carry a Pave Penny laser seeker pod under the nose, vital for laser-guided munitions, and the NAW also has a Ferranti laser ranger, Texas Instruments FLIR (forward-looking infrared), GE low-light TV, and many other items including a Westinghouse multi-mode radar with WSO display. It is possible that at least some of the A-10As will be brought at least close to the NAW standard, with the LANTIRN pod, though the two seat NAW itself was never funded. A-10A funding was abruptly terminated in 1982 at a total of 707 aircraft (not including the six RDT&E (research, development, test and engineering) prototypes), the last one rolling off the assembly line in 1983.

In service with the 57th TTW, four regular TFWs (the 23rd, 18st, 354th and 355th) and the 66th FWS of the USAF, and the 174th TFW and four TFGs (103rd, 104th, 128th and 175th) of the ANG, the A-10A has proved popular and effective with many weapons. Serviceability and manpower burden have been as predicted, and the only cause for worry has been that the sustained attrition rate is rather higher than normal, caused by hitting the ground during operations at very low level.

McDonnell Douglas F-15 Eagle

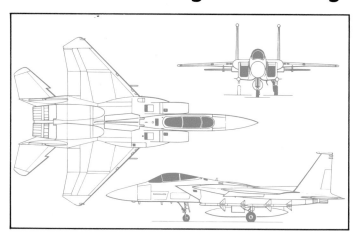

Above: Early F-15As of the 43rd TFS, 21st TFW, helping guard Alaska from Elmendorf AFB.

Origin: McDonnell Aircraft Company, St Louis, Missouri.
Type: Air superiority fighter with attack capability, (E) dual-role fighter/attack.
Engines: Two 23,930lb (10,855kg) thrust Pratt & Whitney F-100-100 afterburning turbofans,(E) two 23,450lb (10,637kg) F100-220.
Dimensions: Span 42ft 9¾in (13.05m); length 63ft 9in (19.43m); height overall 18ft 5½in (5.63m); wing area 608sq ft (56.5m²).
Weights: Empty (A) 27,381lb (12,240kg); takeoff (intercept mission, A) 42,206lb (19,145kg); max (A) 56,000lb (25,401kg), (C, FAST packs) 68,000lb (30,845kg), (E) 81,000lb (36,742kg).
Performance: Max speed (clean, over 45,000ft/13,716m) 1,650mph (2,665km/h, Mach 2.5), (clean, SL) 912mph (1,468km/h, Mach 1.2); combat ceiling (A, clean) 63,000ft (19,200m); time to 50,000ft (15,240m) (intercept configuration) 2.5min; mission radius, no data; ferry range (C) over 3,450 miles (5,560km).

Above: F-15A, typical of early single-seaters. B is two-seater; C and D normally have FAST packs.

Armament: One 20mm M61A1 gun with 940 rounds; four AIM-7 Sparrow AAMs or eight AIM-120A (AMRAAM), plus four AIM-9 Sidewinders; three attack weapon stations (five with FAST packs) for external load of up to 16,000lb (7,258kg), or (E) 24,500lb (11,113kg).
History: First flight 27 July 1972; service delivery (inventory) November 1974; first flight (C) 26 February 1979, (E prototype) November 1982.
Users: AF, ANG.

Most observers in the Western World regard the F-15 as the natural successor to its ancestor, the F-4, as the best fighter in the world. To a considerable degree its qualities rest on the giant fixed-geometry wing, F100 engine and Hughes APG-63 pulse-doppler radar.

Inevitably the F-15 emerged as a large aircraft, costly to buy and to operate. Two of the powerful engines were needed to achieve the desired ratio of thrust/weight, which near sea level in the clean condition exceeds unity. The lower edge of the fuselage is tailored to snug fitting of four medium-range AAMs. The gun is in the bulged strake at the root of the right wing, drawing ammunication from a vertical drum inboard of the duct.

There is no fuel between the engines but abundant room in the integral tank inner wing and between the ducts for 11,600lb (5,260kg, 1,741gal, 6,592lit), and three 600gal (2,270lit) drop tanks can be carried, each stressed to 5g maneuvers when full. An inflight refueling boom receptacle is in the top of the inboard left wing, opposite to the gun. Roll is by ailerons only at low speeds, the dogtoothed slab tailplanes taking over entirely at over Mach 1, together with the twin rudders, which are vertical.

Much of the structure is of steel, titanium, boron-epoxy composite and glassfiber, the tail and giant dorsal airbrake being honeycomb sandwich assemblies.

Avionics and flight/weapon control systems are typical of the 1970 period, with a flat-plate scanner pulse-doppler radar, vertical situation display presenting ADI (attitude/director indicator), radar and EO information in one picture, a HUD, INS and central digital computer. In its integral ECM/IFF subsystems the F-15 was far better than most Western fighters, with Loral radar warning (with front/rear antennas on the left fin tip), Northrop ALQ-135 internal countermeasures system, Magnavox EW warning set and Hazeltine APX-76 1FF with Litton reply-evaluator. High-power jammers, however, must still be hung externally, Westinghouse pods normally occupying an outer wing pylon.

The APG-63 main radar offered excellent capability to track low-level targets, with cockpit switches giving a Hotas (hands on throttle

Beech C-12, U-21 Super King Air

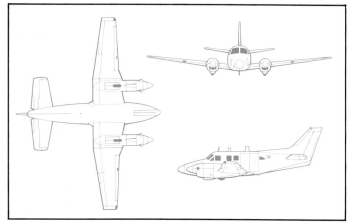

Above: The RU-21J is one of the latest of the Cefly Lancer series of special electronic-warfare models for the Army.

Origin: Beech Aircraft Corporation, Wichita, Kansas.
Type: Pressurized twin-turboprop for various roles.
Engines: Two Pratt & Whitney Canada PT6 turboprops; (most) 850shp PT6A-42, (C-12A) 750shp PT6A-38.
Dimensions: Span (no tip tanks) 54ft 6in (16.61m) (see text for variants); length 43ft 9in

Above: Smaller than the T-tailed Supers, the basic U-21 is derived from the King Air and is known to the Army as the Ute.

(13.34m); height 15ft (4.57m); wing area 303sq ft (28.15m²).
Weights: (Basic B200) empty 7538lb (3,419kg); max 12,500lb (5,670kg) , (B200T) 14,000lb (6,350kg), (RU021J) 15,000lb

(6,804kg).
Performance: (Basic B200) max cruising speed (25,000ft/7,620m) 333mph (536km/h); takeoff run 1,942ft (592m); range (max fuel, 35,000ft 10,570m, full reserves, at

max cruising speed), 2,271 miles (3,654km).
Armament: None.
History: First flight (Super King Air 200) 27 October 1972.
Users: AF, Army, Marine Corps, Navy.

Right at the ''top of the market'', the T-tailed Super King Air 200 has the power and performance

reduced drag and leaving existing pylons free (thus an F-15C can carry 12 bombs, 4 AAMs, 2 IR sensor pods and still carry 3 tanks).

In the late 1970s the USAF began studying an EFT (enhanced tactical fighter), configured equally for surface attack and air superiority roles. McDonnell modified an early F-15B as the Enhanced Eagle and, after prolonged tests, this carried the day over the rival F-16XL. The resulting F-15E offered an astonishing extra capability in the surface attack role, a major advance being the inclusion of a backseater. Though the very powerful GE F110-129 engine was tested in F-15E 87-0180, all USAF aircraft have the F100, but in upgraded versions (see data). The Dash-229 in particular offers welcome extra power to counter the increase in maximum takeoff weight.

Features include the new APG-70 high-resolution radar, with DBS (doppler beam sharpening), totally new computer and programmable armament control system, wide-field HUD, internal ASPJ ECM, LANTIRN all-weather nav/targeting pod, and multifunction displays in the rear cockpit for managing the complete mission. Remarkably few structural changes apart from the landing gears are needed to handle the gross weight, which is almost double that of a B-17.

Production for the USAF terminated with a block of three funded in 1992, but a further six were added with 1996 funds to bring the total up to 215. In 1997 it was expected that a further six might be funded in FY97 and FY98, to make the total 227. Additional sales have been made to Israel (25 F-15I) and Saudi Arabia (72 F-15S).

Above: One of the first recipients of the F-15C was the 32nd TFS. The side bulges of the FAST packs show on the Eagle breaking away. Missiles are AIM-7F Sparrows and -9L Sidewinder.

and stick) capability which dramatically improved dogfight performance. This has since been updated in the F-15C.

The original plan was to procure 769 F-15s, but this number has risen to 1,488, of which 1,000 had been delivered to the USAF and others by early 1986. Current production is centered on the F-15C and two-seat F-15D, which provide updates in mission capability.

A signal processor gives the ability to switch from one locked-on target to another, to switch between air and ground targets and keep searching whilst already locked-on to one or more targets. Increase in memory capacity from 24 to 96K gives a new high-resolution radar mode which can pick one target from a large group at extreme range. Internal fuel is increased by 2,000lb (907kg) and conformal pallets, called FAST (fuel and sensor, tactical) packs fit snugly on each side of the fuselage to increase total fuel by 9,750lb (4,422kg).In 1983 an improved so-called tangential carriage arrangement was introduced which enables 12 bombs of 1,000lb (454kg), or four of twice this size, to be hung on short stub pylons along the lower edges of the FAST packs, giving

Left: An Army C-12A accompanied by a special missions (VIP passenger) VC-12A of the USAF.

UC-12B; utility cargo/passenger model with large (high flotation) tyres, 49 for US Navy, 17 for Marines.

C-12C Huron; uprated C-12A, 14 for Army.

C-12D; uprated utility model with large cargo door and tip tanks (span 55ft 6in, 16.92m), initial order for 33 for US Army and Foreign Military Sales.

UC-12D; as C-12D, six for AF and six for Air National Guard.

RC-12D; special mission US Army aircraft for Guardrail Elint/ECM and battlefield surveillance, with large dipole aerials above and below wings as in earlier RU-21J and ECM tip pods.

Of a total of 380 of all versions for US military customers, the Army had accounted for 208 by 1997. Their latest versions are the RC-12M/N/P/Q, all special sensor and communications platforms. Further purchases are expected.

of many twin-engine attack aircraft of World War II, but cruises in smooth near-silence at altitudes few aircraft of that era could even attain. Maximum accommodation is for a pilot and 14 passengers, one taking the co-pilot's place. the following are major variants.

C-12A; basic Army transport, named Huron, full airways avionics and de-icing, special survival gear carried, usually eight passengers; 60 delivered, plus 30 for USAF which includes VC-12A VIP versions for 89th MAG at Andrews AFB for the President and others, and for overseas embassies and HQs.

General Dynamics F-16 Fighting Falcon

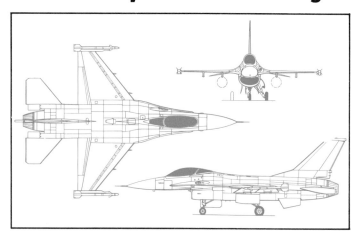

Origin: General Dynamics, today Lockheed Martin Tactical Aircraft Systems, Fort Worth, Texas.

Type: (A, C, N) Multirole fighter, (B, D) operational fighter/trainer (G) reconnaissance.

Engine: (A, B, C, D) One 23,840lb (10,814kg) thrust Pratt & Whitney F100-200 afterburning turbofan, (F) 23,450lb (10,637kg) F100-220 (from 1986) 23,770lb (10,782kg) F100-220E or 28,984lb (13,147kg) General Electric F110-100; (Block 50/52) 29,100lb (13,200kg) F100-229 or 29,588lb (13,421kg) F110-129.

Dimensions: Span 31ft (9.45m) (32ft 10in/10.1m over missile fins); length (all) 49ft 3in (15.01m); height 16ft 8$\frac{1}{2}$in (5.09m); wing area 300sq ft (27.87m²).

Weights: Empty (A) 16,234lb (7,364kg), (D) 17,408lb (7,896kg); loaded (AAMS only) (A) 23,357lb (10,594kg), (B) 22,814lb (10,348kg); (max external load) (A, B) 35,400lb (C, D) 37,500lb (17,010kg); (Block 40/42) 42,300lb (19,187kg).

Performance: Max speed (all versions, AAMs only) 1,350mph (2,173km/h, Mach 2.05) at

Above: Big horizontal stabilizer of this F-16A-25 is also seen on today's C and GE-engined N.

40,000ft (12.192m); max at SL 915mph (1,472km/h, Mach 1.2); initial climb (AAMs only) 50,000ft (15,240m)/min; service ceiling, over 50,000ft (15,240m); tactical radius (A, six Mk 82, internal fuel, Hi-Lo-Hi) 340 miles (547km); ferry range 2,415 miles (3,890km).

Armament: One M61A-1 20mm gun with 500/515 rounds, centerline pylon for 250gal (1,136lit) drop tank of 2,200gal (1,136lit) drop tank of 2,200lb (998kg) bomb, inboard wing pylons for 4,500lb (2,041kg) each, middle wing pylons for 3,500lb (1,587kg) each, outer wing pylons for 700lb (318kg) each (being uprated under MSIP-1 to 3,500lb), wingtip pylons for 425lb (193kg), all ratings being at 9g. Normal max load 11,950lb (5,420kg) for 9g, 20,450lb (9,276kg) at reduced load factor.

History: First flight (YF) 20 January 1974; (production F-16A) 7 August 1978; service delivery (A) 17 August 1978.

Users: AF, ANG, Navy.

Above: The Wolf's head is the badge of the famed 8th TFW, from Kunsan AB, S. Korea.

Starting as a small technology demonstrator, the F-16 swiftly matured into a brilliantly capable multirole fighter which in the eyes of most observers is number one in the Western world. Basic features include a fixed wing tapered on the leading edge, with automatic variable camber from hinged leading and trailing edges, a slab horizontal tail, a single large engine of the type already used in the F-15, fed by a plain ventral inlet without any variable geometry, a modern cockpit with a reclining seat, sidestick force-transducer controller linked to FBW flight controls and an overall concept of relaxed static stability which even today represents an exceptional application of the CCV concept.

At the time of its design the F-16's ability to sustain 9g in prolonged turns was unique, and turns at 5.5g can be made with a theoretical external stores load of 20,450lb (9,276kg), roughly the same as the original clean gross

weight!

It was in January 1975 that the F-16 was selected as a major type for the USAF inventory, suddenly transforming it from a mere demo program (generally regarded as having no place in the inventory of a service which regarded the F-15 as sacrosanct) into a major aircraft program for worldwide deployment. The total includes two-seaters, with full avionics and weapons but 17 per cent less fuel.

In June 1975 the F-16 was selected for Belgium, Denmark, Netherlands and Norway, mainly to replace the F-104. These European countries insisted on substantial industrial offsets, and with remarkable speed a multinational manufacturing program was set up to build production aircraft. All major aircraft, engine, avionics and accessory firms in the four European countries participated in the project and there were assembly lines in Belgium

Below: The first F-16A deliveries went to the 388th TFW, one of whose Falcons is seen here with tanks, bombs, two species of Sidewinder and ALQ-119 jammer.

(SABCA/SONACA) and the Netherlands (Fokker) as well as at Fort Worth. Though this has put up the costs, and still not achieved the potential output of which Fort Worth alone would be capable if working at maximum rate, the multinational program has worked quite well and Fokker continued to supply major airframe portions until the company's collapse in 1996.

By far the largest user is the USAF. This chose the 388th TFW at Hill AFB, Utah, as lead operator, and Hil has also served as a principal logistics center and training base for the international F-16 program. Other F-16 units in the USAF include the 56th and 58th TTWs, the 8th, 363rd and 474th TFWs, the Thunderbirds display team, the 169th TFG of the ANG and the 466th TFS of the AFRes. USAFE deploys the 50th TFW at Hahan, West Germany, and the 401st TFW at Torrejon, Spain.

In 1980 the USAF launched the MSIP (multistaged improvement program), to extend multirole all-weather capability of the basic aircraft. Since late 1981 all aircraft have wiring and avionic system architecture for later updating with LANTIRN night attack pods, one on each side of the inlet duct, the ASPJ (airborne self-protection jammer) EW system and the AIM-120A AMRAAM AAM. The latter rectifies the lack of a radar-guided AAM which cost the F-16 several export sales to the F-18 Hornet.

General Dynamics built an F-16/J79 demonstrator which the Department of Defense is offering to nations supposedly not quali-

Below: Distinguished by its canard underfins, the AFT-TI F-16 points the way for future fighters, with dramatic new air-combat capabilities.

fied for the regular aircraft. GD also flew an F-16 with the F101DFE engine, as a result of which the outstanding F110 engine is now in production to power future F-16s. The F-16XL, two prototypes of which (one with F110 engine) flew in 1982. These aircraft have a giant cranked-arrow wing, of 663sq ft (61.69m^2) area, with no horizontal tail, and the fuselage is lengthened to 54ft 1.86in (16.51m). The XL was a contender in the USAF Enhanced Tactical Fighter competition, and showed its ability to carry 29 weapons on 17 stations and not only beat the regular F-16 in field length but also carry double the weapon load 45 per cent further.

GD also built a research F-16/AFTI (Advanced Fighter Technology Integration) with full CCV capability and large canted controls. Together with modified flight controls these enable the AF-TI to maneuver instantly in any direction, without rotation of the fuselage axis. Features include the wide-field Marconi HUD, pedals for pointing the aircraft in any direction and a throttle to control direct lift, pitch and also vertical translation.

Instead of these visibly different versions, Lockheed Martin has concentrated on more detailed updates centred on avionics and weapons.

F-16A and two seat F-16B were

Above: Though it lost to the F-15E in the EFT contest the XL could well lead to a new family of F-16 aircraft from 1991, with enormously enhanced multirole capabilities.

the original production versions, 1,676 delivered for USAF and 12 export customers, plus 68 embargoed for Pakistan. The F-16C and the two-seat F-16D, the major current versions, were produced in many sub-variants to a total (late 1996) of 2,299 for USAF and seven export customers.

There are 14 research, test or proposed versions, some the result of demands from export customers.

McDonnell Douglas F/A-18 Hornet

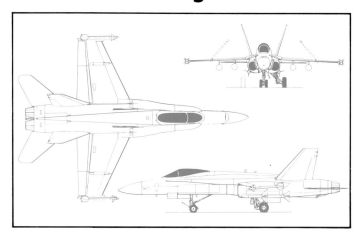

Origin: McDonnell Aircraft Company, St Louis, Missouri, (now a division of Boeing), with Northrop associate contractor.
Type: Carrier-based and land-based dual-role fighter and attack, with reconnaissance capability (RF-18).
Engines: Two General Electric afterburning turbofans, (to January 1992) 16,000lb (7,258kg) F404-400, (later) 17,700lb (8,029kg) F404-402.
Dimensions: Span (with missiles) 40ft 4¾in (12.31m), (without missiles) 37ft 6in (11.42m); length 56ft (17.07m); height 15ft 3½in (4.66m); wing area 400sq ft (36.15m²).
Weights: Empty 23,050lb (10,455kg); loaded (fighter) 36,710lb (16,651kg), (attack) 49,224lb (22,328kg); max loaded (catapult limit) 50,064lb (22,710kg), (airfield) 56,000lb (25,401kg).
Performance: Max speed (clean, at altitude) 1,190mph (1,915km/h, Mach 1.8), (max weight, sea level) subsonic; sustained combat maneuver ceiling, over 49,000ft (14,935m); combat radius (air-to-air mission, high, no external fuel) 461 miles (741km); ferry range, more than 2,300 miles (3,700km).
Armament: One 20mm M61 gun with 570 rounds in upper part of forward fuselage; nine external weapon stations for max load (catapult launch) of 13,400lb (6,080kg), (airfield) 15,500lb (7,031kg), including bombs, sensor pods, missiles (including Sparrow) and other stores, with tip-mounted Sidewinders.
History: First flight (YF-17) 9 June 1974; (first of 11 test F-18) 18 November 1978 (production, F/A-18) 1980; service entry 1982.
Users: Navy, Marine Corps.

It is remarkable that this twin-engined machine designed for carrier operations should have won three major export sales almost entirely because of its ability to kill hostile aircraft at stand-off distance using radar-guided AAMs (which with a few trivial changes could be done by its losing rival, the F-16). From the outset in 1974 the Hornet was designed to be equally good at both fighter and attack roles,

Above: All F/A-18s look alike, but the RF-18 has a different nose with camera pallet. Broken lines show tanks and folded wings.

replacing the F-4 in the first and the A-7 in the second. It was also hoped that the Hornet – strictly the F-18 but usually designated F/A-18 by the Navy to emphasize its dual role – would prove a "cheaper alternative" to the F14, but predictably the long and not wholly successful development process has resulted in an aircraft priced at well over $20 million; indeed the initial Spanish contract for 72 aircraft plus spares and training is priced at $3,000 million, or $41.7 million each.

Where the Hornet is unquestionably superior is in the engineering of the aircraft itself, which is probably the best achieved in any production combat type, and in particular in the detail design for easy routine maintenance and sustained reliability. Though not a large aircraft, with dimensions between those of the compact European Tornado and the F-4, and significantly smaller than the F-15, the F-18 combines the Tornado's advantage of small afterburning engines and large internal fuel capacity with avionics and weapons configured from the start for both F and A missions. Of course, in the low-level attack role it cannot equal Tornado because it has a large wide-span fixed wing, giving severe gust response, and suffers from relatively low maximum speed and lack of terrain-following radar; but in the typical Navy/Marines scenario with a mission mainly over the sea and a dive on target these shortcomings are less important.

Originally it had been planned to buy an F-18 for the Navy and an A-18 for the Marines, still a single seater but with small changes. It proved possible to build a common airplane for both services.

In weapon carriage the Hornet is first class with plenty of pylons and payload capability, and clearance for a wide spectrum of stores. In the fighter mission it is excellent, now that the wing has been redesigned to meet the specified rates of roll, and unlike its most immediate rival, the F-16,

Above: Dive bombing over the Fallon range is routine for Hornets from Lemoore's VFA-113, "The Stingers".

it has from the start carried a high-power liquid-cooled radar, the Hughes APG-65, matched with radar-guided AAMs.

It would be easy to criticize the armament as the only old part of a new aircraft, but in fact the M61 gun is still hard to beat, and the AIM-7 Sparrow and -9 Sidewinder AAMs have been so updated over the years that both remain competitive. The main shortcoming of the Sparrow in requiring continuous illumination of the target – which means the fighter must keep flying towards the enemy long after it has fired its missile – is a drawback to all Western fighters, and will remain so until AIM-120 (AMRAAM) came into service in 1987. In most air-combat situations the Hornet can hold its own, and compared with previous offensive (attack) aircraft is in a different class; it is in the long-range interdiction role that Hornet has shortcomings.

These center chiefly on radius with a given weapon load, though it has been pointed out this can be rectified to some extent by using

larger external tanks and by air refueling, the airplane being equipped with a British-style retractable probe permanently installed in the upper right side of the nose. Forward vision is good, though unlike the F-16 there is a transverse frame. The cockpit will always be a major "plus" for this aircraft, with Hotas controls, up-front CNI controls and three excellent MFDs (multi-function displays) which replace virtually all the traditional instruments. This cockpit goes further than anything previously achieved in enabling one man to handle the whole of a defensive or an offensive mission. But this is not to deny that a second crewmember would not ease the workload, especially in hostile airspace, and there have been studies of a two-seat version since the start of the program, though escalating costs have made its go ahead unlikely.

There is a two-seat dual-plot version for conversion training; this retains weapons capability and the APG-65 radar, but has about 6 per cent less internal fuel. The first two-

Below: The colossal effect of the hinged leading and trailing edges is evident from this landing shot, with hook extended.

seat version was the F/A- 18B.

The first Navy/Marines training squadron, VFA-125, commissioned at NAS Lemoore in November 1980. Three Marine Corps squadrons, VMFA-314, -323 and -531, were equipped by mid-1984, with three others following, while Navy squadrons are now also converting at lower priority. Until 1984 the Hornet was cleared operationally only for the fighter mission, because the Marines needed to replace the F-4 in this role more urgently. The attack mission depends to some degree on adding the laser spot tracker and FLIR on the Sparrow AAM fuselage pylons.

In 1984 cracking of the fin attachments and fin tips resulted in an AoA (angle of attack) limitation while the structure was modified. By this time development was in hand for the first major upgrade, and this went into production in 1986-87 as the F/A-18C and two-seat F/A-18D. This has upgraded avionics linked to a digital bus, and to new weapons which can include up to six AMRAAM missiles or four Imaging-IR Maverick attack missiles. Reconnaissance equipment can also be carried, and from May 1994 the radar was replaced by the more capable APG-73. From 1990 all deliveries have Night Attack capability, with various IR sensors, a laser designator/ranger, new cockpit displays, a new raster HUD and night-vision goggles.By 1997 1,460 Hornets had been ordered. This total does not include the F/A-18E/F Super Hornet described later.

Right: On takeoff and climbout the rudders are toed inward to pull the nose up. This is a training mission by VFA-125 "Rough Raiders" from Lemoore.

Below: Firing a Sidewinder from the right wingtip of a Hornet from Marine squadron VMFA-314 "Black Knights" from El Toro.

Sikorsky S-70 (H-60 Hawk family)

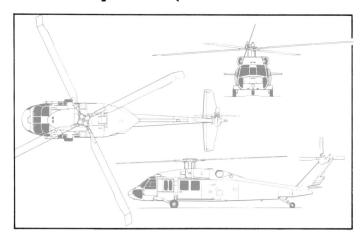

Origin: Sikorsky Aircraft, Division of United Technologies Corporation, Stratford, Connecticut.
Type: (UH) combat assault transport, (EH) electronic warfare and target acquisition, (HH) combat rescue, (SH) ASW and anti-ship helicopter.
Engines: (UH, EH) two 1,560shp General Electric T700-700 turboshafts, (SH, HH) two 1,690shp T700-401.
Dimensions: Diameter of four-blade rotor 53ft 8in (16.36m); length overall (rotors turning) 64ft 10in (19.76m); length (rotors/tail folded) (UH) 41ft 4in (12.6m), (SH) 41ft $\frac{1}{2}$in (12.5m); height overall (UH) 16ft 10in (5.13m), (SH) 17ft 2in (5.23m); main-rotor disc area 2.261sq ft (210.05m²).
Weights: Empty (UH) 10,624lb (4,819kg), (SH) 13,648lb (6,191kg); max loaded (UH) 20,205lb (9,185kg) (normal mission weight 16,250lb, 7,375kg), (HH) 22,000lb (9,979kg), (SH)

Above: Black Hawk has had many mods but is still called UH-60A. Here, ESSS, ECM and exhaust suppression are not installed.

21,884lb (9,925kg).
Performance: Max speed (UH) 184mph (296km/h); cruising speed (UH) 167mph (269km/h), (SH) 155mph (249km/h); range at max weight, 30 min reserves, (UH) 373 miles (600km), (SH) about 500 miles (805km).
Armament: (UH) See below, (EH) electronic only, (SH) two Mk 46 torpedoes and alternative dropped stores, plus offensive avionics.
History: First flight (YUH) 17 October 1974, (production UH) October 1978, (SH) 12 December 1979; service delivery (UH) June 1979.
Users: Army, AF, Navy, Marines.

This helicopter family owes little to any previous Sikorsky type, and when the first version (the UH-60A

Above: Future combat rescue helicopter of the Air Force, the HH-60D is packed with fuel and special mission avionics.

Black Hawk) was designed in the late 1970s it was packed with new technology. The original requirement came from the US Army, which needed a UTTAS (utility tactical-transport aircraft system) for general battlefield supply duties.

The basic role called for a crew of three and a cabin for 11 troops with full equipment, but the UH-60A can readily be fitted with 14 troop seats, or alternatively with six litters. The cargo hook can take a load of 8,000lb (3,629kg), and a typical frontline load can be a 105mm gun, 50 rounds of packaged ammunition and the gun crew of five. The UH-60A can also be used for command and control or for reconnaissance missions. The design was made especially compact so that it would fit into a C-130; a C-5 can carry six.

Right: The ordinary UH-60A has payload capability much greater than its restricted cabin suggests; this shows it off well.

The UHG-60A proved to be a successful machine, with agility and good all-weather avionics. As with all later versions most of its critical parts are designed to withstand 23mm gunfire, and in a gruelling kind of combat life it has proved one of the most "survivable" of all helicopters.

Originally there was no call for armament, apart from provision for the troops to fire a 7.62mm M60 LMG from a pintle mount on each side of the cabin (and standard kit includes chaff/flare dispensers for self defense). In the 1980s, however the Army began re-equipping its Black Hawk fleet with the ESSS (external stores support system) which adds large "wings" with four pylons on which can be hung anything from motorcycles to 16 Hellfire precision missiles. Gun pods are another alternative, as is the M56 mine-dispensing system. For self-ferry duties four external tanks can be attached, giving a range of 1,323 miles (1,230km).

As expected the UH-60A is a big program, with deliveries about 770 at the time of writing, with a predicted eventual total for the Army of 1,715. Another 11 have gone to the USAF, nine being used for recovery and rescue missions at Elgin AFB. The EH-60A BlackHawk is a specialized ECM version packed with 1,800lb (816kg) of equipment designed to detect, monitor and jam enemy battlefield communications. This installation is called Quick Fix II, the main item being the ALQ-151 ECM kit.

The Army plans to buy 132 of this version as its SEMA (special electronics mission aircraft). It also hopes to fund 78 of another version, the EH-60B, fitted with the SOTAS (stand-off target acquisition system), main element of which is a large target-indicating radar whose signals are relayed to a ground station. This program has run into cost and schedule prob-

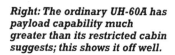

Left: Recovery of a navy SH-60B Seahawk aboard frigate Crommelin (FF-37). The SH-60F will look rather similar.

lems, and was halted in late 1981.

The main USAF model is the HH-60A Night Hawk, which uses almost the same airframe but has uprated engines and transmission more akin to that of the SH-60B Sea Hawk. The Night Hawk is planned as the next-generation all-weather combat rescue and special missions vehicle. Features include external tanks and additional internal fuel to achieve a full-load combat radius of 288 miles (463km), flight-refueling probe, various new weapons provisions in the fuselage, added protection systems, and a mass of avionics including all-weather terrain following with a FLIR and the LANTIRN, as well as special communications and a pilot's helmet display like that of the AH-64A Apache. The USAF hopes to afford 90, the first of which is flying in Europe 1 camouflage, as well as 66 HH-60Es which will save money by having no FLIR, radar-map display or helmet display.

The Marines HMS-1 Executive Flight Detachment flies nine VH-60A (VIP) transports.

Yet another quite different version is the US Navy's SH-60B Seahawk. This, the Sikorsky S-70L, was built to meet the need for a LAMPS III (light airborne multi-purpose system), packaged into a shipboard helicopter. In fact the SH-60B is much larger and more costly than most shipboard machines, because of the strenuous demands for equipment and weapons to handle ASW and

ASST (anti-ship surveillance and targeting) in all weather.

Apart from all the obvious changes needed for operation from destroyers and frigates, the Seahawk has uprated engines and transmission and a totally new fuselage with APS-124 search radar under the cockpit and forward part of the cabin, side chin-mounted ESM pods, a MAD station on the right, a battery of 25 sonobuoy launchers on the left with four more reloads inside the fuselage (125 buoys in all), and an impressive array of sensors, navaids, communications, processing systems and self-defense measures. Normal ASW armament comprises two torpedoes. There is no FR probe, but the Seahawk can be coupled to a refueling hose from a ship and refuel at the hover or while maintaining station at sea.

The basic Black Hawk has given rise to the Enhanced Black Hawk, AH-60A and AH-60L Special Forces penetrators, the related MH-60A and MH-60L, EH-60A electronic detection and jamming platform, MH-60G Pave Hawk and YH-60Q for armed rescue medevac and UH-60V for command/patrol. The Seahawk has led to the SH-60F for close in ASW protection, HH-60H for strike/rescue special warfare and the HH-60J Jayhawk for medium-range recover. There are many variants for export. By 1997 deliveries, totalled 1,823 Black Hawks and 382 Seahawks.

Right: UH-60As exercise in Egypt.

Rockwell International B-1B

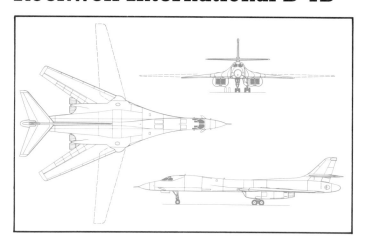

Origin: Rockwell International Corporation, (now Boeing North American), El Segundo, California.
Type: Strategic bomber and ALCM carrier.
Engines: Four General Electric F101-102 turbofans rated at 14,600lb (6,623kg) dry and 30,780lb (13,962kg) with maximum afterburning.
Dimensions: Span (fully spread) 136ft 8½in (41.67m), (fully swept) 78ft 2½in (23.84m); length 147ft (44.81m); height 34ft (10.36m); wing area 1,950sq ft (181.2m²).
Weights: Empty 182,360lb (82,718kg); maximum (low altitude) 422,000lb (191,419kg); maximum taxi weight 470,000lb (213,192kg).
Performance: Maximum speed, clean (low level) over 600mph (966km/h), (high altitude) 825mph (1,330km/h, Mach 1.25); combat ceiling (light) 50,000ft (15,240m), (maximum weight) about 15,000ft (4,572m); combat radius (typical mission) about 1,500 miles (2,414km).
Armament: It is possible to carry three launchers loaded with 24 SRAMs, one in each bay, or a single launcher with eight ALCMs. Other internal load options include 12 B28 or B43 thermonuclear bombs, 24 B61 or B83 bombs, or in a conventional role up to 84 Mk 82 (nominal 500lb/227kg) or 24 Mk 84 (nominal 2,000lb/907kg) GP bombs, all on rotary launchers.

Above: The production B-1B with wings at 15° sweep are shown in broken lines.

Along the underside of the fuselage are hardpoints for eight large stores ejector racks on which can hang an additional 14 ALCMs or SRAMs, eight B28s, 14 B43s/B61s/B83s or Mk 84s, or a further 44 Mk82s.
History: First flight (B-1A) 23 December 1974; final termination of B-1A flight program 30 April 1981; announcement of B-1B program September 1981; first flight (B-1B) 18 October 1984; service delivery July 1985.
User: AF

One views the B-1B with mixed feelings. With a baseline budget of $20,500 million in FY81 dollars, the B-1B is at last providing SAC (now merged into Combat Command) with advanced-technology muscle. It took the pressure off the old B-52s and allows belief in their penetrative capability to be abandoned and instead enables them to serve their twilight years as ALCM carriers and in the anti-ship role.

The B-1B restored the concept of the strategic Triad, composed of ICBMs, SLBMs and bombers. The other side of the coin is that the B-1 has been 23 years in coming, is the end-product of an outrageously long period of specification, argument, discussion, evaluation and

Above: The B-1Bs were originally camouflaged, as here, but today they are all-gray.

policy-change, and finally is entering service in a form that tries to square a basic design of the 1960s with the demands of the next century.

This is not to deny that the stealth qualities of the B-1B are about two orders of magnitude better than the B-52, and in fact remarkably good for so large an aircraft whose design originally paid little heed to this requirement. The B-1 was originally designed to fly at Mach 2 at high altitude (though the primary mission was low-altitude penetration), and some of the larger modifications introduced when the original four prototypes were flying were made possible when it was realized that Mach 2 was of no interest. Among the changes were replacement of a complex crew-escape capsule by four ordinary ejection seats, and simplification of the engine inlets, nacelles and overwing fairings.

A go-ahead had been expected in 1976, for SAC service in 1978. Instead argument raged about whether or not "bombers" were obsolete, and President Carter delayed a decision until, on 30 June 1977, he announced that there was a new weapon called a cruise missile. This had suddenly transformed the effectiveness of the B-52; the B-

1 was therefore no longer needed and would not be put into production. Carter did permit some B-1 test flying to continue. The AF and Rockwell, was well as their main associate contractors, used the the next few years to advantage in making the B-1 a better aircraft. Major changes included a tremendous increase in internal fuel capacity, with corresponding increase in strength of the landing gear; great increase in the number and variety of weapons that can be carried, with a movable fuselage bulkhead in the forward weapons bay and the addition of rows of external stores stations beneath the fuselage; optional weapons-bay tanks; and, most important of all, dramatic improvement in stealth characteristics by modifying both the airframe and the on-board defensive electronics systems.

In October 1981 a new spirit of national confidence enabled President Reagan to announce that 100 of the improved bombers, designated B-1B, would be bought for SAC service from 1986.

In fact the first SAC delivery, to Dyess AFB, took place in June 1985, and this base achieved IOC in June 1986, almost a year ahead of the original schedule. The Palmsdale assembly plant delivered all 100

Below: To add a splash of color, this B-1A prototype served in the B-1B test program at Edwards

aircraft by 1988, and these went to a test wing at Edwards and to Bomb Wings at Dyess, Ellsworth, Grand Forks, McConnell and Mountain Home AFBs. Several units were later inactivated, and by 1997 the total force comprised 82 bombers, plus 11 with the Air National Guards of Georgia and Kansas. Most bases have supporting KC-135s or KC-10s. Program cost (rather more than the baseline figure given previously) is currently on-budget at $28,400 million, or some $40,000 million including all supporting services.

During its low-level penetration the B-1B would have the wings partly or wholly swept, the maximum angle being reached at full speed in the most heavily defended area – this despite the great increase in IR Emission from the engines in afterburner. At a rough estimate, the B-1B RCS (radar cross section) is 1 per cent as large as that of a B-52H, compared with 50 to 10 per cent for the B-1A prototypes. A special subsystem called SMCS (structural mode control system), previously LARC (low-altitude ride control), senses vertical and lateral accelerations of the nose caused by turbulence, and automatically damps the motion out by commanding deflections of two small foreplanes (originally the third rudder section was used as well). This extends structural life and improves crew comfort; indeed some form of ride control is essential for all high-speed attack aircraft of the future.

To fly its mission successfully the B-1B uses both an OAS (offensive avionics system) and a defensive avionics system, each bigger and more advanced than anything previously attempted in the West. The prime contractor for the OAS is BMAC (Boeing Military Airplane Co.), and remarkably enough several of its elements are derived from those fitted to the F-16, one of these being the Singer Kearfott INS. There have to be plenty of unavoidable emissions, three emitters being the radar altimeter, doppler and TFR (terrain following radar), the latter being part of the main APQ-164 multimode nose radar which, again very unexpectedly, is derived from the F-16's APG-66 radar, a small air-cooled radar or low power but in the B-1 modified with a phased-array antenna. Much bigger and more costly, the defensive electronics are the responsibility of Eaton AIL Division and center on AIL's vast ALQ-161 system, developed for the original B-1 and now considerably upgraded and augmented.

Defensive electronics is the responsibility of one of the two backseat crew members, who also look after chaff, flares and other defensive systems. With all subsystems working at full power ALQ-161 power consumption is about 20kW.

When the B-1 was originally designed, the longest item of ordnance to be carried was the AGM-69 SRAM (short-range attack missile), with a length of 14ft (4.27m). The ALCM (air-launched cruise

missile) was at that time planned to be the same length, to fit the same rotary launcher, which accommodates eight missiles and could fit inside one weapon bay of the B-52. The B-1 was designed with three weapon bays each able to accommodate one of these rotary launchers as an alternative to other loads. What threw a major spanner into the works was the decision to stretch the ALCM to increase its range to 1,550 miles (2,500km), the resulting AGM-86B having a length of 20ft 9in (6.32m). This demanded a longer rotary dispenser which can-

not fit in the original triple B-1 weapon bays. The result is an untidy modification which links the front and center bays into a single volume with a length of 31ft 3in (9.53m) with a movable bulkhead between them. Should it be desired to carry ALCMs internally the bulkhead is moved to accommodate a single launcher with up to eight ALCMs.

In its early years these impressive aircraft were trashed by the media. The only factor justifying this treatment was the nightmare of trying to make the complex ALQ-161 work properly, and fail-

Above: For test purposes the first B-1B at one time had the tank boomer guidance pattern painted in high-contrast white. Other white lines picked out the vulnerable windshield glass and SMCS canard fins.

ure to achieve this was one reason why the "Bone" (never called the Lancer) did not participate in the Gulf War. Today a comprehensive and costly defensive upgrade is in progress, which includes towing a powerful radar decoy far astern, with a fiber-optic jamming link.

McDonnell Douglas AH-64A Apache

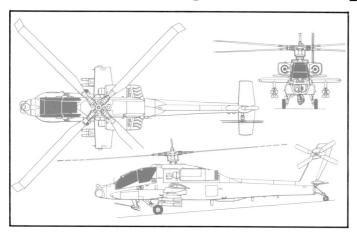

Above: By early 1986 Apaches had flown 5,000hr on development and 10,000 in combat, most under good visual conditions.

Origin: McDonnell Douglas Helicopter Company, Culver City, California.
Type: Anti-armor and attack helicopter.
Engines: Two General Electric T700 turboshafts, (to No 603) 1,696shp T700-701, (from No 604) 1,940shp T700-701C.
Dimensions: Diameter of four-blade main rotor 48ft (14.63m); length (rotors turning) 58ft 3⅛in (17.76m); length of fuselage 48ft 2in (14.68m); height overall 13ft 11¾in (4.26m); wing span 17ft 2in (5.23m); main-rotor disc area 1,809.5sq ft (168.11m²).
Weights: Empty 10,760lb (4,881kg); max 21,000lb (9.525kg), (-701C engines) 22,238lb (10,107kg).
Performance: Maximum speed 182mph (293km/h), (Longbow) 162mph (261km/h); hovering ceiling 11,500ft (3,505m); range

Above: Many years of refinement led to today's AH-64A, shown with Hellfire missiles but not the dorsal pulsed IR jammer.

(internal fuel) 300 miles (483km); ferry range 1,057 miles (1,701km); endurance in anti-tank mission 1h 50min.
Armament: One 30mm Hughes M230A1 Chain Gun with 1,200 rounds in remotely aimed ventral mounting; four wing pylons for 16 Hellfire missiles or four 19-tube FFAR launchers or any combination.
History: First flight 30 September 1975; service delivery March 1984.
User: Army.

A generation later than the cancelled Lockheed AH-56A Cheyenne (the world's first dedicated armed escort and attack helicopter), the AH-64 was selected as

the US Army's standard future attack helicopter in December 1976. This followed competitive evaluation with the rival Bell YAH-63, which had tricycle landing gear and the pilot seat in front of the pilot-gunner. The basic development contract also included the Chain Gun, a lightweight gun (in 30mm calibre in this application) with a rotating lockless bolt. In 1977 development began of the advanced avionics, electro-optics and weapon-control systems, progressively fitted to three more prototypes, followed by a further three – designated Total Systems Aircraft – flown by early 1980. The 56-month development ended in mid-1981. Hughes is responsible

for the rotors and dynamic components, while Teldyne Ryan produces the bulk of the rest of thee airframe (fuselage, wings, engine nacelles, avionic bays, canopy and tail unit). The entire structure is designed to withstand hits with any type of ammunition up to 23mm calibre. The main blades, for example, each have five stainless-steel spars, with structural glass-fiber tube linings, a laminated stainless-steel skin and composite rear section, all bonded together.

Probably the most expensive helicopter in the Western world, the AH-64 – designed and put into production by the former Hughes Helicopters – is the ultimate expression of the US army-s need for an all-can-do attack helicopter. Its two powerful engines enabled it to meet Army needs for sensors, weapons, aiming systems and survivability.

McDonnell Douglas/British Aerospace AV-8B Harrier II

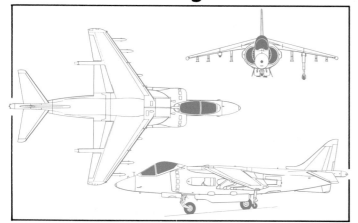

Origin: Joint prime contractors McDonnell Aircraft Company, St Louis, Missouri, and British Aerospace, UK.
Type: Multirole close-support attack fighter.
Engine: One Rolls-Royce vectored-thrust turbofan, (to December 1990) 21,450lb (9,730kg) F402-406A, (later) 23,800lb (10,796kg) F402-408.
Dimensions: Span 30ft 4in (9.25m); length 46ft 4in (14.12m); height 11ft 8in (3.56m); wing area 230sq ft (21.37m²).
Weights: Empty 13,086lb

Above: This AV-8B is shown with plain ventral strakes in place of the GAU-12/U gun.

(5,936kg); max (VTO) 19,185lb (8,702kg), (STO) 31,000lb (14,061kg).
Performance: Max speed (low level) 661mph (1,065km/h), (high) Mach 0.98, 647mph (1,041km/h); combat radius (STO, seven Mk 82 bombs plus tanks, lo profile, no loiter) 748 miles (1,204km); ferry range 2,441 miles (3,929km).
Armament: Seven external pylons, centerline rated at 1,000lb

Above: A Marines pre-production aircraft very similar to those now in squadron service.

(454kg) inboard wing 2,000lb (907kg), centre wing 1,000lb (454kg) and outboard 630lb (286kg), for total external load of 7,000lb (3,175kg) for VTO or 17,000lb (7,711kg) for STO, (GR.5) two additional AAM wing pylons; in addition ventral gun pods for one 25mm GAU-12/U gun and 300 rounds.
History: First flight (YAV-8B rebuild) 9 November 1978, (AV-8B)

Right: This original company prototype demonstrated real bomb-toting capability in 1981.

November 1981; entry into service 1983.
User: Marine Corps.

Though developed directly from the original British Aerospace Harrier, the Harrier II is a totally new aircraft showing improvement and refinement in almost every part. This is the case in radius of action with any given weapon load, but it also extends to the scope and variety of

The chief mission sensors are the TADS (target acquisition and designation sight) and PNVS (pilot's night vision sensor), which are in the nose, normally exposing the entire machine when in use. TADS enables any surface target to be tracked manually or automatically during attack by the gun, rockets or the laser-homing Hellfire.

Both crew have the Honeywell IHADSS (integrated helmet and display sight system) and each can in emergency fly the helicopter and control its weapons. The nose sight incorporates day/night FLIR (forward-looking infra-red), laser ranger/designator and laser tracker.

Avionics and other equipment are more comprehensive than in any other helicopter, in the Western world at least. Navigation systems include a strapdown inertial system, doppler and ADF, which with a digital autostabilization system enables the pilot – who sits above and behind the copilot/gunner – to fly NOE (nap-of-Earth) missions in visual conditions without bothering about location. Protection is enhanced by careful structural design, together with Black Hole IR suppression, an advanced radar warning receiver (RWR), and a laser detector, radar jammer, IR jammer and chaff/flare dispenser.

In the late 1980s various upgrade programmes were schemed, but in 1991 the decision was taken to remanufacture all existing Army Apaches (then about 540) to the standard of the AH-64D, with upgraded avionics. Of this total, 227 are being further upgraded as the Longbow Apache. This is

Above: Though big and costly the Apache is reckoned "the only battlefield helicopter that can fight in any weather".

recognizable by its Westinghouse Longbow radar antenna mounted above the main rotor.

By 1997 the plant at Mesa, Arizona, had halved its rate of output from five per month. Deliveries then totalled 827 to the Army and 104 for export, with another 109 export versions on order and a further 150+ exports expected.

possible loads, and to the comfort and pleasure of flying.

The original Harrier required a lot of attention, especially during accelerating or decelerating transitions, and suffered from poor all-round view and a traditional cockpit, whereas the Harrier II offers a completely new experience which makes full use of technology stemming from the F-15 and F-18. At the same time, apart from the wing, which is a wholly new long-span structure made from graphite composites, the new aircraft is a joint effort with inputs from both partners.

The wing is the most obvious visible difference, compared with earlier Harriers. Apart from giving greater lift, at the expense of extra drag, it houses much more fuel, so that total internal fuel capacity is 50 per cent greater. With eight sinewave spars and composite construction it is virtually unbreakable, with limitless fatigue life, and the curved Lerx (leading-edge root extensions) enhance combat maneuverability and bring turn radius closer to what the customers require. (The only real fault of the Harrier II, in British eyes, is

that it was planned as a "superior bomb truck" for the US Marine Corps, whereas the RAF was more interested in air-combat agility and speed for its GR.5 version).

Under the wing are six stores pylons, four of them plumbed for tanks which in the Marine Corps AV-8B are normally of 300gal (1,136lit) size. The extra pylons on the GR.5 are in line with the outrigger landing gears and will normally carry AIM-9L Sidewinders. The under-fuselage gun pods are configured to serve as LIDs (lift-improvement devices) which, joined across the front by a retractable dam, provide a cushion of high-pressure air under the aircraft which counters the suck-down effect of rising air columns around the fuselage. In the AV-8B a 25mm gun is housed in the left pod with its ammunition fed from the right pod.

In the matter of avionics and EW the Harrier II is updated, the basic kit including INS (Litton ASN-130A or, in the GR.5 a Ferranti set), digital air-data and weapons, computers, large field of view HUD, fiber-optic data highways and comprehensive RWR and ECM systems. The primary weapon-delivery system is the Hughes ARBS (angle/rate bombing system), with dual-wave-length TV/laser target acquisition, and tracking.

The RWR system's forward-looking receivers are in the wingtips, rather than in a fin-tip airing as in early Harriers. The ALQ-164 jammer pod can be attached on the centerline pylon. A bolt-on inflight-refueling probe pack can be added above the left inlet duct, the probe being extended hydraulically when required. The cockpit is redesigned, with a large-angle HUD, UFC as on the F/A-18, MFD and ACES II seat.

Total Harrier II production by 1997 amounted to 428, of which the Marine Corps had received 286 including 24 TAV-8B dual-control trainers. The last 27 are Harrier II Plus, with the nose enlarged to house APG-65 radar, as in the F/A-18A/B, with a FLIR sensor above. This increases empty weight to 14,860lb (6,740kg), but the Dash-408 engine maintains flight performance essentially unchanged. Squadrons VMA-542, -223 and -231 initially each deployed six Plus aircraft alongside 12 regular AV-8Bs, but the Marines are upgrading 73 existing AV-8Bs so that these three squadrons can become fully Plus-equipped. Armament now includes AMRAAM, Maverick and Harpoon cruise missiles.

Lockheed Martin F-117A Nighthawk

Origin: Lockheed (later Lockheed Martin) Skunk Works, Palmdale, California.
Type: Low-observable ('stealth') precision attack bomber.
Engines: Two General Electric F404-F1D2 turbofans each rated in the 10,800lb (4,899kg) thrust class.
Dimensions: Span 43ft 4in (13.21m); length 65ft 11in (20.09m); height 12ft 5in (3.79m); wing area 1,140sq ft (105.9m^2).
Weights: Empty approximately 30,000lb (13,608kg); internal fuel, about 17,000lb (7,711kg); maximum takeoff weight 52,500lb (23,814kg).
Performance: Maximum speed 646mph (1,040km/h); normal cruise Mach number 0.9; unrefueled mission radius with 5,000lb (2,268kg) bomb load 691 miles (1,112km); landing speed (not confirmed by USAF) 172mph (277km/h).

Armament: Two internal bays each with a single door. The standard weapon is the GBU-27A Paveway III LGB (laser-guided bomb), but all other free-fall or guided ordnance in the 2,000lb (907kg) class can be carried, up to a total weight of 5,000lb (2,268kg). Precision-guided weapons are extended prior to release 30in (0.76m) downwards on a trapeze.
History: First flight (XST Have Blue) 1 December 1977, (Senior Trend) 18 June 1981; release of photograph 10 November 1988; public unveiling 21 April 1990; delivery of last F-117A 12 July 1990.
User: USAF.

So weird that it looks like a strange creation from another planet, the F-117A is the first aircraft in the world to enter service whose entire design has been

driven by the objective of making it almost invisible to hostile radars. Lockheed's Skunk Works had pioneered this 'stealth' technology with the SR-71, and began taking it much further in 1974. A year later design began on the proof-of-concept XST-1, using the new technique of faceting, in which the entire external surface is made up of carefully angled flat panels to reflect radar energy away in harmless directions.

Via five full-size Senior Trend development aircraft (79-10780/10784) the 59 production attack aircraft (from 80-10785) emerged from Burbank from April 1982. Coated in RAM (radar-absorbent material) and painted black, they went to the 4450th Test Sqn at Groom Lake, later moving to equally remote Tonopah Test Range in New Mexico. No designation was allocated, and pilots merely wrote the cryptic number

Above: Developed by Lockheed Skunk Works, the F-117A is the first operational aircraft to exploit 'stealth' technology.

'117' on their forms and logbooks. Later the letter F was added, though the Nighthawk has no air-to-air capability.

The 4450th TS became the 4450th Tactical Group and then the 37th Tactical Fighter Wing, made up of the 415th, 416th and 417th TFS. Having avoided action in Libya and the Bekaa Valley, the USAF's amazing "stealth fighter" was sent into action in the most stupid way possible in the US invasion of Panama in December 1989. Six aircraft flew missions that a Congressman said "could have been performed by an Aero Commander"' four turned back and the other two missed their target by wide margins. But on 17 January 1991 the 37th began

Boeing E-6A Mercury

Left: Designed to replace the TACAMO EC-130Q, the E-6A was a larger aircraft with greater range.

cruising speed at 40,000ft (12,192m) 523mph (842km/h); service ceiling 42,000ft (12,802m); patrol altitude 25,000-30,000ft (7,620-9,144m); unrefueled mission range 7,307 miles (11,759km); endurance on station 1,150 miles (1,851km) from base (unrefueled) 10h 30min, (one refuel) 28h 54min, (multiple refuelings) 72h; field length 6,700ft (2,042m).
Armament: None.
History: First flight 1 June 1987; first delivery 2 August 1989; final delivery 28 May 1992.
User: US Navy.

Origin: Boeing Defense & Space Group, Seattle, Washington.
Type: Communications relay platform.
Engines: Four CFM International F108-CF-100

turbofans each rated at 24,000lb (10,886kg) thrust.
Dimensions: Span (over ESM pods) 148ft 2in (45.16m); length 152ft 11in (46.61m); height 42ft 5in (12.93m); wing area 3,050sq ft (283.4m^2).

Weights: Empty, equipped, 172,795lb (78,380kg); internal fuel, 155,000lb (70,308kg); maximum takeoff 342,000lb (155,131kg).
Performance: Maximum (dash) speed 610mph (981km/h);

For over 30 years the vital task of communicating with Navy warships, and especially the SSBN fleet of missile-armed submarines submerged on station around the world, was performed by the TACAMO EC-130Q. By 1980 these aircraft were not only

making a contribution to the Gulf War which was out of all proportion to the number of aircraft deployed (45). In 1,271 sorties they dropped over 2,000 tons of bombs, mainly the GBU-27A, "demonstrating accuracy unmatched in the history of air warfare". Despite the 60 SAM sites and 3,000 guns surrounding Baghdad alone, not one F-117A was so much as hit by a bullet.

The F-117A is almost a flying wing with a fat midships sections like the B-2A though it does have short fins carrying large rudder-vators inclined outwards at 42.5°. These surfaces are sharply swept, like the wings, which have a leading-edge angle of 67.5°. The trailing edges carry four large elevons for pitch and roll, while the tails operate in opposition for pitch and in unison for yaw. The trajectory is sensed by four air-data probes projecting from the nose (despite their small size, even these are faceted) which control the FBW (fly-by-wire) system.

A key feature of faceting is that it even extends to the wings, which have two flat faces underneath and three on top. This obviously is aerodynamically less efficient than conventional aerofoils, though as on Concorde vortices are used to help generate lift. Thus, field length is long and take-off speed high, though there is no truth in the media suggestion – expressed in the name "Wobblin Goblin", which is unknown to the F-117 community – that the aircraft is difficult to fly or lacks agility.

A particularly challenging task was designing the propulsion system. The answer was to put unaugmented versions of a highly

mature turbofan above the wing roots and fit over the inlet a flat grid with a mesh size much smaller than the wavelength of radars. At low speeds additional air is sucked in through doors in the top of the inlet ducts. The jets which are cooled by secondary airflows, emerge through flat two-dimensional 'platypus nozzles' occupying the broad forward-swept inboard trailing edges, each jet being some 4in (100mm) deep and over 5ft (1.5m) wide. Fuel is housed in tanks wherever there is room in the fuselage and wings. Above the fuselage is an air-refueling receptacle which emerges by rotating 180°. At the pointed pinnacle of the fuselage

Above: Designed to penetrate dense threat environments, the F117-A is seen here refueling over the Nevada desert.

(actually on the big upward-hinged canopy) is an air-refueling light.

At various points in the airframe are blade antennas for communications and navigation, all of which are retracted on an operational mission. Weapons are aimed by the IRADS (infra-red acquisition and designation system). This comprises a FLIR (forward-looking infra red) in front of the windscreen and a downward-looking DLIR on the starboard side of the nosewheel bay. Both IR

receivers are mounted in swivelling turrets which also incorporates laser designators to guide smart bombs. The turret doors, like those over the landing gears and weapon bays, have precisely fitting zig-zag edges to minimize any radar signal sent back along its outward path.

In 1992 the operating unit moved to Holloman AFB, New Mexico, and renumbered as the 49th TFW, comprising the 7th, 8th and 9th TFS. Since then the existing aircraft have been put through a series of important upgrades, but proposed versions for the US Navy, RAF and a number of other possible customers have been overtaken by the Joint Strike Fighter.

becoming tired but there was a clear need for a larger aircraft with greater range, higher operating altitude and the ability to carry greater loads of avionics. The first contract for the TACAMO II was placed with Boeing in April 1983.

Altogether Boeing built 16 E-6A Mercury aircraft. They are not conversions but were in fact the last aircraft of basic 707 type to be constructed. A great deal, including the basic interior trim, lighting and nuclear hardening, is the same as the E-3 Sentry. Differences include the engines, absence of radome support structure and addition of ESM (electronic support measures) pods on the wingtips.

The interior furnishing and equipment is totally different. The primary payload is the AVLF (airborne very low frequency) communications system, with a trailing wire antenna 26,000ft (7,925m) long. This has a 90lb (41kg) weight on the end so that, while the E-6 orbits, the antenna stays almost entirely vertical. In

each operational area the aircraft uplinks with the Presidential E-4, with E-4B AABNCP aircraft, with satellites and also with the Emergency Rocket Communications System, and downlinks to the SSBNs on station and with

Above: Boeing E-6A Tacamo, taking off on its first flight in 1987. Altogether 16 of this type of aircraft were built.

VLF ground stations. The main VLF link uses 200kW of power,

and communicates with the submarines via towed buoyant wire antennas. Two operating crews are carried so that, with repeated refueling, a Mercury can remain on station for a period of anything up to 72h.

Northrop Grumman E-8 Joint-STARS

Origin: Northrop Grumman Corporation, Melbourne, Florida.
Type: Reconnaissance and battlefield-management platform.
Engines: Four 18,000lb (8,165kg) thrust Pratt & Whitney JT3D-3B turbofans.
Dimensions: Span 145ft 9in (44.42m); length 152ft 11in (46.61m); height 42ft 6in (12.95m); wing area 3,050sq ft (283.4m²).
Weights: Empty 171,000lb (77,566kg); internal fuel, 155,000lb (70,308kg); maximum takeoff weight 336,000lb (152,410kg).
Performance: Maximum

operating Mach number 0.84, equivalent at high altitude to 554mph (892km/h); patrol height 30,000-40,000ft (9,144-12,192km); service ceiling 42,000ft (12,802m); endurance (unrefueled) 11h (one refuel) 20h.
Armament: None.
History: Launch of concept 1980; FSD (full-scale development) contract to Grumman 27 September 1985; first flight 22 December 1988; final delivery, probably 1999.
User: USAF.

From the late 1970s various

schemes were studied by the Army and USAF for battlefield management, especially in Europe. Eventually this emerged as the Westinghouse Norden APY-3 multimode side-looking phased-array radar. This uses a 24ft (7.32m) antenna in a canoe fairing under the fuselage of the carrier aircraft. This is scanned electronically in azimuth (direction) and steered mechanically in elevation to produce a sharp picture on either side of the aircraft track. In the synthetic-aperture mode this can detect tank-size objects 109 miles (175km) away, while an interleaved doppler

mode can instantly pick out moving objects.

The system became known as Joint [service] STARS, from Surveillance Target Attack Radar system. The choice of platform to carry it fell on the Boeing 707. It was planned to carry out trials with a converted airliner designated EC-18C and then build 22 new aircraft designated E-8B. Experience with the C-18 program revealed that it would be more cost/effective to build new aircraft than refurbish old ones, but budget pressures caused this to be overridden.

The complex test programme

Bell/Boeing V-22 Osprey

Left: The Bell/Boeing V-22 Osprey combines airplane speed with helicopter hovering capability.

Origin: Bell Helicopter Textron teamed with Boeing Helicopters, Joint Program Office at Arlington, Virginia.
Type: Tilt-rotor VTOL multimission aircraft.
Engines: Two 6,150shp Allison T406-AD-400 turboshafts.
Dimensions: Span, including nacelles, 50ft 11in (15.52m); span over turning rotors 83ft 10in (25.55m); diameter of proprotors 38ft 0in (11.58m); length, excluding probe, 57ft 4in (17.47m); length with wing pivoted and blades folded 62ft 7½in (19.09m); height (over tail) 17ft 7¼in (5.38m); (over spinners in hovering mode) 21ft 9in (6.63m); wing area, including center section, 382sq ft; total proprotor disc area 2,268sq ft (210.7m²).
Weights: Typical empty weight 32,628lb (14,800kg); internal fuel 13,700lb (6,215kg); normal take-off weight (VTO) 47,500lb (21,546kg), (STO) 55,000lb (24,948kg); maximum STO weight 60,500lb (27,443kg).
Performance: Maximum cruising speed (in aeroplane mode, at optimum altitude) 397mph (638km/h); (at sea level) 316mph (509km/h); (in helicopter mode) 115mph (185km/h); maximum rate of climb at sea level (vertical) 1,090ft (332m)/min; (inclined) 2,320ft (707m)/min; service ceiling 26,000ft (7,925m); hovering ceiling (out of ground effect) 14,200ft (4,328m); range

(VTO with 12,000lb; 5,443kg payload) 1,382 miles (2,224km), (STO with 20,000lb; 9,072kg payload) 2,073 miles (3,336km); STO run at 55,000lb (24,948kg) less than 500ft (152m).
Armament:: None specified, but basic aircraft designed for nose-mounted cannon.
History: First flight (first prototype) 19 March 1989, (first EMD aircraft) December 1996; start of service evaluation (USMC) June 1999; IOC (initial operational capability) planned for 2001.
Users: US Marine Corps, US Navy and USAF; US Army retains a requirement.

For over 80 years designers have sought a way to combine the high speed and cruising efficiency of the aeroplane with the hovering capability of a helicopter. The first tail-rotor machine to accomplish this was the Bell XV-3 of 1955, which had a rotor pivoted to each tip of its fixed wing. This was followed in 1957 by the Boeing 76 (VZ-2) which had rotors mounted on a pivoting wing. After another 20 years Bell impressed observers with the tilt-rotor XV-15, which reached 346mph (557km/h) in level flight.

This alone interested the US military, who also noted that, for any given fuel burn, doubling the cruising speed automatically doubles the range an aircraft can fly. The result was that in December 1981 the Defense Secretary

announced development of a JVX (Joint-Services Vertical Experimental) aircraft. On 7 June 1982 Bell and Boeing announced a 50/50 teaming agreement to meet the need. The areas of responsibility split neatly into: Boeing, everything below the wing; Bell, the remainder.

The basic fuselage is that of an assault transport. Behind the two-pilot cockpit the cabin is 24ft 2in (7.37m) long, 5ft 11in (1.8m) wide and 6ft 0in (1.83m) high, and has a full-section rear ramp door and a large door at the front on the right, which can have a rescue hoist. It can accommodate 24 troops plus two gunners firing from side windows, or 12 litter casualties and medical attendants, or 20,000lb (9,072kg) of cargo. In the nose are a multifunction radar, a FLIR (Forward-Looking Infra-Red) and retractable inflight-refuelling probe. The twin-wheel landing gears are fully retractable, and at the back is the twin-fin tail with fully powered elevators and rudders.

On top is a turntable mounting, called a carousel, for the wing. A long-stroke actuator can pivot the wing 90° to stow the aircraft in a ship hangar, with proprotor blades folded along the slightly forward-swept leading edge. On each tip is the engine nacelle, with a chin air inlet and variable exhaust doors at the other end downstream of an infra-red emission suppresser. Each drives a proprotor with three almost rectangular blades made of epoxy composite, glassfiber and metal, and notable for the 45° twist along each blade. Each blade is mounted in elastomeric bearings and can not only change pitch in the usual way but also power-fold in the plane of rotation to lie along the leading edge of the wing.

In the VTO or hovering mode the nacelles are vertical and the rotors provide lift. A cross-shaft links the main gearboxes, partly to keep both motors equally powered should either engine fail and also

to enable the engines to be started by a 350hp APU (auxiliary power unit) in the central fairing. After a VTO the nacelles are pivoted slowly down to the cruise position by screwjack actuators. The total available angular movement is 97.5°. As the V-22 accelerates forwards the lift is taken over by the wings, the rotors becoming propellers. Inside the wing are eight of the 13 crash-resistant protected fuel tanks, and on the trailing edge are pairs of powered elevons.

The most urgent need for the Osprey is for the Marine Corps, which has a requirement for 425 (originally 552) MV-22A assault transports. In 1988-92 this unique aircraft was repeatedly threatened with cancellation, but even after they had been forced to downgrade the mission requirement the Marines were able to show that no helicopter could do the job. The basic mission is to carry 24 combat-equipped troops over a radius of 230 miles (370km) at 288mph (463km/h) with a hover at the midpoint at 3,000ft (914m) at 33°C (91.4°F).

The Air Force requirement is for 50 (originally 80) CV-22A special-mission aircraft, for delivery from 2003. These will have complex avionics and equipment, and must carry 12 troops or 2,880lb (1,306kg) of equipment over a radius of 599 miles (964km) with a hover at 4,000ft (1,219m) at 35°C (95°F). The Navy needs 48 (originally 50) HV-22A combat search and rescue aircraft, for delivery from 2010. These will also fly fleet logistics and special-warfare missions.

The Army withdrew its original requirement for 231 aircraft broadly similar to the MV-22A. Nevertheless, it remains in the program as an observer, and retains a future need for these aircraft for medevac, special operations and combat assault support. The target price for production aircraft, without special mission equipment, is $29.4 million. In the long term many export customers, and many derived successors including civil transports, are likely to emerge.

Left: The Joint-STARS provides precise tracking and targeting of ground targets and slow-moving airborne targets for battlefield management.

was carried out by ex-Qantas N770JS and ex-American Airlines N8411, which were initially converted by Boeing Military Airplanes at Wichita and then by Grumman Melbourne Systems Division. By 1990 both were designated as E-8As, engaged in trials in Europe. Since then 20 ex-airline 707s have been converted by Northrop Grumman at Lake Charles and Melbourne. The

planned IOC (initial operational capability) date was in 1997, but in a 'crash' program the two E-8A development aircraft, each with 10 operator consoles, operated in the Gulf War from January 1991.

Since then Northrop Grumman have been producing 20 E-8C aircraft, including the upgraded E-8A testbeds and one permanent E-8C testbed. They have 18 operator consoles and flight refueling receptacles. In 1995 the second E-8A and the E-8C testbed operated over Bosnia. The first fully operational E-8C (92-3289) was delivered on 22 March 1996.

Northrop Grumman B-2A Spirit

Origin: Northrop Grumman Corporation, El Segundo, California.
Type: Strategic penetration bomber.
Engines: Four General Electric F118-GE-100 turbofans each rated at 17,300lb (7,847kg) thrust.
Dimensions: Span 172ft 0in (52.43m); length 69ft 0in (21.03m); height 17ft 0in (5.18m); wing area, just over 5,000sq ft (464.5m^2).
Weights: Empty, about 111,000lb (49,896kg); internal fuel, about 200,000lb (90,720kg); maximum weapon load 40,000lb (18,144kg); normal loaded weight 336lb (152,635kg); maximum takeoff weight 376,000lb (170,550kg).
Performance: Maximum speed not disclosed but probably about 500mph (805km/h); service ceiling, about 50,000ft (15,240m); range with eight AGM-129 cruise missiles and eight B83 nuclear bombs (total 37,300lb, 16,919kg) at maximum takeoff weight, 7,250 miles (11,667km) hi-hi-hi or 5,063 miles (8,149km) with 1,151 miles (1,852km) near target flown at low level; ranges are very similar taking off at

358,000lb (162,386kg) with eight AGM-129s and eight B61 nuclear bombs (total 24,000lb, 10,886kg); range with one air refuelling 11,508 miles (18,520km); landing approach speed 161mph (259km/h).
Armament: Two internal weapon bays side-by-side each equipped with a Boeing rotary launcher assembly with eight store stations. Thus, 16 large weapons can be carried, selected from the AGM-129 advanced cruise missile, B61 or B83 nuclear bombs, Mk 84 conventional bomb, GAM (GPS-Aided Munition) or JDAM (Joint Direct Attack Munition). Other loads, carried on fixed bomb-rack assemblies, can include 36 CBU-87/-89/-97/-98 cluster bombs, 36 M117 fire bombs or 80 Mk 82 bombs or Mk 36 or Mk 62 sea mines.
History: First flight 17 July 1989; first delivery 17 December 1993; final delivery 1999.
User: USAF.

By sheer chance the B-2 looks superficially like the B-35 and B-49 flying-wing bombers and reconnaissance aircraft of 40 years earlier (which never entered service); it also has precisely the same wing span. In every other respect it is utterly different, and demonstrates advanced technology to a greater degree than any other aircraft.

Planning by the USAF for a totally new ATB (Advanced Technology Bomber) began in 1978. The objective was to back up the B-1B by an aircraft possessing such complete stealth (lo-observable) qualities that it could approach its targets at high level without being detected. The first development contract, priced at $7,300 million, was awarded to Northrop in October 1981. Boeing Military Airplanes was assigned the aft center section and outer wing, and Vought various parts including the intermediate fuse-

Left: A B-2 stealth bomber, flies an operational training mission from Whiteman AFB, Missouri.

lage (though there is no fuselage as such). The prime contractor handled assembly at Palmdale and the test programme there and at Edwards.

In 1983 the design was modified for low-level operation, and at that time the USAF planned to acquire 132 ATBs in a $36,600 million program. After the collapse of the Soviet Union this programme was dramatically cut back, partly because costs proved to be much higher than the estimates. By 1994, though the program had been reduced to 21 aircraft, a total of $39,639 million had already been spent, and by 1997 the total was likely to be less than $50 billion. Direct cost per aircraft in 1995 was $2,114 million, but in 1996 Northrop Grumman was offering to build a follow-on batch of 20 B-2As at $566 million each. This has been rejected by the Clinton administration, and an FY96 Congressional injection of an extra $493 million is being used to accelerate upgrading existing aircraft and also bring AV-1 (Air Vehicle 1) up to full production standard.

Stealth design has dominated every part of the B-2A. Though not explicitly denied, there has been no official confirmation of a persistent story that, in cruising flight, the engines are used to generate an overwhelmingly powerful electrostatic field which emits positive ion clouds from the leading edge and negative charges from the engine jets. This effectively both defeats gravity and provides propulsion, whilst making the aircraft effectively invisible to radars of any wavelength. Certainly the seven-segment leading edge has a sharp beaky profile utterly inexplicable by any normal laws of aerodynamics.

From the conventional viewpoint, the flying-wing design of the B-2 represents a stealth concept quite different from the faceted design of the F-117. The entire surface of the aircraft is devoid of discontinuities or projections, and is almost entirely made of RAM (Radar-Absorbent

Material) comprising carefully dimensioned composite honeycombs with special coatings. The straight leading edges have a sweepback of 33°, and every other leading edge – such as the engine inlets and the doors to the landing gears and weapons bays – have a zigzag profile set at precisely the same angle.

The pressurized crew compartment causes a bulge above the centerline, at the front of which are large curved glass windscreens. The crew number only two, seated side-by-side, with a jump seat behind. Aft of this entire amidships section is occupied by the weapons bays, then the engine bays and further out the 767-type main landing gears. Almost all the rest of the wing is occupied by special JP-8 fuel, which can be added in flight via a receptacle on the upper centreline. The four short engines are fed by S-ducts so that their first fan stages cannot be seen even by a radar directly ahead. At the back the jets are expelled over black channels in the upper surface, and there has been speculation on how the formation of contrails is avoided in cold atmospheres.

Flight control is effected by a unique movable surface on the centerline, elevons on the forward-swept trailing edges outboard of the engines, and split "drag rudders" (reminiscent of those of the earlier Northrop flying wings) on the backward-swept outer portions. Each surface is divided into two equal parts able to serve different functions, all controlled by a unique system of avionics.

AV (Air Vehicle) Nos 1 through 6 are test aircraft, which will eventually be brought up to operational standard and delivered. Together with AV-7/AV-16 they form Block 10. AV-17 to -19 are Block 20, the first to be completed to initial operational standard. AV-20 and 21 are Block 30, to which all others will eventually be modified. AV-7 to -16 are named *Spirit of* followed by the name of a state, and serve with the 393rd BS, 509th BW, at Whiteman AFB, Missouri.

Lockheed Martin F-22

Origin: Lockheed Martin Aeronautical Systems, Marietta, Georgia.

Type: Advanced tactical fighter.

Engines: Two Pratt & Whitney F119-PW-100 turbofans each with a maximum augmented rating in the 35,000lb (15,876kg) class.

Dimensions: Span 44ft 6in (13.56m); length 62ft 1in (18.92m); height 16ft 7in (5.05m); wing area 840sq ft (78.0m²).

Weights: Target empty weight 31,670lb (14,365kg); maximum loaded 60,000lb (27,216kg).

Performance: Design target level speeds, 800kt (921mph, 1,482kh/h, M1.2) at sea level, 1,040mph (1,678km/h, M1.58) in supercruise [see below]; M2.2 (about 1,450mph, 2,333km/h) maximum at high altitude; design service ceiling 65,000ft (19,812m); design high-altitude unrefuelled combat radius 750nm (863 miles, 1,389km); design field length 3,500ft (1,067m).

Armament: Main internal bay for four AIM-120A or six AIM-120C AMRAAMs and/or attack weapons (eg, GBU-32 Joint Direct Attack Munitions); two side bays each for a single AIM-9X Sidewinder; four underwing stores stations each rated at 5,000lb (2,268kg); one long-barrel M61A2 20mm gun with 480 rounds.

History: First flight (YF-22) 29 September 1990, (first EMD) due May 1997; (first production delivery) scheduled for August 2000; (decision on full production) due March 2002, for final USAF delivery 2012.

Users: USAF, but exports are expected to friendly nations.

In contrast to fighter programmes of the past, where a new type might enter service two years after the start of design, soon to be replaced in its turn by something else, today a fighter may take 20 years to develop and then serve for up to 50. It was in June 1981 that the USAF issued an RFI (Request for Information) on an Advanced Tactical Fighter to replace the F-15. Concept-definition contracts were awarded in September 1983, and in October 1986 Lockheed (as it then was) and Northrop were awarded Dem/Val (demonstration and validation) contracts under which each built two flight articles, one powered by YF119 engines and the other with the GE YF120. Teamed with Boeing and General Dynamics, Lockheed's YF-22 was announced as the winner over the rival YF-23 on 23 April 1991.

Since then the design has been considerably modified, and from May 1997 nine EMD (Engineering and Manufacturing Development) prototypes, followed by four PPV (Pre-Production Verification) aircraft, will clear the F-22A for production (a two-seat F-22B was abandoned). Though the California "Skunk Works" built the prototypes, the huge Marietta plant will handle assembly and production test, as well as making the forward fuselage and tail. Fort Worth (the F-16 plant previously owned by General Dynamics) makes the centre fuselage. Boeing Military Airplanes makes the wings and aft fuselage, including the powerplant installation, and handles the radar and other subsystems.

Aerodynamically the F-22A is a compromise between the demands of the multiple missions, outstanding combat agility and stealth. It is claimed to be the first production fighter to have super-cruise capability, sustained flight at supersonic speed with the engines in MIL (maximum dry) thrust, without augmentation. The fuselage is extremely broad and boat-like with a chine (sharp edge) along the steeply sloping sides. The large wings are equi-tapered and have leading-edge flaps, outboard ailerons and plain inboard flaperons. The enormous tail comprises sloping fins with rudders and sweptback tailerons. The rudders can flick open 30° outwards to act as the speed-brake, rendering the dorsal air-brake of the prototypes unnecessary.

Structurally the F-22 is designed for 9g, the same as the F-16 but lower than the +10 of the Su-35. About 41 per cent is titanium, 23 per cent composites and 15 per cent aluminum alloys. There are three landing wheels, with high-pressure tires demanding a very high standard of runway (the USAF still has no intention of operating in the absence of runways). The engines have fully variable inlets and two-dimensional nozzles of variable profile and area, which can be vectored 20° in any direction and also provide reverse thrust and variable control of the IR (infra-red) signature. Fuel is housed in two fuselage tanks and the sealed wings, the aerial-refueling socket being just ahead of the fins.

The USAF originally said it had a requirement for 750 ATFs, but this was progressively reduced to 401 F-22As and 50 two-seat F-22Bs. In July 1996 the two-seater was cancelled in order to save money, and by early 1997 it had not been announced how many additional single-seaters, if any, might be ordered instead. In 1991 it was expected that development would cost $13 billion and production (of 648 then planned) $52.5 billion. Unit flyaway price was then expected to be $61.2 million, but the actual figure in 2001 money is likely to nudge $100 million. Thus, export sales are likely to be on a small scale, and in any case few countries are likely to qualify as recipients of such a high-tech weapon.

During the past eight years Lockheed/Lockheed Martin has increasingly searched for a market for derived versions. One would be a two-seater dedicated to electronic warfare. Another would be a two-seat carrier-based version to replace the A-6. So far no niche has emerged, and effort has largely been transferred to the JSF.

*Below: **An artist's rendering of the F-22 in combat. This scene was created entirely on computer, as was the plane's design.***

McDonnell Douglas C-17A Globemaster III

Origin: McDonnell Douglas Aerospace (division of the Boeing Co), Long Beach, California.

Type: Intra-theatre heavy cargo airlifter.

Engines: Four Pratt & Whitney F117-PW-100 turbofans each rated at 40,000lb (18,462kg) thrust.

Dimensions: Span 169ft 10in (51.76m); length 174ft 0in (53.04m); height 55ft 1in (16.79m); wing area 3,800sq ft (353.03m²).

Weights: Empty, equipped 277,000lb (125,645kg); internal fuel 176,190lb (79,920kg); maximum payload (for load factor 2.25g) 170,400lb (77,292kg); maximum takeoff weight 585,000lb (265,352kg).

Performance: Cruising speed at 28,000ft (8,535m) M0.75, equivalent to 512mph (824km/h); maximum cruising speed at low altitude 403mph (648km/h); airdrop speed at low altitude 132-288mph (213-463km/h); service ceiling 45,000ft (13,716m); range without air refuelling 2,877 miles (4,630km) with payload of 160,000lb (72,575kg), 5,408 miles (8,704km) with zero payload; radius with payload of 81,100lb (36,786kg) with takeoff in 975m (3,200ft), landing in 823m (2,700ft), return takeoff in 853m (2,800ft) with same payload and landing back at base in 792m (2,600ft), 575 miles (925km).

Armament: None.

History: First flight 15 September 1991; first delivery 14 June 1993; IOC (Initial Operational Capability) with 17th Airlift Sqn 17 January 1995; final delivery 2003.

After a long period of study, Douglas Aircraft was selected by the USAF to build a C-X heavy cargo aircraft on 28 August 1981. The objective was to combine the fuselage cross-section, range and payload capability of a C-5 with outstanding agility and STOL capability not inferior to that of a C-130, so that, for example, a main battle tank could be delivered direct to a front-line airstrip. Demands included a tough airframe able to slam on to the ground with a vertical velocity of 900ft/min (4.6m/s) with maximum payload, reverse thrust for quick manoeuvres and backing-up on the ground, and modern commercial standards of reliability, easy maintainability and low costs.

The design was planned around the dimensions of box needed to meet the demands, and this turned out to be a length of 68ft 2in (20.78m) (85ft 2in, 25.96m, including the rear ramp door), width of 18ft 0in (5.49m) and unobstructed height of 12ft 4in (3.76m) under and ahead of the wing and 13ft 6in (4.11m) behind it. Apart from an M1 tank, possible loads can include six 5-ton vans, 18 463L cargo pallets, five M2 Infantry Fighting vehicles, two Apache and three Kiowa helicopters (all with rotor hubs in place), 102 passengers on palletized seats or 48 litter casualties, in each case with substantial numbers of supporting personnel. Heavy items can be air-dropped using the LAPES (Low-Altitude Parachute Extraction System), and on each side at the rear are doors specially designed for rapid exit by paratroops.

The wing has a modest 25° sweepback, deep superficial aerofoil profile, 9ft 6in (2.9m) winglets, full-span slats and exceedingly powerful Fowler flaps carrying fixed vanes. These flaps rotate back on fixed hinges until at full deflection they are in the jets from the engines (this EBF, externally-blown flap, idea was proved on the smaller YC-15). The C-17 is expected to spend half its flight time in turbulent air at low level. To provide stability and powerful control, the outboard ailerons and huge tail with two rudders and four elevators are all fully powered by a quad-redundant FBW (fly-by-wire system); all these structural components are supplied by Northrop Grumman, with computers by Lockheed Martin.

The four engines are hung close under the wing in composite nacelles which incorporate directed-flow reversers usable in flight as well as on the ground. A total of 22,572gal (27,086US gal, 102,610lit) of fuel is carried in four independent tanks in the wings, refueled by sockets in the rear of the landing-gear blisters or via an air-refueling receptacle behind the two-man flight deck. Each of the four main landing gears has three wheels in a row. On retraction the units rotate 90° about a vertical axis and then rise vertically, the innermost wheels moving to offset positions. The C-17 is

Above: The C-17 Globemaster III transport, landing at Charleston AFB.

designed to use unpaved strips and can steer sharp corners.

Apart from excessive fuel burn and temperature problems on the slats and flaps (cured by replacing composite structure by titanium) flight testing went well. However, trouble arose from the planned very low rate of production, with funding in small increments. The USAF cut its planned buy from 210 to 120, and then, because of cost overruns and slips in schedule, capped the buy at 40. Lockheed lobbied for a C-5D Galaxy, while Boeing fought for an NDAA (Non-Developmental Airlift Aircraft) based on the 747-400F. In 1992 the sick C-17 program was transferred to McDonnell Douglas Aerospace, which fought to bring the program back on track.

In the winter of 1995 the C-17 performed well in the Bosnian airlift, and the programme was completely revitalized by the award on 2 February 1996 of a single giant multi-year contract for 80 C-17As, completing the purchase of all 120 aircraft. These average out at approximately $250 million each. Now owned by Boeing, McDonnell Douglas forsees little prospect for export sales, except for the United Kingdom which urgently needs such an aircraft to carry the necessary equipment for its Joint Deployment Force. It is also hoped to market a commercial version, designated MD-17.

Boeing Sikorsky RAH-66 Comanche

Origin: USA, first flight of YRAH-66 prototype 4 January 1996.
Type: Reconnaissance and air-combat helicopter.
Engines: Two LHTEC T800-801 turboshafts, each with maximum TO rating of 1,550shp.
Dimensions: Diameter of five-blade main rotor 39ft 0½in (11.90m); length (rotor turning) 46ft 10½in(14.28m), (ignoring rotor and gun) 43ft 3¾in (13.20m); height over stabilizer (tailplane) 11ft 0¾in (3.27m).
Weights: (Estimated figures for production helicopter) empty 7,765lb (3,522kg); TO on primary mission 10,597lb (4,807kg); TO on maximum alternative mission 12,828lb (5,819kg); maximum self-deployment (four external tanks) 17,408lb (7,896kg).
Performance: (Estimated figures for production helicopter at 4,000ft (1,219m and 35°C, 95°F) maximum speed 201mph (324km/h); vertical rate of climb 1,418ft (432m)/min; 180° hover turn on to target 4.7 sec; snap turn to target at 80kt (92mph, 148km/h) 4.5 sec; endurance (standard fuel) 2.5h; ferry range (four tanks) 1,450 miles (2,334km); g limits +3.5/-1.

Background: In 1981 the US Army published a broad plan for a single basic design of helicopter, called LHX (Light Helicopter Experimental), to replace the UH-1, AH-1, OH-58 and OH-6, with a planned production run of 5,000. These were to be equipped for a wide variety of roles. They were planned to incorporate all the latest technology, and in particular have high flight performance and outstanding agility in order to survive in aggressive roles in the front-line of land warfare. In 1987 the missions were reduced in diversity to scout/attack only, and the pro-

Below: The new RAH-66 Comanche reconnaissance/ attack helicopter which is more capable than the Vietnam-era light helicopters.

jected requirement reduced to 2,096. In 1988, a Request for Proposals was issued, and responded to by a "First Team" comprising Boeing Helicopters and Sikorsky Aircraft, and a "Super Team" comprising Bell and McDonnell Douglas. In 1990 the planned buy was further reduced to 1,292, with the possibility of a further 389. In 1991 Boeing Sikorsky was selected, and an order placed for first four YRAH-66 prototypes (RAH = reconnaissance/attack helicopter), plus a propulsion testbed and a static-test article. Progress has since been patchy, with delays and design changes interspersed with bursts of funding and the decision to follow the USAF F-22A fighter management with the addition of three more prototypes for EMD (Engineering and Manufacturing Development) and the closest possible commonality with the F-22A mission-equipment technology. In early 1997 the plan was for the EMD phase to extend from 1998 to 2003. Low-rate production of the first 24 was to take place in 2001, followed by 48 in 2002, 96 in fiscal Year 03, and thereafter 120 per year. In 1995 the program was again torn up, and in 1997 the current plan comprises two prototypes (the second to fly in September 1998), six "early operational capability" Comanches without armament, and full production in FY2004, with the first US Army unit not forming until 2007. This delay is expected to result in an improved production helicopter.

Design features: Initially seen as a powerful but small machine similar in size to the OH-58, the RAH-66 has grown ever larger until its fuselage volume exceeds that of an Apache. Compared with the Apache the Comanche is 12 years later in basic design, reflected in advanced structure, engines and systems. The engines are exceptionally powerful for their weight and size, and have no axial compressor blades. They contribute to the low IR and

acoustic signature. The unique airframe contributes to the low radar and visual signatures. During development it was entirely designed, the original upright-triangular cross-section being replaced by a diamond (lozenge) shape, and the twin-V tails giving way to a T-type tails in 1996 was still being modified. Almost entirely of composites, including the rotors, it is based on a strong box-beam backbone. On this everything else is mounted, and though many of the hinged skin panels can be used as maintenance platforms they do not carry flight loads. The bearingless main rotor has five blades with swept tips, attached to the hub by flexbeams. The tail rotor (called a Fantail, though a copy of the French Fenestron) is designed to run with any one of its eight blades shot off. As far as possible the whole machine is designed to survive 12.7mm fire. Most unusually, the front cockpit is occupied by the pilot. The crew compartment is slightly pressurized, to provide CBW (chemical and biological warfare) protection. The landing gears are of the tailwheel type, and are fully retractable to reduce drag and radar. Visual signatures. The main units can kneel, and the tail folds down in order that, with main rotor unclipped (a quick task), eight can be loaded inside a C-5 Galaxy. Weapons and extra fuel are hung under detach-

Above: The Comanche can quickly convert from stealthy scout to powerful gunship.

able stub wings, which are not used in the armed reconnaissance role. A small Williams gas turbine provides subsystem power.
Avionics: As noted, maximum commonality with the F-22A was a requirement. The pilot flies with a triplex fly-by-wire system with all the expected automatic lock functions, operating through a fiber-optic AHRS. Navaids include GPS, an inertial platform, digital map display and a radar altimeter. Though the collective is conventional, the cyclic is a fighter-type sidestick. Push-buttons on both sticks are used to designate targets and fire weapons. Communications include hf/single-sideband, vhf-FM and uhf/-AM, all with anti-jam features, as well as the Have Quick tactical link and IFF. Both crew have an HMS, and two flat-panel displays, all cockpit facilities being NVG-compatible. Sensors in the nose include "second-generation" FLIR and monochrome LLTV. All US Army Comanches will have provision for Longbow radar, and the present plan is that it will actually be installed (above the main rotor) in every third machine. Defensive systems include RWRs, laser-warning receivers and radar and IR jammers.
Armament: All versions have a Lockheed Martin three-barrel 20mm gun in a GIAT (French) turret fed by up to 500 rounds (320 in the primary mission). For attack, stub wings can be fitted, each of which can support four Hellfire missiles, while six more can be carried internally and fired from outward-hinged bay doors similar in technology to those of the F-22A. In the air combat mission each bay door can carry six Stinger missiles. Exceptionally in this role, stub wings can be fitted, enabling a further 16 Stingers to be carried. By the time this helicopter is in service, something much better than Stinger is likely to be available.
Future: As emphasized, this program has been beset by redesign, delay and budget limitation. Out of it should come a superior front-line helicopter.

McDonnell Douglas F/A-18E/F Super Hornet

Origin: McDonnell Douglas division of Boeing, St Louis, Missouri.
Type: Carrier-based fighter/attack aircraft.
Engines: Two 22,000lb (9,979kg) thrust General Electric F414-400 augmented turbofans.
Dimensions: Span (over missiles) 44ft 8½in (13.62m); length 60ft 1¼in (18.31m); height 16ft 0in (4.88m); wing area 500sq ft (46.45m²).
Weights: Empty (design target) 29,574lb (13,415kg); internal fuel 14,400lb (6,532kg); maximum external stores 17,750lb (8,051kg); loaded (attack mission) 66,000lb (29,938kg).
Performance: Maximum speed (high altitude) over Mach 1.8, equating to 1,888mph (1,912km/h); combat ceiling 50,000ft (15,240m); combat radius (interdiction with four 1,000lb bombs, two 400gal tanks, two AIM-9, two FLIR, hi-lo-lo-hi profile) 449 miles (723km); combat endurance (at 173 miles, 278km, from carrier, six AAMs and three tanks) 2h 15min; approach speed 144mph (232km/h).
Armament: The Super Hornet is designed to carry the entire range of Navy offensive and defensive ordnance, with 2,250lb (1,012kg) greater total weight and "bring back" load almost doubled to 9,000lb (4,082kg). When the first single-seat E-version rolled out it was carrying

(as a demonstration) AIM-9s, AIM-120 AMRAAMS, AGM-88 Harm, AGM-84D Harpoon, AGM-84H SLAM-ER, BLU-109 JDAM, AGM-154 JSOW and AGM-65E Maverick. The M61A1 gun is retained.
History: First flight (E) 29 November 1995, (F) 1 April 1996; service entry 2001; final delivery to USN expected 2015.
User: US Navy.

This greatly stretched and upgraded Hornet was proposed in 1991 to replace the cancelled A-12 Avenger II. Since then the programme has enjoyed one of the highest rates of funding of any current defence programme. In partnership with Northrop

Grumman, McDonnell Douglas has set up a new assembly line at St Louis from which up to 48 aircraft are expected to emerge annually, the Navy requirement being for 1,000 aircraft. These are likely to include the single-seat F/A-18E, two-seat F/A-18F and new variants not yet funded, including an electronic-warfare version to replace the EA-6B Prowler. The only threat to the programme could come from rapid development of the Joint Strike fighter.

Compared with the earlier Hornet, the Super is physically larger, which among other things increases internal fuel capacity from 1,333gal (6,060lit) to 1,774gal (8,065lit). This requires a wing

Above: Larger than the earlier Hornet, the Super will be an important plane of the 21st century.

increased in area by 100sq ft (9.29m²), with large dogteeth on the leading edge, and new engines of 37.5 per cent greater power, fed by oblique four-sides "caret" inlets. Both takeoff and landing weights are increased by 10,000lb (4,536kg) and the big increase in "bring back" stores limit means that wastage of expensive ordnance will be sharply reduced. The radar is the APG-73, the airbrake is replaced by a special rudder/flap mode, the wing leading-edge root extensions are much larger, and many details have been changed to reduce radar cross-section.

JSF (Joint Strike Fighter)

Origin: Either Boeing or Lockheed Martin.
Type: Single-seat multirole multiservice combat aircraft.
Engine: One Pratt & Whitney F119 derivative or General Electric YF120-F.
Dimensions: Similar to F-16.
Weights: Similar to F-16.
Performance: Combat radius specified as 600nm (1,112km, 691 miles) with internal weapons or 350nm (649km, 403 miles) with heavier (about 10t, 22,000lb) external weapon load; one version to have STOVL

performance.
Armament: Fixed gun and provision for every kind of tactical air/air and air/ground store on internal and external ejector racks.
History: Launched 1993; three original bidders were reduced to two (as above) November 1996; each to build two versions with the first flights due in the year 2000.
Users: USAF 2,036, US Navy 300, US Marine Corps 642, Royal Navy 60, plus many export customers.

Left: The Royal Navy variant of Lockheed Martin's Joint Strike Fighter aircraft concept.

By far the biggest combat-aircraft program in the world, the JSF is already a $100 billion project, without taking into account the nine air forces (nearly all European NATO plus Sweden and Australia) which hope to participate. The eventual winner will be built in a CTOL long runway version and an ASTOVL (Advanced Short TakeOff Vertical Landing) form for use from short dispersed strips and various ships. The two forms are expected to replace almost all current tactical aircraft, including the F-14, F-15/15E, F-16,

Above: The Joint Strike Fighter as envisioned by Boeing. This is the next generation fighter that will replace several aircraft which are currently in service.

F/A-18, Sea Harrier and probably the Jaguar, Harrier, Viggen and other types. The RAF is studying whether a version could replace Tornado. All versions are expected to be built on a single production line, though a large number of manufacturers in several countries are expected to contribute. Should the JSF make rapid progress it could replace the F/A-18E/F, which became more likely with Boeing's takeover of McDonnell Douglas.

Index

215

Extra Index Entries

Picture Credits

Photograph research for this book was carried out in Washington DC by Jonathan Scott Arms, whose brief was to collect as many rare action photos as possible, in color if they existed. It is a testament to his endeavors that so many of the photographs on the previous pages have never appeared in any publication before. Most of the photographs were supplied by either the various sections of Defense Audio Visual Agency, Department of Defense (DoD), and also the fabulous National Air and Space Museum (NASM), others were kindly provided by the public relations department of manufacturers, aviation magazines and private collectors. All are credited below.

Endpapers: DoD. Pages **1-3**: DoD. **4-5**: top DoD; bottom NASM. **6-12**: DoD. **13**: NASM. **16-18**: DoD. **19-20**: NASM. **21**: Northrop. **22**: DoD. **23**: McDonnell Douglas. **26**: Grumman. **27**: DoD. **28-42**: NASM. **43**: top NASM; bottom DoD. **44-49**: NASM. **50-51**: top NASM; bottom *Aeroplane Monthly*. **52-61**: NASM. **62-63**: top left DoD; others NASM. **64**: top/center DoD; bottom NASM. **65**: top/center NASM; bottom DoD. **66-67**: NASM. **68**: top DoD; bottom NASM. **69**: top NASM; bottom DoD. **70-71**: NASM. **72-73**: bottom DoD; others NASM. **74**: NASM. **75**: top NASM; bottom DoD. **76-77**: NASM. **78**: DoD. **79**: top/bottom left DoD; others NASM. **80-81**: top left DoD; others NASM. **82-83**: top left DoD; others NASM. **84-85**: NASM. **86-87**: top center DoD; others NASM. **88-89**: bottom right Vought; others NASM. **90-91**: NASM. **92-93**: top right DoD; others NASM. **94-97**: NASM. **98**: center Grumman; others

DoD. **99**: top NASM; bottom DoD. **100-101**: top right DoD; others NASM. **102**: DoD. **103**: NASM. **104-105**: bottom right Lockheed; others NASM. **106-107**: NASM. **108**: top NASM; bottom Grumman. **109**: Lockheed. **110-111**: top right DoD; others NASM. **112-113**: DoD. **114-115**: top right NASM. **116-117**: top right Imperial War Museum; center right NATO; others DoD. **118-119**: NASM. **120-121**: center left DoD; others NASM. **122-123**: DoD. **124**: top McDonnell Douglas; bottom/center NASM. **125**: top McDonnell Douglas; center NASM; bottom Boeing. **126-127**: bottom left Grumman; others DoD. **128**: top/bottom NASM; center DoD. **129-130**: DoD. **131-132**: NASM. **133-141**: DoD. **142-148**: DoD. **149**: top DoD; center/bottom McDonnell Douglas. **150-155**: DoD. **156-157**: top left LTV; others DoD. **158-175**: DoD. **176**: top/center DoD; bottom Bell. **177**: top/center McDonnell Douglas; bottom Bell. **178-179**: DoD; bottom DoD. **180**: top Grumman; bottom DoD. **181**: top left Boeing; others DoD. **182-183**: DoD. **184-185**: top Bell; others DoD. **186-187**: DoD. **188-189**: top left Boeing; others DoD. **190-191**: top Grumman; bottom DoD. **192-193**: DoD. **194-195**: top McDonnell Douglas; bottom Beech. **196-197**: DoD. **198-199**: McDonnell Douglas. **200-201**: top left United Technologies/Sikorsky; others McDonnell Douglas. **202-203**: Rockwell International. **204-205**: top right DoD; others McDonnell Douglas. **206**: top Lockheed; bottom DoD. **207**: top Lockheed; bottom Boeing. **208**: Bell/Boeing. **209**: top/bottom Northrop Grumman. **210**: Lockheed Martin. **211**: McDonnell Douglas. **212**: top/bottom Northrop Grumman. **213**: top Northrop Grumman; center Boeing; bottom Lockheed Martin.

Right and below: Ten men were aboard each of these B-17Gs of the 381st Bomb Group heading out over Europe in late 1944. Forty years later a successor, SAC's FB-111A (inset, taking fuel from a KC-135A) needs a crew of two. But the manned bomber has a long-term future.